THE Way OF Righteousness

Good News for Muslims

The stories and message of God's prophets according to the Torah, the Psalms, and the Gospel

P. D. Bramsen

Published by
CMML
Spring Lake, New Jersey

TWOR@iname.com

Cover artwork by David C. Bramsen

Printed in the United States of America

With gratefulness to
my dad (now in heaven)
and my mom (still on earth)
who (with their lives and their lips)
first pointed me to
God's Way of Righteousness.

CONTENTS

PART 1:
THE WAY OF RIGHTEOUSNESS ACCORDING TO THE TORAH

PART 2:
THE WAY OF RIGHTEOUSNESS ACCORDING TO THE PSALMS AND THE PROPHETS

PART 3:
THE WAY OF RIGHTEOUSNESS ACCORDING TO THE GOSPEL

PART 4:
THE WAY OF RIGHTEOUSNESS SUMMARIZED

Preface

"Yoonu Njub" means *The Way of Righteousness*

The Way of Righteousness is an English translation of ***Yoonu Njub***—a series of radio-programs originally written in the Wolof language for the Muslims of Senegal, West Africa. Beginning with the Torah of Moses, these one hundred 15-minute lessons take the listener on a journey through the Scriptures of the prophets to view God's unchangeable purpose for mankind and to hear God's thrilling answer to the prophet Job's four-thousand-year-old question, ***"How can a man be righteous before God?"*** (Job 9:2)

Double Purpose

The reason for making these lessons available in English is **twofold:**

1. to facilitate translation into other languages **for broadcast** to Muslims around the world;

2. to promote reading by English-speaking Muslims and others who want to deepen their understanding of the stories and, especially, *the message* of God's prophets.

The *"Very Religious"* Wolofs

The Wolof people, for whom this radio series was first produced, are the dominant ethnic group in Senegal—the West African nation on the southern edge of the Sahara Desert. Wolofs are a proud, tall, black people, known for their wit and warmth, their storytelling and hospitality, their farming and fishing, their elegant clothes and excellent cuisine. Patience and peace are considered great virtues.

More than 99% of Wolofs claim to be Muslims. Wolof society revolves around the religion of Islam, with traditional African beliefs mixed in. The widespread use of charms and amulets is one example of their continued allegiance to their ancestral religion. To their Islamic and animistic practices, many Wolofs add the veneration of spiritual guides and intermediaries called *marabouts*, a common phenomenon in much of the Muslim world. As one Senegalese man told me, "To follow the requirements of Islam is good, but it does not provide assurance of salvation. The marabouts mediate for us and will help us get into paradise."

In summary, most Wolofs are syncretists—seeking to satisfy the requirements of Islam, animism and maraboutism. Like the Athenians mentioned in Scripture, the Wolofs are "*in all things very religious*." (Acts 17:22) But being ***religious*** does not make one ***righteous***. As Wolof NDiaye (a fictional character credited as the source of Wolof wisdom) says, "Even if a log soaks a long time in water it will never become a crocodile."

Background Story

In 1981, my wife and I and our one-year-old boy, backed by the fervent prayers of the Lord's people, moved to Senegal—a unique majority-Muslim-nation that grants its people the basic right to choose what they will or will not believe. After spending a year in the capital city of Dakar, we settled in Saint Louis, a large town near the border of the Islamic Republic of Mauritania. Six years, two languages (French and Wolof), two children, and many painful, but profitable experiences later, we rejoiced to see one of our Wolof friends submit to God's way of righteousness. Since then, it has been our privilege to witness God's transforming work in the hearts and lives of several others who have declared their faith in the One about whom all the prophets wrote.

Shredded Scriptures in the Air

I look back to a scorching hot day in 1992 as the day that *The Way of Righteousness* radio-series was born. I, along with two of my Senegalese brothers, were in a town in northern Senegal. We were seeking to reason with folks concerning the message of God's prophets and to distribute some illustrated booklets about the prophet Abraham and his sacrificial ram. After a while, some in the crowd began to tear up the literature and shout religious slogans. As we, with saddened hearts, watched them fling the shredded Scriptures into the air, I thought, "Is this really the best use of our time—watching people tear up the Word of God which they haven't even read? What we need to do is to prepare a series of chronological lessons that clearly present the stories and message of God's prophets and broadcast them on the national radio station. Then people all over the country can hear God's message of salvation and make an intelligent choice whether to accept it or reject it." I returned home that evening with this clear vision—and with a settled confidence that God would somehow open the necessary doors.

Scriptures on the Air

Within a few months, God opened the way for us to sign a two-year contract with Senegal's national radio station for a once-a-week 15-minute-program that would present "the stories of the prophets according to the Bible." It was during that two-year period that the radio-series *Yoonu Njub* came to be.

Today these Wolof programs are being aired eleven times a week on various stations within Senegal. God has so worked that these lessons are also being translated and broadcast in the languages of other Muslim people around the world. *"Great is our Lord, and mighty in power...His Word runs very swiftly!"* (Psalm 147:5,15)

GRATEFUL ACKNOWLEDGMENTS

I cannot claim originality for this series any more than one who arranges a bouquet can take credit for the fragrant aroma and exquisite beauty of the flowers. These lessons are a simple arrangement of the glorious Word of God and a display of the One who is *"altogether lovely."*

While I am deeply indebted to many of God's servants for the preparation of these lessons, I owe the most to **Trevor McIlwain** of Australia, the author of *Firm Foundations* (New Tribes Mission, Sanford, Florida). In his excellent studies, Mr. McIlwain uses the chronological method of presenting God's Good News. Like many others, we have used and adapted many of McIlwain's outlines and illustrations.

Malick, one of my beloved Wolof brothers in Senegal, and the voice of *Yoonu Njub*, has done a superb job of correcting and contributing ideas to the original hundred lessons written in the Wolof language. **Eric and Eithne** of England and **Marilyn** of Hawaii diligently labored to translate the New Testament and much of the Old Testament into the Wolof language which made our task immeasurably easier. **Richard**, a colleague from Australia, is the one who got the proverbial ball rolling so that these Wolof lessons could begin to be translated into other languages. He translated the series into English (almost word for word) while studying Wolof and playing the cassettes of these lessons for the men and women of the village where he and his family live. Richard has been a tremendous encouragement, as have many others, such as my coworker, **Andreas** of Germany, and **Bill** of North Carolina, who helped expand the radio and cassette ministry in Senegal. **Russ and Nancy** in South Carolina proofread the English text and provided helpful critiques and suggestions. **Gerry** in Massachusetts also proofread the lessons despite intense physical pain which has been her companion for more than twenty years. In New Jersey, **Jani** skillfully moved the mouse to format the text into a book. My brother **Dave** did the cover artwork.

I reserve my final expression of heartfelt thanks for my favorite (and only!) wife, **Carol**, and to our three faithful children, **Andy, Corrie and Nathan**, who have been a blessed support to me in this ongoing ministry. I could easily mention **scores of others** who have had a share in this project, but suffice it to say that, in the Lord's work, we do nothing by ourselves. We are truly "*laborers together*" and are all eternally indebted to **the Author and Finisher of the Plan of Salvation** of whom these chronological lessons speak.

Paul Bramsen
Senegal, West Africa
1998

Send correspondence to:
E-mail: TWOR@iname.com

Or: The Way of Righteousness
PO Box 4006
Greenville, SC 29608-4006

NOTE: The English Scripture translation used in these one hundred lessons is the *New International Version* which is chosen for its simpler vocabulary. For personal Bible study, you may prefer a more literal translation such as the *New King James Version* which we have used in the preface and appendixes. All Scripture portions are italicized. Square brackets [ ] indicate that which has been paraphrased in order to express the way the verse was translated in Wolof, or for explanatory purposes. The Scripture references in parentheses and the information enclosed in the squiggly brackets { } are not intended to be read on the radio. This information is only for the reader.

Part 1

The Way of Righteousness According to

The Torah

Some of the people studied in this section:

Adam
Eve
Cain
Abel
Enoch
Noah
Abraham
Lot
Ishmael
Isaac
Jacob
Joseph
Moses
Aaron
Pharoah
Joshua
Ruth

"How can a man be righteous before God?"
The Prophet Job 9:2

LESSON 1

GOD HAS SPOKEN!

INTRODUCTION

Peace be with you {Arabic greeting}, listening friends. We greet you in the name of God, the Lord of peace, who wants everyone to understand and submit to the way of righteousness that He has established, and have true peace with Him forever. We are very happy that we can present to you your program ***The Way of Righteousness***. We call this radio program *The Way of Righteousness* because in it we plan to explore the Writings of the Prophets which reveal how unrighteous people can become righteous before God.

Which way are you following—the way of righteousness or the way of unrighteousness? Do you want to know the way of righteousness that comes from God? The Word of God says, "***Blessed*** *are those who* ***hunger*** *and* ***thirst*** *for* ***righteousness****, for they will be filled.*" (Matt. 5:6)

Perhaps there are those who think, "We already know the way of righteousness. We don't need to be concerned with the writings of the first prophets. What we know is good enough for us!" If this is your attitude, listen to what the prophet of God, Solomon, wrote. He said: "*There is* ***a way that seems right*** *to a man, but in the end* ***it leads to death****!*" (Prov. 14:12)

In God's Book, in the book called *Psalms* {Qur'anic name: *Zabur*}, the prophet David, the father of Solomon, spoke much about our need to know the way of righteousness which God has established. He wrote, "*There is* ***no one righteous****, not even one; All have turned away, they have together become worthless; there is no one who does good, not even one.*" (Psa. 14:1,3; Rom. 3:10,12) That is why David wrote this prayer in the Psalms, saying, "*Show me your ways, O LORD, teach me your paths; guide me in your truth [and lead me by the hand]!*" (Psa. 25:4,5) {Note: words in brackets [ ] reflect the way the verse is translated in Wolof.}

If our Lord God does not guide us in the way of truth, we could never know the way of righteousness. We would be like a child lost in Dakar {Senegal's Capital} or a sheep lost in the desert. But the Word of God tells us that "*God does not want anyone to perish...but wants all men to be saved and to come to a knowledge of the truth.*" (2 Pet. 3:9; 1 Tim. 2:4) **Friends, nothing is more important than to know for sure that you are in the way of truth that leads to God.**

In these *Way of Righteousness* programs, we will study the Scriptures **chronologically**. We will follow the stories of God's prophets one by one, from beginning to end. The Word of God has a beginning and an end {Literally in Wolof: *a head and a tail*}. Therefore we plan to explore the stories found in the Scriptures, beginning where God Himself begins, that is, at the very beginning.

We will learn many important things about God and the prophets. We will see that although **many prophets** wrote the Holy Scriptures, **only one Author** inspired the prophets: **God**. The Scriptures of the Prophets contain **many stories**, but **only one central message: the Good News about how people can be made righteous before God.**

Therefore, we ask you to listen attentively and faithfully to the program *The Way of Righteousness*. Wolof wisdom says: "Slowly, slowly one catches a monkey in the forest" and "A water pail will find the person who waits diligently at the well." Similarly, God tells us in His Word that He *"rewards those who **earnestly** seek him."* (Heb. 11:6) To those who truly seek Him, God makes this promise: *"If you seek me with **all** your heart, **you will find me**!"* (Jer. 29:13)

Here on *The Way of Righteousness*, we will increase our knowledge about God and His Word. Do you know what God is like? Or where Satan came from? Do you know why God created man? Or how sin entered the beautiful world that God made? Have you ever read the amazing story about God's prophet Noah, and the flood? Do you really know what the prophets of God wrote? Do you know why Abraham was called *the Friend of God*? Can you clearly explain to your friends or your children the message of the prophets?

Thousands of years ago, the prophet Job {*Ayyub* in Arabic} asked the question, ***"How can a man be righteous before God?"*** (Job 9:2) Do you know God's answer to Job's question? Do you know how **you** can be righteous before God? If you want to know God's response to this question and many others, we invite you to listen to the program *The Way of Righteousness*. Truly, the Word of God is deep, wonderful, alive and powerful. And something else: the Word of God hides nothing. It shows us what man is really like. Thus the Scriptures say, *"Nothing in all creation is hidden from God's sight. Everything is uncovered and laid bare before the eyes of him to whom we must give account."* (Heb. 4:13)

In the time left today, there is an important truth that we must grasp. It is this: **God has spoken**! God, the Most High, has spoken! God has spoken to man (mankind) and God wants to speak to **you**! If you received a letter from a powerful king in a far off land, would you read it? Would you consider what he wrote to you in the letter? Would you pay attention to the words of the king? How much more ought we to pay attention when it is the Most High God who is speaking to us!

How has God spoken to man? The Holy Scriptures tell us, *"In the past God spoke to our forefathers through* **the prophets** *at many times and in various ways...*" (Heb. 1:1) Yes, one of the main ways God has spoken to man is **through the prophets**. In the past, God appointed certain men to proclaim His Word and to write it down in books (scrolls). The Word of God says, "*You must understand that no prophecy of Scripture came about by the prophet's own interpretation. For prophecy never had its origin in the will of man, but men spoke from God as they were carried along by the Holy Spirit [of God].*" (2 Pet. 1:20,21)

God could have written the Scriptures Himself or He could have used His angels to write it. But He did not do this. God chose **ordinary men** to write it for Him. We call these men prophets. The prophets of God were somewhat like secretaries. God planted in their minds what they were to write, and they wrote it down for God. However, God let each prophet write the Scriptures in his own words. **God inspired every word, yet He did not ignore the individual prophet's personality.** God's Book not only contains the direct words of God, but also the thoughts and prayers and problems of people like you and me. Through the stories of God's dealings with people, God wants to show us what He is like and how we can draw near to Him.

Why did God inspire the prophets to write the Holy Scriptures? He inspired them so that the people of every generation might know what God wants them to know. God spoke to the prophets because **He wants to speak to you and me** through what they have written! All that God has said through His prophets is profitable for us who are living today. God expects each of us to know **the message** of the prophets.

Perhaps some think, "Ha! I don't need to know what the first prophets wrote. Their words are not important to me. Each prophet had his task (mission) to accomplish. A prophet came, performed his task and passed on. Another came, accomplished his task and passed on...and so forth. We who live today don't need to know what the first prophets said!" Are these your thoughts also? God's thoughts do not agree with these thoughts! Listen to what the Lord God says,

> "*I tell you the truth, until heaven and earth disappear, not the smallest letter, not the least stroke of a pen, will by any means disappear from the [Holy Scriptures] until everything is accomplished. Anyone who breaks one of the least of these commandments and teaches others to do the same will be called least in the kingdom of heaven!*" (Matt. 5:18,19) "*All Scripture is God-breathed and is useful for teaching, rebuking, correcting and training in righteousness!*" (2 Tim. 3:16)

Truly, all that the prophets wrote is of great value, because they wrote it so that people in every age might know the way of salvation that God has established. Do you know what God's prophets have written? God wants us to know

His Word, believe it and obey it! The Scripture says: "*We have the word of the prophets made more certain, and you will do well to pay attention to it, as to a light shining in a dark place!*" (2 Pet. 1:19)

Yes, sometimes we hear those who fight against God's Book, saying, "No one can trust it! It is full of errors. It has been changed!" However, **the one who fights with the Word of Truth is fighting with God Himself**. "An egg should not wrestle with a rock!" {Wolof Proverb}. The Word of God is the Rock, and man is the egg! Man cannot change the true Word of God–but the true Word of God can change man! God is great, and is able to protect His Eternal Word. That is what the Lord Himself said in the book known as the *Injil* {The Gospel record is called the "*Injil*" in the Qur'an, Arabic for *the Good News* or *the Gospel.*}: ***"Heaven and earth will pass away, but my words will never pass away!"*** (Matt. 24:35)

Many people try to fight against the Word of God because it exposes the true condition of their hearts. Listen to what God says about His own Word: "*The word of God is **living** and **active**. Sharper than any double-edged sword, it penetrates even to dividing soul and spirit, joints and marrow; **it judges the thoughts and attitudes of the heart.***" (Heb. 4:12)

Yes, God's Word is living and active; it speaks to the heart. The Holy Scriptures are the oldest collection of writings in the world, yet they are still relevant for every person. Nothing is more important than the Word of God. However, the Word of God is like rice and fish {*ceebu jën:* Senegal's national dish}. We all agree that rice and fish is delicious to eat and good for the body. But unless I eat it, it is of no benefit to me. I must eat it. In a similar way, I must partake of the Word of God, which nourishes my heart, if I want benefit from it. This is why God says that "*man does not live on bread alone, but on every word that comes from the mouth of God.*" (Matt. 4:4) It is only those "*who **hunger and thirst** for righteousness*" who will be filled. (Matt. 5:6) Do you hunger for the Word of God? It is food, delicious food. It is not food that nourishes your body, but food that nourishes your heart and soul.

So we say to you who fear God and revere His Word: Make a serious effort to follow regularly the program *The Way of Righteousness.* In this way you will increase your knowledge of what God has said long ago through His prophets and learn how you can be made righteous before God the Holy One. God has spoken–and God wants to speak to you!

Before we leave you today, we need to clarify one more thing. In our programs we will not rely on anything or anyone except that which is found in the writings of God's prophets. We who prepare these programs know nothing about God's Truth apart from that which God has made known in the Scriptures. That which the prophet John, the son of Zachariah, declared in the Gospel {*Injil*} is true: "*A man can receive only what is given him from heaven.*" (John 3:27) We dare not rely on our own knowledge. **We rely on God's Word alone.** Our desire is to make known what God has declared in His Word through His prophets.

Do you know what God has said in the Writings of the Prophets? Are you among those who hunger and thirst for the Word of God and for true righteousness? In His holy Word, God has revealed Himself and His righteous way of salvation. We invite you to explore the Scriptures with us here on *The Way of Righteousness* so that you might really understand what God has said. The Word of God tells us: "*Everything that was written in the past was written to teach us, so that through endurance and the encouragement of the Scriptures we might have* **hope.**" (Rom. 15:4)

May we all be certain of this one thing: **God has spoken and He wants everyone to listen and live**! Old and young, men and women, rich and poor, God is saying to every one of you: "*Listen! Open your ears, and come to me. Listen, and your soul will live!*" (Isa. 55:3)

Friends, thank you for listening. In our next program, God willing, we will present our second lesson which is entitled: "What is God like?" If you have any questions about what you have heard today, we invite you to write to *The Way of Righteousness*, (+ P.O. Box, City, etc.) *The Way of Righteousness*, (+ P.O. Box, City, etc.) {One possible way of concluding a lesson, see lesson #2 for another example.}

God bless you as you meditate upon this great invitation from God to you:

> ***"Listen! Open your ears, and come to me. Listen, and your soul will live!"*** (Isa. 55:3)

Lesson 2

What Is God Like?

Genesis 1

Peace be with you, listening friends. We greet you in the name of God, the Lord of peace, who wants everyone to understand and submit to the way of righteousness that He has established, and have true peace with Him forever. We are happy to be able to return today to present your program *The Way of Righteousness*.

In these programs we will be telling **the stories of God's prophets**, one by one. We also plan to explore the Holy Scriptures that the prophets wrote; these declare the way of righteousness that God has decreed so that people might be counted as righteous before Him.

In our first program, we discussed the Writings of the Prophets. We learned that there are many prophets who wrote the Holy Scriptures, but that there is only one Author. That One is God. In our last lesson, we left you with an important thought. That thought was this: **God has spoken**! God has spoken to mankind through the prophets and He wants each of us to listen to Him. God wants to speak to us through the Writings of the Prophets. God never changes, nor does His Word. In every generation, God has protected His Word. "*The Scripture cannot be broken.*" (John 10:35) "*The world will pass away...but the Word of the Lord endures forever!*" (1 John 2:17; 1 Pet. 1:25) That is what the Scriptures say.

Today we are going to get into **the first section in the Holy Scriptures**. It is called the ***Torah*** {or *Pentateuch*}. God planted this book in the mind of a man named Moses {*Musa* in Arabic}. God told Moses what to write and Moses wrote it down. About three thousand five hundred years have passed since Moses' time. The Torah consists of five books, or **five parts**. The first part is known as ***Genesis*** {Lit. in Wolof: *the Beginning*}. There are fifty chapters in the book of Genesis. The first book is called Genesis (the Beginning) because it tells us what happened in the beginning.

It is important for us to know the first book of the Torah very well, because it is **the foundation that God laid**, so that we might understand what He says in the other books of the prophets that follow. As we study this book, we will deepen our knowledge of many important truths. We will learn about God and what He is like. We will study about the angels and Satan, the heavens and the earth, animals and man. We will see how sin entered the world and brought with it great destruction and sorrow. However, we will also examine carefully the way of salvation which the Lord God has provided so that sinners can return to God and have a wonderful relationship with Him. In the first stories, we will see the first people, the first sin, and the first murderer. We will read about the first false religions, the first prophets, and the first nations. We will reflect on the story of Adam and Eve, Cain and Abel, Noah and the flood, God's prophet Abraham and why he was called *the friend of God*. We will see Ishmael and Isaac, Esau and Jacob and Joseph and his wicked brothers. The first book of the Torah contains all this and much more.

Now therefore, friends, we ask you to listen carefully, because the time for us to begin our (chronological) study of the Scriptures of the Prophets has arrived. In the first book of the Torah, chapter one, verse one, we read: ***"In the beginning God created the heavens and the earth."*** (Gen. 1:1) This is where we must begin our lesson in the Holy Scriptures, because it is here that God Himself begins His Book: "*In the beginning God created the heavens and the earth.*"

In this verse there is something we must consider. What existed before God created the heavens and the earth? What was there before the world existed? The Scriptures show us that nothing existed except God. That is why it says, "*In the beginning…God.*" Everything that we can see and touch has a beginning. Thus, long, long ago, there was a time when there was no sky or earth, no ocean or trees. In the beginning, before God created the heavens and the earth, there was no sun, no moon, no stars. In the beginning, there were no men or angels. There was a time when there was nothing as we know it today—nothing except **God**.

That is why we read in the first verse of the first book of the Holy Scriptures, "*In the beginning* ***God*** *created the heavens and the earth.*" The Scriptures do **not** say, "In the beginning God **and** the angels" or "In the beginning God **and** men." No. The Scriptures tell us, "*In the beginning* ***God***." In the beginning, when nothing yet existed, before any angels or people existed…there was only One who was living. That One is **God**!

In our world some say, "I cannot see God, therefore there is no God." To those people who deny that God exists, we would like to ask a few questions. Have you ever seen an atom? Or the oxygen you breathe? Have you ever seen the wind? You cannot see the wind, yet you know that the wind exists because you can see what it does. You can see the trees that move in the wind, but the wind itself no one can see. You cannot hold the wind in your hand, but you can feel its cooling breeze. That is how it is with God. We cannot see God, because God is invisible to human eyes. However, **we know that God exists because we see what God created**. The Scripture says: "*God's invisible qualities–his eternal power and divine* *nature–have been clearly seen, being understood from what has been made, so that men are* ***without excuse.***" (Rom. 1:20)

Another thing we can learn from the first verse of the Torah is this: **God has no beginning**. God was not created in the beginning. God is the Lord of Eternity. Everything that we know and see here in the world had a beginning. But God had no beginning. He has no origin. He has no equal. Only He existed in the beginning. No one gave birth to Him. No one created Him, and He did not create Himself. That is why we read in the Holy Scriptures "*In the beginning* ***God***." Only He has no beginning. He is the One who has always existed and lives forever. The LORD {Lit. in Wolof: *The Eternal One*} is His name. What He is like today, He was like yesterday. What He was yesterday, He will be forever. **God never changes**.

There is something else which we can learn from the verse that says, "*In the beginning God created the heavens and the earth*." It is this. **God is great!** God who created everything is greater than everything and everyone. He is the Lord of Creation. Truly, with our whole heart we can declare: "*Allahu Akbar!*" {Arabic: *God is greater!*} God is great! He has no equal. He is greater than everything in the world–ocean, wind, sun and stars! He is wiser and more powerful than all spirits and people. He is worthy of glory forever! Just as the one who builds a house is more important than the house, so God is superior to everything, because He created everything. God is great! He lives by His own power. He doesn't depend on anything. He is not dependent on anyone. God is greater than everything. He needs nothing. He needs no one. He is the Great One!

We humans have many needs. Every day we must breathe and sleep, drink and eat. We need the sun and rain, food and water, clothes and housing, father and mother, friends and money and so much more. How many are our needs! However, the LORD who created everything, needs nothing! He does not hunger. He does not thirst. He never gets tired. He does not have a body like man. He has no limits. He has no end. He is the Eternal God. **He is the All-Powerful One**.

Now, here is an important question. If God is not like a man and does not have a body like us, what is God like? The Scripture responds to that question with a clear answer. It says, "*God is* ***spirit****, and his worshipers must worship in spirit and in truth*." (John 4:24) What is God like? **God is spirit**. Man is body and spirit, but God is only spirit. The Spirit of God has no limit. He is everywhere. God is above everything and everyone. He fills everything. He sees everything. Night and day are the same to God. If you hide in your room, God is there and He sees you. **God knows everything**. He knows your thoughts and the intentions of your heart. God is great!

So what is God like? Perhaps we can summarize what we have studied today in this way: **God is not like anyone**. God is God and He has no equal. In future lessons of your program *The Way of Righteousness* we will increase our understanding of the character of God. In the Holy Scriptures, God has hundreds and hundreds of names. He is The LORD. The Most High. The Almighty. The Creator. The Author of Life. The Light. The Righteous One. The Holy One. The Compassionate One. The God of Love. He is the living and true God!

In truth, God, who created the heavens and the earth in the beginning, is **the Great One**. Of Him, the Scriptures say:

> "*Oh, the depth of the riches of the wisdom and knowledge of God!...For from him and through him and to him are all things.*" (Rom. 11:33,36) "*God, the blessed and only Ruler, the King of kings and Lord of lords, who alone is immortal and who lives in unapproachable light, whom no one has seen or can see. To him be honor and might forever. Amen!*" (1 Tim. 6:15,16)

In another chapter, God's prophet, Moses, praises God in a beautiful song saying, "*Great and marvelous are your deeds, Lord God Almighty. Just and true are your ways, King of the ages. Who will not fear you, O Lord, and bring glory to your name? For you alone are holy.*" (Rev. 15:3,4) God is infinitely great! That is what the first verse of God's Word teaches us when it says, "*In the beginning* ***God****!*"

And so friends, may we keep in our minds the truth that we have heard today: "*In the beginning God.*" Only God existed in the beginning–and, therefore, **only God** can reveal to us the truth about what happened in the beginning. **Only God** can reveal to us the truth about what will happen in the hereafter. And **only God** can reveal to us the truth about Himself.

Yes, we know that some people say, "No one can know God or what will happen in the hereafter!" Nevertheless, the Writings of the Prophets tell us that **we can know God**, and that **we can know where we will spend eternity**. For the Word of God says,

> "*I write these things to you...so that you may* ***know*** *that you have eternal life!*" and so that you "*may* ***know*** *him who is true...the true God and eternal life!* (1 John 5:13,20) "*No eye has seen, no ear has heard, no mind has conceived what God has prepared for those who love him, but* ***God has revealed it to us by his Spirit****. The Spirit searches all things, even the deep things of God.*" (1 Cor. 2:9,10)

You who are listening to us today, **do you know God personally**? Or is He, for you, simply the great Creator who is far off and unknowable? Dear friends, God wants you to know Him and to live with Him forever! The Scriptures of the Prophets teach us how we can have a wonderful and close relationship with God. However, we must open our ears, and our minds, and our hearts to what God is saying to us. Listen to what God says in His holy Word: "*Turn to Me and be saved, all you ends of the earth; for I am God, and there is no other!*" (Isa. 45:22)

Friends, this is where we must stop today. However, we want to inform you that these chronological lessons are available on audio-cassettes. If you would like to own a complete set, write to us and we will tell you how to obtain them. Or, if you prefer to have the Holy Scriptures in written form, we will send you some Scripture portions. Our address is *The Way of Righteousness*, (+ P.O. Box, City, etc.) *The Way of Righteousness*, (+ P.O. Box, City, etc.) {We leave this in as another example of the kind of offers that can be given at the end of the lesson. In our Wolof radio programs, on every fourth program, we mention the availability of cassettes. We send two or three cassettes to all who write in, free of charge. Some purchase the whole 20-cassette (100-lesson) series.}

Thank you for being with us today. In our next program, God willing, we will look into a fascinating topic: the angels and Satan. Do you know the true story about where they come from?

God bless you as you consider the verse in the Holy Scriptures that says:

> ***"God is spirit, and his worshipers must worship in spirit and in truth."*** (John 4:24)

Lesson 3

Satan and the Angels

Isaiah 14; Ezekiel 28

Peace be with you, listening friends. We greet you in the name of God, the Lord of peace, who wants everyone to understand and submit to the way of righteousness that He has established, and have true peace with Him forever. We are happy to be able to return today to present your program *The Way of Righteousness.*

In our last program, we read the first verse in the Holy Scriptures, which says: *"In the beginning God created the heavens and the earth."* (Gen. 1:1) We saw that everything has a beginning except God. In the beginning, when there was nothing, only One was living. That One was **God**. Only He existed in the beginning. God is the Lord of Eternity. God is great and has no equal! He has no beginning and no end. He has no needs. He is not limited. God is spirit and can be everywhere at once. He is above everything and everyone. He fills everything. He sees everything. He knows everything. He is unique. God is great! That is why the Holy Scriptures say, *"He alone is immortal and lives in unapproachable light, whom no one has seen or can see. To him be honor and might forever! Amen!"* (1 Tim. 6:16)

Today we begin our third lesson in the Scriptures of the Prophets. We intend to consider what God's Word teaches about **the angels and Satan**. Do you know where angels come from? Or where Satan and demons come from? We could not know about such things if God had not told them to us. But God tells us about them in His Word. Let us therefore carefully examine the Holy Scriptures, so that we might know the truth concerning the angels and Satan.

We remind you that, in *The Way of Righteousness* program, we are doing a chronological study of the Writings of the Prophets–from beginning to end. That is why, in the last broadcast, we studied about God Himself, because God is the One who existed in the beginning. And, God willing, in our next lesson, we will tell the story of how God made the world and all that is in it. However, before God created people and the world in which we live, there was something else He created **first: the angels**.

The Word of God tells us much about angels. Today we will try to summarize the more important truths concerning these created beings. God's Word tells us that long, long ago, God, who is spirit, created **many other spirits** called ***angels***. The Scriptures say, "*[All the angels are spirits.]*" (Heb. 1:14) "*[God] makes his angels winds, His servants flames of fire.*" (Heb. 1:7) Thus, the Scriptures teach us that the angels, like God, are spirits. Their form is compared with wind and fire. We cannot see the wind. No one can touch fire. That is how it is with the angels of God. God did not create them with bodies such as we have. We humans are made of body and spirit. However, the angels are only spirits. That is why we cannot see them.

How many angels did God create? What do the Scriptures say about this? It says that God created many, many spirits beyond what anyone can count. On high, in the presence of God, there are "*many angels, numbering thousands upon thousands, and ten thousand times ten thousand.*" (Rev. 5:11) God our Lord is great! God, who has no limit, created for Himself thousands and thousands of beautiful, good and wise angels. The Scriptures tell us that the angels of God have **great power**. They are more powerful than we are. Yet like all creatures, they have their limitations. They are **not all-powerful.** They cannot be everywhere and they do not know everything. They are merely creatures. Only One is without limits. That One is God.

Something else we must understand about the angels is this: When God created the angels they were **holy creatures**, all of them. In the beginning, there were no evil angels. In the beginning, the Devil {Qur'anic/Arabic: "*Iblis*"} did not yet exist. There were no evil spirits. God did not create any evil angels. We must retain this truth in our minds: God can do anything, except one thing. God cannot do what is evil. Let us not forget this. God cannot create what is bad because He is **good**. God cannot make mistakes because He is **perfect**. Sin cannot come forth from Him because He is **pure and holy**. Everything that God thinks and says and does is good and perfect. That is why the Scriptures say: "*God cannot be tempted by evil, nor does he tempt anyone.*" (Jam. 1:13) Well then, where does evil come from? We will see God's answer shortly. First, however, there is something else we must know about the angels.

Why did God create the angels? The Scriptures teach us that God created them so that they could be with God **to love Him, to praise Him and to serve Him** in the joy of heaven forever. God owned them, all of them, because He created them. They all dwelt in the "house" of God on high, in heaven, far beyond the moon, sun and stars. Did you know that there is **a special place where God dwells**? True, in our last lesson we learned that God is everywhere. However, the Scriptures also teach us about a wonderful place in the universe that is holy, full of light and beauty, where God lives and displays all His glory. This is the place that the prophets of God call *The presence of God* or *Heaven* or ***Paradise***. This is where God dwells with His holy angels.

There is something else which we need to know about the angels. It is this: The angels are **not all the same**. Some angels are more beautiful and more wise than others. Some angels surround the throne of God in heaven. Others help and protect people. Other angels, like **Gabriel** and **Michael**, stand in the presence of God and are sent forth to accomplish special missions on the earth.

Some angels oversee others. Have you ever heard the name **Lucifer**? The Word of God tells us that there was a time when Lucifer was the chief of all the angels. If you know the story of Lucifer, you know where **Satan** himself comes from.

The Scriptures tell us that when God first created the angels, **Lucifer was the most beautiful, the most powerful, and the wisest of them all**. Lucifer means *the shining one*. Lucifer was superior to all the other angels in knowledge and wisdom, and in power and authority. God gave him beauty and intelligence beyond measure. Lucifer should have worshiped God, loved him and obeyed him forever, because God created him and greatly blessed him. However, in the Writings of the Prophets we read that one day Lucifer showed contempt for God, and his heart was filled with **pride**. Lucifer said in his heart, "***I will** ascend to heaven;* ***I will** raise my throne above the stars of God;* ***I will** sit enthroned…* ***I will** ascend above the tops of the clouds;* ***I will** make myself like the Most High [God]!*" (Isa. 14:13,14)

Incredible! Lucifer, who had nothing apart from what God had given him, wanted to steal the glory of God, the Most High! And not only did Lucifer rebel against God, but **one third of the angels** who were in heaven chose to turn their backs on the LORD God, and to follow Lucifer in his sin. (See Revelation 12:4)

However God is God, and God knew everything that Lucifer and his angels intended to do. As we already learned in our last study, no one can do anything in secret before God, because God knows everything before it even happens! God saw the sin that was in the heart of Lucifer and in the hearts of the angels who followed him.

So what happened? What did God do? Would God allow Lucifer, who had rebelled against Him, to take His place? Could God condone sin? **Could God live together with the sin of pride and rebellion?** Never! The Writings of the Prophets teach us that God, our God, is holy and cannot look on evil. God cannot tolerate sin. He will not give His glory to another. God is unique; no one can replace Him! Thus, the Scriptures say that **God expelled Lucifer and his evil angels from His holy presence**. Lucifer and those who followed him could no longer live in heaven, in the house of God, because they had sinned by wanting to replace God. That is why God cast out Lucifer and his evil angels. God, who is holy, must judge and punish everyone who rebels against Him.

After Lucifer sinned, his name was changed. He was no longer called Lucifer, *the shining one*, but ***Satan***. Satan means *Adversary*. Lucifer had become God's enemy. And, as you know, Satan and his angels still reject God and all that is good. They reject the Word of God and deny it. Satan fights against God and tries to ruin and hinder God's plans. However, God is the great Judge, and no one can win against Him! "An egg should not wrestle with a rock!" {Wolof Proverb}

The Holy Scriptures tell us that after God expelled Satan and his angels, He created for them **the fires of hell** which are never extinguished. There is a day coming when God will cast into that fire, Satan and his angels, and all who follow them. Thus, it is written: "*They will be tormented day and night for ever and ever.*" (Rev. 20:10)

However the Scriptures teach us that Satan is not yet in the fire (hell). The Word of God says that **Satan is in the world** and fights against God. He is the Destroyer. He wants to destroy God's work. He wants men, whom God created, to perish and go to hell with him. The Word of God says that **most people are under the control of Satan, but they do not know it** because Satan is a **deceiver**. Thus, the Scripture says, "*Satan himself masquerades as an angel of light.*" (2 Cor. 11:14) He tries to deceive men so that they will not pay attention to the Word of God. That is why one of God's prophets wrote, "*Be alert! Your enemy the devil prowls around like a roaring lion looking for someone to devour.*" (1 Pet. 5:8) Beware! The devil wants to destroy you forever!

But praise be to God! He has given us His Word so that we can escape the power of Satan. The Scriptures say, "*You will know the truth, and the truth will set you free!*" (John 8:32) Do you know the truth that can free you from the terrible devices of Satan? Let us not forget: **Satan** is wiser than we are. **But God** is wiser than Satan. **Satan** is stronger than we are. **But God** is stronger than Satan. Do you know the Word of Truth that can deliver you from Satan's power? Many people do not like to hear God's truth. Why do people refuse to listen to the truth? It is because the devil has deceived them. He encourages them to believe what is not true. To be sure, the truth is not always pleasant to hear. "Truth is a hot pepper." {Wolof proverb} However, if you know the truth of God's Word, and believe it, you will be freed from Satan's power. **God's truth** can free people from **Satan's lies**. But you must know the truth and believe it!

Listen to what the Word of God says: "*Dear friends, do **not** believe every spirit, but **test** the spirits to see **whether they are from God**, because many false prophets have gone out into the world.*" (1 John 4:1). "*Do not treat [the words of the prophets] with contempt. Test everything. Hold on to the good. Avoid every kind of evil.*" (1 Thes. 5:20-22) **Do you really know what the prophets of God have written**? Do you understand the Word of Truth? Do you believe it in your heart?

Friends, thank you for listening. We invite you to join us in the next broadcast when we will study together how God created the world. If you have any questions about anything that we have studied today, write to us at *The Way of Righteousness*, etc.…

We look forward to being with you next time. May God bless you as you consider the wonderful promise in His Word that says,

> ***"You will know the truth, and the truth will set you free!"*** (John 8:32)

Lesson 4

How God Made the World

Genesis 1

Peace be with you, listening friends. We greet you in the name of God, the Lord of peace, who wants everyone to understand and submit to the way of righteousness that He has established, and have true peace with Him forever. We are happy to be able to return today to present your program *The Way of Righteousness*.

In our last program, we read what God's prophets have written concerning the **angels and Satan**. We learned that God, in the beginning, created millions of spirits, calling them angels. Among the angels, one was more intelligent and more beautiful than the others. That angel's name was Lucifer. However, there came a day when Lucifer glorified himself in his heart and showed contempt for God, wanting to take God's place. Also, many other angels chose to follow Lucifer in his sin. Thus God, who cannot tolerate those who rebel against Him, expelled Lucifer and the evil angels from His holy presence. Lucifer's name was changed to *Satan*—meaning *Adversary*. After God expelled Satan and his angels, He created for them the fires of hell which are never extinguished. And one day God will throw Satan and all who follow him into that fire. However, Satan has not yet been put into hell. He is in the world, seeking to deceive whomever he can, so that they too will perish.

Today is our fourth lesson in the Writings of the Prophets. In the first book of the Torah, called *Genesis*, in the first chapter, in the first two verses, the Scripture says, "*In the beginning God created the heavens and the earth. Now the earth was formless and empty, darkness was over the surface of the deep.*" (Gen. 1:1,2)

In the beginning, when God first created the heavens and the earth, nothing was living here on the earth. Everything was formless and dark. Only Satan and his angels were here. However, God planned to create humans, who would have the capacity to know God, to love Him and to obey Him forever. However, before He created man, God planned to make a beautiful world where man could live in true prosperity. Today then, we will see **how God created and prepared the world** for the people whom He planned to create.

What do the Scriptures say about how God created the world? It says, "*In six days the LORD made the heavens and the earth, the sea, and all that is in them.*" (Exod. 20:11) Now let us look in the first chapter of the Torah to see what God created in those six days.

1.) Concerning the first day, the Scriptures say,

> "*The Spirit of God was hovering over the waters. And God said, 'Let there be light,' and there was light. God saw that the light was good, and he separated the light from the darkness. God called the light 'day', and the darkness he called 'night'. And there was evening, and there was morning, the first day.*" (Gen. 1:2-5)

Thus, on the first day, God commanded, "Let there be **light** in the darkness." God ordered the earth, which is like a great ball in the heavens, to rotate once every twenty four hours. That is why we have about twelve hours of daylight and twelve hours of night. What a great thing God did on the first day in separating the light from the darkness!

2.) Concerning the second day, the Scriptures say,

> "*And God said, 'Let there be an expanse between the waters to separate water from water.' So God made the expanse and separated the water under the expanse from the water above it. And it was so. God called the expanse 'sky'.*" (Gen. 1:6-8)

On the second day God created **the sky around the earth** which we call *the atmosphere*. The atmosphere is the sky which surrounds the world and contains the air we breathe. That same atmosphere protects everything and everyone from the heat of the sun and many other calamities. Without this special sky that God created on the second day, man could not live on the earth.

3.) On the third day, God created **the oceans, the dry land, and vegetation**. Listen to what the Scriptures say:

> "*And God said, 'Let the water under the sky be gathered to one place, and let dry ground appear.' And it was so. God called the dry ground 'land', and the gathered waters he called 'seas'. And God saw that it was good. Then God said, 'Let the land produce vegetation: seed-bearing plants and trees on the land that bear fruit with seed in it, according to their various kinds.' And it was so...And God saw that it was good. And there was evening, and there was morning–the third day.*" (Gen. 1:9-11,13)

Thus, on the third day, God the Great Designer, created the oceans and the rivers, along with thousands of different types of trees and plants, each with its own fruit and seeds. What a delicious variety of foods God made: mangoes, bananas, coconuts, melons, tomatoes, cabbages, carrots, rice, millet, peanuts, and thousands of other kinds of food! And God said, concerning everything that He had created, "*It is good!*" Everything that God makes and does is good, wonderful and perfect! We have already seen that there is only one thing that God cannot do. God cannot do that which is bad, because **God is good**!

Perhaps some of you are asking, "If God is good, then why is the world full of evil and strife? Why didn't my field produce well this year? Why is my child sick? If God is good, why does evil come forth from man?" Truly, these are important questions, and the Holy Scriptures give us satisfying answers which we will hear in coming lessons. For today however, let us simply keep in mind this important truth: God is good, and as a result, **everything that God created was good**.

Let us take a moment to consider **the goodness of God**. We just heard how He created the trees on the third day. Do you know **why** God created the trees with their fruit? Did God need them? Did He create the trees full of lovely fruit to satisfy His own hunger? No! God the Creator is never hungry and is in need of nothing! Why, then, did God create the trees? The Scriptures show us that, God, in His goodness, created everything **for man**, whom He planned to create on the sixth day.

Do you recognize the goodness of God? Can you taste a mango with its delicious flavor, or smell a flower with its lovely scent and not recognize the goodness of God? Can you see a tree and not thank the One who made it for you? Without trees–life would be horrible! We would not have any firewood with which to cook, or lumber with which to build a boat or a house. We would not have shade in which to relax during the heat of the day, or leaves for tea and medicine. Without trees–life would be impossible. And the trees that God created are only one of thousands of good things that God made for our happiness. God wants us to recognize His goodness. That is what the prophet David wrote in the Psalms saying, "*Taste and see that the LORD is **good**.*" (Psa. 34:8) But now we must continue in today's lesson, before our time runs out.

4.) On the fourth day, God said, "*Let there be lights in the expanse of the sky to separate the day from the night, and let them serve as signs to mark seasons and days and years.*" (Gen. 1:14) God simply gave the order, and **the sun, the moon and the stars** came into existence in the sky. God spoke another word, and the earth began to orbit the sun. He spoke again and the moon began to orbit the earth.

What did God use to create everything in the world? What does the Scripture say? It says:

> "*The universe was formed **at God's command**, so that what is seen was not made out of what was visible.*" (Heb. 11:3) "*In the beginning was **the Word**, and the Word was with God, and the Word was God. He was with God in the*

> *beginning.* **Through him** *all things were made; without him nothing was made that has been made.*" (John 1:1-3)

We have already read that on the first day God simply **spoke** and said, "*Let there be light*" and there was light. On the second day God **said**, "*Let there be an expanse*" and there was an expanse. On the third day God **spoke** again and what He spoke came into existence, and so forth. Now therefore, what did God use to create everything that is in the world? God used nothing except **His Word!** All He did was speak, and what He spoke came to pass. God created everything by His Word. And the Scripture tells that, not only did God **create** everything by His Word, God also **sustains** everything (holds all things together) by **His powerful Word**. It is by the power of God's word that the moon and the stars stay in the sky in their appointed places. It is by the command of God that the sun rises and sets each day at its appointed times. Just think how difficult our lives would be, if we did not know whether the sun would rise tomorrow or not! The Scriptures say, ***"God is faithful!"*** {In Wolof: *God keeps His covenants*} (1 Cor. 1:9) He can be depended upon. He never goes back on His word. He never changes. "*The word of the Lord stands **forever**!*" (1 Pet. 1:25)

5.) On the fifth day, God created thousands and thousands of species of **fish and birds**. The Scriptures say,

> "*And God said, 'Let the water teem with living creatures, and let birds fly above the earth across the expanse of the sky.' So God created the great creatures of the sea and every living and moving thing with which the water teems, according to their kinds, and every winged bird according to its kind. And God saw that it was good. God blessed them and said, 'Be fruitful and increase in number and fill the water in the seas, and let the birds increase on the earth.' And there was evening, and there was morning, the fifth day.*" (Gen. 1:20-23)

6.) Concerning the sixth day, the Scriptures tell us that God created **animals and man**. Unfortunately, we do not have time today to explain this important event. God willing, in the next program, we will carefully examine what the Scriptures say about **how** God created the first man and **why** He created him.

Today we have considered **the goodness of God**. We have read what the prophet of God, David, wrote saying, "***Taste*** *and see that* **the LORD** *is* ***good***!" Friends, have you really **tasted** the goodness of God? Every day we taste and eat various foods that God has provided for us, but have we really "tasted" and recognized God's goodness? If you really want to taste the goodness of God you must listen to and believe the Word of God. The Holy Scripture says: "*Man does not live on bread alone, but on every word that comes from the mouth of God.*" (Matt. 4:4) In our next lesson, we will discover that man is not just a body, but also the owner of a soul. Our souls must feed on the words of God. God's Word is so good and incomparably wonderful, but we must hunger for it. Does your soul hunger for a knowledge of God and His eternal Word as much as your stomach hungers for food? If you hunger for the Word of God in this way, you will discover the Truth that can give you a perfect peace with God here on earth and an incorruptible inheritance in heaven above! We know that this is true, because God Himself promises it, when He says: "*Blessed are those who hunger and thirst for righteousness, for* ***they will be filled****!*" (Matt. 5:6) Amen.

Thank you for your attention. We urge you to join us next time as we see how God created the first man and, even more important, why God created him....

May God bless you and may you never forget His wonderful invitation to you:

> ***"Taste and see that the LORD is good!"*** (Psa. 34:8)

LESSON 5

WHY GOD CREATED MAN

GENESIS 1,2

Peace be with you, listening friends. We greet you in the name of God, the Lord of peace, who wants everyone to understand and submit to the way of righteousness that He has established, and have true peace with Him forever. We are happy to be able to return today to present your program *The Way of Righteousness*.

In our last program, we read **how God created** the heavens, earth, oceans and all they contain. God the LORD made everything in six days using nothing but His Word. We also saw **why God created** the world. He made it for the people whom He planned to create for His own glory. How kind of God to create a beautiful and wonderful place where man could live in true prosperity!

Today we plan to examine the Scriptures and to learn exactly **how** God created the first man. With God's help, we will also seek to understand **why** He created man. In the Torah, in the book of Genesis, in the first chapter, in verse twenty-six, the Word of God says,

> "*The* LORD {"*YHWH*" in Hebrew; *The Everlasting One* in Wolof} *said, 'Let us make man in our image, in our likeness, and let them rule over the fish of the sea and the birds of the air, over the livestock, over all the earth, and over all the creatures that move along the ground.'* ***So God created man in his own image, in the image of God he created him; male and female he created them.***" (Gen. 1:26,27)

We have before us a profound and awesome truth that everyone needs to understand: **God created the first man and woman in His own image**! Think of it! God made man to be like Him! Truly, man is the most important creature among all the creatures that God made. Only man was created in the image of **God**.

Now then, what does the Word of God mean when it says: "*God created man in His own image*"? In chapter two, verse seven, the Scripture says: "*The* LORD *God formed the man from the dust of the ground and breathed into his nostrils the breath of life, and the man became a living being* (soul)." (Gen. 2:7) We notice in this verse that when God created the first man, He created him with two elements: **a body** and **a soul**. Man is not merely a physical being. He has a body **and** a soul. God created man in two steps. Listen again to what the Scriptures say: **One:** "*The LORD God formed the man from the dust of the ground*" **Two**: God "*breathed into his nostrils the breath of life, and the man became a living [soul].*"

From this Scripture we learn that when God created man, He first formed a **body**. Why did God make the body first? He made the body first because it would be the dwelling place into which He would place man's **soul**. Do you know that your body is your house; the temporary "tent" in which "the real you" (your soul) lives? That is what the Scriptures teach, saying, "*The body we have on earth is like **a tent**.*" (2 Cor. 5:1) God created the human body for the soul to dwell in.

With what did God create the first human body? The Scriptures say that the LORD formed it from **the dust of the ground**. In the modern age in which we live, we know that the dust of the earth is composed of about twenty chemicals. Scientists tell us that all twenty of those chemical substances are found in the human body. That is why God's Prophet David wrote in the Psalms, "*The LORD knows how we are formed, he remembers that we are **dust**!*" (Psa. 103:14) Yes, the body is made of dust, but this does not mean that it is worthless! In the human body, there are more than seventy thousand-thousand-thousand-thousand (70 trillion) parts we call *cells*. And all those parts are woven together and designed to function in perfect harmony. **The human body is a miracle!** In our bodies, God has placed the brain, heart, lungs, stomach, liver, intestines, bones, muscles, skin, eyes, ears, nose, mouth, and many, many other amazing parts. Every part "knows" its role. Only God could have created it! That is why the prophet David also wrote, "*LORD, I praise you because **I am fearfully and wonderfully made**; your works are wonderful, I know that full well!*" (Psa. 139:14)

Yes, the human body is an incredible wonder! Yet was it the body that God created in His own image? No! This cannot be, because God is spirit. God did not create the physical form of man in His own image. What then does the Scripture mean when it tells us that "*God created man **in His own image**?*" It means that God created **the soul of man** in His image.

We already observed that when God first created the body of man from the dust of the earth, it was without life. It was only a corpse. Why did God first create the body of man, before He put the soul in it? Why did God, who is all powerful, not create man in one simple step, as He had done with all the other creatures? Perhaps God did it in this way to teach us that man, in himself, has no power over life. Man cannot give himself life and man cannot create anything that lives. **God is the** LORD **of Life**, and in Him alone can life be found. **Life** does not come from man; it is **a gift from God**! The Scripture says, "*The LORD God...breathed into his nostrils the breath of life, and the man became a living being.*"

The body that God had created began to live. Why was it alive? Because God, the LORD of Life, gave it a soul! God breathed His life into the corpse. **The life that was in God, was now in man**. Thus, man became a living being.

So what was it that God created in His own image? **The soul**. God created the soul of man in His own image. Did you know that there are certain characteristics that are found in the Spirit of God which are also found in the spirit of man? Before we conclude today's lesson, we want to consider **three characteristics**, or attributes (features), found in God, which are also found in man. As we think about these three features that we share with God, we can understand better what the Scriptures mean when they say, "*God created man in His own image*." These three features that God placed in the soul of man are as follows:

One: God gave man a **mind (spirit)**, so that he could **know God**.
Two: God gave man a **heart (emotions)**, so that he could **love God**.
Three: God gave man a **will (freedom of choice)**, so that he could **obey God**.

Just as God is the possessor of a mind, and a heart, and a will, so God placed in the soul of man a mind, a heart, and a will. Let us consider what this means.

1.) First, God gave man **a mind** capable of knowing God and thinking as God thinks. God created man with such a powerful mind, because He planned for man to have **close fellowship** with Himself. When we read about the life of the prophet of God, Abraham, we will see that he was called ***the friend of God***. Abraham knew God personally and had a close relationship with Him. However, Abraham is not the only one who has been offered the privilege of being the friend of God. We too can be "**friends of God**." God wants us to have close fellowship with Him. That is why He placed in man's soul a mind (spirit) that can harmonize with the mind (spirit) of God.

Perhaps we can clarify what we are saying with a question. **What distinguishes a man from an animal**? **The mind**. The mind and spirit of man is very different from the mind of an animal. Why is it that animals cannot understand this radio program? Because they do not have the same kind of mind that we have. Listening friends, why are you able to understand our words? Because you share the same kind of mind–a human mind. In a similar way, man's spirit is designed to harmonize (correspond, fellowship) with God's Spirit.

Of course, in saying this, we must not think that our minds and the mind of God are equal in wisdom and knowledge. Never! The wisdom of God is deep, and His knowledge far surpasses the wisdom of man. What we need to understand is this: God has given to man a spirit that has **the possibility of enjoying a meaningful relationship with the Living God**. God does not want you to be like the animals who cannot know Him! An animal has a brain, but cannot **think**

about God. An animal has a mouth, but it cannot **thank God** for the food that He provides for it each day. It has eyes, but it cannot **study the Holy Scriptures**. It has ears, but it cannot **listen to the Word of God**. However, man, whom God created in His image, can come to know the LORD God. Yes, you who are listening today, **you can know God!** You can have a wonderful relationship with your Creator, if you believe and receive the righteous way of salvation that He has established. We will be explaining God's way of salvation clearly in the coming lessons, but what we must understand today is that God has given man a spirit capable of knowing Him.

2.) God placed something else in the soul of man when He created him in His image. **A heart**. God gave man a heart so that he could **love** God. We are not talking about the heart that pumps blood, but about **what you feel in your soul, your emotions, and your thoughts**. We are talking about the very intentions of your heart. God gave the first man the capacity to feel the emotions that God Himself feels. God can love, hate, rejoice, and feel sorrow and compassion. Therefore God placed within the soul of man a heart capable of feeling emotions such as love and hate. God wants man to love what God loves and hate what God hates. **God wants us to love Him with all our heart.** That is why He created man in His own image, and gave him a heart.

3.) There is something else that God gave to man, whom He created in His own image. He placed in the soul of man **a will**. God permits every person **to choose his own path**. God Himself has authority to choose whether He will do something or not. Thus, God created man with the right and responsibility to make important choices for himself. God could have created man so that he would (automatically) do His will, and not have any choice in the matter. However, God gave to man a free will and the responsibility to choose for himself whether to obey God. God did not want to create a mere machine (robot). God did not create man in the image of the sun that rises every day, but has no choice in the matter. The sun fulfils the will of God every day "automatically." That is not how it is with man. **Man is a special creation.** God created us for Himself. God wants us to choose to love Him and worship Him. God has committed a great responsibility to man! Man must choose for himself whether to follow God or Satan, whether he will cherish the Word of God or despise it. God will not force anyone to believe His Word. He will never force us to love Him and obey Him. Love is not love if it is coerced. God allows each of us to choose for ourselves which path we will follow. But, in the end, God will judge everyone who rejects His kingdom, because God created man **for Himself**. That is what the Scriptures say.

We are here on earth **for God**. We are not here for ourselves or for money, or for anything or anyone else. **God created us for Himself; for His pleasure and glory**. God created us with the capacity to **know Him, love Him and obey Him** forever! Yes...**forever**! The Eternal God has given each of us **an eternal soul**. It is God's will that we have **a deep and wonderful relationship** with Him today, tomorrow and throughout eternity. It is for this reason that God created man in His own image.

We bid you farewell with this verse from the Holy Scriptures which reminds us of God's intention for man: "*The* LORD *our* God, *the* LORD *is one*. ***Love the* LORD *your God*** *with* ***all your heart*** *and with* ***all your soul*** *and with* ***all your strength****!*" (Mark 12:29,30)

Thank you for listening. God willing, in our next program we will learn about the first humans, Adam and Eve….

May God bless you and give you insight into the meaning and importance of the greatest commandment ever spoken:

> ***"Love the* LORD *your God with all your heart and with all your soul and with all your strength!"*** (Mark 12:30)

Lesson 6

Adam and Eve and the Garden of Paradise

Genesis 2

Peace be with you, listening friends. We greet you in the name of God, the Lord of peace, who wants everyone to understand and submit to the way of righteousness that He has established, and have true peace with Him forever. We are happy to be able to return today to present your program *The Way of Righteousness*.

We are continuing our study about what happened in the beginning. In today's lesson we will meet **Adam and Eve**, and learn about their first day on earth.

We already read in the Torah: *"In six days the LORD made the heavens and the earth, the sea, and all that is in them."* (Exod. 20:11) We also observed how God created the first man on the sixth day. God created man with **a body and a soul**. God formed the body of man from the dust of the earth, and then He placed in it an eternal soul. God created the soul of man in His own image. This means that God placed in man's soul a special **mind** (spirit), so that man could **know God**. God also gave man a **heart** (emotions) with which he could **love God**. And He entrusted man with a **will** (free choice), so that he would have to choose for himself whether to **obey God** or to disobey Him.

After God finished creating the first man, He had other things to do before He could rest from His work of creation. These works are what we want to learn about today. Let us continue in the Torah, in the second chapter of the book of Genesis. We begin with verse seven. The Scripture says:

> *"The LORD God formed the man from the dust of the ground and breathed into his nostrils the breath of life, and the man became a living being. Now the LORD* ***God had planted a garden in the east, in Eden; and there he put the man he had formed****."* (Gen. 2:7,8)

The Scriptures relate to us how God prepared a delightful garden for the man whom He had created. The garden was called **Eden** {Lit. *delight*} or ***the Garden of***

Paradise. Some think that this garden in which God placed the first man was in heaven. However the Scriptures show us that it was **located here on earth**, in the east, in Eden, probably where the country of Iraq is today. The Writings of God's prophets **never confuse the Garden of Paradise** (Eden) which was on the earth, **and the heavenly Paradise** which is above, in the presence of God.

In the verses that follow, the Scripture says:

> *"The LORD God made all kinds of trees grow out of the ground, trees that were pleasing to the eye and good for food. In the middle of the garden were the tree of life and the tree of the knowledge of good and evil. A river watering the garden flowed from Eden; from there it was separated into four headwaters.... The LORD God took the man [that is* ***Adam****] and put him in the Garden of Eden to work it and take care of it."* (Gen. 2:9,10,15)

Thus we see that God made for the first man, Adam, a lovely place where he could live in true prosperity. God placed him in a luscious garden full of trees that produced fruit beautiful to behold and delicious to eat. In this enchanting place, **everything was perfect and wonderful**. Adam's senses were alive; his eyes took in the beauty, his ears took in the melody of birds singing in the trees, and his senses absorbed the fragrance of the flowers that permeated the garden. God gave Adam everything for his enjoyment. We also read how God, in His goodness, entrusted Adam with **a satisfying task**: to take care of the garden, so that he would be happily occupied.

The most wonderful thing that took place in Eden, was that **God Himself would come to the garden** in the cool of the evening so that He might talk with the man whom He had created in His own image. (See Gen. 3:8) Why did God come visit Adam? He visited Adam, because, as we have already learned, **God created man for fellowship**. God's intention was that He and humans might fellowship together, talk together, rejoice together, and spend eternity together with unified minds and hearts. Yes, God wanted man {Lit. *humans*} to grow in a deep and wonderful relationship with Him forever.

Now there is something else we need to know about the garden into which God placed the first man. In the middle of the garden, God planted two very important trees. One was called *the tree of life*, and the other *the tree of the knowledge of good and evil.* God placed **the tree of life** in the garden to remind Adam that He intended for man to share His eternal life. As for **the tree of the knowledge of good and evil**, God placed it in the middle of the garden to test Adam. Listen to what the Scriptures say: "*And the LORD God commanded the man, "***You are free to eat** *from any tree in the garden; but* **you must not eat** *from the tree of the knowledge of good and evil, for [in the day that] you eat of it you will surely die."* (Gen. 2:16,17)

Why did God forbid Adam to eat of the tree of the knowledge of good and evil? Is God stingy? No, He is not stingy! In fact, one of His names is "*the Generous One!*" {James 1:5 in Wolof} God told Adam, "You can eat of every tree …except one." Was that a difficult command? No, it was not. God, in His grace, gave Adam everything he needed to be happy. He did not withhold any good thing from him. However, God, in His perfect plan, placed before Adam **a simple test**, so that Adam might have the opportunity to show God that he loved Him enough to obey His command. As the Lord God says in His Word: "*If anyone loves me, he will obey my [word] …He who does not love me will not obey my [word].*" (John 14:23,24) God wanted to test Adam's love and loyalty {Lit. in Wolof: *to see where his heart was*}. That is why He gave him this simple command. God did not create a mechanical man (robot). God created a man with a mind, a heart, and a free will so that he could choose for himself to love and obey God.

What did God tell Adam would happen to him if he ate of the forbidden tree? Let us reread the Scriptures. God said, "*You must not eat from the tree of the knowledge of good and evil, for [in the day that] you eat of it* ***you will surely die****!*" Thus, God informed Adam that disobedience to His command would produce **death**. God loved the man He had created; thus He warned him in unmistakable words, saying: Adam, if you disobey me, you will die because my holy law requires the death of "*the soul that sins.*" (Ezek. 18:20)

Perhaps someone is asking: **What is sin?** The Scriptures say: "*Sin is* ***lawlessness***." (1 John 3:4) "***All wrongdoing*** *is sin.*" (1 John 5:17) "*Anyone…who knows the* **good** *he ought to do and* **doesn't do it**, *sins.*" (Jam. 4:17) Sin is going your "*own way.*" (Isa. 53:6) Sin is anything that does not agree with God. **What will happen to those who sin against God?** The Word of God says, "*The soul that sins must die!*" (Ezek. 18:20). And in another verse, it says, "*the wages of sin is* ***death***." (Rom. 6:23) **What is death?** Some think that to die is to cease existing; everything is finished and you no longer know anything. But if we rely on the Writings of the Prophets, we will see that this is not what death is. In the Holy Scriptures, in the Hebrew language in which it was written, death signifies ***separation***. Death is separation from life.

When God said to Adam: "If you eat of the tree of the knowledge of good and evil you will surely die," this is what He was saying: Adam, if you eat of the tree which I have prohibited, in that day you will die, that is: you will be **separated from Me**. If you disobey me you can no longer have a close relationship with me. I am holy and I cannot tolerate sin or those who reject my way. I expelled Lucifer and his angels when they sinned, and I will expel you too if you sin. Also, if you eat of the fruit of the forbidden tree, **your body** will begin to grow old and, eventually, it will die, that is: your soul will leave your body. And that is not all. If you disobey me, not only will your body die, but **your soul** will go to the place created for Satan and his angels. And there you will be separated from me for ever and ever!

Thus, we see that **sin produces three horrible separations. First,** your soul is **separated from God here on earth**. That is, you have no relationship with God the Holy One because of the sin in your heart. **Second,** your soul will be **separated from your body** on the day you die. That is, your body will die and your soul will meet God for judgment. **Third,** your **soul and body will be separated from God forever** in the lake of fire.

Based on the authority of the Word of God, what is death? In short, **death is separation from the God of Life**. Sin separates man from God, the source of true life. God is holy and cannot coexist with sin. The soul that sins is **like a branch** of a tree that is cut off and cast away. What happens when a branch is no longer part of the tree? A branch that is cut off, is it alive? No, it is dead! The leaves do not become instantly dry, but they have begun to die. Similarly, if you have not received the way of forgiveness of sin which God has provided, you may think that you are alive, but the Scriptures of the Prophets say that, before God, you are "***dead*** *in your transgressions and sins*." (Eph. 2:1) ***"Your iniquities have separated you from your God; your sins have hidden His face from you."*** (Isa. 59:2) You are "***like a branch that is thrown away and withers****; such branches are picked up, thrown into the fire and burned*." (John 15:6)

The branch that is no longer connected to the tree cannot produce fruit. That is how a sinner is before God. He cannot produce anything pleasing to God, because he has **no relationship with God,** who is the "True Tree," **the Source of true life**. Sinners can only expect God's righteous judgment. However, in the Writings of the Prophets, God has declared how we can be made righteous before Him and know for sure that our sins are removed. It is this that we will be considering in coming lessons.

Before we close, we would like to read what is found in the remainder of this chapter. The Scriptures tell us how God created **the first woman**. Listen:

> "*The* LORD *God said, 'It is not good for the man to be alone. I will make a helper suitable for him.' So the* LORD *God caused the man to fall into a deep sleep; and while he was sleeping, he took one of the man's ribs and closed up the place with flesh. Then the* LORD *God made a woman from the rib he had taken out of the man, and he brought her to the man. The man said, 'This is now bone of my bones and flesh of my flesh; she shall be called 'woman', for she was taken out of man.' For this reason a man will leave his father and mother and be united to his wife, and they will become one flesh. The man and his wife were both naked, and they felt no shame*." (Gen. 2:18,21-25)

Thus, we discover that **marriage** was designed by God. God created one man and one woman so that they could love each other, share their lives together, and have a happy family that glorifies God. God, who loved Adam and wanted him to be perfectly happy, gave him a very wonderful gift: **a wife!** God wanted Adam to cherish his wife, provide for her, and love her as he loved himself. Even more important, God wanted the man and the woman to enjoy a deep relationship with Himself–to know Him, love Him and obey Him forever. (See Ephesians 5:21-33; 6:1-4)

Thus, God finished His work of creation. The Scriptures says:

> "*God saw all that he had made, and it was* ***very good****. And there was evening, and there was morning, the sixth day. Thus, the heavens and the earth were completed in all their vast array. By the seventh day God had finished the work he had been doing; so* ***on the seventh day he rested from all his work****. And God blessed the seventh day and made it holy, because on it he rested from all the work of creating that he had done.*" (Gen. 1:31-2:3)

Why did God rest on the seventh day? Was it because He was tired? No, God is never tired! The Scriptures say that God rested because He had "***finished the work****!*" Everything was **perfect**. That is why God rested (ceased) from His work on the seventh day. That is also why there are seven days in a week.

Friends, thank you for listening. Next time, God willing, we will learn how sin entered the world....

God bless you as you ponder this declaration from His Word:

> ***"The wages of sin is death, but the gift of God is eternal life...!"*** (Rom. 6:23a)

Lesson 7

How Sin Entered the World

Genesis 3

Peace be with you, listening friends. We greet you in the name of God, the Lord of peace, who wants everyone to understand and submit to the way of righteousness that He has established, and have true peace with Him forever. We are happy to be able to return today to present your program *The Way of Righteousness.*

In the past two studies, we learned how God created the first two people. The Scripture says, "*God created man in his own image,* ***in the image of God*** *he created him; male and female he created them.*" (Gen. 1:27) Within the soul of the man and the woman, God placed a spirit capable of knowing God, and a heart capable of loving Him. God also entrusted them with a free will, so that they could choose for themselves whether to obey Him or not. We also saw that God placed man in the Garden of Paradise, a delightful garden He had prepared on the earth in a place called *Eden*. God gave the first man, **Adam**, and the first woman, **Eve**, everything they needed to live in peace and true prosperity. **God wanted people to know Him, love Him, and worship Him forever.**

Thus, we saw that God, in keeping with His perfect plan, placed **a simple test** before the man whom He had created. In the middle of the garden, God planted **the tree of the knowledge of good and evil**, and then commanded the man, saying, "*You are free to eat from any tree in the garden; but you must* ***not eat*** *from the tree of the knowledge of good and evil, for [in the day that] you eat of it you will surely die.*" (Gen. 2:16)

Why did God test Adam in this way? God wanted to show the condition of Adam's heart. God did not test Adam to cause him to sin, but to bless and strengthen him. The man whom God created had no faults and was without sin, but that does not mean he possessed a perfect love or a mature character. God placed a test before Adam, **to test his love**. If Adam stood the test and obeyed God, he would prove that he loved God in his heart. Also, if Adam stood the test and refused to sin, that test would strengthen him, because the Scriptures say that "*patience in times of trial produces character.*" (Rom. 5:4)

Today then, we have come to the third chapter in the book of Genesis. This is the chapter which shows us **how sin entered the world**. If we are familiar with the teaching of this chapter, then we know why the heart of man is crooked and evil, and why the world is full of suffering and pain.

We have already seen that, in the beginning, Adam and Eve were in the Garden of Paradise where they were perfectly satisfied and had everything for their enjoyment. The best thing of all, was that **the Lord God visited the garden each day**, in the cool of the evening, so that He might talk with Adam and Eve. God visited them because He wanted to have a meaningful and wonderful relationship with them.

However, the Scriptures tell us that **someone else was also in the garden**. Do you know who it was? It was Satan, God's adversary, **the devil**. When God created the world and all that it contains, Satan was watching. When God gave Adam the commandment not to eat of the tree of the knowledge of good and evil, Satan was listening. And he did not stop at simply watching and listening, but he was also **weaving a plan** to spoil God's wonderful works. Satan planned to tempt man whom God had created so that he would disobey God, commit sin, be separated from God and perish! As for God, He knew all that Satan planned to do, but Adam and Eve knew nothing about it.

One day, when Adam and Eve were standing near the forbidden tree, Satan came as a **serpent**, and began to speak with them. Thus, the Scripture says: "*Now the serpent was more crafty than any of the wild animals the* LORD *God had made. He said to the woman, 'Did God really say: You must not eat from any tree in the garden'?*" (Gen. 3:1)

Let us pause here briefly. Why did Satan appear as a serpent? The Scripture gives us the answer when it says: "*the serpent was* ***more crafty*** *than any of the wild animals the* LORD *God had made.*" Satan is the tempter, and therefore presented himself as one who is very wise. Satan did not come to Adam and Eve in the form of a huge red dragon saying, "Peace be on you, Adam and Eve. I am the devil, the enemy of God! I have come today to tempt you to turn your back on God, the Lord of life, so that you might perish forever!" Satan did not operate like that! How did he appear to them then? As a beautiful and wise creature. He chose to speak to them through a serpent, because at that time, before sin entered the world, the serpent was the craftiest of all the animals.

Satan is still like that. He is crafty. He habitually presents what he has to offer as a good thing. The Scriptures say: "*Satan himself masquerades as an* ***angel of light***." (2 Cor. 11:14) Consequently, God warns us in His Word, saying, "*Watch out for false prophets. They come to you in sheep's clothing, but inwardly they are ferocious wolves.*" (Matt. 7:15) **Satan is a deceiver.** That is why he appeared to Adam and Eve as a wise serpent. That is also why he preferred to talk with Eve, instead of with Adam himself, because he hoped that it would be easier to tempt

Eve than Adam. Satan knew that God had given the commandment about the tree to Adam, before He created Eve. However, Eve also knew about God's commandment. The devil is highly intelligent and he knew exactly what he wanted to achieve. Satan thought if he could convince the woman to eat of the tree of the knowledge of good and evil, perhaps Adam would follow her in disobeying God.

Thus, the Scriptures say: "*The serpent said to the woman, "Did God really say, 'You must not eat from any tree in the garden?'*" (Gen. 3:1) Did you hear what Satan said to Eve? He said, "*Did God really say, 'You must not eat from any tree in the garden?'*" Do you see what Satan was trying to do? He was attempting **to plant doubt** in the mind of Eve concerning the sure Word of God. That is why he said, "***Did*** *God...say?" Did God* ***really*** *say ...?*" Satan still uses this method. He **fights against the Word of Truth**, because he knows that the Word of God has the power to disarm him and discredit his lies. Satan knows that the truth dispels lies, as light dispels darkness.

Now let us listen to the rest of the conversation between the woman and the devil. The Scripture says:

> "*The woman said to the serpent, 'We may eat fruit from the trees in the garden, but God has said, 'You must not eat fruit from the tree that is in the middle of the garden, and you must not touch it, or you will die.'* ***'You will not surely die****,' the serpent said to the woman. 'For God knows that when you eat of it your eyes will be opened, and you will be like God, knowing good and evil.'*" (Gen. 3:2-5)

This is amazing! What did God say would happen to Adam and Eve if they ate of the forbidden tree? He said, "*You* ***will*** *die!*" What did Satan say? He said: "*You* ***will not*** *die!*" Thus, Satan did not stop at merely casting doubt upon God's Word, but he came right out and **denied it**! What do you think about this? Who was speaking the truth, God or Satan? The Holy Scriptures say that God is the True One and cannot lie. As for Satan, he does not hold to the truth, "*for there is no truth in him. When he lies, he speaks* ***his native language****, for he is* ***a liar*** *and* ***the father of lies***." (John 8:44)

However, we must also remember that Satan is not only **a liar**. He is also **a deceiver**. He is crafty; he takes what is **not true** and **mixes it** with what is **true**. We can see that in what Satan said to Eve and Adam, "*When you eat of [this tree] your eyes will be opened, and you will be like God, knowing good and evil.*" When Satan said, "*You will be like God!*" that was **a lie**, because the one who sins is not like God, but like Satan. But when Satan said, "*You will know good and evil*" he was speaking **the truth**, because after Adam and Eve sinned they came to know what evil is. However, Satan did not tell them of the bitterness that such knowledge would bring into their lives. God said, "*If you eat of the tree* ***you will surely***

die! But Satan said, "*If you eat of the tree* ***you will not die!***" Satan is a liar. That is why when God said, "*You will die!*" Satan denied it, saying, "*You will not die!*"

Now the moment had come for Adam and Eve to **choose between the Word of God and the word of Satan**. The choice before them was this: Would they believe the words of God or the words of Satan? Would they accept the truth or the lie? Would they follow the Lord of Light or the Lord of darkness?

Let us read on to see the choice they made. The Scriptures say: "*When the woman saw that the fruit of the tree was good for food and pleasing to the eye, and also desirable for gaining wisdom,* ***she took some and ate it****. She also gave some to her husband, who was with her,* ***and he ate it****.*" (Gen. 3:6)

Amazing! God created man in His own image so that he could know Him, love Him and obey Him forever. But what did man do? Did he love God enough to obey His command? No! **He chose to disobey the God of love, and to follow Satan, the enemy of God and man!**

What a sad day this was! Our ancestors, Adam and Eve, turned their backs on the LORD God by eating the fruit of the tree that He had forbidden. The Wolofs say: "An epidemic is not confined to the one from whom it originates!" In the same way, the Word of God says: "*Sin entered the world through* ***one man****, and death through sin, and in this way* ***death came to all men****, because all sinned!*" (Rom. 5:12) Whether we like it or not, that is the way it is!

"The leaping gazelle doesn't produce burrowing offspring." {Wolof proverb; English equiv. "Like father, like son."} You and I, and all people, take after Adam. We are born sinners and must die, because **we come from Adam**. The first man who disobeyed God's commandment is our forefather and **we are just like him**. Who among us can say that we have never disobeyed the commandments of God? Not a single one of us! So where did we inherit this nature in us that disobeys God's commandments? From Adam. Like a horrible contagious disease, **the sin that was in Adam has spread to us all**. Truly, "an epidemic is not confined to the one from whom it originates!"

However, all hope is not lost, because the Word of God also declares: "*Just as the result of* ***one trespass*** *was* ***condemnation*** *for all men, so also the result of* ***one act of righteousness*** *was* ***justification*** *that brings life for all men.*" (Rom. 5:18) We cannot look into it today, but in future lessons we will study the righteous way of salvation that God has established by which sinners might come back to God.

Friends, this has been your program *The Way of Righteousness*. Next time, we plan to continue in this important chapter to see what happened after Adam and Eve strayed from the way of righteousness, and followed the way of unrighteousness....God bless you as you remember this foundational truth:

> ***"Sin entered the world through one man, and death through sin, and in this way death came to all men, because all sinned!"*** (Rom. 5:12)

Lesson 8

What Adam's Sin Produced

Genesis 3

Peace be with you, listening friends. We greet you in the name of God, the Lord of peace, who wants everyone to understand and submit to the way of righteousness that He has established, and have true peace with Him forever. We are happy to be able to return today to present your program *The Way of Righteousness*.

In our study in the Torah, we learned that the LORD God created the first people in His own image. We also learned why God created them. God wanted them to love Him with all their minds, with all their hearts, and with all their strength, and, as a result, to enjoy a wonderful and profound relationship with Him forever.

Thus, we saw how God placed before Adam **a simple test**, to see if he loved God enough to obey Him. Before the first woman was created, God had commanded Adam: "*You are free to eat from any tree in the garden; but you must not eat from the tree of the knowledge of good and evil, for [in the day that] you eat of it you will surely die.*" (Gen. 2:16,17) Thus God tested Adam and warned him that the punishment for disobedience would be death, and separation from Him. God loved Adam and wanted him to enjoy fellowship with Him forever. However, in our last program, we read that **Adam and Eve** listened to the devil and **disobeyed God** by eating from the tree that God had forbidden.

Today then, we plan to continue our study in the Torah, in the third chapter of the book of Genesis, to see **what happened after Eve and Adam sinned against God**. In verse seven, the Scripture says: "**Then** *the eyes of both of them were opened, and they realized that they were naked; so they sewed fig leaves together and made coverings for themselves.*" (Gen. 3:7)

What is the first thing that Adam and Eve did after they disobeyed God? **They tried to cover their shame and guilt!** We already learned that before Adam and Eve ate from the tree of the knowledge of good and evil, they "*were both naked, and they felt no shame.*" (Gen. 2:25) But now their thoughts concerning their bodies had changed. Now they felt guilty and shameful before the Holy One who must judge them. Thus, in an attempt to hide their shame, they wove together leaves from a fig tree, and covered their naked bodies. However, the covering of leaves they put on their bodies did nothing to erase the guilt in their hearts.

Next, the Scripture says: "*Then the man and his wife heard the sound of the LORD God as he was walking in the garden in the cool of the day, and they hid from the LORD God among the trees of the garden.*" (Gen. 3:8) How different things were for Adam and Eve after they sinned! Before they disobeyed God, they rejoiced whenever the LORD God came into the garden to talk to them. However, now when they heard Him approaching, they trembled with **fear and shame**, and **attempted to hide from God** among the trees of the garden! Why was Adam afraid and hiding? That is not difficult to figure out. If someone is stealing from another's field, what will he do if he hears the voice of the owner of the field? He will try to hide. In the same way, Adam, who had taken what God had forbidden, was trying to hide. Adam knew very well that he had transgressed against God.

Should Adam have been afraid after he had disobeyed God's command? Absolutely! Why? Because God had clearly said to him, "*In the day that you eat of the tree of the knowledge of good and evil, **you will surely die**!*" Would God carry out His word? Would Adam really die? What do you think? **Would God really punish the people He had created?** Wolofs say that one should not answer a question with another question, but we can best answer this question with another question. **What did the LORD do to Lucifer, that is Satan, after he rejected God's rule over him?** Did God acquit Satan and the angels who sinned? No, He did not acquit them! God expelled them from His holy presence. And not only that, He also created for them the eternal fire! Like Satan, Adam had rejected God's rule over him. Could God just say, "It's no big deal!" and let Adam go free without judging him? Never! **God is holy and He must judge sin!** Leonardo da Vinci, one of the most brilliant men that ever lived, said, "He who does not punish evil, commands it to be done!" God can never approve evil. He must punish it. The prophet Habakkuk wrote: "*My God, my Holy One…your eyes are too pure to look on evil; you cannot tolerate wrong!*" (Hab. 1:12,13) Yes, "*The LORD will judge His people! It is a dreadful thing to fall into the hands of the living God!*" (Heb. 10:30,31) God's holy nature requires that He judge and punish every sin. Therefore, it was necessary that He judge Adam and Eve because of their sin. That is why in the next verse we read: "*But the LORD God called to the man, 'Where are you?'*" (Gen. 3:9)

What did God do after Adam sinned? God went seeking after Adam, calling out to him, ***"Where are you?"*** Did Adam go looking for God? No! He was trying to hide from God! Why did God call out to Adam? Didn't He know where Adam was? God, who sees and knows everything, knew exactly where Adam was hiding! God called out to Adam, because He wanted Adam to recognize and confess his sin before Him. God still loved Adam although he had disobeyed Him.

What did Adam reply when God asked, "*Where are you?*" The Scriptures say:

> "*[Adam] answered, 'I heard you in the garden, and I was afraid because I was naked; so I hid.' And the* LORD *God said, 'Who told you that you were naked? Have you eaten from the tree from which I commanded you not to eat?' [Adam] said, 'The woman you put here with me, she gave me some fruit from the tree, and I ate it.' Then the* LORD *God said to the woman, 'What is this you have done?' The woman said, 'The serpent deceived me, and I ate.'*" (Gen. 3:10-13)

Did you hear how Adam and Eve answered God? **Each tried to blame someone else.** Adam accused both God and Eve, saying: It's not my fault! The woman **you** gave me—it's **her** fault! As for Eve, she blamed the serpent saying, Don't blame me—the **serpent** deceived me! However, God who knows the heart of man, knew that they were **both guilty**. God did not make them eat the fruit of the tree. Satan also did not make them eat it. Satan can tempt and deceive people, but he cannot force anyone to sin. Satan deceived Eve, but what she did was still sin before God. As for Adam, the Scripture tells us that he was not deceived. (1 Tim. 2:14) He consciously chose to go his own way. Adam knew exactly what God had commanded, but he chose to stray from the way of righteousness, and follow the way of unrighteousness. And he didn't stop with disobeying God, but added sin to his sin by trying to put the blame on others.

To this day, people still attempt to blame others for their transgressions, but God knows the truth. Through the Holy Scriptures, God is speaking to people, saying: **Where are you?** Answer me! What have you done? Why do you refuse to believe and obey my Word? Why do you despise my goodness? Why do you try to blame others for your own sin? "'*As surely as I live,' says the* LORD*, 'Every knee will bow before me; every tongue will confess to God.' So then, each of us will give an account of himself to God.*"(Rom. 14:11,12)

Let us now continue in the chapter to see how God judged the serpent, Satan, Eve and Adam. The Scriptures say:

> "*So the* LORD *God said to the* ***serpent****, 'Because you have done this, Cursed are you above all the livestock and all the wild animals! You will crawl on your belly and you will eat dust all the days of your life. And I will put enmity between you and the woman, and between your offspring and hers: He will crush your head and you will strike His heel.' To the* ***woman*** *He said, 'I will greatly increase your pains in childbearing; with pain you will give birth to children. Your desire will be for your husband, and he will rule over you.' To* **Adam** *he said, 'Because you listened to your wife and ate from the tree about which I commanded you: You must not eat of it, Cursed is the ground because of you; through painful toil you will eat of it all the days of your life. It will produce thorns and thistles for you,*

> *and you will eat the plants of the field. By the sweat of your brow you will eat your food until you return to the ground, since from it you were taken; for dust you are and to dust you will return.'"* (Gen. 3:14-19)

Do you see what their sin produced? It produced sorrow and pain, thorns and thistles, toil and sweat, sickness and death. Yes, "*the wages of sin is* ***death****!*" (Rom. 6:23) What did God say would happen to Adam and Eve if they ate of the forbidden tree? He said, "**In the day** that you eat of it you will surely **die**." Were Adam and Eve buried on the day they ate it? No. But did they die on that day? Indeed they did! On that very day, **Adam and Eve died in their souls**, because they no longer had a relationship with God.

As we have already learned, **death is *separation from God*.** When Adam and Eve disobeyed God, they separated themselves from God, **the Source of Life.** When they chose to believe the devil and go along with him, they forfeited their friendship with God and lost their share in God's life. They had become God's enemies because they had taken sides with Satan, God's adversary. Their relationship with God had died. To illustrate, if you have an enemy and your friend takes sides with him, then is it not true that your friend has become your enemy? Your relationship with your friend has died. As we say: "Your friend's enemy is your enemy." {Wolof Proverb} In the same way, whoever obeys Satan is the enemy of God. Sin separates man from God.

Before we conclude today, there is something we must understand and remember. It is this: We are all born into this world as those who are "***dead*** *in…transgressions and sins*" (Eph. 2:1) and "***separated*** *from the life of God.*" (Eph. 4:18) We may not like this, but that is what the Word of God says. The day that Adam disobeyed God, he became a **sinner.** Adam, who sinned, is the father of the human race. Thus, the result of Adam's sin is that **all of his descendants are sinners**. "A rat only begets that which digs." {Wolof proverb similar to: "The apple doesn't fall far from the tree."} Also, Adam's sin caused him to be **separated from God**. Adam, who rejected God's rule over him, is the father of all who live. The result is that **all of Adam's descendants are born separated from God**. As the (Wolof) proverb says: "An epidemic is not confined to the one from whom it originates!" This is exactly what the Word of God declares, when it says: "*Sin entered the world through one man, and death through sin, and in this way* ***death came to all men, because all sinned****!*" (Rom. 5:12)

Our forefather Adam, who separated himself from God, is **like a branch cut from a tree**. What happens if the branch is no longer united to the tree? It dries up and dies. And what happens to the branches which are part of the branch that has been cut off? Are they alive? No, they are also dead, because they belong to the dry branch. In the same way, all **the children of Adam are like the small branches** of the branch that has been cut off. Because of his sin, Adam is like the dry branch, and we are one with him. The sin of our ancestor Adam has affected all of us. We all share his character and condemnation.

The Prophet David wrote in the Psalms: "*Surely I was* ***sinful at birth****, sinful from the time my mother conceived me*." (Psa. 51:5) Sin is much like AIDS—a dreadful disease which has spread throughout the world. Once AIDS enters a person's body, it will never leave. The person who has AIDS can spread it to his children. AIDS is a killer and man does not yet have a cure for it. Sin is like that. It is a terrible calamity that has spread throughout the earth. **Sin is a killer**, causing man to perish forever, and **man, in himself, has no remedy for it**.

However, we are praising God today with happy hearts, because God Himself has provided a remedy to save us from the penalty of sin and from the power of sin. However, we must believe God's remedy and receive it. God willing, in our next program, we will see how God gave Adam and Eve, and all their descendants, a wonderful promise concerning a mighty Savior who would come into the world to deliver sinners from sin, Satan and hell.

Thank you for listening....

God bless you as you think about these words penned by the prophet David:

> ***"Surely I was sinful at birth, sinful from the time my mother conceived me."*** (Psa. 51:5)

Lesson 9

The Wonderful Promise

Genesis 3

Peace be with you, listening friends. We greet you in the name of God, the Lord of peace, who wants everyone to understand and submit to the way of righteousness that He has established, and have true peace with Him forever. We are happy to be able to return today to present your program *The Way of Righteousness*.

In our last program, we saw how Adam and Eve strayed from the way of God by eating fruit from the tree that God had forbidden. Thus, man, whom God created in His own image, chose to follow Satan, the enemy of God. Before Adam and Eve sinned, they rejoiced whenever God came to the garden to talk with them, but now, when they heard the voice of God, they were **afraid and ashamed and tried to hide from God** among the trees of the garden! However, God pursued Adam and Eve, spoke with them, and declared to them what their **sin** would bring into the world: trouble and suffering, thorns and thistles, sickness and **death**.

Consequently, from that day until today, the shadow of death hangs over Adam's descendants. All of Adam's children are conceived in sin and born with an evil nature. Whether we like it or not, **we all share the character of our forefather, Adam**. "A rat only begets that which digs." It is because of Adam's sin that we are all born sinners. Truly, "an epidemic is not confined to the one from whom it originates!" {Wolof proverbs} And just as **Adam's sin** separated him from God, so has **our sin** separated us from God. That is what the Scriptures say,

> "*Sin entered the world through one man, and death through sin, and in this way death came to all men, because all sinned. (Rom. 5:12)* "*All have sinned and fall short of the glory of God.*" (Rom. 3:23) "*Your iniquities have separated you from your God; your sins have hidden His face from you.*" (Isa. 59:2)

This message is not pleasant to hear, but that is the way it is. "Truth is a hot pepper." {Wolof proverb}

Thus, we see how **Adam's one sin separated the whole human race from God**. On the day that Adam disobeyed God, Adam (and the whole human race yet to be born) left the kingdom of light and entered the kingdom of darkness. They no longer had any share in the Kingdom of God. Because of their sin, their portion was **with Satan**, who had taken them as his captives and slaves. Now, they couldn't hope for anything in this life, except slavery to sin and fear of death–and in the hereafter, endless punishment in the eternal fire!

If the Scriptures ended here, we could only close the book and weep bitterly like someone lost at sea, with no hope of rescue. If God had not opened a way of salvation to save the children of Adam, we would be doomed forever! But blessed be the LORD our God, the Scriptures of the Prophets do not end with the story of Adam's sin. **God, who is great in mercy, has opened for the children of Adam a door of salvation**! Thus, the Word of God says,

> "*Where sin increased, [God's] grace increased all the more.*" (Rom. 5:20) "*Do not be afraid, because I bring you good news of great joy that will be for all the people!*" (Luke 2:10) "*For the grace of God that brings salvation has appeared to all men!*" (Tit. 2:11)

As we have already learned, God is holy and, therefore must judge sinners. God is righteous and cannot merely "forget" sin. He must punish every sin. The penalty for sin is death and eternal separation from God. God never changes and the penalty of sin never changes. However, today, we will begin to read in the Scriptures how God, the Holy One, designed {Lit. *wove*} **a plan to deliver sinners** from the penalty of sin. Thus, we will learn that God is not only the Holy One, but He is also the Merciful One! **God, our Judge, wants to become our Savior!**

Today we will see how, on the day that Adam and Eve sinned, God began to make known His wonderful plan to save sinners. Let us continue now in the Torah, in the book of Genesis, so that we might learn about this Good News. We are reading in chapter 3, verse 15: God said to Satan who was in the serpent, ***"I will put enmity between you and the woman, and between your offspring and hers; he will crush your head, and you will strike his heel."***

This difficult verse contains many profound and important truths which God's prophets would later explain in detail. The contents of this verse, can be summarized like this: **God was beginning to make known His plan to bring into the world a Savior** {or *Deliverer*} who would redeem the children of Adam from the dominion of Satan. **This is the first verse that mentions the coming of the holy Redeemer** {or *Mediator*}. In this verse, let us consider four truths concerning the Redeemer whom God promised to send.

1.) The first truth is this: God was announcing how this Redeemer would be **born of a woman only**, that is, a virgin. All of us have a male and a female parent. However, the Redeemer who was to come, would be born only of a woman, by the power of God. He would not have an earthly father. The Savior of the world could not come from Adam, because all of Adam's descendants are stained by sin. The Savior of sinners had to be without sin. He had to come forth from God, from heaven. Thus, the first thing we may learn from this verse is this: God promised a holy Redeemer who would be the offspring of a woman, but not the offspring of a man.

2.) There is something else that God announced on the day that Adam and Eve sinned. Concerning the promised Redeemer, God said to Satan: "You will strike his heel." Thus, God began to announce how **Satan would torment the Savior** that God would send from heaven. In coming lessons, we will see that the prophets foretold how Satan would incite men to persecute, torture and kill the Redeemer. A stricken Redeemer would be part of God's plan. In order to bring us back to God, the Savior of the world would have to die as a sacrifice for sin; the Righteous One dying for us, the unrighteous. He would willingly lay down His life to pay sin's penalty: death.

3.) The third truth concerning the Redeemer was that God told Satan, who was in the serpent, that "he (the Redeemer) would crush his (Satan's) head." That was bad news for Satan, but good news for whoever wants to be delivered from the power of Satan, sin and hell! Thus, God began to announce that **the Redeemer would, in the end, defeat the devil** and set free the children of Adam who had become slaves of sin.

4.) Finally, God began to announce that there would be **two lines (groups) of people** in the world: The people of Satan and the people of God. The people of Satan are those who refuse to believe the Word of God. The people of God are those who believe God's Word and put their trust in the promised Redeemer. (John 1:9-13)

Thus, on the day that Adam and Eve sinned, God began to announce His wondrous plan to redeem sinners. In coming programs, little by little, we will see how all of God's prophets announced the coming of a holy Savior who would free sinners from the hand of the devil. If what we have just taught is not yet clear in your mind, do not worry, because as we progress in our chronological study, things will become clearer. Remember the (Wolof) proverb which says: "A water pail will find the person who waits diligently at the well." Are you waiting at the "well" of the Word of God? Good! God says: "*If you look for [the truth] as for silver, and search for it as for hidden treasure...then you will...find the knowledge of God!*" (Prov. 2:4,5)

Now then, let us finish reading the third chapter of the first book of the Torah. The Scriptures say:

"*The LORD God made garments of skin for Adam and his wife and clothed them.*

> *And the* LORD *God said, 'The man has now become like one of us, knowing good and evil. He must not be allowed to reach out his hand and take also from the tree of life and eat, and live forever.' So the* LORD *God banished [Adam] from the Garden of Eden to work the ground from which he had been taken. After he drove the man out, he placed on the east side of the Garden of Eden cherubim and a flaming sword flashing back and forth to guard the way to the tree of life."* (Gen. 3:21-24)

That is where the third chapter ends. Before we conclude today, let us consider some important truths contained in these verses.

The Scriptures say: "*The* LORD *God made garments of skin for Adam and his wife and clothed them.*" Do you remember what Adam and Eve did after they ate of the tree of the knowledge of good and evil? **They wove together fig leaves** and wrapped them around their waists in an attempt to hide their shame before God. Did God accept the clothes they had made for themselves, the clothes they made with leaves? No, He did not! Why did God not accept the clothes they made for themselves? Because God wanted to teach Adam and Eve that He is **perfect** and cannot accept the **imperfect** works of man. Concerning this, the Scriptures say: "*All of us have become like one who is unclean, and* ***all our righteous acts are like filthy rags***." (Isa. 64:6) There is nothing man can do to cover his sins before God.

However, God did something for man. **God killed some animals**, skinned them, and made **clothes of skin** for Adam and Eve. Yes, **God made the first animal sacrifice**. What a shocking sight for Adam and Eve as they watched the blood flow out of the animals that God had killed! Through the shed blood of animals, God wanted to teach Adam and Eve that "*the wages of sin is* ***death***," (Rom. 6:23) and that "*without* ***the shedding of blood*** *there is* ***no forgiveness*** *of sin.*" (Heb. 9:22) We cannot explain this in detail today, except to say that God's basic law of forgiveness states: ***"Without the shedding of blood there is no forgiveness of sin."*** The penalty of sin must be paid. The penalty of sin is death. God can only forgive sins that have been paid for. A pure and innocent victim must die in the place of the guilty sinner. This is the only way that God can forgive people of their sins without compromising His righteousness {Lit. in Wolof: *and still dwell in His righteousness*}.

Thus God established animal sacrifices to remind sinners that the penalty of sin is death. The animal sacrifice symbolized the holy Redeemer who would come into the world to shed His blood as a payment for sin. We will learn more about this later. Today, however, let us remember that God shed the blood of animals to cover the shame of Adam and Eve.

After this, **God expelled Adam and Eve** from the Garden of Paradise in Eden. He placed an angel holding a flaming, flashing sword to guard the way to the tree of life. Adam and Eve had chosen the way of death when they ate the fruit that

God had forbidden. Consequently, they could no longer enjoy the blessings of the wonderful Garden of Paradise. We have already seen how God expelled Lucifer, that is, Satan, from His presence because of his sin. And now we see that God expelled Adam and Eve because of their sin. God is the Holy One, and **He must punish all that is unholy**.

And so dear friends, let us keep two thoughts in mind: **First, God is the Righteous One**. God cannot tolerate sin. That is why He judged Adam and Eve and expelled them from the garden **Second, God is the Merciful One**. Adam and Eve did not deserve God's mercy. They only deserved God's judgment. However, God does not want people to perish. That is why He promised a Savior who could save sinners from the darkness of the kingdom of Satan, and transfer them into the light and glory of the Kingdom of God.

Do not be deceived: **God's mercy can never contradict God's righteousness**. These two characteristics of God must operate together. In future lessons, we will see more clearly how God can show mercy to sinners, without contradicting His righteousness.

Listening friends, this has been your program *The Way of Righteousness*. We have been talking with you about the wonderful promise God made on the day that Adam and Eve strayed from God's way. We hope that you will keep listening to these programs until you have come to understand fully God's wonderful promise about **the Redeemer** He has sent to save you from your sins.

Thank you for listening. We invite you to join us for the next program to learn some important lessons from Adam and Eve's first two sons: Cain and Abel....

God bless you as you carefully consider what the Scripture declares, saying:

> ***"Where sin increased, [God's] grace increased all the more."*** (Rom. 5:20)

Lesson 10

Cain and Abel: The Way of Sacrifice

Genesis 4

Peace be with you, listening friends. We greet you in the name of God, the Lord of peace, who wants everyone to understand and submit to the way of righteousness that He has established, and have true peace with Him forever. We are happy to be able to return today to present your program *The Way of Righteousness*.

Last time, in our study in the Torah, we saw that God, after Adam and Eve sinned, began to announce **His plan** to bring into the world One who would deliver the children of Adam from the power of Satan and sin and hell. We also saw how God refused to accept the clothes of leaves that Adam and Eve made for themselves. God wanted to teach them that sinners have no way of covering their shame before the Holy One who must judge them. Only God can save sinners from their guilt. Thus, we saw how God Himself sacrificed some animals, made clothes of skin, and put them on Adam and Eve. **God made the first blood sacrifice.** We also read how God announced that there would be two lines of people on earth: those who refuse to believe the Word of God, and those who believe it.

Today we will read about Adam and Eve's first two sons: **Cain**, who refused to believe God, and **Abel**, who believed God. As we saw, Adam and Eve were now living outside the Garden of Paradise (Eden). God had expelled them because of their transgression. Because of their sin, they could no longer live in the blessings of the Garden of Paradise. Their sin had spoiled their relationship with God. However, God still loved them and cared for them.

Now then, let us read together from the Torah. In the fourth chapter of the book of Genesis, it is written, "*Adam lay with his wife Eve, and she became pregnant and gave birth to* ***Cain****. She said, 'With the help of the* Lord *I have brought forth a man.' Later she gave birth to his brother* ***Abel****. Now Abel kept flocks, and Cain worked the soil.*" (Gen. 4:1,2)

Adam and Eve bore two sons, Cain and Abel. They were sinners, just like their parents. The sin of Adam spread to his children, like a contagious disease.

Cain and Abel were conceived in sin. Thus, the Scriptures say: "*Adam bore sons in his own likeness.*" (Gen. 5:3). "Like father, like son." **Cain and Abel were born with a sinful nature.** The children grew physically and increased in knowledge. Cain became a farmer. He was a serious laborer and was not afraid of hard work. Abel was a shepherd. **Both knew about God.** They knew that God exists and that He is holy and hates sin. And both should have known that **to approach God, they needed to come by the way of the blood sacrifice which God had ordained.**

There came a day in the lives of Cain and Abel, when they decided to worship God and present to Him a sacrifice. Thus, the Scriptures say:

> "*In the course of time Cain brought some of the fruits of the soil as an offering to the LORD. But Abel brought fat portions from some of the firstborn of his flock.* ***The LORD looked with favor on Abel and his offering, but on Cain and his offering he did not look with favor.*** *So Cain was very angry, and his face was downcast.*" (Gen. 4:3-5)

Let us consider what happened. Two people wanted to worship God. Both presented sacrifices to God. But the Scriptures say: "*The LORD looked with favor on Abel and his offering, but on Cain and his offering he did not look with favor.*" Why did God accept Abel's sacrifice, and refuse Cain's sacrifice? What was the difference between those two sacrifices?

Truly, Cain's sacrifice and Abel's sacrifice were very different. Cain brought to God **beautiful vegetables and delicious fruit**. As for Abel, he brought to God **the blood of a lamb without blemish**. God forgave Abel of his sins, but did not forgive Cain of his sins.

Why did God forgive the sins of Abel, who brought the blood of a lamb, and did not forgive the sins of Cain, who brought vegetables and fruit? Was it because God does not like vegetables and fruit? No, that is not the reason! Why, then, did God judge Abel as righteous, and leave Cain in his sin? Here is the reason: **Abel brought the sacrifice that God required, but Cain brought something else.** What was it that God required so that He could forgive their sins without compromising His righteousness? He required the blood—**the life**—of an unblemished animal. Abel believed God and brought a blood sacrifice, just as God required. Thus, the Scripture says: "***By faith*** *Abel offered God a better sacrifice than Cain did. By faith he was commended as a righteous man, when God spoke well of his [sacrifice].*" (Heb. 11:4) Abel believed God, but Cain did not believe Him.

What does it mean to believe God? To believe God is to have confidence in God to the point of obeying His Word. To believe God is **to accept what God says as true**. If you say, "I believe in God," but you do not believe what God says in the Holy Scriptures, then you do not really believe God. **God and His Word**

are one. If you believe God, you will believe and obey His Word. If you do not believe what God says, it is God Himself you are rejecting.

God accepted Abel because he believed His Word and came with the blood of a lamb, as God had commanded. God did not accept Cain, because he did not honestly believe the Word of God. Cain claimed to believe in God, but his actions denied it, because he did not bring a blood sacrifice, as God had commanded.

Someone may be asking, "Why did God command animal sacrifices? Why did God say, *"Without the shedding of blood, there is no forgiveness of sin"?* Here is the reason: God's holy Law declares that **the payment (wages, penalty) of sin is death**! That is why blood had to be shed. God did not say, "Sin's penalty can be paid with fruits and vegetables." Nor did God say, "The payment for sin is praying and fasting and doing good works." No! What God, in His holiness, did say is: The payment required for sin is **death**!

God, in the Writings of the Prophets, shows us that every person, every child of Adam has sinned and that each sinner has **a great debt** before God, the Holy One. The sinner must die and then pay that debt of sin in hell forever. The debt of sin is huge and you cannot produce enough good works to cancel it before God. **The penalty of sin is death and hell**, which is why good works can never pay it off!

Let us try to illustrate it. Imagine that I owe a huge amount of money to a creditor, and I go to him and say, "I know that I owe you a lot of money. However, I am totally broke, and cannot pay my debt with money, but I have another plan to pay you. Here's my plan: Every day, I will sweep the porch of your house. Thus I will work for you until I pay off my debt." How would the creditor respond to my proposition? Perhaps he would get angry, or perhaps he would laugh at me, however, what is certain is that he would not accept my idea! Why would the creditor not accept my plan? Because there is no way I can pay my huge debt with my feeble "good works."

Similarly, no one can pay off their debt of sin with good works. Only one thing can pay for sin—not money or good works—but **death**. The penalty of sin is death and judgment. Consequently, God could not cancel Cain and Abel's debt of sin based on the works of their own hands. God's plan to cancel their debt of sin was through the blood of a sacrifice. The innocent must die in the place of the guilty.

Forgiveness of sin is not based on man's plan, but on God's plan. On the basis of **the (substitutionary) sacrifice**, God opened a door of forgiveness and salvation for the children of Adam. In earlier generations, God decreed that every sinner must present an animal without blemish and slaughter it. The innocent animal would die as a substitute for the sinner. Because of the blood of such a sacrifice, God could be patient with Adam's descendants and **cover** their sins for a time. But the blood of animals **could not cancel** the debt of man's sin, because the value of an animal is not equal to that of a man. That is why the Scriptures say that animal sacrifices were *"only **a shadow** of the good things that are coming, **not the realities themselves**...because **it is impossible for the blood of [animals] to take away sins**."* (Heb. 10:1,4)

Thus, the most important thing to remember about animal sacrifices is that they were **mere illustrations of the Savior** who was to come into the world to pay the debt of sin for the descendants of Adam. This Savior, whom God promised, would die *"for sins once for all, the righteous for the unrighteous, to bring [them] to God."* (1 Pet. 3:18) As it is written in the Gospel {*Injil*}: *"All the prophets testify about [this Savior] that **everyone who believes in Him receives forgiveness of sins** through His Name."* (Acts 10:43)

However, in past generations, God's plan of salvation required animal sacrifices. But Cain ignored God's plan. Cain came up with another way, a religion of his own making. Cain created **the first false religion**. He brought to God the works of his own hands. He sacrificed to God that which he had cultivated, that is, the produce of the cursed earth, which has no blood. Did God accept such a bloodless "sacrifice"? No, God did not accept it.

As for Abel, he brought to God a lamb without blemish and slaughtered it so that the blood was shed. After that he burned it. Because of that sacrifice, Abel had a clear conscience before God. He knew that, in himself, he deserved to die, but **the innocent lamb had died in his place**. Thus, Abel testified to his faith in the Redeemer who would come into the world, to die in the place of sinners, to bear the punishment for their sin.

We want to summarize today's story by asking a very important question. Why did God not accept Cain's sacrifice? Was Cain a greater sinner than Abel? That is not the reason. They were both sinners. Both presented sacrifices to God. Cain was a religious person. On the surface, perhaps we can even say that Cain's sacrifice was more respectable than Abel's sacrifice. Vegetables and fruits are very beautiful, but a slaughtered lamb and its blood is not a pleasant sight! However, sin is an offensive thing to God and the way of forgiveness that God established declared: ***"Without the shedding of blood, there is no forgiveness of sin!"*** Thus, God refused Cain and his sacrifice, because Cain did not respect God's righteous way of salvation.

No one can come to God, unless he comes by the righteous way that God has ordained! **God's way is perfect and precise!** It is like mathematics. If a teacher asks a student at school, "How much is two plus two?" There is only one correct answer. **Two plus two equals four.** The student who answers three is wrong. The one who says five is wrong. The person who says four and a half is also wrong. Two plus two can only equal four! That is the way it is with the righteous way of salvation that God has established. There is only one God and **one way** for sinners to be reconciled to God, the Holy One! It is **the way of the absolutely perfect Sacrifice**.

You who are listening today, do you know what the Word of God says concerning the holy Sacrifice that God has provided **to cancel your debt of sin permanently**? Do you know that God Himself sent down to earth an almighty Savior so that you can be **forgiven** of your sins and have **a pure heart** before God? In coming lessons, we will be learning much about this wonderful Savior. Concerning Him, the Holy Scriptures say: "*Salvation is found in no one else, for there is no other name under heaven given to men by which we must be saved.*" (Acts 4:12)

Friends, this is where we must stop today. In the will of God, next time we will complete our study about Cain and Abel....

God bless you as you take time to contemplate His basic law which says:

> ***"Without the shedding of blood, there is no forgiveness of sin."*** (Heb. 9:22)

Lesson 11
Unrepentant Cain

Genesis 4

Peace be with you, listening friends. We greet you in the name of God, the Lord of peace, who wants everyone to understand and submit to the way of righteousness that He has established, and have true peace with Him forever. We are happy to be able to return today to present your program *The Way of Righteousness.*

In our last program we learned about the first two sons of Adam and Eve, **Cain and Abel**. We saw how each of them wanted to worship God and present to Him a sacrifice. Cain took some crops that he had cultivated and offered them to God. But Abel offered God a lamb without blemish and slaughtered it as a sacrifice that covers sin. And the Scripture declares: *"The LORD accepted Abel but He did not accept Cain."*

Why did God accept Abel but not Cain? Because God's way of righteousness demanded **a blood sacrifice**. God judged Abel as righteous because he believed the Word of God and brought the offering that God required. As for Cain, he attempted to approach God through his own efforts, which is why God did not accept him.

Today we plan to **conclude our study about Cain and Abel**. Do you know what happened after God refused Cain's sacrifice? In the book of Genesis, chapter four, verse five, the Scripture says: *"So Cain was very angry, and his face was downcast."* (Gen. 4:5) Why was Cain angry? That is not difficult to understand. To illustrate, if I do something bad and someone says to me, "You have done wrong! Change your ways, and do what is right!" how might I respond to the one who rebuked me? Either I will humbly receive his words and **change my ways** or I will get angry with him and **continue in my error**.

God rebuked Cain so that he might realize that the works of his hands, which he had presented as a sacrifice, were worthless before God. **God wanted Cain to repent** and to bring the sacrifice of a lamb without blemish, as Abel had done. God wanted to lead Cain in the right way, the way of forgiveness. However Cain, in his pride, refused to admit his transgression before God. Instead, he became angry and despondent.

Thus, "*the* L*ORD said to Cain, 'Why are you angry? Why is your face downcast? If you do what is right, will you not be accepted? But if you do not do what is right, sin is crouching at your door; it desires to have you, but you must master it.*'" (Gen. 4:6,7) Why did God question Cain in this way? He questioned him because He did not want Cain to perish. God wanted Cain to repent of his sins, and follow the right way. God was warning Cain about a terrible enemy, which threatened to destroy him and his descendants. That enemy is called ***Sin****!*

What is sin? Sin is **the problem of the world**. It is our worst enemy. Sin is like a snake, full of deadly poison. It is like a little spark that can burn up a great forest. Sin is a torch with which Satan is burning up the world! The Word of God says, "*Anyone ...who knows the good he ought to do and doesn't do it, **sins**.*" (Jam. 4:17) "***Sin** is lawlessness.... He who does what is **sinful** is of the devil, because the devil has been **sinning** from the beginning.*" (1 John 3:4,8) Sin is the force that moves in the members of our bodies and fights against what is true and good. Sin is anything that does not agree with the will of God. Sin is refusing to believe and obey the Word of God. **To go my own way is sin.** (See Isaiah 53:6)

What will be the end of those who go their own way and refuse to believe God and obey Him? The Scriptures say, "*They will be **punished with everlasting destruction and shut out from the presence of the Lord** and from the majesty of his power.*" (2 Thes. 1:9) Those who come by the way of salvation that God has decreed will be granted eternal life. But those who harden their hearts against the truth will face God's wrath and judgment. However, the Scriptures say that God does not want "*anyone to perish, but everyone to come to repentance!*" (2 Pet. 3:9) **God did not want Cain to perish in his sin.** What He wanted was for Cain to repent, forsake the way of unrighteousness that he had chosen, and choose the way of righteousness.

As we saw in the last program, the LORD God had revealed a plan by which sinners could be made righteous before Him. **Abel believed in God's plan**, and slaughtered a spotless lamb as a sacrifice that covers sin. Abel believed what God said, "*The [penalty for] sin is death,*" and "*without the shedding of blood there is no forgiveness of sin!*" (Rom. 6:23; Heb. 9:22) Because of the shed blood of the lamb, Abel had a clear conscience before God. Abel knew that he was a guilty sinner deserving God's punishment, but he knew also that he had offered an innocent lamb just as God required. The lamb which Abel sacrificed was an illustration of the Savior who was to come into the world to offer up His life as a sacrifice that would cancel man's debt of sin forever. As for Cain, he pretended to believe God, but his deeds denied it. **Cain honored God with his mouth, but his heart was far from Him.** The blood of a lamb is what God demanded, but Cain offered Him the works of his hands. Cain's worship was absolutely worthless before God, because he did not accept God's way.

Let us now read the next verse to see what Cain did after God rebuked him for his worthless sacrifice. The Scripture says, "*Now Cain said to his brother Abel, 'Let's go out to the field.' And while they were in the field, Cain attacked his brother Abel and killed him.*" (Gen. 4:8) What did Cain do? Did he repent? Did he believe God and bring to Him the blood of a lamb as a sacrifice for sin? No! **Cain added sin to sin by attacking his brother Abel and killing him.**

Incredible! Cain, who refused to shed the blood of a lamb so that God could forgive him his sins, now shed the blood of his righteous brother! What do you think about this? Who placed within the mind of Cain the idea to kill his brother? To whom was Cain listening? Cain was listening to Satan. The Scriptures say that he killed his brother because Cain "*belonged to the evil one.*" (1 John 3:12). We have already seen how God announced that there would be two lines (groups) of people in the world, the people of God and the people of Satan. **Abel belonged to God** because he believed the Word of God enough to obey it. **Cain belonged to Satan** because he did not believe the Word of God.

Let us now listen to what God said to Cain after he killed his younger brother.

> "*Then the LORD said to Cain, '**Where is your brother Abel?**' 'I don't know,' he replied. 'Am I my brother's keeper?' The LORD said, 'What have you done? Listen! Your brother's blood cries out to me from the ground. Now you are under a curse and driven from the ground, which opened its mouth to receive your brother's blood from your hand. When you work the ground, it will no longer yield its crops for you. You will be a restless wanderer on the earth.'*" (Gen. 4:9-12)

Thus, God punished Cain, saying, "*When you work the ground, it will no longer yield its crops for you.*" Wolof wisdom says, "The cow kicks its calf but does not hate it." Similarly, God did not punish Cain to condemn him, but to lead him to repent of his sin, believe the truth, and be saved. Yet what did Cain do? Did he repent? No, he did not. The Scriptures say, "*So Cain **went out from the LORD's presence** and lived in the land of Nod.*" (Gen. 4:16) Cain, who ignored the word of God, turned his back on God, shutting Him out of his life. **It was not God who distanced Himself from Cain, but Cain who distanced himself from God.**

Today, most of Adam's descendants resemble Cain, continuing in their own way and closing their hearts to God's voice. With their lips they say, "God is great!" but in their hearts they think, "God is far away! No one can know Him!" However, the Word of God shows us that **God is not far from any one of us,** because He is the One who gives to everyone life and breath and everything else. He is closer to us than our own heartbeat. God knows you personally, and wants you to know Him personally too! (See Acts 17:24-31; Romans 10:1-13)

Why is it then that most people do not come to know God (personally)? The Word of God answers this question. God says, "*This is the verdict: Light has come into the world, but* **men loved darkness instead of light** *because their deeds were evil. Everyone who does evil hates the light, and will not come into the light for fear that his deeds will be exposed.*"(John 3:19,20)

People do not know God, because like Cain, **they have turned their backs on His Word**. God's prophet David wrote: *"[God's] word is a lamp to my feet and a light for my path."* (Psa. 119:105) If you turn your back on the light of the Word of God, you will remain in the darkness of sin and you will never come to know God. God will seem far from you. Yet, God wants you to know that He is not far away. He is behind you. He is at your side. He is right in front of you. God loves you and wants to have a close relationship with you. But you must not be like Cain, who hardened his heart and refused to accept God's way of righteousness. **God wanted Cain to repent.** To this very day, God is commanding every person to repent, turn to Him, and believe His Word.

Do you know what it means **to repent**? It means *to change your thoughts and your actions*. To repent is **to confess before God**, "I have been wrong in my thinking concerning the way of salvation that you have established!" To repent is **to agree with God** that you have no possible way of saving yourself from His righteous judgment, and then to turn to Him and submit to His way of salvation.

A person who truly repents is like a traveler who wants to take the train from Thies {Senegal's 2nd largest city} to Dakar {the Capital}. He buys a ticket and climbs aboard. Later, as he is traveling along, he discovers that he is on the train going to Bamako {in Mali, the opposite direction}! What must he do if he is ever to get to Dakar? He must "repent"—that is, he must **admit** that he is heading in the wrong direction, **get off** the train at the next stop, and **get on** the train that goes to Dakar. Thus, we see that genuine repentance has two sides: rejecting the wrong and accepting the right. **True repentance involves two actions.** First, you must **turn from** yourself, your sins, your idols and your self-efforts to gain God's favor. Then you must **turn to** God and His Word which tells you how to be saved. That is true repentance.

As for Cain, he never repented. Cain chose to continue in **his own way**. He refused to submit to **the way of salvation** established by God. That is why the Scriptures say: "***Cain perished on the way of unrighteousness***, *which caused God to reserve for him the blackest darkness forever!*" (Jude 11, 13)

Oh dear friends, **may we not be like Cain**! Let us pay attention to the solemn warning from God which says, *"Unless you repent, you too will all perish!"* (Luke 13:3) God's judgment is sure and will fall upon all those who have never been cleansed from their sins.

Let there be no mistake about this: you will never become righteous before God based on your own good works. Like Cain, many people believe that they will escape God's judgment by attempting to follow the rules and regulations of their religion. But being religious does not make one righteous. God's Word says:

> *"No one will be declared righteous in [God's] sight by observing the law.... All of us have become like one who is unclean, and* ***all our righteous acts are like filthy rags****.... For it is by grace you [are] saved,* ***through faith****, and this* ***not from yourselves****, it is* ***the gift of God****,* ***not by works****, so that no one can boast!"* (Rom. 3:20; Isa. 64:6; Eph. 2:8,9)

Thank you for listening. God willing, in the next program, we will study about some of Adam's descendants, including the Prophet of God, Enoch....

God bless you as you thoughtfully consider what you have heard today. The Scriptures say:

> ***"God is patient with you, not wanting anyone to perish, but everyone to come to repentance.... [But if you do not] repent, you will perish!"*** (1 Pet. 3:9; Luke 13:3)

Lesson 12

The Prophet Enoch

Genesis 4, 5

Peace be with you, listening friends. We greet you in the name of God, the Lord of peace, who wants everyone to understand and submit to the way of righteousness that He has established, and have true peace with Him forever. We are happy to be able to return today to present your program *The Way of Righteousness*.

In our last two programs, we learned about the first two sons of Adam and Eve: Cain and Abel. We saw how both of them presented to God a sacrifice in order to worship Him. Abel believed God and brought **the blood of a lamb**, but Cain tried to approach God through **his own efforts**. God accepted Abel's sacrifice, but He rejected Cain's sacrifice. God called on Cain to repent, but Cain only got angry and killed his brother Abel.

Today we plan to continue in the Torah and study chapters four and five of the book of Genesis. The Word of God tells us that Adam and Eve *"had other sons and daughters."* (Gen. 5:4) However, among the descendants of Adam, God has only made known to us the stories of **two family lines**: the family line of Cain and the family line of Seth, one of Cain's younger brothers.

We will first look at **the family line of Cain**. Cain chose a wife from among his relatives and they had children. However, just as "the leaping gazelle doesn't produce burrowing offspring" {Wolof proverb}, neither did Cain's offspring escape their father's way of thinking and speaking and acting. Like their father, **they did not respect God's Word**. They had great knowledge and intelligence, but did not know God. They only valued earthly things. They built a city, made tools, flutes and harps and things like that. One of those who descended from Cain was called Tubal-Cain. He was ingenious and forged bronze and iron. However, beautiful handwork does not make a beautiful heart!

One of Cain's descendants, named **Lamech**, was the seventh generation after Adam. Lamech walked in the footsteps of his ancestor Cain—except he was even worse. Lamech was the first to take two wives and, like Cain, he became a murderer. The Scriptures say that Lamech murdered two people and then boasted that he was more wicked than Cain! Like Cain and all his descendants, Lamech didn't care about the will of God. Lamech was selfish and loved money. He was proud and conceited. He was a lover of pleasure rather than a lover of God. Satan was his master, but he didn't realize it. Lamech was like this because he chose to follow the way of Cain. Let us keep the name of Lamech in our minds, because we will be coming back to him before we finish our lesson today.

Praise God, the Scriptures do not stop with the story of Cain and his unrighteous descendants. The Word also tells us about **the family line of Seth**, saying that God gave Adam and Eve another son *"in place of Abel, since Cain killed him."* (Gen. 4:25) His name was Seth. Seth means *chosen*. God chose Seth to replace Abel. Why did Seth have to replace Abel? Here is the answer. In the Garden of Paradise (Eden), God had promised One who would come into the world to defeat Satan and deliver the descendants of Adam from his power. That Savior could have come through the family line of Abel who believed God. However, Satan led Cain to kill Abel. Satan wanted to hinder God's plan to send the Savior into the world. However, God's wisdom is greater than Satan's. God had a marvelous plan to deliver the children of Adam from their sins and no one could hinder it, not even Satan! Therefore, God, in keeping with His plan, gave Seth to Adam and Eve, to replace Abel, whom Cain had killed. Thus, **God's plan** concerning the Redeemer continued to advance.

Seth was a true believer. Like Abel, his older brother, Seth chose the way of salvation which God had established. Seth, like all of Adam's offspring, was born in sin. However, he believed what God had promised concerning the Savior who was to come and he manifested his faith by bringing before God the blood of a lamb, as a sacrifice to cover sins. Another noteworthy thing concerning Seth was that he raised his children in the knowledge of the truth of God. Therefore the Scriptures say: *"Seth had a son, and ...at that time men began to call on the name of the Lord."* (Gen. 4:26)

Thus, we see two family lines that came forth from Adam: the line of Cain and the line of Seth. Do you know what those two lines illustrate? They **illustrate the two kinds of people** that have been in the world from Adam's time until today. In God's eyes, there are only two kinds of people on earth. He sees no distinction between those with black skin and those with white, nor between Wolof and Sereer {two ethnic groups in Senegal}, men and women, rich and poor. God is not prejudiced; nonetheless, He separates the people of the world into two distinct groups. What are these two groups of people? They are **those who believe the Word of God**, and **those who do not believe it**; those who **know** God and those who **do not know** Him; those who walk in the **light** and those who walk in **darkness**; those who are **forgiven** of their sins and those who are **not forgiven**. Everyone who believes God and chooses the way of righteous which He has established, will be saved (and go to heaven), just as Seth and his family were saved. Whoever does not take God's way of righteousness will perish (and go to hell), just as Cain and his family perished.

The Scriptures say that Adam lived until he was 930 years old and then he died. In those early times, men lived until they were extremely old—but they died as all men die. **Adam and Eve died**, just as God had said they would. When God created the first two people, it was not His will that they should die, but that they should live. Why then did Adam and Eve die? Because they sinned against God—and sin produces death.

Now then, in the time remaining, we will look at the story of a man of God, who was in the family line of Seth, who believed God. This man is ***Enoch*** …the prophet of God, Enoch. Some know him as "*Idris*" {Qur'anic name}. In the fifth chapter of Genesis, we see the ancestry of Enoch. The Scriptures say: **Adam** became the father of Seth; **Seth** became the father of Enosh; **Enosh** became the father of Kenan; **Kenan** became the father of Mahalalel; **Mahalalel** became the father of Jared; **Jared** became the father of Enoch. Thus, **Enoch** was the seventh generation after Adam in the line of Seth.

Like all men, Enoch was **a born sinner.** However, when he was 65 years of age, Enoch repented of his sins, turned to God, and believed what God promised concerning the Redeemer who was to come into the world to die as the Perfect Sacrifice that takes away sin. Enoch showed his faith by offering to God the blood of an animal as a sacrifice that covers sin. Consequently, God credited Enoch's faith to Him as righteousness, forgave him his sins, and purified his heart. Thus, the Scriptures say: "*Enoch walked with God for 300 years.*" (Gen. 5:22)

However, to walk with God in Enoch's day was not easy, because it was a corrupt and wicked period, much like the present day. Most of those living in Enoch's time sought only after pleasure and lived lives of impurity. As for Enoch, he knew that God had not created man to live in impurity, but in holiness. Therefore, Enoch did not allow covetousness to control him, as it did his neighbors who did not know God. Like God Himself, Enoch loved righteousness and hated iniquity. People insulted him and persecuted him because of his righteous lifestyle, but Enoch didn't let it bother him, because he knew that nothing is more important than to have peace with God.

God chose Enoch to be His servant and His prophet during that evil period. **Like all prophets, Enoch testified about the Redeemer who was to come.** He also announced that the Redeemer would one day return to punish all those who refused to repent and believe in Him. Listen to the preaching of Enoch:

> "*See,* ***the Lord is coming*** *with thousands upon thousands of His holy ones* **to judge** *everyone, and to convict all the ungodly of all the ungodly acts they have done in the ungodly way, and of all the harsh words ungodly sinners have spoken against Him!*" (Jude 1:14,15)

One more amazing thing that we need to know about the prophet Enoch is that he did not die. That's right. The Word of God tells us that **Enoch did not die**! It says: "*Enoch walked with God for 300 years and then he was no more, for God took him.*" (Gen. 5:24) God, in His power and His plan, translated Enoch directly to heaven, without making him go through the door of death.

Why did God translate Enoch in that way? Through the life of Enoch, God wants to teach us what He thinks of those who truly believe Him and seek to please Him in all things. The Scriptures say:

> ***"By faith Enoch was taken from this life, so that he did not experience death****; he could not be found, because God had taken him away. For before he was taken,* ***he was commended as one who pleased God****. And* ***without faith it is impossible to please God****, because anyone who comes to Him must believe that He exists and that He rewards those who earnestly seek Him.*" (Heb. 11:5,6)

For three hundred years, Enoch pleased God, because he believed Him, loved Him and obeyed Him during a time in which most people didn't care about what God wanted. Thus, one day God called his name; instantly, Enoch found Himself in Paradise, in the glory of the house of God forever! In this, there is something very important which God wants to show us. It is this: If you do not have faith like Enoch, you will never please God! However, if you have faith like Enoch, God will count you as righteous, and you need no longer fear death. You can know that God has conquered death for you, because if you listen to the Word of God and believe it, when your life on earth is over, you will go to live in the presence of the Lord forever, just like Enoch! However, you must come to understand and believe what God has said concerning the righteous way of salvation that He has provided for sinners.

To summarize our study, we would like to make a few comparisons between the two descendants of Adam we have read about today: **Lamech** and **Enoch**.

Both Lamech and Enoch belonged to the seventh generation after Adam. Lamech descended through **the line of Cain**, and Enoch descended through **the line of Seth**. Lamech and Enoch shared the same generation (era), but they did not share the same interests. Their way of life was totally different, like night from day.

Lamech did not believe God and His word, but **Enoch** believed God and loved His word.

Lamech walked with Satan in impurity, whereas **Enoch** walked with God in holiness.

Lamech ignored the way of salvation decreed by God, while **Enoch** cherished it and brought to God the blood of a lamb to cover his sins.

Lamech craved money, women, food, clothes and pleasure, whereas **Enoch** desired a life of close fellowship with the One who had given him life.

Lamech died in his sins and went down to hell, but God took **Enoch** up to be with Himself in heaven.

In closing, here is an important question: **Are you most like Lamech or Enoch?** Do you belong to the people of Cain and Lamech or the people of Seth and Enoch? Does your life embrace the faith of Enoch, or are you going your own way like Lamech? God's Word says: "***Examine yourselves** to see whether you are in the faith*" ...because "*without faith* (in God and His Word) *it is **impossible** to please God!*" (2 Cor. 13:5; Heb. 11:6)

Friends, this is where we must stop today. Next time, in the will of God, we will begin to study another one of God's prophets–the prophet Noah....

God bless you as you earnestly consider this verse from His holy Word:

> ***"Without faith it is impossible to please God, because anyone who comes to him must believe that he exists and that he rewards those who earnestly seek him."*** (Heb. 11:6)

Lesson 13

The Prophet Noah: God's Patience and Wrath

Genesis 6

Peace be with you, listening friends. We greet you in the name of God, the Lord of peace, who wants everyone to understand and submit to the way of righteousness that He has established, and have true peace with Him forever. We are happy to be able to return today to present your program *The Way of Righteousness*.

In our reflections in the Holy Scriptures, we have already seen that, in the beginning, when God created the world, everything was **good**. However, when our ancestor Adam disobeyed God, **evil** entered the world through him and spread to all men. Truly, "an epidemic is not confined to the one from whom it originates!" {Wolof proverb} In our last program, we learned about the two lines which descended from Adam, the descendants of Cain and the descendants of Seth. The descendants of Cain **did not believe God**. However, among the descendants of Seth, there were those who **believed God's Word**, and, as a result, God forgave them of their sins. One who came from Seth, was named Enoch. Although most who lived in the time of Enoch followed Satan in lives of impurity, Enoch walked with God in holiness.

Today we will begin to learn about another man who walked with God in a crooked and depraved era. This person is **the prophet Noah** {*Noh* in Arabic}, the great grandson of Enoch. We have already learned that, in early times, people lived to be older than we do today. Do you know who lived to be the oldest man in the world? It was Methuselah, the son of Enoch. He lived until he was 969 years old. Methuselah was the father of Lamech who was the father of Noah. This Lamech, Noah's father, is a different man from Lamech, the descendant of Cain about whom we learned last time. Noah, belonged to the tenth generation after Adam. When Noah was five hundred years old, he became the father of Shem, Ham and Japheth.

What we plan to study concerning Noah will be of great value to us, because the days of Noah were similar to the times in which we live today. In the time of Noah, the world was filled to the brim with sin. The Scriptures say that "*the wickedness of man was great on the earth, and that every inclination of the thoughts of his heart was only evil all the time.*" (Gen. 6:5) The hearts of the children of Adam were filled with evil thoughts, greed, deceit, lewdness, envy, slander, arrogance, strife, fighting, adultery, theft, murder, and folly (based on Mark 7:21,22). Men were ruining the world which God had created for them. Many had religion, but it was merely for show. Fleshly pleasure was their god, and their sins just kept piling up!

Listen to what the Scripture says in the Torah, the book of Genesis, chapter six:

> (Gen. 6) [3]*Then the LORD said, "My Spirit will not contend with man forever, for he is mortal; his days will be a hundred and twenty years."* [5]*The LORD saw how great man's wickedness on the earth had become, and that every inclination of the thoughts of his heart was only evil all the time.* [6]*The LORD was grieved that he had made man on the earth, and his heart was filled with pain.* [7]*So the LORD said, "I will wipe mankind, whom I have created, from the face of the earth, men and animals, and creatures that move along the ground, and birds of the air, for I am grieved that I have made them."*

Thus we see how God purposed to wipe out the descendants of Adam from the earth because of their wickedness. However, we also see how God, in His mercy, intended to be patient with sinners for another 120 years to give them **time to repent**, so that they might not perish. However, when that limit was reached, God would judge everyone who refused to repent and accept His way of righteousness.

There is something we can learn about the character of God, from that limit of 120 years. It is this: **God is very patient, but His patience has a limit**! He will speak and strive with man so that he might repent, but not forever. That is why in the time of Noah, God said, "*My Spirit will not contend with man forever. His days will be a hundred and twenty years.*" Thus we see how God planned to be patient with sinners for a time and then judge them if they refused to repent. In this, we can observe two characteristics of God: **His patience** and **His wrath**. God is good and can be very patient; but He is also righteous and can get very angry!

Some think of God as one who hovers over them with a big stick, as though God is quick to anger and takes pleasure in hitting and hurting people. But God is not like that. **Others think** that God is never angry and will merely forgive and forget the sins of people. "God is good! God is good!" is all they know. But God is not like that either.

The Holy Scriptures tell us the truth concerning the character of God. God is good **and** righteous! He can be patient **and** angry. His goodness and His mercy are why He is patient with sinners, but His righteousness and His holiness are why He is also angry with their sins. God is a Savior and a Judge. The prophets wrote a great deal about the **patience and wrath of God**. Let us listen to some of their words.

The Scriptures say:

> "*But do not forget this one thing: With the Lord a day is like a thousand years, and a thousand years are like a day. The Lord is not slow in keeping his promise, as some understand slowness. He is* ***patient*** *with you,* ***not wanting anyone to perish****, but everyone to come to repentance.* ***But the day of the Lord will come*** *like a thief.*" (2 Pet. 3:8-10) "***The Lord will judge*** *his people. It is a dreadful thing to fall into the hands of the living God.... See to it [therefore] that you do not refuse Him who speaks...for our God is a consuming fire!*" (Heb. 10:30,31; 12:25,29)

In the Psalms we read: "*God is* ***a righteous judge****, a God who expresses* ***his wrath*** *every day [toward the sinner who] does not relent.*" (Psa. 7:11,12)

In the Gospel {*Injil*} it is written:

> "***The wrath of God*** *is being revealed from heaven against all the godlessness and wickedness of men who suppress* ***the truth*** *by their wickedness ...[God will judge them and His] judgment...is based on* ***truth****. You then ...do you think you will escape God's judgment? Or do you show contempt for the riches of* ***his kindness, tolerance and patience****, not realizing that God's kindness leads you toward repentance? But because of your stubbornness and your unrepentant heart, you are storing up wrath against yourself for* ***the day of God's wrath****, when* ***his righteous judgment*** *will be revealed. God will give to each person according to what he has done.*" (Rom. 1:18; 2:2-6)

The wrath of God is not like the wrath of man. Man can become very angry, but his anger will diminish little by little until he may even forget what made him angry in the first place. The anger of God is not like that! The passing of time does not cause God's anger to diminish. God is a righteous Judge and He does not forget anything! **His anger does not diminish** toward those who refuse to repent; instead, **it increases**! This is what we just finished reading in the Scriptures: "*Because of your stubbornness and your unrepentant heart,* ***you are storing up wrath*** *against yourself for the day of God's wrath.*"

The people of Noah's time were "*storing up*" for themselves the wrath of God! However, there remained one man at that time who loved God with all his heart, and believed God's word. That man was **Noah**. Thus the Scriptures say: "***But Noah found favor (grace) in the eyes of the*** **LORD.** *Noah was a righteous man, blameless among the people of his time, and he walked with God.*" (Gen. 6:8,9)

Why did God show Noah His grace? Did Noah merit the grace of God? No! Grace which is merited is no longer grace. Grace means "unmerited favor." Why did God extend His grace to Noah and not to the others? What does the Scripture say about that? It tells us that **Noah believed God**, while the others did not believe Him. **Noah believed the word of God.** He believed what God promised concerning the Redeemer who was to come into the world to save sinners. Like all of Adam's descendants, Noah had sin in him, but God counted Noah as a righteous person because he believed God and offered Him the blood of a sacrifice for his sin, as God had commanded. Thus, the Scriptures say "*Noah was a righteous man, blameless among the people of his time.*"

One day God said to Noah:

> (Gen. 6) [13]"*I am going to put an end to all people, for the earth is filled with violence because of them. I am surely going to destroy both them and the earth.* [14]***So make yourself an ark*** *of cypress wood; make rooms in it and coat it with pitch inside and out.* [15]*This is how you are to build it: The ark is to be 150 meters long, 25 meters wide and 15 meters high.* [16]*Make a roof for it...Put a door in the side of the ark and make lower, middle and upper decks.* [17]*I am going to bring floodwaters on the earth to destroy all life under the heavens, every creature that has the breath of life in it. Everything on earth will perish.* [18]*But I will establish my covenant with you, and you will enter the ark, you and your sons and your wife and your sons' wives with you.* [19]*You are to bring into the ark two of all living creatures, male and female, to keep them alive with you...* [21]*You are to take every kind of food that is to be eaten and store it away as food for you and for them.*"

Thus God told Noah how he planned to bring floodwaters on the earth to destroy everyone who refused to repent and believe the truth. God told Noah to build a large **ark** (boat) to escape the flood. The length of the ark had to be 150 meters; the length of one and a half soccer fields. It would be a refuge for Noah and his family and many animals and anyone else who would believe God's Word. God ordered Noah to make **many rooms** on the inside of the ark, but only **one door** on the outside of the ark. Thus, God's message for the people of Noah's time was this: **Anyone who wishes to escape the judgment of the flood must pass through the one door of the ark.** Every person who passes through the door will be **saved**. Those who do not pass through the door will **perish**!

So Noah started to build the ark. It was a huge task. Noah and his three sons had to chop down hundreds and hundreds of large trees, cut them into planks, shape and nail them, and coat them with tar inside and out. Noah's wife and his son's wives also helped them in that hard work. For one hundred years, day after day, Noah and his family worked on building the ark. But Noah did not limit his activity to merely building. He also preached to the people of his day. Perhaps he said something like this: "Listen! The LORD has told me to warn you of His wrath! God's anger boils because of your sin! He has decided to bring a flood on the earth to destroy everyone who refuses to repent. However, I make known to you good news! God, in His mercy, has ordered me to build an ark to be a refuge for anyone who repents of their sin and believes the word of God!" Thus Noah warned the people with many words, and urged them to turn from the evil ways of their corrupt generation.

What do you think? Did the people of Noah's era believe the word which God announced to them through His prophet? We cannot reply now, because our time is gone. Next time, however, in the will of the Lord, we will continue with the story of the prophet Noah and see how God preserved everyone who believed His word, and how He judged those who did not believe His word, letting them drown in the waters of a great flood.

Thank you for listening....God bless you as you think about what we read today in the Scriptures:

> ***"The Lord is not slow in keeping his promise, as some understand slowness. He is patient with you, not wanting anyone to perish, but everyone to come to repentance. But [the day of God's judgment] will come like a thief."*** (2 Pet. 3:9,10)

Lesson 14

Noah and the Great Flood

Genesis 7

Peace be with you, listening friends. We greet you in the name of God, the Lord of peace, who wants everyone to understand and submit to the way of righteousness that He has established, and have true peace with Him forever. We are happy to be able to return today to present your program *The Way of Righteousness*.

In our last program we began to look at the fascinating story of the prophet Noah who was born ten generations after Adam. In a corrupt and depraved era, Noah walked with God. We saw how **the LORD was grieved** in His heart because of the sins of Adam's descendants. The Scriptures say that *"man's wickedness on the earth had become great, and every inclination of the thoughts of his heart was only evil all the time."* (Gen. 6:5) That is why God, in His holy wrath, planned to wipe (unrepentant) sinners from off the face of the earth.

However, **God's grace** was with Noah, because Noah loved God and **believed His word**. Thus, one day God said to Noah: I have purposed the death of all mankind because the earth is filled with wickedness. I will bring a great flood upon the earth, to destroy everything which lives under the heavens. As for you, you are to build a large ark (boat) to be a refuge for you and your family.

For one hundred years, Noah and his family worked to construct that large ark. But Noah did not limit his work merely to building the ark. He also preached to the people around him, saying: Repent of your sins then and return to God! God, the Righteous One, will judge the world!

Did the people of Noah's time repent of their sins and believe the word which God announced to them through His prophet? What do you think? Among the thousands and thousands of children of Adam who were upon the earth, how many of them repented and believed God enough to enter the ark? The Scriptures reply: ***"Only a few people, eight in all, were saved..."*** (1 Pet. 3:20)

How many people believed God? Only eight: Noah and his wife, their three sons and their wives. All the others did not believe the word of God. Some simply ignored Noah's preaching, while others mocked him. They thought he was crazy because of the boat he was building in a place where there was no water.

The people may have mocked Noah like this: "Hey you guys! Come see this fellow who is building a huge boat out here in the wilderness! Noah must be insane! Floodwaters here in the desert? Impossible! Besides, God is good; He wouldn't destroy the people He has created! You're crazy, Noah!" However, Noah ignored their insults because he believed what God had said. He continued right on constructing the ark and preaching, saying, "Repent! God is going to judge the world in righteousness! Why do you refuse to believe the word of God? Why do you want to perish?"

Finally the day came when Noah and his family finished building the ark. In the last verse of the sixth chapter of the book of Genesis we read: "*Noah did everything just as God commanded him.*" (Gen. 6:22) The boat was ready. Everything was complete. Only one thing remained: Noah and his family needed to enter the ark. One more time, we can hear Noah trying to convince the people: "Listen to God! Repent and believe His word! The flood is soon to come! Enter the ark while there is still time! The door is open! Whoever passes through it will be saved. But if you refuse to enter, how will you escape the judgment of God?" Thus, Noah earnestly warned the people. **But they would not listen**.

Consequently, in chapter seven, the Scriptures say:

> (Gen. 7) [1]*The LORD then said to Noah, "Go into the ark, you and your whole family, because I have found you righteous in this generation.* [2]*Take with you seven of every kind of clean animal, a male and its mate, and two of every kind of unclean animal, a male and its mate,* [3]*and also seven of every kind of bird, male and female, to keep their various kinds alive throughout the earth.* [4]*Seven days from now I will send rain on the earth for forty days and forty nights, and I will wipe from the face of the earth every living creature I have made."* [5]*And Noah did all that the LORD commanded him.*

Why did Noah and his family enter the ark? Because they saw a cloudy sky? Because they smelled the coming rain? No! A clear sky is all they saw when they entered the ark. Why then did they go in? There is only one reason. They entered because **they believed what God had said**. Perhaps there were those outside who thought: "I also believe God, but I am not going to go inside that ark! I believe in God, but I cannot accept Noah's preaching!" What can we say about those people? We can say that **they did not really believe God**, because they did not believe what God testified through His prophet. They refused to repent of their sins and they refused to accept the way of escape which God had provided for them through Noah. They may have honored God with their lips, but their hearts were far, far from Him.

Thus, the Scriptures say:

> *"And Noah and his sons and his wife and his sons' wives entered the ark to escape the waters of the flood. Pairs of clean and unclean animals, of birds and of all creatures that move along the ground, male and female, came to Noah and entered the ark, as God had commanded Noah….* ***Then the LORD shut him in.***" (Gen. 7:7-9,16)

Did you hear what God did after Noah and his family entered the ark? The Scriptures say, ***"The LORD shut them in!"*** The day of God's great anger had arrived. God had been patient with the people of that generation for a long time, but now **His patience had run out! Only His wrath remained.** God had closed the door; and when God closes the door, no one can open it.

Thus, God brought the floodwaters on the earth just as He had promised. The sky began to darken; the wind began to blow. There were clouds and thunder and lightning and earthquakes. Now the children of Adam were **trembling with fear**. When everything was peaceful, it had been so easy for them to challenge God with insulting words and works. But now that the judgment of God had begun to descend upon them, their mouths were shut! The hour for them to face God's righteous judgment had arrived and there was no longer anywhere to hide!

A heavy rain fell, the deep springs of the earth gushed forth water, the oceans and rivers overflowed, resulting in a great flood. Torrents of water surged into every town and village. Those who were not immediately swept away fled in terror, seeking higher ground. Those who had mocked Noah and rejected the word of God, now knew that what God had said through His prophet was **the truth**. However, this knowledge was of **no benefit** to them because now the opportunity to repent was gone; the period of salvation was past. Perhaps some were calling to Noah, shouting out, "Noah! Noah! Open the door! Noah, help us! Save us! We believe you Noah! You were right! We believe! We believe!" **But it was to late.** God had closed the door. The day of salvation was past. The day of judgment had come. Praying, weeping, beating on the door, even knowing the truth—nothing could change the mind of God. **When God closes the door of salvation, no one can open it.**

Thus, the Scriptures tell us that for forty days there was a continual downpour of rain and constant flooding until even the mountains were covered. But the ark floated on top of the water.

> *"Every living thing that moved on the earth perished. Every living thing on the face of the earth was wiped out; men and animals and the creatures that move along the ground and the birds of the air were wiped from the earth.* ***Only Noah was left, and those with him in the ark.***" (Gen. 7:21,23)

Did God do what He had promised to do? Of course! Did He judge those sinners who refused to repent? He surely did! He judged everyone who was not in the ark, just as He had said He would do.

Fellow listeners, this is where we must stop today in the story of Noah. God willing, in our next program, we will conclude this story to see what happened to Noah and his family in the ark. However, before we bid you farewell today, there is an important lesson God wants to teach us through the story of the judgment of the great flood. It is this: **God has planned another day when He will judge the people of the world.** And that coming Day of Judgment will be even more terrible than the judgment which came upon Noah's generation!

Listen to what one of God's prophets declares concerning that final day of judgment. He writes:

> "*Then I saw* ***a great white throne*** *and Him who was seated on it. Earth and sky fled from His presence, and there was no place for them. And I saw the dead, great and small, standing before the throne, and books were opened. Another book was opened, which is the book of life. The dead were judged according to what they had done as recorded in the books. If anyone's name was not found written in the book of life, he was thrown into* ***the lake of fire****.*" (Rev. 20:11-12,15)

Listening friend, are you confident as you contemplate that fearful day of judgment? Is your name written in the book of eternal life? Have you passed through the door of salvation which God has opened? The Word of God says: ***"Now is the time of God's favor, now is the day of salvation."*** (2 Cor. 6:2) We saw how God patiently appealed to the people of Noah's day to repent, believe and be saved, but in the end, He closed the door of salvation. Whoever refused to enter through the door of the ark faced God's fierce judgment.

Concerning that **coming Day of Judgment** when God will judge the world in righteousness, the Scriptures say: "*The day of the Lord will come like a thief in the night. While people are saying, 'Peace and safety', destruction will come on them* ***suddenly****, as labor pains on a pregnant woman, and they will not escape!*" (1 Thes. 5:2,3) No one shall escape in that day, except those who have passed through the door of salvation which God has opened for the children of Adam.

Do you know about **the Door** that God has opened for sinners? Do you know the way of escape that God has provided for you? Who escaped the judgment of the flood in Noah's day? Only those who went through the door of the ark! Similarly, concerning the coming judgment day, the Scriptures clearly show us that God has provided only **one door of salvation** for the sinful children of Adam. Do you know about that door of salvation? Then listen to these sure words spoken by the holy Mediator whom God sent into the world. He said: "***I am the [Door]***;

whoever enters through me will be saved!" (John 10:9) "*I tell you the truth, whoever hears my word and believes him who sent me has eternal life and* ***will not [come into judgment]****!*" (John 5:24)

Friends, this is where we must stop today, but, in future programs, we will learn much more about this Savior whom God sent into the world, the One who said, ***"I am the [Door]; whoever enters through me will be saved!"***

Thank you for listening. Next time, God willing, we will conclude the story of the prophet Noah....

May God bless you and teach you as you think about this weighty question found in His Word:

> ***"How shall we escape, if we ignore such a great salvation?"*** (Heb. 2:3)

LESSON 15

NOAH AND THE FAITHFULNESS OF GOD

GENESIS 8, 9

Peace be with you, listening friends. We greet you in the name of God, the Lord of peace, who wants everyone to understand and submit to the way of righteousness that He has established, and have true peace with Him forever. We are happy to be able to return today to present your program *The Way of Righteousness*.

Today we plan to **finish the story of God's prophet, Noah**. First let us review what we have learned in the past two programs about Noah and the great flood. In chapter six of the book of Genesis, we saw that the wickedness of man was very great in the time of Noah; every inclination of the thoughts of man's heart was evil. This is why God purposed to bring a flood upon the earth to wipe out every sinner who refused to turn from his sin and turn to the true and living God.

In that crooked and depraved generation, only one man pleased God. That man was Noah. Noah trusted God and loved Him. That is why, one day, God spoke to Noah, and commanded him to build a great ark (boat), which would be a refuge for him, his family and many animals so that they could escape the flood. For one hundred years, Noah, along with his family, was building the ark and exhorting the people to repent and believe the word of God. Yet **no one paid attention** to the preaching of Noah. No one really believed what Noah was telling them about the coming flood!

Nonetheless, a day came when the ark was ready. The hour for God to judge this evil world had arrived. God had been patient with scoffers for a long time, but now His patience had run out. Thus, the LORD told Noah to enter the ark with his family and take with him seven males and seven females of every kind of clean animal {fit for sacrifice}, and two of each unclean animal, a male and a female. Noah and his family and the animals entered the ark as God had ordered. And the Scriptures say: "*Then the LORD shut them in.*" God, who had opened the door of salvation for the children of Adam, was also the One who closed it. **The day of God's mercy was gone; the day for His fearsome wrath had arrived!**

Then came the lightning, thunder and violent shaking of the earth. Heavy rains fell, causing a great flood. Everyone fled, seeking to go up into the mountains, but no one could escape from God's holy wrath! Those who had mocked Noah and rejected God's word, now knew the truth. But now it was **too late**! The time of salvation was past. God had shut the door.

For forty days and nights rain poured down from the sky and springs gushed up from the earth until even the mountains were covered. But the ark floated on top of the water. The Scripture says:

> *"Every living thing that moved on the earth perished. Every living thing on the face of the earth was wiped out; men and animals and the creatures that move along the ground and the birds of the air were wiped from the earth.* ***Only Noah was left, and those with him in the ark."*** (Gen. 7:21,23)

Thus, the Scripture records that God carried out the punishment just as He had promised. Everyone **outside** the ark perished. **God is faithful to keep His word.**

What happened to those **inside** the ark? Did God forget Noah and his family? God, who feeds the birds of the air, and not one of them falls to the earth except that He wills it, did not forget them. Let us read what is written in the book of Genesis in chapter eight. The Scriptures say:

> *"But* **God remembered Noah** *and all the wild animals and the livestock that were with him in the ark, and he sent a wind over the earth, and the waters receded …And on the seventeenth day of the seventh month the ark came to rest on the mountains of Ararat."* (Gen. 8:1,4)

Thus we see that God remembered Noah and those who were with him inside the ark. He sent a wind to blow over the earth so that the waters would recede. God guided the ark so that it came to rest on a high mountain named *Ararat*. After Noah and his family had been in the ark for one year and a week, much of the water which had covered the earth had dried up. Thus God said to Noah, *"Leave the ark, you and your wife, your sons and their wives."* So Noah and his family went out of the ark, as did all the animals. When he had gone out, he built an altar, took some of the clean animals and birds and offered them to the LORD on the altar as a burnt offering.

Did you hear what Noah first did after he left the ark? **He sacrificed some innocent animals**, burning them on an altar he built. God had not abolished His law which stated: *"Without the shedding of blood there is no forgiveness of sin."* (Heb. 9:22) While **the great flood destroyed most of the sinners** from off the face of the earth, **it did not destroy the root of sin** that remained in the hearts of the children of Adam. That is why Noah and his descendants had to continue offering to God sacrifices for sin. As we have seen, such animal sacrifices were the foundation of the way of salvation that God had decreed. The sacrifices that our ancestors slaughtered in early times, symbolized {illustrated} the Redeemer who was to come and shed His own blood to pay the debt of sin for Adam's descendants. That is why, when Noah left the ark, the first thing he did was to shed animal blood, thus showing his children and grandchildren that the laws of God had not changed–that "*the wages of sin is death*" (Rom. 6:23) and "*without the shedding of blood there is no forgiveness of sin.*" (Heb. 9:22)

Thus, the Scriptures say:

> "*The* LORD *smelled the pleasing aroma (of the sacrifice)...Then God blessed Noah and his sons, saying to them, 'Be fruitful and increase in number and fill the earth...I now establish* **my covenant** *with you and with your descendants after you...Never again will all life be cut off by the waters of a flood; never again will there be a flood to destroy the earth...This is the sign of the* **covenant** *I am making between me and you and every living creature with you, a* **covenant** *for all generations to come: I have set* **my rainbow** *in the clouds, and it will be the sign of the* **covenant** *between me and the earth. Whenever I bring clouds over the earth and the rainbow appears in the clouds, I will remember* **my covenant** *between me and you and all living creatures of every kind. Never again will the waters become a flood to destroy all life.*" (Gen. 8:21; 9:1,9,11-15)

In these verses we have just read, there is a word which God repeated five times to Noah. Did you hear it? The word is "***covenant***." In the Word of God, a covenant is a special promise made by God to man. **God is the Keeper of covenants.** God is faithful, and He wants to show forth His faithfulness to the sons of Adam! That is why, in His goodness, He established a covenant with Noah and those who descended from Him saying, "*Never again will all life be cut off by the waters of a flood.*" That is what God promised. And He did not limit His promise to mere words, but He confirmed it by putting His rainbow in the clouds.

Did you know that the beautiful **rainbow** that we see sometimes in the clouds after it has rained is a sign which declares **the faithfulness of God**? Every time we see a rainbow in the clouds, God wants to remind us of His faithfulness that endures from generation to generation. God put the rainbow in the clouds to confirm His covenant in which He promised that the waters will never again become a flood to destroy all life. Truly, God is the Keeper of covenants! **He is faithful!**

Concerning the rest of Noah's life, there are other events of which we could speak, but we do not have the time. You can read them for yourselves, however, in the Torah, the book of Genesis, chapter nine. You will see that after the flood, Noah lived another 350 years, and when he was very old he went to be with the LORD on high.

In summary, perhaps we can conclude our talk about God's prophet, Noah, with a question or two. What was the difference between Noah and the people of his time? What did Noah do to please God? He did simply one thing. **Noah believed the word of God**. That is why Noah did not perish with the people of his generation. Listen to what God Himself has testified about Noah:

> "***By faith*** *Noah, when warned about* ***things not yet seen****, in holy fear built an ark to save his family.* ***By his faith*** *he condemned the world and became heir of the righteousness that comes* ***by faith****."* But *"without faith it is impossible to please God."* (Heb 11:7,6)

Before we bid you farewell today, there are **two thoughts** which we must keep in our minds. We just considered the first of these two thoughts. What made Noah pleasing to God? **His faith. Noah believed God; he believed what God said**. Noah had confidence in the LORD and obeyed His word even when all others around him rejected it. It was Noah's faith that caused God to deliver him from the evil generation in which he lived. You who are listening to us today, **do you truly believe what God has said**? God's will for each of us is that we believe His Word as Noah did.

The second thing we must remember from the story of Noah is even **more important than Noah's faith**. Do you know what it is? It is **God's faithfulness**. Why is God's faithfulness more important than Noah's faith? Because if God was not faithful to keep His covenants and promises, the faith that Noah had in Him would be of no benefit. We all know what happens when we put our trust in someone who does not keep his promise. Suppose you have a friend who promises you: "Tomorrow I will bring you a sack of rice." You believe him; you have faith in him. What happens if he does not bring it? You will be disappointed (and perhaps hungry!). The faith that you had in your friend was worthless. Why? Because your friend did not do what he had promised. You trusted someone who was unfaithful.

It is not like that with God. The Scriptures say:

> *"If we are faithless,* ***he will remain faithful****, for he cannot disown himself."* (2 Tim. 2:13) *"For, all men are like grass, and all their glory is like the flowers of the field; the grass withers and the flowers fall, but* ***the word of the LORD stands forever****.... and the one who trusts in him will [not be disappointed!]"* (1 Pet. 1:24,25; 2:6) Yes, ***"God is faithful!"*** (1 Cor. 1:9)

He will do what He has promised!

In the story of Noah we clearly see how **God did everything that He promised**. We read how God saved everyone who was inside the ark and judged everyone who was outside, just as He had promised. We also saw how God forgave Noah his sins because he offered up the blood of an animal as a sacrifice, just as God had told him to do. And we learned how God placed His rainbow in the clouds so that Noah and all people would not forget that ***"God is faithful!"***

Oh, fellow listeners, if you should forget everything we have considered today except one thing, remember this: **God is Faithful**! He cannot go back on His Word. He does what He promises, even if it seems He is slow in doing so. "*God is faithful…. and the one who trusts in Him will never be put to shame.*" (1 Cor. 1:9; 1 Pet. 2:6) Let us then believe Him and accept His Word with humility. And may we benefit from the story of the prophet Noah and the great flood—by imitating Noah who believed the Word of God when everyone around him refused to believe it and were destroyed.

This is where we must stop today. We thank you for listening. In our next lesson, God willing, we will see what became of Noah's descendants and learn where the many languages of the world come from….

God bless you as you remember this truth from His Word:

> ***"God is faithful…. and the one who trusts in Him will never be put to shame."*** (1 Cor. 1:9; 1 Pet. 2:6)

Lesson 16

The Tower of Babel

Genesis 10, 11

Peace be with you, listening friends. We greet you in the name of God, the Lord of peace, who wants everyone to understand and submit to the way of righteousness that He has established, and have true peace with Him forever. We are happy to be able to return today to present your program *The Way of Righteousness*.

In our last program we concluded our study of God's prophet, Noah. We saw how God purposed to wipe out the children of Adam with a flood because of their wickedness. For a hundred years **God gave sinners time to repent** while Noah constructed the ark which would be a refuge for those who believed the word of God. Still, no one turned from his or her sin or believed the message of the Lord God, except Noah and his family. Thus, in the end, **God, who is righteous and faithful, did just as He had promised**. He wiped out everyone who did not pass through the door of the ark, and saved those few who did.

Today we will continue in the book of Genesis and learn what happened in **the period following the time of Noah**. In our talks about Noah, we learned that he had three sons, **Shem, Ham and Japheth**. The Scriptures show us that it is from these three men that **all the peoples of the world** come. Shem was the father of the Jews and the Arabs. Most of the people of Africa and China are probably descendants of Ham. Europeans are descendants of Japheth.

If you would like to broaden your knowledge of the origin of the nations, you can study chapters ten and eleven of the first book of the Torah. However, in our lesson today, we have time to explain just one thing about the history of Noah's three sons, Shem, Ham and Japheth. It is this: **Shem** was the one whom God chose to be in **the ancestry of the Redeemer** who would come into the world. That is why the Holy Scriptures follow more closely the story of the descendants of Shem. It is from his line that both the prophets of God and the Savior of the world came.

Thus, all the peoples of the earth come from the three sons of Noah. You and I, all the people of Senegal, the people of Gambia, Mauritania and all of Africa, as well as all the other peoples of the world–everyone living today is a descendant of Noah. Therefore we can say that we are here today because Noah believed God and made an ark to save his family; for when he saved his family from the flood, he also saved you and me along with them (from extinction).

God blessed Noah and his sons, saying to them: "*Be fruitful and increase in number and fill the earth.*" (Gen. 9:1) Thus, hundreds of years after the flood, once again, there were multitudes of people dwelling upon the earth. And again, **the world began to be corrupted by sin**. We have already seen that Noah and his sons were born sinners because they were descendants of Adam. When they entered the ark, their **sinful nature**, which they received from Adam, went along with them. And when they went out of the ark, they went out with the **root of sin** still in their hearts. The flood did not change man's sinful condition. As the (Wolof) proverb puts it: "A rat only begets that which digs." Therefore, all the people of the world continued to be born sinners, because they were all descendants of Noah who was a descendant of Adam.

It is sad, but true, that hundreds of years after the great flood, most of Noah's descendants were no longer concerned about God and His will. **They did not believe the word of God** as did their ancestors Seth, Enoch and Noah. They forgot God and did not thank Him for giving them life and breath and sunshine and rain and food. As for the rainbow that God had placed in the clouds to remind them of His faithfulness, most no longer even knew what it meant. Listen to what the Word of God declares concerning them:

> "*For although they knew God, they neither glorified him as God nor gave thanks to him, but their thinking became futile and their foolish hearts were darkened. Although they claimed to be wise, they became fools. They exchanged the truth of God for a lie, and worshiped and served created things rather than the Creator, who is forever praised. Amen.*" (Rom. 1:21,22,25)

Like Cain and his descendants, most of Noah's descendants chose to bury the truth, and follow unrighteousness. They had religion, but it was a false religion because it did not line up with the way of righteousness established by God. They did not listen to the true word of God. They were listening to Satan.

There was a man by the name of **Nimrod**, who descended from Ham, Noah's second son. Nimrod was a great hunter who lived about five hundred years after the flood. His name means *rebel*. Nimrod was highly intelligent, but he did not know God. He ignored the word of God and followed the way of Satan, the way of Cain, and the way of the people of Noah's generation. Nimrod built several large cities, and planned to build **a great city** in which all the people of the world could live together and be as one.

Let us now read in chapter eleven of the book of Genesis to see what the

Scriptures say concerning the great city which Nimrod and those with him planned to build. The Scripture says:

> (Gen.11) [1]***Now the whole world had one language and a common speech.***
> [2]*As men moved eastward, they found a plain in Shinar and settled there.* [3]*They said to each other, "Come, let's make bricks and bake them thoroughly." They used brick instead of stone, and bitumen for mortar.* [4]*Then they said, "Come, let us build ourselves a city, with* ***a tower that reaches to the heavens****, so that we may make* ***a name for ourselves*** *and* ***not be scattered*** *over the face of the whole earth."*

Thus, we see how the sons of Adam planned to build a great city and **a high tower** that would reach to the heavens. Why did they want to build that high tower? Nimrod and those who went along with him were seeking to make a name for themselves in the world. They planned to gather the people of the world into one place, so that they would become powerful and not be scattered over the earth. However, what they planned to do did not please God. God had told the children of Noah to spread out over the surface of the earth. God, who created man, knew what was best for the people of the world. However, most of Noah's descendants didn't care about the thoughts of God. They thought that they were more intelligent than God. Like Satan himself, their hearts were full of **pride and rebellion against God**. But the Scriptures say: *"Whoever exalts himself will be humbled, and whoever humbles himself will be exalted."* (Matt. 23:12) And *"what is highly valued among men is detestable in God's sight."* (Luke 16:15)

To exalt man or to seek a great name for yourself is **sin** before God, because there is **only one Name worthy of praise and glory**. That is the Name of **the Lord God** who made heaven and earth! As the Scripture says: "***Let him who boasts boast in the Lord****! For it is not the one who [praises] himself who is approved, but the one whom the Lord [praises]."* (2 Cor. 10:17,18)

However, in the time of Nimrod, most of the children of Adam had no respect for the Lord. They thought they didn't need God and His word; they did not need anyone to tell them anything. They were characterized by a **spirit of independence and rebellion**. To this day, that same attitude is found in the hearts of the children of Adam. We even see it in little children when they flip their arm and say, "No, I won't!" {a Wolof expression of stubborn refusal}. And how much more is this same spirit of rebellion found in adults! What is the cause of the strife found in the homes and nations of the world? Is it not this spirit of independence which thinks: "I can take care of myself. My traditions are the best. My religion is good enough for me. My sect is right. My people are superior. My tribe is the smartest. My name is the most important. My things! My will! My works! My money! My! My!! My!!!" How self-centered is man! Everyone pulls for his own interests. That (self-seeking) spirit of independence is why the world is full of quarrels, fights and wars. However, **God hates such a spirit**, for His Name alone is worthy of glory. That is why He says in His Word: "*I am the LORD; that is my name! I will not give my glory to another!*" (Isa. 42:8)

However, those who began to build the tower to reach to the heavens didn't care about God's glory. They only sought their own glory. They had no use for the Name of their Creator. Certainly, many people of that time were religious, but **they ignored the word of God**. They thought they could reach heaven in their own way. Think of it! Just five hundred years after the flood, people were, once again, going their own way and ignoring the Lord who gave them life and breath. They were like a horse that, after it has been washed, goes and rolls in the mud! (See 2 Pet. 2:22) How foolish and wicked of man to want to live his life apart from God and His Word!

So what did God do? Did He ignore the people's plan to live independently of their Creator? Did He accept those who rebelled against Him? No, He did not! Listen to what God did. The Scripture says:

> (Gen.11) [5]*But the LORD came down to see the city and the tower that the men were building.* [6]*The LORD said, "If as one people speaking the same language they have begun to do this, then nothing they plan to do will be impossible for them.* [7]*Come, let us go down and confuse their language so they will not understand each other."* [8]*So the LORD scattered them from there over all the earth, and they stopped building the city.* [9]*That is why it was called Babel, because* ***there the LORD confused the language of the whole world. From there the LORD scattered them over the face of the whole earth****."*

Thus, we see how God upset the plans of Nimrod and the others who had begun to build a great city for their own glory. Until this time, everyone in the world spoke the same language. But on this day, **God mixed up their language** so that they could no longer understand each other. You will remember that God had commanded Noah's descendants "*to fill the earth*"; to spread out all over the world. But Nimrod and his followers wanted to do things their own way and gather all the people of the world into one place. God defeated their intentions by giving them new languages. That is how **God scattered them over the face of the whole earth**. This is the reason we have hundreds of nations and thousands of languages in the world today.

God certainly did a thorough job of mixing up the languages of the world. Think how many languages are spoken in Senegal alone. Oh how great is our God! No one can go against God Almighty and prosper. "An egg should not wrestle with a rock!" {Wolof Proverb} Man tried to "wrestle" with God and lost. Do you know the name of this city which man tried to build in rebellion against

God? Yes, the name of the city is **Babel**. Babel means *confusion*. Life apart from God and His Word is only **confusion**!

That is the story of the city of Babel and the people who tried to exalt their own name. Are we ever like the people of Babel? Do we ever exalt ourselves? God tells us that it is **sin** to do so. Listening friend, **whose name are you seeking to exalt?** Your own name? ...the name of a man, perhaps some marabout {religious leader}? Or are you seeking to exalt the Name of **the Lord God** and Him alone? Whose praise {*thanks*} are you seeking? The praise of man? Or are you seeking the praise of **God**? One thing is absolutely certain. The praise that comes from men will pass away, but the praise that comes from God will endure forever. God's Word says: "*All men are like grass, and all their glory is like the flowers of the field; the grass* ***withers*** *and the flowers* ***fall***, *but the word of the Lord stands* ***forever***!" (1 Pet. 1:24)

Listen to this word from the LORD Himself:

> "'*Let not the wise man boast of his wisdom or the strong man boast of his strength or the rich man boast of his riches, but* ***let him who boasts boast about this***: *that he understands and knows me, that I am the* LORD, *who exercises kindness, justice and righteousness on the earth, for in these I delight,' declares the* LORD." (Jeremiah 9:23,24)

God willing, in our next program, we will review everything that we have studied from the beginning until now....God bless you as you remember:

> ***"It is not the one who commends himself who is approved, but the one whom the Lord commends."*** (2 Cor. 10:18)

Lesson 17
Review of "The Beginning"

Genesis 1-11

Peace be with you, listening friends. We greet you in the name of God, the Lord of peace, who wants everyone to understand and submit to the way of righteousness that He has established, and have true peace with Him forever. We are happy to be able to return today to present your program *The Way of Righteousness*.

Today, with God's help, we plan to **review and summarize** what we have studied up to this point in the Torah of the prophet Moses. The Torah is the first section in the Holy Scriptures of the Prophets. This section is very important because it is **the foundation** which God Himself has laid, by which we can test everything we hear, to know whether it comes from God. The Torah has five parts or books. The first part we call *Genesis*. There are fifty chapters in Genesis. In our chronological lessons, we have studied up to chapter eleven.

Can you remember what is written in the first verse of the Word of God? Let us reread it. It says: "*In the beginning God created the heavens and the earth.*" God is the Lord of Eternity. In the beginning, when the world did not yet exist, only God existed. God is the Eternal Spirit who has no beginning. That is why the first verse of Scripture says: "*In the beginning **God**!*"

Next, we saw how God, before He created the world, created thousands and thousands of powerful spirits, calling them **angels**. Among the angels, there was one who was wiser and more beautiful than all the others. That one was **Lucifer**, whom God appointed chief of the angels. However, the Scriptures say that a day came when Lucifer exalted himself and despised God in his heart, wanting to take God's place. There were also many other angels who chose to follow Lucifer in his sin. That is why God, who cannot tolerate sin, expelled Lucifer and the evil angels and changed Lucifer's name to **Satan**, which means *Adversary*. After God expelled Satan and his angels, he created for them the fires of **hell** which are never extinguished. The Scriptures say that on the day of final judgment, God, the Righteous One, will throw Satan into that fire along with all who follow him.

Next, we read how **the LORD created the heavens and the earth** and everything they contain in **six days** and He used nothing except His word! God created everything for man (whom He planned to create for His pleasure and glory). **Man** {Lit. *A human*} is the most important creature that God created, because man was created in the image of God. God wanted to have a deep and meaningful relationship with man. That is why God placed in the soul of man an intelligent **spirit** (mind) so that he could know God, God gave him a **heart** so that he could love God, and God committed to him a **free will** so that he could choose for himself to obey God or to disobey Him.

In the second chapter of the Torah, we read that God planted **the Garden of Paradise** (Eden) on the earth, and placed in it the man He had created, that is **Adam**. God, in His goodness, gave Adam everything so that he could live in peace and prosperity.

Also, in the day on which God created Adam, God said to him, "*You are free to eat from any tree in the garden; but you must not eat from the tree of the knowledge of good and evil, for [in the day that] you eat of it you will surely die*." (Gen. 2:16,17) Thus, we saw how God put **a simple test** before Adam. God wanted a meaningful relationship with the man whom He had created. Therefore God tested him, giving him the authority to choose either to love Him enough to obey Him, or not to obey Him.

We also read that, on the day that God created Adam, God gave him a very wonderful present, a wife! God created the woman from a rib which He took from Adam and then presented her to Adam. He called her ***Eve***. Thus, in six days, God completed His work. So the Scriptures say: "*God saw all that he had made, and it was very good*." (Gen. 1:31) On the seventh day God rested (ceased from His work of creation) and rejoiced in all that He had made.

In the third chapter, we saw how **sin** came into our world. The Scriptures show us how, one day, when Adam and Eve were near the tree which God had forbidden, Satan came as **a crafty snake**, saying,

> "*Did God really say, 'You must not eat from any tree in the garden?' The woman said to the serpent, 'We may eat fruit from the trees in the garden, but God did say, 'You must not eat fruit from the tree that is in the middle of the garden, and you must not touch it, or you will die.' 'You will not surely die,' the serpent said to the woman. 'For God knows that when you eat of it your eyes will be opened, and you will be like God, knowing good and evil.*'"(Gen. 3:1-5)

Thus, we saw how **Satan contradicted the word of God**! What had God told Adam and Eve would happen to them if they ate of the tree which he had forbidden? He said: "*You will die!*" And what did Satan say? He said: "*You will **not** die!*" Whose word did Adam and Eve choose to believe and follow: the word of God?

Or the word of Satan? Alas, the Scriptures record that Adam and Eve chose to believe the word of Satan and eat the fruit of the tree which God had forbidden! Satan deceived Eve so that she transgressed. **Adam deliberately chose to disobey God's command and to follow Satan**. Thus, the Holy Scriptures say: "*Sin entered the world through one man, and death through sin, and in this way death came to all men.*" (Rom. 5:12)

Consequently, **God expelled Adam and Eve** from the Garden of Paradise, just as He had said He would do. But before He expelled them, **God promised to send a Savior** into the world to redeem the children of Adam from the power of Satan, sin and death! To confirm that promise, God slaughtered some animals and made clothes of the skins and put them on Adam and Eve. By means of those **animal sacrifices**, God was teaching Adam and Eve that "*the wages of sin is death*" (Rom. 6:23) and that "*without the shedding of blood there is no forgiveness of sin.*" (Heb. 9:22)

In chapter four, we read the story of Adam's first two children, **Cain and Abel**. We saw how **Abel offered to God an innocent lamb**, slaughtered it as a sacrifice for sin, just as God had done for Abel's parents. However, **Cain tried to approach God in his own way**, bringing what he had cultivated in the earth which God had cursed. Thus, the Scriptures say: "*The LORD looked with favor on Abel and his offering, but on Cain and his offering He did not look with favor.*" (Gen. 4:4,5) God called Cain to give account so that he would repent and accept God's way of righteousness, but Cain only got angry, and killed Abel, his younger brother.

Afterward, God gave Adam and Eve another child, named **Seth**. Seth, like Abel, believed God and approached Him with the blood of a sacrifice. Thus, we saw the two genealogies which descended from Adam, that is, the line of Cain and the line of Seth. The descendants of Cain did not believe God. But among the descendants of Seth were those who believed God. One, who descended from Seth, was named **Enoch**. Enoch walked with God in a corrupt generation. Enoch had a great grandson by the name of **Noah**. In the days of Noah, God purposed to wipe out the children of Adam with a flood because of their **wickedness**. In that perverse time, **only Noah believed God**, which is why God told him to build a huge ark (boat), which would be **a refuge** for him and his family and many animals, and any who would turn from their sins and believe the word of God. For a hundred years, God patiently endured sinners while Noah constructed the ark. However, no one repented of his sins to the point of believing the message of God, except Noah and his family. Thus, in the end, God did everything that He had promised. He judged everyone who did not believe the truth. All but Noah and his family perished in **the great flood**.

Noah had three sons: **Shem, Ham and Japheth**. From these three men all the peoples of the world descend. However, we saw how most of their descendants quickly forgot God and His word. In our last lesson, we learned how Nimrod and those who went along with him planned to bring all the people of the world to one place and build a great city with a high tower in rebellion against God. However God confused their language, and scattered them throughout the earth. The city became known as **Babel**, which means *confusion*. That, in short, is what we have studied up to this point in the book of Genesis, in chapters one to eleven.

How then can we summarize what we have seen in all these stories? What does God want to teach us from what happened in the beginning of time? There are many lessons to be learned, but today we only have time to explain two of them. One lesson is that **Man is unrighteous**. The other truth to be learned is that **God is righteous!**

In our studies, we have repeatedly seen **the unrighteousness of man**. We saw it begin in the Garden of Paradise (Eden), when Adam ate the fruit of the tree which God had forbidden. We saw it again in Cain, Adam's firstborn son, who refused to follow the way of sacrifice which God had established. We observed this same unrighteousness in Cain's descendants, in the people of Noah's generation, and in those who tried to build the tower of Babel. In short, the story of the children of Adam is: Man is unrighteous! As it is written in the Scriptures: "***All men** are under [the dominion of] sin...**there is no one righteous, not even one**!... **All have turned away**, they have together become worthless; **there is no one who does good, not even one**!*" (Rom. 3:9,10,12)

Just as we have seen the unrighteousness of man, so we have also seen **the righteousness of God**. The Scripture tells us that "*God is **light**; in Him there is no darkness at all!*" (1 John 1:5) We witnessed God's righteousness when He expelled Lucifer because of his pride and rebellion. We saw it again when He expelled Adam and Eve because of their disobedience. Next, God revealed His righteousness by promising to send into the world a holy Redeemer who would pay the debt of sin for the children of Adam. Also, we observed the righteous character of God in His law which stated: "*Without the shedding of blood there is no forgiveness of sin.*" (Heb. 9:22) God displayed His righteousness when He accepted Abel because of the blood of a lamb, and refused Cain, who scorned God's way of forgiveness. We saw God's righteous nature in the time of Noah, when, after giving man a hundred years to repent, He sent a flood to wipe out all who refused His way. And in our last study, we saw how God revealed His righteousness by mixing up the language of the people of the city of Babel who were rebelling against Him.

Yes, God is righteous and must judge people according to **His standard of righteousness**! Unrighteous sinners cannot approach Him on the basis of their imperfect "good deeds." God must judge and condemn anything that is tainted by sin. The Scripture says, "*Our God is a consuming fire!...The Lord will judge his people. It is a dreadful thing to fall into the hands of the living God!*" (Heb. 12:29; 10:30,31)

Thus, in the first eleven chapters of the Torah, God has made known to us the important truth concerning His absolute righteousness. Does this mean that unrighteous man has no hope of being accepted by God? No, praise be to God, there is **hope for sinners**! God, in His grace, has revealed a way by which the unrighteous children of Adam can be made right before Him! Do you know the way of salvation which God has established for sinners? If you do not yet understand **God's way of righteousness**, we invite you to join us in the upcoming programs as we study about the prophet Abraham who was called *the friend of God*. In the amazing story of Abraham we will see how those who are unrighteous can be made righteous before God.

Thank you for listening....May God bless you as you think about all we have studied today. Remember that God's Word says:

> ***"Everything that was written in the past was written to teach us, so that through endurance and the encouragement of the Scriptures we might have hope."*** (Rom. 15:4)

Lesson 18

Why God Called Abraham

Genesis 11,12

Peace be with you, listening friends. We greet you in the name of God, the Lord of peace, who wants everyone to understand and submit to the way of righteousness that He has established, and have true peace with Him forever. We are happy to be able to return today to present your program *The Way of Righteousness.*

In past lessons, we have been learning about God and His way of righteousness. We have seen Adam and Eve, Cain and Abel, Seth and Enoch, Noah and the people of his generation, and Nimrod and the tower of Babel. Only a few of our ancestors followed **God and His way of righteousness**; most followed **Satan and his way of unrighteousness**.

Today we have come to the story of a man whose name is well known in the Word of God, and who had an important place in God's plan to redeem the children of Adam. The Scripture refers to this man as "*the friend of God*" and "*the father of all who believe.*" Do you know who it is? It is the prophet of God, **Abraham** {*Ibrahim* in Arabic}. The Holy Scriptures speak a great deal about Abraham. His name appears in the Writings of the Prophets more than three hundred times. Therefore, God willing, today and in coming lessons, we will search the Scriptures to discover what they teach concerning this man who was called *the friend of God*. Today we intend to look into the beginning of the story of Abraham, to see **how God called him** to follow Him, and **why He called him**.

Before we begin, you should know that, at first, Abraham's name was not *Abraham*, but **Abram**. Two lessons from now we will see why God changed Abram's name to Abraham. Today, however, let us keep in mind that Abraham was first called *Abram*. In chapter eleven of the book of Genesis, we learn that Abram belonged to the **descendants of Shem**. Do you remember Shem, Ham and Japheth? They were the three sons of Noah. Between Shem and Abram, there were ten generations, just as there were ten generations between Adam and Noah. Abram's father's name was Terah. The Scripture says: "*Terah became the father of Abram, Nahor and Haran. And Haran became the father of Lot.*" (Gen. 11:27) Lot was the son of Abram's older brother. Lot's Father had died {Note: in Wolof culture that would make Abram Lot's functional father}. Abram's wife's name was Sarai. "*Now Sarai was barren; she had no children.*" (Gen. 11:30) Abram and Sarai had the same father, but not the same mother.

Abram lived in a city named Ur, which was located in the country of Chaldea, known today as Iraq. This city was not far from where Nimrod tried to build the city of Babel with its tall tower. The people of the land worshiped idols. Like all of Adam's offspring, **Abram was born in the darkness of sin.** Abram's father did not know the true God and neither did Abram.

However the Scriptures tell us that one day **the LORD God revealed Himself to Abram** and spoke with him. You need to know that in early times, God occasionally spoke directly with people, because they did not yet have the Writings of the Prophets. Today God speaks to people through **the Holy Scriptures**. That is why we no longer need words which resound from the sky, or visions, or angels in order to know God's way of righteousness. When we meditate upon the Holy Scriptures, we are listening to **the voice of God**.

Let us listen now to what God said to Abram. In chapter twelve, verse one, we read: "*The LORD had said to Abram, '**Leave your country**, your people and your father's household and go to the land I will show you.'*" (Gen. 12:1) Did you hear what God commanded Abram? He told Abram to leave his father's house, bid farewell to his relatives, leave his country, and move to a country to which God would lead him. To man's way of thinking, what God asked Abram to do was extremely difficult, but God had plans to greatly bless him.

Let us now reread this verse and the two verses which follow, to know **why** God called Abram to leave his home and go to another country.

> "*The LORD had said to Abram, 'Leave your country, your people and your father's household and go to the land I will show you. **I will make you into a great nation** and I will bless you; I will make your name great, and you will be a blessing. I will bless those who bless you, and whoever curses you I will curse; and **all peoples on earth will be blessed through you**.*" (Gen. 12:1-3)

Why did God command Abram to move to another country? This is why: **God planned to make of Abram a new nation from which the prophets of God and the Savior of the world would arise**. That is why God promised Abram saying, "*I will make you into a great nation…and you will be a blessing…and all peoples on earth will be blessed through you.*"

Here is **a great truth**. Do you understand it? God chose Abram to become the father of the ancestors through which the promised Redeemer would come into the world. This Redeemer was destined to be the Savior for all the peoples of the world, so that whoever believes in Him, might be saved from the dominion of sin and Satan, and from the eternal fire. Thus, we see that when God called Abram, He was moving forward with His plan to send the Savior of sinners into the world. Abram himself was not the Savior of the world, but **he was to become the father of a nation from which the promised Savior would come**.

That is the promise {or *covenant*} God made to Abram–on the condition that he leave his country and go to the place that God would show him. Did Abram obey God? What do you think? The Word of God tells us:

> "***So Abram left, as the LORD had told him***...*Abram was seventy-five years old when he set out from Haran. He took his wife Sarai, his nephew Lot, all the possessions they had accumulated and the people they had acquired in Haran, and they set out for the land of Canaan, and they arrived there.*" (Gen. 12:4-5)

Why did Abram obey God, turning his back on his father's home and religion? There is only one reason. **Abram had confidence in God.** Abram did not know where he was going, but he believed the word of the LORD which said, "Move out! If you move, I will greatly bless you!" Abram had confidence in God and left his country as the LORD God had told him. And God, in His faithfulness, led Abram to the land of **Canaan**, which today is called *Palestine* or *Israel.*

Next, the Scriptures say: "*Abram traveled through the land...At that time the Canaanites were in the land. The LORD appeared to Abram and said, '**To your offspring I will give this land**.'*" (Gen. 12:6-7) Thus we learn that God, who promised to make Abram the father of a new nation, also promised him a new country as well. That is what God meant when He appeared to Abram and promised him, "*To your offspring I will give this land.*"

Again, we see something which surpasses human wisdom. The land of Canaan had people living throughout it. How could Abram and his descendants possess it? **Abram was seventy-five years old. His wife was sixty-five and childless.** Could two elderly people have enough children and descendants to fill the land? How could this happen?

Let us try to illustrate what God promised Abram. It is like an elderly man who has no children and comes from a far off land to visit Senegal. He comes with his elderly wife, who has never been able to conceive. When they arrive, someone says to them, "One day you and your descendants will possess the whole land of Senegal!" The old man laughs and says, "You are very funny! My descendants are going to possess the land? I do not even have any descendants! I am an old man; I have no children, and my wife is unable to conceive—and you say to me that my descendants are going to multiply and possess Senegal? Are you ill?"

Perhaps this illustration seems a little absurd; nonetheless, this is the kind of promise God made to Abram–to a man who was old and childless, with a wife who could not conceive. Listen to what God promised Abram in chapter thirteen. He said,

> "*All the land that you see I will give to you and your offspring forever. I will make your offspring like the dust of the earth, so that* ***if anyone could count the dust, then your offspring could be counted****. Go, walk through the length and breadth of the land, for I am giving it to you.*" (Gen. 13:15-17)

Did God do what He promised? Did He make of Abram a great nation? Did He give the land of Palestine to Abram's descendants? He surely did! In future lessons we will see that Abram became the father of the Hebrew nation to which God gave the land that, today, is called *Israel*.

Next, the Scriptures say: "*So [Abram] built* ***an altar*** *there to the LORD, who had appeared to him. From there he went on toward the hills east of Bethel and pitched his tent.... There he built* ***an altar*** *to the LORD and called on the name of the LORD.*" (Gen. 12:7,8) What was the first thing that Abram did, upon arriving in the new country which God had promised to give him? He slaughtered an animal and burned it on an altar he constructed. Just as Abel, Seth, Enoch and Noah did, Abram, in the same way, offered up animal sacrifices to God. Why did Abram do this? He did it because God had not done away with His law which states: "*Without the shedding of blood, there is no forgiveness of sin!*" (Heb. 9:22) **Abram, like all of Adam's offspring, was a sinner.** The only reason God could overlook Abram's sins was because Abram believed God and brought to Him **the blood of a sacrifice**, which was an illustration of **the holy Redeemer** who was to come into the world to die in the place of sinners.

Our time is about up. What we have studied today is very important and must not be forgotten. Do you understand now **why** God called Abram to turn his back on his father's house and move to another country? Yes, God intended to make of Abram **a new nation**, which would be a "*door of blessing*" for all peoples of the earth. What God planned to do with Abram was **part of the wonderful plan** that He announced in the Garden of Paradise on the day that our ancestors, Adam and Eve, sinned. Do you remember how God had promised One who would come into the world to deliver the children of Adam from the power of Satan? Two thousand years later, in the time of Abram, **God had not forgotten His promise**.

Today we have seen how God, in His faithfulness, called Abram so that he might become the father of a nation through which the promised Savior would come into the world. That was why God promised Abram saying, "*I will make you into a great nation and I will bless you; I will make your name great, and you will be a blessing. I will bless those who bless you, and whoever curses you I will curse; and* ***all peoples on earth will be blessed through you.***" (Gen. 12:2,3)

Have you grasped today's lesson? Allow us to ask you a couple of questions which summarize what we have studied today. **First: Why did God call Abram to leave home and go to another country?** Because God planned to make of Abram a new nation. **Second: Why did God want to make of Abram a new nation?** Because it was through this nation that God planned to give us the prophets, the Scriptures and at last, the holy Redeemer Himself. Thus, in summary, we see that when God called Abram, **God was moving forward with His plan to bring into the world the Savior of sinners.**

Friends, we must stop here today. In our next lesson, God willing, we will learn why Abram was called "the friend of God."...God bless you as you meditate on His promise to Abram:

> ***"I will make you into a great nation. You will be a blessing...and all peoples on earth will be blessed through you."*** (Gen. 12:2,3)

LESSON 19

ABRAHAM, GOD'S FRIEND

GENESIS 13-15

Peace be with you, listening friends. We greet you in the name of God, the Lord of peace, who wants everyone to understand and submit to the way of righteousness that He has established, and have true peace with Him forever. We are happy to be able to return today to present your program *The Way of Righteousness*.

In the last lesson, we began to look into what God's Word says about the prophet Abraham. We learned that, at first, Abraham was not called Abraham, but ***Abram***. We saw that Abram was born in the country of Chaldea, which today is called Iraq. The people of that land were idol worshipers. However, the Scriptures say that, one day, the LORD God appeared to Abram and told him to leave his father's house and move to a country which He would show him.

Do you remember **why** God called Abram to move to another country? It was because God planned to make of Abram **a new nation** from which the prophets of God would arise, and ultimately, the Savior of the world Himself. Thus, we discovered that when God called Abram, He was moving forward with **His plan** to bring the Redeemer into the world. That is why God said to Abram, *"You will be a blessing...and **all peoples on earth will be blessed through you**."* (Gen. 12:2,3)

Thus, we read how Abram obeyed God and left his city, not knowing where God would lead him. When Abram left his father's house, he was seventy-five years old. Abram took with him Sarai, his wife, and Lot, the son of his older brother, and all his accumulated wealth and his servants, and headed in the direction of Canaan. Canaan is the land which today is known as Palestine or Israel.

When Abram arrived in the land of Canaan, the LORD appeared to him again and said, *"To your offspring I will give this land."* (Gen. 12:7) Thus we saw how God, who promised to make Abram the father of a new nation, also promised to give him a new land for his offspring to dwell in. Incredible! Abram and his wife were elderly and did not have any children. How then could they have descendants who would fill the land? We will soon see God's answer to this.

Now, let us continue in the story of Abram. We are studying in the Torah, in the book of Genesis, chapter thirteen. In this chapter we will see **what happened between Abram and his nephew Lot**. The Scriptures say:

> (Gen. 13) [2]*Abram had become very wealthy in livestock and in silver and gold.* [3]*...He went from place to place until he came to Bethel, to the place between Bethel and Ai where his tent had been earlier* [4]*and where he had first built an altar. There Abram called on the name of the LORD.* [5]*Now Lot, who was moving about with Abram, also had flocks and herds and tents.* [6]*But the land could not support them while they stayed together, for their possessions were so great that they were not able to stay together.* [7]*And quarreling arose between Abram's herdsmen and the herdsmen of Lot...* [8]*So Abram said to Lot, "Let's not have any quarreling between you and me, or between your herdsmen and mine, for we are brothers.* [9]*Is not the whole land before you? Let's part company.* ***If you go to the left, I'll go to the right; if you go to the right, I'll go to the left.****"*
>
> [10]*Lot looked up and saw that the whole plain of the Jordan was well watered, like the garden of the LORD, like the land of Egypt, toward Zoar. (This was before the LORD destroyed Sodom and Gomorrah.)* [11]*So Lot chose for himself the whole plain of the Jordan and set out toward the east. The two men parted company:* [12]***Abram*** *lived in the land of Canaan, while* **Lot** *lived among the cities of the plain and pitched his tents near Sodom.* [13]*Now the men of Sodom were wicked and were sinning greatly against the LORD.*

Thus we see how Lot chose the more verdant fields, and left his uncle Abram with the drier ones. However the portion which Lot chose was in the region of Sodom–a city which was filled with great wickedness!

Lot chose **his own will**, while Abram chose **God's will**. Two studies from now, Lord willing, we will see what happened to Lot who followed his own desires. In the end, Lot lost everything: his riches, his wife, his family, his happiness, and his testimony! As for Abram, who left everything in the hands of God, he was greatly blessed by God.

How can we profit from the story of Lot and Abram? Perhaps by asking ourselves a simple question. Which of the two am I most like? **Lot** or **Abram**? Am I seeking after **the things of the world**, like Lot? Or **the things of Eternity**, like Abram? Like the two of them, each of us must choose between our own will and God's will. The one who is wise will choose God's will. The Scriptures say: "*What good is it for a man to gain the whole world, yet forfeit his soul?*" (Mark 8:36) "*Do not love the world or anything in the world...[Because] the world and its desires pass away,* ***but the man who does the will of God lives forever****.*" (1 John 2:15,17) What is it that you want more than anything else? The things of the earth which are passing away or things of God which last forever?

Now, let's continue with the story of Abram. The Scriptures say:

> (Gen. 14) [14]*The* LORD *said to Abram after Lot had parted from him, "Lift up your eyes from where you are and look north and south, east and west.* [15]***All the land that you see I will give to you and your offspring forever.*** [16]*I will make your offspring like the dust of the earth, so that if anyone could count the dust, then your offspring could be counted.* [17]*Go, walk through the length and breadth of the land, for I am giving it to you."* [18]*So Abram moved his tents and went to live near the great trees of Mamre at Hebron, where he built an altar to the* LORD.
>
> (Gen. 15) [1]*After this, the word of the* LORD *came to Abram in a vision: "Do not be afraid, Abram. I am your shield, your very great reward."* [2]*But Abram said, "O Sovereign* LORD*, what can you give me since I remain childless and the one who will inherit my estate is Eliezer of Damascus?"* [3]*And Abram said, "You have given me no children; so a servant in my household will be my heir."* [4]*Then the word of the* LORD *came to him: "This man will not be your heir, but a son coming from your own body will be your heir."* [5]*He took him outside and said, "Look up at the heavens and count the stars, if indeed you can count them." Then he said to him, "So shall your offspring be."* [6]***Abram believed the* LORD*, and he credited it to him as righteousness.***

Incredible! Abram and his wife were elderly and had no child. Yet God continued to make promises to Abram concerning a great people that would issue from him. How could this be? How could Abram become the father of a great nation? There is only one answer: The LORD God is the God who can do all things! God is great! Nothing is impossible for Him! What God promises God performs.

What about Abram? Did he believe the LORD, who had promised an "impossible" thing? Listen to what the Scripture says: ***"Abram believed the* LORD*, and He credited it to him as righteousness!"*** What a wonderful thing! God had promised Abram something which, humanly speaking, could not happen. Yet how did Abram respond? He **believed** what God had promised him! And what did God do? **God judged Abram as one who is righteous, because of his faith!**

This truth ought to thrill the hearts of those who want to be counted as righteous before God. Why did God judge Abram as one who is righteous? Was Abram a righteous person in himself? No! In our next lesson we will see how Abram had a sinner's nature, like every descendant of Adam. Why then did God count Abram as righteous? **God counted Abram as one who is righteous, because Abram believed what God said!**

What does it mean to believe God? As you may know, the Scriptures of the Prophets were written in the Hebrew language. In Hebrew, the word for "**believe**" is "**AMAN**" from which we get our word ***Amen***. When you say "Amen" you are simply saying, "Yes! It is true!" or "Yes, I agree!" This is what it means to believe. When God made a promise to Abram, Abram's heart response was: "Amen! Yes! It is true! I believe your words!" **Based on that simple "Amen" to the word of God, God counted Abram as righteous.**

How about you? Do you want God to count {consider} you as one who is righteous, as He counted Abram righteous? Then you must believe God as Abram believed God. **You must believe what God says, even if it is not easy.** You must accept the true Word of God, even if your relatives or your friends do not believe it. God wants to clothe you in His righteousness and give you the right to live in His holy presence forever, but **you must believe His Word**! The Holy Scriptures say:

> "*...without faith it is **impossible** to please* God!" (Heb. 11:6) and that "*it is by grace that you are saved, **through faith**–and this not from yourselves, it is the gift of* God–***not by works****, so that no one can boast.*" (Eph. 2:8,9)
>
> "*What then shall we say that Abraham, our forefather, discovered in this matter? If, in fact, Abraham was justified by works, he had something to boast about–but not before God. What does the Scripture say? '**Abraham believed God, and it was credited to him as righteousness**.'*" (Rom. 4:1-3)

Abram believed what God said. That is the reason that God imparted to him His perfect righteousness. And the most wonderful thing in all of this is that the words "*Abram believed the* LORD*, and he credited it to him as righteousness*" are not just for Abram. We too can have a share in these words. **God will impart to us His perfect righteousness–if we believe the Good News of God** concerning the Redeemer who later came into the world through the lineage of Abraham.

How about you? **Do you really believe God?** We are not asking if you believe that **God exists,** or if you believe that **God is one**. The Scriptures speak of that kind of "faith," saying: "*You believe that there is one God. Good! **Even the demons believe that**–and shudder!*" (Jam. 2:19) Satan himself knows that there is only one God. Believing that there is one God, will **not** cause God to forgive your sins and count you as one who is righteous! What God wants is for you to **believe His Word and receive it**. God wants to speak to you through the Writings of the Prophets. He wants you to know and to believe the news of salvation which shows how you can be made forever righteous before God, the Holy One!

Dear friend, has God clothed you with **His righteousness**? Or are you merely wearing the clothes of religion? Are you listening to the trustworthy **Word of God**? Or to the passing words of men? Do you **know** what the Holy Scriptures declare concerning the righteous way of salvation which God has established? Have you **believed** it?

As for Abram, he believed the word of God, although it meant bidding farewell to his relatives and his father's religion. And that is precisely why he was called ***the friend of God***. That is what the Scriptures say: "*Abraham* ***believed God****, and it was credited to him as* **righteousness***, and he was called* **God's friend**." (Jam. 2:23) How about you? Are you a friend of God?

This is where we must stop today. We thank you for listening and invite you to join us next time as we look at the story of Abram and Ishmael....

God bless you as you think about this great verse from His Book:

> ***"Abraham believed God, and it was credited to him as righteousness, and he was called God's friend."*** (Jam. 2:23)

LESSON 20

ABRAHAM AND ISHMAEL

GENESIS 16,17

Peace be with you, listening friends. We greet you in the name of God, the Lord of peace, who wants everyone to understand and submit to the way of righteousness that He has established, and have true peace with Him forever. We are happy to be able to return today to present your program *The Way of Righteousness.*

Two lessons ago, in our study in the Holy Scriptures, we began to explore the story of the prophet Abraham. At first, Abraham's name was not Abraham, but *Abram*. But in our program today, we will discover **why God changed Abram's name to *Abraham***.

The first part of today's lesson is **a sad story** which reveals something that Abram did which was not pleasing to God. Some think that God's prophets never sinned. But the Word of God declares: *"There is no difference, for **all have sinned** and fall short of the glory of God."* (Rom. 3:22,23) and *"If we claim we have not sinned, we make [God] out to be a liar and his word has no place in our lives."* (1 John 1:10) We have already seen how Adam's sin spread to all people–young and old, men and women, pagan and prophet. Only one Person was not stained by the sin of Adam. That One is **the holy Redeemer** whom God sent to earth to save sinners. He was not stained by sin, because He came from above–from the presence of God the Holy One.

In our last two lessons, we saw how **God promised to make of Abram the father of a great nation**, from which the Redeemer would arise. Both Abram and his wife were elderly and had no children, yet that did not cause Abram to doubt the word of God. However, today we will see that, ten years after God first promised to give Abram a posterity, **Abram tried to "help" God fulfil His promise**. However, what Abram did, in his impatience, produced many problems.

Now then, let us continue in the Torah to see how Abram and Sarai arranged things in an effort to have the son that God promised. In chapter sixteen of the book of Genesis, the Scriptures say:

> (Gen.16) [1]*Now Sarai, Abram's wife, had borne him no children. But she had an Egyptian maidservant named* ***Hagar***; [2]*so she said to Abram, "The LORD has kept me from having children. Go, sleep with my maidservant; perhaps I can build a family through her." Abram agreed to what Sarai said.* [3]*So after Abram had been living in Canaan ten years, Sarai his wife took her Egyptian maidservant Hagar and gave her to her husband to be his wife.* [4]*He slept with Hagar, and she conceived. When she knew she was pregnant, she began to despise her mistress.* [5]*Then Sarai said to Abram, "You are responsible for the wrong I am suffering. I put my servant in your arms, and now that she knows she is pregnant, she despises me. May the LORD judge between you and me."* [6]*"Your servant is in your hands," Abram said. "Do with her whatever you think best." Then Sarai ill-treated Hagar; so she fled from her.*

Thus we see how the sin of Abram produced bitterness and conflict in his household. Sarai was jealous because Hagar was pregnant; Hagar was upset with Sarai who was mistreating her. Thus, Hagar ran away from Sarai.

Next, the Scriptures say:

> (Gen. 16) [7]*The angel of the LORD found Hagar near a spring in the desert...* [8]*And he said, "Hagar, servant of Sarai, where have you come from, and where are you going?" "I'm running away from my mistress Sarai," she answered.* [9]*Then the angel of the LORD told her, "Go back to your mistress and submit to her."* [10]*The angel added, "I will so increase your descendants that they will be* ***too numerous to count****."* [11]*The angel of the LORD also said to her: "You are now with child and you will have a son. You shall name him* ***Ishmael****, for the LORD has heard of your misery.* [12]*He will be a wild donkey of a man; his hand will be against everyone and everyone's hand against him, and* ***he will live in hostility toward all his brothers****."*

So Hagar returned to Sarai, her mistress, as the angel of God had said. "*So Hagar bore Abram a son, and Abram gave the name Ishmael to the son she had borne. Abram was eighty-six years old when Hagar bore him Ishmael.*" (Gen. 16:15,16) Thus, **Ishmael** {*Ishma il* in Arabic} was born, the one who is the father of all the Arabs. As we will see, God cared for Ishmael and had a plan for him, but Ishmael was **not** the son which God had promised Abram. God's wonderful plan to make a new nation of Abram had not changed. God is not in a hurry as was Abram. God always does what He promises, even if it seems to us that He is slow. Thus, the Scripture tells us that for thirteen years after the birth of Ishmael, God remained silent, saying nothing to Abram. But one day God spoke again to Abram.

Let us read in chapter seventeen, and hear what God said to Abram after thirteen long years of silence. What we are going to read is very wonderful. The Scriptures say:

> (Gen. 17) 1*When Abram was* **ninety-nine years old**, *the* LORD *appeared to him and said,* "**I am God Almighty**; *walk before me and be blameless.* 2**I will confirm my covenant between me and you and will greatly increase your numbers**."
>
> 3*Abram fell face down and God said to him,* 4"*As for me, this is my covenant with you: You will be the father of many nations.* 5*No longer will you be called Abram;* **your name will be Abraham**, *for I have made you* **a father of many nations**. 6*I will make you very fruitful; I will make nations of you, and kings will come from you.* 7*I will establish my covenant as an everlasting covenant between me and you and your descendants after you for the generations to come, to be your God and the God of your descendants after you.* 8*The whole land of Canaan, where you are now an alien, I will give as an everlasting possession to you and your descendants after you; and I will be their God.*"
>
> 9*Then God said to Abraham,* "*As for you, you must keep my covenant, you and your descendants after you for the generations to come.* 10*This is my covenant with you and your descendants after you, the covenant you are to keep: Every male among you shall be circumcised.* 11*You are to undergo circumcision, and it will be* **the sign of the covenant** *between me and you.* 12*For the generations to come every male among you who is eight days old must be circumcised…*"
>
> 15*God also said to Abraham,* "*As for Sarai your wife, you are no longer to call her Sarai; her name will be* **Sarah**. 16*I will bless her and will surely give you a son by her. I will bless her so that she will be* **the mother of nations**; *kings of peoples will come from her.*" 17*Abraham fell face down; he laughed and said to himself,* "*Will a son be born to a man a hundred years old? Will Sarah bear a child at the age of ninety?*" 18*And Abraham said to God,*"*If only Ishmael might live under your blessing!*" 19*Then God said,* "*Yes, but your wife Sarah will bear you a son, and you will call him* **Isaac**. **I will establish my covenant with him as an everlasting covenant for his descendants after him**. 20*And* **as for Ishmael**, *I have heard you: I will surely bless him; I will make him fruitful and will greatly increase his numbers. He will be the father of twelve rulers, and* **I will make him into a great nation**. 21**But my covenant I will establish with Isaac**, *whom Sarah will bear to you by this time next year.*"

This is where we must stop today in reading the Scriptures. We have seen how Abram listened to the counsel of his wife and went to bed with Hagar her servant. What Abram did was wrong. Ishmael, the son born to Abram and Hagar, was not part of God's plan to create a new nation which would bring blessing to all the nations of the world. However, **the unfaithfulness of men cannot thwart the faithfulness of God**. Thus, as we just read, when Abram was ninety-nine years old, God reappeared to him to confirm the promise He had made to him so long ago. He said, *"I am God Almighty...You will be the father of many nations. No longer will you be called Abram; your name will be Abraham, for I have made you a father of many nations."* In keeping with His perfect plan, God changed Abram's name to *Abraham*, which means ***the father of many***. God also changed Sarai's name to **Sarah**, which means ***princess***.

Here is something very wonderful. We are looking at an elderly couple who have never had a child of their own; Abram and Sarai. Now God is giving them new names in order to announce what is to take place. Abram is renamed *Abraham*, ***the father of many***, and Sarai is called *Sarah*, meaning ***princess***. God was going to give Abraham and Sarah **a son**, and from that son, **a nation**. Through that nation **many kings and prophets** would arise, and, finally, **the Savior of the world**! Truly, the LORD is great and worthy of praise forever! He did not forget what He had promised to Abraham long before.

So what did Abraham do after God confirmed His promise to give him a child in his old age? The Scriptures say: *"Abraham fell face down; he laughed and said to himself, 'Will a son be born to a man a hundred years old? Will Sarah bear a child at the age of ninety?'"* **Abraham laughed!** But he did not laugh because of unbelief, but because of happiness.

Thus, the Scriptures say:

> *"Against all hope, Abraham in hope **believed** and so became the father of many nations, just as it had been said to him, 'So shall your offspring be.' Without weakening in his faith, he faced the fact that his body was as good as dead–since he was about a hundred years old–and that Sarah's womb was also dead. **Yet he did not waver through unbelief regarding the promise of God, but was strengthened in his faith and gave glory to God, being fully persuaded that God had power to do what he had promised**."* (Rom. 4:18-21)

Nevertheless, Abraham wanted to know what would happen to Ishmael, the child of his servant, Hagar. God replied,

> *"As for Ishmael, I have heard you: I will surely bless him...**I will make him into a great nation. But my covenant I will establish with Isaac,** whom Sarah will bear to you...I will establish my covenant with him as an everlasting covenant for his descendants after him."* (Gen. 17:20,21,19)

Thus, God confirmed His purpose to bring forth the prophets and, at last, the Redeemer Himself through the descendants of Isaac. In the next lesson, God willing, we will see how the LORD gave Abraham and Sarah the son of the promise—Isaac {*Ishaq* in Arabic}.

Truly, **God is faithful**. God does what He promises! Nothing is too difficult for Him! Listen to these beautiful verses from the holy Gospel {*Injil*}:

> *"Oh, the depth of the riches of the wisdom and knowledge of God!*
> *How unsearchable His judgments, and His paths beyond tracing out!*
> *Who has known the mind of the Lord? Or who has been His counselor?*
> *Who has ever given to God, that God should repay Him?*
> *For from Him and through Him and to Him are all things.*
> ***To Him be the glory forever! Amen.***" (Rom. 11:33-36)

Thank you for listening....May God bless you as you consider the meaning of this verse found in the Holy Scriptures:

> ***"If we are [unfaithful to God], He will remain faithful, for he cannot disown Himself."*** (2 Tim. 2:13)

Lesson 21

Abraham: Sodom's Ruin and Isaac's Birth

Genesis 18-21

Peace be with you, listening friends. We greet you in the name of God, the Lord of peace, who wants everyone to understand and submit to the way of righteousness that He has established, and have true peace with Him forever. We are happy to be able to return today to present your program *The Way of Righteousness*.

In our studies in the Torah, we have seen how God promised to make Abraham the father of a new nation from which the prophets of God and the Savior of the world would come. However, up to this point in the story, Sarah, Abraham's wife had not yet borne a son and both she and Abraham were extremely old.

Today we have another amazing story. At the start of the story we will see three men who came to visit Abraham. However, these three men were more than mere humans. Two of them were **angels** and the other was **the LORD God Himself**! Some might say that God could not have appeared to Abraham in the form of man, but they have forgotten that God is great and that nothing is too hard for Him. God can do anything, except that which is unrighteous.

Today we will be reading from four chapters of the Torah. In the book of Genesis, chapter eighteen, the Scripture says:

> (Gen.18) [1]***The*** LORD ***appeared to Abraham*** *near the great trees of Mamre while he was sitting at the entrance to his tent in the heat of the day.* [2]*Abraham looked up and saw* ***three men*** *standing nearby. When he saw them, he hurried from the entrance of his tent to meet them and bowed low to the ground.* [3]*He said, "If I have found favor in your eyes, my lord, do not pass your servant by.* [4]*Let a little water be brought, and then you may all wash your feet and rest under this tree.* [5]*Let me get you something to eat, so you can be refreshed and then go on your way–now that you have come to your servant." "Very well," they answered, "do as you say."*

[6]So Abraham hurried and… [8]brought some curds and milk and the calf that had been prepared, and set these before them. While they ate, he stood near them under a tree. [9]"Where is your wife Sarah?" they asked him. "There, in the tent," he said. [10]Then ***the LORD*** *said,* ***"I will surely return to you about this time next year, and Sarah your wife will have a son."*** *Now Sarah was listening at the entrance to the tent, which was behind him. [11]Abraham and Sarah were already old and well advanced in years, and Sarah was past the age of childbearing. [12]So Sarah laughed to herself as she thought, "After I am worn out and my master is old, will I now have this pleasure?" [13]Then the LORD said to Abraham, "Why did Sarah laugh and say, 'Will I really have a child, now that I am old?' [14]Is anything too hard for the LORD? I will return to you at the appointed time next year and Sarah will have a son." [15]Sarah was afraid, so she lied and said, "I did not laugh." But he said, "Yes, you did laugh."*

*[20]Then the LORD said, "***The outcry against [the cities of] Sodom and Gomorrah is so great*** *and their sin so grievous [21]that I will go down and see if what they have done is as bad as the outcry that has reached me. If not, I will know." [22]The men (that is, the two angels) turned away and went toward Sodom,* ***but Abraham remained standing before the LORD.***

[23]Then Abraham approached Him and said: "Will you sweep away the righteous with the wicked? [24]What if there are fifty righteous people in the city? Will you really sweep it away and not spare the place for the sake of the fifty righteous people in it? [25]Far be it from you to do such a thing–to kill the righteous with the wicked, treating the righteous and the wicked alike. Far be it from you! ***Will not the Judge of all the earth do right?****"*

[26]The LORD said, "If I find ***fifty*** *righteous people in the city of Sodom, I will spare the whole place for their sake." [27]Then Abraham spoke up again: "Now that I have been so bold as to speak to the Lord, though I am nothing but dust and ashes, [28]what if the number of the righteous is five less than fifty? Will you destroy the whole city because of five people?" "If I find* ***forty-five*** *there," he said, "I will not destroy it."*

[29]Once again he spoke to Him, "What if only forty are found there?" He said, "For the sake of ***forty****, I will not do it." [30]Then he said, "May the Lord not be angry, but let me speak. What if only thirty can be found there?" He answered, "I will not do it if I find* ***thirty*** *there." [31]Abraham said, "Now that I have been so bold as to speak to the Lord, what if only twenty can be found there?" He said, "For the sake of* ***twenty****, I will not destroy it." [32]Then he said, "May the Lord not be angry, but let me speak just once more. What if only ten can be found there?" He answered, "For the sake of* ***ten****, I will not destroy it." [33]When the LORD had finished speaking with Abraham, he left, and Abraham returned home.*

(Gen. 19) *[1]The two angels arrived at* **Sodom** *in the evening, and* **Lot** *was* *sitting in the gateway of the city. When he saw them, he got up to meet them and bowed down with his face to the ground.* [2]*"My lords," he said, "please turn aside to your servant's house. You can wash your feet and spend the night and then go on your way early in the morning." "No," they answered, "we will spend the night in the square."*

[3]*But he insisted so strongly that they did go with him and entered his house. He prepared a meal for them, baking bread without yeast, and they ate.* [4]*Before they had gone to bed, all the men from every part of the city of Sodom–both young and old–surrounded the house.* [5]*They called to Lot, "Where are the men who came to you tonight? Bring them out to us so that we can have sex with them."*

Many of the men of Sodom were homosexuals and reveled in a sin God calls perversion. (See Romans 1:26,27)

(Gen. 19) [6]*Lot went outside to meet them and shut the door behind him* [7]*and said, "No, my friends. Don't do* ***this wicked thing****...* [8]*don't do anything to these men, for they have come under the protection of my roof."* [9]*"Get out of our way," they replied. And they said, "This fellow came here as an alien, and now he wants to play the judge! We'll treat you worse than them." They kept bringing pressure on Lot and moved forward to break down the door.* [10]*But the men inside [that is, the two angels] reached out and pulled Lot back into the house and shut the door.* [11]*Then they struck the men who were at the door of the house, young and old, with blindness so that they could not find the door.*

[12]*The two men said to Lot, "Do you have anyone else here–sons-in-law, sons or daughters, or anyone else in the city who belongs to you? Get them out of here,* [13]*because we are going to destroy this place.* ***The outcry to the LORD against its people is so great that he has sent us to destroy it.****"* [14]*So Lot went out and spoke to his sons-in-law, who were pledged to marry his daughters. He said, "Hurry and get out of this place, because the LORD is about to destroy the city!" But his sons-in-law thought he was joking.* [15]*With the coming of dawn, the angels urged Lot, saying, "Hurry! Take your wife and your two daughters who are here, or you will be swept away when the city is punished."* [16]*When he hesitated, the men grasped his hand and the hands of his wife and of his two daughters and led them safely out of the city, for the LORD was merciful to them.* [17]*As soon as they had brought them out, one of them said,* ***"Flee for your lives! Don't look back, and don't stop anywhere in the plain! Flee to the mountains or you will be swept away!"***

[24]***Then the LORD rained down burning sulphur on Sodom and Gomorrah–from the LORD out of the heavens.*** [25]*Thus he overthrew those cities and the entire plain, including all those living in the cities–and also the*

vegetation in the land. [26]***But Lot's wife looked back, and she became a pillar of salt.***

[27]***Early the next morning Abraham got up and returned to the place where he had stood before the LORD.*** [28]*He looked down toward Sodom and Gomorrah, toward all the land of the plain, and he saw dense smoke rising from the land, like smoke from a furnace.* [29]*So when God destroyed the cities of the plain, he remembered Abraham, and he brought Lot out of the catastrophe that overthrew the cities where Lot had lived.*

This is the solemn story of how God judged the cities of Sodom and Gomorrah with burning sulphur from the sky. Today the ruins of Sodom lie under the Dead (Salt) Sea in Palestine (Israel). To pursue sin is never a wise choice. **God is serious about judging sin!**

Now, in the time left today, we want to continue in the Torah and see how **God gave Abraham and Sarah a son**, thus **fulfilling the promise** He had made to them so long ago. In chapter twenty one, the Scriptures say:

(Gen. 21) [1]*Now the LORD was gracious to Sarah* ***as he had said****, and the LORD did for Sarah* ***what he had promised****.* [2]*Sarah became pregnant and bore a son to Abraham in his old age,* ***at the very time God had promised him****.* [3]*Abraham gave the name Isaac to the son Sarah bore him.* [4]*When his son Isaac was eight days old, Abraham circumcised him, as God commanded him.* [5]***Abraham was a hundred years old*** *when his son Isaac was born to him.* [6]*Sarah said, "God has brought me laughter, and everyone who hears about this will laugh with me."* [7]*And she added, "Who would have said to Abraham that Sarah would nurse children? Yet I have borne him a son in his old age."*

Thus did God fulfil the promise He had made to Abraham and Sarah a long time before. Sarah, who was known as one "who can't have children," bore a son **just as God had said**. They called him ***Isaac***, which means *he laughs*. But not everyone was rejoicing over Isaac's birth.

The Scriptures say:

(Gen. 21) [8]*[Isaac] grew and was weaned, and on the day [he] was weaned, Abraham held a great feast.* [9]*But Sarah saw that* ***the son whom Hagar the Egyptian had borne to Abraham was mocking****,* [10]*and she said to Abraham, "Get rid of that slave woman and her son, for that slave woman's son will never share in the inheritance with my son Isaac."* [11]*The matter distressed Abraham greatly because it concerned his son.* [12]*But God said to him, "Do not be so distressed about the boy and your maidservant. Listen to whatever Sarah tells you, because it is through Isaac that your offspring will be reckoned.* [13]*I will make the*

> *son of the maidservant into a nation also, because he is your offspring."* [14]*Early the next morning Abraham took some food and a skin of water and gave them to Hagar. He set them on her shoulders and then* ***sent her off with the boy****.*

Ishmael's departure was painful for Abraham, but it had to be, since God had revealed to him that the new nation, and the Savior of the world, would come through **Isaac**—not though Ishmael. Ishmael, who was about fifteen years old, made fun of Isaac and had **no appreciation for God's plan** to make of Isaac a great nation which would offer salvation to the world.

So what happened to Ishmael? The verses which follow show us how he went with his mother and lived in the desert near Egypt, and married an Egyptian woman. Ishmael became the father of the Arab race, which became enemies of the nation which came from Isaac, just as God had predicted to Abraham. (See Genesis 16:12) To this day there is a rivalry between Arabs and Jews, as you well know! God loves the Arabs and the Jews and all people in every nation and wants them to turn to Him.

Friends, our time is gone. We trust that each of you have again seen that the true and living God is **a faithful God** who cannot go back on His word. That is why He judged Sodom and Gomorrah–**just as He said**. That is why He gave Abraham and Sarah a son in their old age–**just as He had promised He would do**. And that is why He had Abraham send Ishmael away–**that His unchanging purposes might be established**.

Thank you for your attention. We urge you to join us next time, because, God willing, we will be looking into the most significant event in Abraham's life: the story of Abraham's sacrifice of his son….

Until next time, we leave you with this verse from the Word of God:

> ***"Oh, the depth of the riches of the wisdom and knowledge of God! How unsearchable His judgments, and His paths beyond tracing out!"*** (Rom. 11:33)

Lesson 22

Abraham's Sacrifice

Genesis 22

Peace be with you, listening friends. We greet you in the name of God, the Lord of peace, who wants everyone to understand and submit to the way of righteousness that He has established, and have true peace with Him forever. We are happy to be able to return today to present your program *The Way of Righteousness*.

In our studies in the Torah, we have explored many wonderful and important stories about the prophet of God, Abraham. Today we come to the most significant lesson from the life of Abraham: the true story of "*Tabaski*" (**Abraham's sacrifice**) and what it means. {*Tabaski*: a familiar word in Wolof and in some other African languages—as a verb: *to sacrifice a ram on the feast day*; as a noun: *the Muslim feast of* "**Id al-Adha**" *commemorating Abraham's sacrifice of his son*}

In our last lesson, we learned how God gave Abraham and Sarah a child in their old age, thus fulfilling what He had promised long before. Their son's name was Isaac. God had promised Abraham that, through the descendants of Isaac, He would bring forth a new nation, through which all the nations of the world would be blessed. We also saw how Ishmael and his mother, Hagar, left Abraham's household, and went to live in the land of Egypt. Thus, only Isaac remained at home, the one born according to God's promise.

One day God asked Abraham to do an astonishing and difficult thing. In the Torah, the book of Genesis, chapter twenty-two, the Scriptures say:

> (Gen. 22) [1]*Some time later God tested Abraham. He said to him, "Abraham!" "Here I am," he replied.* [2]*Then God said, "Take your son, your only son, Isaac, whom you love, and go to the region of Moriah.* ***Sacrifice him there as a burnt offering on one of the mountains I will tell you about****."*

What!? What was God asking of Abraham? He was commanding Abraham to take his beloved son to a far away mountain, and offer him as a burnt sacrifice! How could this be? Abraham had waited for twenty-five long years to have the son which God had promised him, and now God is telling him to slay his son as a sacrifice! How did Abraham answer God? Did he argue with the words of God because they were difficult to accept? The Scripture says:

> (Gen. 22) [3]***Early the next morning Abraham got up*** *and saddled his donkey. He took with him two of his servants and his son Isaac. When he had cut enough wood for the burnt offering,* ***he set out for the place about which God had told him****.*

For three days, Abraham and his son and two servants walked and walked and walked, heading toward the mountain of which God had spoken. Abraham's heart was ready to break as he neared that fearful place where he would have to slay his beloved son and cremate him! Of course, we who are reading the story today know that God was only testing Abraham's faith, but Abraham didn't know that! What God had asked of him was a terrible and painful trial!

Next the Scriptures say:

> (Gen. 22) [4]*On the third day Abraham looked up and saw the place in the distance.* [5]*He said to his servants, "Stay here with the donkey while I and the boy go over there. We will worship and then we will come back to you."* [6]*Abraham took the wood for the burnt offering and placed it on his son Isaac, and he himself carried the fire and the knife.* [7]*As the two of them went on together, Isaac spoke up and said to his father Abraham, "Father?" "Yes, my son?" Abraham replied. "The fire and wood are here," Isaac said, "but* ***where is the lamb*** *for the burnt offering?"* [8]*Abraham answered, "****God himself will provide the lamb for the burnt offering, my son****." And the two of them went on together.*
>
> [9]*When they reached the place of which God had told him, Abraham built an altar there and arranged the wood on it. He bound his son Isaac and laid him on the altar, on top of the wood.* [10]*Then he reached out his hand and took the knife to slay his son.* [11]*But the angel of the* LORD *called out to him from heaven, "Abraham! Abraham!" "Here I am," he replied.* [12]*"Do not lay a hand on the boy," he said. "Do not do anything to him. Now I know that you fear God, because you have not withheld from me your son, your only son."* [13]*Abraham looked up and there in a thicket he saw* ***a ram caught by its horns****. He went over and took the ram and sacrificed it as a burnt offering instead of his son.* [14]***So Abraham called that place The*** **LORD** ***Will Provide****. And to this day it is said, "****On the mountain of the*** **LORD** ***it will be provided****."*

This story is very important and deserves clarification. The story of Abraham's sacrifice has three sides: ***a historical side****,* ***a symbolic side*** *and* ***a prophetic side****.* In other words, to understand Abraham's sacrifice, we need to understand three things: 1.) What took place, 2.) what the sacrifice symbolized, and 3.) what Abraham prophesied concerning an event that was yet to take place.

Concerning **the historical side**, we have read today how God **tested Abraham's faith** and **saved his son** from death by means of a sacrificial ram. This happened about four thousand years ago in the place where Jerusalem is located today. That, in short, is the "historical" side of the story of Abraham's sacrifice.

Concerning **the symbolic side** of the story, God's Word tells us that **we are all like Abraham's son**. We read that God, in His justice, **condemned Abraham's son to death**. We too are all condemned sinners and deserve God's judgment. But we also read how God, in His grace, **saved Abraham's son from death**. Similarly, God, in His grace, has come to our rescue in providing a means by which we can be saved. What is that way of salvation? The story of Abraham's sacrifice teaches us that **the way of salvation** established by God is the way of **the Perfect Sacrifice**.

In today's story, we saw how God provided a ram (sheep) to die in the place of Abraham's son. Only the horns of the sheep were caught in the bush; the sheep's skin was not torn. If the sheep had a single flaw, it could not have replaced Abraham's son on the altar. But the sacrifice which God provided was **a perfect sheep**, without blemish. In our study in the first chapters of the Torah, we learned about the way of salvation which God established. Do you remember what that way was? After Adam and Eve sinned, God decreed that, since the payment for sin is death, there could be no forgiveness of sin without the shedding of blood. Thus, all who wanted to have their sins forgiven were required to take **an animal without blemish**, slay it, and present it to God as a burnt offering. The innocent animal had to die in the place of the guilty person. This was the only way by which God could forgive the sins of the sons of Adam, without compromising His justice.

Something else we must remember is this: The Scriptures say that sacrificial animals were merely "***symbolic** of that which was to come; a shadow of the good things that are coming–**not the realities themselves**. Because it is impossible for the blood of [animals] to take away sins.*" (Heb. 10:1,4) The blood of animals cannot pay for sin because animals and humans are not of equal value. Thus, we learn that the sheep which replaced Abraham's son on the altar was **an illustration of a greater, more perfect sacrifice**. The Word of God shows us that the sheep which died in the place of Abraham's son was **a symbol of the holy Redeemer** who was to come into the world and **die for all sinners**, so that God could forgive everyone who believes in Him. In short, this is what Abraham's sacrificial sheep symbolizes. It is an illustration of the Savior whom God promised to send into the world to save sinners from His righteous judgment!

Concerning **the prophetic side** of the story, do you remember what Abraham said to his son as they were climbing the mountain? He told him: "***God Himself***

***will provide the lamb** for the sacrifice.*" And do you remember what Abraham announced after he had slain the ram, and burned it in place of his son? He called the place of sacrifice: "*The LORD **will** Provide.*" And the prophet Moses, who wrote the Torah, adds: "*And to this day it is said: 'On the mountain of the LORD it **will** be provided!'*" What was the reason for this? Why did the prophet Abraham say, "*The LORD **will** provide*"? Why did he not say, "Praise be to God! The Lord **has** provided a sacrifice!"? Friends, this is a question of **tremendous importance**, because the answer to it contains the Good News of God's Word, which each of us must understand and believe!

Why did Abraham call the place,"*The LORD **will** provide*"? This is why: **Abraham was announcing an event that was to yet take place on those same mountains** where the sheep had replaced his son on the altar. In short, Abraham was declaring: "I praise God, because he has provided a sheep to replace my son on the altar. However, I am telling you that one day, on this same mountain, **God will provide another sacrifice** which will be far greater than the ram which saved my son today from the knife and the fire. Yes, the Sacrifice which God will provide shall have the power to save the children of Adam from eternal death in the fire which never goes out! God will send down a holy Redeemer who will die as a sacrifice, the innocent for the guilty, so that whoever believes in Him will not perish!" This is God's Good News for all people which Abraham was announcing when he said, "*God Himself **will** provide **the lamb** for the sacrifice!*"

Before we conclude the story of "Abraham's sacrifice" today, each of us needs to know that, approximately two thousand years after Abraham prophesied that God would provide a Sacrifice for sinners, **God fulfilled Abraham's prophecy**. We cannot say much about it today, but those of you who know the Gospel {*Injil*}, know the story of the Redeemer. You know that He was born of a virgin woman who belonged to the family line of Abraham and Isaac, just as God had promised. The Redeemer who was to die in the place of sinners had no earthly father. He came from heaven, and thus, did not inherit Adam's sinful nature. He had no sin; He had no blemish. That is why He was worthy to die as **the Perfect Sacrifice**; as a substitute for the guilty children of Adam. When we come to the Gospel, we will learn that this Savior's name is ***Jesus***. The name *Jesus* means ***God saves***. Some call Jesus "*Isa.*" {see lesson #61 for more on this}

When we come to the Gospel Writings {*Injil*}, we will read how there was a prophet named John {Qur'anic name: *Yahya*} whom God sent to prepare the way before Jesus the Redeemer. One day, John saw Jesus coming toward him and said, "*Look! **the Lamb of God**, who takes away the sin of the world!*" (John 1:29) Why did the prophet John call Jesus "*the Lamb of God*"? Because Jesus was born to shed His blood as a sacrifice which takes away sin. **Like the sheep that died in the place of Abraham's son, the Redeemer came to die for all of Adam's descendants.** Jesus is the perfect and final Sacrifice of whom Abraham prophesied when he said: ***"God Himself will provide the lamb for the sacrifice."***

In the Gospel we will read how Jesus willingly delivered Himself up to his enemies, and how they nailed Him to a cross. **Jesus the Redeemer, whom God provided, fulfilled the prophetic and the symbolic meaning of Abraham's sacrificial sheep**. That is why, just before Jesus died, He cried out, ***"It is finished!"*** (John 19:30) {Wolof: "*All is complete/perfect!*"} And three days later, God confirmed the perfection and power of the Redeemer's sacrifice by raising Him from the dead! **Jesus is the One who perfectly fulfilled the meaning of Abraham's sacrifice.** And did you know that the location where Jesus died in the place of sinners was in the same mountains where Abraham slaughtered the sheep in place of his son? Do you know the location of those two sacrifices? Yes, it is Jerusalem.

Dear friends, whoever you are, wherever you are, God is commanding you to turn from your wrong ideas and futile works, and place your hope completely in the perfect and final Sacrifice that He has provided. For the Scriptures say: "*[Jesus the Redeemer] Himself bore our sins in His body on the tree, so that we might die to sins and live for righteousness; by His wounds you have been healed.*" (1 Pet. 2:24) Today we saw that Abraham's son accepted the sacrifice which God provided for him. How about you? **Have you accepted the Sacrifice which God has provided for you**?

We thank you for listening....God bless you as you carefully consider the meaning of Abraham's words from Mount Moriah when he said,

> ***"God himself will provide the Lamb...On the mountain of the LORD it will be provided!"*** (Gen. 22:8,14)

Lesson 23

Esau and Jacob: The Temporal and the Eternal

Genesis 25

Peace be with you, listening friends. We greet you in the name of God, the Lord of peace, who wants everyone to understand and submit to the way of righteousness that He has established, and have true peace with Him forever. We are happy to be able to return today to present your program *The Way of Righteousness.*

In our last program, we looked into the story of **Abraham's sacrifice** {"*Id al-Adha*"}. The Gospel {*Injil*} gives us an interesting summary of this important story when it says:

> "*By faith Abraham, when God tested him, offered Isaac as a sacrifice. He who had received the promise was about to sacrifice his one and only son* {who was born according to God's promise}, *even though God had said to him, 'It is through Isaac that your offspring will be reckoned.' Abraham reasoned that God could raise the dead, and figuratively speaking, he did receive Isaac back from death.*" (Heb. 11:17-19)

Our last five lessons have been taken up with stories from the life of the prophet Abraham. There are many more stories in the Torah about Abraham which we have not explored. Unfortunately, we do not have time to read them all. However, before we leave Abraham and go on to the stories of his descendants, there is something that God said to Abraham that we should know about. One day, God told Abraham what would happen to his offspring. He said,

> "*Know for certain that your descendants will be* ***strangers in a country not their own****, and they will be* ***enslaved and ill-treated four hundred years****. But* ***I will punish the nation they serve as slaves****, and* ***afterwards they will come out with great possessions****.*" (Gen. 15:13,14)

With those words, God was announcing that the descendants of Abraham would become slaves in the land of Egypt. God also promised that after four hundred years He would deliver them from the dominion of the people of Egypt. Four lessons from now, in the will of God, we will begin to see how these precise prophecies were fulfilled, just as God told Abraham.

Then, in chapter twenty-five, the Scriptures say:

> "***Abraham left everything he owned to Isaac.*** *Altogether, Abraham lived a hundred and seventy-five years. Then Abraham breathed his last and died at a good old age, an old man and full of years; and he was gathered to his people. His sons Isaac and Ishmael buried him in the cave of Machpelah near Mamre, in the field of Ephron…the field Abraham had bought from the Hittites. There Abraham was buried with his wife Sarah.*" (Gen. 25:5,7-10)

Thus, Abraham, the friend of God, entered the presence of the Lord, whom he knew and loved.

How can we conclude and summarize our lesson concerning the prophet of God, Abraham? Perhaps with two questions and their answers. The first question is: **Why did God ask Abraham to move and go to another country?** Answer: Because God planned to make of Abraham a new nation through which the Redeemer would come into the world. The second question is: **Why did God judge Abraham as one who is righteous and accept him into His holy presence forever?** Answer: Because Abraham believed what God said even if it was not easy. Abraham was saved by faith in God's promises and not by his own works. This is what the Scriptures declare when they say: "*Abraham* ***believed God****, and it was credited to him as righteousness, and he was called God's friend.*" (Jam. 2:23)

In chapter twenty-five in the book of Genesis, the Scriptures continue with the history of Abraham's descendants. Let us now continue in the Torah and learn the story of **Isaac and his twin sons**. The Scripture says:

> (Gen. 25) [19]*This is the account of Abraham's son Isaac.* ***Abraham*** *became the*
> *father of Isaac,* [20]*and* ***Isaac*** *was forty years old when he married* ***Rebekah*** *daugh-*
> *ter of Bethuel the Aramean from Paddan Aram and sister of Laban the Aramean.*
> [21]*Isaac prayed to the LORD on behalf of his wife, because she was barren. The*
> *LORD answered his prayer, and his wife Rebekah became pregnant.* [22]*The babies*
> *jostled each other within her, and she said, "Why is this happening to me?" So she*
> *went to enquire of the LORD.* [23]*The LORD said to her, "****Two nations*** *are in your*
> *womb, and two peoples from within you will be separated; one people will be*
> *stronger than the other, and* ***the older will serve the younger****."*
>
> [24]*When the time came for her to give birth, there were* ***twin boys*** *in her womb.*

> [25]*The first to come out was red, and his whole body was like a hairy garment; so they named him* **Esau**. [26]*After this, his brother came out, with his hand grasping Esau's heel; so he was named* **Jacob**. *Isaac was sixty years old when Rebekah gave birth to them.* [27]*The boys grew up, and Esau became a skillful hunter, a man of the open country, while Jacob was a quiet man, staying among the tents.*

Thus, we see that Isaac and Rebecca had twins, whom they named **Esau** and **Jacob** {*Ya'qub* in Arabic}. They were twins, but that doesn't mean they were the same! As Esau grew up, he set his affections only on **the things of the world** which are temporary, but Jacob valued **the things of God** which last forever. Esau did not care about the promises that God had made to Abraham, his grandfather, and to Isaac, his father, concerning the new nation which would arise from them. However, Jacob did care about God's promises.

Esau was the firstborn. Therefore, humanly speaking, he was the one who should have received the inheritance of the firstborn and become the father of the great nation which God had promised to his grandfather, Abraham, and to his father, Isaac. However, even before the twins were born, God told Rebecca, their mother, "*the older will serve the younger.*" (Gen. 25:23) God, in His foreknowledge, was announcing that the inheritance of the firstborn and the descendants of the new nation would come **through Jacob** and not through Esau. As for Jacob, he should have waited for God, leaving all in the hands of the One who had the power to give him the inheritance in His appointed time. However, **Jacob did not wait for God**. Let us read on now to see how Jacob acted in order to take the inheritance from Esau, his older brother.

The Scriptures say:

> (Gen. 25) [29]*Once when Jacob was cooking some stew, Esau came in from the open country, famished.* [30]*He said to Jacob, "Quick, let me have some of that red stew! I'm famished!"...* [31]*Jacob replied, "First sell me your birthright."* [32]*"Look, I am about to die," Esau said.* **"What good is the birthright to me?"** [33]*But Jacob said, "Swear to me first." So he swore an oath to him, selling his birthright to Jacob.* [34]*Then Jacob gave Esau some bread and some lentil stew. He ate and drank, and then got up and left. So Esau despised his birthright.*

Do you understand what Esau did? He exchanged his inheritance as the firstborn son for a little bit of food! Imagine a very rich man who has two sons. The man has fields and houses, and riches and lots of money. The firstborn is the one who should inherit most of his wealth. However one day, the elder comes in from the bush, and sees his younger brother cooking fish and rice {Senegal's national dish} beside the path. The firstborn says to his younger brother. "I am starved, give me some of that rice to eat!" However, the brother replies, "I will not give it to you, but I will sell it to you." The elder asks, "How much will you sell it to me for?" The younger brother says, "Your rights of inheritance as the firstborn." The elder replies, "Sold! I am hungry enough to die. Of what use is my birthright to me?" So the elder swears to hand over to his younger brother his whole inheritance! Then the firstborn sits down, eats and drinks, gets up and goes on his way.

What can we say about this firstborn who exchanged fields and houses, and riches and authority for one bowl of rice and fish? We can say just one thing: "**How stupid**!" Just as this firstborn despised the blessings of his father and the riches of the world, in the same way **Esau despised the blessings of God and the riches of Eternity**. The things that Esau despised were infinitely more valuable than the riches of the world, because that which Esau despised was the right to be a part of the new nation through which the Savior of the world would come.

What does God want to teach us today through the story of Esau and Jacob? God wants to warn us not to follow in the footsteps of Esau by trading the riches of Eternity for the pleasures of the world which are passing away. Listen to what the Word of the Lord declares about this. It says:

> "*What good will it be for a man if he gains the whole world, yet forfeits* ***his soul****? Or what can a man give in exchange for* ***his soul****?*" (Matt 16:26) "*See to it that no one misses the grace of God…or is godless like* ***Esau, who for a single meal sold his inheritance rights as the oldest son***." (Heb. 12:15,16)

Esau missed out on the grace of God, because he did not value the things of God. Thus, God is warning us, saying: Do not walk in the footsteps of Esau! Do not despise the blessings I want to give to you!

How about you? Do you want God's blessings? God loves you and wants to bless you greatly, but you must give Him first place in your life. You must value the Word of God more than food and money. Then you will begin to understand what the Scriptures mean when they say: ***"No eye has seen, no ear has heard, no mind has conceived what God has prepared for those who love him."*** (1 Cor. 2:9) God wants to bless us greatly. He wants to forgive all our sins, change our wicked hearts, purify us and fill us with His love, joy, peace and assurance. And these blessings are only part of the inheritance which God wants to give to every descendant of Adam! However, you must seek the things of Eternity **with all of your heart**. He who does not desperately want God's eternal blessings will never receive them. As we sometimes hear, "Whoever wants honey must brave the bees."{Wolof proverb}

Do you want to receive God's blessings? Then you must seek to understand what God has promised in His Word. Do you know His wonderful promises, which are so great that they surpass human understanding? Do you cherish them? Or are you merely seeking after the things of the world? The Word of God shows us that there are only two kinds of people in the world: Those who **value the**

world and seek after the things of the earth, and those who **value eternity** and seek after things which are above. Which kind of person are you?

Listen to what is written in the Psalms, in the first chapter:

> (Psa. 1) [1]**Blessed is the man** *who does not walk in the counsel of the wicked or stand in the way of sinners or sit in the seat of mockers.* [2]*But his delight is in the law of the* LORD, *and on his law he meditates day and night.* [3]*He is like a tree planted by streams of water, which yields its fruit in season and whose leaf does not wither. Whatever he does prospers.* [4]**Not so the wicked**! *They are like chaff that the wind blows away.* [5]*Therefore the wicked will not stand in the judgment, nor sinners in the assembly of the righteous.* [6]*For the* LORD *watches over the way of the righteous, but the way of the wicked will perish!*

How about you? In which way are you walking? Are you walking in the way of those who **treasure God's promises**? Or are you like Esau who **traded the promises of God** for the passing things of the world? The Word of God warns us, saying:

> *"What good will it be for a man if he gains* **the whole world**, *yet* **forfeits his soul**? *Or what can a man give in exchange for his soul?"* (Matt. 16:26) *"Do not work for* **food that spoils**, *but* **for food that endures to eternal life**, *which the [Redeemer] will give you. On him God...has placed his seal of approval."* (John 6:27) *"See to it that no one misses the grace of God...or is godless like Esau, who for* **a single meal** *sold his inheritance rights as the oldest son."* (Heb. 12:15,16)

Fellow listeners, this is where we must stop today. Next time, in the will of God, we will continue in the Torah with the story of Jacob....

God bless you as you carefully consider this warning from His Word:

> ***"See to it that no one misses the grace of God...like Esau, who for a single meal sold his inheritance rights as the oldest son."*** (Heb. 12:15,16)

Lesson 24

Jacob Becomes Israel

Genesis 28-32

Peace be with you, listening friends. We greet you in the name of God, the Lord of peace, who wants everyone to understand and submit to the way of righteousness that He has established, and have true peace with Him forever. We are happy to be able to return today to present your program *The Way of Righteousness*.

In our last lesson, we read about the twins which Isaac begot, that is, **Esau and Jacob**. Esau despised the promises which God made to his grandfather, Abraham, and exchanged his firstborn inheritance for a bowl of food! As for Jacob, he valued God's promises. However, this does not mean that Jacob was without faults! Jacob's very name means *deceiver*. Today then, we plan to continue in the Torah and see **how God changed Jacob–the deceiver, into Jacob–the man of God**.

Jacob was a real trickster {deceiver}. The Scriptures, which do not hide the shortcomings of the prophets, record for us how Jacob deceived his older brother Esau twice in order to take his birthright from him. It was for this reason that Esau, in his anger, purposed to kill his younger brother. Consequently, their mother, Rebecca, called Jacob in secret, advised him to flee to his (maternal) uncle Laban, who lived in Haran, and to stay there until his brother's anger subsided.

Now, let us read in the book of Genesis, chapter twenty-eight, to see what happened after Jacob left his father Isaac's house and headed for his uncle Laban's house. The Scriptures say:

> (Gen. 28) [10]*Jacob left Beersheba and set out for Haran. (Haran was the country in which Abraham lived before God called him)* [11]*When [Jacob] reached a certain place, he stopped for the night because the sun had set. Taking one of the stones there, he put it under his head and lay down to sleep.*
>
> [12]*He had **a dream** in which he saw **a stairway resting on the earth, with its top reaching to heaven**, and the angels of God were ascending and descending*

> *on it. [13]There above it stood the LORD, and he said: "**I am the LORD, the God of your father Abraham and the God of Isaac. I will give you and your descendants the land on which you are lying.** [14]Your descendants will be like the dust of the earth, and you will spread out to the west and to the east, to the north and to the south. All peoples on earth will be blessed through you and your offspring. [15]I am with you and will watch over you wherever you go, and I will bring you back to this land. **I will not leave you until I have done what I have promised you.**" [16]When Jacob awoke from his sleep, he thought, "Surely the LORD is in this place, and I was not aware of it." [17]He was afraid and said, "How awesome is this place! This is none other than the house of God; this is the gate of heaven." [18]Early the next morning Jacob took the stone he had placed under his head and set it up as a pillar and poured oil on top of it. [19]He called that place Bethel, [which means "the house of God"].*

Thus, **God** appeared to **Jacob** in a dream and **promised the same thing** He had promised his grandfather **Abraham** and his father **Isaac**–that is, to make of his offspring **a great nation**. Therefore, we see that the firstborn inheritance which Jacob stole from his older brother was given to him by God in the end. Jacob did not deserve to become the father of the new nation which would bring the Redeemer into the world. However, God is a God of mercy and grace, who gives good things to those who do not deserve them.

What did Jacob see in his dream? The Scriptures say he "*saw **a ladder** resting on the earth, with its top reaching to heaven, and the angels of God were ascending and descending on it.*" In his dream, Jacob saw **a ladder**. The ladder which Jacob beheld was an unusual ladder, a very tall ladder, reaching from **earth to heaven** and entering the presence of God!

Through the dream of the tall ladder, God was showing Jacob that He wanted to have a wonderful and close relationship with him. God also wanted to show him that **the Redeemer** who was to come into the world would be **like that ladder** which went between heaven and earth—**the Mediator between God and man**.

To this day, many think that a person can climb up and enter Paradise based on his own good works. However, God's Word tells us that there is **only one "ladder" between God and man** and that "ladder" does not come from man but from God. We, the children of Adam, in our own strength, have no means to climb up and enter the presence of God. The reason for this is our sin and our total lack of strength to please God the Holy One. But God, who is full of mercy, because of His great love for people, has opened a way of salvation for Adam's descendants.

Therefore, the ladder which Jacob saw in his dream symbolized the Mediator whom God had promised to send into the world to save sinners. The Mediator is like the ladder which Jacob saw between heaven and earth. That is what the Scriptures teach when they say: "*There is one God and* **one Mediator between God and men**, *the man Christ Jesus, who gave himself as a ransom for all men...so that whoever believes in him shall not perish, but have eternal life.*" (1 Tim. 2:5,6; John 3:16) God's Word is clear on this matter: No one comes to God, except through the holy Mediator that God sent from heaven.

Now, let us see what happened after Jacob arrived at his uncle's house. God's word says that "*a man reaps what he sows.*" (Gal. 6:7) We have already heard how Jacob deceived his older brother. Now we will see how Jacob's uncle deceives him. His uncle's name was Laban and he was a crafty man.

We are reading in chapter twenty-nine. The Scriptures say:

> (Gen. 29) [14]*After Jacob had stayed with [Laban, his maternal uncle] for a whole month,* [15]*Laban said to him, "Just because you are a relative of mine, should you work for me for nothing? Tell me what your wages should be."* [16]*Now Laban had two daughters; the name of the older was Leah, and the name of the younger was Rachel.* [17]*Leah had weak eyes, but Rachel was lovely in form, and beautiful.* [18]*Jacob was in love with* **Rachel** *and said, "I'll work for you seven years in return for your younger daughter Rachel."* [19]*Laban said, "It's better that I give her to you than to some other man. Stay here with me."* [20]*So Jacob served seven years to get Rachel, but they seemed like only a few days to him because of his love for her.* [21]*Then Jacob said to Laban, "Give me my wife. My time is completed, and I want to lie with her."* [22]*So Laban brought together all the people of the place and gave a feast.* [23]*But when evening came, he took his daughter* **Leah** *and gave her to Jacob, and Jacob lay with her...* [25]*When morning came, there was Leah! So Jacob said to Laban, "What is this you have done to me? I served you for Rachel, didn't I? Why have you deceived me?"* [26]*Laban replied, "It is not our custom here to give the younger daughter in marriage before the older one.* [27]*Finish this daughter's bridal week; then we will give you the younger one also, in return for another seven years of work."* [28]*And Jacob did so. He finished the week with Leah, and then Laban gave him his daughter Rachel to be his wife...* [30]*Jacob lay with Rachel also, and he loved Rachel more than Leah. And he worked for Laban another seven years."*

Thus we see how Laban deceived his nephew Jacob. What happened was not a good thing, but you can be sure that God had His hand upon the things happening in the life of Jacob and would make them turn out for Jacob's good. Eventually, Jacob became the father of **twelve sons**. Jacob lived in his uncle's house for twenty years. During those twenty years, God, in His love, allowed Jacob to pass through some very painful trials, so that He might discipline him and purify his faith, just as fire purifies gold.

However, there came a day when God appeared to Jacob and said, "*Return to the land of your grandfather, where you were born. I will be with you.*" (Gen. 31:3). Thus Jacob arose, packed up and moved out, both he and his family. They headed in the direction of the land of **Canaan**–the land which God had promised to give to Abraham, Isaac, Jacob and their descendants.

As Jacob and his family were on the way to Canaan, God appeared to Jacob in a very special way and changed Jacob's name. Listen to what the Scriptures say in chapter thirty-two.

> (Gen. 32) [24]*So Jacob was left alone, and a man wrestled with him till daybreak.* [25]*When the man saw that he could not overpower him, he touched the socket of Jacob's hip so that his hip was wrenched as he wrestled with the man.* [26]*Then the man said, "Let me go, for it is daybreak." But Jacob replied, "I will not let you go unless you bless me."* [27]*The man asked him, "What is your name?" "Jacob," he answered.* [28]*Then the man said, "Your name will no longer be Jacob, but **Israel**, because you have struggled with God and with men and have overcome."* [29]*Jacob said, "Please tell me your name." But he replied, "Why do you ask my name?" Then he blessed him there.* [30]*So Jacob called the place Peniel [which means "face of God"], saying, "It is because I saw God face to face, and yet my life was spared."*

This is an amazing story full of important lessons. We see God appearing to Jacob as a man and wrestling with him. Why did He wrestle with Jacob? Because God wanted Jacob to recognize his weakness before Him. God wanted Jacob to know that all true strength and wisdom comes from God alone! God had wonderful plans for Jacob, but **God's best blessings can only come to those who know that they cannot please God in their own strength**. Jacob was beginning to realize just how weak he was before God. On that night, God gave Jacob a new name, that is, **Israel**. Jacob means *one who deceives*. But Israel means ***one who reigns with God***. Israel would be the name of the new nation God promised to bring forth from the descendants of Abraham, Isaac and Jacob. As you know, it is from the twelve sons of Jacob that the nation of Israel arose. And it is through the people of Israel that the Redeemer came into the world.

Someone might ask: Why did God choose a deceiver like Jacob and make him the father of the nation which would bring the Redeemer into the world? Listen to the answer of the Holy Scriptures:

> "*God chose the foolish things of the world to shame the wise; God chose the weak things of the world to shame the strong. He chose the lowly things of this world and the despised things, and the things that are not, to nullify the things that are,* ***so that no one may boast before Him***." (1 Cor. 1:27-29)

Jacob was a deceiver. In his own strength, there was no way that he could please God. There was nothing good in him, except for one thing: **Jacob believed the Word of God**. Jacob treasured God's promises. Receiving God's blessings was more important to Jacob than anything else in the world. Thus God made Himself known to Jacob and blessed him. God, in His eternal purposes, changed the heart of **Jacob, the deceiver**, into **Israel, the man of God**.

How about you? Like Jacob, have you recognized your inability to please God? Listen to what the Word of God says about this. It says:

> "*Blessed are the* **poor in spirit**, *for theirs is the kingdom of heaven*." (Matt 5:3) {In Wolof, "the poor in spirit" is translated: *you who know your lack of ability to please God*} "*God opposes the proud but gives grace to the humble.* ***Humble yourselves, therefore, under God's mighty hand, that he may lift you up in due time.***" (1 Pet. 5:5,6)

Thank you for listening. In our next study, God willing, we will begin to look at the amazing story of Joseph, one of Jacob's sons....

God bless you. We leave you with this verse from the Word of God:

> ***"Yet the LORD longs to be gracious to you; he rises to show you compassion. For the LORD is a God of justice. Blessed are all who wait for him!"*** (Isa. 30:18)

Lesson 25

Joseph's Humiliation

Genesis 37-39

Peace be with you, listening friends. We greet you in the name of God, the Lord of peace, who wants everyone to understand and submit to the way of righteousness that He has established, and have true peace with Him forever. We are happy to be able to return today to present to you your program *The Way of Righteousness* in which we are recounting the stories of the Prophets of God, one by one. We are continuing to read in the first section of the Word of God called ***the Torah***.

In our last lesson, we learned about the prophet of God, Jacob, Abraham's grandson. We saw how God gave Jacob a new name: **Israel**. Jacob means *deceiver*, but Israel means *one who reigns with God*. Now Jacob had two names: Jacob and Israel. Israel is also the name of the new nation, which God had promised to make from the descendants of Abraham, Isaac and Jacob. Jacob had twelve sons. From these twelve sons arose the people of Israel–the nation through which the Redeemer would come.

Do you know the names of **the twelve sons of Jacob**? They are Reuben, Simeon, Levi, Judah, Zebulun, Issachar, Dan, Gad, Asher, Naphtali, Joseph and Benjamin. Today we begin the captivating story about the sons of Jacob–especially the one named **Joseph**, who was the eleventh son. Now let us get into the wonderful story of Joseph!

We are reading in the Torah, the book of Genesis, in chapter thirty-seven. The Scriptures say:

> (Gen. 37) [2]*This is the account of [the family line of] Jacob.* ***Joseph, a young man of seventeen****, was tending the flocks with his brothers…And [Joseph] brought their father a bad report about them.* [3]*Now Israel loved Joseph more than any of his other sons, because he had been born to him in his old age; and he made a richly ornamented robe for him.* [4]*When* ***his brothers*** *saw that their father loved him more than any of them, they* ***hated him*** *and could not speak a kind word to him.*

5[One day] Joseph had **a dream**, and when he told it to his brothers, they
hated him all the more. 6He said to them, "Listen to this dream I had: 7We were
binding sheaves of corn out in the field when suddenly my sheaf rose and stood
upright, while your sheaves gathered round mine and bowed down to it." 8His
brothers said to him, "Do you intend to reign over us? Will you actually rule us?"
And they hated him all the more because of his dream and what he had said.
9Then he had another dream, and he told it to his brothers. "Listen," he said, "I
had another dream, and this time the sun and moon and eleven stars were bowing
down to me." 10When he told his father as well as his brothers, his father rebuked
him and said, "What is this dream you had? **Will your mother and I and your
brothers actually come and bow down to the ground before you?**" 11His
brothers were jealous of him, but his father kept the matter in mind.

12Now his brothers had gone to graze their father's flocks near Shechem, 13and
Israel said to Joseph, "As you know, your brothers are grazing the flocks near
Shechem. **Come, I am going to send you to them**." "Very well," he replied.
14So he said to him, "Go and see if all is well with your brothers and with the
flocks, and bring word back to me."

17So Joseph went after his brothers and found them near Dothan. 18But they
saw him in the distance, and before he reached them, **they plotted to kill him**.
19"Here comes that dreamer!" they said to each other. 20"Come now, let's kill him
and throw him into one of these cisterns and say that a ferocious animal devoured
him. Then we'll see what comes of his dreams." 21When Reuben heard this, he
tried to rescue him from their hands. "Let's not take his life," he said. 22"Don't
shed any blood. Throw him into this cistern here in the desert, but don't lay a
hand on him." Reuben said this to rescue him from them and take him back to his
father.

23So when Joseph came to his brothers, **they stripped him of his robe**, the
richly ornamented robe he was wearing, 24and **they took him** and threw him into
the cistern. Now the cistern was empty; there was no water in it. 25As they sat
down to eat their meal, they looked up and saw a caravan of Ishmaelites coming
from Gilead. Their camels were loaded with spices, balm and myrrh, and they
were on their way to take them down to Egypt. 26Judah said to his brothers,
"What will we gain if we kill our brother and cover up his blood? 27Come, let's sell
him to the Ishmaelites and not lay our hands on him; after all, he is our brother,
our own flesh and blood." His brothers agreed. 28So when the Midianite merchants came by, his brothers pulled Joseph up out of the cistern and **sold him** for
twenty shekels of silver to the Ishmaelites, who took him to Egypt.

29When Reuben returned to the cistern and saw that Joseph was not there, he
tore his clothes. 30He went back to his brothers and said, "The boy isn't there!
Where can I turn now?" 31Then they got Joseph's robe, slaughtered a goat and
dipped the robe in the blood. 32They took the ornamented robe back to their father

and said, "We found this. Examine it to see whether it is your son's robe." [33]*He recognized it and said, "It is my son's robe! Some ferocious animal has devoured him. Joseph has surely been torn to pieces."* [34]***Then Jacob tore his clothes, put on sackcloth and mourned for his son many days.*** [35]*All his sons and daughters came to comfort him, but he refused to be comforted. "No," he said, "in mourning will I go down to the grave to my son." So his father wept for him.*

(Gen. 39) [1]*Now Joseph had been* ***taken down to Egypt****. Potiphar, an Egyptian who was one of Pharaoh's officials, the captain of the guard, bought him from the Ishmaelites who had taken him there.* [2]***The LORD was with Joseph*** *and he prospered, and he lived in the house of his Egyptian master.* [3]*When his master saw that the LORD was with him and that the LORD gave him success in everything he did,* [4]*Joseph found favor in his eyes and became his attendant. Potiphar put him in charge of his household, and he entrusted to his care everything he owned.* [5]*From the time he put him in charge of his household and of all that he owned, the LORD blessed the household of the Egyptian because of Joseph. The blessing of the LORD was on everything Potiphar had, both in the house and in the field.* [6]*So he left in Joseph's care everything he had; with Joseph in charge, he did not concern himself with anything except the food he ate. Now Joseph was well-built and handsome,* [7]*and after a while his master's wife took notice of Joseph and said, "Come to bed with me!"* [8]*But he refused. "With me in charge," he told her, "my master does not concern himself with anything in the house; everything he owns he has entrusted to my care.* [9]*No one is greater in this house than I am. My master has withheld nothing from me except you, because you are his wife.* ***How then could I do such a wicked thing and sin against God?****"* [10]*And though she spoke to Joseph day after day, he refused to go to bed with her or even to be with her.*

[11]*One day he went into the house to attend to his duties, and none of the household servants was inside.* [12]*She caught him by his cloak and said, "Come to bed with me!" But he left his cloak in her hand and ran out of the house.* [13]*When she saw that he had left his cloak in her hand and had run out of the house,* [14]*she called her household servants. "Look," she said to them, "this Hebrew has been brought to us to make sport of us! He came in here to sleep with me, but I screamed.* [15]*When he heard me scream for help, he left his cloak beside me and ran out of the house."*

[16]*She kept his cloak beside her until his master came home.* [17]*Then she told him this story: "That Hebrew slave you brought us came to me to make sport of me.* [18]*But as soon as I screamed for help, he left his cloak beside me and ran out of the house."* [19]*When his master heard the story his wife told him, saying, "This is how your slave treated me," he burned with anger.* [20]*Joseph's master took him and put him in prison, the place where the king's prisoners were confined. But while Joseph was there in the prison,* [21]*the LORD was with him; he showed him*

> *kindness and granted him favor in the eyes of the prison warden.* [22]*So the warden put Joseph in charge of all those held in the prison, and he was made responsible for all that was done there.* [23]*The warden paid no attention to anything under Joseph's care, because* ***the LORD was with Joseph and gave him success in whatever he did****.*

Thus begins the story of Joseph, the son of Jacob. We can summarize what we have seen today with this statement: **Joseph loved righteousness and hated wickedness.** He would rather suffer in prison than enjoy the passing pleasures of sin. That was why, when the wife of his master invited him to lie with her and commit adultery, Joseph refused, answering her, "How could I do such a wicked thing and sin against God?"

Joseph knew that **serving God** and **serving sin** do not go together! Joseph had presented his heart to God. That is why he loved righteousness and hated wickedness. Like his great-grandfather, Abraham, **Joseph also believed what God had promised concerning the Savior** who was to come to earth to die for the sins of Adam's descendants. God judged Joseph to be righteous because Joseph **believed** the word of God. Because of his faith, God forgave Joseph of his sins and filled his heart with the desire and the power to overcome sin and to live righteously in an evil world.

God "walked" with Joseph because Joseph "walked" with God. Joseph could not enjoy sin, because his heart belonged to God. The one who believes and worships God from the heart will **love what God loves** and **hate what God hates**. That is what the Scripture declares when it says:

> "***No one can serve two masters****. Either he will hate the one and love the other, or he will be devoted to the one and despise the other.*" (Matt. 6:24) "*For what do* ***righteousness*** *and* ***wickedness*** *have in common? Or what fellowship can* ***light*** *have with* ***darkness****?* (2 Cor. 6:14) "*God is* ***light****; in Him there is* ***no darkness*** *at all. If we claim to have fellowship with him yet walk in the darkness, we lie and do not live by the truth.*" (1 John 1:5,6)

Those who truly belong to God believe the Word of God and seek to obey it. But those who do not belong to God are controlled by sin. They may have the **outward form of religion**, but **sin still controls** their thoughts, the intentions of their hearts, their words and their deeds. They may intend to overcome sin, but they are unable to do so, because **sin is stronger** than they are. They do not have in their hearts **the power of God's Holy Spirit**, which God gives to all those who believe His Word and accept the way of salvation which He has established.

You who are listening today, has God renewed your heart by His power? Have you received **the Good News** about the Savior who has the power to cleanse your heart from all sin? Or are you still living under the dominion of sin? The Scripture says: "***Come near to God and he will come near to you***. *Wash your hands, you sinners, and purify your hearts, you double-minded.... Humble yourselves before the Lord, and He will lift you up.*" (Jam. 2:8)

Friends, we thank you for listening. In our next study, in the will of the Lord, we will continue with the story of Joseph and see how he got out of prison and rose to the position of ruler over the whole land of Egypt....

God bless you as you meditate upon this verse found in the Scriptures:

> ***"God is light; in him there is no darkness at all. If we claim to have fellowship with him yet walk in the darkness, we lie and do not live by the truth."*** (1 John 1:5,6)

Lesson 26

Joseph's Exaltation

Genesis 40-42

Peace be with you, listening friends. We greet you in the name of God, the Lord of peace, who wants everyone to understand and submit to the way of righteousness that He has established, and have true peace with Him forever. We are happy to be able to return today to present your program *The Way of Righteousness*.

In our last lesson, we began to learn about Joseph, who was the eleventh of Jacob's twelve sons. We read how Joseph dreamed that his brothers would one day bow down to him. Joseph's brothers did not believe him. However, today we will see how **God fulfilled Joseph's dream** in causing his brothers to come and kneel before him.

As we learned, Joseph's older brothers hated and persecuted him because of his dreams. In their anger and jealousy, they went so far as to sell him as a slave to some merchants who were descendants of Ishmael. The Ishmaelites took Joseph to Egypt and sold him to an official of Pharaoh, king of Egypt. As for Joseph, he was a faithful servant and honest in his work, because he **walked with God**. Joseph was also very handsome, which caused the wife of his master to lust after him, wanting to lie with him. But Joseph refused, answering the woman, "*How could I do such a wicked thing and sin against God?*" When Joseph refused to commit adultery with her, the woman spoke against Joseph and had him locked up. However, Joseph preferred to go to prison rather than to enjoy pleasures of sin for a short time. Joseph put God first in his life. For two years Joseph remained in the dungeon, but God had not forgotten him.

Now then, let us continue in the Torah and see how God changed Joseph's circumstances. We are reading in the book of Genesis, chapter forty-one. The Scriptures say:

> (Gen. 41) [1]*[Thus, two full years after Joseph had been put in prison,* ***Pharaoh****, the king of Egypt,]* ***had a dream****: He was standing by the Nile,* [2]*when out of the river there came up seven cows, sleek and fat, and they grazed among the reeds.*

> [3]*After them, seven other cows, ugly and gaunt, came up out of the Nile and stood beside those on the riverbank.* [4]*And the cows that were ugly and gaunt ate up the seven sleek, fat cows. Then Pharaoh woke up.* [5]*He fell asleep again and had a second dream: Seven ears of corn, healthy and good, were growing on a single stalk.* [6]*After them, seven other ears of corn sprouted–thin and scorched by the east wind.* [7]*The thin ears of corn swallowed up the seven healthy, full ears. Then Pharaoh woke up; it had been a dream.* [8]*In the morning his mind was troubled, so he sent for all the magicians and wise men of Egypt. Pharaoh told them his dreams, but no one could interpret them for him.*
>
> [9]*Then the chief cupbearer said to Pharaoh, "Today I am reminded of my shortcomings.* [10]*Pharaoh was once angry with his servants, and he imprisoned me and the chief baker in the house of the captain of the guard.* [11]*Each of us had a dream the same night, and each dream had a meaning of its own.* [12]*Now a young Hebrew was there with us, a servant of the captain of the guard. We told him our dreams, and he interpreted them for us, giving each man the interpretation of his dream.* [13]*And things turned out exactly as he interpreted them to us: I was restored to my position, and the other man was hanged."*
>
> [14]*So* **Pharaoh sent for Joseph**, *and he was quickly brought from the dungeon. When he had shaved and changed his clothes, he came before Pharaoh.* [15]*Pharaoh said to Joseph, "I had a dream, and no one can interpret it. But I have heard it said of you that when you hear a dream you can interpret it."* [16]*"***I cannot do it**,*" Joseph replied to Pharaoh, "***but God will give Pharaoh the answer he desires**."*

Then Pharaoh recounted to Joseph his dream. After he had told it he said to Joseph,

> [24]*"...I told this to the magicians, but none could explain it to me."* [25]*Then Joseph said to Pharaoh, "The dreams of Pharaoh are one and the same. God has revealed to Pharaoh what he is about to do.* [26]*The seven good cows are seven years, and the seven good ears of corn are seven years; it is one and the same dream.* [27]*The seven lean, ugly cows that came up afterwards are seven years, and so are the seven worthless ears of corn scorched by the east wind: They are seven years of famine.* [28]*"It is just as I said to Pharaoh: God has shown Pharaoh what he is about to do.* [29]**Seven years of great abundance** *are coming throughout the land of Egypt,* [30]*but* **seven years of famine** *will follow them. Then all the abundance in Egypt will be forgotten, and the famine will ravage the land.* [31]*The abundance in the land will not be remembered, because the famine that follows it will be so severe.* [32]*The reason the dream was given to Pharaoh in two forms is that the matter has been firmly decided by God, and God will do it soon.* [33]*And now let Pharaoh look for a discerning and wise man and put him in charge of the*

land of Egypt. 34Let Pharaoh appoint commissioners over the land to take a fifth of the harvest of Egypt during the seven years of abundance. 35They should collect all the food of these good years that are coming and store up the grain under the authority of Pharaoh, to be kept in the cities for food. 36This food should be held in reserve for the country, to be used during the seven years of famine that will come upon Egypt, so that the country may not be ruined by the famine."

*37The plan seemed good to Pharaoh and to all his officials. 38So Pharaoh asked them, "***Can we find anyone like this man, one in whom is the spirit of God?***" 39Then Pharaoh said to Joseph, "Since God has made all this known to you, there is no one so discerning and wise as you. 40You shall be in charge of my palace, and all my people are to submit to your orders. Only with respect to the throne will I be greater than you."*

41So Pharaoh said to Joseph, "I hereby put you in charge of the whole land of Egypt." *42Then Pharaoh took his signet ring from his finger and put it on Joseph's finger. He dressed him in robes of fine linen and put a gold chain around his neck. 43He had him ride in a chariot as his second-in-command, and men shouted before him, "Make way!" Thus he put him in charge of the whole land of Egypt. 44Then Pharaoh said to Joseph, "I am Pharaoh, but without your word no one will lift hand or foot in all Egypt." 45Pharaoh gave Joseph the name* **Zaphenath-Paneah** *[meaning "***Preserver of Life***"]...And Joseph went throughout the land of Egypt. 46Joseph was thirty years old when he entered the service of Pharaoh king of Egypt. And Joseph went out from Pharaoh's presence and traveled throughout Egypt. 47During the seven years of abundance the land produced plentifully. 48Joseph collected all the food produced in those seven years of abundance in Egypt and stored it in the cities. In each city he put the food grown in the fields surrounding it. 49Joseph stored up huge quantities of grain, like the sand of the sea; it was so much that he stopped keeping records because it was beyond measure...*

53The seven years of abundance in Egypt came to an end, 54and the seven years of famine began, just as Joseph had said. There was famine in all the other lands, but in the whole land of Egypt there was food. 55When all Egypt began to feel the famine, the people cried to Pharaoh for food. Then Pharaoh told all the Egyptians, "Go to Joseph and do what he tells you!" 56When the famine had spread over the whole country, Joseph opened the storehouses and sold grain to the Egyptians, for the famine was severe throughout Egypt. 57And **all the countries came to Egypt to buy grain from Joseph**, *because the famine was severe in all the world.*

(Gen. 42) *1When Jacob (the father of Joseph and his brothers) learned that there was grain in Egypt, he said to his sons, "Why do you just keep looking at each other?" 2He continued, "I have heard that there is grain in Egypt. Go down there and buy some for us, so that we may live and not die." 3Then* **ten of**

> ***Joseph's brothers went down to buy grain from Egypt.*** [4]*But Jacob did not send Benjamin, Joseph's brother, with the others, because he was afraid that harm might come to him.* [5]*So Israel's sons were among those who went to buy grain, for the famine was in the land of Canaan also.*
>
> [6]*Now Joseph was the governor of the land, the one who sold grain to all its people. So when Joseph's brothers arrived,* ***they bowed down to him*** *with their faces to the ground.* [7]*As soon as Joseph saw his brothers, he recognized them, but he pretended to be a stranger and spoke harshly to them. "Where do you come from?" he asked. "From the land of Canaan," they replied, "to buy food."* [8]*Although* ***Joseph recognized his brothers, they did not recognize him.*** [9]***Then he remembered his dreams about them.***

Do you understand what happened? We see Joseph's older brothers bowing down before their younger brother Joseph, exactly as he had dreamed long ago! This Joseph whom they had hated, denied, and wanted to kill–in the end, they bowed before him! Joseph immediately recognized his brothers, but they did not recognize him, because they had not seen him for more than twenty years! In our next lesson, God willing, we will finish the story of Joseph and see how he made himself known to his brothers.

But what about our lesson today? What does God want to teach us through the story of Joseph and his brothers? God wants to make known to us that what happened between Joseph and his brothers is **an illustration** of what would happen between the Savior of the world and the descendants of Adam. Friends, if we remember only one thing from our lesson today, let it be this: **Joseph was a shadow** (a picture) **of the Savior** whom God promised to send into the world. There are at least one hundred elements (events, comparisons) in the story of Joseph which foreshadow (typify, illustrate) the story the Redeemer who came into the world some eighteen hundred years later. Obviously, we do not have time on this program to mention all hundred comparisons–but we will mention three.

1.) First, we saw how Joseph's older brothers **rejected** both him and his dreams. They hated him, insulted him and even sold him. The same things happened to the Savior whom God sent into the world. The people of the world rejected both the Redeemer and His message—insulting Him, persecuting Him, selling Him, and even nailing Him to a cross.

2.) The second picture is this: At first, people despised, ignored, mistreated, and imprisoned Joseph. Yet in God's chosen time the king of Egypt **appointed** Joseph as the supreme ruler over the whole land, declaring to all who wanted to be saved from hunger and death: "Go to Joseph, the Preserver of Life!" In the same way, concerning the Savior of the world whom God has sent down, the LORD God says: Go to the Savior whom I have appointed! He is the Preserver of

Life; He is the Source of Life! If you submit yourself to Him, you will never again experience hunger in your heart and your soul shall live forever.

3.) The third comparison between Joseph and the Redeemer is a solemn one. In the end, Joseph's brothers **submitted to** his authority. They had no choice but to prostrate themselves before the very one they had denied and dishonored! In the same way, the Word of God announces that the Redeemer, whom so many deny and dishonor to this very day, will one day return to judge the world in righteousness. In that day all the people of the world will bow before Him; all will know that He is the One whom God has appointed as the Savior and the Judge of the world!

Listening friend, how about you? **Have you submitted yourself to the Savior** whom God has appointed to preserve you from eternal judgment? Or will you wait until it is too late, until the Day of Judgment—when you will be forced to bow before Him?

We must stop here today, but that doesn't mean you need to stop thinking about today's lesson!...

May God bless you and give you insight into all you have heard today. The Word of God says:

> ***"We have the word of the prophets made more certain, and you will do well to pay attention to it, as to a light shining in a dark place."*** (2 Pet. 1:19)

Lesson 27

Joseph: The Rest of the Story

Genesis 42-50

Peace be with you, listening friends. We greet you in the name of God, the Lord of peace, who wants everyone to understand and submit to the way of righteousness that He has established, and have true peace with Him forever. We are happy to be able to return today to present your program *The Way of Righteousness*.

In the past two programs we have been reading about Joseph, the son of Jacob. Today we plan to hear **the rest of the story of Joseph** and, in so doing, to come to the **end of the first section of the Torah**, the book of Genesis. We have already seen that Jacob, Abraham's grandson, had twelve sons. Joseph was the eleventh son. They all lived in the land of Canaan, the land which, as you know, God had promised to give to the descendants of Abraham, Isaac and Jacob. When Joseph was a young man, he dreamed that his older brothers would, one day, bow down before him. But his older brothers despised him and his dreams, and sold him as a slave into the land of Egypt. However, God delivered Joseph from all his troubles, and gave him the wisdom to interpret the dream of Pharaoh, king of Egypt. With God's help, Joseph predicted the severe seven-year famine which was to take place throughout the land. Thus, Pharaoh appointed Joseph supreme ruler over the whole land of Egypt.

After the seven years of plenty ended, we saw that the famine, which Joseph had predicted, came upon Egypt and upon the land of Canaan. However, in the land of Egypt there was grain stored up in abundance because of the grace and wisdom which God gave to Joseph.

When Jacob heard that Egypt had grain {In Wolof: *millet* (Senegal's staple food)}, he sent Joseph's ten older brothers to go buy some. But he did not send Benjamin, Joseph's younger brother, along with them for fear that some harm would come to him. Next, we saw the ten older brothers arrive in Egypt and prostrate themselves before their brother Joseph, thus fulfilling that which

Joseph had dreamed long before. Joseph recognized his older brothers, but they did not recognize him, because they had not seen him for more than twenty years and, in their minds, Joseph was dead.

Today we will conclude the story to see **how Joseph made himself known to his brothers**. Joseph did not immediately reveal himself to his brothers, because he wanted to test them first, to know whether their deceitful and wicked hearts had changed. Thus, the Scriptures say: "*As soon as Joseph saw his brothers, he recognized them, but he pretended to be a stranger and spoke harshly to them. 'Where do you come from?' he asked. 'From the land of Canaan,' they replied, 'to buy food.'*" (Gen. 42:7)

Joseph asked them many questions, accused them of being spies and locked them in prison. **Joseph wanted to make them think about their lives and the condition of their hearts before God.** Three days later, Joseph allowed them to depart, but kept one of them in prison, telling the others to return to Egypt with their younger brother Benjamin, their father's youngest {Lit. *last*} child.

After many months, the older brothers returned to Egypt to buy more grain, bringing Benjamin, their younger brother, along with them. When they arrived, they again met Joseph, the ruler of the land–but still they did not recognize him. Joseph had them brought into his house, which caused them to be very much afraid. He then put on a great feast for them, making them sit around the table in the order of their ages, beginning with the eldest to the youngest, and giving them food from his table. Benjamin received five times more food than the others. Perhaps Joseph was testing his brothers to see if they would be jealous of Benjamin, as they had been jealous of him. However, not one of them showed any jealousy toward their younger brother, Benjamin.

After the feast, Joseph ordered a servant to fill their sacks with grain and to hide his special silver cup in Benjamin's sack. After Joseph's brothers had left, Joseph sent his chief steward to pursue them and to accuse them of stealing. When the chief steward caught up with them, he said, "Why have you repaid good with evil? Did you not take the cup from which my master drinks?" They replied, "We did not take it. Let the one with whom you find the cup die and we ourselves will become your slaves!" The chief steward replied, "Whoever is found to have the cup will become my slave, but the rest of you may go on your way."

The chief steward searched all the sacks, beginning with the sack of the eldest and ending with the sack of the youngest—and found the cup in Benjamin's sack! At this, Joseph's older brothers tore their clothes, and returned to the city, and threw themselves to the ground before Joseph. Joseph then said to them, "What have you done? Did you think you could deceive me?" Judah, the fourth son of Jacob, said to him, "What can we say? How can we clear ourselves? God has revealed our wrongdoings and our unrighteousness! We are your slaves, we and the one with whom you found the cup!"

Joseph replied, "Only the man with whom the cup was found will be my slave.

The rest of you may return in peace to your father." Then Judah came near to Joseph and told him again of the anguish which his father had in letting Benjamin accompany them to Egypt. After this, Judah pleaded with Joseph to have mercy on them and to allow Benjamin to return home to his father. Judah also asked that he, Judah, become Joseph's slave instead of Benjamin. When Joseph saw the anguish which the brothers had because of their past sins, and the pity they had for their father and their younger brother, Joseph knew that **his older brothers had truly repented.** He knew that **the time had come to make himself known** to his brothers!

Thus, the Scriptures say:

> (Gen. 45) [1]*Then Joseph could no longer control himself before all his attendants, and he cried out, "Make everyone leave my presence!" So there was no one with Joseph when he made himself known to his brothers.* [2]*And he wept so loudly that the Egyptians heard him, and Pharaoh's household heard about it.* [3]*Joseph said to his brothers, "**I am Joseph!** Is my father still living?" But his brothers were not able to answer him, because they were terrified at his presence.*
>
> [4]*Then Joseph said to his brothers, "Come close to me." When they had done so, he said, "**I am your brother Joseph, the one you sold into Egypt**!* [5]*And now, do not be distressed and do not be angry with yourselves for selling me here, because **it was to save lives that God sent me ahead of you.*** [6]*For two years now there has been famine in the land, and for the next five years there will not be ploughing and reaping.* [7]*But God sent me ahead of you to preserve for you a remnant on earth and to save your lives by **a great deliverance**.* [8]*"**So then, it was not you who sent me here, but God**. He made me father to Pharaoh, lord of his entire household and ruler of all Egypt.* [9]*Now hurry back to my father and say to him, 'This is what your son Joseph says: God has made me lord of all Egypt. Come down to me; don't delay.* [10]*You shall live in the region of Goshen and be near me– you, your children and grandchildren, your flocks and herds, and all you have.* [11]*I will provide for you there, because five years of famine are still to come. Otherwise you and your household and all who belong to you will become destitute.'* [12]*You can see for yourselves, and so can my brother Benjamin, that it is really I who am speaking to you.* [13]*Tell my father about all the honor accorded me in Egypt and about everything you have seen. And bring my father down here quickly."* [14]*Then he threw his arms around his brother Benjamin and wept, and Benjamin embraced him, weeping.* [15]*And he kissed all his brothers and wept over them. Afterwards his brothers talked with him.*

After this, Joseph's brothers prepared to return to their father's house. Joseph gave them carts, as Pharaoh had commanded, and he also gave them provisions for their journey.

> [25]*So they went up out of Egypt and came to their father Jacob in the land of Canaan.* [26]*They told him, "**Joseph is still alive!** In fact, he is ruler of all Egypt." Jacob was stunned; he did not believe them.* [27]*But when they told him everything Joseph had said to them, and when he saw the carts Joseph had sent to carry him back, the spirit of their father Jacob revived.* [28]*And Israel [that is, Jacob] said, "I'm convinced! My son Joseph is still alive. I will go and see him before I die."*

After this, the Scriptures tell how Jacob and his family moved out of the land of Canaan and headed for Egypt. Jacob offered a sacrifice along the way, and there God spoke to him, saying,

> *"I am God, the God of your father. Do not be afraid to go down to Egypt, for **I will make you into a great nation there**. I will go down to Egypt with you, and **I will surely bring you back again**. And Joseph's own hand will close your eyes."* (Gen. 46:3,4)

After a long journey, Jacob and his family arrived in the land of Egypt. How happy Jacob was to see his beloved son Joseph after so many years! Thus Jacob, who is also called ***Israel***, and his family, settled in Egypt, in the region of Goshen. There they increased greatly in numbers and became a very large tribe. Jacob lived in Egypt for seventeen years. In all, he lived to be 147 years old. Thus, Jacob, the father of the tribes of Israel, died, and went to be with God on high. Joseph and his brothers and all the people of Egypt mourned for him for seventy days. Jacob's sons buried their father in the land of Canaan, in the tomb of Abraham his grandfather.

In the last chapter of the book of Genesis, chapter fifty, the Scripture says:

> (Gen. 50) [15]*When Joseph's brothers saw that their father was dead, they said, "What if Joseph holds a grudge against us and pays us back for all the wrongs we did to him?"...* [19]*But [when Joseph heard this] he said to them, "Don't be afraid. Am I in the place of God?* [20]***You intended to harm me, but God intended it for good to accomplish what is now being done, the saving of many lives.*** [21]*So then, don't be afraid. I will provide for you and your children." And he reassured them and spoke kindly to them.* [22]*Joseph stayed in Egypt, along with all his father's family. He lived a hundred and ten years...* [24]*Then Joseph said to his brothers, "I am about to die. But God will surely come to your aid and take you up out of this land to the land he promised on oath to Abraham, Isaac and Jacob."* [25]*And Joseph made the sons of Israel swear an oath and said, "God will surely come to your aid, and then you must carry my bones up from this place."* [26]*So Joseph died at the age of a hundred and ten. And after they embalmed him, he was placed in a coffin in Egypt.*

This is how the book of Genesis ends. "*So Joseph* ***died****...and...was placed in* ***a coffin*** *in Egypt.*" This book, which began with the story of how God created **life**, ends with a story of **death**. Because of Adam's sin, death has come to all men. Like it or not, "*the wages of sin is death!*" (Rom. 6:23) Even a good man like Joseph, who bore the title *Preserver of Life*, had to die, because he, too, was a descendant of Adam with the roots of sin in his heart. Joseph, with the help of God, was able to **preserve** the people of Egypt, and his family, from starving to death, but he could **not preserve** them from **death itself**. Yet we can praise God with joyful hearts {Lit. in Wolof: *cold hearts*}, because, in the book of Genesis, we also read about **God's wonderful promise** to send us an all-sufficient Savior who would **conquer death itself**. Death is a result of **sin**. The Savior God promised to send would deliver Adam's descendants from **the root of sin** and **the penalty of sin**. The root of sin is the devil and the evil heart of man. The penalty of sin is death and hell. The Savior whom God promised to send has conquered them all and can transform the lives of those who believe in Him.

You who are listening today, do you know this all-sufficient Savior who has defeated Satan and sin, death and hell, and offers eternal life to all who believe in His Name? The holy Gospel {*Injil*} speaks of this Savior saying: "*Praise be to the Lord, the God of Israel, because He has come and has redeemed His people.* ***He has raised up a horn of salvation for us...as he said through His holy prophets of long ago!***" (Luke 1:68-70) Amen!

In our next program, God willing, we will begin the second book contained in the Torah, which is called *Exodus*....

God bless you as you consider this verse of Scripture which summarizes the book of Genesis:

"Where sin increased, [God's] grace increased all the more!" (Rom. 5:20)

LESSON 28

REVIEW OF THE FIRST BOOK OF THE TORAH

GENESIS 1-EXODUS 1

Peace be with you, listening friends. We greet you in the name of God, the Lord of peace, who wants everyone to understand and submit to the way of righteousness that He has established, and have true peace with Him forever. We are happy to be able to return today to present your program *The Way of Righteousness*.

We are still studying in the Torah. As you know, the Torah is the first book in the Writings of the Prophets and is divided into five sections or books. The first section is called *Genesis* (Lit. *the Beginning*). In our last broadcast, we completed our studies in Genesis. Today then, we begin the second section of the Torah, which is called ***The Exodus***. The book of Exodus contains the amazing and wonderful account of how God freed the children of Israel from the bondage of their slavery in the land of Egypt.

Before we get into the book of Exodus, let us **review** what we have studied in the first book of the Holy Scriptures. It is crucial that we have a thorough knowledge of the book of Genesis, because it is the foundation that God has laid so that we might understand and believe all that is written in the other books of the prophets which follow.

Do you remember the first verse of the book of Genesis? It says: "*In the beginning God created the heavens and the earth.*" This is important. "In the beginning **God**!" When nothing yet existed–only One existed. That One was God! Next, we learned how God created millions of holy **angels**, by the power of His Eternal Word and His Holy Spirit. God created the angels so that they might serve Him and praise Him forever. Among the angels was one with superior wisdom and beauty. That one was **Lucifer**, the chief of the angels. However, the Scriptures tell us that there was a day when Lucifer became conceited and despised God in his heart. Lucifer and many other angels began to devise a plan to overthrow God. However, no one can overthrow God. God cannot tolerate those who rebel against Him (Lit. *refuse His rule*). Consequently, God expelled Lucifer and his evil angels and changed the name of Lucifer to **Satan**, which means *Adversary*. And after God expelled Satan and his angels, He created for them the fire of **hell**. The Scriptures say that on the Day of Judgment, God, the Righteous One, will throw Satan into that fire along with all who follow him.

Next we read how the LORD created **the world** for the people whom He planned to create. **Man** {neuter: A human} is the most important creature of all that God created, because man was created in the image of God! God wanted to have a deep and wonderful relationship with man. That is why He placed in the soul of man a **mind** capable of knowing God, gave him a **heart** capable of loving God, and entrusted him with a **will** capable of obeying God.

Next, we saw how God placed **a test** before the man and the women whom He had created. God warned Adam saying, "*You are free to eat from any tree in the garden; but you must not eat from the tree of the knowledge of good and evil, for [in the day that] you eat of it you will surely die!*" that is: you will be separated from me forever!

However, we saw how our ancestors, Adam and Eve, chose to obey Satan by eating from the tree which God had forbidden. Consequently, the Word of God says: "***Sin** entered the world through one man, and **death** through sin, and in this way **death came to all men**.*" (Rom. 5:12) How true it is that "an epidemic is not confined to the one from whom it originates!" {Wolof proverb} Because of Adam's sin, we are all sinners. Because of Adam's sin, we all deserve to die and face God's judgment.

Next, we learned how God expelled Adam and Eve from the Garden of Paradise because of their sin. However, before He expelled them, God announced how He planned to send into the world **a Redeemer** to save the children of Adam from the power of Satan and from the penalty of sin. God, in His wonderful design, had a plan to redeem sinners. His plan was to send into the world a perfect Man who would not be contaminated by the sin of Adam. This righteous Man would willingly shed His blood to pay the debt of sin for the children of Adam. In this way, God could forgive people of their sins, without compromising His justice. Truly, what God promised concerning the coming Redeemer was an amazing promise!

Next we saw how God confirmed that wonderful promise by sacrificing some animals, and making for Adam and Eve clothes of skin. God was teaching Adam and Eve that "*the payment for sin is death*" and that "*without the shedding of blood there is no forgiveness of sin*."

After that, we learned about Adam's first two sons, Cain and Abel. We saw how Abel offered God **a lamb** without blemish and slaughtered it, thus symbolizing **the Redeemer** who was to come into the world and die for sinners. As for Cain, he tried to approach God through his own efforts, offering Him what he had cultivated. Consequently, the Scriptures say: "*the Lord accepted Abel, but He did not accept Cain.*" Why did God not accept the sacrifice of Cain? Because God's law did **not** say: "the payment for sin is **good works**!" Rather, it stated: "*the payment for sin is* ***death****!*" and "*without* ***the shedding of blood*** *there is no forgiveness of sin.*" God pleaded with Cain to repent and accept the way of righteousness that He had ordained, but Cain became furious, and killed his younger brother, Abel.

Most of Adam's descendants followed the footsteps of Cain, so that by the time of Noah, the Scriptures say that God "*saw how great man's wickedness on the earth had become, and that every inclination of the thoughts of his heart was* ***only evil all the time****.*" Because of man's wicked heart, God purposed to send a flood to wipe out rebellious sinners. In that corrupt time, only Noah believed God, which was why God told him to build a large boat, which would be a refuge for all who entered it. God was patient with sinners for a long time while Noah was constructing the boat. However, no one repented and entered the boat, except Noah and his family.

Noah had three sons, Shem, Ham and Japheth. The prophet Abraham descended from Shem. We read how God commanded Abraham to leave his father's house and go to the land of Canaan (Palestine). God planned to make of Abraham **a new nation** from which the prophets of God and **the Savior of the world** would come forth. That is why God said to Abraham, "*You will be a [door of] blessing...and all nations of the earth will be blessed through you.*" (Gen. 12:2,3)

Thus, Abraham became the father of Isaac in his old age, just as God had promised. Isaac then became the father of Jacob, and Jacob, whom God renamed Israel, became the father of twelve sons. And from the twelve sons of Jacob originated the new nation which God had promised Abraham, the nation of Israel.

In the past three programs, we have been looking into the captivating story of the sons of Jacob, particularly the one named Joseph, the eleventh son. The elder brothers of Joseph hated him, but God blessed him and made him the ruler over all the land of Egypt. After that, a famine fell on Egypt and the whole land of Canaan, causing great misery. As a result, Jacob and his sons had nothing to eat. When Jacob heard that Egypt had grain, he sent his sons there. We then saw how Joseph made himself known to his brethren, forgave them, and called his father and all his family to move and settle in Egypt. Thus, at the **end of the book of Genesis,** we see that **the children of Israel** were no longer in the land of Canaan which God had promised Abraham, but **in Egypt**. However, all this happened to fulfil what God had told Abraham a long time previously when he said to him:

> "*Know for certain that* ***your descendants will be strangers in a country not their own****, and they will be enslaved and ill-treated four hundred years. But I*

> *will punish the nation they serve as slaves, and afterwards they will come out with great possessions.*" (Gen. 15:13,14)

God Himself had his hand on all that happened to the children of Israel. Why did God allow Abraham's great grandchildren, the Israelites, to settle in Egypt, when He had promised them the land of Canaan? Because God intended to show forth His glory and His power through what would happen to the Israelites in the land of Egypt. God planned to deliver the children of Israel by His awesome power, **so that everyone might know that He is the King of kings; Lord of lords, the Almighty**!

Now, listening friends, in the few minutes that we have left today, let us read from the first chapter of the book of Exodus. The Scripture says:

> (Exodus 1) [6]*Now Joseph and all his brothers and all that generation died,* [7]*but the Israelites were fruitful and multiplied greatly and became exceedingly numerous, so that the land was filled with them.* [8]*Then a new king, who did not know about Joseph, came to power in Egypt.* [9]*"Look," he said to his people, "the Israelites have become much too numerous for us.* [10]*Come, we must deal shrewdly with them or they will become even more numerous and, if war breaks out, will join our enemies, fight against us and leave the country."*
>
> [11]*So they put slave masters over them to oppress them with forced labor, and they built Pithom and Rameses as store cities for Pharaoh.* [12]*But the more they were oppressed, the more they multiplied and spread; so the Egyptians came to dread the Israelites* [13]*and worked them ruthlessly.* [14]*They made their lives bitter with hard labor in brick and mortar and with all kinds of work in the fields; in all their hard labor the Egyptians used them ruthlessly.*
>
> [15]*The king of Egypt said to the Hebrew midwives, whose names were Shiphrah and Puah,* [16]*"When you help the Hebrew women in childbirth and observe them on the delivery stool, if it is a boy, kill him; but if it is a girl, let her live."* [17]*The midwives, however, feared God and did not do what the king of Egypt had told them to do; they let the boys live.* [18]*Then the king of Egypt summoned the midwives and asked them, "Why have you done this? Why have you let the boys live?"* [19]*The midwives answered Pharaoh, "Hebrew women are not like Egyptian women; they are vigorous and give birth before the midwives arrive."*
>
> [20]*So God was kind to the midwives and the people increased and became even more numerous.* [21]*And because the midwives feared God, he gave them families of their own.* [22]*Then Pharaoh gave this order to all his people: "Every boy that is born you must throw into the Nile, but let every girl live."*

This is where the first chapter of the book of Exodus ends. In the will of God, in the next broadcast, we will get into this extraordinary story and see how God called a man and prepared him to deliver the children of Israel from the hand of Pharoah, the wicked king of Egypt. Do you know the name of this man? Yes, it is Moses—the prophet of God, Moses.

Thank you for listening....God bless you. And remember:

> ***"Everything that was written in the past was written to teach us, so that through endurance and the encouragement of the Scriptures we might have hope."*** (Rom. 15:4)

LESSON 29
THE PROPHET MOSES

EXODUS 1,2

Peace be with you, listening friends. We greet you in the name of God, the Lord of peace, who wants everyone to understand and submit to the way of righteousness that He has established, and have true peace with Him forever. We are happy to be able to return today to present your program *The Way of Righteousness*.

As you should know, there are five books in the Torah which God's prophet, Moses, wrote. In our last program we finished the book of Genesis, and crossed over into the second book which is called *Exodus*. Our prayer to God is that He will enlighten our minds and our hearts in all that we read in this profound book that is full of valuable instruction.

We have already seen how the second book of the Torah begins where the first book ends. Thus, we saw how the descendants of Abraham, Isaac and Jacob, that is, **the Israelites, settled in Egypt**, far from the land of Canaan that God had promised to give them.

In the first chapter of the book of Exodus we read:

> (Exod. 1) [1]*These are the names of* ***the sons of Israel*** *who went to Egypt with*
> *Jacob, each with his family:* [2]*Reuben, Simeon, Levi and Judah;* [3]*Issachar, Zebulun*
> *and Benjamin;* [4]*Dan and Naphtali; Gad and Asher.* [5]*The descendants of Jacob*
> *numbered seventy in all; Joseph was already in Egypt.* [6]*Now Joseph and all his*
> *brothers and all that generation died,* [7]*but the Israelites were fruitful and* ***multi-***
> ***plied greatly*** *and became exceedingly numerous, so that the land was filled with*
> *them.*
>
> [8]*Then* ***a new king****, who did not know about Joseph, came to power in Egypt.*
> [9]*"Look," he said to his people, "the Israelites have become much too numerous*
> *for us.* [10]*Come, we must deal shrewdly with them or they will become even more*
> *numerous and, if war breaks out, will join our enemies, fight against us and leave*
> *the country."* [11]*So they put slave masters over them to oppress them with* ***forced***
> ***labor****, and they built Pithom and Rameses as store cities for Pharaoh.* [12]*But the*

> *more they were oppressed, the more they multiplied and spread; so the Egyptians came to dread the Israelites [13]and worked them ruthlessly. [14]They made their lives bitter with hard labor in brick and mortar and with all kinds of work in the fields; in all their hard labor the Egyptians used them ruthlessly.*

Let us pause here. **More than three hundred years had passed** since the death of Joseph. Another Pharaoh was reigning over Egypt, a king who had forgotten all that Joseph had done for the people of Egypt. This Pharaoh oppressed Israel terribly, making them his slaves. How hard he made them work! Perhaps the Israelites thought that God had forgotten what He had promised their ancestor Abraham about their becoming a powerful nation. However, God hadn't forgotten a thing! God was, in fact, in the process of fulfilling what He had promised so long ago.

Truly, **God is faithful**! He keeps His covenants! What God promises to do, He will do, even if man thinks He is slow! **God was the One who conceived the plan to create a new nation from which the prophets and the Redeemer would come forth—and nothing would hinder the accomplishment of His plan**!

You remember that when God first revealed His plan to create that new nation, He started with an elderly couple, Abraham and Sarah. When Abraham was one hundred years old, he begot Isaac; Isaac begot Jacob; and Jacob begot twelve sons who produced the tribes of Israel. When they moved to the land of Egypt, they numbered seventy people. But now, after some three hundred years, they had become a great multitude, more that a million people! **Did God do what He had promised long ago?** Did God make of Abraham a new and vast nation? Yes, He did! God is faithful, and cannot go back on His Word. He is worthy of glory forever!

In today's reading, we see how **Pharaoh** oppressed the tribes of Israel, making them his slaves. However, we also see that every time Pharaoh tried to dominate and diminish the tribes of Israel, God would cause them to flourish and multiply. Thus, the Scriptures record that Pharaoh became very angry and gave this command to the Israelites: "*Every boy that is born you must throw into the Nile!*" (Exod. 1:22) What do you think about this? Who was leading Pharaoh in this wicked plan? **Satan**, that's who! Why did Satan want to oppress and destroy the people of Israel? Because Satan knew that God had promised to send into the world a Redeemer who would deliver the children of Adam from the power of sin and hell. And Satan knew that this coming Redeemer would descend through **the nation of Israel**! That is the reason Satan incited Pharaoh to persecute the people of Israel and even attempt to wipe them out by having all their baby boys thrown in the Nile river.

But God, who is stronger than Satan, planned to use a man from within the tribes of Israel to deliver His chosen people from the hand of Pharaoh. Do you know the name of this hero? Yes, it is the renowned prophet of God, **Moses** {*Musa* in Arabic}. But Moses parents, *Amram and Jochebed*, were also heros because *"they were not afraid of the king's edict."* (Heb. 11:23; Exod. 6:20). In the second chapter of the book of Exodus, we read about **the early years of Moses' life**.

The Scripture says:

> (Exod. 2) [1]*Now a* ***man*** *of the house of Levi* (Levi was the third son of Jacob) *married a Levite* ***woman***, [2]*and she became pregnant and gave birth to* ***a son****. When she saw that he was a fine child, she hid him for three months.* [3]*But when she could hide him no longer, she got a papyrus* ***basket*** *for him and coated it with tar and pitch. Then she placed the child in it and put it among the reeds along the bank of the Nile.* [4]*His* ***sister*** *stood at a distance to see what would happen to him.*
>
> [5]*Then* ***Pharaoh's daughter*** *went down to the Nile to bathe, and her attendants were walking along the river bank. She saw the basket among the reeds and sent her slave girl to get it.* [6]*She opened it and saw the baby. He was crying, and she felt sorry for him. "This is one of the Hebrew babies," she said.* (The Egyptians called the people of Israel *Hebrews*.)
>
> [7]*Then [Miriam, the sister of the baby, who was hiding among the reeds,] asked Pharaoh's daughter, "Shall I go and get one of the Hebrew women to nurse the baby for you?"* [8]*"Yes, go," she answered. And the girl went and got the baby's mother.* [9]*Pharaoh's daughter said to her, "Take this baby and nurse him for me, and I will pay you." So the woman took the baby and nursed him.* [10]*When the child grew older, she took him to Pharaoh's daughter and he became her son. She named him* ***Moses****, saying, "I drew him out of the water."*

This is the story of the birth of Moses. Think of it! While other male babies were being killed, baby Moses was being nourished by his own mother and protected by Pharaoh, the wicked king! **God** had His hand on all that happened in the life of Moses. God planned to use Moses to deliver the children of Israel from their slavery. How deep is the wisdom of God, far surpassing the wisdom of Satan or man. Do you know where Moses grew up after he was weaned? He grew up in the house of Pharaoh who, as you know, was oppressing the people of Israel! Yet God intended to use Moses to deliver the Israelites from the hand of Pharaoh. God, in His plan, chose to use the daughter of the cruel king to protect Moses. God knew that the king's house would be the safest and best place for Moses. God also knew that there were many things Moses needed to learn and understand so that he would be properly prepared to lead the children of Israel. Thus, the Scriptures say: "*Moses was educated in all the wisdom of the Egyptians and was powerful in speech and action.*" (Acts 7:22) But Moses still had much to learn.

The Scripture says:

> (Exod. 2) [11]*One day,* ***after Moses had grown up****, he went out to where his own people were and watched them at their hard labor. He saw an Egyptian beating a Hebrew, one of his own people.* [12]*Glancing this way and that and seeing no one, he killed the Egyptian and hid him in the sand.* [13]*The next day he went out and saw two Hebrews fighting. He asked the one in the wrong, "Why are you hitting your fellow Hebrew?"* [14]*The man said, "Who made you ruler and judge over us? Are you thinking of killing me as you killed the Egyptian?" Then Moses was afraid and thought, "What I did must have become known."* [15]*When Pharaoh heard of this, he tried to kill Moses, but Moses fled from Pharaoh and went to live in Midian.*

Thus, we see how, at first, Moses tried to deliver the children of Israel by his own power. However, that is not how God wanted it done. God wanted to use Moses as **an instrument** to liberate the children of Israel. **Israel's deliverance was not to come from Moses, but from God**. Moses, in himself, was only a man, and had no power to free the children of Israel from the hand of Pharaoh unless God gave it to him.

Thus, the Scriptures tell us that, for forty years, Moses lived in the desert, in land of Midian. God had many important lessons to teach Moses in that hot and dry wilderness. There is a verse in the Word of God which says: "*Whoever can be trusted with very little can also be trusted with much, and whoever is dishonest with very little will also be dishonest with much.*" (Luke 16:10) Before God could commit to Moses the weighty task of shepherding the whole assembly of Israel, Moses first needed to show himself faithful in little tasks. Thus, the Scriptures relate to us that, there in a land far from Egypt, Moses became a shepherd, got married and had two children. For forty years, Moses was a faithful shepherd. There in the desert–while Moses was shepherding his father-in-law's flock–**God was preparing Moses** for the day when he would shepherd the nation of Israel. God had great plans for Moses and His people Israel!

Next, the Scriptures say:

> (Exod. 2) [23]*During that long period, the king of Egypt died. The Israelites groaned in their slavery and cried out, and their cry for help because of their slavery went up to God.* [24]***God heard their groaning and he remembered his covenant with Abraham, with Isaac and with Jacob.*** [25]*So God looked on the Israelites and was concerned about them.*

The children of Israel remained slaves for a very long time. Oh how great was their oppression! But God had not forgotten them. God planned to deliver the people of Israel from their slavery. We might ask: Why did God plan to free the children of Israel from the hand of Pharaoh? Was it because they were better than others? No! The Israelites were sinners, like the people of Egypt, like all people. **Why then did God have such special plans for the children of Israel?** Simply because of **His faithfulness** and **His mercy**. Let us read again the last verse. We read: "*God heard their groaning and he* ***remembered his covenant*** *with Abraham, with Isaac and with Jacob* **(Observe God's faithfulness!)**. *So God looked on the Israelites and* ***was concerned about them*** **(Observe God's mercy!)**." (Exod. 2:24,25)

Yes, God, in His faithfulness and mercy, remembered His covenant which He had made with Abraham when He said to him,

> ***"I will make you into a great nation. You will be a blessing…and all peoples on earth will be blessed through you."*** (Gen. 12:2,3) *"Your descendants will be strangers in a country not their own, and they will be enslaved and ill-treated four hundred years. But I will punish the nation they serve as slaves, and afterwards they will come out with great possessions."* (Gen. 15:13,14)

In the next lesson, Lord willing, we will see how God appeared to Moses in a very unusual way and called him to go to Egypt to deliver the Israelites from their slavery, just as He had promised Abraham long beforehand.

Thank you for listening….

God bless you. We bid you farewell with this word from the Psalms:

> ***"Give thanks to the LORD, call on his name; make known among the nations what he has done….He remembers his covenant forever, the word he commanded, for a thousand generations, the covenant he made with Abraham, the oath he swore to Isaac."*** (Psa. 105:1,8,9)

Lesson 30

Moses Meets God!

Exodus 3,4

Peace be with you, listening friends. We greet you in the name of God, the Lord of peace, who wants everyone to understand and submit to the way of righteousness that He has established, and have true peace with Him forever. We are happy to be able to return today to present your program *The Way of Righteousness*.

In our last lesson, we saw how Pharaoh, the king of Egypt, oppressed the descendants of Abraham, the Israelites, by making them his slaves, working them ruthlessly. However, we also read, "*the more they were oppressed, the more they multiplied and spread, so the Egyptians came to dread the Israelites*." (Exod. 1:12) Finally, Pharaoh issued a decree that every infant boy born to the Israelites was to be thrown into the river to die.

However, God, who is more powerful than Satan, had a plan to overturn the evil which Pharaoh was doing. Thus, we read how the daughter of Pharaoh took in an Israelite baby that she found in a basket in the river. The daughter of Pharaoh had pity on him and adopted him as her child, naming him **Moses**. Thus, Moses grew up in the house of Pharaoh–the very one who sought to destroy the people of Israel! God, in His wisdom, planned to use Moses to deliver the Israelites from the hand of the wicked king. When Moses was forty years old, he ran from Pharaoh who wanted to kill him. For forty years Moses lived in the wilderness, where he got married and tended the flock of his father-in-law.

Now, let us continue with this story to see **how God revealed Himself to Moses** so that He might send him to Pharaoh to lead the people of Israel out of Egypt. We are reading in the Torah, in the third chapter of the book of Exodus. The Scripture says:

> (Exod. 3) [1]*Now Moses was tending the flock of Jethro his father-in-law…and he*
> *led the flock to the far side of the desert and came to [Sinai], the mountain of*
> *God.* [2]***There the angel of the LORD appeared to him in flames of fire from***
> ***within a bush.*** *Moses saw that though the bush was on fire it did not burn up.*

> 3*So Moses thought, "I will go over and see this strange sight– why the bush does not burn up."*
>
> 4*When the* LORD *saw that he had gone over to look,* God called to him from *within the bush, "Moses! Moses!" And Moses said, "Here I am."* 5*"Do not come any closer," God said. "Take off your sandals, for the place where you are standing is* ***holy ground****."* 6*Then he said, "***I am the God of your father, the God of Abraham, the God of Isaac and the God of Jacob.***" At this, Moses hid his face, because he was afraid to look at God.* 7*The* LORD *said, "***I have indeed seen the misery of my people in Egypt.*** I have heard them crying out because of their slave drivers, and I am concerned about their suffering.* 8*So I have come down to rescue them from the hand of the Egyptians and to bring them up out of that land into a good and spacious land, a land flowing with milk and honey–the home of the Canaanites...* 9*And now the cry of the Israelites has reached me, and I have seen the way the Egyptians are oppressing them.* 10*So now, go. I am sending you to Pharaoh to bring my people the Israelites out of Egypt."*
>
> 11*But Moses said to God, "Who am I, that I should go to Pharaoh and bring the Israelites out of Egypt?"* 12*And God said, "I will be with you. And this will be the sign to you that it is I who have sent you:* **When you have brought the people out of Egypt, you will worship God on this mountain.**" 13*Moses said to God, "Suppose I go to the Israelites and say to them, 'The God of your fathers has sent me to you,' and they ask me, 'What is his name?' Then what shall I tell them?"* 14*God said to Moses, "***I AM WHO I AM***. This is what you are to say to the Israelites: 'I AM has sent me to you.'"* 15*God also said to Moses, "Say to the Israelites, 'The* LORD*, the God of your fathers–the God of Abraham, the God of Isaac and the God of Jacob–has sent me to you!'* **This is my name forever***!"*

We can learn **at least four things about God's character** from what God said to Moses from inside the burning bush on Mount Sinai.

1.) First, we learn that God is **holy**! When Moses saw the flames of the burning bush, he was amazed, drew near to investigate, and heard the voice of God calling out to him. Moses trembled with fear, and did not dare to look. Why was Moses afraid? Because he was standing in the presence of God, the Holy One! God declared His holiness by saying to Moses: *"Do not come any closer. Take off your sandals, for the place where you are standing is holy ground!"*

Truly, God, who appeared to Moses in the fiery flames, is **holy**. God wants everyone to recognize His holiness. Concerning the angels who stand in the presence of God, the Scriptures say: *"Day and night they never stop saying: 'Holy, holy, holy is the Lord God Almighty, who was, and is, and is to come.'"* (Rev. 4:8) The angels recognize the holiness of God. You who are listening today, do you recognize God's holiness?

Let us think a little about what this means. As we have already seen in previous lessons, the holiness of God caused Him to expel Adam and Eve from the Garden of Paradise after they had sinned. The holiness of God caused Him to refuse Cain's sacrifice. It was also God's holiness that caused Him to wipe out the people of Noah's day with a flood. In the period that followed, God confused the language of the world, scattering the people of Babel, those who were trying to rebel against God. And in Abraham's time, the holiness of God caused Him to rain fire from the sky on the people of Sodom, those who were taking pleasure in wickedness.

Tragically, to this very day, most people do not respect the holiness of God. They do not comprehend who God is. They have not recognized His absolute purity. We can see this in the way people practice sin and take pleasure in it. We also see the lack of importance people attach to the holiness of God when they wear religion like a cloak, but do not examine the Holy Scriptures in order to understand God's truth. Many habitually use God's name in insincere talk. They invoke the name of God in vain by saying, *"bi ism Allah"* {Arabic: *in the name of God*}, or *"Insha'a Allah"* {*if God wills it*} when, in reality, the will of God is the farthest thing from their minds. We observe people's failure to understand the holiness of God by the way they seek to establish their own righteousness before God and refuse to accept the way of righteousness which God has established. Some think that they can make themselves pure before God by prolonged fasting, repetitious praying, or ceremonies of washing and purification {ablution}. But, as we clearly see in the Writings of the Prophets, such outward actions do not satisfy **God the Holy One** who requires that a person be pure on the inside. Dear friends, God is holy! That is why He said to Moses, *"Take off your sandals, for the place where you are standing is* ***holy ground****."*

2.) Next, based on what God said to Moses in the burning bush, we discover that God is not only the Holy One, but He is also **the Faithful One**! {Lit. *the One who keeps His covenants*} Did you hear what God first said to Moses? He said, *"I am the God of your forefathers, the God of Abraham, Isaac and Jacob."* (Exod. 3:6) These words should bring joy to the heart of anyone who wants to approach God and enjoy a relationship with Him. God, the Holy One, is the One who established a covenant with Abraham, Isaac and Jacob. God is the Faithful One; He will never leave or betray His friends! Even after hundreds of years, He had not forgotten what He had promised to Abraham, Isaac and Jacob and their descendants.

What about you? Do you appreciate the faithfulness of God? Do you enjoy a close relationship with the God who spoke with Abraham, Isaac and Jacob? This is an important question for anyone who wants to be truly happy in this life and in the life to come. We are not asking: Do you have religion?–because following the rules of religion will never make anyone righteous before God. What we are asking is: Do you have a right relationship with God? Have you believed the message of the way of salvation which God has established? Have you come to see that following **a religion** and having **a relationship** with God Himself are two different things?

Today there are thousands and thousands of religions in the world. For example, the experts tell us that in the country of Brazil alone, there are more than four thousand different religions and sects! Four thousand religions!?! Amazing! Are there four thousand gods? Or four thousand ways which lead to God? No! The Scriptures say: "*There is* ***one God and one Mediator*** *between God and men.*" (1 Tim. 2:5) Why then are there thousands of religions and thousands of different sects in the world today? It is because most of Adam's descendants have ignored the foundation of truth that God established with Abraham, Isaac, and Jacob. They do not know about the promises which God made to Abraham and his descendants concerning the Mediator, who was to come into the world to deliver the children of Adam from the penalty and power of sin. They do not know the Word of the God who never changes. They do not know **the Faithful One**!

3.) God manifested another characteristic when He appeared to Moses in the fire that blazed in the bush. The characteristic is **mercy**. God is not only the Holy One and the Faithful One, but He is also **the Merciful One**. That is why God said to Moses concerning the people of Israel,

> "*I have indeed* ***seen*** *the misery of my people in Egypt. I have* ***heard*** *them crying out because of their slave drivers, and I am* ***concerned*** *about their suffering. So I have* ***come*** *down to rescue them from the hand of the Egyptians and to bring them up out of that land into a good and spacious land...*" (Exod. 3:7,8)

Why did God plan to liberate the people of Israel and lead them to a good land? Did the Israelites deserve God's mercy? Were they better than other nations? No, they were not! Why then did God purpose to deliver them and bless them so? Only because of His faithfulness and His mercy. As the Scriptures say: "*God heard their groaning and He remembered His covenant with Abraham, with Isaac, and with Jacob. So God looked on the Israelites and [had mercy on] them.*" (Exod. 2:24,25) Yes, God is **the Merciful One**!

4.) Finally, there is one more aspect of God that we can observe in the story of the burning bush. We heard Moses ask God what His name is. Can the nature of the eternal God be described in a single name? This God who is so great and holy, faithful and merciful; this God whom man cannot see with his eyes; this God who created everything, sees everything, knows everything, and can do anything—**What is His name?** Some think God's name is simply "*God*" {*Allah*}. Truly, God is God. However, *God* is not His **name**. God is who He is. I am a man, but *Man* is not my name. Each of us has a name by which we are known. What is

God's name? What answer did God give to Moses? Let us read it again. God said to Moses,

> "**I AM WHO I AM**. *This is what you are to say to the Israelites:* '**I AM** *has sent me to you.*'" *God also said to Moses, "Say to the Israelites,* '**The LORD,** *the God of your fathers–the God of Abraham, the God of Isaac and the God of Jacob–has sent me to you!*' **This is my name forever***!*" (Exod. 3:14-15) {Note: Hebrew "*YHWH*" & English "*LORD*" translates in Wolof as *The Eternal One*}

What is the name of God which describes His eternal nature? Did you hear it? It is: **the LORD! {The Eternal One**}! In the Holy Scriptures, the prophets ascribe to God hundreds and hundreds of names and titles, but this name, *the* LORD, is used more than any other—over six thousand, five hundred times. God is the LORD, the Eternal "I AM," the One who was, who is, who will exist forever! He is the Eternal One! He has no beginning. He has no end. He has no limits. He has no equal. He is the One who exists by His own power! What He was yesterday and is today, He will be forever. He never changes. The LORD {The Eternal One} is His Name!

Listening friend, do you know **the LORD?** Do you recognize His **holiness**? Are you rejoicing in His **faithfulness** (in relationships; in keeping His covenants)? Have you received His **mercy**? Do you believe His Word? Have you entered into a close relationship with the God of Abraham, Isaac and Jacob? Do you know the LORD who spoke to Moses from the burning bush?

Thank you for listening. God willing, next time we will continue the story of Moses and see how God sent him to Pharaoh, the wicked king of Egypt....

God bless you as you continue to ponder these words God spoke to Moses:

> **"I AM WHO I AM!...I AM *the* LORD!...*This is my name forever!*"** (Exod. 3:14,15; 6:2)

LESSON 31

PHARAOH: WHO IS THE LORD?

EXODUS 4-7

Peace be with you, listening friends. We greet you in the name of God, the Lord of peace, who wants everyone to understand and submit to the way of righteousness that He has established, and have true peace with Him forever. We are happy to be able to return today to present your program *The Way of Righteousness*.

Today we are continuing in the second book of the Torah which tells the story of **God's prophet, Moses, and the people of Israel in Egypt**. In past lessons, we saw how Pharaoh, the king of Egypt, persecuted the Israelites, making them his slaves. However, God had a plan to overturn the evil that Pharaoh was doing. God planned to use Moses, a man from among the children of Israel, to deliver the Israelites from the hand of Pharaoh.

We learned that Moses was educated in all the knowledge of Egypt. When Moses was forty years old, he attempted to deliver his people by his own methods. Moses' efforts, however, produced only problems, forcing him to flee from Pharaoh and hide in the wilderness. Moses had to learn that in himself, he was only a man and that he had no power to deliver the people of Israel unless God gave it to him. Thus, Moses lived in the wilderness for forty years, caring for his father-in-law's flock.

One day, **when Moses was eighty years old, God appeared to him on a mountain called Sinai**, in the flames of a burning bush. The bush was on fire, but it did not burn up. When Moses saw it, he was amazed. As he drew near to investigate, he heard the voice of God saying, "*I am the God of your forefathers, the God of Abraham, Isaac and Jacob.*" Moses trembled with fear and did not dare to look. Then God said, "*Take off your sandals, for the place where you are standing is holy ground. I have indeed seen the misery of my people in Egypt. I have heard them crying out because of their complaints. So I have come down to rescue them. So now, go.* ***I am sending you to Egypt.***"

Now, let us continue in the Torah to see how God concluded His talk with Moses and sent him to the king of Egypt. In chapter three, we heard how God promised to be with Moses, to give him wisdom and authority before Pharaoh and the people of Egypt. Yet in chapter four we will see that Moses was afraid to go.

In the book of Exodus, chapter four, the Scripture says:

> (Exod. 4) [1]*Moses answered, "What if they do not believe me or listen to me and say, 'The LORD did not appear to you'?"* [2]*Then the LORD said to him,* "**What is that in your hand?**" *"A staff," he replied.* [3]*The LORD said, "Throw it on the ground." Moses threw it on the ground and it became a snake, and he ran from it.* [4]*Then the LORD said to him, "Reach out your hand and take it by the tail." So Moses reached out and took hold of the snake and it turned back into a staff in his hand.* [5]***"This," said the LORD, "is so that they may believe that the LORD, the God of their fathers–the God of Abraham, the God of Isaac and the God of Jacob–has appeared to you."***
>
> [10]*Moses said to the LORD, "O Lord, I have never been eloquent, neither in the past nor since you have spoken to your servant. I am slow of speech and tongue."* [11]*The LORD said to him,* "**Who gave man his mouth?** *Who makes him deaf or mute? Who gives him sight or makes him blind? Is it not I, the LORD?* [12]*Now go; I will help you speak and will teach you what to say."* [13]*But Moses said, "O Lord, please send someone else to do it."* [14]*Then the LORD's anger burned against Moses and he said, "What about your brother,* **Aaron** *the Levite? I know he can speak well. He is already on his way to meet you, and his heart will be glad when he sees you.* [15]*You shall speak to him and put words in his mouth;* ***I will help both of you speak and will teach you what to do****...* [17]*But take this staff in your hand so that you can perform miraculous signs with it."*
>
> [18]*Then Moses went back to Jethro his father-in-law and said to him, "Let me go back to my own people in Egypt to see if any of them are still alive." Jethro said, "Go, and I wish you well."* [19]*Now the LORD had said to Moses in Midian, "Go back to Egypt, for all the men who wanted to kill you are dead."* [20]*So Moses took his wife and sons, put them on a donkey and started* **back to Egypt**. *And he took the staff of God in his hand.* [21]*The LORD said to Moses, "When you return to Egypt, see that you perform before Pharaoh all the wonders I have given you the power to do...* [22]*Then say to Pharaoh, 'This is what the LORD says: Israel is my firstborn son,* [23]*and I told you, "Let my son go, so that he may worship me."*
>
> [27]*The LORD said to Aaron, "Go into the desert to meet Moses." So he met Moses at the mountain of God and kissed him.* [28]*Then Moses told Aaron everything the LORD had sent him to say, and also about all the miraculous signs he had commanded him to perform.* [29]***Moses and Aaron brought together all the elders of the Israelites***, [30]*and Aaron told them everything the LORD had said to Moses. He also performed the signs before the people,* [31]*and they believed.* ***And when they heard that the LORD was concerned about them and had seen their misery, they bowed down and worshiped.***

Chapter five. (Exod. 5) [1]*Afterwards Moses and Aaron went to Pharaoh and said, "This is what the* LORD, *the God of Israel, says:* '**Let my people go**, *so that they may hold a festival to me in the desert.'"* [2]*Pharaoh said,* "**Who is the** LORD, *that I should obey him and let Israel go?* **I do not know the LORD and I will not let Israel go***!"*

Let us stop here briefly. We see how God spoke to Pharaoh through the mouth of Moses and Aaron {*Harun* in Arabic}. Did Pharaoh believe the word of God? No, he did not! Did you hear how he answered Moses and Aaron? He said, "**Who is the** LORD, *that I should obey him and let Israel go? I do not know the* LORD *and I will not let Israel go!"*

Pharaoh did not know the LORD {Lit. *the Eternal One*}. Pharaoh and all the people of Egypt **had a religion**, but **they did not know God**. They only cared about following the religion of their ancestors. They did not care about knowing the living and true God–the God of Abraham, Isaac and Jacob. Pharaoh and the Egyptians put their confidence in their customs, their idols, their fetishes and their religious leaders, but they did **not** put their confidence **in the LORD and His Eternal Word.**

Thus, in chapter six we read:

(Exod. 6) [1]*Then the* LORD *said to Moses,* "**Now you will see what I will do to Pharaoh**: *Because of my mighty hand he will let them go; because of my mighty hand he will drive them out of his country."* [2]*God also said to Moses,* "**I am the LORD.** [3]*I appeared to Abraham, to Isaac and to Jacob as God Almighty, but by my name the* LORD *I did not make myself known to them.* [4]*I also established my covenant with them to give them the land of Canaan, where they lived as aliens.* [5]*Moreover, I have heard the groaning of the Israelites, whom the Egyptians are enslaving, and I have remembered my covenant.* [6]*"Therefore, say to the Israelites:* '**I am the LORD,** *and I will bring you out from under the yoke of the Egyptians. I will free you from being slaves to them, and I will redeem you with an outstretched arm and with mighty acts of judgment.* [7]*I will take you as my own people, and I will be your God. Then you will know that* **I am the LORD** *your God, who brought you out from under the yoke of the Egyptians.* [8]*And I will bring you to the land I swore with uplifted hand to give to Abraham, to Isaac and to Jacob. I will give it to you as a possession.* **I am the** LORD.'"

(Exod. 7) [4]**Pharaoh will not listen to you**. *Then I will lay my hand on Egypt and with mighty acts of judgment I will bring out my divisions, my people the Israelites.* [5]*And the Egyptians will know that* **I am the LORD** *when I stretch out my hand against Egypt and bring the Israelites out of it."* [6]*Moses and Aaron did just as the* LORD *commanded them.* [7]*Moses was eighty years old and Aaron eighty-three when they spoke to Pharaoh.*

Thus, we see how the LORD planned to judge Pharaoh and the people of Egypt with mighty acts of judgment. God, in His righteousness, purposed to pay back the Egyptians for the hundreds of years of suffering which they had brought on the Israelites. Also, through the miracles that God planned to perform by the hand of Moses, the LORD wanted to display His glory and power. Thus, He would show the people of Egypt and the whole world, that **the LORD God who spoke to Abraham, Isaac, Jacob and Moses is the living and true God**!

As we have already learned, God is the Merciful One and does not want anyone to perish, but wants everyone to repent and to know and receive the truth. That was why He planned to perform miracles that would confirm the word He spoke through Moses. The LORD wanted everyone **to know beyond any doubt** that the God who was speaking through Moses is **the one true God**!

We need to remember that in Egypt there were hundreds of idols which the Egyptians considered gods. However, God wanted them to know that there is only one true God. God wanted them to know that **the one true God is the God who established His covenant with Abraham, Isaac and Jacob**—promising to make of them a nation through which God would channel the prophets, the Scriptures and the Savior of the world.

However, Pharaoh was not interested in knowing the one true God. That is why, when God sought to speak to Pharaoh through His prophets, Moses and Aaron, Pharaoh answered them, saying, "***Who is the LORD,** that I should obey him and let Israel go? I do not know the LORD and I will not let Israel go!*" (Exod. 5:2)

Pharaoh spoke the truth when he said that he did not know the LORD! He did not know the God who established an eternal covenant with Abraham, Isaac and Jacob. Pharaoh had **a religion**, but he did not have **a relationship** with God. Pharoah's heart was closed to the truth that came from the one true God. Thus, he ignored the message which God spoke to him through Moses and Aaron.

To this very day, most people in the world follow the way of Pharaoh. They talk about God, but they pay no attention to the Word of the LORD. Consequently, **they do not know God**. They know some things **about God**, but they do not know **God Himself**. They have a **religion** handed down to them by their ancestors, but they do not have a true **relationship** with the living God who revealed Himself to Moses.

How about you? **Do you know the LORD?** Do you really know what He has said through His prophets? Have you ever sincerely looked into the Writings of God's prophets? Do you really know the LORD God? Do you love Him with all your heart? Do you want to obey Him? Or are you, like Pharaoh, just following the religion of your ancestors?

Oh dear friends, may not even one of us be like Pharaoh who refused to listen to and believe the Word of the Eternal God! Listen to this warning from God's Word: ***"See to it, brothers, that none of you has a sinful, unbelieving heart***

that turns away from the living God!" (Heb. 3:12) Today, if you hear his voice, do not harden your hearts as did Pharaoh who said, *"Who is the* LORD, *that I should obey him?"*

Thank you for listening. God willing, in our next study we will continue this captivating story and see how God brought upon Pharaoh and the Egyptians ten plagues so that they might know that He is the LORD!...

God bless you as you heed this solemn warning from His holy Word:

> ***"Today, if you hear his voice, do not harden your hearts!"*** (Heb. 3:15)

ST#33

LESSON 32

THE PLAGUES

EXODUS 7-10

Peace be with you, listening friends. We greet you in the name of God, the Lord of peace, who wants everyone to understand and submit to the way of righteousness that He has established, and have true peace with Him forever. We are happy to be able to return today to present your program *The Way of Righteousness.*

"An egg should not wrestle with a rock!" This (Wolof) proverb summarizes what we will study today in the Holy Scriptures. What happens when an egg and a rock collide? The egg breaks; the rock remains unchanged. Today we will see what happened when Pharaoh, the king of Egypt, tried to fight against the LORD God of whom the prophet Moses writes: "*He is **the Rock**, his works are perfect, and all his ways are just.*" (Deut. 32:4).

Last study, we saw how God sent Moses and Aaron to Pharaoh to free the children of Israel from their slavery in Egypt. They said to Pharaoh: "The LORD, the God of Israel, says, 'Let my people go worship me in the wilderness!'" However, Pharaoh replied to them: "*Who is the LORD, that I should obey him and let Israel go? I do not know the LORD and I will not let Israel go!*" (Exod. 5:2) In brief, God determined to free the people of Israel, whereas Pharaoh was determined to keep them as his slaves. However, "an egg should not wrestle (*fight, contend*) with a rock!"

Let us now return to the second part of the Torah, the book of Exodus, chapter seven, to see how Pharaoh tried to "wrestle" with God. The Scripture says:

> (Exod. 7) [10]*So Moses and Aaron went to Pharaoh and did just as the LORD commanded. Aaron threw his staff down in front of Pharaoh and his officials, and it became a snake.* [11]*Pharaoh then summoned the wise men and sorcerers, and the Egyptian magicians also did the same things by their secret arts:* [12]*Each one threw down his staff and it became a snake. But Aaron's staff swallowed up their staffs.*

Notice the start of the "wrestling match" {Note: wrestling is the traditional sport of Senegal} between **Pharaoh and God. On one side, we see Pharaoh with his wise men and sorcerers.** {Lit. in Wolof: *marabouts*, *spiritual guides*} **On the other side we see Moses and Aaron.** After Aaron's staff miraculously changed into a snake, Pharaoh's sorcerers {*marabouts*} imitated the miracle with their incantations. "*Each one threw down his staff and it became a snake.* ***But Aaron's staff swallowed up their staffs.***"

What can we say about all this? We know that the wonders which Moses and Aaron performed came **from God**. However, Pharaoh's marabouts also performed wonders. From where did they get their power? Did they get it from God? No! God does not fight against Himself. So where did their power come from? Pharaoh's marabouts relied on the art of deception and on the power that comes **from Satan**.

The Holy Scriptures show us that Satan is very crafty and loves to deceive people; he is also very powerful and can perform miracles. However, what is certain is that God is more powerful than Satan. Thus, Aaron's staff swallowed the staffs of Pharaoh's marabouts. However, all of this did not cause Pharaoh to repent and to listen to the word of God.

Listen to what the Scripture says:

> (Exod. 7) [14]*Then the LORD said to Moses, "Pharaoh's heart is unyielding; he refuses to let the people go.* [15]*Go to Pharaoh in the morning as he goes out to the water. Wait on the bank of the Nile to meet him, and take in your hand the staff that was changed into a snake.* [16]*Then say to him, 'The LORD, the God of the Hebrews, has sent me to say to you: Let my people go, so that they may worship me in the desert. But until now you have not listened.* [17]*This is what the LORD says:* ***By this you will know that I am the*** *LORD: With the staff that is in my hand I will strike the water of the Nile, and it will be changed into blood...* [20]*Moses and Aaron did just as the LORD had commanded. He raised his staff in the presence of Pharaoh and his officials and struck the water of the Nile, and all* ***the water was changed into blood****.* [21]*The fish in the Nile died, and the river smelled so bad that the Egyptians could not drink its water. Blood was everywhere in Egypt.* [22]***But the Egyptian magicians did the same things by their secret arts****, and* ***Pharaoh's heart became hard****; he would not listen to Moses and Aaron, just as the LORD had said.* [23]*Instead, he turned and went into his palace, and did not take even this to heart.* [24]*And all the Egyptians dug along the Nile to get drinking water, because they could not drink the water of the river.*
>
> [25]*Seven days passed after the LORD struck the Nile.* [8:1]*Then the LORD said to Moses, "Go to Pharaoh and say to him, 'This is what the LORD says: Let my people go, so that they may worship me.* [2]*If you refuse to let them go, I will plague your whole country with frogs.* [3]*The Nile will teem with frogs. They will come up*

into your palace and your bedroom and onto your bed, into the houses of your officials and on your people, and into your ovens and kneading troughs.

However, Pharaoh did not listen to the warnings from Moses. (Exod. 8)
5Then the LORD said to Moses, "Tell Aaron: 'Stretch out your hand with your staff over the streams and canals and ponds, and make frogs come up on the land of Egypt.'" 6So Aaron stretched out his hand over the waters of Egypt, and the ***frogs came up and covered the land. 7But the magicians did the same things by their secret arts****; they also made frogs come up on the land of Egypt.*
8Pharaoh summoned Moses and Aaron and said, "Pray to the LORD to take the frogs away from me and my people, and I will let your people go to offer sacrifices to the LORD."... 12Then Moses cried out to the LORD about the frogs he had brought on Pharaoh...The frogs [all] died... 14They were piled into heaps, and the land reeked of them. 15But when Pharaoh saw that there was relief, ***he hardened his heart*** *and would not listen to Moses and Aaron, just as the LORD had said.*

16Then the LORD said to Moses, "Tell Aaron, 'Stretch out your staff and strike the dust of the ground,' and throughout the land of Egypt the dust will become gnats." 17They did this, and when Aaron stretched out his hand with the staff and struck the dust of the ground, ***gnats came upon men and animals****. All the dust throughout the land of Egypt became gnats.* ***18But when the magicians tried to produce gnats by their secret arts, they could not****. And the gnats were on men and animals. 19The magicians said to Pharaoh, "This is the finger of God."* ***But Pharaoh's heart was hard*** *and he would not listen, just as the LORD had said.*

Did you see what happened with the sorcerers, Pharaoh's marabouts? We already saw how they had a certain power, which they received from Satan. That is why, through their secret arts, they managed to imitate God's power and change a little water into blood, and make a few frogs appear (as if the Egyptians needed more blood in their water and frogs in their beds!). However, **their power was limited.** Pharaoh's marabouts were unable to remove the plagues which Almighty God had brought down upon the land of Egypt. After Aaron struck the ground with his staff and the dust became gnats, the sorcerers performed their secret arts, trying to change the dust into gnats, but they could not. Thus, they told Pharaoh, ***"This is the finger of God!"***

Clearly, the sorcerers' power was limited. Certainly, Satan has power and can give man certain powers, but those powers will never exceed the limits that God has fixed. God alone is the All-Powerful One. Only He can do all things! He alone is the One without limitations! Pharaoh's marabouts were beginning to learn about the unlimited greatness of God, but **Pharaoh still refused to submit to God.** Pharaoh continued to harden his heart and think that he could wrestle with the God of Israel and win!

Thus, the Scriptures tell how God brought upon Pharaoh and upon the land of Egypt another seven plagues, by the hands of Moses and Aaron. Unfortunately, we do not have time to read about each plague. We can only name them.

The **fourth plague** consisted of **clouds of flies** which filled the land, even the people's houses, causing much destruction. In the **fifth plague**, a terrible **sickness fell on the livestock**, and many died. However, not one died among the herds of the children of Israel. Nevertheless, Pharaoh hardened his heart and refused to let the people of Israel go. **Next**, terrible **boils** broke out on men and animals. And the Scripture says: "*The magicians could not stand before Moses because of the boils that were on them and on all the Egyptians.*" (Exod. 9:11) In the **seventh plague** a terrible **hailstorm**, of proportions never before seen in Egypt, rained down and ruined all the fields. **After that** was over, the land was filled with **locusts**, which ate all that the hailstorm had left. This was the eighth plague.

In the **ninth plague**, God said to Moses, "*Stretch out your hand toward the sky so that* ***darkness*** *will spread over Egypt–darkness that can be felt.*" (Exod. 10:21) Thus, for three days no one could see anything. However, in the district where the children of Israel lived, there was light. Not one plague broke out on them. Yet all of this did not cause Pharaoh to repent and let the people of Israel go. The Scripture says: "*Pharaoh said to Moses, "Get out of my sight! Make sure you do not appear before me again! The day you see my face you will die.*" (Exod. 10:28)

There is **one more plague** that God brought down on Pharaoh and the Egyptians, but we will wait until next time to look at it, because our time is almost gone.

How can we summarize our lesson today? Perhaps like this: Pharaoh tried to fight with the LORD God. Did Pharaoh and his marabouts overcome the Almighty One? Could they overpower Him? No! No one can grapple with God and overpower Him! An egg does not fight with a rock and win!

What does God want to say to us through what we have read today? The Scripture says: "*These things happened to them as* ***examples*** *and were written down as* ***warnings*** *for us.*" (1 Cor. 10:11) God wants to warn us. God wants us to take a good look at ourselves and to heed His warnings.

You who are listening today, **are you paying attention to the Word of God?** Are you obeying it? Or, are you, like Pharaoh, fighting with God? Let your own heart answer. Are you submitted to the Word of God? This does not mean, are you submitted to the customs of your ancestors and their religion–but have you received with humility the Word of the LORD God? Or are you attempting to fight with God?

"An egg should not wrestle with a rock!" **Man** is like ***a fragile egg*** and the **Word of God** is like ***a solid rock***. The Scripture says: "***All men*** *are like grass, and all their glory is like the flowers of the field; the grass withers and the flowers fall,* ***but the word of the Lord*** *stands forever!*" (1 Pet. 1:24,25) The Word of the Eternal

God is a solid Rock and everyone who builds his life upon this Rock has placed his life on a solid foundation. However, if you refuse to build your life on that rock–one day the Rock of the Word of God will fall on you and crush you. An egg cannot fight with a rock and win. Neither can man contend with God's eternal Word and escape punishment.

This is where we must stop. Thank you for listening. God willing, in our next study, we will see what the LORD did to cause Pharaoh to allow the children of Israel to leave Egypt....

God bless you as you think about what the prophet Moses wrote in the Torah, saying:

> ***"The LORD God is the Rock, His works are perfect, and all His ways are just. A faithful God who does no wrong, upright and just is He."*** (Deut. 32:4)

LESSON 33

THE PASSOVER LAMB

EXODUS 11,12

Peace be with you, listening friends. We greet you in the name of God, the Lord of peace, who wants everyone to understand and submit to the way of righteousness that He has established, and have true peace with Him forever. We are happy to be able to return today to present your program *The Way of Righteousness.*

In our last lesson, we saw how Pharaoh tried to fight against God. The LORD purposed to deliver the people of Israel who were slaves in Egypt, but the king of Egypt was determined to keep them as his slaves. However, "an egg should not wrestle with a rock!" {Wolof Proverb}. Thus, we saw how God brought upon Egypt **nine terrible plagues** by the word of Moses and Aaron. Yet all these miracles and signs did not cause Pharaoh to submit to the word of God and let the Israelites leave his country.

Today we plan to continue in the story and see how God brought upon Pharaoh **one final plague**, the tenth, so that Pharaoh would allow the Israelites to leave Egypt. In our last lesson, we heard Pharaoh, after the ninth plague, say to Moses and Aaron, "*Get out of my sight! Make sure you do not appear before me again! The day you see my face you will die!*" (Exod. 10:28) Now let us read in chapter eleven and hear how God Himself answered Pharaoh, through the mouth of Moses.

The Scripture says:

> (Exod. 11) 4*So Moses said [to Pharaoh], "This is what the LORD says: 'About*
> *midnight I will go throughout Egypt.* 5***Every firstborn son in Egypt will die****,*
> *from the firstborn son of Pharaoh, who sits on the throne, to the firstborn son of*
> *the slave girl, who is at her hand mill, and all the firstborn of the cattle as well.*
> 6*There will be loud wailing throughout Egypt, worse than there has ever been or*
> *ever will be again.* 7*But among the Israelites not a dog will bark at any man or*
> *animal.' Then you will know that the LORD makes a distinction between Egypt*
> *and Israel.* 8*All these officials of yours will come to me, bowing down before me*

> *and saying, 'Go, you and all the people who follow you!' After that I will leave." Then Moses, hot with anger, left Pharaoh.*

Thus, we see how God planned to bring a plague upon the land of Egypt which was to be worse than all the other plagues that had already happened. God announced the impending death of every firstborn son in Egypt. What a terrible plague! And what would happen to the firstborn of the Israelites? Would they die along with those of the Egyptians? Certainly, they did not deserve to escape God's judgment, because they also were sinners, just as all the people of Egypt were. However, God who is faithful and merciful, designed **a plan** to protect the people of Israel from that plague.

Let us continue in chapter twelve and hear what God told Moses to instruct the Israelites to do so that their firstborn would escape death. The Scripture says:

> (Exod. 12) [1]*The LORD said to Moses and Aaron…,* [3]*"Tell the whole community of Israel that on the tenth day of this month each man is to take* ***a lamb*** *for his family, one for each household…* [5]*The animals you choose must be year-old males* ***without defect****, and you may take them from the sheep or the goats.*
> [6]*Take care of them until the fourteenth day of the month, when all the people of the community of Israel must slaughter them at twilight.* [7]*Then they are to take some of* ***the blood*** *and put it* ***on the sides and tops of the doorframes*** *of the houses where they eat the lambs.* [8]*That same night they are to eat the meat roasted over the fire, along with bitter herbs, and bread made without yeast.* [9]*Do not eat the meat raw or cooked in water, but roast it over the fire: head, legs and inner parts…* [46]*It must be eaten inside one house; take none of the meat outside the house. Do not break any of the bones."*
>
> [11]*"This is how you are to eat it: with your cloak tucked into your belt, your sandals on your feet and your staff in your hand. Eat it in haste; it is* ***the LORD's Passover****.* [12]*On that same night I will pass through Egypt and strike down every firstborn, both men and animals, and I will bring judgment on all the gods of Egypt.* ***I am the LORD****.* [13]*The blood will be a sign for you on the houses where you are; and* ***when I see the blood, I will pass over you****. No destructive plague will touch you when I strike Egypt."*

Let us pause here. Do you see the plan that God decreed to save the firstborn sons of Israel from death and redeem all the people of Israel from their bondage of slavery in Egypt? It was an amazing plan; a plan which, to man's way of thinking, was utterly ridiculous. He purposed to redeem them with **the blood of a lamb**–the blood of a lamb without blemish–blood with which they would stain the doorframes of their houses. Only the blood of the lamb could save their firstborn from death.

After God had finished speaking to Moses and Aaron, they assembled all the elders of Israel, telling them the word which God had spoken concerning the sacrifice of the lamb. When the elders of Israel heard how the LORD planned to save their firstborns from the plague of the death, they prostrated themselves and worshiped the LORD. After that, the elders and all the people of Israel did exactly what God had commanded Moses.

Thus, the Scripture says:

> (Exod. 12) [29]***At midnight the*** **LORD** ***struck down all the firstborn in Egypt****,
> from the firstborn of Pharaoh, who sat on the throne, to the firstborn of the prisoner, who was in the dungeon, and the firstborn of all the livestock as well.* [30]*Pharaoh and all his officials and all the Egyptians got up during the night, and there was loud wailing in Egypt, for there was* ***not a house without someone dead****.*

Did you hear what happened on that dreadful night? Did God judge the land of Egypt as He said He would? Yes He did! At midnight, the angel of destruction passed through the land of Egypt, striking all the firstborn, from the firstborn of king Pharaoh to the firstborn of those in prison. On that night, great crying and wailing echoed throughout Egypt, because there was not one Egyptian house without someone dead!

But what happened in the houses of the Israelites? Did God save their firstborn from the plague of death? What do you think? God had promised them, saying, ***"When I see the blood, I will pass over you."*** The people of Israel had stained the doors of their houses with the blood of a lamb, just as God commanded them. Consequently, there was **not one death** among their firstborn. However, in the houses of the Egyptians, **every firstborn died** because they did not take part in God's way of deliverance, the way of the blood of a lamb.

Thus, the Scripture says:

> (Exod. 12) [31]*During the night* ***Pharaoh*** *summoned Moses and Aaron and said, "****Up! Leave my people, you and the Israelites!*** *Go, worship the* LORD *as you have requested.* [32]*...and also bless me!"* [33]***The Egyptians urged the people to hurry and leave the country****. "For otherwise," they said, "we will all die!"*

Finally, Pharaoh had no choice but to give in and let the Israelites go. We have already seen how, at first, Pharaoh said to Moses and Aaron, "*Who is the* LORD*, that I should obey Him and let Israel go? I do not know the* LORD *and I will not let Israel go!*" But, in the end, Pharaoh and all the Egyptians were forced to admit that the God of Abraham, Isaac and Israel is the Almighty God, more powerful than any of their idols, fetishes, and marabouts! "An egg should not wrestle with a rock!" No one can fight with God and win!

On that night, the Israelites made their exodus from Egypt, and left with much wealth that the Egyptians gave them. The Scripture says:

> (Exod. 12) [35]*The Israelites did as Moses instructed and asked the Egyptians for articles of silver and gold and for clothing.* [36]*The LORD had made the Egyptians favorably disposed toward the people, and they gave them what they asked for; so they plundered the Egyptians...* [40]*Now the length of time the Israelite people lived in Egypt was 430 years.*

All this took place to fulfill what God had promised Abraham hundreds of years earlier, saying,

> *"Know for certain that your descendants will be strangers in a country not their own, and they will be enslaved and ill-treated four hundred years. But I will punish the nation they serve as slaves,* ***and afterwards they will come out with great possessions."*** (Gen. 15:13,14)

The story we have seen today, known as *the Passover*, is like a deep and wide ocean full of hidden treasures. There is so much that we could say about the story of the Passover. Obviously, we do not have time to explain all the truths contained in this story. However, there is one very important truth which we must retain in our minds. It is God's promise to the Israelites: ***"When I see the blood I will pass over you!"***

Why did the firstborn of Israel not die along with those of the people of Egypt? They did not die because God opened for them **a way of salvation through the blood of a lamb**. God decreed that the firstborn would be **spared from death** in every house where the door was stained with the blood of a lamb. But every firstborn found in a house where the blood had **not** been applied would **die**!

If a youth from among the firstborn of Israel questioned his father, saying, "Father, why does our innocent lamb have to die?" The father would reply something like this, "My son, as you know, God has condemned every firstborn son in the land. Because of our sins, we all deserve God's judgment. However, God, in His mercy, has told us that if we sacrifice a lamb without defect, and apply {Lit. in Wolof: *stain*} the blood to our doors, the plague will not strike us. The lamb must die, because the payment of sin is death. God is righteous and cannot simply overlook our sins. The lamb will replace you. We will sacrifice it in your place, as our forefather Abraham sacrificed the ram in his son's place. Our God is righteous and does not take sin lightly! His word to us is clear. He will only pass over our house if **the blood** is on the doorframes!"

Dear friends, what we need to realize today is that, before God, all of Adam's descendants are like the firstborn sons of the people of Egypt and Israel. **God's**

holy law condemns every one of us to die and face God's righteous judgment. That is what the Scripture says: *"There is no difference, for* ***all have sinned and fall short*** *of the glory of God."* (Rom. 3:22,23) The payment of sin is eternal condemnation, *"shut out from the presence of the Lord and from the majesty of his power!"* (2 Thes. 1:9)

What then must we do to be saved? How can God save sinners from the penalty of their sins without compromising His righteousness? We cannot take it very far today, but what we need to know is this: **The lambs** which the Israelites sacrificed to escape the plague of death **symbolized the Redeemer** who was to come and pour out his blood to pay the debt of sin for all the descendants of Adam. Concerning that Redeemer, the Scripture says: *"He died for sins once for all,* ***the righteous for the unrighteous*** *to bring you to God...[****like a sacrificial lamb*** *offered up to God on the day of the Passover]."* (1 Pet. 3:18; 1 Cor. 5:7). Thus, the blood of the lamb, which the Israelites applied to their doors to save their firstborn from death, was **an illustration**. It pictured the blood which the Savior of the world would shed upon the cross, so that whoever believes in Him, might escape God's everlasting punishment.

How about you? **Do you know** what God's prophets have written concerning the blood of the Redeemer? The Redeemer shed His blood so that God might forgive you of your sins without compromising His righteousness. **Do you believe** what is written concerning the blood that has the power to save you from the punishment of hell and guarantee you a place in God's presence forever? In the Day of Judgment, will God's terrible judgment pass over you? Or will it fall upon you as it did upon the Egyptians?

Friends, our time is gone. We thank you for listening. In our next program, God willing, we will continue with the story of the Israelites and see how God opened a path through the middle of the sea....

May God bless you and reveal to your hearts the deeper meaning of the words which He spoke to Israel, saying,

"When I see the blood I will pass over you!" (Exod.12:13)

Lesson 34

A Path Through the Sea

Exodus 13-15

Peace be with you, listening friends. We greet you in the name of God, the Lord of peace, who wants everyone to understand and submit to the way of righteousness that He has established, and have true peace with Him forever. We are happy to be able to return today to present your program *The Way of Righteousness*.

In our last lesson, we saw how God delivered the people of Israel from their slavery by slaying all the firstborn of the Egyptians. However, He delivered the firstborn of the Israelites from death, because of the blood of the lamb, which they put on the doors of their houses. For God Himself had said, "*The blood will be* ***a sign*** *for you on the houses where you are; and* ***when I see the blood, I will pass over you***." (Exod. 12:13)

Thus, on that night, all the tribes of Israel made their exodus from Egypt. That night of the Passover was a night of great joy for them. Think about it! For hundreds of years the people of Egypt had mistreated them and oppressed them with hard work to the point where there was no happiness left in their lives. But now…now they were **free**! On that night of the Passover, the LORD God delivered them! Their chains of slavery were broken! And now **God promised** to guide them through the wilderness and take them **back to the land of Canaan**, the land which, as you know, God had sworn long beforehand to give to the descendants of Abraham, Isaac and Jacob. Canaan was the land in which Jacob and his sons lived before they moved to Egypt to live with Joseph. Today this land is called *Palestine* or *Israel*.

Today we have before us the amazing story about **how God delivered the Israelites from the armies of Pharaoh**. Most of our reading is found in chapter fourteen of the book of Exodus. Listen to the story which the prophet Moses has recorded in the Torah:

> (Exod. 12) [37]*The Israelites journeyed from Rameses to Succoth. There were about* ***six hundred thousand men on foot, besides women and children***.

> [38]***Many other people*** *went up with them, as well as large droves of* ***livestock****, both flocks and herds.* [13:19]*Moses took the* ***bones of Joseph*** *with him because Joseph had made the sons of Israel swear an oath. He had said, "God will surely come to your aid, and then you must carry my bones up with you from this place."...* [21]*By day the LORD went ahead of them in* ***a pillar of cloud*** *to guide them on their way and by night in* ***a pillar of fire*** *to give them light, so that they could travel by day or night.* [22]*Neither the pillar of cloud by day nor the pillar of fire by night left its place in front of the people.*
>
> (Exod. 14) [1]*Then the LORD said to Moses,* [2]*"Tell the Israelites to turn back...to camp by the [Red] sea...* [3]*Pharaoh will think, 'The Israelites are wandering around the land in confusion, hemmed in by the desert.'* [4]*And I will harden Pharaoh's heart, and he will pursue them.* ***But I will gain glory for myself through Pharaoh and all his army, and the Egyptians will know that I am the*** *LORD." So the Israelites did this.*
>
> [5]*When the king of Egypt was told that the people had fled,* ***Pharaoh and his officials changed their minds*** *about them and said, "What have we done? We have let the Israelites go and have lost their services!"* [6]*So he had his chariot made ready and took his army with him.* [7]*He took six hundred of the best chariots, along with all the other chariots of Egypt, with officers over all of them.*
>
> [9]***The Egyptians–all Pharaoh's horses and chariots, horsemen and troops–pursued the Israelites*** *and overtook them as they camped by the [Red] Sea...* [10]*As Pharaoh approached, the Israelites looked up, and there were the Egyptians, marching after them. They were* ***terrified*** *and cried out to the LORD.* [11]*They said to Moses, "Was it because there were no graves in Egypt that you brought us to the desert to die? What have you done to us by bringing us out of Egypt?* [12]*Didn't we say to you in Egypt, 'Leave us alone; let us serve the Egyptians'? It would have been better for us to serve the Egyptians than to die in the desert!"*

What were the people of Israel saying? Why were they not trusting God? Could not the God who had delivered them from the bondage of slavery again deliver them from Pharaoh's troops? Of course He could! However the Israelites did not think about this because they were so terrified. The **sea** was in front of them. **Mountains** were on their right and on their left. Behind them, Pharaoh's **troops** were advancing to recapture them or even kill them! What should they do? What could they do? How could they be saved? Let's listen to what Moses said and see what God did.

> (Exod. 14) [13]*Moses answered the people, "****Do not be afraid. Stand firm and you will see the deliverance the LORD will bring you today.*** *The Egyptians you see today you will never see again.* [14]*The LORD will fight for you; you need*

> *only to be still."* [15]*Then the* LORD *said to Moses, "Why are you crying out to me? Tell the Israelites to move on.* [16]*Raise your staff and stretch out your hand over the sea to divide the water so that the Israelites can go through the sea on dry ground.* [17]*I will harden the hearts of the Egyptians so that they will go in after them. And I will gain glory through Pharaoh and all his army, through his chariots and his horsemen.* [18]***The Egyptians will know that I am the*** **LORD***..."* [19]*Then the angel of God, who had been traveling in front of Israel's army, withdrew and went behind them. The pillar of cloud also moved from in front and stood behind them,* [20]*coming between the armies of Egypt and Israel. Throughout the night the cloud brought darkness to the one side and light to the other; so neither went near the other all night long.*
>
> [21]*Then Moses stretched out his hand over the sea, and all that night the* LORD *drove the sea back with a strong east wind and turned it into dry land.* ***The waters were divided****,* [22]*and the Israelites went through the sea on* **dry ground***, with a wall of water on their right and on their left.* [23]*The Egyptians pursued them, and all Pharaoh's horses and chariots and horsemen followed them into the sea.* [24]*During the last watch of the night the* LORD *looked down from the pillar of fire and cloud at the Egyptian army and threw it into confusion.* [25]*He made the wheels of their chariots come off so that they had difficulty driving. And the Egyptians said, "Let's get away from the Israelites! The* LORD *is fighting for them against Egypt."* [26]*Then the* LORD *said to Moses, "Stretch out your hand over the sea so that the waters may flow back over the Egyptians and their chariots and horsemen."* [27]*Moses stretched out his hand over the sea, and at daybreak the sea went back to its place. The Egyptians were fleeing toward it, and the* LORD *swept them into the sea.* [28]*The water flowed back and covered the chariots and horsemen–****the entire army of Pharaoh*** *that had followed the Israelites into the sea.* ***Not one of them survived.*** [29]*But the Israelites went through the sea on dry ground, with a wall of water on their right and on their left.* [30]*That day the* LORD *saved Israel from the hands of the Egyptians, and Israel saw the Egyptians lying dead on the shore.* [31]***And when the Israelites saw the great power the*** **LORD** ***displayed against the Egyptians, the people feared the*** **LORD** ***and put their trust in him and in Moses his servant.***

Then Moses and the Israelites sang this song to the LORD: "*I will sing to the* LORD, *for he is highly exalted...The* LORD *is my strength and my song; he has become my salvation*" (Exod. 15:1,2). Thus, they began to sing, and thank God for **the great salvation** which he had accomplished for them. Miriam, the sister of Aaron and Moses, took a tambourine, and all the women followed her, beating tambourines and singing and dancing. Miriam struck up a song, saying, "***Sing to the Lord for He is highly exalted!*** *The horse and its rider He has hurled into the sea!*" (Exod. 15:21).

Friends, that is the true and wonderful story about how God made a path through the sea for the people of Israel. Now then, how can we conclude our lesson today? Perhaps we can conclude with a simple question. Here is the question: **Who could save the Israelites from Pharaoh's troops**? Could they save themselves? We saw how **the sea** was in front of them. **The mountains** were on their right and left. And **Pharaoh's troops** were behind them. Could the people of Israel save themselves? Could they cause the sea to dry up? Or level the mountains? Or perhaps battle the troops of Pharaoh? No, they could not! Who then could save them? **God alone!** Only the LORD God could deliver them. That is why Moses said to them, *"Do not be afraid. Stand firm and you will see* ***the deliverance the LORD will bring you*** *today!"* Only God could save them! And He did save them. That is why, after they had arrived on the other side of the sea, they sang, *"The LORD is my strength and my song;* ***He*** *has become* ***my salvation****."*

God Himself had become **their salvation**. There was nothing that the Israelites could do to save themselves from Pharaoh's troops—nothing, except to follow the path which God had opened for them in the midst of the sea, and then thank Him and worship Him for delivering them from certain death!

Dear friends, God wants everyone to know that all the children of Adam are like the children of Israel. Like them, we have no hope of escaping the disaster that will soon befall us unless God delivers us! Perhaps the sea is not before us, but **death and hell** await us. Perhaps the mountains are not at our sides, but **the holiness of God** fences us in and condemns us. Pharaoh and his troops are not behind us, but **Satan and our sins** are upon us and threaten to destroy us forever!

Who can save the children of Adam from God's righteous judgment? Who can save the sinner from the fire that never goes out? Who can save man from the power of Satan? Who can save us from all of this? Who can get us to the other side of the sea of sin and bring us into the holy place called Paradise? **God alone!** Only God can save us! Man has no possibility of saving himself nor of saving another person. This is what the Scriptures declare: "***It is by [the grace of God that] you have been saved****, through faith, and this* ***not from yourselves****, it is the gift of God, not by works, so that no one can boast.*" (Eph. 2:8,9)

God, who is great in mercy, has opened a way of salvation for all the children of Adam, to deliver us from the power of Satan and sin and hell. God wants us to escape the judgment of raging fire that awaits all who die in their sins, but **we must come through the way of salvation which He has opened for us**! Do you know the way of salvation, which God has opened for you so that you can **escape** the power of **Satan**, the horrible consequences of **sin** and the punishment of **hell**? Are you in the way of righteousness which God has established so that you can be blessed in His holy presence forever?

The way of salvation which God has opened for the children of Adam is not based upon good deeds which man can do, nor is it based upon following the requirements of a religion. God says, It is "**not** *by works, so that* **no one** *can boast.*" What is the way of salvation that God has established for us? It is **the way of the Redeemer**, who came from heaven to die for our sins and rise again—to free all those who believe in Him—those of us who were **like slaves** because of the power of sin and the fear of death. The Holy Scriptures speak of this mighty Deliverer, saying: "*Salvation is found in* **no one else**, *for there is* **no other name** *under heaven given to men by which we must be saved.*" (Acts 4:12)

Yes, God has opened for you a way in the "sea of sin" so that you can escape the punishment of sin and get to the other side—into the safe and holy presence of God. But you must cross over by the way that God has opened for you. Concerning this way of salvation, the Redeemer said,

> "***I am the way*** *and the truth and the life. No one comes to [God] the Father except through me....I tell you the truth, whoever* **hears** *my word and* **believes** *him who sent me has eternal life and will not be condemned;* ***he has crossed over from death to life***." (John 14:6; 5:24)

Dear friend, have you "*crossed over from* **death** *to* **life**"?

Thank you for listening. Next time, Lord willing, we will see how God fed the Israelites in the desert....God bless you as you reflect on Moses' word to the Israelites,

> ***"Do not be afraid. Stand firm and you will see the deliverance the LORD will bring you today!"*** (Exod. 14:13)

ST#36

Lesson 35

Food in the Desert

Exodus 16,17

Peace be with you, listening friends. We greet you in the name of God, the Lord of peace, who wants everyone to understand and submit to the way of righteousness that He has established, and have true peace with Him forever. We are happy to be able to return today to present your program *The Way of Righteousness*.

In our last lesson, we saw how **God saved** the people of Israel from the hand of Pharaoh and his troops. When the Israelites arrived at the shore of the Red Sea, they had no possible means of escaping from Pharaoh's army. However, we saw how God pushed the waters aside for them so that they could walk through the middle of the sea, on dry ground. But when the troops of Egypt tried to cross, they were drowned. Thus, on that day the LORD God saved Israel from the hand of the people of Egypt. And when they saw the great power of the LORD, they feared Him and sang to Him, "*I will sing to the LORD, because He is my Salvation. The LORD is great!*"

We are presently looking in the book of Exodus, where the Israelites are in the wilderness **between Egypt and Canaan**. Canaan is the country which God had promised to give to their forefather Abraham and his descendants, so that they could own it. Today we are going to see **how God fed the Israelites in the desert**. The Scriptures show us how God Himself "walked" before them, in a great cloud during the day and in a flame of fire during the night. One thing is sure, if God did not guide them and care for them, they would perish in the wilderness.

Let us try to imagine for a moment the circumstances in which the Israelites found themselves. They were a huge crowd–a multitude bigger than the whole population of Dakar (more than two million people)! They were passing through a bone-dry desert—a desert without water or food. Think about it! A great multitude walking through a barren wilderness of sand and thorny trees! How would the tribes of Israel survive? Who could save them from the threat of hunger and thirst? How could that multitude and their many herds find enough water and food to stay alive in the wilderness? Could they feed themselves? No! Who could feed them then? There is only one answer. **God alone** could feed them and preserve them!

Did the Israelites **trust God**? Or did they worry about what they would eat and what they would drink? Surely the people of Israel should have trusted the LORD God. God had done so many great things for them. He freed them from their bondage of slavery by means of the ten plagues. He delivered their firstborn from death, by means of the blood of the lamb. He opened a dry path through the middle of the sea. And now He was going before them in a cloud to lead them back to the land of Canaan, as He had promised to their forefather, Abraham, so long ago. What do you think? Did the people of Israel have confidence in their God? Did they believe that God could do what He had promised? Let's turn back to the Scriptures now and discover the answer.

We are reading in chapter sixteen, in the book of Exodus, in the Torah of Moses. The Scripture says:

> (Exod. 16) [1]*The whole Israelite community set out from Elim and came to the Desert of Sin, which is between Elim and Sinai, on the fifteenth day of the second month after they had come out of Egypt.* [2]*In the desert the whole community* ***grumbled*** *against Moses and Aaron.* [3]*The Israelites said to them, "If only we had died by the LORD's hand in Egypt! There we sat round pots of meat and ate all the food we wanted, but* ***you have brought us out into this desert to starve this entire assembly to death****."*

Well, did the tribes of Israel have confidence in God? No, they did not! They were grumbling against Him and His prophet Moses. Listen to how God answered them.

> (Exod. 16) [11]*The LORD said to Moses,* [12]*"I have heard the grumbling of the Israelites. Tell them, 'At twilight you will eat meat, and in the morning you will be filled with bread.* ***Then you will know that I am the LORD your God****.'"* [4]*Then the LORD said to Moses, "I will rain down bread from heaven for you. The people are to go out each day and gather enough for that day. In this way I will test them and see whether they will follow my instructions.*
>
> [13]*That evening quail came and covered the camp, and in the morning there was a layer of dew around the camp.* [14]*When the dew was gone, thin flakes like frost on the ground appeared on the desert floor.* [15]*When the Israelites saw it, they said to each other,* **"What is it?"** *For they did not know what it was. Moses said to them, "It is the bread the LORD has given you to eat.* [31]*The people of Israel called the bread* ***manna****. It was white like coriander seed and tasted like wafers made with honey.*

That is how God fed the tribes of Israel in the wilderness, until the day they arrived at the land of Canaan. Did you hear where the food came from? It came **from heaven**. It came **from God**. Did the Israelites deserve the food that God sent down for them? No! They didn't deserve anything except God's punishment for all their unbelief and ungratefulness. It was only because of God's mercy that they didn't die of hunger in the desert.

Now let's continue reading to see what happened another time, when **the Israelites ran out of water**. We are reading in chapter seventeen. The Scripture says:

> (Exod. 17) [1]*The whole Israelite community set out…traveling from place to place as the LORD commanded. They camped at Rephidim, but there was* ***no water*** *for the people to drink.* [2]*So they* ***quarreled*** *with Moses and said, "Give us water to drink." Moses replied, "Why do you quarrel with me? Why do you put the LORD to the test?"* [3]*But the people were thirsty for water there, and they grumbled against Moses. They said, "Why did you bring us up out of Egypt to make us and our children and livestock die of thirst?"* [4]*Then Moses cried out to the LORD, "What am I to do with these people? They are almost ready to stone me."* [5]*The LORD answered Moses, "Walk on ahead of the people. Take with you some of the elders of Israel and take in your hand the staff with which you struck the Nile, and go.* [6]*I will stand there before you by the rock at Horeb. Strike the rock, and water will come out of it for the people to drink." So Moses did this in the sight of the elders of Israel."*

Thus, a great flow of water came gushing from the rock, flowing in the desert, and all the people drank, they and their herds.

Let us stop here and think a little about the story we are reading today. After all that God had done for the Israelites, did they have faith in Him? Were their hearts full of praise and thankfulness because of all that He had done for them? No! They did not trust God. Instead they complained and spoke against the God who had already saved them from so many, many dangers.

What did God do? The LORD God, in His patience and His goodness, gave them food and water in the desert. Did the people of Israel deserve God's goodness? No! They only deserved God's judgment. Why did God show them His goodness? Because God is **faithful** and **merciful**. He is God, the Faithful One, the Merciful One. Because of **His mercy** He provided food and water for the Israelites, even though they were ungrateful sinners! If salvation from hunger and thirst depended on the goodness and merit of the people themselves, God surely would have let them die in the desert.

Also, we should realize that God did not protect them simply because of His mercy, but also **to keep His Word**. God is faithful to keep all His promises—and

He had made an important promise concerning the nation of Israel. As we have already learned, **God had promised to bless all the nations of the world through the nation of Israel**, because it was to be through them that the prophets, the Holy Scriptures and the Savior of the world would come. Yes, God is faithful and full of mercy! He is the **God of truth** and the **God of love**. Surely the tribes of Israel did not deserve God's love. Yet even when they disobeyed God and spoke against Him, God proved His faithfulness and His love by giving them food from heaven.

Perhaps someone asks, "Of what value are the stories of the Israelites to us today?" The Word of God says: "*These things happened to them* ***as examples*** (or *illustrations*) *and were written down* as warnings **for us**, *on whom the fulfillment of the ages has come*." (1 Cor. 10:11) As God delivered the children of Israel from the power of the desert, in a similar way, God wants to deliver every child of Adam from **the power of sin**.

We ask you: What did the Israelites have to do so they would not perish in the desert? They simply had **to gather and eat the food that God sent down from the sky**. From where did their deliverance come? Did it come from their own efforts? No, their deliverance came from God. They had no power to save themselves from hunger and death. They couldn't do anything but **gather and eat the food that God had sent down for them**.

The Holy Scripture shows us that we are all sinners like the people of Israel and have **no means of saving ourselves**—neither from the power of sin nor from the righteous judgment of God. Perhaps we are not walking through a dry desert as were the Israelites, but the shadow of death still hangs over us as it hung over them. The Word of the LORD is clear: Anyone who refuses to receive the means of salvation that God has provided will die in his sin and fall into the eternal fire of hell. These are not pleasant thoughts. Die in sin! Come into judgment! Fall into hell! These are **terrible tragedies**! The **good news**, however, is that no one needs to die in his (or her) sin. Just as God gave the Israelites food so that they could live and not die of hunger in the wilderness, in a similar way God has given us "Food" so that we can be blessed in this life and forever in the life to come!

What is the "Food" which gives eternal life? Can we buy a food in the market that can give us the power to live forever in God's presence? No, no such food is available in the market! Well then, where and what is this "Food" which gives eternal life?

Friends, you must know that about one thousand five hundred years after the Israelites ate manna (bread) in the wilderness, God sent down **the Redeemer**, the Savior of the world. He is the "Food" which God has provided to save the people of the world from the power of sin, death, judgment and hell. Let us listen and think carefully about what the Redeemer Himself said when He was upon the earth. He said,

> *"I tell you the truth, he who believes has everlasting life. I am the bread* {Lit. *food, sustenance*} *of life. Your forefathers ate the manna in the desert, yet they died. But here is the bread that comes down from heaven, which a man may eat and not die.* ***I am the living bread that came down from heaven...He who comes to me will never go hungry, and he who believes in me will never be thirsty****!"* (John 6:47-51,35)

Dear friends, this is where we must stop today. In our next program, God willing, we will begin to see how God gave Israel the Ten Commandments....

God bless you as you ponder what the Redeemer declared, saying,

> ***"I am the bread of life. He who comes to me will never go hungry, and he who believes in me will never be thirsty!"*** (John 6:35)

ST# 37

Lesson 36

Fiery Mount Sinai!

Exodus 19, 20

Peace be with you, listening friends. We greet you in the name of God, the Lord of peace, who wants everyone to understand and submit to the way of righteousness that He has established, and have true peace with Him forever. We are happy to be able to return today to present your program *The Way of Righteousness*.

In our last lesson, we saw how God cared for the tribes of Israel in the arid desert, giving them **food from the sky** so that they would not die of hunger. We saw also how the Israelites provoked God time after time because of their lack of belief and their lack of faithfulness.

Today we are going to see how God appeared to the people of Israel in the desert and gave them **His holy law**. We are reading in the Torah, the book of Exodus, chapter nineteen. It begins like this: "*In the third month after the Israelites left Egypt, on the very day, they came to the Desert of Sinai.*" (Exod. 19:1) Where were Moses and the Israelites now in their journey through the desert? They had come to the mountain of **Sinai**. Do you remember where Moses was when God first called him and spoke to him from the bush which was on fire but didn't burn up? It was on that same mountain of Sinai. Do you remember the story? We heard how God spoke to Moses on Mount Sinai saying,

> "*I have indeed seen the misery of my people in Egypt…so I have come down to rescue them…So now, go. I am sending you to Egypt…I will be with you. And this will be the sign to you that it is I who have sent you:* ***When you have brought the people out of Egypt, you will worship God on this mountain.***" (Exod. 3:7,8,10,12)

Did God do for Moses what He had promised? He surely did! Where is Moses in our reading in the Torah today? We see Moses and the multitude of Israel **at the base of Mount Sinai, just as God had promised Moses forty years earlier** when He spoke to him in the burning bush, saying, "*When you have brought the people out of Egypt, you will worship* God on **this mountain**!"

Now let us continue reading to see how God reappeared to Moses and spoke to all the people of Israel at Mount Sinai. The Scripture says:

> *(Exod. 19) [3]Then Moses went up to God, and the LORD called to him from the mountain and said, "This is what you are to say to the house of Jacob and what you are to tell the people of Israel: [4]'You yourselves have seen what I did to Egypt, and how I carried you on eagles' wings and brought you to myself. [5]***Now if you obey me fully and keep my covenant, then out of all nations you will be my treasured possession.** *Although the whole earth is mine, [6]you will be for me a kingdom of priests and a holy nation.' These are the words you are to speak to the Israelites." [7]So Moses went back and summoned the elders of the people and set before them all the words the LORD had commanded him to speak. [8]The people all responded together, "***We will do everything the LORD has said***!"*

Did you hear how the Israelites answered God? They said, "*We will do* ***everything*** *that the LORD has said!*" Was what they said true? Could they keep **all** the commandments of God? God knew very well that the Israelites could not do everything that He commanded them. What God really wanted was that they recognize their inability to please God, acknowledge their sinful condition before Him, and believe the Good News concerning the Redeemer who was to come into the world to redeem sinners. God had forgiven the sins of their ancestors Abraham, Isaac and Jacob based on their **faith in God's promises**. God wanted to forgive the people of Israel through faith alone also. God's way of salvation has always been by **faith alone**—faith in God and His plan of salvation. The Scripture says: "*Clearly no one is justified before God by the law, because 'The righteous will live* ***by faith****.'*" (Gal. 3:11)

However, up to this point, the people of Israel hoped that they could achieve righteousness before God through **their own efforts**. How foolish of them! {Lit. *How short on wisdom!*} They had forgotten how many times they had offended God! They did not yet realize just how great their sin was before God! In their thoughts, sin was **not** such a serious affair, but in the sight of God who must judge them, **sin is a terrible affair**! {Lit. *injurious*} **God is holy and perfect**; He cannot approve any works that are less than perfect! However, up to this point, the Israelites had not yet recognized this. That is why they said (presumptuously), "*We will do everything the LORD has said!*" However, God had a plan by which He would show them that they could **not** do "*everything the LORD has said!*" Now let us continue in the Scriptures to see how God came down on Mount Sinai, revealed His glory and holiness, and gave **the Ten Commandments** to the tribes of Israel.

The Scripture says:

(Exod. 19) [10]*And the* LORD *said to* Moses, *"Go to the people…[and tell them that in three days] the* LORD *will come down on* Mount Sinai *in the sight of all the people.* [12]*Put* **limits** *for the people around the mountain and tell them, 'Be careful that you do not go up the mountain or touch the foot of it. Whoever touches the mountain shall surely be put to* **death**. [13]*He shall surely be stoned or shot with arrows; not a hand is to be laid on him. Whether man or animal, he shall not be permitted to live.'…* [16]*On the morning of the third day there was* **thunder** *and* **lightning**, *with a* **thick cloud** *over the mountain, and a* **very loud trumpet blast**. *Everyone in the camp trembled.* [17]*Then* Moses *led the people out of the camp to meet with* God, *and they stood at the foot of the mountain.* [18]*Mount Sinai was covered with* **smoke**, *because the* LORD *descended on it in* **fire**. *The* ***smoke billowed up from it like smoke from a furnace, the whole mountain trembled violently***, [19]*and the* ***sound of the trumpet grew louder and louder***… [20]**The** LORD **descended** *to the top of* Mount Sinai…

(Exod. 20) [1]*And* God *spoke all these words:* [2]"***I am the*** LORD *your* God, *who brought you out of Egypt, out of the land of slavery.*

1.) *You shall have* **no other gods** *before me. (v.3)*

2.) *You shall* **not make for yourself an idol**…*for I, [am] the* LORD *your* God. *(v.4,5)*

3.) *You shall* **not misuse the name of the** LORD *your* God, *for the* LORD *will not hold anyone guiltless who misuses his name. (v.7)*

4.) ***Remember the Sabbath day*** *by keeping it holy. (v.8)*

5.) ***Honor your father and your mother***. *(v.12)*

6.) *You shall* **not murder**. *(v.13)*

7.) *You shall* **not commit adultery**. *(v.14)*

8.) *You shall* **not steal**. *(v.15)*

9.) *You shall* **not give false testimony** *against your neighbor. (v.16)*

10.) *You shall* **not covet** *your neighbor's house. You shall not covet your neighbor's wife, or his manservant or maidservant, his ox or donkey, or anything that belongs to your neighbor." (v.17)*

[18]*When the people saw the thunder and lightning and heard the trumpet and saw the mountain in smoke,* ***they trembled with fear***. ***They stayed at a distance*** [19]*and said to* Moses, *"Speak to us yourself and we will listen. But do not have* God *speak to us or we will die!"* [20]Moses *said to the people, "Do not be afraid.* God *has come to test you, so that* ***the fear of God*** *will be with you to keep you from sinning."* [21]***The people remained at a distance…***

This is where we will stop in the Scriptures today. God willing, in the next program we will look at each of the Ten Commandments which God gave to the Israelites on Mount Sinai. But before we bid you farewell today, there is something that God wants to teach us through what we have just read. What we must understand is this: **God is Holy and we can never approach Him based on our own efforts**. The Scriptures teach that "*all men are like* ***grass***" (1 Pet. 1:24) and "*God is a* ***consuming fire***!" (Heb. 12:29) We all know what happens to grass that happens to be in the path of a wild fire!

In the beginning of our lesson today, we heard how the Israelites said to Moses, "*Everything that the* LORD *has said we will do*." They said that because **they did not recognize the holiness of God**. They somehow thought that they could please God through their own efforts. However, after God had appeared to them on Mount Sinai, their thoughts changed drastically! When the Israelites witnessed the thunder, the lightning and the mountain erupting with smoke and heard the voice of the LORD echoing out to them with ten holy commandments, "***they trembled with fear***. *They stayed at a distance and said to Moses, 'Speak to us yourself and we will listen. But do not have God speak to us or* ***we will die!'***"

Thus the people of Israel began to recognize God's absolute holiness and their utter inability to approach Him. At the base of Mount Sinai they became aware of the truth of Scripture: "*All men are like grass*" and "*God is a consuming fire!*" (1 Pet. 1:24; Heb. 12:29) In the presence of God the Holy One, could the Israelites honestly say, "No problem! Everything the LORD has said we will do!"? No, they could not! Now the Israelites recognized that **they had a problem; a very serious problem**! They sensed the holiness of God and the strictness of His commandments; they sensed their own unholiness and inability to keep God's perfect law. They felt **like dry grass in the path of a wild fire**!

How about you? Do you recognize the holiness of the LORD? Do you see that God and His law are righteous and perfect? Do you realize that your heart and your works are unrighteous and imperfect before God? Or are you like the Israelites who thought, "No problem! We will do everything that God requires! We will draw near to God by our good deeds!" Truly, such thoughts do not agree with God's thoughts. Can those who are filthy and stained with sin dwell with the One who is pure and holy? No, they cannot! Can God approve that which is half good and half evil? No, He cannot and He will not! God is holy and cannot tolerate that which is unholy! He demands perfection! **Do you realize this?** Or are you hoping that, in the Day of Judgment, your "**good deeds**" will somehow wipe out your **evil deeds**? If that were so, then **God would not be a righteous judge**! To illustrate, what would we think about a judge who tells a murderer, "You are guilty of murder, however, because of the good deeds that you have done in the past, I won't sentence you. You may go free." What would we say of a judge who did that? We would declare him to be an unrighteous, unjust judge.

Friends, **God is a righteous Judge!** He cannot overlook sin! The Lord God who must judge the world can only do what is righteous! **The righteousness of God demands a payment for sin.** And that payment is **death** and **eternal separation from God**! The good works which we do cannot cancel our debt of sin.

Concerning our good deeds, the Scripture says: "*All of us have become like one who is unclean, and all our righteous acts are like filthy rags!*" (Isa. 64:6) **God** is like a **consuming fire** and the **good works** of the sons of Adam are like **dry grass**. In our own righteousness, we cannot stand before the flame of God's holy judgment!

Did the Israelites dare get close to the fire of God which descended on Mount Sinai? Did they try to climb the mountain up to where God was? Were they bold enough to approach the mountain which quaked and rumbled with thunder and lightning; the mountain from which billowed up smoke like smoke from a furnace? No! They did not approach it! They **stood afar off** and **trembled with fear**! Not one person among them dared to approach the mountain because of the fear they felt before the holiness of the LORD God and His awesome power. But that fear was very good for them, because the Word of God says: ***"The fear of the LORD is the beginning of wisdom!"*** (Prov. 1:7)

Friends, our time is gone today. However, we encourage you to remember what we have just heard and seen: that **God is holy** and **must judge people** according to **His standard** of holiness. **God is holy** and He cannot ignore sin. **God is holy** and we cannot approach Him on the merits of our own efforts!

In the next lesson, in the will of God, we will examine and interpret the Ten Commandments which God gave the Israelites there on the mountain of Sinai. Thank you for listening....

God bless you and instruct you as you think about this foundational truth from His Word:

"The fear of the LORD is the beginning of wisdom!" (Prov. 1:7)

LESSON 37

TEN HOLY COMMANDMENTS

EXODUS 20

Peace be with you, listening friends. We greet you in the name of God, the Lord of peace, who wants everyone to understand and submit to the way of righteousness that He has established, and have true peace with Him forever. We are happy to be able to return today to present your program *The Way of Righteousness*.

In our last lesson, we saw how **the whole mountain of Sinai was billowing with smoke** because the LORD God had descended upon it in fire, thunder and lightning in order to give His Ten Commandments to the children of Israel. God warned the Israelites not to touch the mountain where He was lest they die. God wanted to teach them just how **holy** He is!

Today we plan to look more closely at each of the Ten Commandments, and compare them with our lives to know how we stand before God, the Holy One. We are reading in the Torah, the book of Exodus, chapter twenty. After God descended on Mount Sinai in the midst of the fire and smoke, He spoke these words: "*I am the LORD your God, who brought you out of Egypt, out of the land of slavery.*" (Exod. 20:1,2)

1.) ***"You shall have no other gods before me."*** (Exod. 20:3) This is the first commandment. The LORD God said, "*You shall have no other gods before me.*" He **alone** must be our God. He will not share His glory with another. God, the Creator, is the only One we must worship. However, what we see in this country and throughout the world is quite another thing. People exalt other men to a place of which God alone is worthy. Only His name is holy and awesome. He alone deserves our total devotion and confidence. Yet, when people have a problem or face an obstacle, their first thought is not to turn to God and pray to Him who created everything and can do anything. Instead, they put their hope in other human beings like themselves, and give to them the place that belongs to God alone. Those who do that have another god before them. To have another god is sin!

2.) In the second commandment God said: ***"You shall not make for yourself an idol...You shall not bow down to them or worship them; for I, the LORD***

your God, am a jealous God!" (Exod. 20:4,5) In this commandment, God tells us to keep ourselves from idols. Idols are not limited to sculptured images which are worshiped in certain locations or in the niches of houses. An idol is **anything** that comes between us and God. For some people, soccer is their god, because soccer is more important to them than God. For others, the television comes between them and God. They don't care about looking into the Word of God to understand it; they don't have time for anything except watching television. Then there are others who, as you know, wear charms–implying that God Himself is not enough for them. For others, it is their wealth that replaces God. God doesn't have first place in their lives; money does. They will even get involved with that which is not pleasing to God to get more money. For such people their god is money. Anything which replaces God is an idol.

3.) In the third commandment, God said: ***"You shall not misuse the name of the LORD your God, for the LORD will not hold anyone guiltless who misuses His name."*** (Exod. 20:7) Truly, God does not want us to use His holy name in vain. However, almost every day you can hear someone making a promise to his neighbor, saying, "'*Insh'a Allah*'{Arabic: *If God wills it*}, I will do this or that, or I will go to such and such a place," while, in his heart, he has no intention of doing it. The will of God is the farthest thing from his mind. He only **uses** the name of God to make his neighbor believe his lies. This is sin. Others say, "*Bilaay* {Arabic: *By God*}, I did not do such and such!" when they know perfectly well that they did that very thing! Someone else says, "God knows that I will not do this or that," but they are only lying. Such are misusing the name of God. The Word of God says: "*Simply let your 'Yes' be 'Yes', and your 'No', 'No'; anything beyond this comes from the evil one.*" (Matt. 5:37)

4.) In the fourth commandment, God spoke to the children of Israel saying: ***"Remember the Sabbath day by keeping it holy. Six days you shall labor and do all your work...For in six days the LORD made the heavens and the earth, the sea, and all that is in them, but he rested on the seventh day."*** (Exod. 20:8,9,10) In this we see that God wanted the children of Israel to rest every seventh day to **honor Him**.

5.) In the fifth commandment which God gave, He said: ***"Honor your father and your mother, so that you may live long in the land the LORD your God is giving you."*** (Exod. 20:12) Here we can see that our parents are very special and worthy of honor, and that we should give them the **respect** that they deserve. However, this is not what we see in today's generation. We see children who talk back to their parents when their parents speak to them, turn their noses up at them and go their way. They do not honor their parents. They only irritate them. However, this is not the way of living that we learn from the fifth commandment. The will of God for children is that they love their parents, honor them and obey them in everything that pleases God and agrees with His will.

6.) In the sixth commandment, God said: ***"You shall not murder."*** (Exod. 20:13) Here God says: He who kills a man, sins against God, because God is the One who gives to every person his life and soul. To murder a man is to hate God, because God made man in His own image. The Word of God also shows us that murder is not limited to killing a person, because the Scripture says: "*Anyone who **hates** his brother is a murderer.*" (1 John 3:15) What many ignore is that God does not merely judge a person according to what he has done, but also according to what he wants to do, that is, according to his intentions! Since God looks at the heart, hatred and murder are equally sinful in His sight.

7.) In the seventh commandment, God said: ***"You shall not commit adultery."*** (Exod. 20:14) Marriage is a precious gift from the LORD. God knows what is best for us, which is why, after He gives a man a wife to marry, He wants him to **limit** himself to his wife and refuse to have a single lustful desire for any other women. God's Word says that "*husbands ought to love their wives as their own bodies.*" (Eph. 5:28) and that "*anyone who divorces his wife, except for marital unfaithfulness, and marries another woman commits adultery.*" (Matt. 19:9) When people disobey God's law and do what is forbidden to them, they often receive in their bodies the consequences of their acts. That is why many deadly diseases fall on those who have sexual relations outside the limits of marriage decreed by God. You should know another thing: Adultery is not limited to what we do with our bodies, but it also includes what is in our minds. Concerning this, the Scripture says: "*Anyone who looks at a woman lustfully has already committed adultery with her in his heart.*" (Matt. 5:28)

8.) In the eighth commandment God said: ***"You shall not steal."*** (Exod. 20:15) This command is clear. However, you should also know that, before the eyes of God who must judge us, stealing is not limited to **taking** money or some object that doesn't belong to you. Even if you simply want to take the things of another, but do not take them, you are a thief in your heart! God looks at the heart. Stealing has many sides to it. For example, if your employer commits to you a job, and he pays you to do that job, and he believes that you are working when in reality you are just wasting time, then you are stealing! Yes, you have stolen from your employer's profits. And what is the punishment for stealing and for every other sin? It is to die and enter the fire of hell which is never extinguished!

9.) The ninth commandment says: ***"You shall not give false testimony against your neighbor."*** (Exod. 20:16) This also is perfectly clear. The LORD God is the God of truth and has nothing to do with lies! Man thinks it is permissible to tell little lies to avoid problems and keep peace. But with the God of Truth there are no "little lies!" God says: Everyone who lies takes on the character of **Satan**, "*for he is a liar and the father of lies.*" (John 8:44) Satan lied to our ancestors, Adam and Eve, and he continues to deceive people with his lies! Whoever tells a lie is like Satan.

10.) In the tenth commandment God says: ***"You shall not covet your neighbor's house. You shall not covet your neighbor's wife, or his manservant or maidservant, his ox or donkey, or anything that belongs to your neighbor."*** (Exod. 20:17) This commandment shows us clearly that God knows just how crooked and wicked the heart of man is. Covetousness and greed are found in the **hearts** of the children of Adam. Our wicked hearts cause us to lust after another man's wife or to set our eyes on something that someone else has which we do not have. This is sin, because God's Word says: "*We brought nothing into the world, and we can take nothing out of it. But if we have food and clothing, we will be content with that.*" (1 Tim. 6:7,8)

These are the Ten Commandments which God entrusted to Moses and to the children of Israel.

How should we conclude our lesson today? Perhaps with a question. Here is the question which each of us must answer: "Have **I** obeyed **all** of the Ten Commandments?" You may already know that when the holy Redeemer came into the world, He summarized the Ten Commandments in two phrases. He said:

1.) "***Love the Lord your God with all your heart and with all your soul and with all your mind!*** *and,*

2.) ***Love your neighbor as yourself.*** *All the Law and the Prophets hang on these two commandments.*" (Matt. 22:37,39,40)

Now, if you want to examine yourself to know whether you have kept the Ten Commandments which God gave to Moses, you can ask yourself two questions:

First: What is my relationship with **God** like? **Do I love God with all my heart?**

Second: What are my relationships with **people** like? **Do I love my neighbor as I love myself?**

What is your relationship with **God** like? Let your heart answer honestly. Do you love God with your whole mind? Do you love him with all your heart? Do God and His Word have first place in your life?

How about your relationship with **people**? Do you love your neighbor as you love yourself? Do you put others before yourself in everything? Do you care for your fellowman as you care for yourself? Do you do for others everything that you want them to do for you?

If you cannot answer "yes" to all these questions, know that, before God, you are a **transgressor**. By your own efforts, you cannot hope for anything except the damnation of God's righteous judgment! The Scripture says: "*The cowardly, the unbelieving, the vile, the murderers, the sexually immoral, those who practice magic arts, the idolaters and all liars–their place will be in the fiery lake of burning sulphur.*" (Rev. 21:8)

God is holy and cannot tolerate that which is unholy. God is perfect and cannot accept any works which are imperfect. That is why the Scripture says:

"Whoever keeps the whole law and yet stumbles at just one point is guilty of breaking all of it!" (Jam. 2:10) Trying to keep the Ten Commandments will not cause anyone to be *"declared righteous in [the sight of God]! For* ***all*** *have sinned and fall short of the glory of God!"* (Rom. 3:20, 23). Yes, dear friends, the Word of God is clear: "***All*** *have sinned!"* and "***All*** *who rely on observing the law are under a curse."* (Gal. 3:10)

Perhaps someone asks, "Well then, **why did God give these Ten Commandments to us** if none of us can keep them?" This is a very important question and, in the will of the Lord, in our next program we will hear how God answers it....

May God bless you and reveal to you the important truth contained in this statement from His Word:

> ***"Whoever keeps the whole law and yet stumbles at just one point is guilty of breaking all of it."*** (Jam. 2:10)

Lesson 38

Purpose of the Commandments

Exodus 20

Peace be with you, listening friends. We greet you in the name of God, the Lord of peace, who wants everyone to understand and submit to the way of righteousness that He has established, and have true peace with Him forever. We are happy to be able to return today to present your program *The Way of Righteousness*.

In our last two lessons we saw how God descended on Mount Sinai in fire, thunder and lightning to deliver His ten holy commandments to the tribes of Israel. In the first commandment God said to them: **You shall have no other gods before me.** In the second: **You shall not make for yourself an idol.** Third: **You shall not use the name of the LORD your God in vain.** Fourth: **Remember the Sabbath day by keeping it holy.** Fifth: **Honor your father and your mother.** Sixth: **You shall not murder.** Seventh: **You shall not commit adultery.** Eighth: **You shall not steal.** Ninth: **You shall not lie.** Tenth: **You shall not covet the things of your neighbor.**

These are the Ten Commandments which God sent down to Moses and to the Israelites. God laid on them a heavy burden, saying to them: Whoever can **perfectly** keep **everything** that the Ten Commandments demand, is worthy to live with Me forever. However, whoever keeps the whole law but fails in just **one point** is guilty of breaking **all of it**, and will be separated from Me **forever**!

That was the way of holiness God delivered to the tribes of Israel on Mount Sinai. God commanded that they obey Him in everything! Yes, **everything**! Are sinners able to keep **all** of God's commandments? No, they are not! Nevertheless, that is exactly what God, the Holy One, requires! Therefore, **the big question** before us today is this: **Why did God give His Ten Commandments to the children of Israel, when He knew that no one could keep them perfectly?** Why did God place such a heavy burden on Adam's descendants?

We have already seen how the children of Israel said, "*We will do everything the LORD has said!*" However, God knew that they could not do all that He required. The Israelites did not realize that they lacked the strength to fulfil the will of

God perfectly. They did not recognize just how far they were from God and His great glory. That is precisely why God gave the Israelites ten perfect commandments, saying to them: **Keep them all, if you can! But whoever fails in even one point will be separated from Me forever!**

God intended, through those burdensome commandments, **to reveal to the tribes of Israel their lack of ability to please Him**. God knew that the children of Israel could not follow all His commandments, but they themselves had not yet discerned this. The Israelites were like religious people of our day, who wrongly think that God simply wants us to try to do good and on Judgment Day, if our "good works" outweigh our "bad works," then God will say to us, "Come, and dwell in My presence forever!" However, those who think this are mistaken and do not know the Scriptures or the holiness of God. God is perfect, and cannot overlook even one sin!

By way of illustration, how many sins did our ancestor Adam have to commit before God expelled him from the Garden of Paradise? Ten sins? Or one hundred? Perhaps a thousand? No! Just **one sin** and Adam had to get out!

One sin and Adam was no longer perfect before God!

One sin and he could no longer approach God!

One sin and he had to die!

One sin and he earned for himself a place in the eternal fire!

Yes, God is holy and does not take sin lightly! That is why He told the children of Israel: "*Whoever keeps the whole law and yet stumbles at just **one point** is guilty of breaking **all of it**.*" (Jam. 2:10)

Therefore, if this is what the holiness of God is like, what we want to know is: **Why did God give the Ten Commandments to the Israelites when He knew that no one could keep them perfectly?** Listen to God's answer: "*No one will be declared righteous in [God's] sight by observing the law; rather, [**the purpose of the commandments is to reveal sin**!]*" (Rom. 3:20) So what is the purpose of the Ten Commandments? To remove sin? "No," God says, "the purpose of the commandments is to **reveal** sin!" {or as NIV translates it: to make us "*conscious of sin*."}

Did you get that? Why did God give His ten holy commandments to Moses and the children of Israel? Did He give them those commands so that by keeping them they could earn the right to enter Paradise? No! That cannot be because God says, "If you fail to keep **all**, you are condemned!" Can the children of Adam perfectly obey God in **all** that He has commanded? Can one draw pure, clean water from a dirty, polluted water pot? Impossible!

What is the purpose of the Ten Commandments? The Scripture says: "The purpose of the commandments is **to reveal sin**!" God did not give the commandments to save us from His judgment. God gave them to show us that **we are condemned sinners** and that **we need a Savior**! Is this clear in your mind?

The Ten Commandments are somewhat like an **X-ray** machine at the hospital. If I am sick and I do not know what is wrong with me, perhaps the doctor will examine me by taking some X-rays. What is the purpose of an X-ray photo? It has just one purpose: **to reveal what is wrong inside my body**. In a similar way, the holy commandments which God entrusted to Moses are like the hospital's X-ray machine. Their purpose is **to reveal what is wrong—the sin that is in my heart and soul**. How can the Ten Commandments reveal the sin that is in me? They reveal my sin in this way: If I compare my conduct with God's holy law, I will see how far I am from God—in my thoughts, my words and my deeds. When **I look at God's law** and then **I look at myself**, I know that I have sinned against God and sinned against man and that **I cannot be admitted into the pure and uncontaminated presence of a holy God**!

Just as the hospital X-ray machine is useful for **showing** what is not right in a person's body, so the Ten Commandments are useful for **showing** what is not right in a person's heart. And just as the X-ray **cannot cure** the one who is sick, likewise the Ten Commandments **cannot cure** my heart which is full of sin. In order for that to happen, I must go back to the Great Physician, that is, to God. Only God has a plan to save me from the death and condemnation that await me due to the sin that is inside me.

Perhaps someone says, "Wait a minute, my friend! I'm a good person! I am not like others who steal, cheat, and commit adultery!" If that is your attitude, clearly you have not yet fathomed God's holiness! What you need to know is that, on the Day of Judgment, **God will not compare you with your sinful neighbor. He will compare you with His holy and perfect law**, which states: "*Whoever keeps the whole law and yet stumbles at just* ***one point*** *is guilty of breaking* ***all of it****!*" (Jam. 2:10) The God who says: "You shall not commit adultery" also says, "You shall not lie!" Thus, if you have not committed adultery, but have told just one lie, then you have transgressed the whole law (see James 2:11) and cannot enter the presence of God in Paradise, because the Scripture says: "***Nothing impure will ever enter it****, nor will anyone who does what is shameful or deceitful.*" (Rev. 21:27) What is certain is that we can never please God through our own efforts! That is what the Word of God declares when it says:

> "*All of us have become like one who is* ***unclean****, and all our righteous acts are like* ***filthy rags****.*" (Isa. 64:6) "*God condemns all as sinners. There is no one righteous, not even one. All have turned away. There is no one who does good, not even one. There is no difference, for all have sinned and fall short of the glory of God!*" (Rom. 3:19,10,12,22,23)

Now then, if that is what we are like before the One who must judge us, how can we escape His punishment? What must we do to be saved? Are we without hope? Based on **our own efforts** we have no hope. But thanks be to God, He has designed **a plan to rescue** the children of Adam from the punishment of sin!

Let us now continue in the Torah, in the book of Exodus, chapter twenty, and see the way God provided for the children of Israel to deliver them from the curse which His holy law brought upon them. After God gave the Ten Commandments to the Israelites, the Scripture says:

> (Exod. 20) [18]*When the people saw the thunder and lightning and heard the trumpet and saw the mountain in smoke, they trembled with fear. They stayed at a distance...* [21]*while Moses approached the thick darkness where God was.* [22]*Then the* LORD *said to Moses, "Tell the Israelites this: 'You have seen for yourselves that I have spoken to you from heaven...* [24]*[Therefore,] make* **an altar** *of earth for me and* **sacrifice** *on it your burnt offerings and fellowship offerings, your sheep and goats and your cattle.* ***Wherever I cause my name to be honored, I will come to you and bless you.***"

Thus, Moses wrote in a book everything that God instructed him. Then early in the morning Moses arose, made an altar at the base of Mount Sinai as God had commanded. When Moses finished making it, he ordered some young men to sacrifice some bulls, collect the blood in bowls, and burn the flesh on the altar. Then Moses took the blood of the bulls and sprinkled it on the altar, on the book in which he had written the Ten Commandments, and on all the crowd, and said, "*This is* **the blood of the covenant** *that the* LORD *has made with you.*" (Exod. 24:4-7)

Thus we see Moses, at the commandment of God, making an altar, sacrificing some animals, and sprinkling the blood upon the whole multitude of Israel. What was the reason for all of this? God wanted to remind the Israelites of what He had taught their ancestors Adam, Abel, Noah, Abraham, Isaac and Jacob, that "***without the shedding of blood there is no forgiveness of sin.***" (Heb. 9:22) Everyone who wished to approach God had to approach Him in the perfection of a spotless sacrifice.

Why did God command those animal sacrifices? God commanded them because He is righteous, and His holy law states that **the penalty** of even the "smallest" of sins is death and eternal condemnation, far from God and His great glory. And since the children of Israel could not keep all His holy commandments, they had to bring to God a sacrifice without blemish, so that the **innocent** victim could replace the one who was **guilty**. However, as we have already learned, animal sacrifices could not **remove** sin, they could only **cover** man's sin, until God sent **the holy Redeemer** into the world. The Redeemer would willingly offer Himself as the final Sacrifice for sin.

How glad we are today to know that this Savior has come and has paid for our sins once for all. Do you know His name? Yes, it **Jesus**. The name *Jesus* means ***the LORD saves***. Jesus had no earthly father. He came from heaven. He did not inherit the sin nature found in all of Adam's descendants. Jesus perfectly obeyed the Ten Commandments and fulfilled all of God's righteous requirements. Because He was without sin, He was qualified to give His life as a sacrifice which takes away the sin of all who believe in Him. Based on the Redeemer's perfect sacrifice, God can declare you and I as righteous, because the One who had no sin, suffered the penalty for your sin and mine.

Dear friends, based on what we have studied today, let us remember two very important thoughts.

1.) First, know for sure that **no one can save themselves by keeping the Ten Commandments**! Listen again to what the Scripture says about this: "*All who rely on observing the law are under a curse, for it is written: 'Cursed is everyone who does not continue to do everything written in the Book of the Law!'*" (Gal. 3:10) "*For whoever keeps the whole law and yet stumbles at just one point is guilty of breaking all of it.*" (Jam. 2:10) No one will be saved by trying to keep the Ten Commandments! The purpose of the commandments is to reveal sin.

2.) The second thought that we must keep in our minds is that **God alone has a plan to save sinners**! Listen to what the Scripture says: "*There is one God and one Mediator between God and men, the man Christ Jesus, who gave Himself as a ransom for all!*" (1 Tim. 2:5,6) Truly, only God has a plan to save sinners.

And so, listening friends, we leave you with these two thoughts: **No one** will be saved by trying to keep the Ten Commandments! And: **God alone** has a plan to save sinners!

Thank you for listening....

May God bless you and give you insight into what we have studied today, for His Word says:

> ***"No one will be declared righteous in [God's] sight by observing the law; rather, through the law we become conscious of sin!"*** (Rom. 3:20)

Lesson 39

Broken Commandments

Exodus 32

Peace be with you, listening friends. We greet you in the name of God, the Lord of peace, who wants everyone to understand and submit to the way of righteousness that He has established, and have true peace with Him forever. We are happy to be able to return today to present your program *The Way of Righteousness*.

In our last three lessons, we have seen how God spoke with the Israelites from Mount Sinai in the midst of the fire, thunder and lightning, and gave them His ten **holy** commandments. We also saw how God commanded the people of Israel to make an **altar** at the base of Sinai and offer some spotless animals as sacrifices.

Why did God order those animal sacrifices? God ordered them because He is righteous, and His holy law declares: "*Whoever keeps the whole law and yet stumbles at just one point is* ***guilty*** *of breaking all of it.*" Whoever breaks God's law has sinned...and the payment of sin is death! (Jam. 2:10; 1 John 3:4; Rom. 6:23) Since the Israelites could not keep all of God's commandments, they had to present to God sacrifices without blemish, so that the innocent animal might die as **a substitute** for the guilty person. The animal forfeited its life so the sinner would not have to. In this way God proved that He is righteous and that He cannot excuse sin based on man's efforts. God can only forgive sin based on the blood of a perfect sacrifice.

Our lesson today is called "**Broken Commandments**." At this point in the story of the prophet Moses and the tribes of Israel, they are still camping in front of Mount Sinai in the desert. Let us now return to the Torah to see what happened after God gave them the Ten Commandments. We are reading in chapter twenty-four in the book of Exodus.

The Scripture says:

> (Exod. 24) [12]*The LORD said to* Moses, "**Come up to me** *on the mountain and stay here, and I will give you the tablets of stone, with the law and commands I have written for their instruction.*" [13]*Then* **Moses set out with Joshua his**

> ***assistant***, *and* **Moses went up on the mountain of God**. [14]*He said to the elders, "Wait here for us until we come back to you. Aaron and Hur are with you, and anyone involved in a dispute can go to them."* [15]*When Moses went up on the mountain, the cloud covered it,* [16]*and the glory of the* LORD *settled on Mount Sinai. For six days the cloud covered the mountain, and on the seventh day the* LORD *called to Moses from within the cloud.* [17]*To the Israelites the glory of the* LORD *looked like a consuming fire on top of the mountain.* [18]*Then Moses entered the cloud as he went on up the mountain. And he stayed on the mountain* ***forty days and forty nights***.

Let us pause here. In the next study, Lord willing, we will learn what God told Moses on Mount Sinai during that forty day period. Today, however, we are going to see what happened to the Israelites who were in the camp at the base of the mountain waiting for Moses to return. We all know that waiting for God patiently is not easy for the children of Adam. It is much easier for us to give up; to forget God's Word and go our own way. Thus, what we are going to read now about the Israelites is important for us–very important. God wants **to warn us** through this shocking story.

In chapter thirty-two, we read:

> (Exod. 32) [1]*When the people saw that Moses was so long in coming down from the mountain, they gathered round Aaron and said, "* ***Come, make us gods who will go before us.*** *As for this fellow Moses who brought us up out of Egypt, we don't know what has happened to him."* [2]*Aaron answered them, "Take off the gold earrings that your wives, your sons and your daughters are wearing, and bring them to me."* [3]*So all the people took off their earrings and brought them to Aaron.* [4]*He took what they handed him and made it into an idol cast in the shape of a calf, fashioning it with a tool. Then they said, "These are your gods, O Israel, who brought you up out of Egypt."*

Do you see what the Israelites were doing? Not many days after they had said, "*Everything that the* LORD *has said we will do!*" we see them breaking the first and second commandments which God had just given them on Mount Sinai! God had said to them: One:"*You shall have no other gods before me!*" Two: "*You shall not make for yourself an idol!*" But what did the Israelites do? They turned their backs on God and made for themselves an idol in the shape of a calf like the idols they had seen in Egypt.

Why did the Israelites so quickly turn their backs on God and His Word? Because what they wanted was **a god which they could see and touch**. They were like people today who choose to ignore the Word of God and follow men and their traditions. Following a **man** whom the eye can see is easier than following **God** whom no one can see. That is why most of the children of Adam substitute **the ideas of men,** which have no solid basis, for **the true Word of God**.

Let us see now what happened after the Israelites made for themselves the golden calf. The Scripture says:

> (Exod. 32) [5]*When Aaron saw this, he built an altar in front of the calf and announced, "Tomorrow there will be a festival to the LORD."* [6]*So the next day the people rose early and sacrificed burnt offerings and presented fellowship offerings. Afterwards they sat down to eat and drink and got up to indulge in revelry.*

Did you hear what Aaron did? The Scriptures tell us that "*he built an altar in front of the calf and announced, 'Tomorrow there will be a festival to the LORD!'*" Was that the truth? Could the Israelites worship the LORD in that way? Definitely not! We know that **God did not have any part of the worship festival that they were organizing.** Now they had not only broken the first and second commandments, but also the third commandment which says: "*You shall not use the name of the LORD your God in vain.*" "God the LORD! God, God, God!" was in their mouths, but their hearts were far from Him. Their worship was in vain. Their words about God were worthless. Their prayers were only a lot of meaningless bowing down that could only make God angry!

Now, let's finish the story:

> *(Exod. 32)* [7]*Then the LORD said to* Moses, "*Go down, because your people, whom you brought up out of Egypt, have become corrupt.* [8]*They have been* ***quick to turn away*** *from what I commanded them and have made themselves an idol cast in the shape of a calf. They have bowed down to it and sacrificed to it and have said, 'These are your gods, O Israel, who brought you up out of Egypt.'* [9]"*I have seen these people," the LORD said to Moses, "and they are a stiff-necked people.* [10]*Now leave me alone so that my anger may burn against them and that I may destroy them. Then I will make you into a great nation."*
>
> [11]*But Moses sought the favor of the LORD his God. "O LORD," he said, "why should your anger burn against your people, whom you brought out of Egypt with great power and a mighty hand?* [12]*Why should the Egyptians say, 'It was with evil intent that he brought them out, to kill them in the mountains and to wipe them off the face of the earth'? Turn from your fierce anger; relent and do not bring disaster on your people.* [13]*Remember your servants Abraham, Isaac and Israel, to whom you swore by your own self: 'I will make your descendants as numerous as the stars in the sky and I will give your descendants [the land of Canaan] I promised them, and it will be their inheritance forever.'"* [14]*Then the LORD relented and did not bring on his people the disaster he had threatened.* [15]*Moses turned and*

> *went down the mountain with the two tablets of the Testimony in his hands. They were inscribed on both sides, front and back. [16]The tablets were the work of God; the writing was the writing of God, engraved on the tablets. [17]When Joshua [who accompanied Moses] heard the noise of the people shouting, he said to Moses, "There is the sound of war in the camp." [18]Moses replied: "It is not the sound of victory, it is not the sound of defeat; it is the sound of singing that I hear."*
>
> *[19]When Moses approached the camp and saw the calf and the dancing, his anger burned and he threw the tablets out of his hands,* **breaking them to pieces** *at the foot of the mountain. [20]And he took the calf they had made and burned it in the fire; then he ground it to powder, scattered it on the water and made the Israelites drink it. [21]He said to Aaron, "What did these people do to you, that you led them into such great sin?" [22]"Do not be angry, my lord," Aaron answered. "You know how prone these people are to evil. [23]They said to me, 'Make us gods who will go before us. As for this fellow Moses who brought us up out of Egypt, we don't know what has happened to him.' [24]So I told them, 'Whoever has any gold jewelry, take it off.' Then they gave me the gold, and I threw it into the fire, and out came this calf!" [25]Moses saw that the people were running wild and that Aaron had let them get out of control and so become a laughingstock to their enemies. [26]So he stood at the entrance to the camp and said, "Whoever is for the LORD, come to me." And all the Levites rallied to him. [27]Then he said to them, "This is what the LORD, the God of Israel, says: 'Each man strap a sword to his side. Go back and forth through the camp from one end to the other, each killing his brother and friend and neighbor.'" [28]The Levites did as Moses commanded, and that day* **about three thousand of the people died**. *[35]And the LORD struck the people with a plague because of what they did with the calf Aaron had made.*

After this, the LORD told Moses to chisel out **two stone tablets** to replace the ones which he had broken. On these the LORD rewrote **the commandments** which the children of Israel had already broken. What a great sin the Israelites committed! They had **broken** God's holy law. The evil heart of man showed itself again. In spite of all the LORD had done for the people of Israel, we see how quickly they left the way of righteousness which God had established. They chose to follow another way, to create for themselves **their own religion**. They chose the path of the works of their hands. They turned their back on the way that God had established and rejoiced in a religion they chose for themselves. The Name of God was on their lips, but their hearts were far from Him! That is why they went as far as to have a calf forged, taking pleasure in the works of their hands, and turning their backs on the living and true God.

What does God want to teach us through this shocking story? God wants us to think about where we stand in our relationship with Him. Perhaps there are those who are thinking: "I am not like the Israelites. I have never turned my back on God and worshiped an idol." You who think this way, are you positively sure that you have never worshiped an idol? Perhaps you have not had an idol forged for yourself. However, an idol is not limited to sculptured images to be worshiped. An idol is anything which comes between us and God. An **idol** can be money, clothes, sex, soccer, television, self, another person like yourself, or the traditions of your ancestors. Some cling to idols of fetishes and amulets. For others, their religious obligations are their idols; they put more importance on praying and fasting than on listening to the Word of God! **Anything that replaces God and His truth is an idol.**

Who is your God? Whom do you really worship, the LORD God, or an idol? Is the name of God merely on your lips or is His Name inside your heart? There is something that distinguishes those who truly worship God from those who worship idols. It is **the Word of God**. What is your attitude toward the true Word of God? Do you know God's Word? Do you believe it? Do you love it with all your heart? Or are you like the Israelites of whom God said, *"These people honor me with their lips, but their hearts are far from me. They worship me* ***in vain****; their teachings are but rules taught by men."*? (Matt. 15:8,9)

How about you? Whom do you really worship, the LORD God who gave His righteous law to Moses? Do you believe His Word? Or are you placing your hope in the way of your own religious works as the Israelites did? Whatever the case may be, the Scripture says:

> *"These things happened to [the Israelites] as examples and were written down as warnings for us...Therefore, my dear friends,* ***flee from idolatry****. I speak to sensible people."* (1 Cor. 10:11,14,15) *"But the cowardly, the unbelieving, the vile...those who practice magic arts, [and all]* ***idolaters****...their place will be in the fiery lake of burning sulfur."* (Rev. 21:8) *"We accept man's testimony, but God's testimony is greater because it is the testimony of God which he has given about [the Redeemer, who] has come and has given us understanding, so that we may know him who is true....Dear children,* ***keep yourselves from idols****!"* (1 John 5:9,20,21)

Thank you for listening....

Next time, God willing, we will look at the unusual plan God designed so that He might dwell among the sinful Israelites without compromising His righteousness.

God bless you as you remember this important warning from His Word:

> ***"Keep yourselves from idols!"*** (1 John 5:21)

Lesson 40

The Tent of Meeting

Exodus 24-40, Leviticus 16

Peace be with you, listening friends. We greet you in the name of God, the Lord of peace, who wants everyone to understand and submit to the way of righteousness that He has established, and have true peace with Him forever. We are happy to be able to return today to present your program *The Way of Righteousness.*

In our last lesson, we saw how the Israelites turned from the LORD who had redeemed them from their slavery in Egypt. While Moses was receiving God's Word on Mount Sinai, the Israelites made a calf of gold to be worshiped as an idol. Today, however, we are going to hear a much more pleasant story. But we must listen to it very carefully because it is very profound. We are going to see how God told Moses and the Israelites to make a very special tent so that He might teach them how they might approach Him, meet with Him and worship Him. Our lesson today is called **"The Tent of Meeting."**

Reading in the Torah, the book of Exodus, chapter twenty-four, the Scripture says:

> (Exod. 24) 16***The glory of the LORD settled on Mount Sinai****. For six days*
> *the cloud covered the mountain, and on the seventh day the LORD called to Moses*
> *from within the cloud.* 17*To the Israelites the glory of the LORD looked like a*
> *consuming fire on top of the mountain.* 18*Then Moses entered the cloud as he*
> *went on up the mountain. And he stayed on the mountain forty days and forty nights.*
>
> (Exod. 25) 1*The LORD said to Moses,* 2*"Tell the Israelites to bring me an*
> *offering. You are to receive the offering for me from each man whose heart prompts*
> *him to give.* 3*These are the offerings you are to receive from them: gold, silver and*
> *bronze;* 4*blue, purple and scarlet yarn and fine linen; goat hair;* 5*ram skins dyed*
> *red and hides of sea cows; acacia wood;* 6*olive oil for the light; spices for the*
> *anointing oil and for the fragrant incense;* 7*and onyx stones and other gems to be*
> *mounted on the ephod and breast-piece.* 8*Then have them* ***make a sanctuary***

> ***for me, and I will dwell among them.*** [9]***Make this tabernacle and all its furnishings exactly like the pattern I will show you.***"

Did you hear what God told Moses? He told him something very amazing and wonderful! God planned to dwell among the Israelites, among those who had sinned against Him so many, many times! Why would God, who is so great and holy, want to live with such sinners? Why would God, who is spirit and has need of nothing, bother to talk to the descendants of Adam who had turned away from Him? As we have already seen, God created man in the image of God because He wanted to have fellowship with man. Man's sin spoiled that fellowship, but God established a righteous way by which man could come back to Him. It was because of His eternal purposes and His great compassion for sinners that the LORD God planned to place His glorious presence in the midst of the Israelites. By means of **a very special tent** (tabernacle) and **very special laws**, God planned to illustrate how Adam's descendants can draw near to God. As we have already learned, because God is holy, sinners cannot have fellowship with Him in just any way. For this reason, God commanded the Israelites to make a special tent for Him so that He could be in their midst–in a way worthy of His holiness and glory. Also, by means of this special tent, God planned to teach future generations many important lessons about Himself and about the Savior He planned to send into the world.

Before we examine what God commanded Moses concerning the dwelling place which the Israelites were to build for Him, we must first understand that God did not tell them to build a tent for Him because He needed a place to live! No! God, the Most High, who created the world and everything in it, does not live in houses made by men! In the Writings of the Prophets, the LORD Himself declares: "*Heaven is my throne, and the earth is my footstool. Where is the house you will build for me? Where will my resting place be? Has not my hand made all these things, and so they came into being?*" (Isa. 66:1,2; Acts 7:48,49)

Why then, did God command the Israelites to make a tent in which His Spirit and glory would dwell? As we have already said, God wanted to teach the Israelites and all the descendants of Adam how much He longs to have **fellowship** with them. God also wanted to put before them **an illustration** of the way by which people can be forgiven of their sins and have the right to live with God in heaven forever!

Thus, God commanded Moses and the Israelites to make for Him a tent so that He could dwell in their midst. However, that Tent of Meeting was not to be like any ordinary tent. In fact, the Scriptures contain fifty chapters which describe how the work of the Tent of Meeting was to proceed! They are profound chapters and we do not have time to speak of all they contain. We can only attempt to summarize the most important things.

What you must know first about this Tent of Meeting is that God told Moses that it must have **two rooms**. The Tent of Meeting was one tent, but a beautiful and heavy **curtain** (veil) was made to divide the tent into two rooms.

The first room was called ***the Holy Place***. No one could enter that room except the priests {Wolof: *priest, marabout, spiritual leader*}. The priests were those whom God had chosen from the descendants of Aaron to kill the animals as sacrifices which cover sin. There were three things in that room. A gold table on which they burned incense, an oil lamp, and a table on which to place special bread which was presented before God in worship.

The second room of the tent was named ***the Holiest Place*** (The Holy of Holies). It was called the Holiest Place because after the tent was finished God planned to come down and fill that room with His majestic glory. The Holiest Place was an illustration of heaven (Paradise). Consequently, that room belonged to God alone! That is why God told Moses that anyone who tried to enter the Holiest Place would die! No one was to enter the Holiest Place except the High Priest and he could only enter once a year. Furthermore, he had to enter with the blood of a sacrifice for his own sins and for the sins of the people, as God had decreed.

Inside the Holiest Place, God commanded Moses to place a chest made of acacia wood, and overlay it with pure gold. That chest was called ***the Ark (chest) of the Covenant***. Inside the ark of the covenant, they were to keep the two tablets of stone on which the Ten Commandments were written. Above the ark (chest) they placed a lid of gold which the High Priest had to sprinkle with the blood of an animal once every year so that God could forgive the Israelites their sins. That is why God called this lid ***the Atonement Cover*** (or *Mercy Seat*) {Lit. in Wolof: *the means, instrument or place of forgiveness*}.

After that, God showed Moses how they must make a high curtain to surround the Tent of Meeting. That wall, **the wall of the courtyard**, was to be made of a white curtain. In the curtain surrounding the tent, they were to make **one door**. Thus no one could enter the courtyard of the Tent of Meeting unless he passed through the door of the courtyard. Inside the courtyard, in front of the door of the courtyard, God commanded Moses and the Israelites to place **an altar** made of bronze. Everyone who passed through the door of the courtyard had to pass by the altar first. God wanted to teach the Israelites and all of Adam's descendants the way by which they must approach God. How were the Israelites to approach God? By the way of the blood sacrifice.

Everyone who wanted to enter the courtyard of "God's dwelling place" had to enter with an animal sacrifice as a payment for sin. God was teaching the Israelites that **no one can ever approach Him except on the basis of the blood of the sacrifice**. That is why God told Moses, saying, "*The life of a creature is in the blood, and I have given it to you to make atonement for yourselves on the alter;* ***it is the blood***

***that makes atonement for one's life*.**" (Lev. 17:11) {"*atonement*" in Wolof: "*the means by which sins can be paid for.*"}

Therefore, if someone wanted to worship God, he had to offer an animal sacrifice first for the forgiveness of his sin. The worshiper had to bring a bull, a sheep, or a bird into the courtyard of the Tent of Meeting. In front of the altar, he was required to place his hands on the head of the sacrifice he had brought, confess to God that he was a sinner and that he deserved to die for his sins. Next, he would slay the animal. After that, a priest would take the blood of the sacrifice, sprinkle it on the altar and on the ground around the altar, and then burn the sacrifice on the altar. In this way God could forgive (*cover*) the guilty person's sins, because the innocent animal had died in his place.

The Israelites had to repeat these sacrifices over and over every year. **Animal sacrifices could not satisfy God's holiness forever**. They were **temporary illustrations of the Redeemer** who was to come and die in the place of sinners—so that God could **permanently** forgive the descendants of Adam their debt of sin without compromising His righteousness.

To illustrate what the Redeemer would do for sinners, God established for the Israelites one day each year when the High Priest would enter the second room, the Holiest Place, of the Tent of Meeting. That day was called ***The Day of Atonement*** {Lit. in Wolof: *the Day when God covered sins*}. On that one day (in October), the High Priest had the authority to enter the Holiest Place, and sprinkle blood on the atonement cover of the ark of the covenant. He could never enter the Holiest Place without bringing with him the blood of a spotless animal, which he consecrated to God for his own sins and for those of the multitude. In this way, God was showing how the Redeemer would come, shed His blood so that God could forgive sinners, and welcome them into His presence forever!

Ah, fellow listeners, our lesson today is incredibly deep and wonderful. And there is so much more that we would like to say, but our time is almost gone. However before we bid you farewell, there is something else which you should understand about the Tent of Meeting. In the last chapter of the book of Exodus, the Scripture says:

> "*The Israelites had done all the work just as the* LORD *had commanded Moses. Moses inspected the work and saw that they had done it just as the* LORD *had commanded. So Moses blessed them...Then the cloud covered the Tent of Meeting, and* ***the glory of the*** LORD ***filled the tabernacle****. Moses could not enter the Tent of Meeting because the cloud had settled upon it, and the glory of the* LORD *filled the tabernacle.*" (Exod. 39:42,43; 40:34,35)

Do you see what happened? After the Tent of Meeting was ready, the glory of God descended on the tent and filled the Holiest Place, and the light of the glory of God shone forth, even surpassing the light of the sun! What we must remember is that, in all of this, God was illustrating the greater blessings which were to come when the Redeemer of the world descended from heaven and came to dwell among the sons of Adam. **The Redeemer Himself is the true "Tent of Meeting"** which God gave so that we can have a close and wonderful relationship with Him forever! As it is written in the holy Gospel {*Injil*}:

> "*In the beginning was the Word, and the Word was with God, and the Word was God....* ***The Word became flesh and made His dwelling among us!*** *And we beheld His glory!...[He is] the Lamb of God who takes away the sin of the world!*" (John 1:1,14,29)

Yes, the Redeemer is the One who **fulfilled everything** symbolized by the Tent of Meeting and by the animal sacrifices, for He not only came into our world and **lived among men**, but He also **shed His blood** as the Perfect Sacrifice for sinners so that we might have a close relationship with God forever!

Is what we have studied today hard to understand? Then let us remember that sometimes there are things in the Word of God that are difficult to understand, but that does not keep them from being true! May we never forget that the LORD Himself says: "*My thoughts are not your thoughts, neither are your ways my ways!...As the heavens are higher than the earth, so are* ***my ways higher than your ways and my thoughts than your thoughts****!*" (Isa. 55:8,9)

Our time is up today....

May God bless you. We bid you farewell with these verses from the Holy Scripture:

> ***"Oh, the depth of the riches of the wisdom and knowledge of God! How unsearchable his judgments, and His paths beyond tracing out! Who has known the mind of the Lord? Who has been his counselor?...for from him and through him and to him are all things. To him be the glory forever! Amen."*** (Rom. 11:33-36)

Lesson 41

The Israelites' Unbelief

Numbers 13, 14

Peace be with you, listening friends. We greet you in the name of God, the Lord of peace, who wants everyone to understand and submit to the way of righteousness that He has established, and have true peace with Him forever. We are happy to be able to return today to present your program *The Way of Righteousness*.

We continue to explore the Torah. As you know, the Torah is the first part of the Writings of the Prophets and contains five sections or books. In the first book, called **Genesis**, we learned how sin entered the world, bringing with it suffering, death and condemnation. However, we also saw how God designed a plan to save Adam and his descendants from the penalty of sin, the eternal fire of hell. We learned how God promised to send a Redeemer to die for sinners so that God could forgive them of their sins without compromising His own righteousness. The book of Genesis also taught us how God chose Abraham and promised to make of him a great nation, the nation from which the prophets would come and, at last, the Redeemer of the world.

In the second book of the Torah, that is, **Exodus**, we saw how God delivered Abraham's descendants, the Israelites, from their chains of slavery in the land of Egypt, through the hands of Moses, His prophet. God led the tribes of Israel out of Egypt and into the wilderness, bringing them to Mount Sinai where He gave them His commandments and taught them about the way of blood sacrifice by which He could forgive their sins.

In the last lesson, we saw how God commanded Moses and the Israelites to build for Him the beautiful and amazing **Tent of Meeting** (Tabernacle) so that He might dwell in their midst. Once everything was ready "*the cloud covered the Tent of Meeting, and the glory of the LORD filled the tabernacle*." (Exod. 40:34) God was showing the Israelites how He wanted to have a wonderful relationship with them, but that no one could approach Him except by means of the blood of a sacrifice offered on the altar of the Tent of Meeting. The Tent of Meeting with its animal sacrifices were mere **shadows and illustrations of the Redeemer** who was to come from heaven, dwell on earth, and shed His blood as a sacrifice to take away sin.

In the **third section of the Torah,** called ***Leviticus*** {Lit. *The laws of the tribe of Levi*}, God inspired Moses to write the laws that explain in detail how the Israelites were to present to God sacrifices which cover sin. This book is very profound, and we do not have time to look at all it contains. If you study it for yourself, you should note two words which appear some two hundred times. These two words summarize the message of the whole book. The two prominent words are "***Holy***" and "***Blood***." Why do these two words appear repeatedly in this book? Because one of the most important messages a person can ever grasp is that **God is holy**, and that "*without the shedding of* ***blood*** *there is no forgiveness of sin!*" (Heb. 9:22) The value of the third book of the Torah was to teach the Israelites how an impure sinner stained with sin could approach God who is pure and holy. God showed clearly that no one could approach Him, except by the blood of a sacrifice, a sacrifice which foreshadowed the holy Redeemer who would come into the world and die for sinners, to pay their debt of sin.

With the time remaining today, let us cross over now into **the fourth section** of the Torah of Moses, the book of **Numbers**. In this book, we read how the Israelites lived at the base of Mount Sinai for about one year. During that year, God taught them many things, and inspired Moses to write much of the holy Torah from which we are reading today.

However, God did not intend for the Israelites to live in the wilderness forever. That is why, one day, God directed them to get up and move out, and continue onward to the abundant land He had promised them, the land of Canaan. The Scriptures tell us that, on the day they were to depart from Sinai, the cloud of the glory of God, which covered the Tent of Meeting, arose and began to move out in front of them. **The LORD Himself** was leading them, in a **cloud** during the day to show them the way, and in a **pillar of fire** every night.

Thus, the Israelites followed the cloud during the day and the pillar of fire at night until they arrived at the border of Canaan, the land God had promised to Abraham and his descendants a long time before. God did not forget His promises. **Because of God's faithfulness and power, the Israelites had arrived at the border of the land of Canaan,** which we call today Palestine or Israel.

However, Canaan was filled with inhabitants. The people of Canaan were many and mighty. How then could the Israelites possess it? There was only one way: **God would give them the land.** Nothing is too hard for God! God promised Abraham: "*This land of Canaan I will give to your descendants!*" God planned to exterminate the people of Canaan and turn the land over to the descendants of Abraham, the Israelites. It is important to understand that the sins of the people of Canaan were very great. They were guilty of gross immoralities, even sacrificing their children to their false gods. God had been very patient with the people of Canaan, but they continued in their shameful desires and sinful ways. Therefore, God planned to give their land to the tribes of Israel.

Now then, let us read in the fourth section of the Torah to see what happened when the Israelites arrived at the border of the land of Canaan. In chapter thirteen, the Scripture says:

> (Num. 13) [1]*The LORD said to Moses,* [2]*"Send some men to explore the land of Canaan, which* **I am giving to the Israelites**. *From each ancestral tribe send one of its leaders."* [3]*So at the LORD's command Moses sent [twelve men] out from the Desert of Paran...* [21]*So they went up and explored the land...*
>
> [25]*At the end of forty days they returned from exploring the land.* [26]*They came back to Moses and Aaron and the whole Israelite community at Kadesh in the Desert of Paran. There they reported to them and to the whole assembly and showed them the fruit of the land.* [27]*They gave Moses this account: "We went into the land to which you sent us, and* **it does flow with milk and honey**! *Here is its fruit.* [28]**But the people who live there are powerful**, *and the cities are fortified and very large. We even saw descendants of giants called Anak there!*
>
> [30]*Then* **Caleb** *(one of the men who explored the land) silenced the people before Moses and said, "We should go up and take possession of the land, for we can certainly do it!"* [31]**But the men** *who had gone up with him said, "We can't attack those people; they are stronger than we are!"* [32]*And they spread among the Israelites a bad report about the land they had explored. They said, "The land we explored devours those living in it. All the people we saw there are of great size.* [33]*We saw the Nephilim (giants) there...We seemed like grasshoppers in our own eyes, and we looked the same to them."*
>
> (Num. 14) [1]*That night all the people of the community raised their voices and* **wept aloud**. [2]*All the Israelites* **grumbled** *against Moses and Aaron, and the whole assembly said to them, "If only we had died in Egypt! Or in this desert!* [3]*Why is the LORD bringing us to this land only to let us fall by the sword? Our wives and children will be taken as plunder. Wouldn't it be better for us to go back to Egypt?"* [4]*And they said to each other, "We should choose a leader and go back to Egypt!"* [5]*Then Moses and Aaron fell face down in front of the whole Israelite assembly gathered there.* [6]**Joshua** *son of Nun and* **Caleb** *son of Jephunneh, who were among those who had explored the land, tore their clothes* [7]*and said to the entire Israelite assembly, "The land we passed through and explored is exceedingly good.* [8]*If the LORD is pleased with us, he will lead us into that land, a land flowing with milk and honey, and will give it to us.* [9]*Only do not rebel against the LORD. And do not be afraid of the people of the land, because we will swallow them up. Their protection is gone,* **but the** LORD **is with us.** *Do not be afraid of them."*

> [10]**But the whole assembly talked about stoning them.** *Then the glory of the LORD appeared at the Tent of Meeting to all the Israelites.* [11]*The LORD said to Moses,* "**How long will these people treat me with contempt? How long will they refuse to believe in me**, *in spite of all the miraculous signs I have performed among them?"*

Let us pause here. Do you hear how Israel transgressed and offended God? Do you see their unbelief? Do you notice how they accused God of going back on His word? Yes, on that day, the Israelites sinned greatly because they did not believe God's promise to give them the land of Canaan. **They did not believe** what God had promised Abraham, Isaac, Jacob, Joseph, and Moses. They were like so many today who say, "We believe in God and the prophets!" yet they do not really believe God and they do not believe the prophets, because they do not believe what God has promised through His prophets in the Holy Scriptures! Unbelief is a terrible sin before God.

Enough said. Let us continue the story.

> (Num. 14) [26]*The LORD said to Moses and Aaron:* [27]*"How long will this wicked community grumble against me? I have heard the complaints of these grumbling Israelites.* [28]*So tell them, 'As surely as I live, declares the LORD, I will do to you the very things I heard you say:* [29]**In this desert your bodies will fall**, *every one of you twenty years old or more who was counted in the census and who has grumbled against me.* [30]*Not one of you will enter the land I swore with uplifted hand to make your home, except* **Caleb** *son of Jephunneh and* **Joshua** *son of Nun.* [31]**As for your children** *that you said would be taken as plunder, I will bring them in to enjoy the land you have rejected.* [32]*But you, your bodies will fall in this desert...* [35]*I, the LORD, have spoken, and I will surely do these things to this whole wicked community, which has* **banded together against me.** *They will meet their end in this desert; here they will die."*
>
> [36]*So the men Moses had sent to explore the land, who returned and made the whole community grumble against him by spreading a bad report about it,* [37]*these men responsible for spreading the bad report about the land were struck down and died of a plague before the LORD.* [38]*Of the men who went to explore the land, only Joshua...and Caleb...survived* (because they believed the word of the LORD).

Thus we see how the Israelites refused to believe the LORD even though He had redeemed them from the hand of Pharaoh and brought them to the border of the land of Canaan. What did God do with those who did not believe His Word? He condemned them to die in the wilderness! Why did this generation of Israelites not enter the land of Canaan? **Because they would not believe the Word of God!**

Friends, to refuse to believe the Word of God is a terrible tragedy. God must punish everyone who refuses to believe Him! Whoever despises and treats with indifference what God says in His holy Word is calling God a liar and can have no part in His eternal kingdom! It is not God's will that anyone perish in unbelief. God wants all **to believe** the Good News about the way of salvation which He has established. But each person must decide for himself. All who refuse to believe God's Word will perish. Listen to this warning from the Holy Spirit of God through the prophets:

> *"Today, if you hear his voice, do not harden your hearts as you did in the rebellion, during the time of testing in the desert....See to it, brothers, that none of you has* ***a sinful, unbelieving heart*** *that turns away from the living God!"* (Heb. 3:7,8,12; Psa. 95:7-11)

Fellow listeners, thank you for listening. Next time, God willing, we will see how all those who refused to believe God perished in the wilderness, just as God pledged...God bless you as you heed this warning from the Holy Scriptures:

> ***"See to it, brothers, that none of you has a sinful, unbelieving heart that turns away from the living God."*** (Heb. 3:12)

LESSON 42

THE BRONZE SNAKE

NUMBERS 20, 21

Peace be with you, listening friends. We greet you in the name of God, the Lord of peace, who wants everyone to understand and submit to the way of righteousness that He has established, and have true peace with Him forever. We are happy to be able to return today to present your program *The Way of Righteousness*.

Last time, in the fourth section of the Torah, in the book of Numbers, we saw how the Israelites arrived at the border of Canaan, the land God had promised to Abraham, Isaac, Jacob and their descendants. God planned to drive out the wicked giants which lived in the land and turn everything over to the Israelites. However most of the people of Israel were afraid of the giants and **would not believe God's promise** to give them the land of Canaan.

Thus, we read how God judged the Israelites because of their unbelief. He said to them,

> ***"Not one of you will enter the land I swore with uplifted hand to make your home, except Caleb...and Joshua...because they have a different spirit and follow me wholeheartedly****. Their descendants will inherit it. And also, as for your children that you said would be taken as plunder, I will bring them in to enjoy the land you have rejected! But you, your bodies will fall in this desert!"* (Num. 14:30-32)

What we must understand is that God wanted to bless the Israelites abundantly, but **He could not bless them because of their unbelief**. Since they refused to believe what the LORD had promised them, God condemned the Israelites to wander in the desert for forty years, until all those over twenty years old who had not believed Him died.

Now, let us continue in the book of Numbers to see what happened at the end of the forty years which the Israelites wasted in the wilderness due to their unbelief. In chapter twenty, we read:

> (Num. 20) [1]*After the Israelite community had walked in the wilderness for about forty years, they arrived at the Desert of Zin, and they stayed at Kadesh [where they had first refused to believe God and enter the land of Canaan which He had promised to them]. There Miriam* (the elder sister of Moses) *died and was buried.*
>
> [2]*Now there was no water for the community, and the people gathered in opposition to Moses and Aaron.* [3]*They* ***quarreled*** *with Moses and said, "If only we had died when our brothers fell dead before the LORD!* [4]*Why did you bring the LORD's community into this desert, that we and our livestock should die here?* [5]*Why did you bring us up out of Egypt to this terrible place? It has no grain or figs, grapevines or pomegranates. And there is no water to drink!"*

Do you hear what the Israelites were saying? After all that God had done for them and their fathers in Egypt and in the wilderness, were their hearts full of thankfulness and trust? No! They were doing exactly as their fathers had done. They were grumbling! Of course, they were weary of the wilderness, but they should have remembered that it was because of their unbelief that they had not yet entered the land of Canaan. True, the Israelites did not have water. But why then did they not pray to God? The One who had cared for them for forty years in the parched wilderness–could He not give them water to drink? Of course He could! God wanted to supply all their needs! However, the Israelites did not yet fully trust the Lord their God.

Let us continue in the chapter to see what happened. The Scripture says:

> (Num. 20) [6]*Moses and Aaron went from the assembly to the entrance of the Tent of Meeting and fell face down, and the glory of the LORD appeared to them.* [7]*The LORD said to Moses,* [8]*"Take the staff, and you and your brother Aaron gather the assembly together.* ***Speak to that rock*** *before their eyes and it will pour out its water. You will bring water out of the rock for the community so that they and their livestock can drink."*
>
> [9]*So Moses took the staff from the LORD's presence, just as he commanded him.* [10]*He and Aaron gathered the assembly together in front of the rock and Moses said to them, "Listen, you rebels, must we bring you water out of this rock?"* [11]*Then Moses raised his arm and* ***struck the rock*** *twice with his staff. Water gushed out, and the community and their livestock drank.* [12]*But the LORD said to Moses and Aaron, "Because you did not trust in me enough to honor me as holy in the sight of the Israelites, you will not bring this community into the land I give them."*

Did you grasp what happened? What did God command Moses to do so that the multitude of Israel would have water to drink? He said, "*Speak to that rock!*"

Did Moses obey God by speaking to the rock? No! In his anger Moses hit it twice. This did not prevent God, in His goodness, from causing the rock to spout forth water, but what Moses did displeased God. That is why God punished him, saying, "*Because you did not trust in me enough to honor me* ***as holy*** *in the sight of the Israelites,* ***you will not*** *bring this community into the land I give them.*"

Perhaps in our thinking, the punishment that God imposed on Moses was too severe. However, we must remember that what pleases God is faith in His word and obedience to His word. God cannot accept anything that is against His word–even if it came from the prophet Moses!

God does not show favoritism. Moses was a great prophet, but he was a human like all of us. Therefore, he was a sinner like all of Adam's offspring. Even the prophet of God, **Moses, could not save himself** because of his good works. Like all of Adam's descendants he had defects and did not fulfil all that is righteous. The prophet Moses, like all the Israelites, had to come by the way of salvation which God had established, by the way of the blood sacrifice. Through the sin of Moses, God wants to remind us that **all** have sinned and fall short of the glory of God. All are guilty before God. Everyone has sinned. No one is righteous! There is no one who has not strayed from the way of God–except for the perfectly righteous Redeemer who came from heaven to save sinners!

Continuing with the story of the Israelites, in the end of chapter twenty we read how Aaron, Moses' older brother, died on the mountain called Hor, and the community of Israel mourned for him there for thirty days.

After that, in chapter twenty-one, the Scripture says:

> (Num. 21) [4]*They traveled from Mount Hor along the route to the Red Sea...But the people grew* ***impatient*** *on the way;* [5]*they spoke against God and against Moses, and said, "Why have you brought us up out of Egypt to die in the desert? There is no bread! There is no water! And we detest this miserable food!"*
>
> [6]*Then the LORD sent* ***venomous snakes*** *among them; they bit the people and many Israelites died.* [7]*The people came to Moses and said, "We sinned when we spoke against the LORD and against you. Pray that the LORD will take the snakes away from us." So Moses prayed for the people.* [8]*The LORD said to Moses, "Make a snake and put it up on a pole; anyone who is bitten can look at it and live."* [9]*So Moses made a bronze snake and put it up on a pole. Then when anyone was bitten by a snake and* ***looked*** *at the bronze snake, he* ***lived****.*

Let us think about this amazing story. Why did God send venomous snakes among the Israelites? He sent the snakes because of their **sin**. We heard how they spoke against God and Moses, and despised the food which God sent down to them. That is why God sent venomous snakes to bite them, causing many to **die**.

What could the Israelites do to escape death? Could they save themselves from the plague of snakes? Could they heal themselves of the deadly poison? Impossible! What could they do then? They could cry out to God! And that is what they did. We saw how the Israelites repented and went to Moses, saying to him, "We have sinned! We have transgressed against you and against God! Pray to the LORD for us that He might have mercy on us and take away these snakes!"

Did God take the snakes away from them? He did something even better than that! God told Moses to make a bronze snake and raise it up on a pole so that "*anyone who is bitten can* ***look*** *at it and* ***live***." This was **God's remedy**. If a snake bit someone, all that a person had to do was to look at the bronze snake which was hung on the pole and he would be healed! This was the way of deliverance that God arranged: **Look and live**!

God promised to heal **whoever looked** at the bronze snake which Moses suspended on the pole. What happened then to those who **refused to look**? They died a painful death. But whoever believed God and looked at the bronze snake was delivered from death, because God had promised them, saying, "***Anyone*** *who is bitten can* ***look*** *at it and* ***live***."

Truly, this is a fascinating story, but it is more than fascinating. It was written to instruct us. God wants to show us that **we all** are like the Israelites. We too are sinners, which is why we often grumble against God and man, and offend God in our thoughts, in our words and in our deeds. **Satan** is like the venomous snakes that were biting the Israelites. And **sin** is like the poison that was killing them. Satan has bitten all of the children of Adam and the poison of sin will cause us to perish forever, unless God provides for us **a remedy**! The payment of sin is to perish in the eternal fire and, in ourselves, we have no means of escape! However, we praise God, because just as He designed a plan to save the Israelites from **the poison of the snakes**, so also He has designed a plan to save the children of Adam from **the poison of sin**!

You who are listening today, do you know what God has done to save you from the curse which sin has brought? **Listen to what the holy Redeemer said** about fifteen hundred years after Moses raised the bronze snake in the wilderness. He said, "*Just as Moses lifted up the snake in the desert, so the Son of Man* (the Redeemer of the world), *must be lifted up…that whoever believes in Him shall not perish but have eternal life!*" (John 3:14,16)

From this verse in the holy Gospel {*Injil*}, we learn that the bronze snake, which Moses raised up in the desert, was **an illustration** {shadow, picture, symbol} of the Redeemer who was to come and die on a cross so that He might defeat the devil who holds the power of death. (Heb. 2:14) Oh, how wonderful this message is! As we will discover in coming lessons, through the death and resurrection of the Redeemer, God has opened for the children of Adam a door of salvation, peace and joy forever! All God wants is for you to admit that you cannot save yourself from the power of sin, and believe in your heart what God has testified concerning the Savior who died on the cross to pay for you your debt of sin. God says: **Look to the Redeemer and you will live!** Believe on Him and God will heal you, save you from the poison of sin and reserve for you an eternal dwelling place in His presence in heaven!

Old and young, men and women, rich and poor, God is saying to everyone: **Look and live!** Look to the mighty Redeemer whom God has sent and you will be **saved**! But God is also saying: **If you refuse to look**, if you do not believe in the Savior through whom God has provided the only cure for sin, then "*you will die in your sins!*" (John 8:24) God's righteous law declares that whoever does not accept the remedy that He has provided **will perish**. God has no other remedy by which the sons of Adam can be cured from the poison of sin. Have you looked to the Redeemer of whom all the prophets have written? He will cleanse you and give you eternal life if you will simply put your trust in Him alone. Listen again to what the Scripture says: "*Just as Moses lifted up the snake in the desert, so the Son of Man* (the Redeemer of the world), *must be lifted up...**that whoever believes in Him shall not perish but have eternal life**!*" (John 3:14,16)

Fellow listeners, our time is up today. Thank you for listening. Next time, God willing, we will consider the final words of the prophet Moses, and thus complete our study in the holy Torah....God bless you as you ponder this promise from Him:

> ***"[Look to Me, and you will be saved!]"*** (Isa. 45:22)

Lesson 43

Moses' Final Message

Deuteronomy

Peace be with you, listening friends. We greet you in the name of God, the Lord of peace, who wants everyone to understand and submit to the way of righteousness that He has established, and have true peace with Him forever. We are happy to be able to return today to present your program *The Way of Righteousness.*

Over the past forty-two lessons, we have been looking into the first book of the Holy Scriptures, the book we call the Torah. As you know, it is God who implanted His words in the mind of the prophet Moses, inspiring him to write them in a book. Approximately three thousand five hundred years have gone by since Moses wrote the Torah, yet it is still of immeasurable value to us today. The Torah is **the foundation** that God Himself laid, so that we can test everything that we hear and **discern whether it comes from God or not**. The teaching contained in the Torah is **pure truth** from God. Any teaching that contradicts it is **false**. All of God's truth is in perfect harmony with what is written in the Torah. There is one thing that Almighty God cannot do. Do you know what it is? That's right, **God cannot contradict Himself**! In the Torah, Moses penned these words, ***"God is not a man, that he should lie, nor a son of man, that he should change his mind. Does he speak and then not act? Does he promise and not fulfil?"*** (Deut. 23:19)

Through our study in the Torah of Moses, God has revealed to us many profound mysteries. Today we plan to **conclude our journey through the holy Torah**. But before we look at the final chapters, let us review what we have seen from the beginning until today.

In the first chapter of the Torah, we saw how God created the first man in His own image. God wanted to have a wonderful and meaningful **relationship** with man whom He had created. That is why He placed in the soul of man a mind (spirit) so that he might know God, gave him a heart so that he could love God and entrusted to him a will so that he could choose for himself whether to obey God or to disobey Him.

In the third chapter, we saw how the first man, Adam, chose to obey Satan and eat of the tree which God had prohibited. Thus, the Scripture says: "***Sin** entered the world through one man, and **death** through sin, and in this way death came to all men, because all sinned.*" (Rom. 5:12) The penalty of sin is death and eternal separation from God.

Thus, we saw how God expelled Adam and Eve from the Garden of Paradise because of their sin. But before He put them out, God announced how He planned one day to send **a Redeemer** into the world, to open a door of salvation for Adam's offspring; to free them from the dominion of Satan and the penalty of sin.

Next, we learned how God called Abraham, promising to make of him **a special nation** from which the prophets and the Redeemer would descend. Thus, Abraham begot Isaac; Isaac begot Jacob; and Jacob begot twelve sons. Later, God changed Jacob's name to **Israel**. The twelve sons of Israel formed the new nation which God had promised Abraham. The ten older sons sold their younger brother, Joseph, as a slave who was taken to Egypt. However, "*a man reaps what he sows.*" (Gal. 6:7) Consequently, we saw how all the children of Israel became slaves in Egypt. Nevertheless, God did not forget His promise to Abraham and his descendants. In the book of Exodus we learned how God fulfilled His promise to Abraham by calling Moses to free the Israelites from their bonds of slavery.

In studying the story of Moses, we read the amazing and wonderful account of how God delivered the multitude of Israel from the oppression of Pharaoh and the people of Egypt. We also read how God protected them in the desert and brought them to the border of Canaan, the land which He had promised their forefather Abraham long before. However, most of the Israelites were afraid of the giants of Canaan and did not trust God to do for them what He had promised them. That is why they did not enter the abundant land of Canaan at that time.

Because of their unbelief, the Israelites wandered in the wilderness for forty years, until all those who did not believe what God had promised concerning Canaan passed away. That was the punishment that God brought upon them because of their unbelief. Surely "*the LORD is…a faithful God who does no wrong, upright and just is He!*" (Deut. 32:4)

Now, let's **complete our journey in the Torah**. Remember, the Israelites were in the desert because God was chastening them for their unbelief. Every one of those more than twenty years old who had refused to believe what God had promised concerning the land of Canaan had died. Not one remained alive. Now their children were at the border of Canaan. After forty long years in the wilderness, the children of Israel were now very anxious to get settled in the land their parents had failed to enter!

Our study today is from the fifth section of the Torah, the book of **Deuteronomy** {Lit. *Second Law*}. In this final section Moses reviews God's holy law and teaches it to the tribes of Israel. This profound book contains **the final message** that

Moses preached to the people to prepare them to enter the land which God had promised them. We do not have time to read Moses' entire sermon today, but we can summarize Moses' words in these few words: **"Do not forget!"**

In brief, Moses said something like this to the Israelites: Be careful not to forget that you were slaves in Egypt! Do not forget all that God did for you on the way, between Egypt and the new land which you are about to enter! Do not forget the sins that you committed against the Lord your God! Do not forget how the LORD judged your parents because of their unbelief, which is why all their corpses remain in the desert. Do not forget that God was good to your parents, but they were hardheaded and refused to believe Him. **Do not forget it!**

Today, when you hear the voice of God, do not harden your hearts, as your parents did in the wilderness. Will you be like your ancestors who refused to believe the Word of God, or will you believe the LORD your God? If you refuse to believe the Word of God as your ancestors did, God will punish you as He punished them. **Do not forget it!**

The LORD God will bring you into the land, which flows with milk and honey, which He swore to your ancestors. Do not forget your God who gave you the land, because man does not live on bread alone, but on every word that comes from the mouth of the LORD! **Do not forget it!**

After Moses had finished his sermon, the LORD said to Moses:

> (Deut. 32) [49]*Go up into the Abarim Range…across from Jericho, and view Canaan, the land I am giving the Israelites as their own possession.* [50]*There on the mountain that you have climbed you will die…* [51]*This is because both of you broke faith with me in the presence of the Israelites…in the desert and because you did not uphold my holiness among the Israelites.* [52]*Therefore, you will see the land only from a distance; you will not enter the land I am giving to the people of Israel."*
>
> (Deut 34) [1]*Then Moses climbed Mount Nebo from the plains of Moab…There the LORD showed him the whole land…all the land of Judah as far as the western sea…* [4]*Then the LORD said to him, "This is the land I promised on oath to Abraham, Isaac and Jacob when I said, 'I will give it to your descendants.' I have let you see it with your eyes, but you will not cross over into it."* [5]*And* ***Moses the servant of the LORD died there*** *in Moab, as the LORD had said.* [6]*He buried him in Moab…but to this day no one knows where his grave is.* [7]*Moses was a hundred and twenty years old when he died, yet his eyes were not weak nor his strength gone.* [8]*The Israelites grieved for Moses in the plains of Moab thirty days, until the time of weeping and mourning was over.* [9]*Now* ***Joshua*** *[who replaced Moses as the leader of the Israelites]…was filled with the spirit of wisdom because Moses had laid his hands on him. So the Israelites listened to him and did what the LORD had commanded Moses.*

> [10]*Since then, no prophet has risen in Israel like Moses, whom the LORD knew face to face,* [11]*who did all those miraculous signs and wonders the LORD sent him to do in Egypt, to Pharaoh and to all his officials and to his whole land.* [12]*For no one has ever shown the mighty power or performed the awesome deeds that Moses did in the sight of all Israel."* Amen.

So dear friends, this is where the Torah concludes. Everything written in the Torah is recorded so that we might gain knowledge, knowledge that will lead us to faith in God's way of salvation. Truly, Moses was **a great prophet.** He knew the LORD God face to face. He performed miraculous signs from God. By the hand of Moses, God delivered the Israelites from the oppression of Pharaoh. Also by his hand, God has given us the Torah, the first book in the Holy Scriptures. Everyone should know what the prophet Moses wrote. Whoever does not know the Torah of Moses will be mistaken in much and is in great danger of perishing in the way of unrighteousness. Remember, the Torah is the foundation which God Himself laid, the foundation upon which God, through all the other prophets, would build the rest of His holy book.

Truly, the prophet Moses wrote amazing, profound and wonderful words. Yet of all that Moses did and wrote, nothing is more important than what he announced in the fifth section of the Torah, in chapter eighteen. In this chapter Moses told the Israelites how God planned to raise up **another, even greater, prophet who would speak directly for God**. Listen to what Moses told the people of Israel:

> (Deut. 18) [15]***The LORD your God will raise up for you a prophet like me from among your own brothers. You must listen to him.*** [16]*For this is what you asked of the LORD your God at Horeb (Mount Sinai) on the day of the assembly when you said, "Let us not hear the voice of the LORD our God nor see this great fire anymore, or we will die."* [17]*The LORD said to me:* ***"What they say is good.*** [18]***I will raise up for them a prophet like you from among their brothers; I will put my words in his mouth, and he will tell them everything I command him.*** [19]***If anyone does not listen to my words that the prophet speaks in my name, I myself will call him to account."***

By this declaration from the mouth of Moses, God was announcing the coming of another prophet who would come forth from the Hebrew nation (verses 15,18), a Man who would speak forth the Word of God in all fulness and purity (vs.18,19), a Prophet who would be a Mediator between God and man (vs.16,17). Do you know who that Prophet was? Do you know which Prophet spoke with even greater authority than Moses? Do you know which Prophet displayed works which were greater than the miracles performed by Moses? Yes, the Prophet of whom Moses spoke is **the righteous Redeemer**, who was born of a Jewish virgin. Concerning Him, Moses issued an early warning to the nation of Israel: ***"You must listen to him!...If anyone does not listen to my words that the prophet speaks in my name, I myself will call him to account."***

Friends, this is where our study of the Torah must end. How can we conclude our journey in this vast and wonderful book? Let us finish with what Moses himself proclaimed to the Israelites on the day he died. In chapter thirty-two Moses said:

> "***Listen, O heavens, and I will speak; hear, O earth, the words of my mouth....I will proclaim the name of the LORD. Oh, praise the greatness of our God! He is the Rock, His works are perfect, and all His ways are just. A faithful God who does no wrong, upright and just is He!***" (Deut. 32:1,3,4)

With those words of God from the mouth of Moses we bid you farewell today. Thank you for listening. Next time, God willing, we will begin the holy book which comes after (and is connected with) the Torah of Moses and see how God brought the Israelites into the land flowing with milk and honey just as He had promised them long before....

May God, who alone is worthy of glory and majesty forever, bless you! The prophet Moses said it perfectly:

> ***"The LORD...is...a faithful God who does no wrong! Upright and just is He!"*** (Deut. 32:4) Amen!

LESSON 44

JOSHUA AND THE LAND OF CANAAN

JOSHUA

Peace be with you, listening friends. We greet you in the name of God, the Lord of peace, who wants everyone to understand and submit to the way of righteousness that He has established, and have true peace with Him forever. We are happy to be able to return today to present your program *The Way of Righteousness*.

In our last program we concluded our study of the Torah of Moses, the first book in the Writings of the Prophets. In the holy Torah, we learned how sin entered the world and brought along with it a curse. However, we also saw how the LORD God, in His wonderful plan, promised to send into the world a Savior who would redeem the children of Adam from the curse which sin brought. To move forward with His plan to send the Savior into the world, God called Abraham to leave his father's house and country and move to the faraway land of Canaan. God planned to make of Abraham a new nation through which the Redeemer would descend. After Abraham arrived in the land of Canaan, God appeared to him again and promised him, saying, "*The land of Canaan in which you are now a stranger, I am going to give it to your descendants, as a possession forever!*" Today we will see **how God fulfilled what He promised Abraham** long beforehand, and **delivered the land of Canaan to Abraham's descendants**, the Israelites. Canaan is the land that today is called **Israel**.

Last time, in the final chapter of the Torah, we heard how **Moses** died on the mountain overlooking Canaan. After Moses died, **Joshua**, his assistant, became the new leader. {Lit. in Wolof: *inherited the burden*} Joshua was designated by God to replace Moses. We have seen Joshua several times already. The distinguishing characteristic of Joshua was that he believed all that God promised, even when most of the Israelites did not believe. Joshua was one of the two spies who believed God when the Israelites first arrived at the border of the land of Canaan. The Israelites were ready to throw stones and kill him, simply because he encouraged them to believe the LORD and possess the land of Canaan. Today we will see that this same Joshua, whom the Israelites rejected forty years earlier was the very one whom God chose to be the leader who would take them into the land of Canaan!

The book of Joshua, which we are reading today, is found in the Holy Scriptures, between the Torah {*Taurat*} and the Psalms {*Zabur*}. The book of Joshua recounts how God fulfilled what He had promised Abraham long ago when He said to him, "*I will give to [you and your descendants] the whole land of Canaan as an everlasting possession!*" (Gen. 17:8)

At this point in our chronological study, the Israelites did not yet have a country of their own. They were still wanderers in the desert. Moreover the land of Canaan in which they were to live was full of giants who were mighty warriors. However, the Almighty God planned to expel the inhabitants of Canaan and to exterminate them because of their many repulsive sins, and entrust that abundant land to the Israelites.

Now let us see how Joshua and the Israelites entered the land, conquered it and possessed it. In the first chapter, the Scripture says:

> (Josh. 1) [1]*After the death of Moses the servant of the LORD, the LORD said to Joshua, son of Nun, Moses' assistant:* [2]*"Moses my servant is dead. Now then, you and all these people, get ready to cross the Jordan River into the land I am about to give to them, to the Israelites.* [3]***I will give you every place where you set your foot, as I promised Moses.*** [4]*Your territory will extend from the great river…to the Great Sea on the west.* [5]*No one will be able to stand up against you all the days of your life. As I was with Moses, so I will be with you; I will never leave you nor forsake you."*
>
> [6]*"Be strong and courageous, because you will lead these people to inherit the land I swore to their forefathers to give them.* [9]***Have I not commanded you? Be strong and courageous. Do not be terrified; do not be discouraged, for the LORD your God will be with you wherever you go.*** *"* [10]*So Joshua ordered the officers of the people:* [11]*"Go through the camp and tell the people, 'Get your supplies ready. Three days from now you will cross the Jordan here to go in and take possession of the land the LORD your God is giving you for your own.'"*

After this, the Scriptures tell how Joshua sent **two spies**, saying to them, "Go, look over the land, especially **Jericho.**" The two spies went and investigated the city of Jericho and the tall, solid walls which surrounded the city. At night the two spies hid in Jericho, staying in the house of a prostitute named **Rahab**. However, some people of Jericho saw the Israeli spies enter the house of Rahab. They immediately informed the king, telling him, "Some of the Israelites are in the city to spy." The king sent soldiers to the house of Rahab to arrest them, but Rahab hid them on the roof.

After the soldiers left, Rahab called the spies, saying to them, "I know that the LORD, your God, is the true God. I know too that your God will deliver into your hands my city and all the land of Canaan. All the people of the land are greatly afraid of you, because they have heard how your God opened the Red Sea before you and how He has destroyed all your enemies. I believe that the LORD your God is the true God! Therefore, I ask you to swear to me that when you come and conquer our city, that you will protect me and my family, and deliver us from death!" The two spies answered, "When God delivers your city into our hands, we will protect you and all those who are in the house with you."

In chapter three, the Scriptures recount how the people of Israel needed to cross the **Jordan River** to enter the land of Canaan, but the river was deep and wide. How could a multitude of two or three million cross the wide river? Ah, that is easy to answer, because the LORD God Almighty who opened a path for them through the Red Sea had not changed! God again opened a path for the Israelites, this time through the Jordan River. Thus, they passed through the midst of the waters on dry ground. All the Israelites crossed the river, arriving in front of the great city of Jericho. The people of Jericho had closed the gates of the city. No one could enter the city; no one could leave.

In chapter five, the Scriptures tell us that, when Joshua was near Jericho, he lifted his head and saw a man with a drawn sword in his hand standing before him. Joshua asked him, "Are you our friend or our foe?" He answered him, "I am **the commander of the army** of the LORD God!" Joshua fell face down to the ground. Then He who was called the commander of the army of God said to Joshua, "Take off your sandals, for the place where you are standing is holy." Joshua did as he was told.

Friends, do you know who was talking with Joshua? It was the LORD Himself who was making a brief appearance! We have already seen how God appeared to Abraham as a man and spoke with him, and how He appeared to Moses in the flames of a fire in a bush. And now we see how God appeared to Joshua as a mighty commander holding a sword!

Thus, the LORD God told Joshua,

> *"See, I have delivered Jericho into your hands, along with its king and its fighting men. March around the city once with all the armed men. Do this for six days. Make seven priests carry trumpets of rams' horns in front of the ark. On the seventh day, march around the city seven times, with the priests blowing the trumpets. When you hear them sound a long blast on the trumpets, make all the people give a loud shout; then the wall of the city will collapse and the soldiers will go up, every man straight in."* (Josh. 6:2-5)

Then the LORD finished speaking to Joshua and left.

Joshua immediately went to the Israelites and told them everything the LORD had commanded him. Then Joshua ordered them to take the ark (chest) of the covenant and march around the city once. But he told them, "Do not say a word until the day I give you the command to shout. Then you can shout." After they had marched around the city one time, they went back to the camp and spent the night there. On the second day, they marched around the city once and returned to camp. This is what they did for the first six days.

But on the seventh day, at daybreak they arose and marched around the city seven times. After they had circled the city the seventh time, the priests sounded the trumpet blast. Then Joshua commanded the multitude, "*Shout! for the* LORD *has given you the city!*" (Josh. 6:16)

When the Israelites heard the trumpet sound, they shouted a great shout, and the walls around the city collapsed! The men of Israel then entered the city, every man going straight in. Thus we see how Joshua and the Israelites conquered the first city in the land of Canaan. On that day all the people of Jericho died, except Rahab and her family, just as the two spies had promised her. The house of Rahab did not collapse, because she had turned from idols and placed her trust in the God of Israel.

Why were Joshua and the Israelites able to conquer that heavily fortified city and enter the land which God had promised them? They conquered it because they **believed** the Word of God. God is with those who believe His Word. Why did Rahab not die with the people of Jericho when the city fell? She survived because she did not stop at merely being amazed by God's power; she **believed** Him to the point of taking sides with the people of God. That is what the Scripture declares when it says:

> "*By* ***faith*** *the walls of Jericho fell, after the people had marched around them for seven days. By* ***faith*** *the prostitute Rahab, because she welcomed the spies, was not killed with those who were disobedient....And* ***without faith it is impossible to please God****, because anyone who comes to him must* ***believe*** *that he exists and that he rewards those who earnestly seek him.*" (Heb. 11:30,31,6)

We wish we could share with you more of the stories contained in the Book of Joshua, but time does not allow us to do so. In summary, you should know that this book describes in detail how God was with Joshua and the Israelites, and how He delivered to them the land of Canaan, city by city, just as He had promised. Thus, in chapter twenty-one, the Scripture says: "*God gave the Israelites all the land!...God gave them rest on every side!...God handed all their enemies over to them!*" (Joshua 21:43,44)

Friends, did God fulfil what He had promised Abraham and his descendants long beforehand? Did God give the land of Canaan to the Israelites as He said He would? Yes He did! God is faithful (to keep His covenants)! Everything

He promises, He will do, even if man thinks He is slow in doing so. The LORD God longed to be gracious to the children of Israel and give them the plentiful land of Canaan, but He was waiting for them to trust Him. As we saw, the Israelites **wasted many years before they began to believe** what God had promised them. Their parents did not inherit the blessings of the land of Canaan, because they did not believe the promises of God.

How about you? Do you believe God? We are not asking you if you believe in the existence of God or in the oneness of God. The devil himself knows that God exists and that God is One! The question you must answer today is: Do you believe **God Himself**? Do you **love** Him? Do you trust **the Word of God** with all your heart? Do you **know** what God has reserved for those who believe Him? Do you **possess** the everlasting life and the Holy Spirit which God gives to every person who believes His Good News? Most of the children of Adam believe that God exists. Yet, sadly, those who **know** and **believe** the great and precious promises of God are few. Listening friend, God loves you and wants to bless you beyond what you can even imagine, but you must **know** His word, **believe** it and **receive** it! Concerning this, the Holy Scripture declares:

> *"No eye has seen, no ear has heard, no mind has conceived what God has prepared for those who love Him."* (1 Cor. 2:9) *"We do not want you to become lazy, but to imitate those who through **faith and patience** inherit what **has** been promised!"* (Heb. 6:12)

Thank you for listening....God bless you as you consider this exhortation from the Word of God:

> ***"We do not want you to become lazy, but to imitate those who through faith and patience inherit what has been promised!"*** (Heb. 6:12)

Lesson 45

Judges and Ruth

Judges & Ruth

Peace be with you, listening friends. We greet you in the name of God, the Lord of peace, who wants everyone to understand and submit to the way of righteousness that He has established, and have true peace with Him forever. We are happy to be able to return today to present your program *The Way of Righteousness.*

Today, in the last half of our program, we plan to look at a touching "**love story**" recorded in the Holy Scriptures–so don't go away! In our last program we saw how Joshua the servant of Moses led the Israelites into Canaan. We read how God went before Joshua and the Israelites to expel their enemies and bring them into the abundant land of Canaan, just as He had promised their ancestor Abraham long beforehand. Today we plan to look at the two holy books which follow the book of Joshua. They are the books of **Judges and Ruth**. These two books show us what happened **between** the time of the **prophet Joshua** and the time of **the prophet David**.

Before we get into the book of Judges, we should read the message Joshua entrusted to the Israelites before he died. In the last chapter of the book of Joshua, Joshua met with all the leaders of the Israelites to warn them and encourage them to love and obey the LORD their God who had freed them from Egypt and given them the beautiful land in which they were now living. In His last speech to them, Joshua said to them,

> *"If serving the* LORD *seems undesirable to you, then* ***choose for yourselves this day whom you will serve****, whether the gods your forefathers served beyond the River, or the gods of the Amorites, in whose land you are living.* ***But as for me and my household, we will serve the*** **LORD***." Then the multitude of the Israelites answered Joshua saying, "We too will serve the* LORD*, because He is our God!"* (Josh. 24:15,18)

Now let's look at what really happened. In Judges, chapter two, the Scripture says:

> (Judg. 2) [7]***The people served the LORD throughout the lifetime of Joshua*** *and of the elders who outlived him and who had seen all the great things the LORD had done for Israel.* [8]*Joshua...the servant of the LORD, died at the age of a hundred and ten.* [9]*And they buried him...in the hill country of Ephraim.* [10]*After that whole generation had been gathered to their fathers, another generation grew up, who knew neither the LORD nor what he had done for Israel.* [11]***Then the Israelites did evil in the eyes of the LORD*** *and served the Baals.* [12]*They forsook the LORD, the God of their fathers, who had brought them out of Egypt. They followed and worshiped various gods of the peoples around them. They provoked the LORD to anger* [13]*because they forsook him and served Baal.*

Thus, the Israelites forgot the LORD their God, turned their back on Him, and **began to follow the religions of the nations around them**. However, those nations did not know the true God and did not have His Word. They worshiped Baal. Baal was an idol which the people of Canaan claimed was God. They made for themselves images which were representations of Baal and worshiped them. The nations who gave praise to Baal **thought they were worshiping God**. But in reality, they were worshiping their own desires and Satan; however they did not know it because Satan had deceived them. Satan also deceived many Israelites, which was why they turned from the LORD God and began to worship Baal as the nations around them did.

Thus we see how most of the Israelites turned their back on the way which God had established, which was the way of the Law of Moses and the animal sacrifice on the altar to cover sin. Instead of following God's way of righteousness, they followed a false way, that is, the way of the religion of Baal. The first commandment of the Ten Commandments which God spoke to Moses on Mount Sinai, says:

> *"You shall have no other gods before me...for I, the LORD your God, am a jealous God, punishing the children for the sin of the fathers to the third and fourth generation of those who hate me, but showing love to a thousand [generations] of those who love me and keep my commandments."* (Exod. 20:3,5,6)

But most of the Israelites did not honor the LORD God, which is why God punished them.

Continuing in chapter two of the book of Judges, the Scripture says:

> (Judg. 2) [11]*Then* ***the Israelites did evil*** *in the eyes of the LORD and served the Baals...* [14]*In his anger against Israel* ***the LORD handed them over*** *to raiders who plundered them. He sold them to their enemies all around, whom they were no longer able to resist.* [15]*Whenever Israel went out to fight, the hand of the*

> *LORD was against them to defeat them, just as he had sworn to them. They were in great distress.*

Thus, the book of Judges recounts how the Israelites hardened their hearts and turned from the LORD, again and again. That is why God handed them over to their enemies time after time, to punish them, so that they would acknowledge their sin and repent and be saved from destruction. Every time the Israelites truly repented, God raised up for them leaders (judges) to save them from their enemies. We would like to tell you about such heroes as Gideon who defeated a huge, powerful army with just three hundred men, or about Samson who singlehandedly overcame a thousand soldiers, but time does not allow us to do so. Perhaps you will read their fascinating stories for yourselves in the book of Judges.

In summary, the book of Judges shows us that each time the Israelites strayed from God and His Word, the LORD would punish them so that they would turn from their sin and return to Him. When they repented, God would provide for them a leader to rescue them from their enemies. That is the story of **the book of Judges** in brief.

Yes, the Israelites transgressed against God again and again. But could their unfaithfulness hinder God's faithfulness? Never! Truly, God punished every individual who sinned, but He preserved the nation of Israel as a whole, because God could not forget what He had promised Abraham long beforehand when He said to him, "*All peoples on earth will be blessed through your offspring.*" God planned to make of Abraham's descendants a nation which would bring to the earth **the Savior of the world**. Nothing could hinder God's wonderful design: not the sin of the Israelites, not Pharaoh, not the people of Egypt, not the people of Canaan, not a false religion like that of Baal, not even Satan himself. **Nothing could hinder God's plan to send down the Savior of the world through the nation of Israel**!

Now, we must look at the short book that follows the book of Judges: **the book of Ruth**. The story of this book is a marvelous story. It is like a lovely flower growing in the midst of a smelly garbage dump, because it tells **the story of a woman who loved God in the midst of a crooked and depraved generation**.

We cannot read to you the whole book of Ruth today, but we can summarize it for you. What you must first know is that **Ruth** was a widow and that she did not belong to the nation of Israel. She belonged to the people of **Moab** and lived in the land of Moab, which was situated south of the land of Israel. Also, you should know that the people of Moab were idolaters and despised both the God of Israel and the Israelites.

Ruth belonged to the nation of Moab, but this did not cause her to despise the God of Israel. No, in fact, **Ruth believed in the God of Israel with all**

her heart. Ruth had heard how the LORD God had performed awesome miracles in delivering the multitude of Israel from the hands of the Egyptians. Also, Ruth had heard the reliable words which the prophet Moses had written in the Torah concerning the way of salvation which God had established. Ruth believed in the LORD with all her heart, and accepted the message that He sent down to the Israelites.

So then, what we must observe concerning Ruth is this: she lived in Moab among idolaters. Ruth's parents were idolaters. And Ruth was born into their religion. But now **Ruth no longer believed the religion of her father**. The God of Israel was the One in whom Ruth believed. Thus we see that Ruth had a choice to make and it was not easy! Should Ruth remain in her father's house, continue in her father's religion and marry a man who did not know the God of Israel? Or should she turn her back on her father's house and religion and move to Israel? That is the difficult choice that Ruth had to make!

Before we find out which path Ruth chose, you should also know that Ruth had a sister-in-law named **Orpah**. Like Ruth, Orpah also knew about the God of Israel. Thus, Ruth's sister-in-law also **had to choose** between continuing in the religion of her father or following the LORD God of Abraham, Isaac and Jacob.

Which path did Ruth and Orpah chose? Orpah chose **the easier path**, that is, to remain in her father's house and marry a man who shared her father's religion. But Ruth chose **the difficult path**, that is, to leave her father's house and move to the land of Israel. Ruth knew that no one can worship two gods. One could not mix worshiping the God of Israel and worshiping the idols of Moab. That is why Ruth turned her back on her father's religion. Ruth decided, **it is better to obey God than to obey man.** Ruth was willing to be misunderstood by her family and friends in order to follow the true and living God. As the Wolofs say, "Whoever wants honey must brave the bees." Thus Ruth left her father's house, and moved to the land of Israel, to a small town called ***Bethlehem***.

Now a man lived in Bethlehem whose name was **Boaz**. Boaz was **the son of Rahab**, the woman who escaped from the disaster which fell on the city of Jericho (as we saw in our last lesson). Boaz was a righteous man, and greatly treasured the Word of God. Boaz also had riches and many fields of grain, but he did not yet have a wife.

The Scriptures recount how Ruth, who now lived in the city of Bethlehem, had the habit of leaving early in the morning every day to go to the fields to gather (glean) the barley {Wolof: *millet*} which the harvesters had dropped. Ruth was a poor peasant and according to the law which God gave Moses for the Israelites, the poor were allowed to glean in this way, so that they might not go hungry. Thus the Scriptures tell us how God led Ruth to go and glean in the field of Boaz, the son of Rahab.

Boaz noticed Ruth gleaning in his field and spoke with her. Boaz quickly recognized the beauty of Ruth's character. Boaz was a righteous man and saw that Ruth was a virtuous woman. Can you guess what happened? It isn't too hard to figure out! Yes, Boaz and Ruth **fell in love** with each other and eventually got married. Ruth put God and His Word first in her life and God blessed her for it. Thus, the Scripture says: Boaz and Ruth had a son named **Obed**. Obed became the father of **Jesse**, and Jesse became the father of **David** who became the great king of the nation of Israel, and the prophet who wrote many of the **Psalms**. And from David's offspring **the Redeemer** arose, that is, the Savior of the world, of whom all the prophets prophesied.

Thus we see today how God worked in the life of Ruth, a woman who was not of the nation of Israel. **While the Israelites turned their backs on the LORD their God to follow the religions of the surrounding nations, Ruth turned her back on the religion of her father to follow the God of Israel!** Thus, God led Ruth to live in Bethlehem to marry Boaz, and to become the great-grandmother of David, king of Israel. In all of this, we can see how God was moving forward with His plan to bring **the Redeemer** into the world, because it was from **the descendants of David** and **in the town of Bethlehem** that the Savior of the world was destined to be born.

This is where we must stop. Next time, God willing, we will get into the book that recounts the life of the prophet David who was born in Bethlehem and descended from Ruth and Boaz. Today we bid you farewell with a question: **Who are you most like?** Are you more like Orpah, Ruth's sister-in-law, who chose **the easy path**? Or are you like courageous Ruth, who turned her back on her father's religion to follow **the One true God**?

Thank you for listening....God bless you as you remember what the prophet Joshua told the Israelites before he died:

> ***"Choose for yourselves this day whom you will serve...As for me and my household, we will serve the LORD!"*** (Josh. 24:15)

PART 2

THE WAY OF RIGHTEOUSNESS
ACCORDING TO

THE PSALMS AND THE PROPHETS

Some of the people studied in this section:

Samuel
Saul
David
Goliath
Bathsheba
Solomon
Elijah
Jonah
Isaiah
Jeremiah
Daniel
Zechariah
Malachi

"Do you believe the prophets?"
ACTS 26:27

LESSON 46

SAMUEL, SAUL, AND DAVID

1 SAMUEL 1-16; PSALMS 8,23

Peace be with you, listening friends. We greet you in the name of God, the Lord of peace, who wants everyone to understand and submit to the way of righteousness that He has established, and have true peace with Him forever. We are happy to be able to return today to present your program *The Way of Righteousness*.

In our last program, we saw that the time following the prophet Joshua was a **dark and corrupt period** in the history of the nation of Israel. But even in that dark time we observed the light of the faithfulness of God. The LORD had not forgotten what He had promised to Abraham and his descendants concerning the Redeemer who was to come forth from the nation of Israel.

Thus we saw how God was at work in the life of a woman called **Ruth**. Ruth was not an Israelite, but she believed in the God of Israel with all her heart. And while many Israelites turned from the LORD their God to follow the religions of the surrounding nations, Ruth chose to turn from the religion of her father to follow the God of Israel. Ruth moved to the land of Israel and settled in the town of Bethlehem where she married an Israelite named Boaz. Boaz and Ruth had a son named Obed; and Obed begot Jesse, the father of the prophet **David**. Thus God's plan to redeem the children of Adam from their sins was moving ahead, because it was **through the descendants of David** that **the Redeemer** would come into the world. It was in **Bethlehem**, David's hometown, that the Savior was to be born. In future lessons, we will hear how God's prophets predicted all these things and then how the Redeemer fulfilled them hundreds of years later. Only God could do such a thing!

The prophet David {*Dawud* in Arabic} is very prominent in the Holy Scriptures. His name appears more than one thousand times. What do **you** know about the prophet David? Perhaps you know that he was the young man who defeated Goliath, the giant, with just a sling and stone. You probably also know that David was a great king in Israel and the prophet who wrote much of the book of Psalms {*Zabur*}. If you know these things, that is great, but your knowledge of David should not end there. If we know that David was a great king, but do not know **what made him great**–of what use to us is such knowledge? Or if we know that David wrote the Word of God in the Psalms, but do not know **what he wrote**–of what use is that to us?

Friends, if you want to increase your knowledge concerning **the prophet David** and hear some of the wonderful and powerful words that he wrote in **the Psalms,** then we invite you to join us for today's study and for the next five lessons.

Do you know the name of the prophet of God who preceded the prophet David? It is the prophet **Samuel**. God chose Samuel to turn the people of Israel back to the LORD their God, because their hearts were very far from God. Today we will read from **the book of Samuel.** This holy book is important among the Writings of the Prophets, because it contains valuable stories from the life of Samuel and the first three kings of Israel: Saul, David and Solomon.

As we have seen, God gave the Israelites **leaders** such as Moses, Joshua and Samuel to guide and judge them. However, the LORD God, who delivered them from their bonds of slavery in Egypt, was **their rightful King.** God, who commanded them to make a special tent so that He could place His glory in their midst, wanted to be their Ruler. They were to obey and follow Him alone. However, most of the Israelites were not content to have just the LORD as their King. **They wanted to be like all the nations** of the world and have a son of Adam to reign over them as their king!

In chapter eight of the first book of Samuel, the Scripture says:

> (1 Sam. 8) [4]*So all the elders of Israel gathered together and came to Samuel at Ramah.* [5]*They said to him, "You are old, and your sons do not walk in your ways; now appoint* ***a king*** *to lead us,* ***such as all the other nations have****."* [6]*But when they said, "Give us a king to lead us," this displeased Samuel; so he prayed to the* LORD. [7]*And the* LORD *told him: "Listen to all that the people are saying to you; it is not you they have rejected, but they have rejected me as their king.* [8]*As they have done from the day I brought them up out of Egypt until this day, forsaking me and serving other gods, so they are doing to you.* [9]*Now listen to them; but warn them solemnly and let them know what the king who will reign over them will do."*

Thus, God told Samuel to give the people what they wanted and to appoint a king for them. God did not want the Israelites to have another king besides Him, but since they had rejected God's reign, God would not rule over them by force. In the next chapter, we see how Samuel appointed for the Israelites a man by the name of **Saul**. The Scripture says: "*Then Samuel took a flask of oil and poured it on Saul's head.*" (1 Sam. 10:1) That is what the Israelites did whenever they appointed someone. They poured oil on the head of the prophet, priest or king to set him apart. After Samuel poured oil on Saul's head, he said to all the people, "'*Do you see the man the LORD has chosen? There is no one like him among all the people.' Then the people shouted, 'Long live the king!*" (1 Sam. 10:24)

At first, the Israelites rejoiced greatly in their king, Saul. He was strong and brave, and young and handsome, and taller than all the other children of Israel. By outward appearances, Saul should have been an excellent king. But God does not evaluate things as man does. Man looks at the **outward appearance**, but God looks at the **heart**. King Saul started out well, but, in time, he became proud and jealous and self-sufficient. Saul honored God with his lips, but his heart was far from Him. Saul did not respect and obey the Word of God. He did what he wanted to do instead of what God wanted him to do.

Thus, the Scripture tells us that some years after Saul was appointed king,

> (1 Sam. 15) [10]*...the word of the LORD came to Samuel:* [11]*"I am grieved that I have made Saul king, because* ***he has turned away from me and has not carried out my instructions****." Samuel was troubled, and he cried out to the LORD all that night.* [12]*Early in the morning Samuel got up and went to meet Saul...*[13]*When Samuel reached him, Saul said, "The LORD bless you! I have carried out the LORD's instructions."...* [22]*But Samuel replied: "Does the LORD delight in burnt offerings and sacrifices as much as obeying the voice of the LORD? To obey is better than sacrifice, and to heed is better than the fat of rams.* [23]*For rebellion is like the sin of divination, and arrogance like the evil of idolatry.* ***Because you have rejected the word of the LORD, he has rejected you as king****!"*

Thus, Samuel told Saul that the kingdom would be taken from him and given to another. In the next chapter, the Scripture says,

> (1 Sam. 16) [1]*The LORD said to Samuel, "How long will you mourn for Saul, since I have rejected him as king over Israel? Fill your horn with oil and be on your way; I am sending you to* **Jesse of Bethlehem**. *I have chosen* **one of his sons** *to be king."* [2]*But Samuel said, "How can I go? Saul will hear about it and kill me." The LORD said, "Take a heifer with you and say, 'I have come to sacrifice to the LORD.'* [3]*Invite Jesse to the sacrifice, and I will show you what to do. You are to anoint for me the one I indicate."* [4]*Samuel did what the LORD said. When he arrived at Bethlehem, the elders of the town trembled when they met him. They asked, "Do you come in peace?"* [5]*Samuel replied, "Yes, in peace; I have come to sacrifice to the LORD. Consecrate yourselves and come to the sacrifice with me." Then he consecrated Jesse and his sons and invited them to the sacrifice.* [6]*When they arrived, Samuel saw Eliab and thought, "Surely the LORD's anointed stands here before the LORD."* [7]*But the LORD said to Samuel,*

> *"Do not consider his appearance or his height, for I have rejected him.* ***The LORD does not look at the things man looks at. Man looks at the outward appearance, but the LORD looks at the heart****."*
>
> [8]*Then Jesse called Abinadab and made him pass in front of Samuel. But Samuel said, "The LORD has not chosen this one either."* [9]*Jesse then made Shammah pass by, but Samuel said, "Nor has the LORD chosen this one."* [10]*Jesse made seven of his sons pass before Samuel, but Samuel said to him, "The LORD has not chosen these."* [11]*So he asked Jesse, "Are these all the sons you have?" "There is still* ***the youngest****," Jesse answered, "but he is tending the sheep." Samuel said, "Send for him; we will not sit down until he arrives."* [12]*So he sent and had him brought in. He was ruddy, with a fine appearance and handsome features. Then the LORD said, "Rise and anoint him; he is the one."* [13]*So Samuel took the horn of oil and anointed him in the presence of his brothers, and from that day on the Spirit of the LORD came upon* ***David*** *in power.*

Thus we see how God appointed **David** to be the king of Israel after Saul. But you must understand that David did not become the king of Israel on that day. David was only a youth and the time which God ordained for him to reign over the nation of Israel had not yet come. In fact, David would have to wait ten years before he would sit on the throne of Israel.

So David returned to the fields surrounding Bethlehem to tend and guard his father's flocks. David was a good and faithful shepherd. He feared nothing because **he trusted in the LORD**. For example, one day, when David was tending his father's sheep, a lion snatched up one of them. David went after the lion, struck it and rescued the sheep from its mouth. When the lion turned on him, David seized it by its hair, struck and killed it. (1 Sam. 17:35)

David was not only an excellent shepherd; he could play the harp and sing too. The Spirit of God inspired David to compose many hymns and to write them in the book of **Psalms** {Zabur}. Oh, how David loved the Lord God and His Word!

We would like to conclude today's program with a few excerpts from the Psalms of David. Try to imagine David in the lush fields, among the sheep, playing the harp and praising God with songs and thanksgivings produced by the Spirit of God. Listen:

> "**O LORD, *our Lord, how majestic is your name in all the earth***!...*When I consider your heavens, the work of your fingers, the moon and the stars, which you have set in place, what is man that you are mindful of him, the son of man that you care for him? You made him a little lower than the heavenly beings and crowed him with glory and honor....O LORD, our Lord, how majestic is your name in all the earth!" (Psa. 8:1,3-5,9)*
>
> "***Your word is a lamp*** *to my feet and a light for my path! I have hidden your*

word in my heart that I might not sin against you!" (*Psa. 119:105,11*) *"The law of the LORD is perfect, reviving the soul! The statutes of the LORD are trustworthy, making wise the simple! The precepts of the LORD are right, giving joy to the heart. The commands of the LORD are radiant, giving light to the eyes! They are more precious than gold, than much pure gold; they are sweeter than honey, than honey from the comb! By them is your servant warned; in keeping them there is* great reward!" (Psa. 19:7,8,10,11)

"**The LORD is my shepherd**, *I shall not be in want. He makes me lie down in green pastures; he leads me beside quiet waters; he restores my soul. He guides me in paths of righteousness for his name's sake. Even though I walk through the valley of the shadow of death, I will fear no evil, for you are with me; your rod and your staff, they comfort me. You prepare a table before me in the presence of my enemies. You anoint my head with oil; my cup overflows. Surely goodness and love will follow me all the days of my life, and I will dwell in the house of the LORD forever!"* (Psa. 23) Amen!

Friends, thank you for listening. In the next lesson, we plan to continue the story of David and see how God was with him as he faced Goliath, the giant....

God bless you as you think about what God told Samuel:

> ***"The LORD does not look at the things man looks at. Man looks at the outward appearance, but the LORD looks at the heart."*** (1 Sam. 16:7)

Lesson 47

David and Goliath

1 Samuel 17; Psalm 27

Peace be with you, listening friends. We greet you in the name of God, the Lord of peace, who wants everyone to understand and submit to the way of righteousness that He has established, and have true peace with Him forever. We are happy to be able to return today to present your program *The Way of Righteousness*.

In the last program we began to look at the prophet David. Listen to what God testified concerning him: "*I have found* ***David*** *son of Jesse a man after my own heart; he will do everything I want him to do.*" (Acts 13:22) We saw how God appointed David to be the second King of Israel, because the first king, Saul, did not obey the word of God. However, David did not become the king of Israel on the day that God appointed him. He was still a youth, and God's time for him to receive the kingdom had not yet arrived. After being anointed as king, David returned to the fields outside the town of Bethlehem to tend his father's flocks.

Today we will read a wonderful story that shows how God was with David, because David walked with God. Our lesson is called "**David and Goliath.**" Let us now continue in the first book of Samuel, chapter seventeen. The Scripture says:

> (1 Sam. 17) [1]*Now the* ***Philistines*** *[who were the most vicious enemies of Israel] gathered their forces for war…* [2]***Saul and the Israelites*** *assembled and camped in the Valley of Elah and drew up their battle line to meet the Philistines.* [3]*The Philistines occupied one hill and the Israelites another, with the valley between them.*
>
> [4]*A champion named* ***Goliath****, who was from Gath, came out of the Philistine camp. He was over three meters tall.* [5]*He had a bronze helmet on his head and wore a coat of scale armor of bronze weighing 60 kilos;* [6]*on his legs he wore bronze greaves, and a bronze javelin was slung on his back.* [7]*His spear shaft was like a weaver's rod, and its iron point weighed seven kilos. His shield-bearer went ahead of him.*
>
> [8]*Goliath stood and shouted to the ranks of Israel, "Why do you come out and*

line up for battle? Am I not a Philistine, and are you not the servants of Saul? Choose a man and have him come down to me. [9]*If he is able to fight and kill me, we will become your subjects; but if I overcome him and kill him, you will become our subjects and serve us."* [10]*Then the Philistine said, "This day I defy the ranks of Israel! Give me a man and let us fight each other."* [11]*On hearing the Philistine's words,* ***Saul and all the Israelites were dismayed and terrified.***

While Goliath was taunting Israel, **David** was tending his father's flocks in peace, far from the war, meditating upon the Word of God, playing his harp and singing to the LORD. However, David had three older brothers who were soldiers in the army of Israel. One day David's father came to him and said, **"Go and visit your brothers** on the battlefront and bring me word about how things are going." So David left his sheep with another shepherd, arose early in the morning and left for the battlefield.

While David was greeting his older brothers and speaking with them, Goliath, the champion of the Philistines, stepped out from his lines facing the soldiers of Israel and threatened them as he had been doing for the past forty days. When the Israeli soldiers saw him, they ran from him in fear. Then someone said to David, "Do you see that man? He keeps defying us. Whoever kills him, king Saul will give him great wealth and will also give him his daughter in marriage and his father's family will not have to pay taxes."

Then David said, "That uncircumcised Philistine, who is he that he should defy the armies of the living God?" When he said that, David's older brother became angry with him and said, "Why have you come here? And with whom did you leave those few sheep in the desert? I know why you have come here. You only want to watch the battle!" However, one of the Israeli soldiers heard the courageous words which David spoke concerning the giant, and went and reported them to Saul, the king. Then Saul sent for David and questioned him.

Thus, the Scripture says:

(1 Sam. 17) [32]***David said to Saul*, "Let no one lose heart** *on account of this Philistine; your servant will go and fight him."* [33]*Saul replied, "You are not able to go out against this Philistine and fight him; you are only a boy, and he has been a fighting man from his youth."* [34]*But David said to Saul, "Your servant has been keeping his father's sheep. When a lion or a bear came and carried off a sheep from the flock,* [35]*I went after it, struck it and rescued the sheep from its mouth. When it turned on me, I seized it by its hair, struck it and killed it.* [36]*Your servant has killed both the lion and the bear; this uncircumcised Philistine will be like one of them, because he has defied the armies of the living God.* [37]*The LORD who delivered me from the paw of the lion and the paw of the bear will deliver me from the hand of this Philistine." Saul said to David, "Go, and the LORD be with*

> *you."* [38]*Then Saul dressed David in his own tunic. He put a coat of armor on him and a bronze helmet on his head.* [39]*David fastened on his sword over the tunic and tried walking around, because he was not used to them. "I cannot go in these," he said to Saul, "because I am not used to them." So he took them off.*
>
> [40]*Then he took his staff in his hand, chose* ***five smooth stones*** *from the stream, put them in the pouch of his shepherd's bag and, with his* ***sling*** *in his hand, approached the Philistine.* [41]*Meanwhile, the Philistine, with his shield-bearer in front of him, kept coming closer to David.* [42]*He looked David over and saw that he was only a boy, ruddy and handsome, and he despised him.* [43]*He said to David, "Am I a dog, that you come at me with sticks?" And the Philistine cursed David by his gods.* [44]*"Come here," he said, "and I'll give your flesh to the birds of the air and the beasts of the field!"*
>
> [45]*David said to the Philistine, "You come against me with sword and spear and javelin, but* ***I come against you in the name of the LORD Almighty****, the God of the armies of Israel, whom you have defied.* [46]*This day the LORD will hand you over to me, and I'll strike you down and cut off your head. Today I will give the carcasses of the Philistine army to the birds of the air and the beasts of the earth, and the whole world will know that there is a God in Israel.* [47]*All those gathered here will know that it is not by sword or spear that the LORD saves;* ***for the battle is the LORD's****, and he will give all of you into our hands."*
>
> [48]*As the Philistine moved closer to attack him, David ran quickly toward the battle line to meet him.* [49]*Reaching into his bag and taking out a stone, he slung it and struck the Philistine on the forehead. The stone sank into his forehead, and he fell face down on the ground.* [50]*So* ***David triumphed*** *over the Philistine with a sling and a stone; without a sword in his hand he struck down the Philistine and killed him.* [51]*David ran and stood over him. He took hold of the Philistine's sword and drew it from the scabbard. After he killed him, he cut off his head with the sword. When the Philistines saw that their hero was dead, they turned and ran.* [52]*Then the men of Israel and Judah surged forward with a shout and pursued the Philistines to the gates of Ekron.*

Thus, we see today how young David saved his nation from their enemies with a **sling**, a **stone**, and a **solid faith in the living God**. Truly, the story of David and Goliath is an amazing story with many important lessons.

We saw how Saul and the Israeli soldiers feared Goliath greatly. None of them dared to fight with him, but David was not afraid of the giant; he knocked him to the ground and killed him! Why were Saul and his soldiers afraid, but David was not afraid? What was the difference between David and the Israeli soldiers? We can summarize the difference between them in this way: David was not afraid of the giant, because he had **confidence in the LORD God**. Saul and his soldiers did not have confidence in God. Therefore, they were afraid of the giant.

Saul and his soldiers only saw **the powerful giant**. David saw **the Almighty God**! Saul and the Israeli soldiers had a form of religion, but that did not cause them to have a real relationship with God. Belonging to a religion does not cause you to belong to God. Saul and his soldiers knew very well that God exists, that God is one, and that He is great and powerful. But that knowledge could not save them from Goliath. However, David had a genuine relationship with the Living God, the Almighty! David knew God and walked with Him. David believed the promises of God. That is why David was not afraid of Goliath.

You who are listening today, who are you most like? David? Or Saul and his soldiers? Do you know God personally? Or have you just heard a few things about Him? Do you know the Word of God so well that it fills your heart with joy? Or are you only trying to fulfil your religious obligations? Do you have a solid and happy relationship with the living God? Or do you only have dry religion?

Listen to what the prophet David wrote in the Psalms, concerning the relationship he had with God. He said:

> "***The LORD is my shepherd***, *I shall not be in want. Even though I walk through the valley of the shadow of death, I will fear no evil, for you are with me…Surely goodness and love will follow me all the days of my life, and I will dwell in the house of the LORD forever!*" (Psa. 23:1,4,6)

How about you? Do you have a close relationship with the LORD God? Do you know Him as your Shepherd? Are you certain that you will dwell in His house in heaven forever? David had that confidence, because he knew the wonderful and precious promises of the LORD God. And he didn't just know them **in his head**; he believed them **in his heart**.

David had a genuine faith. His faith was not based upon the unreliable words of men. His faith was based upon the trustworthy Word of the LORD God who never abandons His people! Listen to what David wrote in the Psalms:

> "***The LORD is my light and my salvation, whom shall I fear?*** *The LORD is the stronghold of my life, of whom shall I be afraid?…Though an army besiege me, my heart will not fear; though war break out against me, even then will I be confident. One thing I ask of the LORD, this is what I seek: that I may dwell in the house of the LORD all the days of my life, to gaze upon the beauty of the LORD and to seek him in his temple….Hear my voice when I call, O LORD; be merciful to me and answer me. My heart says of you, 'Seek his face!'"* ***Your face, O LORD, I will seek!***" (Psa. 27:1,3,4,7,8)
>
> "***I love you, O LORD, my strength.*** *The LORD is my rock, my fortress and my deliverer; my God is my rock, in whom I take refuge. He is my shield….With your help I can advance against a troop; with my God I can scale a wall.* ***As for***

> ***God, his way is perfect; the word of the LORD is flawless. He is a shield for all who take refuge in him!*** (Psa. 18:1,2,29,30)

Thank you for listening. In our next lesson, Lord willing, we will continue with the story of the prophet David and see how he began to reign as the king of Israel....God bless you. We bid you farewell with this word from David in the book of Psalms:

> ***"Taste and see that the LORD is good; blessed is the man who takes refuge in Him!"*** (Psa. 34:8)

Lesson 48

King David and God's Promise

1 Samuel 18 – 2 Samuel 7

Peace be with you, listening friends. We greet you in the name of God, the Lord of peace, who wants everyone to understand and submit to the way of righteousness that He has established, and have true peace with Him forever. We are happy to be able to return today to present your program *The Way of Righteousness*.

Today we are continuing in the story of **the prophet David**. Two lessons ago, we saw how God chose young David to be the second king of Israel, though he did not begin to reign the day God appointed him. God rejected Saul, the first king, because he was unconcerned about doing the will of God. However, God testified concerning David, saying, "*I have found David, son of Jesse, a man after my own heart; he will do everything I want him to do.*" (Acts 13:22) In our last lesson, we saw David kill the giant, Goliath, defeating him with a sling and a stone and **a solid faith in the living God**. Now let us continue the story of David and see how David replaced Saul as the king of Israel.

Continuing in the first book of Samuel, the Scripture says:

> (1 Sam. 18) [6]*When the men were returning home after David had killed [Goliath] the Philistine, the women came out from all the towns of Israel to meet King Saul with singing and dancing, with joyful songs and with tambourines and lutes.* [7]*As they danced, they sang: "Saul has slain* ***his thousands****, and David* ***his tens of thousands****."* [8]*Saul was very angry; this refrain galled him. "They have credited David with tens of thousands," he thought, "but me with only thousands. What more can he get but the kingdom?"* [9]*And from that time on Saul kept* ***a jealous eye*** *on David.*

Thus, the Scriptures relate how the Israelites dearly loved David. But the more they loved David, the more Saul hated him. **Jealousy filled Saul's heart** and controlled him so that all he could think of was what he must do to get rid of David. Consequently, David fled and hid in the desert, together with the four hundred men of Israel who accompanied him. Saul and his soldiers hunted for David and his men in the wilderness. Saul did everything in his power to catch David and kill him. However, he could not do so because the LORD was with David. But Saul did cause David a lot of distress. For eight long years, David and his men had to run from an angry King Saul.

However, the jealousy and anger that Saul displayed toward David did not cause David to hate him. Why didn't David hate Saul, the man who was trying to kill him? David could not hate Saul, because **David walked with the God who causes His sun to rise on the righteous and the unrighteous**. As the Scripture says:

> *"Everyone who loves has been born of God and knows God. Whoever does not love does not know God, because* ***God is love****. We love because He first loved us. If anyone says, 'I love God,' yet hates his brother, he is a liar. For anyone who does not love his brother, whom he has seen, cannot love God, whom he has not seen."* (1 John 4:7,8,19,20)

We do not have time to read all that happened between Saul and David, but we do want to look at one story and observe **David's humility and love**. Reading in the first book of Samuel, chapter twenty-four, the Scripture says:

> (1 Sam. 24) [1]*[Some people came to Saul and said to him], "David is in the*
> *Desert of En Gedi."* [2]*So* ***Saul*** *took three thousand chosen men from all Israel and*
> ***set out to look for David*** *and his men near the Crags of the Wild Goats.* [3]*He*
> *came to the sheep pens along the way; a cave was there, and Saul went in to relieve himself. David and his men were far back in the cave!*
>
> [4]*The men said, "This is the day the LORD spoke of when he said to you, 'I will give your enemy into your hands for you to deal with as you wish.'" Then* ***David***
> ***crept up unnoticed and cut off a corner of Saul's robe****.* [5]*Afterwards, David*
> *was conscience-stricken for having cut off a corner of his robe.* [6]*He said to his*
> *men, "The LORD forbid that I should do such a thing to my master, the LORD's*
> *anointed, or lift my hand against him; for he is the anointed of the LORD."* [7]*With*
> *these words David rebuked his men and did not allow them to attack Saul. And Saul left the cave and went his way.*
>
> [8]*Then David went out of the cave and called out to Saul, "My lord the king!"*
> *When Saul looked behind him, David bowed down and prostrated himself with*
> *his face to the ground.* [9]*He said to Saul, "Why do you listen when men say,*
> *'David is bent on harming you'?* [10]*This day you have seen with your own eyes*
> *how the LORD gave you into my hands in the cave. Some urged me to kill you, but I spared you; I said, 'I will not lift my hand against my master, because he is*
> *the LORD's anointed.'* [11]*See, my father, look at this piece of your robe in my*

hand! I cut off the corner of your robe but did not kill you. Now understand and recognize that I am not guilty of wrongdoing or rebellion. I have not wronged you, but you are hunting me down to take my life. [12]*May the LORD judge between you and me. And may the LORD avenge the wrongs you have done to me, but my hand will not touch you.* [13]*As the old saying goes, 'From evildoers come evil deeds,' so my hand will not touch you.*

[16]*When David finished saying this, Saul asked, "Is that your voice, David my son?" And he wept aloud.* [17]*"You are more righteous than I," he said. "You have treated me well, but I have treated you badly.* [18]*You have just now told me of the good you did to me; the LORD gave me into your hands, but you did not kill me.* [19]*When a man finds his enemy, does he let him get away unharmed? May the LORD reward you well for the way you treated me today.* [20]*I know that you will surely be king and that the kingdom of Israel will be established in your hands."*

After that, Saul returned home, but it wasn't long before jealousy took hold of his heart again and incited him to go back into the wilderness and resume his hunt for David. Saul did this for eight years, all because of **jealousy**! Yet, every time, God rescued David from the hands of Saul. In the end, Saul reaped the evil he had sown. Listen to what is written in chapter thirty-one.

The Scripture says:

(1 Sam. 31) [1]*Now the Philistines fought against Israel; the Israelites fled before them, and many fell slain on Mount Gilboa.* [2]*The Philistines pressed hard after Saul and his sons, and they killed his sons Jonathan, Abinadab and Malki-Shua.* [3]*The fighting grew fierce around Saul, and when the archers overtook him, they wounded him critically.* [4]*Saul said to his armorbearer, "Draw your sword and run me through, or these uncircumcised fellows will come and run me through and abuse me." But the armorbearer was terrified and would not do it; so* ***Saul took his own sword and fell on it****.*

On that day, Saul and his three sons died. Thus, the descendants of Saul were completely exterminated, just as God had said they would be. In the chapters that follow, the Scriptures relate how **God turned the kingdom of Israel over to David**. David was a just king who loved righteousness and hated iniquity. David loved the LORD God with his whole heart. The Word of God and the glory of God occupied first place in David's thoughts. Therefore, when David began to rule over Israel, the first thing that he wanted to do was to bring the Tent of Meeting (Tabernacle) and the ark (chest) of the covenant to Jerusalem. Jerusalem had become the capital of Israel, which is why David wanted to set up the tent of worship and the altar of sacrifice there.

After David had moved the tent of worship to Jerusalem, the Scriptures relate how he planned to build a beautiful temple to honor the name of the LORD. David wanted to build a temple in which the ark of the covenant could be placed and where sinners could present to God sacrifices which cover sin. However, the LORD told David that he was not the one to build a house for God, but that God would build for him a house, that is, **a posterity which would endure forever**! Listen to **the covenant God made with David.** He said to him:

> (2 Sam. 7) [12]"*When your days are over and you rest with your fathers, I will raise up your offspring to succeed you, who will come from your own body, and I will establish his kingdom.* [13]*He is the one who will build a house for my Name, and I will establish the throne of his kingdom forever.* [14]*I will be his father, and he shall be my son.* [16]***Your house and your kingdom shall endure forever before me; your throne shall be established forever.***"

Do you understand the covenant God established with King David on that day? It was a tremendous promise that surpasses human comprehension! God promised David, "*Your house and your kingdom shall endure forever before me;* ***your throne shall be established forever****!*"

What?! How would David's kingdom endure **forever**? How could this be? How could David, who was only a man, have a government that would last forever? Here is the answer: God promised David that **one of his descendants** would establish an everlasting government. A Man would be born in David's royal family line who would receive the authority to reign in heaven and on earth forever. He would be called the King of kings, the Lord of lords, the Prince of Peace. Hundreds of years after David's time, and about seven hundred years before this King of kings was born, the prophet Isaiah penned these words:

> "*For to us a child is born, to us a son is given, and* ***the government will be on his shoulders****. And he will be called* ***Wonderful Counselor, Mighty God, Everlasting Father, Prince of Peace****.* ***Of the increase of his government and peace there will be no end****! He will reign on David's throne and over his kingdom, establishing and upholding it with justice and righteousness from that time on and* ***forever****. The zeal of the* LORD *Almighty will accomplish this!*" (Isa. 9:6,7)

Do you know who, among the descendants of David, has been given the authority to establish an eternal government? Do you know who will judge the children of Adam on the Day of Judgment and reign throughout eternity? Yes, it is **the Redeemer, the King from heaven**, who was born of a virgin, a virgin who belonged to the descendants of David. Concerning this King, the Scripture says:

"***God exalted Him to the highest place and gave Him the name that is above every name!***" (Phil. 2:9)

When David understood God's plan to send the Redeemer through his family line, David kneeled and worshiped the Lord saying,

> (2 Sam. 7) [18]"***Who am I, O Sovereign LORD, and what is my family, that you have brought me this far****?* [19]*And as if this were not enough in your sight, O Sovereign LORD, you have also spoken about* ***the future*** *of the house of your servant. Is this your usual way of dealing with man, O Sovereign LORD?* [22]"***How great you are, O Sovereign LORD! There is no one like you, and there is no God but you****, as we have heard with our own ears.* [28]*O Sovereign LORD, you are God!* ***Your words are trustworthy****, and you have promised* ***these good things*** *to your servant.* [29]*Now be pleased to bless the house of your servant, that it may continue* ***forever*** *in your sight; for you, O Sovereign LORD, have spoken, and with your blessing the house of your servant will be blessed* ***forever****.*"

That is how David thanked the LORD for His promise concerning **the King** who would come forth through his descendants. You who know the Holy Scriptures know that God has already fulfilled part of this promise. For in the Gospel {*Injil*} we read that, a thousand years after David's time, God sent an angel to some shepherds who were tending their flocks in the same hills of Bethlehem where David had tended his father's flock. The angel of the LORD said to the shepherds, "*I bring you good news of great joy that will be* ***for all the people****. Today* ***in the town of David*** *a Savior has been born to you; he is Christ* ***the Lord****.*" (Luke 2:10,11) Yes, **the King** God promised to bring forth through David's posterity has been born. Presently, He is back in heaven, awaiting that terrible and glorious day when He will return to judge the world in righteousness. In that day, everyone will know that the promise God made to David concerning his **eternal kingdom** is true. In that day it will be said, "*The kingdom of the world has become the kingdom of our Lord and of his Christ, and* ***he will reign for ever and ever****!*" (Rev.11:15)

We must stop here today. Thank you for listening. Next time, in the will of God, we will continue the story of King David and hear about an event that will make your ears tingle. Thank you for listening....

God bless you. We leave you with this verse from the Holy Scriptures:

> ***"Oh, the depth of the riches of the wisdom and knowledge of God!...For from him and through him and to him are all things. To him be the glory forever! Amen!"*** (Rom. 11:33,36)

Lesson 49

David and Bathsheba

2 Samuel 11,12; Psalm 51,32

Peace be with you, listening friends. We greet you in the name of God, the Lord of peace, who wants everyone to understand and submit to the way of righteousness that He has established, and have true peace with Him forever. We are happy to be able to return today to present your program *The Way of Righteousness*.

In our last program, we saw how David became the King of Israel. David was a just and compassionate king who sincerely cherished the Word of God. Today, however, we are going to read **something about David which is not pleasant** to hear. David did something that was abominable in God's sight; he coveted his neighbor's wife, committed adultery with her, and then added sin to sin by attempting to cover it up. Some may ask, "Why is such an awful story found in the Holy Scriptures?" The Scripture answers this question when it says: "*Everything that was written in the past was written **to teach us**!*" (Rom. 15:4) "*These things...were written down **as warnings for us**...So, if you think you are standing firm, be careful that you don't fall!*" (1 Cor. 10:11,12) In the Holy Scriptures, God does not hide the sins of the prophets because God wants to teach us valuable lessons.

Now then, let us return to the second book of Samuel and see how David fell into sin. In chapter eleven, the Scripture says:

> (2 Sam. 11) [1]*In the spring, at the time when kings go off to war,* ***David*** *sent* ***Joab*** *out with the king's men and the whole Israelite army. They destroyed the Ammonites and besieged Rabbah. But David remained in Jerusalem.* [2]*One evening David got up from his bed and walked around on the roof of the palace. From the roof he saw a woman bathing. The woman was very beautiful,* [3]*and David sent someone to find out about her. The man said, "Isn't this* ***Bathsheba****...the wife of* ***Uriah*** *the Hittite?"* [4]*Then David sent messengers to get her. She came to him, and he slept with her...then she went back home.* [5]*The woman conceived and sent word to David, saying, "I am pregnant."*

Next, the Scriptures describe how David tried to cover up his sin. When David heard that Bathsheba was pregnant, he sent word to Joab, the leader of his army, and ordered him to send to him Uriah, Bathsheba's husband. Now Uriah was a mighty man in the army of Israel. And so Joab sent Uriah to David.

> (2 Sam. 11) *7When Uriah came to him, David asked him how Joab was, how the soldiers were and how the war was going. 8Then David said to Uriah, "Go down to your house and wash your feet." So Uriah left the palace, and a gift from the king was sent after him. 9But Uriah slept at the entrance to the palace with all his master's servants and did not go down to his house. 10When David was told, "Uriah did not go home," he asked him, "Haven't you just come from a distance? Why didn't you go home?" 11Uriah said to David, "The ark and Israel and Judah are staying in tents, and my master Joab and my lord's men are camped in the open fields. How could I go to my house to eat and drink and lie with my wife? As surely as you live, I will not do such a thing!"*
>
> *12Then David said to him, "Stay here one more day, and tomorrow I will send you back." So Uriah remained in Jerusalem that day and the next... 14In the morning David wrote a letter to Joab and sent it with Uriah. 15In it he wrote, "Put Uriah in the front line where the fighting is fiercest. Then withdraw from him so that he will be struck down and die." 16So while Joab had the city under siege, he put Uriah at a place where he knew the strongest defenders were. 17When the men of the city came out and fought against Joab, some of the men in David's army fell; moreover, Uriah the Hittite died. 18Joab sent David a full account of the battle [...with the news:] 21"Your servant Uriah the Hittite is dead."*
>
> *26When Uriah's wife heard that her husband was dead, she mourned for him. 27After the time of mourning was over, David had her brought to his house, and she became his wife and bore him a son.* ***But the thing David had done displeased the LORD.***
>
> (2 Sam. 12) *1[Thus, one day] The LORD sent [a prophet by the name of]* ***Nathan*** *to David. When he came to him, he said, "There were two men in a certain town, one rich and the other poor. 2The rich man had a very large number of sheep and cattle, 3but the poor man had nothing except one little ewe lamb that he had bought. He raised it, and it grew up with him and his children. It shared his food, drank from his cup and even slept in his arms. It was like a daughter to him. 4Now a traveler came to the rich man, but the rich man refrained from taking one of his own sheep or cattle to prepare a meal for the traveler who had come to him. Instead, he took the ewe lamb that belonged to the poor man and prepared it for the one who had come to him."*
>
> *5[When David heard this story, he] burned with anger against the man and said to Nathan, "As surely as the LORD lives,* ***the man who did this deserves to***

> ***die**! [6]He must pay for that lamb four times over, because he did such a thing and had no pity!" [7]Then Nathan said to David, "**You are the man!** This is what the LORD, the God of Israel, says: 'I anointed you king over Israel, and I delivered you from the hand of Saul. [8]...I gave you the house of Israel and Judah. And if all this had been too little, I would have given you even more. [9]Why did you despise the word of the LORD by doing what is evil in his eyes? You struck down Uriah the Hittite with the sword and took his wife to be your own. You killed him with the sword of the Amonites. [10]Now, therefore, the sword shall never depart from your house, because you despised me and took the wife of Uriah the Hittite to be your own.' [11]This is what the LORD says: 'Out of your own household I am going to bring calamity upon you. Before your very eyes I will take your wives and give them to one who is close to you, and he will lie with your wives in broad daylight. [12]You did it in secret, but I will do this thing in broad daylight before all Israel!'" [13]Then David said to Nathan, **"I have sinned against the LORD!"** Nathan replied, "**The LORD has taken away your sin. You are not going to die**. [14]But because by doing this you have made the enemies of the LORD show utter contempt, the son born to you will die." [15]Nathan went home.*

In the following chapters, the Scriptures show us how David's sin produced great trouble and many tragedies within his family. But the Word of God also says: "*Where **sin** increased, **grace** increased all the more.*" (Rom. 5:20) Thus, in the remaining time today, we will see how God showed David His **grace**, and forgave him all his **sins**.

Why did God forgive David of his sins? Did you hear how David responded when Nathan said to David, "*You are the man!*"? God's prophet, Nathan, had great courage to say such a thing to the great King of Israel. How did David answer Nathan? Did he lock Nathan in prison or even have him executed, as many kings might have done? No, he did not do this. Did David try to justify his sins by saying, "God willed it!" or "God is good, perhaps He will erase my evil deeds because of my good deeds!"? Did David answer Nathan like that? No, David did not! Then how did David respond? David said, "*I have sinned!*" "***I have sinned against the LORD!***"

To better understand how David confessed his sin before God, we need to read what David wrote in the Psalms after the prophet Nathan rebuked him for his sin with Bathsheba. In Psalm fifty-one, David said:

> (Psa. 51) [1]***Have mercy on me, O God, according to your unfailing love**; according to your great compassion blot out my transgressions. [2]Wash away all my iniquity and cleanse me from my sin. [3]For I know my transgressions, and my sin is always before me. [4]Against you, you only, have I sinned and done what is evil in your sight, so that you are proved right when you speak and justified when*

> *you judge.* [5]*Surely I was sinful at birth, sinful from the time my mother conceived me.* [6]*Surely you desire truth in the inner parts; you teach me wisdom in the inmost place.* [7]***Cleanse me with hyssop, and I shall be clean; wash me, and I shall be whiter than snow***. [10]*Create in me a pure heart, O God, and renew a steadfast spirit within me.* [17]***The sacrifices of God are a broken spirit; a broken and contrite heart, O God, you will not despise!***

This is how David repented. David mourned greatly because of his sin. He had a broken and crushed heart before God. **David was not like those who have religion, but continue in sin every day.** Truly, David had fallen into the pit of sin, but he could not live in it, because David loved God, and knew that "*God is light; in him there is no darkness at all.*" (1 John 1:5)

So then, after David repented, what did God say to him through the mouth of the prophet Nathan? Did God tell him, "Go and do some good works and I will erase your sins!"? No, God did not say that! Nathan simply said to him, "*The* LORD *has taken away your sin. You are not going to die!*"

After this, David wrote in the Psalms, describing the blessedness of the man whom **God has forgiven, apart from his own works.** He said: "*Blessed is he whose transgressions are* ***forgiven****, whose sins are* ***covered****. Blessed is the man whose sin* ***the Lord does not count against him*** *and in whose spirit is no deceit!*" (Psa. 32:1,2; Rom. 4:7,8) Yes, God forgave David and judged him as righteous! That does not mean that God removed the tragedies that David's sin produced. What it means is that, in the Day of Judgment, God would not remember David's sins. He had **erased** them all from His book!

How could God do that? How could God forgive all the sins of David and yet remain a righteous judge? Could God simply forget, just like that, all the evil which David had done? No! God is a righteous judge, and He cannot merely close His eyes to the sins of the children of Adam. Well then, how could God forgive David, and still maintain His righteousness?

Do you remember what David prayed to God after he recognized his sin? He prayed, "*Wash away all my iniquity…Cleanse me with* ***hyssop****, and I shall be clean; wash me, and I shall be whiter than snow!*" (Psa. 51:2,7) God had commanded the Israelites to use the branch of the hyssop plant for sprinkling the blood of the sacrifices. The sprinkled blood illustrated the great sacrifice of **the coming Redeemer** who would willingly die, shedding His blood as a **payment** for sins.

God could forgive David his sins because David had **repented** (turned from sin to God) and **believed** in God's power to cleanse him by the work of the coming Redeemer. David might have offered to God a prayer something like this: "Oh God, I am grieved over my sin and ask you to forgive me! I know that you can forgive me of my sins, because one day you will send the Redeemer, who has no sin, and He Himself will endure for me the punishment for my sin once and forever. Therefore Lord, have mercy on me, a sinner! Wash me in the blood of the holy Redeemer, and I shall be completely pure!"

Did God, in His grace, forgive David all his sins? Did God cleanse David's heart and judge him as righteous? Yes, He did! On what basis did God do this? God forgave David because he **confessed** his sinful condition before God, and **believed** what God had promised concerning the Redeemer, who would come and bear the punishment for sin. The faith he had in the promises of God is the reason David could rejoice, and write in the Psalms: ***"Blessed is he whose transgressions are forgiven, whose sins are covered! Blessed is the man whose sin the Lord does not count against him and in whose spirit is no deceit!"*** (Psa. 32:1,2)

Friends, thank you for listening. In our next two lessons, in the will of God, we will look into the holy book of Psalms to see what the prophet David testified concerning the Redeemer, who would bear our punishment, so that God could forgive us our sins forever....

God bless you as you think about this verse David wrote in the Psalms concerning one of God's greatest blessings:

> ***"Blessed is he whose transgressions are forgiven, whose sins are covered! Blessed is the man whose sin the Lord does not count against him and in whose spirit is no deceit!"*** (Psa. 32:1,2)

Lesson 50

The Prophet David and the Messiah

Psalms 1,2

Peace be with you, listening friends. We greet you in the name of God, the Lord of peace, who wants everyone to understand and submit to the way of righteousness that He has established, and have true peace with Him forever. We are happy to be able to return today to present your program *The Way of Righteousness.*

In the past four lessons we have been examining the story of **the prophet David.** We have seen how David was a shepherd, harpist, hymn writer, student of God's Word, hero in battle, king of Israel, and a prophet of God. In our last lesson, we saw that David was also **a sinner**; that he did something which greatly displeased God. However, we also saw how God forgave David his sins, because David truly turned from his sins with a repentant heart and believed what God had promised concerning the Redeemer who was to come into the world and bear the punishment for the sins of the people of the whole world.

Today we plan to meditate on the wonderful book found in the middle of the Holy Scriptures. Do you know the name of this book? Yes, it is the **Psalms** {*Zabur*}. The Book of the Psalms contains one hundred and fifty chapters or hymns. Over a period of hundreds of years, God used several prophets to write the Psalms, including Moses, Solomon, Asaph and the sons of Korah. However, David wrote more of the Psalms than any other prophet. Today we want to immerse ourselves in the first two hymns (or chapters) of the Psalms.

The first hymn shows us the two categories of people that are in the world: Those who walk in **the way of righteousness**, and those who walk in **the way of unrighteousness**. In the first Psalm, it is written:

> (Psa. 1) [1]***Blessed is the man who does not walk in the counsel of the wicked*** *or stand in the way of sinners or sit in the seat of mockers.* [2]*But his delight is in the law of the LORD, and on his law he meditates day and night.* [3]*He is like a tree planted by streams of water, which yields its fruit in season and whose leaf does not wither. Whatever he does prospers.* [4]**Not so the wicked!** *They are like chaff that the wind blows away.*

> [5]*Therefore the wicked will not stand in the judgment, nor sinners in the assembly of the righteous.* [6]***For the LORD watches over the way of the righteous, but the way of the wicked will perish!***

We see here **the way of those who are blessed** and **the way of those who are perishing.** Everyone wants to be blessed. No one wants to perish. God wants everyone to be blessed. But you must come by the way of blessing which God has ordained. What is that way of blessing? This first hymn of the Psalms summarizes it in two thoughts. **First:** Do not follow in the way of those who mock the Word of God. **Second:** Meditate upon God's Word with the goal of understanding, believing and receiving the way of salvation that God has established.

If you believe and follow God's way of righteousness, the Scripture says that you will be *"like a tree planted by streams of water"*; your life will be established in God Himself, yielding *"fruit in season"* such as love, joy and peace. However, if you do not follow God's way of righteousness, you will perish like *"like chaff that the wind blows away."*

Now let us move into the second hymn in the Psalms. In this chapter, God inspired David to write about **the Redeemer** who was to come into the world. Let us listen carefully to the message that God has spoken to us through the pen of His prophet, David. The Scripture says:

> (Psa. 2) [1]*Why do the nations conspire and the peoples plot in vain?* [2]*The kings of the earth take their stand and the rulers gather together against the LORD and against* **his Anointed One (Messiah)**. [3]*"Let us break their chains," they say, "and throw off their fetters."* [4]*The One enthroned in heaven laughs; the Lord scoffs at them.* [5]*Then he rebukes them in his anger and terrifies them in his wrath, saying,* [6]*"I have installed* **my King** *on Zion, my holy hill."* [7]*I will proclaim the decree of the LORD: He said to me, "You are* **my Son**; *today I have become your Father.* [8]*Ask of me, and I will make the nations your inheritance, the ends of the earth your possession.* [9]*You will rule them with an iron scepter; you will dash them to pieces like pottery."* [10]*Therefore, you kings, be wise; be warned, you rulers of the earth.* [11]*Serve the LORD with fear and rejoice with trembling.* [12]***Kiss the Son, lest he be angry and you be destroyed in your way, for his wrath can flare up in a moment. Blessed are all who take refuge in him.***

Do you understand what the LORD God has declared in the second chapter of the Psalms? It is extremely important! In this hymn, God makes known **three wonderful names of the Redeemer** who would come into the world to bring salvation to the children of Adam. Did you hear the three names? They are: **The Messiah, the King,** and **the Son.** Let us think a little about these three names by which God refers to the Savior of the world.

1.) First, we see that God calls the Redeemer "**the Messiah**." Messiah is a Hebrew word meaning *the One whom God has selected* {Lit. *the Anointed One*}. With the name *Messiah*, God was announcing to the children of Adam that everyone must believe and accept the Redeemer who was to come into the world, because He is the One whom God Himself has selected as the Savior and Judge of the world. However, in the first three verses of this hymn, God predicted that most of the children of Adam would reject the Messiah whom God was going to send into the world. Let us read those verses again.

> "*Why do the nations conspire and the peoples plot in vain? The kings of the earth take their stand and the rulers gather together against the* LORD *and against his Anointed One (Messiah). 'Let us break their chains,' they say, 'and throw off their fetters!'*" (Psa. 2:1-3)

Why would the people of the world refuse to accept the Messiah whom God sent? They would reject the Messiah because He would be a holy person, unstained by sin, and the Scripture tells us that "*everyone who does evil hates the light and will not come into it* ***because they fear that their deeds will be exposed***." (John 3:20) Thus, God was predicting in these verses how the Jews and the nations of the world would work together to try to destroy the holy Man whom God had selected as the Savior and Judge of the world. But God knew everything which wicked men would attempt to do. God planned to use the evil plans of men to accomplish His righteous plan to redeem sinners. That is why we read: "*The One enthroned in heaven laughs; the Lord scoffs at them!*" (Psa. 2:4) Thus, the first name that God gave to the Redeemer in this chapter is ***the Messiah.*** You might be interested to know that the Hebrew word *Messiah* is the same as the Greek word *Christ*. Both mean "*the One whom God has selected.*"

2.) The second name is "**the King.**" The Messiah is also the King. Through that name, God wants everyone to know that the Messiah will, in the end, be the Judge and Ruler of the world even though most people would reject Him. On the great Day of Judgment, everyone will kneel before Him, because He is the One whom God has selected to be the King of kings, the Lord of lords. Consequently, the Messiah will be either **your Savior or your Judge**–because, like it or not, **He is the King** whom God has selected to reign forever!

3.) Third, we heard in this chapter another name which God gives the Messiah. It is a name we must consider very carefully. It is "**the Son**." Before we explain what this name means, perhaps we should remember that everything that David wrote in the Psalms, he wrote with the wisdom that God imparted to him. Also, we must remember that in the Writings of the Prophets there are sometimes things which are difficult to understand, but that does not prevent them from being true! God warns us in His Word saying: "*[The Scriptures] contain* *some things that are hard to understand, which ignorant and unstable people distort…to their own destruction!*" (2 Pet. 3:16) Ignorance is a terrible thing, especially when it concerns the Messiah whom God has selected to deliver the children of Adam from eternal destruction! The (Wolof) proverb states it well: **"Before you know it, ignorance will kill you!"** Let us keep that thought in mind as we think about the third name which God Himself has given to the Messiah.

Now back to Psalm two. In verse seven we read that the Messiah says, "*I will proclaim the decree of the LORD: He said to me, "You are **my Son**; today I have become **your Father**.*" (Psa. 2:7) Did you hear what the LORD says to the Messiah? He said, "*You are **my Son**…I have become **your Father**.*" Do you know **why** God called the Messiah **His Son**? Do you know **what** this name means? We hope that all of you know what the name does **not mean.** It does not mean that God took a wife to have a child by her! Never! Such a thought is blasphemy! God is spirit and He does not beget a son as man begets one.

So then, why did God say to the Messiah, "*You are **my Son**!*"? We can thank God, because the LORD God Himself has told us why. We do not have time to go very far into this subject today, but we would like to give you **three reasons** {Lit. *thoughts*} from the Writings of the Prophets **why** God called the Messiah **His Son**.

First, you must know that God called the Messiah *His Son*, because **the Messiah came from above**; from heaven. Everyone who believes the Writings of the Prophets, knows that the Messiah did not come from a man, but from the presence of God. As you know, **the Messiah did not have an earthly father**. Concerning His earthly existence, He came through the descendants of David, because the Messiah was born of a virgin woman who was a relative of king David. But on His Father's side, the Messiah came forth uniquely from the Spirit of God. That is why God could say to Him, "*You are **my Son**; today I have become your Father!*"

Second, God called the Messiah *His Son* because the Scripture says that **God and the Messiah share the same holy character**. Like father, like son. The promised Redeemer had to be pure and holy just as God is pure and holy. We cannot go far with this now, but when we come to the Gospel record {*Injil*}, we will see that the Messiah was not like the sons of Adam who are stained with sin! As we have seen, even the greatest of the prophets committed sin. However, the Messiah never sinned. He always did the will of God. It was necessary that the Messiah be without sin since He came into the world to save sinners from their sin! Can those with great debts pay the debts of others? No, they cannot! The Messiah had no debt of sin. The Scripture calls Him the "*one who is holy, blameless, pure, set apart from sinners, exalted above the heavens.*" (Heb. 7:26) **Yes, the Redeemer was holy, just as God who sent Him is holy!** That is why God was not ashamed to call him **His Son**.

Third, you should know that God called the Messiah *His Son* **to distinguish Him from all the other prophets.** We have already seen how Abraham was called *"the friend of God."* The prophet Moses was called *"the man of God."* Of David, God said, *"I have found a man after my own heart."* But to which prophet did God say, *"You are **my Son**; today I have become **your Father**"*? That could only be said to the Messiah, because the Messiah is the only one who came from above, who was born of a virgin, and was unstained by sin.

You who are listening today, do you know **the Messiah, the King** whom God calls **His Son**? God wants everyone to know Him, listen to Him, believe in Him and receive Him. That is why the prophet David finished this chapter with these words:

> *"Therefore, you kings, **be wise**; **be warned**, you rulers of the earth. Serve the LORD with fear and rejoice with trembling. Kiss the Son, lest he be angry and you be destroyed in your way, for his wrath can flare up in a moment. **Blessed are all who take refuge in him!**"* (Psa. 2:10-12)

This is where we must stop today. Next time, in the will of God, we will meditate upon another great hymn which the prophet David wrote in the book of Psalms....

God bless you as you give serious thought to what the prophet David wrote in the Psalms saying:

> ***"Be wise; be warned...Serve the LORD with fear and rejoice with trembling. Kiss the Son, lest he be angry and you be destroyed in your way, for his wrath can flare up in a moment. Blessed are all who take refuge in him!"*** (Psa. 2:10-12)

Lesson 51

More from the Psalms

Psalm 22

Peace be with you, listening friends. We greet you in the name of God, the Lord of peace, who wants everyone to understand and submit to the way of righteousness that He has established, and have true peace with Him forever. We are happy to be able to return today to present your program *The Way of Righteousness*.

Last time we examined the first two chapters in **the book of Psalms** {*Zabur*}. It would be great if we had the time on our broadcast to read and discuss every chapter in the Psalms–but since the book of Psalms contains one hundred and fifty chapters that will not be possible.

However, before we close the book of Psalms, we would like to study with you another hymn that God put into the mind of David: **chapter twenty-two**. This chapter is very important, because it **predicts how the Messiah would die in agonizing pain to pay the debt of sin** for all the children of Adam. In this chapter, David, who preceded the Messiah's coming by one thousand years, prophesied some thirty events which would take place on the day that the Messiah was to die. When we read the Gospel {*Injil*} which contains the story of the Messiah, we will see that **everything took place exactly as God's prophet, David, had predicted**. Thus, we can be certain that this hymn did not come from the mind of man, but from the mind of God. **Only God** can predict the future with such precise accuracy.

Now let us listen to what the prophet David wrote in the twenty-second Psalm. In this chapter, David wrote the thoughts which would be in the mind of the Messiah on the day He would shed his blood as a payment for sin. He said:

> (Psa. 22) [1]*My God, my God, why have you forsaken me? Why are you so far from saving me, so far from the words of my groaning?* [3]*Yet you are enthroned as the Holy One; you are the praise of Israel.* [6]*But I am a worm and not a man, scorned by men and despised by the people.* [14]*I am poured out like water, and all my bones are out of joint. My heart has turned to wax; it has melted away within*

> *me.* [15]*My strength is dried up like a potsherd, and my tongue sticks to the roof of my mouth; you lay me in the dust of death.* [16]*Dogs have surrounded me; a band of evil men has encircled me,* ***they have pierced my hands and my feet!***

Let us pause here briefly. Did you grasp what the prophet David wrote about the Messiah? One thousand years before the Messiah came into the world, David writes: "*A band of evil men has encircled me,* ***they have pierced my hands and my feet!***" With these words David predicted how the sons of Adam would pierce the hands and feet of the Messiah by nailing Him to a cross. Why did the prophet David write in the Psalms that evil men would pierce the Messiah's hands and feet? Why should the Messiah die such a painful death? Why would God allow men to murder the holy Redeemer whom He sent?

The Word of God gives us the answer. It was necessary for the Redeemer to suffer excruciating pain and die such a horrible death, so that He might **take our place** and bear for us the punishment of God. Since the payment of sin is death and eternal condemnation in hell, it was necessary that the Messiah taste the torments of hell which we deserve because of our sin. God, in His grace, planned to send the Redeemer who was unstained by sin, so that He might, of His own free will, "*taste death for everyone.*" (Heb. 2:9) This is how God could open for the children of Adam a way of forgiveness from sin and a door to eternal life, without compromising His justice! The Messiah would pay the penalty for our sins. The **death of the righteous Messiah** is the reason that God, the Righteous One, can **judge as righteous everyone who believes in Him**.

What the prophet David wrote concerning the Messiah's death is truly amazing. Think of it! One thousand years before the Messiah's birth, David wrote in detail how the Messiah would suffer upon the cross to which He would be nailed. Perhaps what we need to understand and remember is this: The Romans are the ones who devised nailing a person to a cross–that painful death called *crucifixion*. Yet when David wrote about it in the Psalms, the nation of Rome did not yet exist and nobody knew about putting a person to death in this way, that is, by crucifixion; by nailing him to a cross. However, God put the message of the Messiah's death on a cross in the mind of David, and inspired him to write it in the Psalms, **so that we might know for sure** that the Messiah's death upon the cross was **God's plan** to save us from the penalty of our sin.

The truth which this chapter contains is perfectly clear, and we should pay attention to it. However, **everyone does not accept this message from God**. To this day, some contradict what God's prophet, David, wrote in the Psalms concerning the Messiah's death on the cross. They say, "God would not allow the Messiah to die such a shameful and painful death!" But those who say this are ignorant of the Scriptures of the Prophets and of God's plan to save sinners. Dear listening friends, be careful not to ignore God's way of salvation! Wolof wisdom says, "Before you know it, **ignorance** will kill you!" And God's Word says, "*How shall we escape **if we ignore** such a great salvation?*" (Heb. 2:3) "*The message of the cross is foolishness to those who are perishing, but to us who are being saved it is the power of God!*" (1 Cor. 1:18)

Now let us look farther at what David wrote concerning the circumstances of the Messiah's death on a cross. We hear how the Messiah says:

> (Psa. 22) [1]**My God, my God, why have you forsaken me?** [7]**All who see me mock me; they hurl insults, shaking their heads**: [8]"**He trusts in the LORD; let the LORD rescue him. Let him deliver him, since he delights in him**." [14]*I am poured out like water, and all my bones are out of joint. My heart has turned to wax; it has melted away within me.* [15]*My strength is dried up like a potsherd, and* ***my tongue sticks to the roof of my mouth****; you lay me in the dust of death.* [16]*Dogs have surrounded me; a band of evil men has encircled me, they have* ***pierced my hands and my feet****.* [17]*I can count all my bones;* ***people stare*** *and gloat over me.* [18]***They divide my garments among them and cast lots for my clothing.***

With these words, David was predicting that after men nailed the Messiah to the cross, they would insult Him, mock Him, stare at Him and divide his garments between them and cast lots for his clothes. This is exactly what happened one thousand years after David wrote it. Listen to what is written in the Gospel {*Injil*} concerning the death of the Messiah. The Scripture says:

> "*When they had crucified him, they divided up his clothes by casting lots. And sitting down, they kept watch over him there....Those who passed by hurled insults at him, shaking their heads and saying, '...Come down from the cross, if you are the Son of God!' In the same way the chief priests, the teachers of the law and the elders mocked him. "He saved others," they said, "but he can't save himself! He's the king of Israel! Let him come down now from the cross, and we will believe in him. He trusts in God. Let God rescue him now if he wants him, for he said, 'I am the Son of God!'*" (Matt. 27:35,36,39,40)

Thus the Gospels record how the words of God's prophet, David, were fulfilled.

We also read today that David predicted that the Messiah would thirst and suffer greatly in His body and in the depths of His soul and spirit. That is why the Messiah cries out in the first verse saying, "My God, my God, *why have you forsaken me?*" When we study the Gospel, we will see that everything happened exactly as David predicted in this Psalm. Why did the Messiah cry out on the cross, saying, "My God, *my God, why have you forsaken me?*" Because God is "*the Holy One*" (Psa 22:3), and cannot tolerate sin. God Himself had to turn His back on the Messiah who was nailed to the cross, and separate Himself from Him, because **God laid on Him the punishment for all our sins**. That is why the Scriptures say: "*God made [the Messiah] who had no sin to be sin* ***for us****, so that in him we might become the righteousness of God!*" (2 Cor. 5:21)

God be praised, there is something else that the prophet David predicted in the Psalms—some very good news! In the sixteenth chapter, David writes of the Messiah, saying: "*You, God,* ***you will not abandon me to the grave, nor will you let your Holy One see decay.*** *You have made known to me the path of life.*" (Psa. 16:10,11) In this way David predicted how God planned to raise the Messiah from the grave, so that whoever believes in Him, might live with Him in the holy presence of God forever! Thus, the Gospel {*Injil*} declares: "*[The Messiah]* ***died for our sins*** *according to the Scriptures…He* ***was buried****, [and] He* ***was raised*** *on the third day according to the Scriptures!*" (1 Cor. 15:3,4)

David also predicted that after the Messiah rose from the dead, God would take Him up to heaven, and tell Him to sit at His right hand, until He returns to judge the people of the earth. That is what David wrote in the Psalms, chapter one hundred and ten, when he says: "*The LORD says to my Lord: 'Sit at my right hand until I make your enemies a footstool for your feet.'*" (Psa. 110:1)

In the end of chapter twenty-two, David writes:

> (Psa. 22) [27]*All the ends of the earth will remember and turn to the LORD, and all the families of the nations will bow down before him…* [30]*Posterity will serve him; future generations will be told about the Lord.* [31]*They will proclaim his righteousness to a people yet unborn, for* ***He has done it****!*

This Psalm concludes with these words: "***He has done it****!*" What would the Messiah do? He would die in the place of all sinners! He would fulfil all that God had promised Adam and Eve concerning the Redeemer who would save them and their descendants from the penalty of their sin. The Messiah would die as the final sacrifice. Through His death on the cross, the Messiah would fulfil and abolish the symbolic animal sacrifices which God required from sinners in earlier times. Like the ram that died in the place of Abraham's son, the Redeemer would die in the place of sinners as the final and perfect Sacrifice—for all—forever! This is God's Good News to the world: The Messiah died in **your place**! Believe in Him and you will be saved from God's judgment! The way of salvation is wide open to all who believe it. That is why, just before the Messiah died, He cried out, ***"It is finished!"*** (John 19:30) "***He has done it****!*" (Psa. 22:31) And God confirmed the Messiah's perfect sacrifice by raising Him from the dead on the third day! We will see all this in detail when we study the book of the Gospel.

Meanwhile, may we remember this: **One thousand years before the birth of Jesus Christ, the prophet David predicted that sinners would pierce the Messiah's hands and feet**! And let us not forget the reason for the Messiah's painful death. He died for **you** and for **me**, and for **all sinners**, so that whoever believes in Him will not perish, but have eternal life! The Messiah allowed wicked men to pierce His hands and His feet because of His desire to do the will of God—and because of His great love for you and me! Listen to what Jesus the Messiah says in the Gospel {*Injil*}:

> "***I lay down my life–only to take it up again. No one takes it from me, but I lay it down of my own accord***. *I have authority to lay it down and authority to take it up again. This command I received from my Father [in heaven].*" (John 10:17,18)

Listening friends, are you thanking and praising God for sending the Messiah to save you from your sins? The Holy Scripture says: "*[Jesus, the Messiah] suffered for* ***you****! He himself bore our sins in his body on the tree, so that we might die to sins and live for righteousness; by his wounds you have been healed.…He was delivered over to death for our sins and was raised to life for our justification…* ***so that everyone who believes in him shall not perish but have eternal life!***" (1 Pet. 2:21,24; Rom. 4:25; John 3:16)

May God make clear to you everything we have read today. Thank you for listening. God willing, in our next program, we will continue in the Writings of the Prophets and move on to the story of David's son, Solomon.…

God bless you as you ponder why He inspired the prophet David to write:

> ***"They have pierced my hands and my feet!"*** (Psa. 22:16)

Lesson 52

The Prophet Solomon

1 Kings 2-10; Psalm 72

Peace be with you, listening friends. We greet you in the name of God, the Lord of peace, who wants everyone to understand and submit to the way of righteousness that He has established, and have true peace with Him forever. We are happy to be able to return today to present your program *The Way of Righteousness*.

If God appeared to you and said to you, "Ask for whatever you want, and I will give it to you," what would you choose? A long life? Great riches? Fame? Or something else? One day God appeared to Solomon, the son of David, in a dream and said to him, ***"Ask for whatever you want me to give you."*** Do you know what Solomon chose? We will hear today how he answered God.

In the past six lessons we have been looking into the story of the prophet of God, **David**. We have read some of the hymns he wrote in the book of **Psalms**. In our last lesson we saw how David prophesied that the sons of Adam would kill the Messiah by piercing His hands and His feet. David also foretold that God would raise the Messiah from the dead. Today we plan to leave the story of David and move on to the story of his son, **Solomon** {*Suliman* in Arabic}.

In the first book of Kings chapter two, the Holy Scripture says:

> (1 Kings 2) [1]*When the time drew near for David to die, he gave a charge to Solomon his son.* [2]*"I am about to go the way of all the earth," he said. "So be strong, show yourself a man,* [3]*and observe what the LORD your God requires:* ***Walk in his ways...as written in the Law of Moses, so that you may prosper in all you do and wherever you go.*** [10]*Then David rested with his fathers and was buried in the City of David.* [11]*He had reigned for forty years over Israel...* [12]*So Solomon sat on the throne of his father David, and his rule was firmly established.*
>
> (1 Kings 3) [3]*Solomon showed his love for the LORD by walking according to the statutes of his father David...the LORD appeared to Solomon during the night in a dream, and God said,* ***"Ask for whatever you want me to give you."***

*[6]Solomon answered, "…O LORD my God, you have made your servant king in place of my father David. But I am only a little child and do not know how to carry out my duties… [9]**So give your servant a discerning heart** to govern your people and to distinguish between right and wrong. For who is able to govern this great people of yours?" [10]**The Lord was pleased** that Solomon had asked for this. [11]So God said to him, "Since you have asked for this and not for long life or wealth for yourself, nor have asked for the death of your enemies but for discernment in administering justice, [12]I will do what you have asked. I will give you a wise and discerning heart, so that there will never have been anyone like you, nor will there ever be. [13]Moreover, I will give you what you have not asked for, both riches and honor, so that in your lifetime you will have no equal among kings. [14]And if you walk in my ways and obey my statutes and commands as David your father did, I will give you a long life." [15]Then Solomon awoke, and he realized it had been a dream. He returned to Jerusalem, stood before the ark of the Lord's covenant and sacrificed burnt offerings and fellowship offerings. Then he gave a feast for all his court.*

[16]Now two prostitutes came to the king and stood before him. [17]One of them said, "My lord, this woman and I live in the same house. I had a baby while she was there with me. [18]The third day after my child was born, this woman also had a baby. We were alone; there was no one in the house but the two of us. [19]"During the night this woman's son died because she lay on him. [20]So she got up in the middle of the night and took my son from my side while I your servant was asleep. She put him by her breast and put her dead son by my breast. [21]The next morning, I got up to nurse my son, and he was dead! But when I looked at him closely in the morning light, I saw that it wasn't the son I had borne." [22]The other woman said, "No! The living one is my son; the dead one is yours." But the first one insisted, "No! The dead one is yours; the living one is mine." And so they argued before the king.

[23][Then King Solomon] said, "This one says, 'My son is alive and your son is dead,' while that one says, 'No! Your son is dead and mine is alive.'" [24]Then the king said, "Bring me a sword." So they brought a sword for the king. [25]He then gave an order: "Cut the living child in two and give half to one and half to the other."

*[26]The woman whose son was alive was filled with compassion for her son and said to the king, "Please, my lord, give her the living baby! Don't kill him!" But the other said, "Neither I nor you shall have him. Cut him in two!" [27]Then the king gave his ruling: "Give the living baby to the first woman. Do not kill him; she is his mother." [28]When all Israel heard the verdict the king had given, **they held the king in awe, because they saw that he had wisdom from God to administer justice**.*

(1 Kings 4) *[29]God gave Solomon wisdom and very great insight, and a breadth*

> *of understanding as measureless as the sand on the seashore.* [30]***Solomon's wisdom was greater*** *than the wisdom of all the men of the East, and greater than all the wisdom of Egypt.* [31]*He was wiser than any other man...And his fame spread to all the surrounding nations.* [32]*He spoke three thousand proverbs and his songs numbered a thousand and five.* [34]*Men of all nations came to listen to Solomon's wisdom, sent by all the kings of the world, who had heard of his wisdom.*

Next, the Scriptures record that at that time there was a queen, **the queen of Sheba**, who had heard of the profound wisdom and great majesty of Solomon. The queen made plans to go to Jerusalem to visit Solomon, to know whether what she had heard about him was **the truth or not**. This queen lived in a land very far from Jerusalem, in the land of Sheba, which lies south of Saudi Arabia. The country of Sheba is known today as Yemen. Between that country and Jerusalem is a distance of about two thousand kilometers. However, that great distance did not discourage the queen of Sheba from traveling to visit Solomon.

In chapter ten, the Scripture says:

> (1 Kings 10) [1]*When the queen of Sheba heard about the fame of Solomon and his relation to the name of the LORD, she came* ***to test him with hard questions.*** [2]*Arriving at Jerusalem with a very great caravan, with camels carrying spices, large quantities of gold, and precious stones, she came to Solomon and talked with him about all that she had on her mind.* [3]*Solomon answered all her questions; nothing was too hard for the king to explain to her.* [4]*When the queen of Sheba saw all the wisdom of Solomon and the palace he had built,* [5]*the food on his table, the seating of his officials, the attending servants in their robes, his cupbearers, and the burnt offerings he made at the temple of the LORD, she was overwhelmed.*
>
> [6]*She said to the king, "The report I heard in my own country about your achievements and your wisdom is true.* [7]*But I did not believe these things until I came and saw with my own eyes.* ***Indeed, not even half was told me; in wisdom and wealth you have far exceeded the report I heard.*** [8]*How happy your men must be! How happy your officials, who continually stand before you and hear your wisdom!* [9]*Praise be to the LORD your God, who has delighted in you and placed you on the throne of Israel. Because of the LORD's eternal love for Israel, he has made you king, to maintain justice and righteousness."*

This is where we must stop in our reading today. However, what the Word of God says about the queen of Sheba does not end here. Less than one thousand years after that time, the Messiah had something to say about the queen of Sheba and King Solomon. He said, "*The Queen of the South will rise at the judgment with this generation and condemn it; for she came from the ends of the earth to listen to Solomon's wisdom, and* ***now one greater than Solomon is here.***" (Matt. 12:42)

Did you hear what the Messiah said? He said that **the queen of Sheba's investigation of the glory of Solomon will condemn all those who refuse to investigate the glory of the Messiah**. The queen of Sheba did everything in her power to discover the glory of Solomon and listen to his wisdom. She even traveled four thousand kilometers, round trip, to know whether what she had heard was the truth! There is an important lesson for us here. **The Messiah**, who came from heaven, far exceeds Solomon in glory, in wisdom, in knowledge and in power, yet most of the children of Adam **do not recognize** His glory, **nor are they willing to investigate** the matter to know the truth! That was why the Messiah said: "*The Queen of the South will rise at the judgment with this generation and condemn it; for she came from the ends of the earth to listen to Solomon's wisdom, and now one greater than Solomon is here!*" (Matt. 12:42)

You who are listening today, **do you recognize the glory of the Messiah** whom God sent? Or do you put Him on the same level as the prophets? Do you remember what the title *Messiah* means? Yes, it means *the One whom God has selected*. The Messiah is the One whom God has selected as the Savior and Judge of the world. Yet, to this very day, most people ignore the Messiah. They do not know who He is, because they have never searched for Him in the Writings of the Prophets.

Our time is almost up, but before we bid you farewell, you should know that King Solomon wrote three wonderful and profound books which are a part of the Holy Scriptures. Those books are: *Proverbs*, *Ecclesiastes* {Lit. *the Preacher*}, and *the Song of Songs*. Like his father David, Solomon wrote some hymns which are part of the book of Psalms. To conclude today's program, we would like to read chapter seventy-two which the prophet Solomon wrote in the Psalms. In this hymn, **Solomon predicts that the Messiah will return to earth one day to judge mankind in righteousness.** Let us listen to what King Solomon wrote concerning the perfect King who surpassed him in wisdom and glory.

Concerning the Messiah, Solomon wrote:

> (Psa. 72) [2]*He will judge your people in righteousness, your afflicted ones with justice.* [8]*He will rule from the sea…to the ends of the earth.* [9]*The desert tribes will bow before him and his enemies will lick the dust.* [10]*…the kings of Sheba and Seba [in Arabia] will present him gifts.* [11]***All kings will bow down to him** and all nations will serve him.* [15]*Long may he live!…* [17]*May his name endure forever; may it continue as long as the sun! All nations will be blessed through him, and they will call him blessed.* [18]*Praise be to the LORD God, the God of Israel, who alone does marvelous deeds!* [19]*Praise be to his glorious name forever; may the whole earth be filled with his glory! Amen and Amen.*

Thus King Solomon predicted that one day all the people of the world will submit to the Messiah, the King of kings and the Judge of the world! Of course, what God wants is for each of us to submit to Him today! How about you? Are you truly submitted to God? Do you recognize the glory and authority of the Messiah whom God has sent and will send again? Or do you merely place Him on the same level as the prophets? If you will take the time to investigate the Writings of the Prophets, you will discover that the Messiah is the Savior and Judge of the world; the One to whom all the prophets bear witness. That is what the Holy Scriptures declare when they say: "*All the prophets testify [of the Messiah] that everyone who believes in him receives forgiveness of sins through His name!…* ***Do you believe the prophets?***" (Acts 10:43; 26:27)

Friends, thank you for listening. God willing, next time, we will study about the prophet of God, Elijah, who called down fire from heaven….

God bless you as you carefully consider what the Messiah declared, saying,

> ***"The Queen of the South will rise at the judgment with this generation and condemn it; for she came from the ends of the earth to listen to Solomon's wisdom, and now one greater than Solomon is here!"*** (Matt. 12:42)

LESSON 53

THE PROPHET ELIJAH

1 KINGS 6-18

Peace be with you, listening friends. We greet you in the name of God, the Lord of peace, who wants everyone to understand and submit to the way of righteousness that He has established, and have true peace with Him forever. We are happy to be able to return today to present your program *The Way of Righteousness*.

In the last lesson, we studied the story of Solomon, son of the prophet David. We saw how **God gave Solomon exceptional wisdom and discernment**. In the time of King Solomon, Jerusalem was the most beautiful city in the world. But of all the things which Solomon constructed in Jerusalem, nothing surpassed the beauty of **the Temple of the LORD God**. King Solomon built the Temple to replace the Tent of Meeting, the special tent of worship, that Moses and the Israelites had constructed in the wilderness. Solomon employed two hundred thousand workers for seven years to build this beautiful place of worship. Today one can still see in Jerusalem the great stones of the foundation of the temple that Solomon built.

When the temple was finished, the priests sacrificed **thousands of sheep and bulls to symbolize the Redeemer** who would come and shed His precious blood for sinners. This is how they consecrated (offered, devoted) to God the temple that they had built for His name. After they had offered those animals and burnt them on the bronze altar of the temple, the priests carried the ark of the covenant (which had been in the Tent of Meeting) and placed it in the Holiest Place (Holy of Holies) of the new temple. When the priests left the Holy of Holies, immediately the glory of the LORD filled the room. Just as the glory of God filled the Holy of Holies in the tent of worship which Moses and the Israelites made in the wilderness, so the glory of God filled the Holy of Holies in the temple that Solomon built in Jerusalem.

Concerning the rest of Solomon's life, the Scriptures tells us the latter part of his reign was not like the beginning. Listen to what is written in the first book of Kings, chapter eleven. Again, we will notice that the holy Word of God does not hide the sins of the prophets. The Scripture says: "*King Solomon, however, loved many foreign women...As Solomon grew old, his wives turned his heart after other gods, and* ***his heart was not fully devoted to the LORD his God, as the heart of David his father had been***." (1 Kings 11:1,4)

Then Solomon built on the hills east of Jerusalem high places for all of his foreign wives, to burn incense and offer sacrifices to their gods. When he did this, God was angry with Solomon, because he had turned his back on the Word of the true and living God. Then God said to Solomon,

> "***Since this is your attitude*** *and you have not kept my covenant and my decrees, which I commanded you,* ***I will most certainly tear the kingdom away from you*** *and give it to one of your subordinates. Nevertheless, for the sake of David your father, I will not do it during your lifetime. I will tear it out of the hand of your son. Yet I will not tear the whole kingdom from him, but will give him one tribe for the sake of David my servant and for the sake of Jerusalem, which I have chosen.*" (1 Kings 11:11-13)

Thus the Scriptures tell us that after Solomon died, there was fighting and strife within the nation of Israel. The twelve tribes of Israel which came from the children of Jacob, **split in two**, just as God had told Solomon. They were no longer one nation; they became two nations, **Israel** and **Judah**. The ten tribes of Israel in the north of the land formed the kingdom of Israel. The tribe of Judah, joined by the little tribe of Benjamin, formed the southern kingdom of Judah. **Judah** was the tribe of King David and the lineage through which God had promised to bring **the Messiah** into the world.

The Scripture relates how those two nations had many kings. Most of the kings of Israel and Judah were wicked leaders; they turned their backs on the LORD and followed the religions of the nations around them. Among all those kings of Israel, one was more evil and wicked than all the others. Do you know who it was? It was **King Ahab**. Ahab was the eighth king after Solomon.

Concerning Ahab, the Scripture says: "*Ahab son of Omri did more evil in the eyes of the LORD than any of those before him.*" (1 Kings 16:30) He also married **Jezebel**, an evil woman who rejected the Word of the LORD. Furthermore, Ahab built in Israel a temple to the name of **Baal** whom the surrounding nations considered to be God. Thus Ahab greatly angered the LORD by leading the Israelites to follow an empty, false religion and its lying, false prophets.

However, in that time there was a man in Israel who walked with God. His name was **Elijah**. One day, God sent Elijah to King Ahab. "*Elijah...said to Ahab, "As the LORD, the God of Israel, lives, whom I serve, there will be neither dew nor rain in the next few years except at my word.*" (1 Kings 17:1)

Thus, for three and a half years no rain fell on the land of Israel. The famine became severe throughout the land. In chapter eighteen, the Scripture says:

(1 Kings 18) [1]*After a long time, in the third year, the word of the LORD came to Elijah: "Go and present yourself to Ahab, and I will send rain on the land."* [2]*So Elijah went to present himself to Ahab.…* [17]*When he saw Elijah, he said to him, "Is that you, you troubler of Israel?"* [18]*"I have not made trouble for Israel," Elijah replied. "But you and your father's family have. You have abandoned the LORD's commands and have followed the Baals.* [19]***Now summon the people from all over Israel to meet me on Mount Carmel**. And bring the four hundred and fifty prophets of Baal and the four hundred prophets of Asherah, who eat at Jezebel's table."*

[20]*So Ahab sent word throughout all Israel and assembled the prophets on Mount Carmel.* [21]*Elijah went before the people and said, "**How long will you waver between two opinions? If the LORD is God, follow him; but if Baal is God, follow him!"** But the people said nothing.*

[22]*Then Elijah said to them, "I am the only one of the LORD's prophets left, but Baal has four hundred and fifty prophets.* [23]*Get **two bulls** for us. Let them choose one for themselves, and let them cut it into pieces and put it on the wood but not set fire to it. I will prepare the other bull and put it on the wood but not set fire to it.* [24]*Then you call on the name of your God, and I will call on the name of the LORD. **The God who answers by fire, he is God.**"*

Then all the people said, "What you say is good." [25]*Elijah said to **the prophets of Baal**, "Choose one of the bulls and prepare it first, since there are so many of you. Call on the name of your God, but do not light the fire."* [26]*So they took the bull given them and prepared it. Then they called on the name of Baal from morning till noon. "O Baal, answer us!" they shouted. But there was no response; no one answered. And they danced around the altar they had made.* [27]*At noon Elijah began to taunt them. "Shout louder!" he said. "Surely he is a god! Perhaps he is deep in thought, or busy, or traveling. Maybe he is sleeping and must be awakened."* [28]*So they shouted louder and slashed themselves with swords and spears, as was their custom, until their blood flowed.* [29]*Midday passed, and they continued their frantic prophesying until the time for the evening sacrifice. But there was no response, no one answered, no one paid attention.*

[30]***Then Elijah** said to all the people, "Come here to me." They came to him, and he repaired the altar of the LORD, which was in ruins.* [31]*Elijah took twelve stones, one for each of the tribes descended from Jacob, to whom the word of the LORD had come, saying, "Your name shall be Israel."* [32]*With the stones he built an altar in the name of the LORD, and he dug a trench round it large enough to hold two seahs of seed.* [33]*He arranged the wood, cut the bull into pieces and laid it on the wood. Then he said to them, "Fill four large jars with water and pour it on the offering and on the wood."*

[34]*"Do it again," he said, and they did it again. "Do it a third time," he or-*

dered, and they did it the third time. [35]*The water ran down around the altar and even filled the trench.*

[36]*At the time of sacrifice, the prophet Elijah stepped forward and prayed: "O* LORD*, God of Abraham, Isaac and Israel, let it be known today that you are God in Israel and that I am your servant and have done all these things at your command.* [37]*Answer me, O* LORD*, answer me,* ***so these people will know that you, O*** **LORD*****, are God, and that you are turning their hearts back again****."*

[38]*Then the fire of the* LORD *fell and burned up the sacrifice, the wood, the stones and the soil, and also licked up the water in the trench.* [39]*When all the people saw this, they fell prostrate and cried,* **"The LORD, he is God! The LORD, he is God!"**

[40]*Then Elijah commanded them, "Seize the prophets of Baal. Don't let anyone get away!" They seized them, and Elijah had them brought down to the Kishon Valley and slaughtered them there.* [41]*And Elijah said to Ahab, "Go, eat and drink, for there is the sound of a heavy rain."* [42]*So Ahab went off to eat and drink, but Elijah climbed to the top of Carmel, bent down to the ground and put his face between his knees.* [45]*Meanwhile, the sky grew black with clouds, the wind rose, a heavy rain came on.*

This amazing story is full of the glory and power of God, and does not really need our comments. However, before we bid you farewell, we ought to take note of what the prophet Elijah said to the people of Israel. Before he challenged the four hundred and fifty false prophets of Baal, Elijah said to the people, ***"How long will you waver between two opinions? If the*** **LORD** ***is God, follow him; but if Baal is God, follow him!"***

At first, the Israelites gave no response. However, when they saw how the LORD God answered the prayer of Elijah in causing fire to rain down from heaven upon his altar, the whole crowd fell down prostrate and cried, ***"The*** **LORD*****, He is God! The*** **LORD*****, He is God!"*** Thus, in a single day, God's prophet, Elijah, exposed and discredited the false prophets of Baal before everyone and turned the hearts of the Israelites back to the LORD their God!

Why did God answer Elijah's prayer? Because Elijah loved the LORD God and believed His Word. **Why did God ignore the prayer of the prophets of Baal?** Because they were not praying to the one true God who had revealed Himself to Abraham, Isaac, and the nation of Israel. The prophets of Baal ignored God's Word and followed their own religious traditions. They were zealous in observing their rituals, but they did not serve the living God—therefore, all their religious zeal was meaningless. They were like the men in the (Wolof) proverb: "Ten men dig a deep hole, ten men fill it—there is plenty of dust, but no hole!"

Like that, the prophets of Baal had plenty of religion, they made a lot of noise with their prayers and sacrifices, but it was all in vain—because it was not founded upon the Word of the Living God. "Plenty of dust, but no hole!"

Thus, on that momentous day, the prophet Elijah commanded the Israelites to choose either:

The LORD God of Abraham, Isaac and Jacob or **the empty religion of Baal;**
The truth or **a lie;**
The way of righteousness or **the way of unrighteousness;**
The reliable Word of God or **the unreliable words of man's religion.**

What would be your response to Elijah's question: ***"How long will you waver between two opinions?"*** How long will you waver between the true Word of God and the worthless traditions established by men? The Holy Scripture says: **"*No one can serve two masters*.** *Either he will hate the one and love the other, or he will be devoted to the one and despise the other. You cannot serve both God and money.*" (Matt. 6:24) You cannot mix serving the LORD God and serving an empty religion. ***"How long will you waver between two opinions?"***

Friends, thank you for listening. Next time we plan to look at the story of a prophet who spent three days inside a huge fish. Do you the name of this prophet? Join us next time for his amazing story....

God bless you as you ponder what Elijah told the Israelites, when he said,

> ***"How long will you waver between two opinions? If the LORD is God, follow him!"*** (1 Kings 18:21)

LESSON 54

THE PROPHET JONAH

JONAH

Peace be with you, listening friends. We greet you in the name of God, the Lord of peace, who wants everyone to understand and submit to the way of righteousness that He has established, and have true peace with Him forever. We are happy to be able to return today to present your program *The Way of Righteousness*.

In our last program, we looked into the story of God's prophet, **Elijah**. Elijah was a great prophet because the power of the Spirit of God was upon him. He prayed to God that it would not rain and there was no rain in Israel for three and a half years. Also, Elijah confronted the false prophets of Baal, exposing their false religion before all the Israelites. Thus God used the prophet Elijah to turn the hearts of many Israelites back to the LORD their God.

Today then, we want to consider the story of another prophet who came after Elijah. We will see how God chose an Israelite by the name of **Jonah** {*Yunus* in Arabic} and ordered him to **go and preach to foreigners** who were enemies of the Israelites.

We are reading in the book of Jonah, in the first chapter. The Scripture says: (Jonah 1) [1]*The word of the LORD came to Jonah, son of Amittai:* [2]"**Go** *to the great city of Nineveh and preach against it, because its wickedness has come up before me*."

Did you hear what the LORD commanded Jonah? God told him to go and warn the people of the city of Nineveh to repent of their sins–even though Nineveh was the capital of the nation of Assyria, and the people of Assyria were a wicked people who wanted to destroy the Israelites!

Why did the LORD God want to send Jonah to those foreigners who despised and hated the Israelites? Did God also care about Israel's enemies? Yes, He did! God was about to judge the people of Nineveh because their sin had reached to heaven. However, **God takes no pleasure in destroying sinners**. God wants everyone to repent of his sin, believe God's Word and be saved. **That is why the LORD commanded Jonah to go** to the people of Nineveh, and warn them so that they could repent of their sin, turn to God, and be saved.

However, **Jonah did not want to go** and warn his enemies! Jonah did not want to be a prophet to the city of Nineveh! God wanted the people of Nineveh to repent so that He could have mercy on them, but Jonah wanted God to punish them! Thus, Jonah refused his assignment and tried to run away from the LORD God. But where could he flee to get away from the presence of God?

Let us continue the story to see what Jonah did. The Scripture says:

> (Jonah 1) [3]***But Jonah ran away*** *from the* LORD *and headed for Tarshish* (that is, a place very far from Nineveh). *He went down to Joppa, where he found a ship bound for that port. After paying the fare, he went aboard and sailed for Tarshish to flee from the* LORD. [4]*Then* **the LORD sent *a great wind*** *on the sea, and such a violent storm arose that the ship threatened to break up.* [5]*All the sailors were afraid and each cried out to his own God. And they threw the cargo into the sea to lighten the ship. But Jonah had gone below deck, where he lay down and fell into a deep sleep.* [6]*The captain went to him and said, "How can you sleep? Get up and call on your God! Maybe he will take notice of us, and we will not perish."* [7]*Then the sailors said to each other, "Come, let us cast lots to find out who is responsible for this calamity." They cast lots and the lot fell on Jonah.*
>
> [8]*So they asked him, "Tell us, who is responsible for making all this trouble for us? What do you do? Where do you come from? What is your country? From what people are you?"* [9]*He answered, "I am a Hebrew and I worship the* LORD, *the God of heaven, who made the sea and the land."* [10]*This terrified them and they asked, "What have you done?" (They knew he was running away from the* LORD, *because he had already told them so.)* [11]*The sea was getting rougher and rougher. So they asked him, "What should we do to you to make the sea calm down for us?"* [12]*"Pick me up and throw me into the sea," he replied, "and it will become calm. I know that it is my fault that this great storm has come upon you."* [13]*Instead, the men did their best to row back to land. But they could not, for the sea grew even wilder than before.*
>
> [14]*Then they cried to the* LORD, *"O* LORD, *please do not let us die for taking this man's life. Do not hold us accountable for killing an innocent man, for you, O* LORD, *have done as you pleased."* [15]*Then they took Jonah and threw him overboard, and the raging sea grew calm.* [16]*At this the men greatly feared the* LORD, *and they offered a sacrifice to the* LORD *and made vows to him.* [17]*But* ***the LORD provided a great fish*** *to swallow Jonah, and Jonah was inside the fish three days and three nights.*

Let us pause here. To this point, we see how God pursued Jonah, His fleeing prophet! Jonah could run, but he could not escape the hand of God. Why did God pursue Jonah? God pursued him because He loved Jonah and wanted him to do His will. That is why God sent a huge fish to swallow him but not kill him.

Poor Jonah! Now he found himself in the belly of a great big fish! What could Jonah do to save himself? Nothing! Nothing except call out to the LORD God. Only God could save him. In chapter two, the Scripture tells how Jonah prayed to the LORD from inside the fish and confessed his sin of refusing to obey God. For three days, God protected Jonah inside the sea creature. What an important lesson Jonah had learned! On the third day, Jonah cried out, ***"Salvation comes from the LORD!"*** (Jonah 2:9) When Jonah said, *"Salvation comes from the LORD,"* the Scripture says: *"the LORD commanded the fish, and it vomited Jonah onto dry land."* (Jonah 2:10)

In chapter three, the Scriptures continues:

> (Jonah 3) [1]*Then the word of the LORD came to Jonah a second time:* [2]*"**Go** to the great city of Nineveh and proclaim to it the message I give you."* [3]***Jonah obeyed*** *the word of the LORD and went to Nineveh. Now Nineveh was a very important city, a visit required three days.* [4]*On the first day, Jonah started into the city. He proclaimed: "Forty more days and Nineveh will be overturned!"*
>
> [5]***The Ninevites believed God****. They declared a fast, and all of them, from the greatest to the least, put on sackcloth.* [6]*When the news reached the king of Nineveh, he rose from his throne, took off his royal robes, covered himself with sackcloth and sat down in the dust.* [7]*Then he issued a proclamation in Nineveh: "By the decree of the king and his nobles: Do not let any man or beast, herd or flock, taste anything; do not let them eat or drink.* [8]*But let man and beast be covered with sackcloth. Let everyone call urgently on God. Let them give up their evil ways and their violence.* [9]*Who knows? God may yet relent and with compassion turn from his fierce anger so that we will not perish."* [10]***When God saw what they did and how they turned from their evil ways, he had compassion and did not bring upon them the destruction he had threatened****.*

Thus we see that **God had mercy** on the people of Nineveh, because they believed the word which He sent them. The Ninevites repented of their sin with a broken and crushed heart and turned to the LORD. However, **Jonah was not happy** that God showed mercy to the people of Nineveh. Listen to what is written in the fourth and final chapter of the book of Jonah.

The Scripture says:

> (Jonah 4) [1]*But **Jonah was greatly displeased** and became angry.* [2]*He prayed to the LORD, "O LORD, is this not what I said when I was still at home? That is why I was so quick to flee to Tarshish. I knew that you are a gracious and compassionate God, slow to anger and abounding in love, a God who relents from sending calamity.* [3]*Now, O LORD, take away my life, for it is better for me to die than to live."* [4]*But the LORD replied, "Have you any right to be angry?"* [5]*Jonah*

went out and sat down at a place east of the city. There he made himself a shelter, sat in its shade and waited to see what would happen to the city.
[6]Then the LORD God provided a vine and made it grow up over Jonah to give shade for his head to ease his discomfort, and Jonah was very happy about the vine.

[7]But at dawn the next day God provided a worm, which chewed the vine so that it withered.
[8]When the sun rose, God provided a scorching east wind, and the sun blazed on Jonah's head so that he grew faint. He wanted to die, and said, "It would be better for me to die than to live."
[9]But God said to Jonah, "Do you have a right to be angry about the vine?" "I do," he said. "I am angry enough to die."
[10]But the LORD said, "You have been concerned about this vine, though you did not tend it or make it grow. It sprang up overnight and died overnight.
[11]But Nineveh has more than a hundred and twenty thousand people who cannot tell their right hand from their left, and many cattle as well. Should I not be concerned about that great city?" That is how the book of Jonah ends.

Fellow listeners, there is much that we can learn about the nature of man and the nature of God in the story of the prophet Jonah. One thing we see is that **God is no respecter of persons** {Lit. God does not show one-sidedness, favoritism}. Jonah showed favoritism, but God did not show favoritism. **God's heart was very different from Jonah's heart.**

Jonah's heart was full of favoritism, but **God's heart** is full of compassion for all people. Jonah loved his own people and hated his enemies, but God loved the people of Israel **and** the people of Nineveh. Jonah wanted the people of Nineveh **to perish** because they were enemies of Israel, but God wanted them **to repent** of their sin, accept His word, and be saved. **God does not show favoritism.** Whoever you are, whatever you are like, **God loves you**. He does not love your sin and rebellion, but He loves **you. God loves every individual in every nation** and wants everyone to confess their sin to Him, to hear the Truth, understand it, believe it and be saved.

Some people think that God doesn't care about each individual on earth; that He has (arbitrarily) chosen some to burn in hell and others to bask in Paradise. While it is true that most people will die in their sins and face God's righteous wrath, it is wrong to think that God doesn't care about those who are perishing in ignorance. The Holy Scriptures tell us that God "***wants all men to be saved and to come to a knowledge of the truth**!*" (1 Tim. 2:4) "*The Lord [does not want] anyone to perish, but everyone to **come to repentance**.*" (2 Pet. 3:9) However, for those who refuse to repent–God will judge them, because they "***refused to love the truth and be saved**....All will be condemned who have not believed the truth but have delighted in wickedness!*" (2 Thes. 2:10,12) That is what the word of the LORD God declares. **God is good and merciful** and has provided a way of salvation for every person. But **God is also holy and righteous** and will judge every person who does not accept His righteous way of salvation.

Friends, let no one deceive you. God never shows favoritism, nor does He take pleasure in the destruction of sinners. **God wants each person on earth to know the truth, believe it and be saved!** That is why God, in the past, inspired the prophets to write His Word, so that we can **know** the way of salvation that God has ordained, **accept** it and be **saved**! Whoever accepts God's way of salvation will go to heaven. Whoever rejects it or neglects it will perish! God is no respecter of persons. As it is written: God *"wants all men to be saved!...But unless you repent, you...will all perish!"* (1 Tim 2:4; Luke 13:3)

In the next program, God willing, we will learn about a great prophet who made many, many predictions about the Redeemer who was to come into the world to save sinners. That great prophet is Isaiah, a prophet of God who lived seven hundred years before the Messiah entered the world....

God bless you as you remember these two lessons God wanted to teach His unfaithful prophet, Jonah:

> [One:] ***"Salvation comes from the LORD!"*** (Jonah 2:10) [Two:] ***"God does not show favoritism!"*** (Acts 10:34)

LESSON 55

THE PROPHET ISAIAH

ISAIAH

Peace be with you, listening friends. We greet you in the name of God, the Lord of peace, who wants everyone to understand and submit to the way of righteousness that He has established, and have true peace with Him forever. We are happy to be able to return today to present your program *The Way of Righteousness.*

In our last program, we studied the story of the prophet **Jonah** who tried to run away from the LORD. However, trying to run from the presence of God is like trying to run away from your shadow. God accompanied Jonah, even inside the great fish!

Today we plan to read about a prophet who came after the time of Jonah and whose name is well known in the Holy Scriptures. This is **the prophet Isaiah** who lived seven hundred years before the Messiah was born. Isaiah was a priest who worked for God in the temple which Solomon had built in Jerusalem. Every day, Isaiah and the rest of the priests had to present to God animal sacrifices on the altar. These sacrifices were symbolic of the Messiah who was to shed His blood for the sin of the world.

Listen to what happened to Isaiah one day when he was offering sacrifices in the Temple of the LORD. In the book of Isaiah, chapter six, Isaiah writes:

> (Isa. 6) [1]*In the year that King Uzziah died,* ***I saw the Lord seated on a throne, high and exalted****, and the train of his robe filled the temple.* [2]*Above him were seraphs, each with six wings: With two wings they covered their faces, with two they covered their feet, and with two they were flying.* [3]*And they were calling to one another:* "**Holy, holy, holy is the LORD Almighty; the whole earth is full of his glory**." [4]*At the sound of their voices the doorposts and thresholds shook and the temple was filled with smoke.* [5]"**Woe to me!**" *I cried.* "**I am ruined! For I am a man of unclean lips, and I live among a people of unclean lips, and my eyes have seen the King, the LORD Almighty**." [6]*Then one of the seraphs flew to me with a live coal in his hand, which he had*

> *taken with tongs from the altar. [7]With it he touched my mouth and said, "See, this has touched your lips; your guilt is taken away and your sin atoned for." [8]Then I heard the voice of the Lord saying, "Whom shall I send? And who will go for us?" And I said, "Here am I. Send me!"*

Thus the LORD God revealed His glory and His holiness to Isaiah and called him to announce His Word to the Israelites, that is, the Jews, and to write it in a book for the benefit of generations to come. The book of Isaiah is lengthy and profound and we do not have time to look into all it contains. However, we can summarize the prophet Isaiah's message with two important thoughts.

First, Isaiah told the Jews **the bad news** about their sin and the punishment that they deserved.

Second, Isaiah presented to them **the Good News** concerning the Messiah who was to come into the world to bear the punishment of their sin.

Therefore, in brief, the message of the prophet Isaiah is:

1.) **the bad news about sin and its penalty;** and

2.) **the Good News about a Savior who would pay the penalty of sin for sinners.**

Let us first cite a few verses which show **the bad news** that God communicated to Isaiah, so that he might announce it both to the Jews and to anyone who has ears to hear. In chapter one, the prophet Isaiah wrote:

> (Isa. 1) [2]***Hear, O heavens! Listen, O earth! For the LORD has spoken:*** *"I reared children and brought them up, but they have rebelled against me. [3]The ox knows his master, the donkey his owner's manger, but Israel does not know, my people do not understand." [4]Ah, sinful nation, a people loaded with guilt, a brood of evildoers, children given to corruption! They have forsaken the LORD; they have spurned the Holy One of Israel and turned their backs on him.* [13]***Stop bringing meaningless offerings! Your incense is detestable to me. New Moons, Sabbaths and convocations–I cannot bear your evil assemblies.*** [14]***Your New Moon festivals and your appointed feasts my soul hates. They have become a burden to me; I am weary of bearing them.*** [15]***When you spread out your hands in prayer, I will hide my eyes from you; even if you offer many prayers, I will not listen!***

That was how the prophet Isaiah rebuked the Jews because of their hypocrisy. He summarized their sin with these words: ***"The LORD says: 'These people honor me with their lips, but their hearts are far from me. They worship me in vain; their teachings are but rules taught by men!'"*** (Matt. 15:8; Isa. 29:13)

After Isaiah rebuked the Jews for their stubbornness and sinfulness, he began to tell them **the Good News,** which has the power to purify the hearts of all who believe it. In the remaining time, let us listen to some of the wonderful words which Isaiah wrote about the Messiah who would come into the world to save sinners. He writes:

> ***"Come now, let us reason together," says the LORD. "Though your sins are like scarlet, they shall be as white as snow; though they are red as crimson, they shall be like wool!"*** (Isa. 1:18)
>
> (Isa. 40) [1]*Comfort, comfort my people, says your* God. [3]*A voice of one calling: "In the desert* ***prepare the way for the LORD****; make straight in the wilderness a highway for our* God. [4]*Every valley shall be raised up, every mountain and hill made low; the rough ground shall become level, the rugged places a plain.* [5]*And the glory of the LORD will be revealed, and all mankind together will see it. For the mouth of the LORD has spoken."* [9]*You who bring good tidings to Zion, go up on a high mountain. You who bring good tidings to Jerusalem, lift up your voice with a shout, lift it up, do not be afraid; say to the towns of Judah,* "***Here is your God!***" [10]***See, the Sovereign LORD comes with power!***
>
> *"The Lord himself will give you a sign:* **The virgin will be with child and *will give birth to a son*,** *and will call him Immanuel–which means* '***God with us***'*!"* (Isa. 7:14; Matt. 1:23).

God was revealing **a great mystery** through the prophet Isaiah! God planned to send **His Spirit** into the womb of a virgin–a woman who had never been intimate with a man! This is how the Messiah would be born into the world. As you know, the Messiah had no earthly father. Before He was born, He was in heaven, because He is **the Word** which was with God in the beginning. According to Isaiah's prophecy, the Messiah would be **God in a human body.** What an awesome truth! God, who is Spirit, planned to place His own Spirit and Word into the womb of a virgin and then to be born into the world as a baby! That is what Isaiah prophesied, saying: "*The virgin will be with child and will give birth to a son, and will call him Immanuel–which means,* '***God with us***'*!*"

In the chapters which follow, Isaiah writes much about the coming of the Messiah. In one place he says:

> *"The people walking in darkness have seen* ***a great light****; on those living in the land of the shadow of death a light has dawned. For to us* **a child is born***, to us* ***a son is given****...And he will be called* **Wonderful Counselor, Mighty God, Everlasting Father, Prince of Peace***!"* (Isa. 9:2,6) *"Then will the eyes of the blind be opened and the ears of the deaf unstopped. Then will the lame leap like a deer, and the mute tongue shout for joy!"* (Isa. 35:5,6)

In these verses, Isaiah prophecies that the Messiah would bring the holiness and mercy of God to the earth. He also foretold how the Messiah would do mighty works that no one had ever done, so that everyone could know that He was the holy Messiah who came from the presence of God! That is why the prophet Isaiah wrote that the Messiah would be called: ***"Wonderful Counselor! Mighty God! Everlasting Father! Prince of Peace!"*** Obviously, Isaiah was not like people today who attempt to put the Messiah on the same level as the prophets. The prophet Isaiah recognized the glory of the Redeemer, who would come forth from the presence of God.

Before we bid you farewell today, we must read one more chapter: **chapter fifty-three.** This chapter is **the most wonderful chapter among all that the prophet Isaiah wrote**, because in it he prophesies how the Messiah would shed His blood like a sacrificed sheep, to bear the punishment of the sin of the world. Listen carefully to the Good News God gave His prophet Isaiah, seven hundred years before the time of the Messiah.

The Holy Scripture says:

> (Isa. 53) [1]***Who has believed our message and to whom has the arm of the LORD been revealed?*** [2]***He (that is, the Messiah) grew up before him like a tender shoot, and like a root out of dry ground. He had no beauty or majesty to attract us to him, nothing in his appearance that we should desire him.*** [3]***He was despised and rejected by men, a man of sorrows, and familiar with suffering. Like one from whom men hide their faces he was despised, and we esteemed him not.*** [4]***Surely he took up our infirmities and carried our sorrows, yet we considered him stricken by God, smitten by him, and afflicted.*** [5]***But he was pierced for our transgressions, he was crushed for our iniquities; the punishment that brought us peace was upon him, and by his wounds we are healed.*** [6]***We all, like sheep, have gone astray, each of us has turned to his own way; and the LORD has laid on him the iniquity of us all.***
>
> [7]***He was oppressed and afflicted, yet he did not open his mouth; he was led like a lamb to the slaughter, and as a sheep before her shearers is silent, so he did not open his mouth.*** [8]***By oppression and judgment he was taken away. And who can speak of his descendants? For he was cut off from the land of the living; for the transgression of my people he was stricken.*** [9]***He was assigned a grave with the wicked, and with the rich in his death, though he had done no violence, nor was any deceit in his mouth.*** [10]***Yet it was the LORD's will to crush him and cause him to suffer, and though the LORD makes his life a guilt offering, he will see his offspring and prolong his days, and the will of the LORD will prosper in his hand.*** [11]***After the suffering of his soul, he will see the light [of life] and be satisfied; by his knowledge my righteous servant will justify many, and***

> ***he will bear their iniquities.*** [12]***Therefore I will give him a portion among the great, and he will divide the spoils with the strong, because he poured out his life unto death, and was numbered with the transgressors. For he bore the sin of many, and made intercession for the transgressors.***

That is what Isaiah wrote concerning the suffering, which the Messiah would endure to pay for our sins. Yes, the Redeemer had to suffer and shed His blood for all sinners so that God could forgive our sin without compromising His righteousness. That is why Isaiah wrote: "*But he was pierced for our transgressions, he was crushed* ***for our iniquities****...We all, like sheep, have gone astray, each of us has turned to his own way; and* ***the LORD has laid on him the iniquity of us all****.*" (Isa.53:5,6) This awesome verse summarizes the message of the book of Isaiah: the **bad news** and the **Good News**.

1.) First, **the bad news** is that we are all sinners and we have no way of saving ourselves! That is why Isaiah wrote: "***We all, like sheep, have gone astray, each of us has turned to his own way***!"

2.) Second, **the Good News** is that God designed a plan to save sinners, and that plan is through the death and resurrection of the Messiah. That is why Isaiah wrote: "***But he was pierced for our transgressions, he was crushed for our iniquities...and the LORD has laid on him the iniquity of us all***."

Friends, do you **recognize** how great your sin is before God, the Holy One? Do you **believe** that the Messiah who was born of a virgin was "*God with us*"? Do you **know why** the Messiah had to shed His blood like a sacrificed sheep?

Meditate upon these life-giving words of the prophet Isaiah. God wants to help you to understand all that Isaiah wrote in chapter fifty-three. If anything is unclear to you in what we studied today, write to us....

Thank you for listening. God bless you as you think deeply about this message from the LORD to you though the prophet Isaiah:

> ***"Come now, let us reason together," says the LORD. "Though your sins are like scarlet, they shall be as white as snow; though they are red as crimson, they shall be like wool!"*** (Isa. 1:18)

Lesson 56

The Prophet Jeremiah

Jeremiah

Peace be with you, listening friends. We greet you in the name of God, the Lord of peace, who wants everyone to understand and submit to the way of righteousness that He has established, and have true peace with Him forever. We are happy to be able to return today to present your program *The Way of Righteousness*.

In the last program, we heard that the prophet **Isaiah** wrote much about the Messiah who was to come. Seven hundred years before the birth of the Messiah, God put into Isaiah's mind how this Savior of sinners would come from the presence of God, be born of a virgin, live a holy life, and do miracles that no one else could do. However, Isaiah also prophesied that the Messiah would shed His blood, like a sacrificed lamb, to pay for the sins of the world. And once His sacrifice was completed, He would conquer death and rise from the grave, providing eternal life to all who believe in Him. Today we plan to study about another great prophet of God—**the prophet Jeremiah**.

Jeremiah lived about a hundred years after the prophet Isaiah. As we have seen already, the nation of Israel was no longer a unified nation. It had become two nations: Israel and Judah. In Jeremiah's day, the kingdom of **Israel**, which was to the north, was destroyed. God delivered the people of Israel into the hands of their enemies, because they did not believe the message of the prophets and repent of their sin. Thus, of the nations of the Jews, **only Judah remained**. Judah was the nation to the south; its capital was Jerusalem where the temple that Solomon had built was located. As we have already learned, Judah was the tribe through which God had promised to bring the Messiah into the world.

Jeremiah was a Jew. He was born in a small town just five kilometers from Jerusalem. Jeremiah's father served as a priest in the temple in Jerusalem. In that time, most of the Jews in Jerusalem were still **very religious**, following the traditions of their ancestors, but **they did not heed the Word of the LORD God**. Jeremiah, however, was a man who cherished the Word of God and obeyed it; he was looking forward to the day when God would send the Messiah into the world.

Now let us hear how God called Jeremiah to be a prophet. In chapter one of the book of Jeremiah, Jeremiah wrote:

> (Jer. 1) [4]*The word of the* LORD *came to me, saying,* [5]"***Before I formed you in the womb I knew you, before you were born I set you apart; I appointed you as a prophet to the nations***." [6]"*Ah, Sovereign* LORD," *I said,* "*I do not know how to speak; I am only a child.*" [7]*But the* LORD *said to me,* "*Do not say, 'I am only a child.' You must go to everyone I send you to and say whatever I command you.* [8]*Do not be afraid of them, for I am with you and will rescue you,*" *declares the* LORD. [9]*Then the* LORD *reached out his hand and touched my mouth and said to me,* "*Now, I have put my words in your mouth.* [10]*See, today I appoint you over nations and kingdoms to uproot and tear down, to destroy and overthrow, to build and to plant.*"

Thus God called Jeremiah to be His prophet. God appointed him to go to his fellow Jews, and tell them that God would judge them if they did not repent of their sin and turn back to the LORD and His holy Word. Jeremiah's task was heavy and difficult, because **the Jews did not want anyone to tell them that their religious works did not please God**. However, the prophet Jeremiah was not a man-pleaser. Thus, for twenty-four years, Jeremiah preached in Jerusalem and throughout the land of Judah, saying: "God wants me to warn you that if you do not repent of your sins and obey the word of the LORD—God will allow the army of the nation of Babylon to come, enter Jerusalem, destroy and burn both the city and the temple! And they will take you as captives to a faraway land!" That is the message Jeremiah proclaimed to the Jews living in Judah.

Let us read a few excerpts from the writings of Jeremiah where he warned his fellow Jews. In the book of Jeremiah, chapter seven, we read:

> (Jer. 7) [1]*This is the word that came to Jeremiah from the* LORD: [2]"***Stand at the gate of the LORD's house and there proclaim this message:***
>
> "'*Hear the word of the* LORD, *all you people of Judah who come through these gates to worship the* LORD. [3]*This is what the* LORD *Almighty, the God of Israel, says: Reform your ways and your actions, and I will let you live in this place.* [4]*Do not trust in deceptive words and say,* "*This is the temple of the* LORD, *the temple of the* LORD! *[God will never judge us because the temple of the* LORD *is here!]*" [5]*If you really change your ways and your actions and deal with each other justly,* [6]*if you do not oppress the alien, the fatherless or the widow and do not shed innocent blood in this place, and if you do not follow other gods to your own harm,* [7]*then I will let you live in this place, in the land I gave to your forefathers for ever and ever.* [8]***But look, you are trusting in deceptive words that are worthless.***

> [9]*"'Will you steal and murder, commit adultery and perjury,...and follow other gods you have not known,* [10]*and then come and stand before me in this house, which bears my Name, and say, "We are safe" safe to do all these detestable things?'"*

Thus Jeremiah rebuked the Jews who **pretended to know God** but denied Him by their actions. In chapter seventeen, Jeremiah adds:

> (Jer. 17) [5]*This is what the LORD says: "Cursed is the one who trusts in man, who depends on flesh for his strength and whose heart turns away from the LORD...* [9]***The heart [of man] is deceitful above all things and beyond cure.*** *Who can understand it?* [10]*"I the LORD search the heart and examine the mind, to reward a man according to his conduct, according to what his deeds deserve."*

Thus Jeremiah warned the people of Judah, informing them: "If you do not repent of your sins and return to God, the armies of Babylon will destroy the city of Jerusalem and this temple, and you will become their slaves!"

What do you think about this? Do you think the people of Judah respected and heeded the word which the LORD had spoken to them through the mouth of Jeremiah? **Most of them did not heed the warning**! Not even the priests believed the words of Jeremiah. In fact, when the priests heard what he said, they arrested him, whipped him, and put his feet in chains for the day. The priests could not believe that God would allow their enemies, the Babylonians, to enter Jerusalem and destroy the city and the temple that Solomon had built. In their thinking, this could never happen! They were angry with Jeremiah because he predicted the destruction of Jerusalem and wrote God's words in a book.

Not only did the people and the priests refuse to accept the words of God's prophet, Jeremiah. The king of Judah also rejected them. In fact, when the king read the book which Jeremiah had written, **he cut up the book** with a knife and threw it into the firepot in the courtyard so that the entire book was consumed! That is what the king of Judah did. He did not repent of his sin, and he did not accept the word of the LORD. Yes, the king burned the book of Jeremiah, **but he could not change God's decree**. God simply directed Jeremiah to rewrite all His words in another book.

If you study the book of Jeremiah, you will see how **the king and the priests and the people of Judah greatly persecuted Jeremiah,** imprisoning him often. Once they put Jeremiah in a deep, muddy pit. But God came to his rescue, sending to him an African man who pulled him out of the pit.

Something important to consider is that although most Jews **refused to listen** to the prophet Jeremiah, this does not mean that they were not listening to anyone! **They were listening** to men who called themselves prophets—but they were

false prophets! The Scriptures tell us about many men who made themselves out to be prophets of God, but in reality they were hypocrites and deceivers, because **their messages did not come from God**. Consequently, while Jeremiah was proclaiming God's judgment which was to befall Jerusalem, the false prophets were speaking to the people of Judah, saying, "No, no! The disaster Jeremiah is predicting will not happen! Babylon cannot destroy Jerusalem! No one can destroy the temple of God! You will not see disaster! You will only have peace! Nothing but Peace!" {Note: in Wolof culture "Peace" is everything. Their standard reply to "How are you doing?" is, "Nothing but peace!"}

But Jeremiah spoke to all the Jews saying,

> (Jer. 23) [16]*This is what the LORD Almighty says:* ***"Do not listen to what the prophets are prophesying to you; they fill you with false hopes****. They speak visions from their own minds, not from the mouth of the LORD.* [21]***I did not send these prophets, yet they have run with their message; I did not speak to them, yet they have prophesied****.* [22]*But if they had stood in my counsel, they would have proclaimed my words to my people and would have turned them from their evil ways and from their evil deeds!"*

Thus Jeremiah warned the Jews to beware of the words of those who preached falsehood. However, unfortunately, most of the people of Judah did not heed the warning of God's prophet, Jeremiah. Instead **they believed the words of the false prophets**. Nevertheless, in the end, after it was **too late**, the king, the priests, the people, and the false prophets found out who had proclaimed **the true word of God**! They found out because everything that Jeremiah had announced concerning the destruction of Jerusalem came to pass. God's Word always comes true.

Listen to what the Scripture says:

> (Jer. 52) [4]*So in the ninth year of the reign of Zedekiah, [King of Judah]...***Nebuchadnezzar** *king of Babylon marched against Jerusalem with his whole army. They camped outside the city and built siege works all around it.* [5]*The city was kept under siege...* [6]*By the ninth day of the fourth month the famine in the city had become so severe that there was no food for the people to eat.* [7]***Then the city wall was broken through****...[Thus the soldiers captured the king of Judah]...* [9]*He was taken to the king of Babylon...where he pronounced sentence on him.* [10]*There at Riblah the king of Babylon slaughtered the sons of [the king of Judah] before his eyes...* [11]*Then he put out Zedekiah's eyes, bound him with bronze shackles and took him to Babylon...* [13]*[Then Nebuchadnezzar, king of Babylon and his soldiers] set fire to the temple of the LORD, the royal palace and all the houses of Jerusalem. Every important building he burned down.*

> [14]*...and broke down all the walls around Jerusalem.* [15]*Nebuzaradan the commander of the guard carried into exile some of the poorest people and those who remained in the city, along with the rest of the craftsmen and those who had gone over to the king of Babylon.* [16]*But Nebuzaradan left behind the rest of the poorest people of the land to work the vineyards and fields.* [27]*...**So Judah went into captivity, away from her land!***

Thus we see how **God fulfilled everything** that He had predicted through the mouth of Jeremiah, His prophet. Now all the Jews knew that the words of Jeremiah had been **the words of truth**. However, this knowledge was of little benefit to them, because they were now captives in the hands of the Babylonian soldiers!

How should we conclude our lesson today? Perhaps we can finish with this thought: In the Day of Judgment, every descendant of Adam will finally know what is true and what is false. However, **God wants you to discern what is true and what is false *now*—because on Judgment Day it will do you no good to know the truth which you disdained during your lifetime on earth!** On the Day of Judgment it will be too late to repent, because you will have perished in your sins! That is why the word of God says: "***Now** is the time of God's favor, **now** is the day of salvation!" (2 Cor. 6:2)*

"Dear friends, do not believe every spirit, but test the spirits to see whether they are from God, because many false prophets have gone out into the world!" (1 John 4:1)

In the next lesson, we will see what happened to the Jews who were carried away to Babylon....

God bless you as you consider this promise from the LORD, penned by the prophet Jeremiah. The LORD God says,

> ***"You will seek me and find me when you seek me with all your heart."*** (Jer. 29:13)

Lesson 57

The Prophet Daniel

Daniel 1,6

Peace be with you, listening friends. We greet you in the name of God, the Lord of peace, who wants everyone to understand and submit to the way of righteousness that He has established, and have true peace with Him forever. We are happy to be able to return today to present your program *The Way of Righteousness*.

In the last program, we examined the book of **Jeremiah**. The prophet Jeremiah lived some six hundred years before the coming of the Messiah. We saw how Jeremiah warned his fellow Jews, telling them that if they did not repent of their sins and turn back to God, the army of the nation of Babylon would destroy the city of Jerusalem and take them captive. Sadly, most of the Jews listened to **the false prophets** and refused to heed Jeremiah's message. Thus we read how the Babylonian army came, destroyed Jerusalem, and carried the Jews far away to Babylon. Everything happened exactly as God had predicted through the mouth of Jeremiah, His prophet.

But the destruction of Jerusalem did not mean that God had abandoned the Jews, the people He had chosen long beforehand. God could not forget **the covenant** that He had made with Abraham, Isaac and Jacob, when He said to them, "*All the peoples of the world will be blessed through you.*" God had not forgotten **His plan** to send the Redeemer into the world through the nation of Jews which descended from Abraham. Thus the Scriptures relate how God took care of the Jews in Babylon for **seventy years** until He brought them back to Jerusalem, just as He had promised. However, to hear that story, you must wait until our next program.

Today we plan to read about a young Jewish man, who was one of the captives taken to Babylon. That young man is **Daniel**–the prophet of God, Daniel. The name Daniel means ***God is my judge***. That was Daniel's testimony in short. Daniel feared no one except Almighty God before whom every person must give an account one day. Daniel wasn't concerned about what men thought of him. Only God's thoughts mattered to him. God was Daniel's judge. Daniel believed what the prophet Solomon had written long before, saying: ***"Fear of man** will prove to be a **snare**, but **whoever trusts in the LORD** is kept **safe**."* (Prov. 29:25)

God inspired Daniel to write a very profound book. **The book of Daniel** contains many revelations (prophecies) which the human mind could not invent. Only God knows what will happen in the future. Yet the prophet Daniel wrote about **the history of many nations** of the world–and he wrote their history before those nations even existed! For example, Daniel wrote how the kingdoms of Persia, and Greece and Rome would come into existence and what their kings would do. And he wrote it hundreds of years before most of these nations even existed! Also, like so many of God's prophets, Daniel wrote concerning **the first coming and the second coming of the Messiah**. Daniel prophesied that at the Messiah's first coming He would be "*cut off*"— that is, killed as a sacrifice for sin (Dan. 9:26), but when the Messiah returns to earth He will judge the world in righteousness. Listen to the vision the prophet Daniel had concerning the Messiah's second coming:

> "*As I looked, thrones were set in place, and* **the Ancient of Days** *took his seat. His clothing was as white as snow; the hair of his head was white like wool. His throne was flaming with fire, and its wheels were all ablaze. A river of fire was flowing, coming out from before him. Thousands upon thousands attended to him; ten thousand times ten thousand stood before him. The court was seated, and the books were opened!*
>
> *In my vision at night I looked, and there before me was one like* ***a son of man****, coming with the clouds of heaven. He approached the Ancient of Days and was led into his presence. He was given authority, glory and sovereign power; all peoples, nations and men of every language worshiped him. His dominion is an everlasting dominion that will not pass away, and his kingdom is one that will never be destroyed."* (Dan. 7:9,10,13,14)

Now then, since time doesn't allow us to delve into the deepest thoughts of God contained in the book of Daniel, we will spend the rest of our time today looking at **the story of the prophet Daniel** himself.

In the first chapter of the book of Daniel, we see how Nebuchadnezzar, the King of Babylon, selected some of the **Jewish young men** in order to train them to serve in his government. He chose those who were the most handsome and intelligent—with an aptitude for every kind of learning, capable of learning the difficult alphabet and language of Babylon. **Daniel** was one of the young men whom the king chose.

Thus, Daniel began to study in the schools of Babylon. However, on the very first day, Daniel faced **a dilemma**. The great King of Babylon had decided that the young men who were part of his school must drink the best wine and eat the best food. However, this wine and food had been offered to idols. Could Daniel participate in the worship of idols? Absolutely not! Why not? Because Daniel feared **God**. Daniel preferred death to doing something that was not pleasing to God, his Lord. Thus, the Scripture says: "*But* ***Daniel resolved not to defile himself*** *with the royal food and wine, and he asked the chief official for permission not to defile himself in this way.*" (Dan. 1:8)

The Scriptures relate how God rescued Daniel from that dilemma, blessed him and gave him deep knowledge and wisdom, so that the Scripture says: "*So [Daniel] entered the king's service. In every matter of* ***wisdom and understanding*** *about which the king questioned them, he found [Daniel]* ***ten times better*** *than all the magicians and enchanters in his whole kingdom.*" (Dan. 1:20) Thus, for about seventy years, Daniel worked for four different kings, and God was with him.

In the time remaining today, we would like to look at **a story from the life of Daniel**–a story that shows how Daniel feared no one but God alone. We will see how Daniel was very different from the other officials who worked for the King. They were the kind of men who habitually twisted the truth and received bribes–because the fear of God was far from their heart. However, Daniel refused all unrighteousness and falsehood, because the fear of God filled his heart. He preferred to be thrown into a den of lions rather than to displease God.

Where our story begins, Daniel was now an old man and was serving faithfully under his fourth king. The Kingdom of Babylon was no longer called Babylon, but Persia, because two nations, that is, the Medes and the Persians, had conquered Babylon and divided it in two, just as the prophet Daniel had prophesied.

In chapter six, the Scripture says:

> (Dan. 6) [1]*It pleased Darius [the King] to appoint 120 satraps to rule throughout the kingdom,* [2]*with three administrators over them, one of whom was Daniel. The satraps were made accountable to them so that the king might not suffer loss.* [3]*Now* ***Daniel so distinguished himself among the administrators and the satraps by his exceptional qualities*** *that the king planned to set him over the whole kingdom.*
>
> [4]*At this, the administrators and the satraps tried to find grounds for charges against Daniel in his conduct of government affairs, but they were unable to do so. They could find no corruption in him, because he was trustworthy and neither corrupt nor negligent.* [5]*Finally these men said,* ***"We will never find any basis for charges against this man*** *Daniel unless it has something to do with the law of his God."*
>
> [6]*So the administrators and the satraps went as a group to the king and said: "O King Darius, live forever!* [7]*The royal administrators, prefects, satraps, advisers and governors have all agreed that the king should issue an edict and enforce the*

decree that ***anyone who prays to any God or man during the next thirty days, except to you, O king, shall be thrown into the lions' den****.* [8]*Now, O king, issue the decree and put it in writing so that it cannot be altered, in accordance with the laws of the Medes and Persians, which cannot be repealed."* [9]*So King Darius put the decree in writing.*

[10]***Now when Daniel learned that the decree had been published, he went home to his upstairs room where the windows opened toward Jerusalem. Three times a day he got down on his knees and prayed, giving thanks to his God, just as he had done before.*** [11]*Then these men went as a group and found Daniel praying and asking God for help.* [12]*So they went to the king and spoke to him about his royal decree: "Did you not publish a decree that during the next thirty days anyone who prays to any God or man except to you, O king, would be thrown into the lions' den?" The king answered, "The decree stands, in accordance with the laws of the Medes and Persians, which cannot be repealed."* [13]*Then they said to the king, "Daniel, who is one of the exiles from Judah, pays no attention to you, O king, or to the decree you put in writing. He still prays three times a day."*

[14]*When the king heard this, he was greatly distressed; he was determined to rescue Daniel and made every effort until sundown to save him.* [15]*Then the men went as a group to the king and said to him, "Remember, O king, that according to the law of the Medes and Persians no decree or edict that the king issues can be changed."* [16]*So the king gave the order, and they brought Daniel and* ***threw him into the lions' den****. The king said to Daniel, "May your God, whom you serve continually, rescue you!"* [17]*A stone was brought and placed over the mouth of the den, and the king sealed it with his own signet ring and with the rings of his nobles, so that Daniel's situation might not be changed.* [18]*Then the king returned to his palace and spent the night without eating and without any entertainment being brought to him. And he could not sleep.*

[19]*At the first light of dawn, the king got up and hurried to the lions' den.* [20]*When he came near the den, he called to Daniel in an anguished voice, "Daniel, servant of the living God, has your God, whom you serve continually, been able to rescue you from the lions?"* [21]*Daniel answered,* ***"O king, live forever!*** [22]***My God sent his angel, and he shut the mouths of the lions. They have not hurt me, because I was found innocent in his sight. Nor have I ever done any wrong before you, O king."*** [23]*The king was overjoyed and gave orders to lift Daniel out of the den. And when Daniel was lifted from the den, no wound was found on him, because he had trusted in his God.* [24]*At the king's command, the men who had falsely accused Daniel were brought in and thrown into the lions' den, along with their wives and children. And before they reached the floor of the den,* ***the lions overpowered them*** *and crushed all their bones.*

> [25]*Then King Darius wrote to all the peoples, nations and men of every language throughout the land: "May you prosper greatly!* [26]*"I issue a decree that in every part of my kingdom people must fear and reverence the God of Daniel. For he is the living God and he endures forever; his kingdom will not be destroyed, his dominion will never end.* [27]***He rescues and he saves; he performs signs and wonders in the heavens and on the earth. He has rescued Daniel from the power of the lions!***" Amen.

Did you hear what the heathen king said, after he saw how God had saved Daniel from the lions? He said, "*I issue a decree that in every part of my kingdom people must* ***fear the God of Daniel****. For He is the living God and he endures forever!*"

You who are listening today, do you fear the God of Daniel? Perhaps you are asking, **"Who is the God of Daniel?"** The God of Daniel is the God of Abraham, Isaac and Jacob. The God of Daniel is the God of the prophets Moses and David. The God of Daniel is the God who has given us the Holy Scriptures. He is the God who promised to send down a Redeemer who would save sinners from a power that is stronger than the power of lions, that is, the power of Satan, and sin, and hell! The God of Daniel is **God**—the One True God!

Do you fear the God of Daniel? We are **not** asking whether you fear your friends and their thoughts, or whether you fear your ancestors and their customs, or your marabouts and their demands! What we are asking you is: Do you fear **God**? Do you want to please the LORD God and obey His holy Word? Daniel feared **God**, which was why he did not fear man. Daniel preferred to spend a night in the den of lions than to displease the LORD his God! How about you? Do you fear God? Do you fear Him as Daniel feared Him? Do you hate unrighteousness as Daniel hated it? Do you cherish the Word of God like Daniel cherished it? Or are you like most of the sons of Adam who twist the truth, love money, and neglect the Holy Scriptures? **Do your fear God**?

Thank you for listening. In our next lesson, we plan to look at some amazing prophecies written by Zechariah, a prophet who came after Daniel....

God bless you as you meditate on this important truth:

> ***"Fear of man will prove to be a snare, but whoever trusts in the LORD is kept safe!"*** (Prov. 29:25)

Lesson 58

The Prophet Zechariah

Zechariah

Peace be with you, listening friends. We greet you in the name of God, the Lord of peace, who wants everyone to understand and submit to the way of righteousness that He has established, and have true peace with Him forever. We are happy to be able to return today to present your program *The Way of Righteousness*.

Two programs ago, we learned how the prophet of God, Jeremiah, warned his fellow Jews that if they did not heed the Word of God and repent of their sins, God would allow the soldiers of Babylon to come in, destroy their country, and carry them far away. Most of the Jews paid no attention to Jeremiah's warnings. Consequently, the army of Babylon came from the east, destroyed Jerusalem, broke down the temple and took the Jews captives, transporting them to Babylon, just as the prophet Jeremiah had predicted. **Thus the Jewish people were dispersed, because they refused to obey the word of God's prophets.**

But could the Jew's unfaithfulness frustrate God's faithfulness? Never! Listen to what the prophet Jeremiah told the Jews, who were now captives in Babylon because of their sins. He said to them:

> (Jer. 29) [4]*This is what the LORD Almighty, the God of Israel, says to all those I carried into exile from Jerusalem to Babylon:* [10]*..."When seventy years are completed for Babylon, I will come to you and fulfil my gracious promise to bring you back to [Jerusalem].* [11]***For I know the plans I have for you...plans to prosper you and not to harm you, plans to give you hope and a future.***

With this declaration, the prophet Jeremiah was informing the Jews that even if they had forgotten God, **God had not forgotten them**! After seventy years, God planned to bring them back to the land of their ancestors. That is what Jeremiah told the Jews who were captives in Babylon. Truly, **God is faithful** {Lit. the keeper of covenants}. God had not forgotten that He had promised to bless all the nations of the world through the descendants of Abraham, Isaac and

Israel. God had not forgotten that He purposed to entrust His Word to the Israelites so that they might pass it on to all the descendants of Adam. In our study we have seen how God chose His prophets from among the Jews, inspiring them to proclaim His holy Word and write it down for the people of future generations. We know how God placed the book of the Torah in the mind of Moses and the hymns of the Psalms in the heart of David. We have seen similarly how God inspired other Jews like Joshua, Samuel, Solomon, Isaiah, Jeremiah, and Daniel to write the Word of God. We have observed how all the Writings of God's prophets announce the wonderful plan which God designed to send forth the Savior of the world through the nation of Israel.

Today we will see how **God brought the Jews back** to the land of Judah where the Messiah was to be born, thus moving forward with His plan to bring the Messiah into the world. We will learn how the Jews returned to Jerusalem after seventy years of captivity, just as the prophet Jeremiah had predicted.

As we begin reading, let us remember that the land of Babylon was now called Persia, because Persia had conquered Babylon. Reading in the book of Ezra, chapter one, the Scripture says:

> (Ezra 1) [1]*In the first year of Cyrus king of Persia,* ***in order to fulfil the word of the LORD spoken by Jeremiah, the LORD moved the heart of Cyrus king of Persia*** *to make a proclamation throughout his realm and to put it in writing:* [2]*"This is what Cyrus king of Persia says: 'The LORD, the God of heaven, has given me all the kingdoms of the earth and he has appointed me* ***to build a temple for him at Jerusalem*** *in Judah.* [3]*Anyone of his people among you, may his God be with him, and let him go up to Jerusalem in Judah and build the temple of the LORD, the God of Israel…* [5]*Then the family heads of Judah and Benjamin, and the priests and Levites, everyone whose heart God had moved, prepared to go up and build the house of the LORD in Jerusalem.* [6]*All their neighbors assisted them with articles of silver and gold, with goods and livestock, and with valuable gifts, in addition to all the freewill offerings.* [7]*Moreover, King Cyrus brought out the articles belonging to the temple of the LORD, which Nebuchadnezzar had carried away from Jerusalem and had placed in the temple of his god.*

Did God fulfil what He had promised long beforehand through the mouth of Jeremiah, His prophet? Of course He did! We have already seen how God allowed the king of Babylon to **destroy** Jerusalem, and break down the temple of God–**precisely as Jeremiah had prophesied**. And now we see how Cyrus, the king of Persia, commanded any of the Jews who so desired, to return to their land and **rebuild** the temple and the city of Jerusalem–**again precisely as the prophet Jeremiah had prophesied**. Truly, the LORD is the King of kings. He is the One who controls the times and the seasons. All that He declares will happen! The prophet Solomon wrote: "*The king's heart is in the hand of the LORD; he directs it like a watercourse wherever he pleases*." (Prov. 21:1)

Next, the Scriptures describe how a group of Jews left the land of Persia and traveled back to the land of Judah and the city of Jerusalem. A Jew named **Zerubbabel** was their leader. When they came to Jerusalem, they were troubled greatly because the whole city was destroyed, and the temple of the LORD which Solomon had built was in ruins. Nothing was left there except broken pieces of stone and ashes.

Thus the Scriptures relate how the Jews first had a meeting in the place where the temple of the LORD had been. There they rebuilt the altar of sacrifice and sacrificed some animals. Together they thanked and praised the LORD for protecting them in Babylon and Persia for seventy years and for bringing them back to their homeland. God was with those Jews, to help them and strengthen them—so that after many trials and many years of hard work—**they were able to rebuild the temple of the LORD, the city of Jerusalem, and the walls that surrounded it.**

Perhaps some of you are asking, "What relevance does the story of the return of the Jews to Jerusalem have for us?" Friends, the return of the Jews to their land is very important because it was in that land of **Judah**, the southern part of Palestine, that **the Messiah** would be born. It was necessary that the Jews return to the land of Judah so that the Redeemer of the world—**your Redeemer**—could be born there!

At the time of the Jews' return to Jerusalem, God provided a prophet by the name of **Zechariah** {*Zakaria* in Arabic}. This Zechariah is different from Zechariah, the father of the prophet John {*Yahya* in the Qur'an}. God sent Zechariah to strengthen the Jews' faith in God and His promises. Zechariah had an important message to deliver. The time appointed by God to send forth the Messiah was drawing closer! Only five hundred years remained before the Redeemer would come into the world.

Let us examine some of the words which God placed in the mind of Zechariah. Reading in the book of Zechariah, chapter one, the Scripture says:

> (Zech. 1) [1]*The word of the LORD came to the prophet Zechariah son of Berekiah, the son of Iddo:* [2]*"The LORD was very angry with your forefathers.* [4]***Do not be like your forefathers****, to whom the earlier prophets proclaimed: This is what the LORD Almighty says: 'Turn from your evil ways and your evil practices.' But they would not listen or pay attention to me, declares the LORD.* [5]*Where are your forefathers now? And the prophets, do they live forever?* [6]*But did not my words and my decrees, which I commanded my servants the prophets, overtake your forefathers?"*

Did you hear **the warning** the prophet Zechariah gave to the Jews? He said to them, "*The LORD was very angry with your forefathers! Do not be like your forefathers!*" Why was God angry with the Jews' forefathers? God was angry with them because **they did not heed the words of the prophets** that He had sent to them. That was why they ended up as captives in Babylon. Their forefathers were religious, but God was not happy with them because they ignored the words of the prophets. The Jews of that time were like people of today who say, "Of course we believe all the prophets!" However, it is obvious that they do not really believe God's prophets, because they do not heed **what the prophets have written** in the Holy Scriptures. They have a **religion**, but they have no personal **relationship** with God Himself. That is what most of the Jewish ancestors were like. They did not appreciate the words of the prophets. They honored God with their **lips** but they did not receive His Word into their **hearts.** Therefore, God sent His servant Zechariah to the Jews, to warn them so that they would not follow the example of their ancestors who had "God, God, God!" on their lips, but ignored the Word which God had sent to them through His prophets.

After Zechariah warned the Jews, he began to tell them about **the Redeemer** who was to come. We do not have time today to read everything that the prophet Zechariah wrote concerning the Messiah, but we can read a few excerpts.

In the book of Zechariah, chapter nine, the prophet Zechariah prophesied that **the Messiah would enter Jerusalem, riding on a donkey**. He said, "*Rejoice greatly, O Daughter of Zion! Shout, Daughter of Jerusalem! See, your king comes to you, righteous and having salvation, gentle and **riding on a donkey**, on a colt, the foal of a donkey.*" (Zech. 9:9)

In chapter eleven, Zechariah penned a remarkable prophecy which we do not have time to explain in detail. One of the events Zechariah predicted was that **the Messiah would be sold for thirty pieces of silver**. The prophet Zechariah wrote: "*I told them, 'If you think it best, give me my pay; but if not, keep it.' So they paid me **thirty pieces of silver**...So I took the **thirty pieces of silver and threw them in to the house of the LORD**...*" (Zech. 11:12,13)

In chapter twelve, Zechariah prophesied that the Jews would not only sell the Messiah, but would even kill Him! He said: The LORD says,

> "*And I will pour out on the house of David and the inhabitants of Jerusalem a spirit of grace and supplication. They will look on me, **the one they have pierced,** and they will mourn for him as one mourns for an only child, and grieve bitterly for him as one grieves for a firstborn son....If someone asks him, '**What are these wounds on your [hands]**?' he will answer, '**The wounds I was given at the house of my friends**.'*" (Zech. 12:10; 13:6)

With those words Zechariah predicted that the Messiah would have wounds (scars) in His hands. Where would He get these wounds? His fellow Jews would persuade the Romans to crucify Him. The Romans would then nail His hands and feet to a cross and later pierce His side with a spear. Everything happened exactly as Zechariah predicted. What the prophet Zechariah wrote is in **perfect harmony** with what the prophet David prophesied hundreds of years earlier in the Psalms, when He wrote concerning the Messiah: "*They have pierced my hands and my feet.*" (Psa. 22:16)

Friends, God wants us to know that **the death of the Messiah on the cross is the most important part of the plan** that He had designed long ago to save the children of Adam from the penalty of their sin. **The righteous Messiah had to suffer and die for the unrighteous! That is the message of all of God's prophets.** Is all of this clear to you? Do you understand what Zechariah prophesied about the Messiah some five hundred years before the Messiah was born? Do you really believe **the message** of the prophets—that the Messiah would suffer and die and, as the first to rise from the dead, would proclaim forgiveness of sins and a place in Paradise to all who believe in His name? **Do you believe the prophets?** (See Acts 26:18-27) Or are you like the Jews, who honored God's prophets with their lips, but did not believe their message?

Concerning the message of the prophets, the Scriptures declare:

> "***Do not treat prophecies with contempt***." (1 Thes. 5:20) "*We have the word of the prophets made more certain, and* ***you will do well to pay attention*** *to it, as to a light shining in a dark place, until the day dawns and the morning star rises in your hearts*." (2 Pet. 1:19) ***"Do you believe the prophets?"*** (Acts 26:27)

Fellow listeners, thank you for listening. God willing, in our next program we will hear a word from the prophet who wrote the last book of Holy Scripture before the Messiah came into the world....

God bless you as you seek to give an honest answer to this important question from the Word of God:

> ***"Do you believe the prophets?"*** (Acts 26:27)

LESSON 59

THE MESSAGE OF THE PROPHETS SUMMARIZED

MALACHI

Peace be with you, listening friends. We greet you in the name of God, the Lord of peace, who wants everyone to understand and submit to the way of righteousness that He has established, and have true peace with Him forever. We are happy to be able to return today to present your program *The Way of Righteousness*.

For a long time now we have studied the first section of the Holy Scriptures. This section is called ***the First Covenant.*** It is also known as the *Old Testament*. This first section contains the Torah, the Psalms, and the other Writings of the Prophets. As we have seen, God used more than thirty prophets over a period of one thousand five hundred years to write the book of the First Covenant.

Today we will complete our journey in the first section of the Holy Scriptures. However, before we look at the last chapters of the book of the First Covenant, we would like to talk a little about what we have gleaned from this holy book from the first day until now. **We can summarize the message of all the prophets with three great thoughts:**

One: God is **holy** and must judge every sin.
Two: All the children of Adam are born in **sin** and must face God's judgment.
Three: God planned to send down a holy **Redeemer** who would bear the punishment of sin for the children of Adam.

Those are the three truths which all the prophets of God preached. Let us repeat these three points.

First: **God is holy**, and cannot overlook sin.
Second: **Man is unholy**, full of sin, and has no way of saving himself from the penalty of sin.
Third: **God has a plan** to cleanse sinners and save them from judgment.

Have you grasped these three truths? Have these truths grasped you? Do you realize how holy God is? Do you recognize how great your sins are in the eyes of the One who must judge you? Do you know that God has a plan to cleanse you from your sins?

Indeed, **God is holy** and **man is unholy**. We have seen those **two truths** often in our studies in the Holy Scriptures. The holiness of God was the reason that God created the unquenchable fire for Satan and everyone who follows him. The holiness of God was the reason that He expelled Adam and Eve from the garden of Paradise on the day that they ate of the forbidden tree. The holiness of God was the reason that God commanded the sons of Adam to sacrifice animals as a burnt offering to cover sin. His holiness was also the reason He did not accept Cain's offering. Because God is holy He destroyed sinners in Noah's time with a flood of water and rained fire in Abraham's time on the people of Sodom and Gomorrah. The holiness of God is the reason that God has prepared a day when He will judge the world in righteousness.

Listen to what God's prophets wrote about the holiness of God and the unholiness of man. They said: "*O LORD, are you not from everlasting?... Your eyes are too pure to look on evil; you cannot tolerate wrong!*" (Hab. 1:12,13) "*All of us have become like one who is unclean, and all our righteous acts are like filthy rags!*" (Isa. 64:6) If God is so holy and man is so unclean, who then can be saved? How can we be saved from the eternal fire of hell? How can the children of Adam spend eternity in the presence of the God who is pure and holy?

The response to that question is the **third point** in the message of the prophets. After the prophets preached that God is **holy** and that the children of Adam are **unholy**, they went on to declare that God Himself had **a plan** to cleanse the children of Adam from their sin.

The most important message of the book of the First Covenant (*the Old Testament*) is that God promised to send into the world **a righteous Redeemer who would die in the place of the unrighteous children of Adam** to redeem all those who believe in Him. This was and is God's plan to save sinners. Only through the Redeemer's shed blood can God forgive sin and reconcile sinners to Himself, without compromising His holiness.

To advance His plan to send the Savior into the world, God called **Abraham** to make of him a new nation, from whom the prophets of God and the Messiah would come. God spoke to Abraham, saying: "*You will be a blessing and **all the peoples of the earth** will be blessed through you.*" And so Abraham begot **Isaac** in his old age, and Isaac begot **Jacob**, and Jacob begot **twelve sons** who produced the tribes of **Israel**. Thus, we learned that when God called Abraham, He was continuing forward with His plan to send the Savior into the world, because it was from the lineage of Abraham, through the nation of Israel, that the Messiah was to be born.

Next we saw how the children of Israel moved from the land of Canaan and settled in Egypt where they became slaves of the Egyptians. But God did not forget the descendants of Abraham, the Israelites. God called **Moses** to free the Israelites and lead them to the land which God had promised to their ancestor Abraham long before. God also used the prophet Moses to give us the book called **the Torah,** which is the foundation of everything that God has made known since then.

After the time of Moses, we saw how God sent many prophets to the Israelites, but most did not heed the words of the prophets. However, the unfaithfulness of the Israelites did not hinder the faithfulness of God and the plan He had designed to send the Messiah into the world! Thus we saw how God chose **David** as king of Israel and the prophet who would write most of the lovely and profound hymns found in the book of **Psalms**. The prophet David wrote much concerning the Messiah and how the children of Adam would persecute Him and even pierce His hands and His feet. But David also prophesied that after the Messiah had shed His blood as a sacrifice that removes sin, He would conquer death and rise from the grave!

In our journey through the Scriptures, we also discovered that it was not only Moses and David who wrote about the Messiah. **All of God's prophets announced the Messiah's coming**. For example, the prophet **Isaiah** announced that the Messiah would be born in a way which, as you know, no one had ever been born. He said: "*The virgin will be with child and will give birth to a son, and they will call him Immanuel, which means, 'God with us.'*" (Isa. 7:14; Matt. 1:23) The prophet Isaiah wrote this seven hundred years before the Messiah was born.

There was another prophet who lived at the same time as Isaiah. His name was **Micah**. God revealed to Micah the name of the town in which the Messiah would be born. Listen carefully to what the prophet Micah wrote. In the book of Micah, chapter five, we read: "*But you, **Bethlehem** Ephrathah, though you are small among the clans of Judah, out of you will come for me one who will be ruler over Israel, whose origins are from of old, from ancient times!*" (Micah 5:2) Thus, Micah announced that the Messiah would be born in the town of Bethlehem, the hometown of King David! Three programs from now, we will learn how God fulfilled this prophecy, for it was in the town of Bethlehem that the Messiah was born, just as God's prophet, Micah, declared it hundreds of years beforehand.

Surely God prepared the arrival of the Savior of the world very carefully! God's holy Book contains **hundreds of references by the prophets about the coming of the Messiah**. Perhaps you are asking: Why did God place in the minds of the prophets all these thoughts concerning the Messiah **before** He came into the world? There is one very important reason. God inspired the prophets to write much about the Messiah before He came, so that when He came and fulfilled all that the prophets wrote concerning Him, we might know **beyond any**

doubt that He and He alone is the Savior whom God sent. God does not want anyone to deceive you! God wants you to know who the Messiah, the Savior of sinners, is, so that you can believe in Him and follow Him and be saved from your sins. That is one of the reasons He gave us this wonderful, reliable Book called the First Covenant—so we might **distinguish** the **truth** from **error**.

Now to finish our journey in the First Covenant, we would like to read from the book of **Malachi**, the final book of the First Covenant. The words of the prophet Malachi are important for us, because they are the final words which God sent down to the children of Adam before the Messiah visited the earth. Only four hundred years remained before the Redeemer would be born.

Listen to what the prophet Malachi wrote in the last chapter of the First Covenant. He said,

> "'*See, I will send my messenger, who will* ***prepare the way before me.*** *Then suddenly the Lord you are seeking will come to his temple; the messenger of the covenant, whom you desire, will come,' says the* LORD *Almighty....'I the* LORD *do not change...But for you who revere my name,* ***the Sun of Righteousness*** *will rise with healing in [his] wings!*'" (Mal. 3:1,6; 4:2)

Thus the prophet Malachi prophesied that God planned to send a prophet before the Messiah to prepare His way. Do you know who that prophet was? In our next lesson, we will see that the one who would prepare the way before the Messiah was the prophet **John** {*Yahya*}

However, Malachi also wrote: The LORD Almighty says: ***"The messenger of the covenant, whom you desire, will come...I the LORD do not change!"*** (Mal. 3:1) About two hundred years earlier, the prophet Jeremiah had prophesied:

> "'*The time is coming when I will make* ***a new covenant*** *with the house of Israel, and the house of Judah. It will not be like the covenant I made with their forefathers when I took them by the hand to lead them out of Egypt, because they broke my covenant, though I was a husband to them,' declares the* LORD. *This is the covenant I will make with the house of Israel after that time, declares the* LORD. *'I will put my law in their minds and write it on their hearts....I will forgive their wickedness and will remember their sins no more!*'" (Jer. 31:31-34)

With these words, God was announcing that the Messiah would bring a New Covenant which would fulfill the promises and conditions of the First Covenant. The New Covenant would not depend on man who had failed to respect God's covenant; it would depend on God who, in His faithfulness and mercy, would send forth the Messiah, the Messenger of the Covenant.

For thousands of years, God had required the sacrifice of animals so that He might forgive the sins of the children of Adam. **Animal sacrifices** were an important part of **the First Covenant** which God gave to mankind through **His prophets**. However, **the Messiah** would bring to the world **the New Covenant,** because He would **fulfil the symbolism of all the animal sacrifices,** thus setting aside the First Covenant.

The Messiah would not come to **abolish** the words of the prophets, but to **fulfil** them. That is why the prophet Malachi calls the Messiah "***the Sun of Righteousness***." How would the Messiah be like the sun? The prophets were like the moon or a candle which diffuses a little light in a dark world. However, the Messiah is the rising sun, because He came to drive out the darkness of our sin and set us on **the way of righteousness forever**! Who needs the light of the moon or a candle once the sun has arisen? The Messiah is **the Sun of Righteousness**! In our next lesson, we will hear that Zechariah, the father of the prophet John, spoke of the Messiah in a similar way, saying: "*Because of the tender mercy of our God...****the rising sun will come to us from heaven to shine on those living in darkness and in the shadow of death****, to guide our feet into the path of peace.*" (Luke 1:78,79) Amen!

And so, friends, we have come to the end of our journey in the books of the First Covenant. Next time, God willing, we will begin the wonderful section which follows, that is, the New Covenant—the book of the Gospel {*Injil*}. It is in the Gospel that we discover how the Messiah fulfilled the words of the prophets....God bless you as you heed this warning:

> ***"We have the word of the prophets made more certain, and you will do well to pay attention to it, as to a light shining in a dark place, until the day dawns and the morning star rises in your hearts!"*** (2 Pet. 1:19)

Part 3

The Way of Righteousness According to The Gospel About Jesus the Messiah

Jesus asked His disciples,
"Who do the crowds say that I am?"
They replied, "Some say…one of the prophets…"
"But what about you? Who do you say that I am?"
Gospel of Luke 9:18-20

"What do you think about the Messiah?"
Gospel of Matthew 22:42

LESSON 60

THE PROPHET JOHN

LUKE 1

Peace be with you, listening friends. We greet you in the name of God, the Lord of peace, who wants everyone to understand and submit to the way of righteousness that He has established, and have true peace with Him forever. We are happy to be able to return today to present your program *The Way of Righteousness*.

Last time, we finished our journey through the first section of the Holy Scriptures, the section that contains the Torah {*Taurat*}, the Psalms {*Zabur*} and Writings of the Prophets. That first section is called ***the First Covenant***, also known as *the Old Testament*. Today we will begin our study of the second section of the Word of God, called *the New Testament, or* **the New Covenant**.

Why did God separate His holy Book into two sections, a First Covenant (Old Testament) and a New Covenant (New Testament)? God had many reasons for doing this. Perhaps the first thing we need to understand is that all the words in the **First Covenant** were written **before the Messiah was born**, while the words of the **New Covenant** were written **after the Messiah was born**. Thus, the message of God's prophets in the First Covenant was: "God **will send** the Messiah!" But the message of the New Covenant is: "God **has sent** the Messiah, just as He promised through His prophets in the First Covenant!"

Is this important difference between the First Covenant and the New Covenant clear in your mind? Some people criticize the Holy Scriptures because it has an ***Old** Testament* and a ***New** Testament*. They think that *New Testament* means that someone has attempted to nullify and replace the original Writings of the Prophets with another book! But that is not the way it is. The New Testament, that is, the New Covenant, **does not nullify** what the prophets wrote in the First Covenant—it **confirms** what the prophets wrote! The New Covenant shows how God fulfilled the promises and prophecies and symbols of the First Covenant. In the First Covenant, all the prophets were announcing: "The Messiah **will** come! **He will come! He will come!**" But the message of the book of the New Covenant is: "The Messiah **has** come! **The Messiah, of whom all the prophets spoke and wrote, has come! He has come!**"

Yes, we should **thank God** with a joyful heart that the Holy Scriptures contain a First Covenant **and** a New Covenant. Because in those two sections, we can see that what God promised so long ago—He has accomplished! God has sent us a Savior, **just as He promised our ancestors in the Torah, the Psalms and the other books of the prophets.** As the seed of the baobab {the most common tree in Senegal} grows up into a mighty baobab tree, in a similar way the First Covenant comes to maturity in the New Covenant.

As you may know, the second section of the Holy Scriptures, **the New Covenant**, has another name. That name is the "***Injil***." *Injil* is an Arabic word which means ***the Good News*** {the Gospel}. Truly, the message of the book of the Gospel is **extremely good news**, because it tells how the Messiah accomplished (fulfilled) what the prophets announced (prophesied), thus opening for the children of Adam a door of peace with God forever!

Concerning the Book of the Gospel {*Injil*}, you need to understand that the Messiah Himself did not write it. Just as God used many men to write the book of the First Covenant, so He used many men to write the book of the New Covenant. God used **four men** to write the story of the Messiah who came to earth. Those four men were named *Matthew*, *Mark*, *Luke*, and *John*. **Why did God inspire four people to write the story of the Messiah?** Why did He not just use one person to write the book of the Gospel? Here is the reason: God wanted to communicate to us a message which would be beyond doubt and worthy of full confidence. He used four writers in order **to confirm His word.** Just as a table with four legs is more stable than a table with one leg, so four witnesses are more reliable than a single witness. God employed four witnesses, so that we might know that everything written in the Book of the Gospel concerning the Messiah is absolutely true! Just as God placed His words in the minds of the prophets, so God guided four men who lived in the same era as the Messiah to write what they had seen and heard concerning the Savior of the world. {Note: Actually, God inspired *eight men* to write about the Messiah. The letters of the apostles Paul, Peter, James and Jude are also part of the *Injil*—the Gospel Writings—and everything they wrote is in perfect and glorious harmony!}

Do you know in which language Matthew, Mark, Luke and John wrote the holy book of the Gospel? They wrote it in the Greek language. However, we will be reading it in English {Lit. *Wolof*} since most of us do not understand Greek! We thank God that He put it into the hearts of scholars to translate the Gospel from Greek into English as well as some two thousand other languages from around the world.

Yes, sometimes we hear those who try to fight against the book of the Gospel, saying, "No one can trust it. It has been tampered with! It contains errors and contradictions!" Friends, the one who fights with the holy Gospel is fighting with God Himself. "An egg should not wrestle with a rock!" {Wolof Proverb}.

The Holy Scriptures are worthy of our full confidence and obedience. Just as the Word of God is perfect in the Torah and the Psalms, so it is also perfect in the Gospel. The Holy Scriptures cannot be broken. God is great and is able to protect His Eternal Word! He has preserved His Truth for all those who seek after it with all their heart. No one can actually alter the living and enduring Word of God! That is what the Lord Himself declares in the Gospel when He says: ***"Heaven and earth will pass away, but my words will never pass away!"*** (Matt 24:35)

Now then, the moment for us to **begin our journey through the book of the Gospel**, the New Covenant, has arrived. In our last program, we read about the prophet Malachi who lived four hundred years before the Messiah. During those four hundred years following the time of Malachi, God did not send to the Jews any more prophets to write the Word of God. Why did God not send any more prophets? He sent no more prophets because the book of the First Covenant was complete. **God had said everything He wanted to say through the prophets.** Now God was waiting for the appointed hour when He would bring the Messiah into the world so that He might establish the New Covenant.

We have already read what the prophets Isaiah and Malachi foretold concerning God's plan to send a prophet before the Messiah to prepare the way before Him. Do you know which prophet that was? Yes, it was the prophet John {Qur'anic name: *Yahya*}. John's father was Zechariah {Arabic: *Zakaria*}. Zechariah was a priest who served God and the people by offering animal sacrifices on the alter of the temple in Jerusalem.

Let us now open the holy Gospel {*Injil*} and hear what Luke wrote concerning the prophet John's birth. Reading in chapter one, the Scripture says:

> (Luke 1) [5]*In the time of Herod king of Judea there was a priest named* ***Zechariah****, who belonged to the priestly division of Abijah; his wife* ***Elizabeth*** *was also a descendant of Aaron.* [6]*Both of them were upright in the sight of God, observing all the Lord's commandments and regulations blamelessly.* [7]*But they had no children, because Elizabeth was barren; and they were both well on in years.*
>
> [8]*Once when Zechariah's division was on duty and he was serving as priest before God....* [10]*And when the time for the burning of incense came, all the assembled worshipers were praying outside.* [11]***Then an angel of the Lord appeared to him, standing at the right side of the altar of incense.*** [12]*When Zechariah saw him, he was startled and was gripped with fear.* [13]*But the angel said to him: "Do not be afraid, Zechariah; your prayer has been heard. Your wife Elizabeth will bear you a son, and you are to give him the name John.* [14]*He will be a joy and delight to you, and many will rejoice because of his birth,* [15]*for he will be great in the sight of the Lord. He is never to take wine or other fermented drink, and he will be filled with the Holy Spirit even from birth.* [16]*Many of the people of Israel will he bring back to the Lord their God.* [17]*And he will go on*

before the Lord, in the spirit and power of Elijah, to turn the hearts of the fathers to their children and the disobedient to the wisdom of the righteous, to make ready a people prepared for the Lord." [18]*Zechariah asked the angel, "How can I be sure of this? I am an old man and my wife is well on in years."* [19]*The angel answered, "I am* ***Gabriel****. I stand in the presence of God, and I have been sent to speak to you and to tell you this good news.* [20]***And now you will be silent and not able to speak until the day this happens, because you did not believe my words, which will come true at their proper time****."*

[21]*Meanwhile, the people were waiting for Zechariah and wondering why he stayed so long in the temple.* [22]*When he came out, he could not speak to them. They realized he had seen a vision in the temple, for he kept making signs to them but remained unable to speak.* [23]*When his time of service was completed, he returned home.* [24]*After this his wife Elizabeth became pregnant...* [25]*"The Lord has done this for me," she said. "In these days he has shown his favor and taken away my disgrace among the people."*

We see how God sent the angel Gabriel to Zechariah to announce to him how Elizabeth his wife would have a son. This son would become a great prophet who would prepare the way before the Messiah. Thus in the end of the chapter, the Scripture says:

(Luke 1) [57]*When it was time for Elizabeth to have her baby, she gave birth to a son.* [58]*Her neighbors and relatives heard that the Lord had shown her great mercy, and they shared her joy.* [59]*On the eighth day they came to circumcise the child, and they were going to name him after his father Zechariah,* [60]*but his mother spoke up and said, "No! He is to be called* ***John****."* [61]*They said to her, "There is no one among your relatives who has that name."* [62]*Then they made signs to his father, to find out what he would like to name the child.* [63]*He asked for a writing tablet, and to everyone's astonishment he wrote, "His name is John."* [64]*Immediately his mouth was opened and his tongue was loosed, and he began to speak, praising God.* [65]*The neighbors were all filled with awe, and throughout the hill country of Judea people were talking about all these things.* [66]*Everyone who heard this wondered about it, asking, "What then is this child going to be?" For the Lord's hand was with him.*

[67]*His father Zechariah was filled with the Holy Spirit and prophesied:* [68]*"Praise be to the Lord, the God of Israel, because* ***he has come and has redeemed his people****.* [69]***He has raised up a horn of salvation*** *{Wolof: a mighty Savior}* ***for us in the house of his servant David*** [70]***as he said through his holy prophets of long ago,*** [71]*salvation from our enemies and from the hand of all who hate us–* [72]*to show mercy to our fathers and* ***to remember his holy covenant****,* [73]***the oath he swore to our father Abraham****:* [74]*to rescue us from the hand of our*

> *enemies, and to enable us to serve him without fear [75]in holiness and righteousness before him all our days."*
>
> *After Zechariah had said this, he turned toward John, the baby, and said, [76]"And you, my child, will be called a prophet of the Most High;* ***for you will go on before the Lord to prepare the way for him****, [77]to give his people the knowledge of salvation through the forgiveness of their sins, [78]because of the tender mercy of our God, by which* ***the rising sun will come to us from heaven*** *[79]to shine on those living in darkness and in the shadow of death, to guide our feet into the path of peace."*

Thus did Zechariah praise God following the birth of John because he knew that **the time for the Messiah to be born had arrived**! John, the son of Zechariah, was not the Messiah, but the one who would come before the Messiah, in order **to announce the Messiah's arrival** and prepare the way before Him.

Thank you for listening. We urge you to tune in next time as we read the story about how God sent His angel Gabriel to a virgin by the name of Mary to announce to her a very important message. The next lesson is loaded with valuable truth. Don't miss it!...

God bless you as you meditate on these words of Zechariah:

> ***"Praise be to the Lord!...He has raised up [a mighty Savior] for us in the house of His servant David, as he said through his holy prophets of long ago!"*** (Luke 1:68-70)

Lesson 61

The Announcement

Luke 1; Matthew 1

Peace be with you, listening friends. We greet you in the name of God, the Lord of peace, who wants everyone to understand and submit to the way of righteousness that He has established, and have true peace with Him forever. We are happy to be able to return today to present your program *The Way of Righteousness*.

Over the past sixty lessons, we have been studying the Scriptures of the First Covenant, that is, the Torah {*Taurat*} of Moses, the Psalms {*Zabur*} of David, and the Writings of the other prophets. In the last broadcast we began to study the Scriptures of the **New Covenant**, that is, the "*Injil*." ***Injil*** is an Arabic word meaning ***Good News***. Truly, the message of the Gospel {*Injil*} is very good news for all who believe it, because it tells us that **God has sent a mighty Savior to earth, just as He promised through His prophets of long ago**.

Before we begin our study in the Gospel, it would be good for us to remember **why God planned to send a Savior** to the descendants of Adam. Can you remember what happened the day that Adam and Eve disobeyed God? In the Torah, we saw how Adam's disobedience led the whole human race away from the kingdom of God and into the kingdom of Satan. Adam's sin is the reason every one of us is born in crookedness. Just as "a rat only begets that which digs" {Wolof proverb}, in the same way Adam and his offspring can only beget children that sin! Sinners produce sinners. Our sin condemns us so that we have no possible way of making ourselves right before the One who must judge us!

However, we praise God that the Scriptures of the Prophets do not conclude with the story of Adam's transgression! As we have already seen, on the very day that Adam and Eve sinned, God began to make known **His wonderful plan to send a Redeemer into the world** who could deliver the descendants of Adam from the dominion of Satan and sin. On that dark day when sin entered world, God announced that this holy Redeemer would be born exclusively of "*a woman.*" (Gen. 3:15; Gal. 4:4) The Messiah, who was to shed His blood as the Perfect Sacrifice for sinners, could not descend from an earthly father tainted with sin.

He had to be perfect and holy even as God is perfect and holy. That is why the prophet Isaiah (who lived seven hundred years before the Messiah came) wrote: "***The virgin will be with child and will give birth to a son****, and will call him Immanuel–which means 'God with us'!*" (Isa. 7:14; Matt 1:23)

Let us now return to the book of the Gospel so that we might see **how God fulfilled what He promised concerning this perfect and holy Redeemer** who was to be born of a virgin–a young woman who had never been intimate with a man. In our last lesson, we saw how God's angel, Gabriel, appeared to a Jew by the name of Zechariah. Gabriel told Zechariah that he and his wife would have a son by the name of John, who was to prepare the way before the Redeemer.

Now let us continue in the Gospel {*Injil*} of Luke, chapter one, and see how God sent His angel to a virgin by the name of Mary. The Scripture says:

> (Luke 1) [26]*[When Elizabeth, the mother of John, was] in her sixth month, God sent the angel Gabriel to Nazareth, a town in Galilee,* [27]*to* ***a virgin*** *pledged to be married to a man named Joseph,* ***a descendant of David****. The virgin's name was* ***Mary****.* [28]*The angel went to her and said, "Greetings, you who are highly favored! The Lord is with you."* [29]*Mary was greatly troubled at his words and wondered what kind of greeting this might be.* [30]*But the angel said to her, "Do not be afraid, Mary, you have found favor with God.* [31]*You will be with child and give birth to a son, and you are to give him the name* ***Jesus****.* [32]*He will be great and will be called* ***the Son of the Most High****. The Lord God will give him the throne of his father David,* [33]*and he will reign over the house of Jacob forever; his kingdom will never end."* [34]*"How will this be," Mary asked the angel, "since I am a virgin?"* [35]*The angel answered, "The Holy Spirit will come upon you, and the power of the Most High will overshadow you. So the holy one to be born will be called the Son of God.* [36]*Even Elizabeth your relative is going to have a child in her old age, and she who was said to be barren is in her sixth month.* [37]*For nothing is impossible with God."* [38]*"I am the Lord's servant," Mary answered. "May it be to me as you have said." Then the angel left her.*

Let's stop here and talk a little about what happened when God's angel, Gabriel, appeared to Mary. Mary was a young woman who esteemed the Word of God. She was promised in marriage to a man named *Joseph*, but they were not yet living together. Both Joseph and Mary were descendants of King David. You will remember that God's prophets not only prophesied that the Messiah would be **born of a virgin**, but also that **He would belong to the family line of King David**.

So that no one misunderstands, there is something else which you should know about Mary. It is this: Mary was a descendant of Adam. Like us all, she was born with a sinful nature. It is necessary that we say this, because many elevate

Mary to the place of God and worship her and pray to her. To do so is **idolatry**! Certainly, Mary is **worthy of honor** since she was the woman through whom God chose to bring the Messiah into the world. But this favor that God bestowed upon her **does not make her worthy of worship**, because the Scripture says: "*Worship the Lord your God and serve* ***him only****!*" (Matt. 4:10)

Now then, in the verses we just read, we see how Gabriel visited Mary to inform her that she was the virgin through whom God intended to bring the Savior of sinners into the world. Gabriel also told Mary the name of the Child that she was to bear. He said to her, "*You are to give him the name* ***Jesus****.*" The name *Jesus* means ***the LORD saves***. {Note: the Qur'an calls Jesus *Isa*. The Arabic New Testament calls Him *Yasu* which is in keeping with His rightful name. *Jesus* is a transliteration of the Greek form of the Hebrew *Joshua*, which means *the* LORD *saves*.} However, there was another name by which Gabriel referred to the Messiah. Did you hear it? He called Him ***"the Son of the Most High."*** Like it or not, that is what Gabriel said. We have already read in the Psalms of David that God called the Messiah *His Son*. Now we hear how God's angel Gabriel also calls the Messiah "*the Son of God*."

Friends, we know that many who hear the name "**Son of God**," reply, "That's impossible! *Astaghferullah!* {Islamic maxim carrying this idea: *May God forgive you for uttering such blasphemy!*} But as the old (Wolof) proverb says: "Before you slap the shepherd on the mouth, you should find out what he is whistling about." Similarly, before you despise the name "Son of God," you should make an effort to find out what the term *Son of God* means! In the Holy Scriptures, the Messiah is called **God's Son** more than one hundred and twenty times. Thus, we who believe the Writings of the Prophets do not dare deny that God calls the Messiah **His Son**. What we want to know is **why** God calls Jesus **His Son**.

First, we need to know what the name *Son of God* does **not** mean. **It does not mean that God took a wife and had a son**! Anyone who thinks such thoughts is blaspheming God! God is the Highest One and does not produce children as a man produces them. Never! That must be perfectly clear in our minds. We do not have time today to explain all that the name *Son of God* means, but what you must understand is that the name does **not** mean that God took a wife and bore a son by her! This should not be difficult to understand, because here in Senegal we often call anyone who has lived a long time in the country "a son of Senegal," although Senegal obviously cannot have a wife and bear a son. Also, if you travel outside the country, people may call you "a son of Senegal," but that does not mean that Senegal is your father! It simply means that you come from Senegal, your place of origin.

That is how it is with Jesus the Messiah. God calls Him His Son **because He came forth from God**. The Messiah came from heaven. Before He was born He was with God; He was in God. He is the "**Ruh Allah**"; *the Spirit of God*. {Note:

"*Ruh Allah*" is Arabic for Spirit/Soul of God; like the Hebrew "*Ruah*." This is a Qur'anic title for Jesus consistent with who the Messiah is: God's Eternal *Spirit* Son: the second *Spirit* in the One Triune God.}. The Messiah is also the "***Kalimat***"; *the Word* which was with God in the beginning. {"*Kalimat Allah*" is Arabic meaning *the Word/Verb of God*: a title attributed uniquely to the Messiah both in the Bible and the Qur'an.} That is what the Scriptures declare when they say:

> "*In the beginning was* ***the Word****, and* ***the Word was with God****, and* ***the Word was God****. He was with God in the beginning. Through him all things were made; without him nothing was made that has been made.* ***The Word became flesh and made his dwelling among us.***" (John 1:1-3,14)

Yes, the Messiah is **the Word of God** which came from heaven, and was born as a man. We all know that the Messiah had no earthly father. Well now, if He did not have an earthly father, then where did He come from? Whose Son is He? Listen again to what Gabriel told Mary. He said to her, "***The Holy Spirit will come upon you, and the power of the Most High will overshadow you. [That is why] the holy one to be born will be called the Son of God.***" (Luke 1:35)

Perhaps you have heard some say, "Oh yes, we know that Jesus had no earthly father, but Jesus' birth of a virgin isn't so important. God merely wanted to show His power. God created Adam without father or mother. Next, He created Eve with only a father, that is, He formed her from the rib He took from Adam. Then to display His power further, God created a man using only a woman. That is the only reason Jesus was born without an earthly father."

Dear friends, it is true that God is the Almighty One and nothing is impossible for Him! But concerning Jesus' birth of a virgin, you must know that the reason for it was infinitely more important than merely to display God's power! Do not let anyone deceive you! There is a very, very important reason Jesus was born of a virgin thousands of years after God created Adam and Eve! Do you know the reason? The Holy Scripture tell us the reason, when it says: "*[Jesus the Messiah] came into the world* ***to save sinners.***" (1 Tim. 1:15) **Jesus was born into the world to redeem the lost, sinful, contaminated, condemned descendants of Adam—therefore He could not originate from a man tainted with sin!** As we have already seen, according to God's plan, the Messiah had to shed His blood as a sacrifice to pay for sin. To be **the Perfect Sacrifice**, the Redeemer had to be without a single sin or fault, like the healthy, innocent sheep sacrificed every year at the Feast of Sacrifice {*Id al-Adha*}.

Think about it! Can a person with a great debt pay the debts of others? No! Only the one who has no debt is qualified to pay the debts of others. Similarly, the Messiah had to be a man who had no debt of sin, so that He might pay the debt of sin for the children of Adam. God wants us to know that the Messiah and the children of Adam are very different. We are sons **of Adam**, but Jesus is the Son **of God**! We, as children of Adam, are **like the dirty earth** because of our sin. However, Jesus is **like the rain that comes from heaven**. He is pure and holy, just as God is pure and holy. That is why God is not ashamed to call Him ***His Son***! And so friends, we hope that as you leave here today, your minds are clearer and that you better understand why Jesus the Messiah had to be born of a virgin and **what the name "*Son of God*" means and does not mean.**

We conclude today's broadcast by reading in the Gospel of Matthew about the birth of the Messiah. Several months after Mary became pregnant by the power of the Spirit of God, God sent His angel to Joseph, who was to become Mary's husband. The Scripture says:

> (Matt. 1) [18]*This is how the birth of Jesus Christ came about: His mother Mary was pledged to be married to Joseph, but before they came together, she was found to be with child through the Holy Spirit.* [19]*Because Joseph her husband was a righteous man and did not want to expose her to public disgrace, he had in mind to divorce her quietly.* [20]*But after he had considered this, an angel of the Lord appeared to him in a dream and said, "Joseph son of David, do not be afraid to take Mary home as your wife, because what is conceived in her is* ***from the Holy Spirit***. [21]*She will give birth to a son, and you are to give him the name* ***Jesus***, *because* ***he will save his people from their sins***." [22]***All this took place to fulfil what the Lord had said through the prophet***: [23]*"The virgin will be with child and will give birth to a son, and they will call him Immanuel" which means, '****God with us.****'* [24]*When Joseph woke up, he did what the angel of the Lord had commanded him and took Mary home as his wife.* [25]*But he had no union with her until she gave birth to a son. And he gave him the name* ***Jesus***.

We must stop here today. In the will of God, next time we will continue in the Gospel to read the amazing story about the birth of Jesus, the Messiah....

God bless you as you remember what the angel told Joseph concerning the Messiah:

> ***"You are to give him the name Jesus, because he will save his people from their sins!"*** (Matt. 1:21)

LESSON 62

THE MESSIAH IS BORN

LUKE 2; MATTHEW 2

Peace be with you, listening friends. We greet you in the name of God, the Lord of peace, who wants everyone to understand and submit to the way of righteousness that He has established, and have true peace with Him forever. We are happy to be able to return today to present your program *The Way of Righteousness*.

In the last lesson, in our study in the holy Gospel {*Injil*}, we saw how God sent His angel, Gabriel, to the land of Palestine, to the city of Nazareth, to a virgin named Mary. The angel appeared to that virgin to tell her that she would become pregnant by the power and Spirit of God, and give birth to a son and name Him ***Jesus***. Jesus means ***the LORD saves***. Thus, we saw that the time had arrived for which God's people had been long awaiting! **The Redeemer**, whom God had promised on the day that Adam and Eve sinned, **was in the womb of a virgin**, about to come into the world!

Our program today is called "**The Messiah is Born**!" Before we return to the Gospel to see how Jesus the Messiah was born, let us describe **the time** in which He was born. The emperor {king} of Rome, Caesar Augustus, was ruling over many countries including the land of the Jews. However, the Roman empire {kingdom} would not hinder God's plan to send the Redeemer into the world. In fact, God planned to use the Romans to fulfil the words of the prophets.

Can you remember the words of the prophet Micah who came seven hundred years before the Messiah? Micah announced that the Messiah would be born in **Bethlehem**, the hometown of King David. However, Mary, who would give birth to Jesus, did not live in Bethlehem, but in **Nazareth**, a city found approximately one hundred and fifty kilometers north of Bethlehem. How then would the Messiah be born in Bethlehem?

Ah, friends, as you know, nothing is too hard for the LORD God! He is God, and has the final word concerning everything that takes place on earth. He knows everything that is going to happen. Today we will read that, as the time for Mary to give birth drew near, the great emperor of Rome issued a decree, saying: "Let every man and woman go to the city of his ancestors to register there and pay a tax!" This meant that both Mary and Joseph would have to go to Bethlehem, to the city of King David, because they belonged to the descendants of David. Now let us return to the Gospel of Luke, chapter two, and hear how Jesus the Messiah was born in **Bethlehem**, exactly as God had promised long before.

The Scripture says:

> (Luke 2) [1]*In those days* **Caesar Augustus issued a decree** *that a census should be taken of the entire Roman world...* [3]*And everyone went to his own town to register.* [4]*So Joseph also went up from the town of* **Nazareth** *in Galilee to Judea, to* **Bethlehem** *the town of David, because he belonged to the house and line of David.* [5]*He went there to register with Mary, who was pledged to be married to him and was expecting a child.* [6]*While they were there, the time came for the baby to be born,* [7]*and* **she gave birth to her firstborn, a son**. *She wrapped him in cloths and placed him in a manger, because there was no room for them in the inn.*

We must pause here. Did you notice the circumstances in which the Messiah was born? The Messiah was born as a **peasant**, in very lowly circumstances. He was born in an animal stable, because the inn in Bethlehem was full. The One who was to be the Savior and the Judge of the world was born in a smelly stable! Perhaps some are thinking: "This is incredible! If Jesus is the Savior of the world and the Lord of glory who will judge all the children of Adam, why was He not born in a palace, with great glory, so that everyone might know that He is the King of kings and the Lord of lords?"

Friends, we must remember: **God's thoughts are different from man's thoughts,** and the glory of God is different from the glory of the world. Surely, the birth of Jesus was accompanied by great glory, but most of the children of Adam did not recognize it, because **God's glory** and **the world's glory** are so different.

To illustrate, perhaps you have seen rich people who live in large and beautiful houses, wearing expensive clothes and living a life of luxury with servants attending to their every desire. That is the glory of the world. However, **God's glory** is different from the **world's glory**. That is why the Messiah, who came from the presence of God, was not born in comfort and luxury. He was not like many rich people who do not understand the misery and hardships of the poor. No. The One whom God sent to rescue the children of Adam from the power of Satan and sin was born in lowly circumstances, even in a stable! Thus, no one can say that the Messiah came only to save the wealthy, or that He doesn't understand the feelings of the poor. God wants everyone to know that the Redeemer whom He sent came into the world to deliver **everyone** who believes in Him–old and young, men and women, rich and poor, free and slave. Thus the

Scripture says: "*For you know the grace of our Lord Jesus Christ, that though he was rich, yet* ***for your sakes he became poor****, so that you through* ***his poverty*** *might become* ***rich****!*" (2 Cor. 8:9) The Messiah is the only one who ever **chose** to be born. And He chose to be born as a poor man! {Note: Perhaps another reason Jesus was born in a stable was to remind us that He is the "Lamb of God." Lambs are born in stables. We'll learn more about Jesus' title as the "Lamb of God" in lesson #64.}

Now let us continue the story of the birth of the Messiah and read the most wonderful part. On the night that Jesus was born in a stable, God sent His angels to some shepherds who were watching their flocks in the fields surrounding Bethlehem. Listen to how God made known to them the good news about the birth of the Messiah.

The Scripture says:

> (Luke 2) [8]*And there were shepherds living out in the fields near by, keeping watch over their flocks at night.* [9]***An angel of the Lord*** *appeared to them, and the glory of the Lord shone around them, and they were terrified.* [10]*But the angel said to them, "Do not be afraid. I bring you good news of great joy that will be for all the people.* [11]***Today in the town of David a Savior has been born to you; he is Christ, the Lord!*** *{Christ* is the Greek form of the Hebrew word *Messiah*, meaning *the Anointed One}* [12]*This will be a sign to you: You will find a baby wrapped in cloths and lying in a manger."*
>
> [13]*Suddenly* ***a great company of the heavenly host*** *appeared with the angel, praising God and saying,* [14]***"Glory to God in the highest, and on earth peace to men on whom his favor rests!"***
>
> [15]*When the angels had left them and gone into heaven, the shepherds said to one another, "Let's go to Bethlehem and see this thing that has happened, which the Lord has told us about."* [16]*So they hurried off and found Mary and Joseph, and the baby, who was lying in the manger.* [17]*When they had seen him, they spread the word concerning what had been told them about this child,* [18]*and all who heard it were amazed at what the shepherds said to them...* [20]***The shepherds returned, glorifying and praising God for all the things they had heard and seen, which were just as they had been told***. Amen.

To whom did God first make known the good news about the birth of the Messiah? Did He give the good news to the Roman emperor, the wealthy, or the religious leaders? No. God first announced the news of the Messiah's birth to peasants; to humble shepherds who were waiting for Him to come! How thrilled the shepherds were to see the baby Jesus! What an awesome privilege! **They had seen the One about whom all the prophets wrote: the Messiah, the Savior of the world, the Eternal Word of God wrapped in the tiny body of a baby!**

Continuing in the Gospel, let us see what happened about one year after Jesus was born. We have just heard how God announced the birth of Jesus to some **peasants** by His **angels** which appeared in the sky. Now we are going to hear how God announced the Messiah's birth to some **Magi** {or *wisemen* / in Wolof: *masters of knowledge*} by a large and beautiful **star** which appeared in the sky. Listen to what is written in the Gospel of Matthew, chapter two.

The Scripture says:

> (Matt. 2) [1]*After Jesus was born in Bethlehem in Judea, during the time of King Herod, Magi from the east came to Jerusalem* [2]*and asked, "Where is the one who has been born king of the Jews?* ***We saw his star in the east and have come to worship him.*** *"* [3]*When King Herod heard this he was disturbed, and all Jerusalem with him.* [4]*When he had called together all the people's chief priests and teachers of the law, he asked them where the Christ was to be born.* [5]*"In Bethlehem in Judea," they replied, "**for this is what the prophet has written**:* [6]*'But you, Bethlehem, in the land of Judah, are by no means least among the rulers of Judah; for out of you will come a ruler who will be the shepherd of my people Israel.'"* [7]*Then Herod called the Magi secretly and found out from them the exact time the star had appeared.* [8]*He sent them to Bethlehem and said, "Go and make a careful search for the child. As soon as you find him, report to me, so that I too may go and worship him."* (However, in his heart, King Herod planned to kill the child, for he did not want anyone to be king, except himself!)
>
> [9]*After [the Magi] had heard the king, they went on their way, and the star they had seen in the east went ahead of them until it stopped over the place where the child was.* [10]*When they saw the star, they were overjoyed.* [11]*On coming to the house, they saw the child with his mother Mary, and they bowed down and worshiped him. Then they opened their treasures and presented him with gifts of gold and of incense and of myrrh.* [12]*And having been warned in a dream not to go back to Herod, they returned to their country by another route.*

That, in brief, is the story of the birth of the Messiah. What can we say about all we have heard today? One thing we can say with certainty is that the birth of Jesus, the Messiah, is **unequaled** in the history of the world! Among all the prophets and kings and peoples of the world, never has another been born as Jesus was born!

- We have seen today that the Messiah was born of **a virgin, by the power of God, exactly as God's prophets had prophesied.**
- We have heard that Jesus was born in the town of **Bethlehem**, just as the prophet Micah had announced some seven hundred years earlier.
- We also saw how **God sent His angel and a glorious radiance from heaven** to some shepherds to make the good news known to them, saying: "*I bring you*

good news of great joy that will be for all the people. Today in the town of David a Savior has been born to you; he is Christ, the Lord!"

• Then we saw how **a multitude of angels appeared with the first angel, praising God** and saying, *"Glory to God in the highest, and on earth peace to men on whom his favor rests!"*

• We also saw that **God placed a great star in the sky** to announce to some wisemen who lived in a far away land, that the Messiah, the King of kings, the Savior of sinners had been born!

Friends, what then shall we say about all of this? We can say this: No man has ever been born like this Man. Jesus' birth is unique. Concerning His birth, **Jesus is incomparable**! We cannot compare Him with others. Jesus was more than a prophet. **He is the One of whom all the prophets spoke. He is the Messiah from heaven!**

Friends, if Jesus were simply a prophet among many prophets, then **why** did all of God's prophets announce His coming before He was born? **Why** did the angels come down from heaven to celebrate His birth? If Jesus were merely a prophet among many prophets, then **why** did God place a great star in the sky to proclaim His birth? And **for what reason** was He born of a virgin? **May you carefully consider these important questions.**

Thank you for listening. In the next lesson, God willing, we will see how Jesus the Messiah began His ministry upon earth....

God bless you as you reflect upon the angel's message to the shepherds:

> ***"Do not be afraid. I bring you good news of great joy that will be for all the people! Today in the town of David a Savior has been born to you; he is Christ the Lord!"*** (Luke 2:10,11)

Lesson 63

The Holy Son

Luke 2; Matthew 3,4

Peace be with you, listening friends. We greet you in the name of God, the Lord of peace, who wants everyone to understand and submit to the way of righteousness that He has established, and have true peace with Him forever. We are happy to be able to return today to present your program *The Way of Righteousness*.

In our last study in the holy book of the Gospel {*Injil*}, we heard the thrilling story of the Messiah's birth. **No one has ever been born as Jesus was.** He was born of a virgin, by the power of God, in the town of Bethlehem, exactly as prophesied. On the night that Jesus was born, God sent a multitude of shining angels to some shepherds who were spending the night in the fields surrounding Bethlehem. One of the angels said to the shepherds, *"I bring you good news of great joy that will be for* ***all the people****! Today in the town of David* ***a Savior*** *has been born to you; he is Christ, the Lord!"* (Luke 2:10,11)

Today we plan to study **what Jesus was like as a child and as He became an adult**. The book of the Gospel shows us that following the birth of Jesus, Joseph and Mary had four sons and some daughters. The child Jesus grew up with his younger siblings in a crowded house in northern Palestine, in the town of Nazareth. As you know, Joseph did not beget Jesus, but in the eyes of men, Jesus was the son of Joseph. Since Joseph was a carpenter, Jesus also worked as a carpenter while He lived at home. Consequently, Jesus was accustomed to hard work. Thus the Scripture says: *"And Jesus grew in wisdom and stature, and in favor with God and men."* (Luke 2:52)

Like all children, Jesus ate and slept, played and studied. However, there was something about Him that made Him different from other children. Do you know what it was? It is this: **Jesus never committed sin**! No unjust word ever came out of His mouth. (1 Pet. 2:22) He never told anyone, "Forgive my faults" {Wolof formula/cliché for asking forgiveness}, because He never wronged anyone. He could not commit sin, because there was **no root of sin** in Him! He had a holy nature (character). Evil was not a part of Him. He only did what pleased God.

He had a physical body like ours, but He did not have an evil nature like ours! That is what the Scriptures declare, when they say: "*We do not have a high priest {mediator, spiritual leader} who is unable to sympathize with our weaknesses, but we have one who has been tempted in every way, just as we are, yet was* ***without sin****.*" (Heb. 4:14,15)

When Jesus was thirty years old, **the time for Him to begin His work** {mission, ministry} as the Savior of the world had come. One day He bid farewell to his family, left the town of Nazareth, and headed for the Jordan River where the prophet John {*Yahya*} was preaching and baptizing the people in water.

Do you remember John? He was born six months before Jesus. John was the prophet whom God sent to prepare the hearts of people, so that they might repent of their sins and welcome the Messiah whom God had sent. Listen to what is written in the Gospel concerning the prophet John and how he prepared the way of the Messiah.

In the Gospel of Matthew, chapter three, the Scripture says:

> (Matt. 3) [1]*In those days John the Baptist came, preaching in the Desert of Judea*
> [2]*and saying, "***Repent, for the kingdom of heaven is near***." [3]This is he who was spoken of through the prophet Isaiah: "A voice of one calling in the desert,* ***'Prepare the way for the Lord, make straight paths for him****!'" [4]John's clothes were made of camel's hair, and he had a leather belt round his waist. His food was locusts and wild honey. [5]People went out to him from Jerusalem and all Judea and the whole region of the Jordan. [6]Confessing their sins, they were baptized by him in the Jordan River.*

Let us pause here to think about what we are reading. Did you hear John's message? In brief, John preached: "Repent of your sins! Turn from your evil deeds, and prepare to meet the holy Messiah who has come to you from heaven!" Those who confessed their sins before God were baptized by John in the river. Thus, the prophet John became known as *John the Baptizer*. Being baptized in water could not wash away the people's sins. It was only a sign {mark, demonstration} which showed that they had repented of their sins and were ready to receive the Messiah as their Savior.

Some of those who responded to John so that he might baptize them, belonged to the two most famous Jewish sects, *the Sadducees* and *the Pharisees*. **The Sadducees** were the wealthiest Jews and had influence in the Roman government. But in their hearts they did not care about the Writings of the Prophets. **The Pharisees** were the religious experts who were very zealous in praying, fasting, giving alms and paying tithes. However, their worship was worthless, because they were trying to become righteous before God by their own efforts. Also, the Pharisees mixed their traditions with the true Word of God. Consequently, their worship of God had become nothing more than a flashy show combined with contempt for those who did not belong to their group. In short, the Pharisees and the Sadducees honored God with their **lips**, but their **hearts** were far from Him.

Now then, let us continue to read in the Gospel and hear how John rebuked these religious experts because of their hypocrisy. The Scripture says:

> (Matt. 3) [7]*But when [John] saw many of the Pharisees and Sadducees coming to where he was baptizing, he said to them: "You brood of vipers! Who warned you to flee from the coming wrath?* [8]*Produce fruit in keeping with repentance.* [9]*And do not think you can say to yourselves, 'We have Abraham as our father.' I tell you that out of these stones God can raise up children for Abraham.* [10]*The axe is already at the root of the trees, and every tree that does not produce good fruit will be cut down and thrown into the fire.* [11]*"I baptize you with water for repentance.* ***But after me will come one who is more powerful than I, whose sandals I am not fit to carry. He will baptize you with the Holy Spirit and with fire****.* [12]*His winnowing fork is in his hand, and he will clear his threshing-floor, gathering his wheat into the barn and burning up the chaff with unquenchable fire!"*
>
> [13]*Then* ***Jesus*** *came from Galilee to the Jordan to be baptized by John.* [14]*But John tried to deter him, saying, "I need to be baptized by you, and do you come to me?"* [15]*Jesus replied, "Let it be so now; it is proper for us to do this* ***to fulfil all righteousness****." (Then John consented.)*

Thus John baptized the Lord Jesus in the Jordan River. Perhaps some might ask, "Why did Jesus, who was without sin, ask John to baptize Him?" It is true, the Lord Jesus did not need to repent of anything, because He had never committed sin. Why then did Jesus come to John, so that John might baptize Him as he was baptizing sinners? What did Jesus say about this? Jesus said to John, *"Let it be so now; it is proper for us to do this to fulfil all righteousness."* By being baptized, Jesus not only put before us an example to follow, but He also showed us that He came to live as one of us and to die for us.

In the end of the chapter, the Scripture says:

> (Matt. 3) [16]*As soon as* ***Jesus*** *was baptized, he went up out of the water. At that moment heaven was opened, and he saw* ***the Spirit of God*** *descending like a dove and lighting on him.* [17]*And* ***a voice from heaven*** *said, "This is my Son, whom I love; with him I am well pleased!"*

Friends, whose voice echoed from the sky? It was the voice of the LORD God! What did God say? God said of Jesus, ***"This is my Son, whom I love; with him I am well pleased!"*** We have already read in the Holy Scriptures how the prophet

David and the angel Gabriel called the Messiah "*God's Son.*" Now we hear how God Himself calls Jesus, "*my Son, whom I love!*" Why did God call Jesus His Son? As we have already seen, Jesus is called *the Son of God* because He came directly from heaven. Jesus had no earthly father. God placed His Eternal Word in the womb of a virgin. Here we see another reason Jesus is called the Son of God. **God called Jesus His Son to set Him apart from all others.**

How is Jesus different from the children of Adam? Everyone descended from Adam has a nature stained by sin, but **Jesus' nature was unstained by sin**. He did not have a single sin, because He came from the holy Spirit of God. The Messiah took on a **physical form** like ours, but He did not take on our **sinful nature**. He had a holy and perfect nature! That is why God, the Holy One, could take pleasure in Jesus, as a father takes pleasure in an obedient, faithful son. It is said that the son is the shadow of the father. Whoever sees the son knows what his father is like. Similarly, whoever knows Jesus, knows what God is like, because Jesus is the One who came from God **to display God's nature**. No one has ever seen God, but the Messiah has made Him known! Jesus is the only human who had a holy nature, because He is the only One to come from the holy Spirit of God! That is why God was not ashamed to make His voice echo from heaven, saying, "*This is my Son, whom I love;* ***with him I am well pleased****!*"

In the remaining time today, we will begin reading in chapter four to hear what happened after John baptized Jesus. The Scripture says:

> (Matt. 4) [1]*Then Jesus was led by the Spirit into the desert to be tempted by the devil.* [2]***After fasting for forty days and forty nights, he was hungry****.* [3]*The tempter (that is Satan) came to him and said, "**If you are the Son of God**, tell these stones to become bread."* [4]*Jesus answered, "**It is written**: 'Man does not live on bread alone, but on every word that comes from the mouth of God.'"* [5]*Then the devil took him to the holy city and had him stand on the highest point of the temple.* [6]*"**If you are the Son of God**," he said, throw yourself down…For it is written: 'He will command his angels concerning you, and they will lift you up in their hands…"* [7]*Jesus answered and said, "**It is also written**: 'Do not put the Lord your God to the test.'"* [8]*Again, the devil took him to a very high mountain and showed him all the kingdoms of the world and their splendor.* [9]*"All this I will give you," he said, "if you will bow down and worship me."* [10]*Jesus said to him, "Away from me, Satan! For **it is written**: 'Worship the Lord your God, and serve him only."* [11]*Then the devil left him, and angels came and attended him.*

Three times Satan tried to entice Jesus to obey him and sin. All three times Jesus answered the devil by quoting the Word of God. As Satan tempted Adam and Eve to sin in the Garden of Paradise {Eden}, so also, Satan tempted the Lord Jesus to sin in the wilderness. **But Jesus did not sin.**

Why did the devil tempt Jesus? Because he knew that Jesus was the holy Redeemer who had come from heaven to earth to save the children of Adam from his dominion. Satan also knew that if Jesus were to commit a single sin, Jesus could not save the children of Adam from the dominion of sin. Thus Satan harassed Jesus, attempting to deceive Him. But Jesus did not fall for the devil's trap.

Yes, Satan overcame and corrupted our ancestors, Adam and Eve, but he could not overcome the holy Son of God. **The Lord Jesus could not sin because God cannot sin.** Like Father, like Son. Jesus was the living and powerful Word of God in a human body. God sent Him into the world to deliver the children of Adam from the power of Satan and the penalty of sin. Only the Lord Jesus can deliver us from Satan and sin, because only He overcame Satan and sin. That is why the Scripture says of the Messiah:

> ***"Such a high priest meets our need–one who is holy, blameless, pure****, set apart from sinners, exalted above the heavens.* ***Unlike the other high priests****, [The Lord Jesus] does not need to offer sacrifices day after day, first for his own sins, and then for the sins of the people. He sacrificed for their sins once for all when he offered himself.*" (Heb. 7:26,27)

Friends, we thank you for listening. Plan to meet with us in our next study to hear why the disciples of the prophet John left him to follow Jesus....

May God give you insight into what we have read today. We leave you with this verse from Holy Scripture:

> ***"[Jesus Christ] appeared so that he might take away our sins. And in him is no sin."*** (1 John 3:5)

Lesson 64

The Lamb of God

John 1,3

Peace be with you, listening friends. We greet you in the name of God, the Lord of peace, who wants everyone to understand and submit to the way of righteousness that He has established, and have true peace with Him forever. We are happy to be able to return today to present your program *The Way of Righteousness*.

In the past two programs, we saw that Jesus the Messiah was unique in His birth and His character (nature).

• Concerning **His birth**, we discovered that no one has ever been born like Jesus, because He had no earthly father. He was born of a virgin, by the power of the Holy Spirit of God.

• Concerning **His character**, Jesus was unique. Never has another been born with a holy nature like His. He had a body like ours, but He did not have our evil nature. Jesus was unstained by sin, because He was the Savior that God sent into the world to bear for us the punishment for our sin.

Today we plan to continue in the Gospel {*Injil*} and hear **what the prophet John** {*Yahya*} **testified concerning Jesus**. John was the prophet whom God sent to prepare the way before the Messiah.

Reading in the Gospel of John {Note: in the Wolof New Testament, the prophet John (the Baptist) is called *Yahya*, and the apostle John is called *Yowanna*, thus, there is no confusion between these two men}, chapter one, the Scripture says:

> (John 1) 19*Now this was* **John's testimony** *when the Jews of Jerusalem sent priests and Levites to ask him who he was.* 20*He did not fail to confess, but confessed freely, "I am not the Christ (the Messiah)."...* 22*Finally they said, "Who are you? Give us an answer to take back to those who sent us. What do you say about yourself?"* 23*John replied in the words of Isaiah the prophet, "I am the voice of one calling in the desert, 'Make straight the way for the Lord.'"...* 26*"I baptize with water," John replied, "but among you stands one you do not know.* 27***He is the one who comes after me, the thongs of whose sandals I***

> ***am not worthy to untie.*** *"* [28]*This all happened at Bethany on the other side of the Jordan, where John was baptizing.* [29]*The next day John saw* **Jesus** *coming toward him and said,* ***"Look, the Lamb of God, who takes away the sin of the world!*** [30]***This is the one I meant when I said, 'A man who comes after me has surpassed me because he was before me.'"***

Let us pause here and think about the testimony of the prophet John. Did you hear how he referred to the Messiah? Let us listen again to the Scripture. It says: *"John saw Jesus coming toward him and said, 'Look,* ***the Lamb of God,*** *who takes away the sin of the world!'"* We have already read how the prophets of God called the Messiah by many names such as the Redeemer, the Savior, the King, the Lord, the Word of God and the Son of God. Now we hear that He was called "***the Lamb of God***." This is a very important title which deserves clarification.

Why did John call Jesus the Lamb of God? Was Jesus a lamb? No, Jesus was not an actual lamb, just as we who are Senegalese are not actual lions, although we sometimes call ourselves such. {Senegal's mascot is the lion} All of us know clearly that this is only a manner of speech, because we would like to have the strength and courage of a lion. But why did the prophet John call Jesus **the Lamb of God**? Why would anyone want to be like a lamb? Why did John point to Jesus, and say to his disciples, *"Look! Here is the Lamb of God, who takes away the sin of the world!"*?

To understand what the title *"Lamb of God"* means, we should remember what God decreed after Adam and Eve had sinned. God decreed that the payment for sin is death and hell and that if the blood of a spotless sacrifice is not shed, there would be no forgiveness of sin. Thus, we read how Adam and Eve's second son, Abel, believed God, slaughtered **a lamb** and offered it to God on an altar as a sacrifice to cover his sin. When God saw the blood of the lamb, He annulled the punishment for Abel's sin, and judged him as righteous, because **an innocent lamb had died in his place.** Nevertheless, God also said that the blood of a lamb could not be accepted as a sufficient payment for sin forever, because the value of an animal and the value of a man are not equal. **The lamb was only a shadow and an illustration of the holy Redeemer who was to come into the world and shed His blood to deliver sinners from God's righteous judgment.**

Seven hundred years before the birth of Jesus, the prophet Isaiah wrote how the Messiah would be *"led like* ***a lamb*** *to the slaughter"* as a sacrifice to take away our sins (Isa. 53:7). Thus, between the time of Abel and the time of the Messiah, all who believed God respected and participated in the sacrifices of lambs. Noah, Abraham, Moses, David, Solomon and all the prophets, and all who believed the Word of God, had the habit of presenting to God sacrifices of spotless lambs. In this way they were all looking ahead to the day when God would send down the final sacrifice, that is, the holy Redeemer, who would shed His blood as a sacrifice that takes away sin forever.

That is why, dear friends, when the prophet John saw Jesus coming toward him, he pointed to Him and said to his disciples, "***Look, the Lamb of God, who takes away the sin of the world!***" Thus did John make known to his disciples that this Jesus standing before them was the Messiah, "*the Lamb*" which God sent down from heaven, the Perfect Sacrifice of which all the prophets prophesied. Jesus is the holy sacrifice who came into the world to die in the place of the children of Adam so that God can forgive us of our sins forever!

After this, the Scripture says:

> (John 1) 35*The next day John was there again with two of his disciples.* 36*When he saw Jesus passing by, he said,* "**Look, the Lamb of God!**" 37*When the two disciples heard him say this, they followed Jesus.* 38*Turning round, Jesus saw them following and asked, "What do you want?" They said, "Rabbi" (which means Teacher), "where are you staying?"* 39*"Come," he replied, "and you will see." So they went and saw where he was staying, and spent that day with him. It was about the tenth hour.* 40*Andrew, Simon Peter's brother, was one of the two who heard what John had said and who had followed Jesus.* 41*The first thing Andrew did was to find his brother Simon and tell him,* "***We have found the Messiah!***"*…* 42*And he brought him to Jesus. Jesus looked at him and said, "You are Simon son of John. You will be called Cephas" (which, when translated, is Peter, that is, rock).* 43*The next day Jesus decided to leave for Galilee. Finding Philip, he said to him, "Follow me."* 44*Philip, like Andrew and Peter, was from the town of Bethsaida.* 45*Philip found Nathanael and told him,* "***We have found the one Moses wrote about in the Law, and about whom the prophets also wrote, Jesus of Nazareth, the son of Joseph!***" 46*"Nazareth! Can anything good come from there?" Nathanael asked. "Come and see," said Philip.*

Thus, we see how John's disciples began to follow Jesus. Why did the prophet John's disciples leave him to follow the Lord Jesus? They began to follow Jesus because they believed what John told them when he said that **Jesus was the Messiah and the Lamb of God of whom all of God's prophets prophesied**! Thus, when one of John's disciples, that is, Andrew, recognized that Jesus was the Messiah, he went to find his brother Simon Peter and said to him: "***We have found the Messiah!!!***" And when another disciple by the name of Philip recognized who Jesus was, he was overjoyed and told Nathanael, his friend, "***We have found the one Moses wrote about in the Law, and about whom the prophets also wrote, Jesus of Nazareth!***"

Yes, Andrew and Peter, Philip and Nathanael rejoiced greatly when they saw Jesus, because they knew that **for thousands of years the prophets had been predicting the coming of the Messiah. Now they were seeing the Messiah with their own eyes**! Praise be to God! The mighty Redeemer of whom all of God's prophets had been prophesying was in their midst! Praise God, at last, the Messiah had come! Thus, these four disciples of John began to follow Jesus, becoming His first disciples.

After that, the Scripture says:

> (Matt. 4) [21]*Going on from there, [Jesus] saw two other brothers, James son of Zebedee and his brother John. They were in a boat with their father Zebedee, preparing their nets. Jesus called them, [*[19]*saying to them,* ***"Come, follow me, and I will make you fishers of men****."]* [22]*And immediately they left the boat and their father and followed him.* [23]*Jesus went throughout Galilee, teaching in their synagogues, preaching the good news of the kingdom, and healing every disease and sickness among the people.* [24]*News about him spread all over Syria, and people brought to him all who were ill with various diseases, those suffering severe pain, the demon-possessed, those having seizures, and the paralyzed, and he healed them.* [25]*Large crowds from Galilee, the Decapolis, Jerusalem, Judea and the region across the Jordan followed him."*

God willing, in the next lesson, we will venture further into the stories that show how the Lord Jesus taught the crowds and how He worked great miracles. We will see that by His words and His works Jesus proved that **He was who He claimed to be**—the Messiah about whom all the prophets had written! However in the remaining time today, we will read ahead to see what happened to **the prophet John**. As we just saw, after John proclaimed that Jesus was the Messiah, John's disciples began to leave him, one by one, so that they might follow **the Lord Jesus**. Did that please John? **Was the prophet John pleased that his disciples had left him to follow Jesus?** What do you think?

Listen to what is written in the Gospel of John, chapter three.

> (John 3) [26]*[Thus, some people] came to John and said to him, "Rabbi, that man who was with you on the other side of the Jordan, the one you testified about, well, he is baptizing, and everyone is going to him."* [27]*To this John replied, "A man can receive only what is given him from heaven.* [28]*You yourselves can testify that I said, 'I am not the Christ but am sent ahead of him.'* [29]*The bride belongs to the bridegroom. The friend who attends the bridegroom waits and listens for him, and is full of joy when he hears the bridegroom's voice.* ***That joy is mine, and it is now complete.*** [30]***He must become greater; I must become less!***

What do you think about this? John expressed **great joy** when his disciples left him to follow the Messiah! John's joy was complete, because **he had accomplished his mission**; he had prepared the way before the Messiah. Like **a true prophet of God**, John's only desire was to lead people to **the Messiah**. How different the prophet John was from so many religious leaders today! **A true spiritual leader will always point you to the Lord Jesus, because Jesus is the only One who can get you into the holy presence of God in Paradise.** John knew that there were **many prophets of God**, but only **one Savior**! That is why John said: "*Whoever believes in the Son* (Jesus the Messiah) *has eternal life, but whoever rejects the Son will not see life, for God's wrath remains on him!*" (John 3:36)

Concerning the end of John's life, the Scripture says:

> "*And with many other words John exhorted the people and preached the good news [about the Messiah] to them. But...John rebuked Herod the tetrarch [for marrying Herodias, his brother's wife, and for] all the other evil things he had done.*" (Luke 3:18,19)

That is why Herod gave orders to have John arrested, bound and put in prison. In the end, Herod had John beheaded in order to please his wife. (See Mark 6:17,27) Thus, John entered the glory of the presence of God in heaven.

The Scripture tells us that John was a great prophet, even greater than the prophets who came before him. What made John greater than the other prophets? Here is the answer. **All the other prophets** proclaimed: "**The Messiah is going to come**! He will come! He will come!" However, the proclamation of **the prophet John** was: "**The Messiah is here!** His Name is Jesus! Look! The Lamb of God who will be killed to take away the sin of the world has come! Follow Him!" Thus John accomplished his task as the illustrious prophet who prepared the way for the Messiah.

Thank you for listening. In the will of God, in our next program, we will continue in the holy Gospel and discover why Jesus is called the Great Physician....

May God give you insight into what we have studied today. Nothing is more important than what the prophet John proclaimed concerning Jesus the Messiah, when he said,

> ***"Look, the Lamb of God, who takes away the sin of the world!"*** (John 1:29)

Lesson 65

The Great Healer

Mark 1,2

Peace be with you, listening friends. We greet you in the name of God, the Lord of peace, who wants everyone to understand and submit to the way of righteousness that He has established, and have true peace with Him forever. We are happy to be able to return today to present your program *The Way of Righteousness*.

As most of you know, in our journey through the Holy Scriptures, we are now studying in the Gospel {*Injil*}. This is the holy book which relates the Good News about the Messiah who came into the world to free the children of Adam from the dominion of Satan and sin. In our last program, we read that Jesus the Messiah began to visit the towns, **teaching** the multitudes and **healing** every disease and sickness among the people. His name became famous throughout the land.

Today we continue the narrative of Jesus the Messiah to see how **His teachings and His works** were very different from all who preceded Him. Jesus did not have a wife, a house, or worldly riches. He was unique among men. Only one thing was important to Him: to do the will of the One who sent Him; to finish the work which God had given Him to do.

In the Gospel of Mark, chapter one, the Scripture says:

> (Mark 1) [21]*[Jesus and his disciples] went to [the city of] Capernaum, and when the Sabbath came, Jesus went into the synagogue and began to teach.* [22]*The people were amazed at his teaching, because* ***he taught them as one who had authority, not as the teachers of the law****.* [23] *ust then a man in their synagogue who was possessed by an evil spirit cried out,* [24]*"What do you want with us, Jesus of Nazareth? Have you come to destroy us? I know who you are, the Holy One of God!"* [25]*"Be quiet!" said Jesus sternly. "Come out of him!"* [26]*The evil spirit shook the man violently and* ***came out of him*** *with a shriek.* [27]*The people were all so amazed that they asked each other, "What is this? A new teaching, and with authority! He even gives orders to evil spirits and they obey him."* [28]*News about him spread quickly over the whole region of Galilee.*

The teachings of Jesus were very different from the teachings of the teachers of the law {scribes, religious teachers}. All who were listening to Jesus in the synagogue {special building for worship and instruction in the Scriptures} were amazed at His words because He taught them with an authority which their teachers of the law did not have.

You know about **the teachers of the law**. They were supposed to explain the Torah, {*Taurat*}, the Psalms {*Zabur*} and the other books of the prophets. However, most of them could not correctly explain the Writings of the Prophets, because they did not really understand them! They knew all about their religious duties and the traditions of their ancestors, but they did not know the Word of the LORD. These religious "experts" honored God with their lips, but did not love His Word. Thus, when Jesus (who had never studied in their schools of religious training) entered their synagogue and began to explain the Scriptures with authority and clarity, these teachers were greatly embarrassed. To add to their humiliation, the people in the synagogue were totally amazed by Jesus words and works and were asking each other, "Who is this? Where does He get this new teaching? How can He teach with such authority? He even commands evil spirits, and they obey Him! We have never seen anything like this! No one has ever taught like this man! No one has ever done such things as He!"

Truly, since the day that Adam sinned until the day that Jesus began to do miracles, people had never seen anyone who was so powerful. But now they were seeing One who could speak a single word, and Satan and his demons would flee! Only the Messiah who came from heaven could do that! Did you hear what the demon possessed man said to Jesus? He cried out saying, "*What do you want with us, Jesus of Nazareth? Have you come to destroy us?* ***I know who you are, the Holy One of God!***" **The demons** knew exactly where Jesus came from and who He was. However, most of **the people** did not know who Jesus really was. Satan and his evil angels greatly feared the Lord Jesus, because they knew with certainty that He was the Word by which God had created the heavens and the earth in the beginning. They knew that Jesus was the Holy One who had the authority to throw them into the eternal fire! That is why they trembled with fear at the name of Jesus.

Now then, let us continue in chapter one. The Scripture says:

> (Mark 1) [29]*[After Jesus and His disciples] left the synagogue, they went with*
> *James and John to the home of Simon [Peter] and Andrew.* [30]*Simon's mother-in-*
> *law was in bed with a fever, and they told Jesus about her.* [31]*So he went to her,*
> *took her hand and helped her up. The* ***fever left her*** *and she began to wait on*
> *them.* [32]*That evening after sunset the people brought to Jesus all the sick and*
> *demon-possessed.* [33]*The whole town gathered at the door,* [34]*and Jesus healed many*

who had various diseases. He also drove out many demons, but he would not let the demons speak because they knew who he was. [35]*Very early in the morning, while it was still dark, Jesus got up, left the house and went off to a solitary place, where he prayed.* [36]*Simon and his companions went to look for him,* [37]*and when they found him, they exclaimed: "Everyone is looking for you!"* [38]*Jesus replied, "Let us go somewhere else, to the nearby villages, so that I can preach there also. That is why I have come."* [39]*So he traveled throughout Galilee, preaching in their synagogues and driving out demons.* [40]*A man with leprosy came to him and begged him on his knees, "If you are willing, you can make me clean."* [41]*Filled with compassion, Jesus reached out his hand and touched the man. "I am willing," he said. "Be clean!"* [42]*Immediately the* ***leprosy left him*** *and he was cured.*

Thus Jesus healed people of every disease and sickness, showing **compassion** to the descendants of Adam, because they were weary and helpless, like sheep without a shepherd. But there was another reason for the many great miracles which Jesus did. Jesus healed every kind of disease and drove out demons to **prove** to the children of Adam that He was the Messiah whom God had promised so long ago through His prophets. For instance, we have already read that the prophet Isaiah, hundreds of years before Jesus was even born, wrote that when the Messiah comes, "*the eyes of the blind will be opened and the ears of the deaf unstopped. Then will the lame leap like a deer, and the mute tongue shout for joy!*" (Isa. 35:5,6) With these words, the prophet Isaiah announced that the Messiah would do miracles that no one had ever done. We have already read how God gave Moses and Elijah the ability to do great miracles. But the miracles which those two prophets did were few compared to the miracles which the Messiah did. Also, Moses and Elijah did not have any power of their own to perform miracles. However, Jesus the Messiah overflowed with the power of God, because He Himself is the very power of God!

Continuing in Gospel of Mark, chapter two, the Scripture says:

(Mark 2) [1]*A few days later, when Jesus again entered Capernaum, the people heard that he had come home.* [2]*So many gathered that there was no room left, not even outside the door, and he preached the word to them.* [3]*Some men came, bringing to him a paralytic, carried by four of them.* [4]*Since they could not get him to Jesus because of the crowd, they made an opening in the roof above Jesus and, after digging through it, lowered the mat the paralyzed man was lying on.* [5]*When Jesus saw their faith, he said to the paralytic, "**Son, your sins are forgiven**."* [6]*Now some teachers of the law were sitting there, thinking to themselves,* [7]*"Why does this fellow talk like that? He's blaspheming! Who can forgive sins but God alone?"* [8]*Immediately Jesus knew in his spirit that this was what they were thinking in their hearts, and he said to them, "Why are you thinking these things?*

> [9]*Which is easier: to say to the paralytic, 'Your sins are forgiven,' or to say, 'Get up, take your mat and walk'?* [10]*But that you may know that the Son of Man [that is, the Messiah] has authority on earth to forgive sins..." He said to the paralytic,* [11]*"**I tell you, get up, take your mat and go home**."* [12]*He got up, took his mat and walked out in full view of them all. This amazed everyone and they praised God, saying, "We have never seen anything like this!"*

In this narrative, we see that the power of Jesus was not limited to healing a person's **sick body**, but He also had the power to heal a person's **sinful heart**! Jesus, who is the Great Physician (Healer), knew that **the most critical problem** the lame man had was not his impotent legs, but the **sin** that was in his heart. That is why Jesus first said to him, "*Son, your sins are forgiven.*"

What were the teachers of the law thinking when Jesus said this? They were saying to themselves, "Jesus is blaspheming! No one can forgive sins but God alone!" Their thoughts were partly **true** and partly **false**. It is true that **no one can forgive sins except God alone**. However, when the teachers of the law thought that Jesus was blaspheming God, they were mistaken because they did not comprehend was that **Jesus was the Mediator whom God had sent down to make sinners right with God**. Jesus was the Word of God; thus when **Jesus** said "*Your sins are forgiven,*" it was **God** Himself saying, ***"Your sins are forgiven!"*** The Lord Jesus was the voice of God on earth! And not only that, Jesus is also the One who was born to give His life as **the perfect Sacrifice** which takes away sin forever. As a father grants his son the authority to work for him and to speak for him, so God gave Jesus the authority to forgive sins. Forgiveness of sin is found only in the Lord Jesus. But the teachers of the law did not believe this.

We only have a little time left. Therefore, let us read on a little farther in the verses that follow.

> "*As Jesus went on from [the house where he healed the paralytic], he saw a man named Matthew sitting at the tax collector's booth. '**Follow me**,' he told him, and Matthew got up and followed him.*" (Matt 9:9) "*While Jesus was having dinner at [Matthew's] house, many tax collectors and 'sinners' were eating with him and his disciples, for there were many who followed him. When the teachers of the law who were Pharisees saw him eating with the 'sinners' and tax collectors, they asked his disciples: 'Why does he eat with tax collectors and 'sinners'?' On hearing this, Jesus said to them, **'It is not the healthy who need a doctor, but the sick. I have not come to call the righteous, but sinners**.'*" (Mark 2:15-17)

With those words, Jesus, the Great Physician, wanted to show the teachers of the law that they were **sick** before God because of their **sin**. But these religious teachers did not recognize their sin. In fact, they were criticizing Jesus because He was eating with tax collectors and those who were known as "sinners." However, to be with **sinners** and to heal them of their ***sin*** is the very reason for which Jesus was born!

How about you, do you realize that you were born with a terrible disease called **sin**? The sin within you is why you must die and come before the judgment of God the Holy One. But praise God, **there is One who can heal you of the sin in your heart**! Do you know who that One is? Yes, it is **Jesus the Messiah**—the One who was without sin and who came into the world to save the children of Adam from their sins. However, before the Lord Jesus can cure your heart of sin, you must first recognize that you are sick with sin. Only those who know they are sick will go to the doctor. Likewise, only those who know they are sinners will turn to Jesus, the Savior of sinners. **Jesus did not come for those who imagine that they are righteous, but for those who know that they are sinners.** That is why He said to the teachers of the law, "*It is not the healthy who need a doctor, but the **sick**. I have not come to call the righteous, but **sinners**.*"

Friends, this is where we must stop today. In our next program, in the will of God, we will continue in the Gospel and hear some wonderful and profound words which came from the mouth of Jesus, the Healer of sinners....

God bless you as you ponder the Lord's words to the teachers of the law:

> ***"It is not the healthy who need a doctor, but the sick. I have not come to call the righteous, but sinners!"*** (Mark 2:17)

LESSON 66

THE GREAT TEACHER

MATTHEW 5-7

Peace be with you, listening friends. We greet you in the name of God, the Lord of peace, who wants everyone to understand and submit to the way of righteousness that He has established, and have true peace with Him forever. We are happy to be able to return today to present your program *The Way of Righteousness.*

In the last program, we saw that Jesus the Messiah was visiting the towns in Palestine, teaching the multitudes, healing the sick, and driving out demons. People were amazed and asked each other, "***Who is this?*** *A new teaching, and with authority! He even gives orders to evil spirits and they obey him!*" (Mark 1:27)

Today we plan to continue in the Gospel {*Injil*} and hear **the wonderful words which came from the mouth of the Lord Jesus** one day when He was on a mountainside with His disciples and a great crowd. We do not have time to read everything that Jesus taught His disciples on that day; however, anyone who wants to, can read the whole message in the Gospel of Matthew, chapter five to chapter seven.

Friends, wherever you are right now, we invite you to listen to "The Sermon on the Mount"—a sermon which the Lord Jesus preached almost two thousand years ago.

The Scripture says:

> (Matt. 5) [1]*Now when [Jesus] saw the crowds, he went up on a mountainside*
> *and sat down. His disciples came to him,* [2]*and he began to teach them, saying:*
> [3]"***Blessed*** *are the poor in spirit, for theirs is the kingdom of heaven.*
> [4]***Blessed*** *are those who mourn, for they will be comforted.*
> [5]***Blessed*** *are the meek, for they will inherit the earth.*
> [6]***Blessed*** *are those who hunger and thirst for righteousness, for they will be filled.*
> [7]***Blessed*** *are the merciful, for they will be shown mercy.*
> [8]***Blessed*** *are the pure in heart, for they will see God.*

*[9]**Blessed** are the peacemakers, for they will be called sons of God.*

*[10]**Blessed** are those who are persecuted because of righteousness, for theirs is the kingdom of heaven.*

*[11]**Blessed** are you when people insult you, persecute you and falsely say all kinds of evil against you because of me. [12]Rejoice and be glad, because great is your reward in heaven, for in the same way they persecuted the prophets who were before you.*

*[17]"Do not think that I have come to abolish the Law or the Prophets; I have not come to **abolish** them but to **fulfil** them. [18]I tell you the truth, until heaven and earth disappear, not the smallest letter, not the least stroke of a pen, will by any means disappear from the Law **until everything is accomplished**. [19]Anyone who breaks one of the least of these commandments and teaches others to do the same will be called least in the kingdom of heaven, but whoever practices and teaches these commands will be called great in the kingdom of heaven. [20]**For I tell you that unless your righteousness surpasses that of the Pharisees and the teachers of the law, you will certainly not enter the kingdom of heaven**.*

*[21]"**You have heard** that it was said to the people long ago, 'Do not murder, and anyone who murders will be subject to judgment.' [22]**But I tell you** that anyone who is angry with his brother will be subject to judgment. [27]"**You have heard** that it was said, 'Do not commit adultery.' [28]**But I tell you** that anyone who looks at a woman lustfully has already committed adultery with her in his heart. [33]"Again, **you have heard** that it was said to the people long ago, 'Do not break your oath, but keep the oaths you have made to the Lord.' [34]**But I tell you**, Do not swear at all: either by heaven, for it is God's throne; [35]or by the earth, for it is his footstool… [37]Simply let your 'Yes' be 'Yes', and your 'No', 'No'; anything beyond this comes from the evil one.*

*[38]"**You have heard** that it was said, 'Eye for eye, and tooth for tooth.' [39]**But I tell you**, Do not resist an evil person. If someone strikes you on the right cheek, turn to him the other also. [40]And if someone wants to sue you and take your tunic, let him have your cloak as well. [41]If someone forces you to go one mile, go with him two miles. [43]"**You have heard** that it was said, 'Love your neighbor and hate your enemy.' [44]**But I tell you**: Love your enemies and pray for those who persecute you, [45]that you may be sons of your Father in heaven. He causes his sun to rise on the evil and the good, and sends rain on the righteous and the unrighteous. [46]If you love those who love you, what reward will you get? Are not even the tax collectors doing that? [47]And if you greet only your brothers, what are you doing more than others? Do not even pagans do that? [48]**Be perfect, therefore, as your heavenly Father is perfect.***

(Matt. 6) [1]**"Be careful not to do your 'acts of righteousness' before men, to be seen by them**. *If you do, you will have no reward from your Father in heaven.*

2“So ***when you give*** *to the needy, do not announce it with trumpets, as* ***the hypocrites*** *do in the synagogues and on the streets, to be honored by men. I tell you the truth, they have received their reward in full. 3But when you give to the needy, do not let your left hand know what your right hand is doing, 4so that your giving may be in secret. Then your Father, who sees what is done in secret, will reward you.*

5“And ***when you pray, do not be like the hypocrites****, for they love to pray standing in the synagogues and on the street corners to be seen by men. I tell you the truth, they have received their reward in full. 6But when you pray, go into your room, close the door and pray to your Father, who is unseen. Then your Father, who sees what is done in secret, will reward you. 7And when you pray, do not keep on babbling like pagans, for they think they will be heard because of their many words. 8Do not be like them, for your Father knows what you need before you ask him.*

9“This, then, is how you should pray:

‘Our Father *in heaven, hallowed be your name,*
10your kingdom come, your will be done on earth as it is in heaven.
11Give us today our daily bread.
12Forgive us our debts, as we also have forgiven our debtors.
13And lead us not into temptation, but deliver us from the evil one.
For yours is the kingdom and the power and the glory forever. Amen!

*16“****When you fast****, do not look somber as* ***the hypocrites*** *do, for they disfigure their faces to show men they are fasting. I tell you the truth, they have received their reward in full. 17But when you fast, put oil on your head and wash your face, 18so that it will not be obvious to men that you are fasting, but only to your Father, who is unseen; and your Father, who sees what is done in secret, will reward you.*

*19“****Do not store up for yourselves*** *treasures on earth, where moth and rust destroy, and where thieves break in and steal. 20But store up for yourselves treasures in heaven, where moth and rust do not destroy, and where thieves do not break in and steal. 21For where your treasure is, there your heart will be also.*

*22“The eye is the lamp of the body. If your eyes are good, your whole body will be full of light. 23But if your eyes are bad, your whole body will be full of darkness. If then the light within you is darkness, how great is that darkness! 24****No one can serve two masters****. Either he will hate the one and love the other, or he will be devoted to the one and despise the other. You cannot serve both God and Money.*

25“Therefore I tell you, ***do not worry about your life****, what you will eat or drink; or about your body, what you will wear. Is not life more important than food, and the body more important than clothes? 26Look at the birds of the air; they do not sow or reap or store away in barns, and yet your heavenly Father* *feeds them. Are you not much more valuable than they? [27]Who of you by worrying can add a single hour to his life?*

*[28]"And why do you worry about clothes? See how the lilies of the field grow. They do not labor or spin. [29]Yet I tell you that not even Solomon in all his splendor was dressed like one of these. [30]If that is how God clothes the grass of the field, which is here today and tomorrow is thrown into the fire, will he not much more clothe you, O you of little faith? [31]So do not worry, saying, 'What shall we eat?' or 'What shall we drink?' or 'What shall we wear?' [32]For the pagans run after all these things, and your heavenly Father knows that you need them. [33]**But seek first his kingdom and his righteousness, and all these things will be given to you as well.***

(Matt. 7) *[1]"**Do not judge, or you too will be judged**. [2]For in the same way as you judge others, you will be judged, and with the measure you use, it will be measured to you. [3]"Why do you look at the speck of sawdust in your brother's eye and pay no attention to the plank in your own eye? [4]How can you say to your brother, 'Let me take the speck out of your eye,' when all the time there is a plank in your own eye? [5]You hypocrite, first take the plank out of your own eye, and then you will see clearly to remove the speck from your brother's eye. ([12]So in everything, **do to others what you would have them do to you**, for this sums up the Law and the Prophets.)*

*[7]"Ask and it will be given to you; **seek and you will find**; knock and the door will be opened to you. [8]For everyone who asks receives; he who seeks finds; and to him who knocks, the door will be opened.*

*[13]"**Enter through the narrow gate.** For wide is the gate and broad is the road that leads to destruction, and many enter through it. [14]But small is the gate and narrow the road that leads to life, and only a few find it.*

*[15]"**Watch out for false prophets**. They come to you in sheep's clothing, but inwardly they are ferocious wolves. [16]By their fruit you will recognize them. Do people pick grapes from thornbushes, or figs from thistles? [17]Likewise every good tree bears good fruit, but a bad tree bears bad fruit. [18]A good tree cannot bear bad fruit, and a bad tree cannot bear good fruit. [19]Every tree that does not bear good fruit is cut down and thrown into the fire. [20]**Thus, by their fruit you will recognize them.***

*[21]"**Not everyone who says to me, 'Lord, Lord,' will enter the kingdom of heaven**, but only he who does the will of my Father who is in heaven. [22]Many will say to me on that day, 'Lord, Lord, did we not prophesy in your name, and in your name drive out demons and perform many miracles?' [23]Then I will tell them plainly, 'I never knew you. Away from me, you evildoers!'*

*[24]"Therefore **everyone who hears these words of mine and puts them into practice** is like **a wise man** who built his house on the rock. [25]The rain came down, the streams rose, and the winds blew and beat against that house;*

> *yet it did not fall, because it had its foundation on the rock.* [26]*But* ***everyone who hears these words of mine and does not put them into practice*** *is like* ***a foolish man*** *who built his house on sand.* [27]*The rain came down, the streams rose, and the winds blew and beat against that house, and it fell with a great crash."*
>
> [28]*When Jesus had finished saying these things,* ***the crowds were amazed at his teaching,*** [29]*because* ***he taught as one who had authority, and not as their teachers of the law.***

Friends, we must stop here today, because our time is up. We hope you will join us in the next lesson, so that we might think together about the profound and wonderful words which we have heard today, the words of Jesus, the Great Teacher from heaven. If you would like to have what you heard today on cassette, you can write to us and we will send it to you—free of charge....

May God give you understanding in what you have heard today. We leave you with this wonderful word spoken by the Lord Jesus on the mountain:

> ***"Seek first [God's] kingdom and his righteousness, and all these things will be given to you as well."*** (Matt. 6:33)

LESSON 67

YOU MUST BE BORN AGAIN!

JOHN 3

Peace be with you, listening friends. We greet you in the name of God, the Lord of peace, who wants everyone to understand and submit to the way of righteousness that He has established, and have true peace with Him forever. We are happy to be able to return today to present your program *The Way of Righteousness*.

In our study in the holy Gospel {*Injil*}, we have seen that Jesus the Messiah was unique in **His birth**, in **His character**, and in **His works**. And in our last program, we recognized that Jesus was unique in **His teaching**. Never has there been another who has spoken such clear and profound words as He. Those who heard Him were astonished, because He taught them with an authority which their priests {*marabouts*} and teachers of the law {*imams*} did not have. A few words from the mouth of Jesus were of greater value than a multitude of words from their religious leaders. Because of this, most of the leaders of the Jews were not pleased with Jesus. Not only did He teach that which **contradicted their traditions**, but He also **exposed their hypocrisy** before all!

In our last lesson we heard Jesus' sermon which He taught while up on a mountain with His disciples. His sermon can be summarized with six words. Those six words are: ***"Do not be like the hypocrites!"*** Hypocrisy is repulsive to God and destructive to man. That is why Jesus said to the crowd, "*Do not be like the hypocrites!*" You know what it means to be a hypocrite. If someone pretends to have a character trait which is not consistent with what is in his heart, he is a hypocrite. Jesus said that a hypocrite is like a whitewashed tomb; beautiful on the outside but full of uncleanness on the inside (Matt. 23:27).

No one can deceive God. The Word of God says: "*Everything is uncovered and laid bare before the eyes of him to whom we must give account*." (Heb 4:13) Jesus, who knew the heart of man, saw the hypocrisy which was in the religious leaders, the Pharisees and the teachers of the law. On the outside they were zealous in praying, fasting, and giving alms, but in their hearts they really did not love God and His Word. Consequently, all their "righteous"deeds and rituals were worthless. Thus, **Jesus taught His disciples, saying:**

> *"And when you* ***pray****, do not be like the* ***hypocrites****, for they love to pray standing in the synagogues and on the street corners to be seen by men. I tell you the truth, they have received their reward in full."* (Matt. 6:5) *"When you* ***give*** *to the needy, do not announce it with trumpets, as the* ***hypocrites*** *do in the synagogues and on the streets, to be honored by men. I tell you the truth, they have received their reward in full."* (Matt. 6:2) *"When you* ***fast****, do not look somber as the* ***hypocrites*** *do, for they disfigure their faces to show men they are fasting. I tell you the truth, they have received their reward in full."* (Matt. 6:16)
>
> *"****Do not be like the hypocrites****. For I tell you that unless your righteousness surpasses that of the Pharisees and the teachers of the law, you will certainly not enter the kingdom of heaven."* (Matt. 6:5; 5:20) *"Blessed are the* ***poor in spirit****, for theirs is the kingdom of heaven. Blessed are those who* ***hunger and thirst for righteousness****, for they will be filled. Blessed are the* ***pure in heart****, for they will see God. Be* ***perfect****, therefore, as [God] your heavenly Father is perfect!"* (Matt. 5:3,6,8,48) *"Enter through the narrow gate. For wide is the gate and broad is the road that leads to destruction, and* ***many*** *enter through it. But small is the gate and narrow the road that leads to life, and only a* ***few*** *find it."* (Matt. 7:13,14)

Thus the Lord Jesus exhorted the people to choose the narrow way that leads to eternal life. Did you grasp what Jesus said concerning the way of salvation? It is extremely important! What must a person be like if he (or she) is ever to see God, and live in God's presence forever? What did Jesus say about this? In short, He said: **"You must have a pure and perfect heart!"**

But how can a child of Adam who was conceived in sin have a pure and perfect heart? Is there something he can do to cause his evil heart to be transformed into the pure heart that God requires? No! Man, by himself, has no means of purifying his heart. "Even if a log soaks a long time in water it will never be transformed into a crocodile." {Wolof proverb} Similarly, we sinners cannot **do** anything **to make ourselves** pure before God. However, in the remaining time today, we will see that **what is impossible for man is possible for God**!

Now let us continue reading in the Gospel to see how a certain religious ruler from Jerusalem by the name of **Nicodemus** came to talk with Jesus at night. Jesus showed him how a sinner can receive a pure heart and God's gift of eternal life. We are reading in the Gospel of John, chapter three. The Scripture says:

> (John 3) [1]*Now there was a man of the Pharisees named Nicodemus, a member of the Jewish ruling council.* [2]*He came to Jesus at night and said, "Rabbi, we know you are a teacher who has come from God. For no one could perform the miraculous signs you are doing if God were not with him."* [3]*In reply Jesus declared,* ***"I tell you the truth, no one can see the kingdom of God unless he is born again****."*

> 4*"How can a man be born when he is old?" Nicodemus asked. "Surely he cannot enter a second time into his mother's womb to be born!"* 5*Jesus answered, "I tell you the truth, no one can enter the kingdom of God unless he is born of water and the Spirit.* 6***Flesh gives birth to flesh, but the Spirit gives birth to spirit.*** 7***You should not be surprised at my saying, 'You must be born again!'*** 8*The wind blows wherever it pleases. You hear its sound, but you cannot tell where it comes from or where it is going. So it is with everyone born of the Spirit."*
>
> 9*"How can this be?" Nicodemus asked.* 10*"You are Israel's teacher," said Jesus, "and do you not understand these things?* 11*I tell you the truth, we speak of what we know, and we testify to what we have seen, but still you people do not accept our testimony.* 12*I have spoken to you of earthly things and you do not believe; how then will you believe if I speak of heavenly things?* 13*No one has ever gone into heaven except the one who came from heaven, the Son of Man [that is, the Messiah].* 14***Just as Moses lifted up the snake in the desert, so the Son of Man must be lifted up,*** 15***that everyone who believes in him may have eternal life.*** 16***For God so loved the world that he gave his one and only Son, that whoever believes in him shall not perish but have eternal life."*** Amen.

Let us think a little about what the Lord Jesus told the religious ruler, Nicodemus. **What did Jesus tell Nicodemus must happen before he could have eternal life and the right to live with God forever?** He said, "*I tell you the truth, no one can see the kingdom of God unless he is born again.* ***You must be born again!***" Did Nicodemus know what it meant to be born again? No! That is why Jesus said to him, "*You are Israel's teacher, and do you not understand these things? Flesh gives birth to flesh, but the Spirit gives birth to spirit. You should not be surprised at my saying, '**You must be born again**!'*" (John 3:10,6,7)

In brief, Jesus was telling Nicodemus that anyone who wants to see God and live in His holy presence throughout eternity **must be born twice**! That does not mean that you must enter a second time into your mother's womb and be born again (physically). Being born again means that **the Spirit of God must remake you**, washing your heart and renewing you by His power (Titus 3:5). You must be born by **the power that comes from heaven**, which is **completely different from the outward form of religion**. You must be changed on the **inside**—in your **heart**! Whoever is born of Adam is stained with sin and cannot have a part in the Kingdom of God. The children of Adam are powerless to remove the root of sin which grows in their hearts. Just as spending a long time in water does not transform a log into a crocodile, so also spending time performing religious rituals and doing good deeds can never make an evil heart pure. God Himself must work a miracle in your heart and renew it, because that which is perishable cannot inherit that which is imperishable! (See 1 Cor. 15:50) In short, "*You must be born again!*"

That is what Jesus taught the religious ruler, Nicodemus. But Nicodemus had difficulty understanding this. Thus, he asked Jesus: How can this be? **How** can I be born again and receive a new and pure heart?

Jesus answered him,

> *"Just as Moses lifted up the snake in the desert, so the Son of Man must be lifted up, that **everyone who believes in him** may have eternal life. For God so loved the world that he gave his one and only Son, that **whoever believes in him** shall not perish but have eternal life."* (John 3:14-16)

To show Nicodemus how he could escape the judgment of hell and receive eternal life, Jesus reminded him what had happened to his ancestors in the wilderness in the time of the prophet Moses. As we saw in the Torah, once when the children of Israel complained against God and Moses, God sent poisonous snakes among them to bite them so that many died. However, after the children of Israel repented, God commanded Moses to make **a bronze snake and suspend it on a pole**, so that **everyone who looked at it would be healed** and not die.

Thus, Jesus was telling Nicodemus that just as the children of Israel had only to look in faith at the bronze snake on the pole to be saved from death, so the children of Adam only have **to believe** in the remedy that God has provided to save them from eternal punishment. **We** are all like the children of Israel who were bitten by the snakes. **Satan** is like a poisonous snake, and **sin** is like the poison which causes man to perish. Satan has bitten all the children of Adam, and the poison of sin will cause us to perish in hell forever if God does not give us a remedy! We have no possible means of saving ourselves from God's judgment, because the wages of sin is death and hell. But praise be to the LORD God—for just as He provided a remedy to save the children of Israel from the poison of the snakes—so also He has provided **a remedy** to save the children of Adam from "the poison" of sin.

Do you know God's plan to restore and renew the hearts of the children of Adam, which are filled with sin? What did the Lord Jesus say about this? He said that the holy Redeemer must be lifted up on a pole (cross) in order to endure the penalty of sin for sinners—"*that everyone who believes in Him may have eternal life…and not perish!*"

Who then can be saved? What does the Scripture say? It says: "***Everyone who believes in Him**…shall not perish!*" In whom must we believe? We must believe in the Redeemer whom God has sent. Do you believe in Him? Do you believe in your heart that God, who does not want anyone to perish, sent Jesus the Savior down to earth for **you**, to bear **for you** your debt of sin? God's righteous remedy for our problem of sin is Jesus' death on the cross. The Scripture says: ***"God made [Jesus the Messiah] who had no sin to be sin for us, so that in him we might become the righteousness of God."*** (2 Cor. 5:21)

Friends, God has not changed. What the Lord Jesus said to Nicodemus about two thousand years ago, He still says to you today: ***"You must be born again!"*** God wants to cleanse and remake your heart and renew you by His power. However, you must believe His Good News. You must believe in the Messiah whom He sent. You must believe that Jesus, who never sinned, paid for your debt of sin, so that you can live in the presence of God forever. ***"You must be born again!...No one can see the kingdom of God unless he is born again!"*** Amen.

Thank you for listening. In the next study, God willing, we will continue in the Gospel and hear a conversation the Lord Jesus had with a woman who had five husbands....

God bless you as you ponder what Jesus the Messiah declared, saying,

> ***"You should not be surprised at my saying, 'You must be born again!'"*** (John 3:7) ***"Blessed are the pure in heart, for they will see God!"*** (Matt. 5:8)

Lesson 68

The Savior of the World

John 4; Luke 4

Peace be with you, listening friends. We greet you in the name of God, the Lord of peace, who wants everyone to understand and submit to the way of righteousness that He has established, and have true peace with Him forever. We are happy to be able to return today to present your program *The Way of Righteousness*.

Thus far in our study in the holy Gospel, we have seen that Jesus the Messiah was unique in **His birth**, in **His character**, in **His works** and in **His teachings**.

- Concerning **His birth** we saw that no one has ever been born like Jesus, because He was born of a virgin, by the power of the Holy Spirit of God.
- We saw also that Jesus was unique in **His character**, because no one else has ever been born with a holy nature like His.
- Jesus was also incomparable in **His works**, because no one has ever done miracles like He did. He would simply speak a word, and the sick were healed, Satan and his demons fled, and sins were taken away.
- We also discovered that Jesus was unique in **His teaching**. We observed this in our last program in the conversation that took place between Jesus and a religious ruler named Nicodemus. Jesus showed Nicodemus that unless the Spirit of God renewed his heart, he could never enter the presence of God. That is why the Lord Jesus said to him, ***"You must be born again!"***

Today we will hear how Jesus the Messiah spoke to **someone who was very different** from Nicodemus. Nicodemus was a Jew; however, the person we will see in our lesson today was **not a Jew**. Nicodemus was a man; the person we will see today was **a woman**. Nicodemus was a very religious person, but this woman was **a great sinner** who had had five husbands. In the eyes of man, the religious ruler, Nicodemus, was better than the immoral woman. But that is not how God sees it, because all of Adam's offspring—religious folk and great sinners alike, are under the dominion of sin. That is why all of Adam's children must be born again by the power that comes from above.

Now let us return to the Gospel and listen to **the conversation which Jesus**

had with the immoral woman from Samaria. Samaria was the region between Judea and Galilee in the land of the Jews. Many Samaritans were foreigners; the Jews considered them pagans, which is why they did not get along with each other. However, Jesus the Messiah did not show favoritism because God does not show favoritism. **Jesus came into the world to seek and to save every sinner who wants to have a new and pure heart.** That is why Jesus was not ashamed to talk to the Samaritan woman who had had five husbands.

Now let us listen to what is written in the Gospel of John, chapter four. The Scripture says:

> (John 4) 4*Now [Jesus] had to go through Samaria.* 5*So he came to a town in Samaria called Sychar, near the plot of ground Jacob had given to his son Joseph.* 6*Jacob's well was there, and Jesus, tired as he was from the journey, sat down by the well. It was about the sixth hour.* 7*When a Samaritan woman came to draw water, Jesus said to her, "Will you give me a drink?"* 8*(His disciples had gone into the town to buy food.)* 9*The Samaritan woman said to him, "You are* ***a Jew*** *and I am a Samaritan woman. How can you ask me for a drink?" (For Jews do not associate with Samaritans)* 10*Jesus answered her, "If you knew the gift of God and who it is that asks you for a drink, you would have asked him and he would have given you* ***living water****."* 11*"Sir," the woman said, "you have nothing to draw with and the well is deep. Where can you get this living water?* 12*Are you greater than our father Jacob, who gave us the well and drank from it himself, as did also his sons and his flocks and herds?"* 13*Jesus answered, "Everyone who drinks this water will be thirsty again,* 14*but* ***whoever drinks the water I give him will never thirst****. Indeed, the water I give him will become in him a spring of water welling up to eternal life."* 15*The woman said to him, "Sir, give me this water so that I won't get thirsty and have to keep coming here to draw water."* 16*He told her, "Go, call your husband and come back."* 17*"I have no husband," she replied. Jesus said to her, "You are right when you say you have no husband.* 18*The fact is, you have had five husbands, and the man you now have is not your husband. What you have just said is quite true."* 19*"Sir," the woman said, "I can see that you are* ***a prophet****.* 20*Our fathers worshiped on this mountain, but you Jews claim that the place where we must worship is in Jerusalem."* 21*Jesus declared, "Believe me, woman, a time is coming when you will worship the Father neither on this mountain nor in Jerusalem.* 22*You Samaritans worship what you do not know; we worship what we do know, for salvation is from the Jews.* 23*Yet a time is coming and has now come when the true worshipers will worship the Father in spirit and truth, for they are the kind of worshipers the Father seeks.* 24***God is spirit, and his worshipers must worship in spirit and in truth****."* 25*The woman said, "I know that Messiah" (called Christ) "is coming. When he comes, he will explain everything to us."* 26*Then Jesus declared, "****I who speak to you am he."***

> [27]*Just then his disciples returned and were surprised to find him talking with a woman. But no one asked, "What do you want?" or "Why are you talking with her?"* [28]*Then, leaving her water jar, the woman went back to the town and said to the people,* [29]**"Come, see a man who told me everything I ever did. Could this be the [Messiah]?"** [30]*They came out of the town and made their way toward him.*
>
> [39]*Many of the Samaritans from that town believed in him because of the woman's testimony, "He told me everything I ever did."* [40]*So when the Samaritans came to him, they urged him to stay with them, and he stayed two days.* [41]*And because of his words many more became believers.* [42]*They said to the woman, "We no longer believe just because of what you said;* ***now we have heard for ourselves, and we know that this man really is the Savior of the world****."*

This is where the story of the Samaritan woman ends. Truly it is an important story, because it shows how an immoral woman discovered that Jesus is the Savior whom God sent to earth. That discovery transformed her life. At the beginning of the conversation, the woman did not know who was speaking with her. She viewed Jesus as just **another Jew among** many Jews. However, during the conversation, Jesus told her some things that a mere man could not know, which was why she concluded that Jesus must be **a prophet**. However, she finally came to see that this Jesus who was talking with her was **more than a prophet**. He was **the Messiah—the One about whom all the prophets had prophesied, the Savior of the world**!

Once the woman recognized that this Man who was sitting on the edge of the well and speaking with her was the Messiah, she put down her water jar and ran into town, telling them, "*Come, see a man who told me everything I ever did. Could this be the Messiah?*"

After that, the people of the town came out to Jesus and asked Him to stay. Jesus stayed there for two days, teaching them how they could have a new and pure heart and become true worshipers of God. Thus, the Scripture says:

> "*And because of his words many more became believers. They said to the woman,* ***'We no longer believe just because of what you said; now we have heard for ourselves, and we know that this man really is the Savior of the world!'*** " (John 4:41)

Now let us continue in the Gospel and see what happened a few days after Jesus' visit to Samaria. We will see that **not everyone received Jesus as the Savior of the world**. In the Gospel of Luke, chapter four, the Scripture says:

> (Luke 4) [14]*Jesus returned to Galilee in the power of the Spirit, and news about*

him spread through the whole countryside. [15]*He taught in their synagogues, and everyone praised him.* [16]*[Jesus] went to* **Nazareth, where he had been brought up**, *and on the Sabbath day he went into the synagogue, as was his custom. And he stood up to read.* [17]*The scroll of the prophet Isaiah was handed to him. Unrolling it, he found the place where it is written:* [18]*"The Spirit of the Lord is on me, because he has anointed me to preach good news to the poor. He has sent me to proclaim freedom for the prisoners and recovery of sight for the blind, to release the oppressed,* [19]*to proclaim the year of the Lord's favor."* [20]*Then he rolled up the scroll, gave it back to the attendant and sat down. The eyes of everyone in the synagogue were fastened on him,* [21]*and he began by saying to them, "***Today this scripture is fulfilled in your hearing***."*

With these words, Jesus claimed that He was the Messiah and the Savior about which the prophet Isaiah wrote seven hundred years earlier. However, the Jews who lived in Nazareth could not accept that this Jesus, who had grown up among them, was the Savior of the world sent from heaven! That is why they scorned Him, saying, *"Is he not the son of Joseph?"*

The Scripture goes on to say how Jesus warned the people of Nazareth not to despise the Messiah whom God had sent to them. But that only made them more angry. Thus, the Scripture says:

(Luke 4) [28]*All the people in the synagogue were furious when they heard this.* [29]*They got up, drove [Jesus] out of the town, and took him to the brow of the hill on which the town was built, in order to throw him down the cliff.* [30]*But he walked right through the crowd and went on his way.*

Thus the people of Nazareth tried to kill Jesus! Why did they try to kill Him? They tried to kill Him because Jesus claimed to be **the Messiah** about whom all God's prophets had written. "Truth is a hot pepper." {Wolof proverb} Jesus' words of truth made the people of Nazareth so angry that they tried to throw Him off the cliff. But they could not do it, because the time appointed by God for Jesus to die had not yet come. Wolof wisdom says: "The woodcutter does not cut down the main tree in the village (under which folks meet)." Jesus the Messiah is God's "Main Tree!" How foolish and evil of men to want to "cut down" the One whom God appointed as the Savior and Judge of the world! Later, men would kill Him—but God would raise Him from the dead three days later. We will learn more about this in a future lesson.

Now then, how can we summarize our lesson today? We have heard two narratives about **two groups of people.** Both groups heard that Jesus claimed to be the Messiah, but their responses to His claim were very different.

1.) First, we heard about the sinner woman that Jesus met at the well and the people of Samaria. They received the words of Jesus with great joy and **believed** that Jesus is the Messiah, the Savior of the world.

2.) However, in our second narrative, we saw the religious people of Nazareth. They despised the words of Jesus. They did **not believe** that Jesus, who had grown up in their town, was the Messiah.

In brief, we see that the sinners living in the town of Samaria accepted Jesus as the Savior sent from heaven, but the religious people living in Nazareth did not accept Him.

How about you? Which of these two groups do you more closely resemble? Are you like the people of Samaria **who received Jesus as their Lord and Savior**? Or are you like the people of Nazareth, **who refused to believe that Jesus was the Messiah sent from heaven to save them from their sins**? Do you recognize that Jesus is the Redeemer of whom all the prophets wrote? Have you received Him as your Savior?

Listen to what the Holy Scripture says concerning Jesus the Messiah. It says:

> "*The light shines in the darkness, but the darkness has not understood it.... He was in the world, and though the world was made through him, the world did not recognize him. He came to that which was his own, but his own did not receive him.* ***Yet to all who received him, to those who believed in his name, he gave the right to become children of God****—children born not of natural descent, nor of human decision or a husband's will, but born of* ***God****!*" (John 1:5,10-13)

Listening friend, Have you been born of God? Do you really believe in Jesus? Have you received Him as your Lord and Savior?

We must stop here today. We invite you to join us in our next study to see the signs which Jesus showed, so that everyone might know that He is the One true Savior of the world....

God bless you as you remember what the people of Samaria testified concerning Jesus, saying,

> "***This man really is the Savior of the world****!*" (John 4:42)

Lesson 69

The Authority of Jesus

Matthew 12; John 5

Peace be with you, listening friends. We greet you in the name of God, the Lord of peace, who wants everyone to understand and submit to the way of righteousness that He has established, and have true peace with Him forever. We are happy to be able to return today to present your program *The Way of Righteousness*.

As most of you know, right now, in our journey through the Holy Scriptures, we are looking into the book of the Gospel, which relates the Good News about Jesus the Messiah. He is the Savior who visited the world to free the children of Adam from the dominion of Satan, sin and eternal judgment.

In the past few programs, we have seen how Jesus traveled throughout the land of the Jews, **teaching** the multitudes, and **healing** their sick. Thus, a great crowd followed Him. However, most of **the religious rulers were jealous of Him**, because they could not refute the wisdom with which He spoke, nor could they deny the wonders He performed.

Today we will continue in the Gospel and see how **the Lord Jesus was confronted by the religious rulers** regarding **the day of rest** (Sabbath). The Sabbath was the seventh day of the week, the day which God gave the Jews as a day of rest, after they had worked six days. However, the religious rulers of that time, the Pharisees, accused Jesus of violating the Sabbath because He did good works on the Sabbath. They were using this as a pretext to discredit Him, because they could not find anything bad of which to accuse Him.

Let us read the Gospel of Matthew, chapter twelve. The Scripture says:

> (Matt. 12) 1 *At that time Jesus went through the cornfields* ***on the Sabbath****. His disciples were hungry and began to pick some ears of corn and eat them.* 2 *When the Pharisees saw this, they said to him, "Look! Your disciples are doing what is unlawful on the Sabbath."* 3 *He answered, "Haven't you read what [the prophet], David, did when he and his companions were hungry?* 4 *He entered the house of God, and he and his companions ate the consecrated bread which was not lawful*

for them to do, but only for the priests. [5]Or haven't you read in the Law that on the Sabbath the priests in the temple desecrate the day and yet are innocent? [6]I tell you that ***one greater than the temple is here****. [7]If you had known what these words mean, '****I desire mercy, not sacrifice****,' you would not have condemned the innocent. [8]For* ***the Son of Man*** *is* ***Lord of the Sabbath****."*

Jesus has hundreds of names and titles in the Holy Scriptures. One of those titles by which He often called Himself is "***the Son of Man***." This title, the Son of Man, reminds us that the Messiah humbled Himself to take on the form of a son of Adam. It also reveals His glory, because this One, who humbled Himself by becoming a man, is the same One who possesses all authority and all judgment over all the children of Adam. Think of it! The Word and Spirit and power and glory of God—came to earth and took on a human body! Yes, Jesus Christ is the Son of Man, the Lord of the Sabbath and the Lord over all. However, the Pharisees did not accept Jesus for who He really was.

Let us hear what happened next. The Scripture says:

(Matt. 12) [9]*Going on from that place, [Jesus] went into their synagogue, [10]and* ***a man with a shriveled hand*** *was there. Looking for a reason to accuse Jesus, they asked him, "Is it lawful to heal on the Sabbath?" [11]He said to them, "If any of you has a sheep and it falls into a pit on the Sabbath, will you not take hold of it and lift it out? [12]How much more valuable is a man than a sheep!* ***Therefore it is lawful to do good on the Sabbath****." [13]Then he said to the man, "Stretch out your hand." So he stretched it out and it was completely restored, just as sound as the other. [14]But the Pharisees went out and plotted how they might kill Jesus. [15]Aware of this, Jesus withdrew from that place. Many followed him, and he healed all their sick…*

We see how the Pharisees accused Jesus of wrongdoing because He did not respect their traditions. What hypocrisy! These religious rulers had no compassion for the hungry or for the sick, yet they wanted to make people believe that their traditions, which prohibited good works on the Sabbath, came from God! However, Jesus, who knew their evil hearts, reminded them of what God declared in the Scriptures, saying, "*If you had known what these words mean, 'I desire mercy, not sacrifice,' you would not have condemned the innocent. For the Son of Man is Lord of the Sabbath.*"

Reading on, the Scripture says:

(Matt. 12) [22]*Then they brought him* ***a demon-possessed man*** *who was blind and mute, and Jesus healed him, so that he could both talk and see. [23]All the people were astonished and said, "Could this be the Son of David?" [24]But when* *the Pharisees heard this, they said, "It is only by Beelzebub, [that is, Satan] the prince of demons, that this fellow drives out demons." [25]Jesus knew their thoughts and said to them, "Every kingdom divided against itself will be ruined, and every city or household divided against itself will not stand. [26]If Satan drives out Satan, he is divided against himself. How then can his kingdom stand? [27]And if I drive out demons by [Satan], by whom do your people drive them out? So then, they will be your judges. [28]But if I drive out demons by the Spirit of God, then the kingdom of God has come upon you.*

(John 5) *[1]Sometime later, Jesus went up to Jerusalem for a feast of the Jews. [2]Now there is in Jerusalem near the Sheep Gate a pool, which in Aramaic is called Bethesda and which is surrounded by five covered colonnades. [3]Here a great number of disabled people used to lie: the blind, the lame, the paralyzed. And they waited for the moving of the waters. [4]From time to time an angel of the Lord would come down and stir up the waters. The first one into the pool after each such disturbance would be cured of whatever disease he had.*

[5]One who was there had been ***an invalid*** *for thirty-eight years. [6]When Jesus saw him lying there and learned that he had been in this condition for a long time, he asked him, "Do you want to get well?" [7]"Sir," the invalid replied, "I have no one to help me into the pool when the water is stirred. While I am trying to get in, someone else goes down ahead of me." [8]Then Jesus said to him, "Get up! Pick up your mat and walk." [9]At once the man was cured; he picked up his mat and walked.*

The day on which this took place was a Sabbath, [10]and so the Jews said to the man who had been healed, "It is the Sabbath; the law forbids you to carry your mat." [11]But he replied, "The man who made me well said to me, 'Pick up your mat and walk.'" [12]So they asked him, "Who is this fellow who told you to pick it up and walk?" [13]The man who was healed had no idea who it was, for Jesus had slipped away into the crowd that was there.

*[14]Later Jesus found him at the temple and said to him, "See, you are well again. Stop sinning or something worse may happen to you." [15]The man went away and told the Jews that it was Jesus who had made him well. [16]So, because Jesus was doing these things on the Sabbath, the Jews persecuted him. [17]Jesus said to them, "My Father is always at his work to this very day, and I, too, am working." [18]****For this reason the Jews tried all the harder to kill him; not only was he breaking the Sabbath, but he was even calling God his own Father, making himself equal with God.***

Let us pause here. Why did the religious rulers harass Jesus and seek to kill Him? Was it because Jesus healed the invalid on the Sabbath? That was not the real reason. They were seeking to kill Jesus because **He said that God was His Father**. They could not accept that Jesus was the Messiah, who came from the presence of God. Thus they accused Jesus of blasphemy {Lit. *insulting* God} and sought to destroy Him.

But the Scripture says:

> (John 5) [19]*Jesus gave them this answer: "I tell you the truth,* **the Son** *can do*
> *nothing by himself; he can do only what he sees his Father doing, because what-*
> *ever the Father does the Son also does.* [20]*For the Father loves the Son and shows*
> *him all he does. Yes, to your amazement he will show him even greater things*
> *than these.* [21]*For just as the Father raises the dead and gives them life, even so the*
> *Son gives life to whom he is pleased to give it.* [22]*Moreover, the Father judges no*
> *one, but has entrusted all judgment to the Son,* [23]*that all may honor the Son just*
> *as they honor the Father. He who does not honor the Son does not honor the*
> *Father, who sent him.*
>
> [24]***"I tell you the truth, whoever hears my word and believes him who***
> ***sent me has eternal life and will not be condemned; he has crossed over***
> ***from death to life.***
>
> [31]*"If* **I testify** *about myself, my testimony is not valid.* [32]*There is another who*
> *testifies in my favor, and I know that his testimony about me is valid.* [33]*"You have*
> *sent to* **John** *and he has testified to the truth.* [34]*Not that I accept human testi-*
> *mony; but I mention it that you may be saved.* [35]*John was a lamp that burned*
> *and gave light, and you chose for a time to enjoy his light.* [36]*I have testimony*
> *weightier than that of John. For* **the very work** *that the Father has given me to*
> *finish, and which I am doing, testifies that the Father has sent me.* [37]*And* **the**
> **Father** *who sent me has himself testified concerning me. You have never heard*
> *his voice nor seen his form,* [38]*nor does his word dwell in you, for you do not*
> *believe the one he sent.* [39]*You diligently study the Scriptures because you think*
> *that by them you possess eternal life. These are* **the Scriptures** *that testify about*
> *me,* [40]*yet you refuse to come to me to have life.* [41]*I do not accept praise from men,*
> [42]*but I know you. I know that you do not have the love of God in your hearts.* [43]*I*
> *have come in my Father's name, and you do not accept me; but if someone else*
> *comes in his own name, you will accept him.* [44]*How can you believe if you accept*
> *praise from one another, yet make no effort to obtain the praise that comes from*
> *the only God?*
>
> [45]*"But do not think I will accuse you before the Father. Your accuser is Moses,*
> *on whom your hopes are set.* [46]*If you believed* **Moses***, you would believe me, for*
> *he wrote about me.* [47]*But since you do not believe what he wrote, how are you*
> *going to believe what I say?"*

Did you hear how the Lord Jesus reproved the Pharisees who wanted to kill Him? He told them that **whoever rejects the Messiah** whom God sent from heaven **is rejecting** the testimony of the Messiah's incomparable **words** and **works**; he is rejecting the testimony of the prophet **John**, the testimony of the prophet **Moses** and the testimony of the **Scriptures**. In short, whoever rejects the Messiah is rejecting **God Himself**. He who dishonors the Son is dishonoring the Father who sent Him. To refuse the word and authority of Jesus is to refuse the word and authority of God—for Jesus is the very Word of God and the Person to whom God has entrusted all judgment and authority.

Whoever truly believes God and His prophets will also believe that Jesus is the Messiah who came from heaven, because all of God's prophets testified of Him. Those who know and believe the Writings of the prophets also know and believe that Jesus, the son of Mary, is the One whom God has chosen to be the Savior of the world. That was what Jesus told the religious rulers when He said,

> (John 5) [39]*You diligently study the Scriptures because you think that by them you possess eternal life.* ***These are the Scriptures that testify about me****,* [40]*yet you refuse to come to me to have life.* [45]*...do not think I will accuse you before the Father. Your accuser is [the prophet]* Moses*, on whom your hopes are set.* [46]*If you believed* Moses*, you would believe me, for he wrote about me.* [47]***But since you do not believe what he wrote, how are you going to believe what I say?***"

Oh that each of us might carefully consider these words, because God wants to give us insight into their full meaning. God wants the truth to be in our hearts. **If we say that we believe the prophets, then we must believe the One of whom they testified**, that is, **Jesus the Messiah**! Friends, we leave you with this question: Do you **really** believe the prophets? {Emphasis on the "s"} Many are quick to believe the testimony of one man, but, strangely, few believe **the confirmed testimony of God's many prophets** who wrote the Holy Scriptures. How about you? "*Do you believe the prophets?*" (Acts 26:27)

Fellow listeners, this is where we must bid you farewell today because our time is up. However, we invite you to join us in the coming study as we continue in the wonderful story of Jesus the Messiah....

May God bless you and speak to you as you consider what the Lord Jesus told the Pharisees:

> ***"Since you do not believe what [the prophet Moses] wrote, how are you going to believe what I say?"*** (John 5:47)

Lesson 70

The Power of Jesus

Mark 4-6; Matthew 9,10

Peace be with you, listening friends. We greet you in the name of God, the Lord of peace, who wants everyone to understand and submit to the way of righteousness that He has established, and have true peace with Him forever. We are happy to be able to return today to present your program *The Way of Righteousness*.

In our last program, we saw that **the religious rulers of the Jews sought to destroy Jesus because He said that God was His Father, thus claiming to be equal with God**. A great crowd followed the Lord Jesus wherever He went. Among the crowd were some who believed the words of Jesus and others who did not believe Him. Jesus chose twelve apostles (or *messengers*) from among those who believed Him, so that He might be with them, teach them and send them out to proclaim the Good News of salvation.

The **twelve apostles** whom Jesus chose were named Simon who was also called *Peter*, and *Andrew*, his brother; *James* the son of Zebedee, and his younger brother *John*–those four were fishermen. The other apostles were *Philip*, *Bartholomew*, *Thomas*, *Matthew* the tax collector, *James son of Alphaeus*, *Thaddaeus*, *Simon the Canaanite*, and *Judas Iscariot*, who would betray Him. (See Matt. 10:2-4) Those were the twelve disciples who accompanied Jesus. **Several women** also followed Jesus everywhere He went: *Mary Magdalene*, from whom Jesus had driven out seven demons; *Joanna*, the wife of Chuza and the manager of Herod's household; *Susanna* and *other women*. These women helped to support Jesus out of their own means. (See Luke 8:2,3)

As we have already seen, the people were amazed at the teaching of the Lord Jesus, because He taught them with an authority which their religious teachers did not have. The authority of Jesus was not limited to mere words, but was proven by His mighty works. For the Scripture says: "*The kingdom of God is not a matter of talk* ***but of power***." (1 Cor. 4:20) In today's lesson we will see how **the Lord Jesus possessed power and authority** over every creature and every force on earth.

We begin our reading in the Gospel of Mark, chapter four. The Scripture says:

> (Mark 4) [35]*That day when evening came, [Jesus] said to his disciples, "Let us go over to the other side."* [36]*Leaving the crowd behind, they took him along, just as he was, in the boat. There were also other boats with him.* [37]***A furious squall came up****, and the waves broke over the boat, so that it was nearly swamped.* [38]*Jesus was in the stern, sleeping on a cushion. The disciples woke him and said to him, "Teacher, don't you care if we drown?"* [39]*He got up, rebuked the wind and said to the waves,* ***"Quiet! Be still!"*** *Then the wind died down and it was* ***completely calm****.* [40]*He said to his disciples, "Why are you so afraid? Do you still have no faith?"* [41]*They were terrified and asked each other,* ***"Who is this? Even the wind and the waves obey him!"***
>
> (Mark 5) [1]*They went across the lake to the region of the Gerasenes.* [2]*When Jesus got out of the boat,* ***a man with an evil spirit*** *came from the tombs to meet him.* [3]*This man lived in the tombs, and no one could bind him any more, not even with a chain.* [4]*For he had often been chained hand and foot, but he tore the chains apart and broke the irons on his feet. No one was strong enough to subdue him.* [5]*Night and day among the tombs and in the hills he would cry out and cut himself with stones.* [6]*When he saw Jesus from a distance, he ran and fell on his knees in front of him.* [7]*He shouted at the top of his voice, "What do you want with me, Jesus, Son of the Most High God? Swear to God that you won't torture me!"* [8]*For Jesus had said to him, "Come out of this man, you evil spirit!"* [9]*Then Jesus asked him, "What is your name?" "My name is Legion," he replied, "for we are many."* [10]*And he begged Jesus again and again not to send them out of the area.* [11]*A large herd of pigs was feeding on the nearby hillside.* [12]*The demons begged Jesus, "Send us among the pigs; allow us to go into them."* [13]*He gave them permission, and the evil spirits came out and went into the pigs. The herd, about two thousand in number, rushed down the steep bank into the lake and were drowned.* [14]*Those tending the pigs ran off and reported this in the town and countryside, and the people went out to see what had happened.* [15]***When they came to Jesus, they saw the man who had been possessed by the legion of demons, sitting there, dressed and in his right mind; and they were afraid.*** [16]*Those who had seen it told the people what had happened to the demon-possessed man–and told about the pigs as well.* [17]*Then the people began to plead with Jesus to leave their region.* [18]*As Jesus was getting into the boat, the man who had been demon-possessed begged to go with him.* [19]*Jesus did not let him, but said, "Go home to your family and tell them how much the Lord has done for you, and how he has had mercy on you."* [20]*So the man went away and began to tell in the Ten Cities how much Jesus had done for him.* ***And all the people were amazed****.*
>
> [21]*When Jesus had again crossed over by boat to the other side of the lake, a*

large crowd gathered round him while he was by the lake. [22]Then one of the synagogue rulers, named Jairus, came there. Seeing Jesus, he fell at his feet [23]and pleaded earnestly with him, "My little daughter is dying. Please come and put your hands on her so that she will be healed and live." [24]So Jesus went with him. A large crowd followed and pressed around him. [25]And **a woman was there who had been subject to bleeding for twelve years**. [26]She had suffered a great deal under the care of many doctors and had spent all she had, yet instead of getting better she grew worse. [27]When she heard about Jesus, she came up behind him in the crowd and **touched his cloak**, [28]because she thought, "If I just touch his clothes, I will be healed." [29]Immediately **her bleeding stopped** and she felt in her body that she was freed from her suffering. [30]At once Jesus realized that power had gone out from him. He turned around in the crowd and asked, "Who touched my clothes?" [31]"You see the people crowding against you," his disciples answered, "and yet you can ask, 'Who touched me?'" [32]But Jesus kept looking around to see who had done it. [33]Then the woman, knowing what had happened to her, came and fell at his feet and, trembling with fear, told him the whole truth. [34]He said to her, "Daughter, your faith has healed you. Go in peace and be freed from your suffering."

[35]While Jesus was still speaking, some men came from the house of Jairus, the synagogue ruler. **"Your daughter is dead**," they said. "Why bother the teacher anymore?" [36]Ignoring what they said, Jesus told the synagogue ruler, "Don't be afraid; just believe." [37]He did not let anyone follow him except Peter, James and John the brother of James. [38]When they came to the home of the synagogue ruler, Jesus saw a commotion, with people crying and wailing loudly. [39]He went in and said to them, "Why all this commotion and wailing? The child is not dead but asleep." [40]But they laughed at him. After he put them all out, he took the child's father and mother and the disciples who were with him, and went in where the child was. [41]He took her by the hand and said to her, "Talitha koum!" (which means, "**Little girl, I say to you, get up!**"). [42]**Immediately the girl stood up** and walked around (she was twelve years old). **At this they were completely astonished**. [43]He gave strict orders not to let anyone know about this, and told them to give her something to eat.

(Matt. 9) [27]As Jesus went on from there, **two blind men** followed him, calling out, "Have mercy on us, Son of David!" [28]When he had gone indoors, the blind men came to him, and he asked them, "Do you believe that I am able to do this?" "Yes, Lord," they replied. [29]Then he touched their eyes and said, "According to your faith will it be done to you"; [30]and **their sight was restored**. Jesus warned them sternly, "See that no one knows about this." [31]But they went out and spread the news about him all over that region.

[32]While they were going out, **a man who was demon-possessed and could not talk** was brought to Jesus. [33]And when the demon was driven out, **the man**

> ***who had been mute spoke*. *The crowd was amazed* and said, "Nothing like this has ever been seen in Israel." [34]But the Pharisees said, "It is by the prince of demons that he drives out demons."**

> (Mark 6) *[1]Jesus left there and went to his hometown, accompanied by his disciples. [2]When the Sabbath came, he began to teach in the synagogue, and many who heard him were amazed.* **"Where did this man get these things?"** *they asked.* **"What's this wisdom that has been given him, that he even does miracles**! *[3]Isn't this the carpenter? Isn't this Mary's son and the brother of James, Joseph, Judas and Simon? Aren't his sisters here with us?" And they took offence at him. [4]Jesus said to them, "Only in his hometown, among his relatives and in his own house is a prophet without honor." [5]He could not do any miracles there, except lay his hands on a few sick people and heal them.* ***[6]And he was amazed at their lack of faith.***

> *Then Jesus went round teaching from village to village. [7]Calling the Twelve to him, he sent them out two by two and gave them authority over evil spirits. [8]These were his instructions:* (Matt. 10) *[16]"I am sending you out* **like sheep among wolves**. *Therefore be as shrewd as snakes and as innocent as doves. [17]Be on your guard against men; they will hand you over to the local councils and flog you in their synagogues.* ***[28]Do not be afraid of those who kill the body but cannot kill the soul. Rather, be afraid of the One who can destroy both soul and body in hell.*** *[34]Do not suppose that I have come to bring peace to the earth. I did not come to bring peace, but a sword. [35]For I have come to turn 'a man against his father, a daughter against her mother, a daughter-in-law against her mother-in-law—[36]a man's enemies will be the members of his own household.' [37]"Anyone who loves his father or mother more than me is not worthy of me; anyone who loves his son or daughter more than me is not worthy of me… [39]Whoever finds his life will lose it, and whoever loses his life for my sake will find it."* Amen.

Thus, we have seen today that the Lord Jesus was filled with the power of God both in **His words** and in **His works**. The multitudes that followed Him were amazed, saying, ***"Where did this man get these things? What's this wisdom that has been given him, that he even does miracles!"*** (Mark 6:2)

From where did Jesus get His power and wisdom? He didn't "get it" from anywhere, because He Himself **is** the Power and Wisdom of God. The Lord Jesus did all the mighty works of God upon the earth, to show people **where He came from and who He was**. He had authority over every created being and every kind of power because He was the **"*Ruh Allah*"** and the **"*Kalimat Allah*"** {Arabic}, that is: He is **the Spirit of God** and **the Word of God**. That is why Jesus could calm the furious storm and heal the wild, demon-possessed man by simply speaking a word. All of God's unlimited power resided in the Lord Jesus. That is the reason He could heal the woman who had suffered with bleeding for twelve years. This woman had wasted all her money on many doctors and their medicines, but the moment she touched Jesus' cloak she was healed. Similarly, when Jesus touched the eyes of the two blind men immediately their sight was restored. And Jesus' authority was not limited to those who were alive. He also had authority over the dead! That is why He could bring back to life the child who had died. Jesus' power surpassed that of a mere prophet, because He Himself was **the Word of God in a human body**.

Yes, God's Word tells us that **all** power and **all** authority have been given to Jesus the Messiah. That is why if you trust in Jesus as your Savior and your Lord, you will no longer need to fear anything: not death, not life, not evil spirits, not sorcerers, not the present, nor the future! You will **no longer need to wear charms** or pour out an offering to a personal protector spirit because **the Lord Jesus will protect you**. That is what the Scripture says: "*In [Jesus] Christ* ***all the fullness of the Deity lives in bodily form****, and you have been given fullness in Christ, who is* ***the head over every power and authority****!*" (Col. 2:9,10)

Dear friends, are you trusting in the One who is "*who is the head over every power and authority*"? Or are you still trying to appease the lesser powers and authorities of this world?

Thank you for listening. In the next study, Lord willing, we will continue in the Gospel and hear how Jesus taught the multitudes with parables....

May God bless you and teach you the deep meaning of what He has declared concerning the Messiah:

> ***"In [Jesus] Christ all the fullness of the Deity lives in bodily form!"*** (Col. 2:9,10)

Lesson 71

Two Important Parables

Luke 8; Matthew 13

Peace be with you, listening friends. We greet you in the name of God, the Lord of peace, who wants everyone to understand and submit to the way of righteousness that He has established, and have true peace with Him forever. We are happy to be able to return today to present your program *The Way of Righteousness*.

In our last program, we discovered that Jesus the Messiah possessed authority which surpassed the authority of a mere prophet. Jesus was full of the power of God. **He was the very Power of God in a human body!** That was why He could calm the storm, cast out demons, heal the sick and the blind, and even raise the dead to life!

Today we will continue in the book of the Gospel {*Injil*}, and hear how the Lord Jesus taught the crowd using **parables** (stories). Jesus often presented the truth in parables because most people who followed Him around did not really want to know the Word of God. What they wanted was for Jesus to heal their bodies of **sickness**, but they did not want Him to heal their souls of **sin**. Also tagging along behind Jesus, like a pack of hyenas, were the religious rulers who listened to Him only to find an opportunity to accuse Him. When they were around, Jesus would speak to the crowd in parables. He would wait until He was alone with His true followers to explain the meaning of the parables.

God wants everyone to know the truth and to be saved, but if our hearts are stubborn, God will not reveal His truth to us. God wants us to seek after the truth, as most people seek after riches! The prophet Solomon wrote, ***"If you look for the truth as for silver and search for it as for hidden treasure, then you will understand the fear of the LORD and find the knowledge of God."*** (Prov. 2:4,5)

How about you? Do you cherish **God's truth** more than money or any other kind of wealth? Does the true Word of God occupy the most important place in your mind and heart? Perhaps you do not know the true condition of your heart before God. Then listen carefully to the Lord Jesus' **Parable of the Sower**.

We are reading in the Gospel of Luke, chapter eight. The Scripture says:

(Luke 8) [4]*While a large crowd was gathering and people were coming to Jesus from town after town, he told this parable:* [5]*"**A farmer went out to sow his seed**. As he was scattering the seed, some fell along the path; it was trampled on, and the birds of the air ate it up.* [6]*Some fell on rock, and when it came up, the plants withered because they had no moisture.* [7]*Other seed fell among thorns, which grew up with it and choked the plants.* [8]*Still other seed fell on good soil. It came up and yielded a crop, a hundred times more than was sown." When he said this, he called out, "**He who has ears to hear, let him hear.**"*

[9]*His disciples asked him what this parable meant.* [10]*He said,...* [11]*"This is the meaning of the parable: **The seed** is the word of God.* [12]*Those **along the path** are the ones who hear, and then the devil comes and takes away the word from their hearts, so that they may not believe and be saved.* [13]*Those **on the rock** are the ones who receive the word with joy when they hear it, but they have no root. They believe for a while, but in the time of testing they fall away.* [14]*The seed that fell **among thorns** stands for those who hear, but as they go on their way they are choked by life's worries, riches and pleasures, and they do not mature.* [15]*But the seed on **good soil** stands for those with a noble and good heart, who hear the word, retain it, and by persevering produce a crop."*

Do you grasp the meaning of the parable of the sower? In this parable, we see the seed and the soil. What does the seed illustrate? What did the Lord Jesus say? He said: **The seed illustrates the true Word of God**. How about the soil? What does it illustrate? **The soil illustrates the heart of man.**

Yes, the Word of God is like good seed, because it is alive and has power to bring forth eternal life and true blessing in your heart, in your life. However, man's heart is like soil which can be very hard and dry. Let us think a little about this. How many kinds of soil do we see in the parable? We saw how the seed fell upon four kinds of soil.

1.) There was seed which fell upon a **hard path**.

2.) There was that which fell on an **area with many rocks**.

3.) There was that which fell among **thorns**. {Lit. in Wolof: *a kind of grass with burrs*}

4.) There was also that which fell upon **good soil**.

First, Jesus taught that many in the world have a heart like **a hard path** upon which people walk. Some people's hearts are as hard as concrete. If a seed falls onto a hard path–what will happen? Will it spring to life and bear fruit? Never! It cannot even begin to take root. People will just walk on it, and the birds of the air will eat it. This is what the hearts of many are like. People with hearts like the hard soil are **those who do not pay attention to the Writings of the Prophets** and consequently they do not believe that Jesus is the Savior of the world. They only care about their own ideas or the traditions of their ancestors. The true

Word of God cannot produce life in their hearts, just as a seed which falls on a hard path cannot produce life.

The **second** kind of soil about which Jesus spoke had many **rocks and thin soil**. The soil with many rocks illustrates the heart of the one who listens to the Word of God and accepts it immediately with joy, but it **does not last**, because the Word of God did not really take root in the person's heart. This kind of person says he believes, but when some trial comes or he is persecuted because of the Word of Truth, he turns away from the truth. Many are like this. The Word of God does not have deep roots in their hearts, because they prefer the praise of man to the praise of God. Consequently, the Word of God is worthless to them, just as the seed which fell in the rocky place is worthless.

The **third** kind of soil was **full of thorns**. What happens when seed falls among thorns? Will it bear fruit? No, it will not! The thorns will choke it before it can bear fruit. The soil with thorns illustrates the heart of the one who listens to the Word of God, but the cares of the world, and **the deception of riches and greed overwhelm him** (or her), choking the Word so that it is unproductive. Many children of Adam have hearts like thorny soil. They think: "Yes, one day, I will begin to look into the Writings of the Prophets. When I have time, I will listen to the Word of God, *'insha'a Allah!'*" {Arabic: *if God wills it*}. However, Satan knows very well that such people will never take time to understand the Word of God. Everyday problems and needs will dominate their hearts and minds. They must work, make money, go to the market, buy, sell, study, sleep and so forth. Is this your experience? Is your life so full of needs and concerns that you have never yet taken time to seek after the Truth of God with your whole heart? Remember that one day death will suddenly come and usher you into eternity. On that day you will know what was the truth and what was a lie, but knowing the truth which you neither sought nor obeyed during your life will be of no value to you, because the time of repentance will be gone and you will be eternally lost!

The **fourth** kind of soil was **good soil**. The seed that the farmer sowed in the good, well-cultivated soil took root, grew and produced an abundant crop so that the farmer reaped a hundred times more than he had sowed. The good soil that received the seed illustrates the one who hears the Word of God, and **retains it in an honest heart**, thus producing righteousness and eternal life. God's Word is living and powerful and will produce eternal life and righteousness living in all those who receive it with a humble and honest heart.

That, in brief, is what Jesus taught in the parable of the sower. The Word of God is like **the good seed**, and our hearts are like **hard soil**. What must happen before seed can be sown into hard soil? One must plough it, as any farmer knows. Similarly, the heart that pleases God is a broken and contrite heart, prepared to accept the Good Seed of the Word of God. The heart that pleases God is the heart that receives His Word in humility and faith. That is what the Scripture declares when it says: "*Everyone should be quick to listen, slow to speak...Get rid of all moral filth and the evil that is so prevalent, and* ***humbly accept the word planted in you, which can save you***." (James 1:19,21)

What is the condition of your heart? Do you have a humble heart, prepared to accept what God says in the Holy Scriptures through His prophets? Is the Word of God growing in your heart? Or do you have a heart like soil that is hard, rocky and thorny? God's Word is Good Seed, but it will only produce life and blessing in the hearts of those who truly believe it and obey it.

Now let us listen to another "farmer parable" which Jesus spoke to the crowd. It is **the Parable of the Weeds.** The Scripture says:

> (Matt. 13) [24]*Jesus told them another parable:* "***The kingdom of heaven is like a man who sowed good seed in his field.*** [25]***But while everyone was sleeping, his enemy came and sowed weeds among the wheat, and went away***.
> [26]*When the wheat sprouted and formed ears, then the weeds also appeared.* [27]*The owner's servants came to him and said, 'Sir, didn't you sow good seed in your field? Where then did the weeds come from?'* [28]*'An enemy did this,' he replied. The servants asked him, 'Do you want us to go and pull them up?'* [29]*'No,' he answered, 'because while you are pulling the weeds, you may root up the wheat with them.* [30]*Let both grow together until the harvest. At that time I will tell the harvesters: First collect the weeds and tie them in bundles to be burned; then gather the wheat and bring it into my barn.'"*
>
> [36]*Then he left the crowd and went into the house. His disciples came to him and said, "Explain to us the parable of the weeds in the field."* [37]*He answered, "The one who sowed the good seed is* ***the Son of Man*** *(That is the* Messiah, *himself).* [38]*The field is* ***the world****, and the good seed stands for* ***the sons of the kingdom****. The weeds are* ***the sons of the evil one****,* [39]*and the enemy who sows them is* ***the devil****. The harvest is* ***the end of the age****, and the harvesters are* ***angels****.* [40]*As the weeds are pulled up and burned in the fire, so it will be at the end of the age.* [41]*The Son of Man will send out his angels, and they will weed out of his kingdom everything that causes sin and all who do evil.* [42]*They will throw them into the fiery furnace, where there will be weeping and gnashing of teeth.*
> [43]*Then the righteous will shine like the sun in the kingdom of their Father.* ***He who has ears, let him hear***." Amen.

In the parable of the weeds, the Lord Jesus compared the world to a field of wheat. The **Sower** illustrates **Jesus the Messiah.** The **wheat** which grew in the field illustrates those who are **children of God** because of their faith in the Good News of the Messiah. The **enemy** who sowed weeds among the wheat is **the devil.** The **weeds** are **those who do not belong to God** because they have not accepted the Good News of the Messiah. The **harvest** is **the Day of Judgment.**

The **wheat stored in the grain house** illustrates **those who have the right to live in the presence of God forever**. However, the **weeds which one gathers and burns** illustrate **those who will be cast into the eternal fire**.

Listening friends, how about you? Are you like **the wheat**? Or like **the weeds**? Search your heart! The Day of Judgment is coming! The Judge is at the door! Do you have confidence to face the Judge in the Day of Judgment? You need not fear that day if you will believe in your heart the Good News of the One who came to save you from eternal hell. Listen to what Jesus the Messiah declared concerning the Day of Judgment. He said, "*I tell you the truth, whoever* ***hears*** *my word and* ***believes*** *him who sent me has eternal life and* ***will not be condemned****; he has crossed over from* ***death to life****!*" (John 5:24) Amen!

Thank you for listening. Next time, God willing, we will continue in the Gospel and see how Jesus miraculously fed more than five thousand men with just five loaves of bread and two fish....

May God give you insight into all that you have heard today as you remember the words of the Lord Jesus:

> ***"He who has ears, let him hear!"*** (Matt. 13:43)

Lesson 72

The Bread of Life

Mark 6; John 6

Peace be with you, listening friends. We greet you in the name of God, the Lord of peace, who wants everyone to understand and submit to the way of righteousness that He has established, and have true peace with Him forever. We are happy to be able to return today to present your program *The Way of Righteousness*.

In our last lesson, we saw the Lord Jesus speaking to the crowds. He presented His teaching in parables which were loaded with eternal truth. However, **most of the crowd did not grasp the meaning of the parables because their hearts were hardened**. They did not appreciate the things of heaven, but only the things of earth. Most did not follow Jesus because He was the Savior of sinners; they accompanied Him only because of the physical benefits they received from Him.

Today we will listen to more words spoken by the Lord Jesus. We will also see how He confirmed His words by performing a miraculous sign. Our lesson today is called "**The Bread of Life**." {Lit. in Wolof: *The Food which gives Eternal Life*}

Now let us continue in the holy book, the Gospel of Mark, chapter six. The Scripture says:

> (Mark 6) 30*The apostles gathered round Jesus…* 31*Then, because so many people were coming and going that they did not even have a chance to eat, he said to them, "Come with me by yourselves to a quiet place and get some rest."* 32*So they went away by themselves in a boat to a solitary place.* 33*But many who saw them leaving recognized them and ran on foot from all the towns and got there ahead of them.* 34*When Jesus landed and saw a large crowd, he had compassion on them, because they were like sheep without a shepherd. So he began teaching them many things.*
>
> 35*By this time it was late in the day, so his disciples came to him. "This is a remote place," they said, "and it's already very late.* 36*Send the people away so that they can go to the surrounding countryside and villages and buy themselves something to eat."* 37*But he answered, "You give them something to eat." They*

> *said to him, "That would take eight months of a man's wages! Are we to go and spend that much on bread and give it to them to eat?"* 38*"How many loaves do you have?" he asked. "Go and see." When they found out, they said, "Five - and two fish."* 39*Then Jesus directed them to have all the people sit down in groups on the green grass.* 40*So they sat down in groups of hundreds and fifties.*
>
> 41*Taking the five loaves and the two fish and looking up to heaven, he gave thanks and broke the loaves. Then he gave them to his disciples to set before the people. He also divided the two fish among them all.* 42***They all ate and were satisfied**,* 43*and the disciples picked up twelve basketfuls of broken pieces of bread and fish.* 44*The number of the men who had eaten was **five thousand**.* 45*Immediately Jesus made his disciples get into the boat and go on ahead of him to Bethsaida, while he dismissed the crowd.* 46*After leaving them, he went up on a mountainside to pray.* 47*When evening came, the boat was in the middle of the lake, and he was alone on land.* 48*He saw the disciples straining at the oars, because the wind was against them. About the fourth watch of the night he went out to them, walking on the lake. He was about to pass by them,* 49*but when they saw him walking on the lake, they thought he was a ghost. They cried out,* 50*because they all saw him and were terrified. Immediately he spoke to them and said, "Take courage! It is I. Don't be afraid."* 51*Then he climbed into the boat with them, and the wind died down. They were completely amazed,* 52*for they had not understood about the loaves; their hearts were hardened.* 53*When they had crossed over, they landed at Gennesaret and anchored there.*
>
> (John 6) 22*The next day the crowd that had stayed on the opposite shore of the lake realized that only one boat had been there, and that Jesus had not entered it with his disciples, but that they had gone away alone...* 24*Once the crowd realized that neither Jesus nor his disciples were there, they got into the boats and went...in search of Jesus.* 25*When they found him on the other side of the lake, they asked him, "Rabbi, when did you get here?"* 26*Jesus answered, "I tell you the truth, you are looking for me, not because you saw miraculous signs but because you ate the loaves and had your fill.* 27***Do not work for food that spoils, but for food that endures to eternal life**, which the Son of Man will give you. On him God the Father has placed his seal of approval."*

Let us pause here. Why did Jesus say to the crowd, "***Do not work for food that spoils***"? Does that mean we should not work in order to have something to eat? No, it does not mean that, because the Word of God also says: "*If a man will not work, he shall not eat.*" (2 Thes. 3:10) Why then did Jesus say, "*Do not work for food that spoils*"? What Jesus was saying was this: If you work only for your stomach, and merely seek after the things of the world, you will end up losing everything, because your body is going to die and return to dust. However, there is something in your body that will never perish. It is **your soul**. The soul of man will exist forever–either in the glorious place called **Heaven** (Paradise) or in the horrifying place called **Hell**. That is why Jesus said, "*Do not work for food that spoils, but for food that endures to eternal life!*" That was how Jesus warned the crowd, so that they might not merely seek perishable food, but that they might seek the Word of God which never passes away. Because "*man does not live on bread alone, but on every word that comes from the mouth of God.*" (Matt. 4:4) That is what the Lord Jesus said.

Sadly, most of those who surrounded Jesus did not care about the Word of God, nor did they believe in the One whom God had sent! Filling their stomachs with food was more important to them than filling their hearts with the truth that could save them from God's judgment. That is why Jesus said to them, (John 6) [27]*Do not work for food that spoils, but for food that endures to eternal life...*[28]*Then they asked him, "What must we do to do the works God requires?"* [29]*Jesus answered, "The work of God is this:* ***to believe in the one he has sent****."*

Did you hear Jesus' answer? How can a child of Adam, who is conceived in sin, please God? Can we work and accomplish deeds that please God? Can we somehow save ourselves from the power of Satan and sin and hell? Can we produce the perfect and pure heart that God requires? Never! "Even if a log soaks a long time in water it will never become a crocodile." {Wolof proverb} How then can a descendant of Adam please God? What did the Lord Jesus say about this? He said, "*The work of God is this:* ***to believe in the One He has sent****.*" No person can ever begin to please God until he (or she) believes in the holy Redeemer whom God has sent.

Sadly, most of the crowd did not believe that Jesus was the Savior, whom God had sent. That is why they said to Him,

> (John 6) [30]*"What miraculous sign then will you give that we may see it and believe you? What will you do?* [31]*Our forefathers ate the manna in the desert; as it is written: 'He gave them bread from heaven to eat.'"* [32]*Jesus said to them, "I tell you the truth, it is not Moses who has given you the bread from heaven, but it is my Father who gives you the true bread from heaven.* [33]*For the bread of God is he who comes down from heaven and gives life to the world."* [34]*"Sir," they said, "from now on give us this bread."* [35]*Then Jesus declared, "****I am the bread of life. He who comes to me will never go hungry, and he who believes in me will never be thirsty!****"*

With those words Jesus was saying: As God sent food down from heaven to feed the children of Israel for forty years so that they would not die in the wilderness, so God has sent to all the children of Adam "Food" which gives eternal life so that we might not perish in our sin!

Where is this "Food"? Is there a food on earth which if you eat of it you can live in the presence of God forever? No, there is not! What is this "Food" which gives eternal life? What did the Lord Jesus say? He said,

> (John 6) [35]**I am the bread of life**. *He who comes to me will never go hungry, and he who believes in me will never be thirsty.* [36]*But as I told you, you have seen me and still you do not believe.* [37]*All that [God] the Father gives me will come to me, and whoever comes to me I will never drive away...* [40]*For my Father's will is that everyone who looks to the Son and believes in him shall have eternal life, and I will raise him up at the last day."*
>
> [41]*At this the Jews began to grumble about him because he said, "I am the bread that came down from heaven."* [42]*They said, "Is this not Jesus, the son of Joseph, whose father and mother we know? How can he now say, 'I came down from heaven'?"*
>
> [43]*"Stop grumbling among yourselves," Jesus answered....* [45]*Everyone who listens to the Father and learns from him comes to me.* [46]*No one has seen the Father except the one who is from God; only he has seen the Father.* [47]*I tell you the truth, he who believes has everlasting life.* [48]*I am the bread of life.* [49]*Your forefathers ate the manna in the desert, yet they died.* [50]*But here is the bread that comes down from heaven, which a man may eat and not die.* [51]**I am the living bread that came down from heaven**. *If anyone eats of this bread, he will live forever...."*
>
> [60]*On hearing it, many of his disciples said, "This is a hard teaching. Who can accept it?"* [61]*Aware that his disciples were grumbling about this, Jesus said to them, "Does this offend you?* [62]*What if you see the Son of Man ascend to where he was before!* [63]*The Spirit gives life; the flesh counts for nothing. The words I have spoken to you are spirit and they are life.* [64]*Yet there are some of you who do not believe." (For Jesus had known from the beginning which of them did not believe and who would betray him.)...*
>
> [66]*From this time many of his disciples turned back and no longer followed him.* [67]*"You do not want to leave too, do you?" Jesus asked the Twelve.* [68]*Simon Peter answered him,* **"Lord, to whom shall we go? You have the words of eternal life.** [69]**We believe and know that you are the Holy One of God**."

Thus, many disciples turned away, no longer accompanying Jesus because of His difficult teachings. However, among those who followed Jesus were some who would not leave Him, because they were convinced that Jesus was the Messiah, the Holy One from God—**the Bread of Life—the "True Food" which gives eternal life**!

Yes, that is the way it is. Once you know who Jesus really is and what He is like and what He has done for you—you will never be satisfied with another master! Jesus is the only Source of eternal life. He alone can satisfy the heart that hungers for assurance of salvation and a close relationship with God.

How about you? Do you hunger and thirst for eternal life? Do you long to have confidence before God here on earth and in the life to come? Then consider this great invitation from the Lord Jesus Christ who says, ***"Come to me, all you who are weary and burdened, and I will give you rest....I am the bread of life. He who comes to me will never go hungry, and he who believes in me will never be thirsty!"*** (Matt. 11:28; John 6:35) Amen.

Friends, thank you for listening. Next time, God willing, we will continue in the Gospel and hear how the crowd was divided because of Jesus....

God bless you as you remember these words of the Lord Jesus:

> ***"I am the bread of life. He who comes to me will never go hungry, and he who believes in me will never be thirsty!"*** (John 6:35)

LESSON 73

JESUS CAUSES DIVISION

MATTHEW 15,16; JOHN 7

Peace be with you, listening friends. We greet you in the name of God, the Lord of peace, who wants everyone to understand and submit to the way of righteousness that He has established, and have true peace with Him forever. We are happy to be able to return today to present your program *The Way of Righteousness*.

In our last program, we saw the Lord Jesus multiply five loaves of bread and two fish to feed a crowd of more than five thousand men. On the following day, a great crowd surrounded Jesus, but Jesus, who knew their hearts, said to them,

> *"You are looking for me because you ate the loaves and had your fill. Do not work for food that spoils, but for food that endures to eternal life!* ***I am the bread of life****. He who comes to me will never go hungry, and he who believes in me will never be thirsty!"* (John 6:26,27,35)

Sadly, many people turned away and no longer followed Jesus because they valued the food that could nourish their bodies more than the food that could nourish their souls. But some continued to follow Jesus because they believed in their hearts that Jesus was the Holy One from God and the source of eternal life.

Today we plan to continue in the holy Gospel and see how Jesus was **confronted by the religious rulers** of the Jews, and how the Jews were **divided because of Jesus**. Before we begin, it is helpful to know that the religious experts known as the Pharisees, and most of the Jews, followed the customs that they and their ancestors had established. For example, when they returned from a public place, they would not eat until they had washed themselves in a certain way. They also had many other traditions, such as how they were to wash cups, water pots, and kettles so that they would be "clean."

Listen to what is written in the Gospel of Matthew, chapter fifteen. The Scripture says:

> (Matt. 15) [1]*Then some Pharisees and teachers of the law came to Jesus from Jerusalem and asked,* [2]*"Why do your disciples break the tradition of the elders?*

> *They don't wash their hands before they eat!" 3Jesus replied, "***And why do you break the command of God for the sake of your tradition?** *4For God said, 'Honor your father and mother' and 'Anyone who curses his father or mother must be put to death.' 5But you say that if a man says to his father or mother, 'Whatever help you might otherwise have received from me is a gift devoted to God,' 6he is not to 'honor his father' with it.* **Thus you nullify the word of God for the sake of your tradition**. *7You hypocrites! Isaiah was right when he prophesied about you: 8'***These people honor me with their lips, but their hearts are far from me. 9They worship me in vain; their teachings are but rules taught by men.***'"*

Did you notice how Jesus exposed the hypocrisy of the Pharisees and the teachers of the Law in front of everyone? The religious leaders were trying to be righteous before men, but the Lord Jesus knew what was in their hearts. Their **hands, feet and faces** may have been **clean**, but their **hearts** were **contaminated** with sin! **A clean heart is more important than clean hands**. Ceremonial washings (Ablutions) do not purify your heart. If you have a cooking pot that is dirty on the inside, will merely washing the outside make the pot clean? No, it will not! Similarly, the religious ceremonies which the Jews followed could not remove **the sin** that was in their hearts. That is why Jesus said to them:

> (Matt. 15) *7"***You hypocrites***! [The prophet] Isaiah was right when he prophesied about you: 8'These people honor me with their* **lips**, *but their* **hearts** *are far from me. 9They worship me in vain; their teachings are but rules taught by men.'"*
>
> *10[Then] Jesus called the crowd to him and said, "Listen and understand. 11What goes into a man's mouth does not make him 'unclean', but what comes out of his mouth, that is what makes him 'unclean'." 12Then the disciples came to him and asked, "Do you know that the Pharisees were offended when they heard this?" 13He replied, "Every plant that my heavenly Father has not planted will be pulled up by the roots. 14Leave them; they are blind guides.* ***If a blind man leads a blind man, both will fall into a pit.****"*
>
> *15Peter said, "Explain the parable to us." 16"Are you still so dull?" Jesus asked them. 17"Don't you see that whatever enters the mouth goes into the stomach and then out of the body? 18But the things that come out of the mouth come from the heart, and these make a man 'unclean'. 19For out of the heart come evil thoughts, murder, adultery, sexual immorality, theft, false testimony, slander. 20***These are what make a man 'unclean'***; but eating with unwashed hands does not make him 'unclean'."*
>
> *29Jesus left there and went along the Sea of Galilee. Then he went up on a mountainside and sat down. 30Great crowds came to him, bringing the lame, the blind, the crippled, the mute and many others, and laid them at his feet; and he*

> *healed them.* [31]*The people were amazed when they saw the mute speaking, the crippled made well, the lame walking and the blind seeing. And they praised the God of Israel."*
>
> (Matt. 16) [1]*[After that,] the Pharisees and Sadducees came to Jesus and tested him by asking him to show them a sign from heaven.* [2]*He replied, "When evening comes, you say, 'It will be fair weather, for the sky is red,'* [3]*and in the morning, 'Today it will be stormy, for the sky is red and overcast.' You know how to interpret the appearance of the sky, but you cannot interpret the signs of the times.* [4]*A wicked and adulterous generation looks for a miraculous sign, but none will be given it except the sign of Jonah."*
>
> (Matt. 12) [40]*"For as Jonah was three days and three nights in the belly of a huge fish, so the Son of Man will be three days and three nights in the heart of the earth.* [41]*The men of Nineveh will stand up at the judgment with this generation and condemn it; for they repented at the preaching of Jonah, and now* ***one greater than Jonah is here****."*

Thus Jesus predicted that, as the prophet Jonah was in the belly of the great fish for three days, similarly, Jesus would spend three days in the tomb. And as Jonah came out of the fish on the third day, Jesus would rise from the dead on the third day, thus giving an undeniable proof that He is the Messiah from heaven, the One who came to save us from the power of sin and death and hell!

In the remaining time let us continue in the Gospel and see how the religious experts persisted in their unbelief. In the Gospel of John, chapter seven, the Scripture says:

> (John 7) [1]*After this, Jesus went around in Galilee, purposely staying away from Judea because the Jews there were waiting to take his life.* [2]*But when the Jewish Feast of Tabernacles was near,* [3]*Jesus' brothers said to him, "You ought to leave here and go to Judea, so that your disciples may see the miracles you do.* [4]*No one who wants to become a public figure acts in secret. Since you are doing these things, show yourself to the world."* [5]*For* ***even his own brothers did not believe in him.***
>
> [6]*Therefore Jesus told them, "The right time for me has not yet come; for you any time is right.* [7]*The world cannot hate you, but it hates me because I testify that what it does is evil.* [8]*You go to the Feast. I am not yet going up to this Feast, because for me the right time has not yet come."* [9]*Having said this, he stayed in Galilee.* [10]*However, after his brothers had left for the Feast, he went also, not publicly, but in secret.* [11]*Now at the Feast the Jews were watching for him and asking, "Where is that man?"* [12]*Among the crowds there was widespread whispering about him. Some said, "He is a good man." Others replied, "No, he*

deceives the people." [13]But no one would say anything publicly about him for fear of the Jews.

[14]Not until halfway through the Feast did Jesus go up to the temple courts and begin to teach. [15]The Jews were amazed and asked, "How did this man get such learning without having studied?" [16]Jesus answered, "My teaching is not my own. It comes from him who sent me. [17]If anyone chooses to do God's will, he will find out whether my teaching comes from God or whether I speak on my own.... [19]Has not Moses given you the law? Yet not one of you keeps the law. Why are you trying to kill me?"

*[20]"You are demon-possessed," the crowd answered. "Who is trying to kill you?" [21]Jesus said to them, "I did one miracle, and you are all astonished. [22]Yet, because Moses gave you circumcision (though actually it did not come from Moses, but from the patriarchs), you circumcise a child on the Sabbath. [23]Now if a child can be circumcised on the Sabbath so that the law of Moses may not be broken, why are you angry with me for healing the whole man on the Sabbath? [24]**Stop judging by mere appearances, and make a right judgment!**" [30]At this they tried to seize him, but no one laid a hand on him, because his time had not yet come. [31]**Still, many in the crowd put their faith in him. They said, "When the Christ comes, will he do more miraculous signs than this man?"** [32]The Pharisees heard the crowd whispering such things about him. Then the chief priests and the Pharisees sent temple guards to arrest him.*

*[37]On the last and greatest day of the Feast, Jesus stood and said in a loud voice, "**If anyone is thirsty, let him come to me and drink. [38]Whoever believes in me, as the Scripture has said, streams of living water will flow from within him.**" [40]On hearing his words, some of the people said, "Surely this man is the Prophet." [41]Others said, "He is the Christ." Still others asked, "How can the Christ come from Galilee? [42]Does not the Scripture say that the Christ will come from David's family and from Bethlehem, the town where David lived?" [43]Thus the people were divided because of Jesus. [44]Some wanted to seize him, but no one laid a hand on him.*

*[45]Finally the temple guards went back to the chief priests and Pharisees, who asked them, "Why didn't you bring him in?" [46]"**No one ever spoke the way this man does**," the guards declared. [47]"You mean he has deceived you also?" the Pharisees retorted. [48]"Has any of the rulers or of the Pharisees believed in him? [49]No! But this mob that knows nothing of the law - there is a curse on them." [50]**Nicodemus**, who had gone to Jesus earlier and who was one of their own number, asked, [51]"Does our law condemn a man without first hearing him to find out what he is doing?" [52]They replied, "Are you from Galilee, too? Look into it, and you will find that a prophet does not come out of Galilee." [53]Then each went to his own home.*

This is where we will stop today. We have seen how the priests, the teachers of the law and the Pharisees harassed Jesus. They wanted to arrest Him and have Him put to death, but they could do nothing to Him, because the time which God planned for Jesus to die as a sacrifice for sin had not yet come.

Sadly, most of the Jewish religious leaders had **hard hearts**. They despised Jesus and they threatened to expel from the synagogue anyone who acknowledged that Jesus was the Messiah. Thus there was **a division** among the crowd because of Jesus. No one would say anything openly about Jesus because they were afraid of the religious leaders and the priests {marabouts}. Secretly, among themselves, some whispered, "He is a good man." Others retorted, "No, he deceives the people!" The rest wondered, "When the Messiah comes will He do more miraculous signs than this man?"

Friends, what do **you** say about Jesus? What do **you** think about Him? Do you believe that Jesus is the Messiah of whom all the prophets have written? Or do you think that Jesus was just one of the prophets? Let no one misleads you in this matter. Your destiny in the hereafter depends on your response to this question! **Do you know who Jesus really is?** Do you know why He came into the world? Listen to what Jesus said about Himself:

> *"I am* **the** *way and* **the** *truth and* **the** *life. No one comes to [God] the Father except through me!...For this reason I was born, and for this I came into the world, to testify to the truth.* ***Everyone on the side of truth listens to me!****"* (John 14:6; 18:37)

Dear friend, on whose side are you? Are you willing to side with the Truth—even if means being rejected by your own family? Wolof wisdom says, "Whoever wants honey must brave the bees." The Lord Jesus said,

> *"Do not suppose that I have come to bring peace to the earth....I have come to turn a man against his father, a daughter against her mother, a daughter-in-law against her mother-in-law—a man's enemies will be the members of his own household.* ***Anyone who loves his father or mother more than me is not worthy of me!****"* (Matt. 10:34-37)

Thank you for listening. Join us next time when, God willing, we continue in the Gospel to see how Jesus healed a man who was blind from birth....

God bless you as consider these words of Jesus the Messiah:

> ***"Everyone on the side of truth listens to me!"*** (John 18:37)

LESSON 74

THE LIGHT OF THE WORLD

JOHN 8,9

Peace be with you, listening friends. We greet you in the name of God, the Lord of peace, who wants everyone to understand and submit to the way of righteousness that He has established, and have true peace with Him forever. We are happy to be able to return today to present your program *The Way of Righteousness*.

In the last program, we saw how the priests, the teachers of the Law and the Pharisees **harassed Jesus** and tried to arrest Him so that they could have Him put to death. However, no one could take Jesus, because God's appointed time for Him to die as a sacrifice for sin had not yet come. Today we will continue in the book of the Gospel and hear how Jesus reproved those who opposed Him, and how He healed a man who had been blind from birth. Our lesson today is called **"The Light of the World."**

In the Gospel of John, chapter eight, we read:

> (John 8) [2]*At dawn [Jesus] appeared again in the temple courts, where all the people gathered round him, and he sat down to teach them....* [12]*[And Jesus said to them,]* "***I am the light of the world. Whoever follows me will never walk in darkness, but will have the light of life***." [13]*The Pharisees challenged him, "Here you are, appearing as your own witness; your testimony is not valid."* [14]*Jesus answered, "Even if I testify on my own behalf, my testimony is valid, for I know where I came from and where I am going. But you have no idea where I come from or where I am going...* [23]*..."You are from below; I am from above. You are of this world; I am not of this world.* [24]*I told you that you would die in your sins;* ***if you do not believe that I am the one I claim to be, you will indeed die in your sins***." [25]*"Who are you?" they asked. "Just what I have been claiming all along," Jesus replied....* [28]*"When you have lifted up the Son of Man, then you will know that I am, and that I do nothing on my own but speak just what the Father has taught me....* [32]*Then you will know the truth, and* ***the truth will set you free***."

[33]They answered him, "We are Abraham's descendants and have never been slaves of anyone. How can you say that we shall be set free?" [34]Jesus replied, "I tell you the truth, **everyone who sins is a slave to sin**. [35]Now a slave has no permanent place in the family, but a son belongs to it forever. [36]So if the Son sets you free, you will be free indeed. [37]I know you are Abraham's descendants. Yet you are ready to kill me, because you have no room for my word. [38]I am telling you what I have seen in the Father's presence, and you do what you have heard from your father." [39]"Abraham is our father," they answered. "If you were Abraham's children," said Jesus, "then you would do the things Abraham did. [40]As it is, you are determined to kill me, a man who has told you the truth that I heard from God. Abraham did not do such things. [41]You are doing the things your own father does."

"We are not illegitimate children," they protested. "The only Father we have is God himself." [42] Jesus said to them, "**If God were your Father, you would love me**, for I came from God and now am here. I have not come on my own; but he sent me. [43]Why is my language not clear to you? Because you are unable to hear what I say. [44]You belong to your father, the devil, and you want to carry out your father's desire. He was a murderer from the beginning, not holding to the truth, for there is no truth in him. When he lies, he speaks his native language, for he is a liar and the father of lies. [45]Yet because I tell the truth, you do not believe me! [46]Can any of you prove me guilty of sin? If I am telling the truth, why don't you believe me? [47]He who belongs to God hears what God says. The reason you do not hear is that you do not belong to God."

[48]The Jews answered him, "Aren't we right in saying that you are a Samaritan and demon-possessed?" [49]"I am not possessed by a demon," said Jesus, "but I honor my Father and you dishonor me. [50]I am not seeking glory for myself; but there is one who seeks it, and he is the judge. [51]I tell you the truth, if anyone keeps my word, he will never see death." [52]At this the Jews exclaimed, "Now we know that you are demon-possessed! Abraham died and so did the prophets, yet you say that if anyone keeps your word, he will never taste death. [53]Are you greater than our father Abraham? He died, and so did the prophets. Who do you think you are?" [54]Jesus replied, "If I glorify myself, my glory means nothing. My Father, whom you claim as your God, is the one who glorifies me. [55]Though you do not know him, I know him. If I said I did not, I would be a liar like you, but I do know him and keep his word. [56]Your father Abraham rejoiced at the thought of seeing my day; he saw it and was glad." [57]"You are not yet fifty years old," the Jews said to him, "and you have seen Abraham!" [58]"I tell you the truth," Jesus answered, "**before Abraham was born, I am**!" [59]At this, **they picked up stones to stone him,** but Jesus hid himself, slipping away from the temple grounds.

(John 9) [1]As [Jesus] went along, he saw **a man blind from birth**. [2]His disciples asked him, "Rabbi, who sinned, this man or his parents, that he was *born blind?" 3"Neither this man nor his parents sinned," said Jesus, "but this happened so that the work of God might be displayed in his life. 4As long as it is day, we must do the work of him who sent me. Night is coming, when no one can work. 5While I am in the world, I am the light of the world."*

6Having said this, he spat on the ground, made some mud with the saliva, and put it on the man's eyes. 7"Go," he told him, "wash in the Pool of Siloam" (this word means "Sent"). So the man went and washed, and came home **seeing**. *8His neighbors and those who had formerly seen him begging asked, "Isn't this the same man who used to sit and beg?" 9Some claimed that he was. Others said, "No, he only looks like him." But he himself insisted, "I am the man." 10"How then were your eyes opened?" they demanded. 11He replied, "The man they call Jesus made some mud and put it on my eyes. He told me to go to Siloam and wash. So I went and washed, and then I could see." 12"Where is this man?" they asked him. "I don't know," he said.*

13They brought to the Pharisees the man who had been blind. 14Now the day on which Jesus had made the mud and opened the man's eyes was a Sabbath. 15Therefore the Pharisees also asked him how he had received his sight. "He put mud on my eyes," the man replied, "and I washed, and now I see." 16Some of the Pharisees said, "This man is not from God, for he does not keep the Sabbath." But others asked, "How can a sinner do such miraculous signs?" So they were divided. 17Finally they turned again to the blind man, "What have you to say about him? It was your eyes he opened." The man replied, "He is a prophet."

18The Jews still did not believe that he had been blind and had received his sight until they sent for the man's parents. 19"Is this your son?" they asked. "Is this the one you say was born blind? How is it that now he can see?" 20"We know he is our son," the parents answered, "and we know he was born blind. 21But how he can see now, or who opened his eyes, we don't know. Ask him. He is of age; he will speak for himself." 22His parents said this because they were **afraid of the Jews**, *for already the Jews had decided that anyone who acknowledged that Jesus was the Christ would be put out of the synagogue. 23That was why his parents said, "He is of age; ask him."*

24A second time they summoned the man who had been blind. "Give glory to God," they said. "We know this man is a sinner." 25He replied, "Whether he is a sinner or not, I don't know. **One thing I do know. I was blind but now I see**!" *26Then they asked him, "What did he do to you? How did he open your eyes?" 27He answered, "I have told you already and you did not listen. Why do you want to hear it again? Do you want to become his disciples, too?" 28Then they hurled insults at him and said, "You are this fellow's disciple! We are disciples of Moses! 29We know that God spoke to Moses, but as for this fellow, we don't even know where he comes from."*

*30The man answered, "***Now that is remarkable! You don't know where**

> **he comes from, yet he opened my eyes**. [31]*We know that God does not listen to sinners. He listens to the godly man who does his will.* [32]*Nobody has ever heard of opening the eyes of a man born blind.* [33]*If this man were not from God, he could do nothing."* [34]*To this they replied, "You were steeped in sin at birth; how dare you lecture us!" And they threw him out.*
>
> [35]*Jesus heard that they had thrown him out, and when he found him, he said, "Do you believe in the Son of Man?"* [36]*"Who is he, sir?" the man asked. "Tell me so that I may believe in him."* [37]*Jesus said, "You have now seen him; in fact, he is the one speaking with you."* [38]**Then the man said, "Lord, I believe," and he worshiped him.** [39]*Jesus said, "For judgment I have come into this world, so that the blind will see and those who see will become blind."*
>
> [40]*Some Pharisees who were with him heard him say this and asked, "What? Are we blind too?"* [41]*Jesus said, "If you were blind, you would not be guilty of sin; but now that you claim you can see, your guilt remains."*

Thus the Lord Jesus healed the man who was born blind and rebuked the Pharisees because of their blinded minds. These religious experts had a blindness that was worse than ordinary blindness. They could see, but **they did not want to see,** which is why they picked up rocks to throw at Jesus. These religious men had closed their minds to the truth about Jesus. **They did not want to believe** that He was the Messiah and the Light of the world. They did not want to believe that Jesus existed before the prophet Abraham; that He was the Word that was with God in the beginning. **They did not want to see the truth.**

In today's story we have seen **two kinds of blind people**: Those who are blind in the **eyes**; and those who are blind in the **mind**. The darkness of a blind mind is worse than the darkness of blind eyes. If your eyes are blind, you cannot see the things of the world, but if your heart and mind are blind, then you cannot see or understand the things of eternity!

The Word of God teaches us that all of Adam's children are **blind from birth**–blind in their minds and in their hearts. Because of Adam's sin, all of us have been born in the darkness of sin and ignorance. We have no knowledge of God and no natural desire for His truth. Like cockroaches that scatter when a light is turned on, we avoid the light of God's Word, content to live out our lives in the darkness. Sadly, most of Adam's offspring die in the darkness of sin and ignorance. Wolof wisdom says, "Before you know it, ignorance {Lit. lack of knowledge} will kill you!" Similarly, the prophet Hosea wrote: "*Hear the word of the LORD…My people are* ***destroyed*** *from* ***lack of knowledge****. Because you have rejected knowledge, I also reject you…!*" (Hos. 4:1,6)

The **good news** is that God does not want any of us to perish in the darkness of sin and ignorance. That is why He visited our world by sending to us the Lord Jesus Christ. The prophet Zachariah spoke of the Lord Jesus as "***the Rising Sun***" whom God would send *"from heaven to* ***shine*** *on those living in darkness and in the shadow of death, to* ***guide*** *our feet into the path of peace."* (Luke 1:79) The prophets were like the stars that illumine the night, but Jesus Christ is like the rising sun, bringing light and life to all who believe in Him. How many suns did God create to illuminate our world? Only one. How many Saviors has God sent from heaven to deliver sinners from the darkness of sin and eternal hell? Only one. However, most of Adam's children do not understand this, which is why they are still stumbling in the darkness of sin. That is what the Scripture declares concerning the Lord Jesus Christ, saying: "*The light shines in the darkness, but* ***the darkness has not understood it****. He was in the world, and though the world was made through him,* ***the world did not recognize him.***" (John 1:5,10)

Listening friends, has the Lord Jesus opened "the eyes" of your mind and heart? Or are you still stumbling in the darkness of sin and ignorance?

Thank you for listening. In our next study, God willing, we will continue in the Gospel and see how the glory of God shone out of Jesus like the sun....

God bless you as you ponder this declaration by the Lord Jesus:

> ***"I am the light of the world. Whoever follows me will never walk in darkness, but will have the light of life."*** (John 8:12)

LESSON 75

THE LORD OF GLORY

MATTHEW 16,17

Peace be with you, listening friends. We greet you in the name of God, the Lord of peace, who wants everyone to understand and submit to the way of righteousness that He has established, and have true peace with Him forever. We are happy to be able to return today to present your program *The Way of Righteousness*.

In the last lesson, in our study in the book of the Gospel, we heard how Jesus the Messiah opened the eyes of a man who was born blind. Nothing is impossible for Jesus because He is the very Word of God which appeared on earth as a man. That is why Jesus could control every force upon earth–the wind, the sea, demons, disease and death. Everywhere Jesus went the crowds pressed in on Him, but **few recognized who He really was**. They considered Him a prophet, but did not recognize that all the fullness of God dwelt in Him. They did not understand that Jesus was the Lord of Glory, who came from heaven. In our lesson today, God willing, we will see how **the Lord Jesus was full of the light of the glory of God**, and how He displayed it for a brief moment one day when He was on a mountain with three of His disciples.

Now let us return to the holy Gospel. The Scripture says:

> (Luke 9) [18]*Once when Jesus was praying in private and his disciples were with him, he asked them, "Who do the crowds say I am?"* [19]*They replied, "Some say John the Baptist; others say Elijah; and still others, that one of the prophets of long ago has come back to life."* (Matt. 16) [15]*"But what about you?" he asked.* ***"Who do you say I am?"*** [16]*Simon Peter answered, "You are the Christ* (the Messiah), *the Son of the living God."* [17]*Jesus replied, "Blessed are you, Simon son of Jonah, for this was not revealed to you by man, but by my Father in heaven."*

Let us stop here and consider the question Jesus asked His disciples one day when He was alone with them. Jesus asked them, "Who do **people** say that I am?" The disciples answered Jesus that most people said that He was one of the prophets. Then Jesus questioned them again, saying, "But who do **you** say that I am?"

One of the disciples, Simon Peter, answered Jesus, ***"You are the Messiah, the Son of the Living God!"***

Truly, what Jesus asked His disciples is an important question which every one of us must answer! You who are listening today, who do you consider Jesus to be? What do you think about Him? Do you merely classify Him with the prophets? Or do you agree with Peter who declared that Jesus is "the Messiah, the Son of the Living God"? **Who do you think Jesus is?** Do you believe that Jesus is the Messiah—the Redeemer whom God promised long ago on that day when our ancestors, Adam and Eve, sinned? Do you believe that Jesus is "the Son of the Living God"—the Word of God which came down from heaven?

As you know, to this very day, **many people deny that Jesus is the Son of God**, because they think that this name means that God took a wife and had a child by her! But it does not mean that. God's glory is greater than that! God is Spirit and does not beget as a man begets, **but that does not keep God from calling Jesus His Son**. We have already illustrated it like this: If I {the Senegalese radio speaker} go outside the country, and folks call me "a son of Senegal," that does not mean that Senegal took a wife and had a son! No, I am called "a son of Senegal" because Senegal is where I come from.

That is how it was with Jesus, the Messiah, who was born of a virgin. Even before He was born, He was in heaven. He is the "*Kalimat Allah*" and the "*Ruh Allah*"—the very Word and Soul of God. {See lesson #61 for explanation of these Arabic terms.} Only Jesus is worthy to be called the Son of the Most High, because He alone is the Word that was with God in the beginning. This is **a great mystery**, but more than that, it is **a great truth**! God sent His Son into the world not only to save us from our sins, but also to show us what He is like. Jesus displayed God's character on earth. Whoever sees the Son knows what the Father is like. Whoever sees Jesus knows what God is like. Jesus is called the Son of God, because **He came from God**, because **He is like God**, and because **He is the very Word of God and Soul of God**. Dear friends, whether we believe it or whether we refuse to believe it, the truth remains: **Jesus is the Son of the Living God**!

Let us now continue in the Gospel of Matthew and listen to what happened after Peter declared Jesus to be the Messiah, the Son of the Living God. The Scripture says:

> (Matt. 16) [21]*From that time on* ***Jesus began to explain to his disciples that he must go to Jerusalem and suffer*** *many things at the hands of the elders, chief priests and teachers of the law, and that he must* ***be killed*** *and on the third day be* ***raised to life****.* [22]*Peter took him aside and began to rebuke him. "Never, Lord!" he said. "This shall never happen to you!"* [23]*Jesus turned and said to Peter, "Get behind me, Satan! You are a stumbling-block to me;* ***you do not have in mind the things of God, but the things of men****."*

Did you hear what Jesus said to His disciples? He told them that He must go to Jerusalem and suffer many things at the hands of the elders, chief priests and teachers of the law, and that He must be killed and then be raised to life again on the third day. Thus Jesus announced that He would pour out His blood to pay the debt for our sin.

But **Peter could not accept** that the Lord Jesus, who possessed all power and all authority, would allow the evil rulers of the Jews to arrest Him, torture Him and kill Him. That was why Peter said to Jesus, "*Never, Lord! This shall never happen to you!*" However Jesus knew that He had come into the world to shed His blood as a sacrifice that takes away sin. That is the reason He said to Peter, "*Get behind me, Satan! You are a stumbling-block to me; you do not have in mind the things of God, but the things of men!*"

Jesus knew why He had come into the world. He came to give His life by shedding His holy blood for sinners, just as God's prophets had predicted long beforehand. Jesus came so that the symbol of the sacrificial sheep might be fulfilled in Him. Ah, fellow listeners, if we remember only one thing from our lesson today, let it be this: **Jesus the Messiah came into the world to die as a sacrifice to pay for sin—my sin and yours**! God willing, a few lessons from now, we will see how Jesus' prophecy about His own death was precisely fulfilled in Jerusalem. And so friends, even if some proclaim another message which does not agree with what the Lord Jesus and the prophets prophesied so long ago, the truth concerning Jesus' death and resurrection does not change. **God Himself is the One who decreed the death of the Messiah on the cross**, and no one can change the decrees of God! **Jesus chose to die as the supreme Sacrifice**. He did it because He loves you and me and does not want us to perish.

Now let us see what happened one week after Jesus made known to His disciples that He would offer up His life in Jerusalem. The Scripture says:

> (Matt. 17) [1]*After six days Jesus took with him Peter, James and John the brother of James, and led them up a high mountain by themselves.* [2]*There* ***he was transfigured*** *before them.* ***His face shone like the sun, and his clothes became as white as the light.***
>
> (Luke 9) [30]*Two men, Moses and Elijah,* [31]*appeared in glorious splendor, talking with Jesus. They spoke about his departure, which he was about to bring to fulfillment at Jerusalem.* (Matt. 17) [4]*Peter said to Jesus, "Lord, it is good for us to be here. If you wish, I will put up three shelters–one for you, one for Moses and one for Elijah."* [5]*While he was still speaking, a bright cloud enveloped them, and a voice from the cloud said, "**This is my Son, whom I love; with him I am well pleased. Listen to him!**"* [6]*When the disciples heard this, they fell face down to the ground, terrified.* [7]*But Jesus came and touched them. "Get up," he said. "Don't*

be afraid." [8]When they looked up, they saw no one except Jesus. [9]As they were coming down the mountain, Jesus instructed them, "Don't tell anyone what you have seen, until the Son of Man has been raised from the dead."

Did you grasp what happened on that high mountain? It was an amazing and wonderful event! We read that Jesus' outward appearance was transformed—His face shone like the sun and His clothes radiated a sparkling white light. The same awesome, dazzling pure light that shines out of God and surrounds the throne of God in heaven was now shining out of Jesus! The glorious light that filled the Holiest Place in the Tent of the Meeting in the days when Moses and the Israelites were in the wilderness—that same glory was in Jesus, though men could not see it. But for a few brief moments, in the presence of Jesus' three disciples, God unveiled His awesome glory which was hidden in Jesus' body! And at the same moment, God sent down from heaven two prophets, Moses and Elijah, to talk with Jesus concerning His death in Jerusalem. We also read that a bright cloud covered the mountain, and the voice of the Almighty echoed forth from the cloud, saying, ***"This is my Son, whom I love; with him I am well pleased. Listen to him!"***

What was the reason for all this? Why did God do all these glorious things in the presence of Peter, John and James? This is the reason. God wanted to give those three witnesses an unshakable proof that, in truth, Jesus is the Eternal Son of God from heaven, and that all must listen to Him! That is what the Scripture proclaims, saying:

*"He who does not honor **the Son** does not honor **the Father, who sent him**."* (John 5:23) *"In the past God spoke to our forefathers through **the prophets** at many times and in various ways, but in these last days he has spoken to us by **his Son**, whom he appointed heir of all things, and through whom he made the universe. **The Son is the radiance of God's glory and the exact representation of his being**, sustaining all things by his powerful word. After he had provided purification for sins, he sat down at the right hand of the Majesty in heaven."* (Heb. 1:1-3)

You who are listening today, what do you think of Jesus? What do you say about Him? Do you believe that Jesus is the Lord of Glory, who came from heaven? Or do you merely classify Him with the prophets as most people in the world do? Before we bid you farewell today, let us listen to some excerpts from Jesus' apostles, Peter and John, who wrote in the Holy Scriptures several years after they saw the glory of God shine out of Jesus on top of the mountain.

The apostle Peter wrote:

> *"We did not follow cleverly invented stories when we told you about the power and coming of our Lord Jesus Christ, but* ***we were eyewitnesses of his majesty****. For he received honor and glory from God the Father when the voice came to him from the Majestic Glory, saying, 'This is my Son, whom I love; with him I am well pleased.'* ***We ourselves heard this voice*** *that came from heaven when we were with him on the sacred mountain!"* (2 Pet. 1:16-18)

The apostle John wrote:

> *"That which was from the beginning, which we have* ***heard****, which we have* ***seen*** *with our eyes, which we have* ***looked at*** *and our hands have touched–this we proclaim concerning the Word of life. The life appeared; we have seen it...We have seen his glory, the glory of the One and Only, who came from the Father, full of grace and truth!"* (1 John 1:1,2; John 1:14)

And in the end of the Gospel of John, he wrote,

> *"Jesus did many other miraculous signs in the presence of his disciples, which are not recorded in this book.* ***But these are written that you may believe that Jesus is the Christ, the Son of God, and that by believing you may have life in his name****!"* (John 20:30,31)

Do you find all this hard to understand? God wants to give you insight into these marvelous truths. The Scripture says:

> *"The man without the Spirit* ***does not accept*** *the things that come from the Spirit of God, for they are foolishness to him, and he cannot understand them, because they are spiritually discerned...We do, however, speak a message of wisdom among the mature, but not the wisdom of this age or of the rulers of this age, who are coming to nothing. No, we speak of* ***God's secret wisdom****, a wisdom that has been hidden and that God destined for our glory before time began. None of the rulers of this age understood it, for if they had, they would not have crucified the Lord of glory!"* (2 Cor. 2:14,6-8)

May God make clear what we have read today....

Until next time, keep thinking about what Almighty God declared on top of the mountain concerning the Lord Jesus, when He said,

> ***"This is my Son, whom I love; with him I am well pleased. Listen to him!"*** (Matt. 17:5)

Lesson 76

The Good Shepherd

John 10

Peace be with you, listening friends. We greet you in the name of God, the Lord of peace, who wants everyone to understand and submit to the way of righteousness that He has established, and have true peace with Him forever. We are happy to be able to return today to present your program *The Way of Righteousness*.

In the last lesson, we heard the Lord Jesus tell His disciples that **He must die in Jerusalem and rise from the dead on the third day**. Jesus knew that He had been born into the world to shed His blood as a sacrifice that takes away sin. Last time, we also saw the Lord Jesus display His great glory when He was on the mountain with three of His disciples. The face of Jesus shone like the sun, and His clothes radiated a shining pure white light. Thus, the glory of God which resided in Jesus revealed itself.

Today we would like to continue in the holy Gospel and hear how the Lord Jesus compared those who followed Him with **contented sheep**. We have already seen in the Writings of the Prophets that God repeatedly compares the children of Adam to **lost sheep without a shepherd**. However, God does not want the children of Adam to perish like sheep without a shepherd. That is the reason He sent down from heaven a mighty Shepherd to guide us in the way of peace and to save us from our most vicious enemies: Satan, sin, death and hell. **Do you know the Good Shepherd**, whom God sent to the children of Adam? If you do not, we invite you to listen carefully to today's lesson.

We are reading in the Gospel of John, chapter ten. One day, Jesus said to the crowd gathered around Him:

> (John 10) [1]*I tell you the truth, the man who does not enter the sheep pen by the gate, but climbs in by some other way, is a* ***thief*** *and a* ***robber***. [2]*The man who enters by the gate is the shepherd of his sheep….* [6]*Jesus used* ***this figure of speech***, *but they did not understand what he was telling them.* [7]*Therefore Jesus said again, "I tell you the truth, I am the gate for the sheep…* [9]***I am the gate***; *whoever*

*enters through me will be saved. He will come in and go out, and find pasture. [10]The thief comes only to steal and kill and destroy; I have come that they may have life, and have it to the full. [11]***I am the good shepherd***. The good shepherd lays down his life for the sheep. [12]The hired hand is not the shepherd who owns the sheep. So when he sees the wolf coming, he abandons the sheep and runs away. Then the wolf attacks the flock and scatters it. [13]The man runs away because he is a hired hand and cares nothing for the sheep. [14]I am the good shepherd; I know my sheep and my sheep know me—[1]5just as [God] the Father knows me and I know the Father–and I lay down my life for the sheep… [17]The reason my Father loves me is that I lay down my life–only to take it up again. [18]No one takes it from me, but I lay it down of my own accord. I have authority to lay it down and authority to take it up again. This command I received from my Father."*

[19]At these words the Jews were again divided. [20]Many of them said, "He is demon-possessed and raving mad. Why listen to him?" [21]But others said, "These are not the sayings of a man possessed by a demon. Can a demon open the eyes of the blind?"

*[24]The Jews gathered round him, saying, "How long will you keep us in suspense? If you are the Christ, tell us plainly." [25]Jesus answered, "I did tell you, but you do not believe. The miracles I do in my Father's name speak for me, [26]but you do not believe because you are not my sheep. [27]My sheep listen to my voice; I know them, and they follow me. [28]I give them eternal life, and they shall never perish; no one can snatch them out of my hand. [29]My Father, who has given them to me, is greater than all; no one can snatch them out of my Father's hand. [30]***I and the Father are one***." [31]Again the Jews picked up stones to stone him, [32]but Jesus said to them, "I have shown you many great miracles from [God] the Father. For which of these do you stone me?"*

[33]"We are not stoning you for any of these," replied the Jews, "but for blasphemy, because you, a mere man, ***claim to be God****." [34]Jesus answered them, "Is it not written in your Law, 'I have said you are gods'? [35]If he called them 'gods', to whom the word of God came–and the Scripture cannot be broken—[36]what about the one whom the Father set apart as his very own and sent into the world? Why then do you accuse me of blasphemy because I said, 'I am God's Son'? [37]Do not believe me unless I do what my Father does. [38]But if I do it,* ***even though you do not believe me, believe the miracles, that you may know and understand that the Father is in me, and I in the Father****." [39]Again they tried to seize him, but he escaped their grasp.*

Did you hear what Jesus said to the Jews? Since our time does not allow us to explain all the words of Jesus in detail, we will center our thoughts upon **two of the names** by which Jesus referred to Himself. Did you hear them? Those two names are: **The Gate for the sheep** and **the Good Shepherd**.

First we heard that, after Jesus compared the children of Adam with **sheep**, He said to the crowd, "***I am the gate for the sheep****…whoever enters through me will be saved.*" Why did Jesus call Himself "***the Gate for the sheep***"? In those days, a shepherd would make an enclosure of thorny branches or rocks, constructed with a single doorway by which the flock could enter. When evening came and the sheep had entered, the shepherd himself would sleep in the doorway of the sheep pen to guard his sheep. Thus, before any wild animal could enter the pen and kill a sheep, it would have to come through the doorway where the shepherd lay. The shepherd would then chase the wild animal away before it could harm the sheep. In this way the shepherd himself was "*the gate for the sheep.*"

The Lord Jesus called Himself "***the Gate for the sheep***." This means that Jesus cares for all those who belong to Him. This also means that before you can become a part of God's "flock," **you must come through Jesus**. Whoever wants to be saved from the snares of Satan, from the penalty of sin, from the power of death and the punishment of eternal hell must pass through Jesus. He alone is the door that can admit sinners into eternal life. That is why God's Word says: "*Salvation is found in* ***no one else****, for there is* ***no other name*** *under heaven given to men by which we must be saved.*" (Acts 4:12) Jesus is the one and only door to Salvation.

Can you remember what we read some time ago concerning the prophet Noah and the flood? How many doors did God command Noah to make in the boat which would be a refuge to all who wanted to escape the judgment of the flood? **Only one door**. Anyone who wanted to escape the flood had to go through the one door of the boat. Whoever entered through the door was **saved**. Whoever did not enter through the door **perished**! Similarly, concerning the Day of Judgment, the Holy Scriptures confirm to us that God has opened only one door of salvation for the children of Adam. The Messiah Himself is the Door that can admit people into eternal life. That is why Jesus said, "***I am the gate; whoever enters through me will be saved****…but the man who does not enter the sheep pen by the gate, but climbs in by some other way, is a thief and a robber!*" (John 10:9,1)

The second name by which Jesus referred to Himself is much like the first one. Jesus is not *only* "*the Gate for the sheep,*" He is also "***the Good Shepherd***." Jesus is the **Good** Shepherd, because He is the One who loved us and gave His life for us. Oh, what a wonderful Shepherd He is! Concerning Him, the prophet David, wrote in the twenty-third Psalm {*Zabur*}, saying:

> *"The LORD is my shepherd, I shall not be in want. He makes me lie down in green pastures, he leads me beside quiet waters, he restores my soul. He guides me in paths of righteousness for his name's sake. Even though I walk through the valley of the shadow of death, I will fear no evil, for you are with me; your rod and your staff, they comfort me. You prepare a table before me in the presence of*

> *my enemies. You anoint my head with oil; my cup overflows. Surely goodness and love will follow me all the days of my life, and I will dwell in the house of the* LORD *forever!*" (Psa. 23)

What we need to realize is that the Messiah Himself is the Good Shepherd of whom David wrote. That is why Jesus could say, "*I am the good shepherd!*" and, "*I and [God] the Father are* ***one****!*" (John 10:11,30) However, when Jesus declared that He was **one with God**, the Jews accused Him of blasphemy and picked up stones to throw at Him. They could not accept the idea that Jesus was God in a human body. To this very day, most of the children of Adam stumble over these words of Jesus. Some mistakenly think that to say Jesus is one with God must mean that there are two Gods. But that is not the way it is, for the Scriptures of the Prophets clearly declare the unity of God, saying: "*The* LORD *our God is* ***One****!*" (Deut. 6:4) **But the fact that "*God is One*" did not prevent God from revealing Himself on earth as a man.**

Perhaps **an illustration** will help. Think about the sun which shines on the earth giving us light and heat. How many such suns do we have? Only one. Where is the sun? It is far out in space, yet it is also here on earth, penetrating our lives with its life-giving sunshine. The fiery sun and the warm sunshine are one. Similarly, God and Jesus are one. Jesus said, "*I and [God] the Father are* ***one****!*" The Lord Jesus came into our world to communicate the light of God's love and salvation to us. Listen to what the Holy Scriptures declare about God and Jesus:

> "*Our* ***God*** *is a consuming fire…who lives in unapproachable light!…No man has ever seen* ***God****, but* ***God*** *the only* ***Son****, who is at the Father's side, has made him known.…The* ***Son*** *is the radiance of God's glory and the exact representation of his being, sustaining all things by his powerful word. After he had provided purification for sins, he sat down at the right hand of the Majesty in heaven!…God was pleased to have all his fullness dwell in [Jesus Christ]!…* ***In Christ all the fullness of the Deity lives in bodily form****!*" (Heb. 12:29; 2 Tim 6:16; John 1:18; Heb. 1:3; Col. 1:19; 2:9)

Yes, that is what the Word of God declares: "***In Christ all the fullness of the Deity lives in bodily form****!*" (Col. 2:9) Thus, the Lord Jesus could say, "*I and [God] the Father are* ***one****!*" Christ Jesus is **the Good Shepherd** who came from heaven, became a man, lived on earth, and laid down His holy life in order to redeem us from the curse which our sin brought. He is also the One who rose from the dead and offers eternal life to all who believe in Him. That is why Jesus could say:

> "*I am the good shepherd…I lay down my life for the sheep…only to take it up again. No one takes it from me, but I lay it down of my own accord. I have*

> *authority to lay it down and authority to take it up again. This command I received from my Father."* (John 10:14-18)

Beyond all question, Jesus is *"the* **Good** *Shepherd,"* because **He is the One who loved us enough to give His life for us!**

Before we say goodbye today, let us listen once more to the wonderful words of the Lord Jesus, who said:

> (John 10) [9]***I am the gate****; whoever enters through me will be saved....* [10]*but the man who does not enter the sheep pen by the gate, but climbs in by some other way, is a thief and a robber.* [11]**I am the good shepherd.** *The good shepherd* **lays down his life** *for the sheep.* [12]*The hired hand is not the shepherd who owns the sheep. So when he sees the wolf coming, he abandons the sheep and runs away....* [14]*I am the good shepherd...* [27]***My sheep listen to my voice; I know them, and they follow me.*** [28]***I give them eternal life, and they shall never perish; no one can snatch them out of my hand!"***

Listening friends, **who are you following**? Are you following **the Good Shepherd**? Or are you following someone else?

We thank you for listening and invite you to join us for the next program to hear what Jesus taught about the compassion which fills the heart of God....

God bless you as you remember what Jesus the Messiah said about Himself:

> ***"I am the gate; whoever enters through me will be saved!...I am the good shepherd. The good shepherd lays down his life for the sheep!"*** (John 10:9,11)

LESSON 77

THE HEART OF GOD

LUKE 18,15

Peace be with you, listening friends. We greet you in the name of God, the Lord of peace, who wants everyone to understand and submit to the way of righteousness that He has established, and have true peace with Him forever. We are happy to be able to return today to present your program *The Way of Righteousness*.

Throughout our studies in the Writings of the Prophets, we have seen that God is **holy and righteous** and that He cannot tolerate sin. Yet we have also seen that He is also **merciful and compassionate**. That is wonderful news for us, because we desperately need His mercy, since we have all greatly offended God. Our trespasses and our sins are abhorrent to God, and they will condemn us forever unless He has mercy on us! Today we plan to read **two parables** which the Lord Jesus spoke to the crowds. Through these two interesting stories we will learn about **the great mercy that fills God's heart, and how sinners can receive that mercy**.

In **the first parable**, we will see **two men**: one who did not receive God's mercy and one who received it. One belonged to the sect of the Pharisees and was very zealous in prayer, in fasting, and in giving alms. He was exceedingly religious in the eyes of man. The other man was a tax collector, and thus a great sinner in the eyes of man, because most tax collectors were dishonest.

Listen to the story of the Pharisee and the tax collector. We are reading in the Gospel of Luke, chapter eighteen. The Scripture says:

> (Luke 18) 9*To some who were confident of their own righteousness and looked down on everybody else, Jesus told this parable:* 10*"**Two men** went up to the temple to pray, one a Pharisee and the other a tax collector.* 11***The Pharisee** stood up and prayed **about himself**: 'God, I thank you that I am not like other men–robbers, evildoers, adulterers–or even like this tax collector.* 12*I fast twice a week and give a tenth of all I get.'* 13*But **the tax collector** stood at a distance. He would not even look up to heaven, but beat his breast and said, '**God, have***

> ***mercy on me, a sinner**!' [14]I tell you that this man, rather than the other, went home justified before God. **For everyone who exalts himself will be humbled, and he who humbles himself will be exalted**." (Luke 18)*

What did Jesus want to teach through this short parable? In brief, Jesus taught that God shows mercy to those who **acknowledge** their unrighteousness before Him and that He condemns those who **imagine** themselves to be righteous before Him. That is what the Scripture declares when it says: ***"God opposes the proud but gives grace to the humble."*** (1 Pet. 5:5) What man esteems, God despises. Can God accept those who praise themselves, thinking, "I am a righteous person! **I** say my prayers! **I** fast! **I** give alms! **I** go to the mosque! **I** go to church! **I** do this and that!"? Are all these "I"s pleasing to God? Not at all! The heart of God cannot be happy with works that originate from pride.

God loathes the proud heart. Do you remember Cain, Adam's firstborn son, who tried to approach God by his own efforts? Did God accept his sacrifice? No, God did not accept it. Friends, God has not changed. To this day, the heart of God cannot be happy with the **self-efforts of man,** because our efforts are not perfect before Him. What God wants is for us to **recognize our sinful condition**, like the tax collector who beat his breast saying, ***"God, have mercy on me, a sinner!"*** It is such a broken heart that causes God to rejoice. But He abhors those who compare themselves with their fellowman, like the Pharisee, who said to himself, "*God, I thank you that I am not like other men–robbers, evildoers, adulterers–or even like this tax collector.*"

What the Pharisee failed to realize was that on the Day of Judgment, God will not compare us with our sinful fellowman. Instead, God will compare us with His own holy and perfect law which declares: "*Whoever keeps the whole law and yet stumbles at just one point is guilty of breaking all of it!*" (James 2:10) The God who said, "*You shall not commit adultery*" also said, "*You shall not lie.*" If you have not committed adultery, but you have told a lie, then you have broken God's law. You cannot enter Paradise, the presence of God, because the Scripture says: "*Nothing impure will ever enter it, nor will anyone who does what is shameful or deceitful.*" (Rev. 21:27) That is why the children of Adam need **the mercy of God**. Dear friend, have you, like the tax collector in the parable, received **God's mercy**? Or are you, like the Pharisee, still trying to become righteous by **your own efforts**?

Now let us read **the second parable** which shows that the heart of God is full of love and mercy, like a father who loves his children. In the Gospel of Luke, chapter fifteen, we read:

> (Luke 15) [1]*Now the tax collectors and "sinners" were all gathering round to hear [Jesus]. [2]But the Pharisees and the teachers of the law muttered, "This man welcomes sinners, and eats with them." [3]Then Jesus told them this parable…*

11“***There was a man who had two sons.*** 12*The* ***younger one*** *said to his father, ‘Father, give me my share of the estate.’ So he divided his property between them.* 13*Not long after that, the younger son got together all he had, set off for a distant country and there squandered his wealth in wild living.* 14*After he had spent everything, there was a severe famine in that whole country, and he began to be in need.* 15*So he went and hired himself out to a citizen of that country, who sent him to his fields to feed pigs.* 16*He longed to fill his stomach with the pods that the pigs were eating, but no one gave him anything.*

17*When he came to his senses, he said, ‘How many of my father’s hired men have food to spare, and here I am starving to death!* 18*I will set out and go back to my father and say to him: Father, I have sinned against heaven and against you.* 19*I am no longer worthy to be called your son; make me like one of your hired men.’* 20*So he got up and went to his father. But while he was still a long way off,* **his father** *saw him and was filled with compassion for him; he ran to his son, threw his arms around him and kissed him.* 21*The son said to him, ‘Father, I have sinned against heaven and against you. I am no longer worthy to be called your son.’* 22*But the father said to his servants, ‘Quick! Bring the best robe and put it on him. Put a ring on his finger and sandals on his feet.* 23*Bring the fattened calf and kill it. Let’s have a feast and celebrate.* 24*For this son of mine was dead and is alive again; he was lost and is found.’ So they began to celebrate.*

25*Meanwhile,* **the older son** *was in the field. When he came near the house, he heard music and dancing.* 26*So he called one of the servants and asked him what was going on.* 27*‘Your brother has come,’ he replied, ‘and your father has killed the fattened calf because he has him back safe and sound.’* 28*The older brother became angry and refused to go in. So his father went out and pleaded with him.* 29*But he answered his father, ‘Look! All these years I’ve been slaving for you and never disobeyed your orders. Yet you never gave me even a young goat so I could celebrate with my friends.* 30*But when this son of yours who has squandered your property with prostitutes comes home, you kill the fattened calf for him!’* 31*‘My son,’ the father said, ‘you are always with me, and everything I have is yours.* 32*But we had to celebrate and be glad, because this brother of yours was dead and is alive again; he was lost and is found.’”*

What does God want to teach us through this fascinating parable? In it, we saw three men: the father, the younger son and the older son.

• **The father** in the story represents **God**.

• **The younger son** illustrates **sinners who repent** of their sins and turn to God for mercy.

• **The elder son** illustrates **religious people who deceive themselves** by thinking they are righteous before God.

First, let us think a little about **the younger son** who followed his sinful nature in wild living in a faraway land. What became of him? We saw how he eventually recognized that he had offended God and man. He was grieved because of his sins and repented, saying, "*I will set out and go back to my father and say to him: Father,* ***I have sinned*** *against heaven and against you. I am no longer worthy to be called your son; make me like one of your hired men.*" Thus, we saw how the younger son turned his back on the pig pen and headed for his father's house.

What about **the father**–what did he do? Was he angry with his son who had wasted his wealth? Did he merely take him back as a slave? No! Jesus said,

> "*But while [the son] was still a long way off, his father saw him and was filled with compassion for him; he ran to his son,* ***threw his arms around him and kissed him****. The father said to his servants, 'Quick! Bring the best robe and put it on him. Put a ring on his finger and sandals on his feet. Bring the fattened calf and kill it. Let's have a feast and celebrate. For this son of mine was dead and is alive again; he was lost and is found!'*"

What are we to learn from this? We can learn that God is exactly like that father who was full of mercy! **God loves sinners**, and wants to show them mercy, **but He waits** for each sinner to repent of his sins and follow the way of righteousness that He has established.

Concerning **the elder son**, we saw an amazing thing. The elder son did not have the heart of compassion of his father. Instead, he became angry and refused to enter the house, saying to his father, "*Look!* ***All these years I've been slaving for you*** *and never disobeyed your orders. Yet you never gave me even a young goat so I could celebrate with my friends!*" Did you hear what the elder son said? He said, "Look! All these years I've been working for you, like a slave!" However, what the elder son did not understand was that the father did not want a son who worked for him like **a slave**. What he wanted was a son who would **love him from the heart** and take pleasure in doing his will.

To this day, many children of Adam are like that elder son. They consider themselves to be nothing more than "**slaves of God**." But God does not want us to be like **mere slaves**. He wants us to be like **sons and daughters** to Him. That is what the Holy Scripture declares concerning those who receive Jesus as their Lord and Savior, saying: "*For you did not receive a spirit that makes you a* ***slave*** *again to fear, but you received the Spirit of* ***sonship****. And by him we cry, 'Abba* (Papa), *Father!'*" (Rom. 8:15)

Dear friend, do you view yourself as a **slave of God** or **a son of God**? How do you see yourself in the parable we just read? Are you like the younger son who recognized his sin and received his father's mercy? Or are you like the elder son who worked for his father like a slave? God doesn't want you to be like **a slave who fears his master**. What God wants is for you to be like **a son who loves his**

father, happy to do his will. God loves you and longs to show you mercy, but He is waiting for you to repent and turn to Him. That is what the prophet Isaiah wrote, saying: ***"Yet the LORD longs to be gracious to you; he rises to show you compassion. For the LORD is a God of justice. Blessed are all who wait for him!"*** (Isa. 30:18)

God, the Compassionate, the Merciful, waits for you to come to Him, just as the father in the parable waited for his younger son to come back home. God wants you to repent with a broken and humble heart. If you come like this to God and seek Him with your whole heart, then you can be certain that you will meet the God who has a father's heart, full of compassion and mercy. But the one who is proud and scorns God's great mercy can hope for nothing except God's judgment which will be without mercy!

Thank you for listening. In our next program, God willing, we will continue in the Gospel to see how Jesus restored to life a dead man who had been in the tomb for four days!...

May God give you insight into what we have studied today. And remember:

"God opposes the proud but gives grace to the humble." (1 Pet. 5:5)

Lesson 78

The Resurrection and the Life

John 11,12

Peace be with you, listening friends. We greet you in the name of God, the Lord of peace, who wants everyone to understand and submit to the way of righteousness that He has established, and have true peace with Him forever. We are happy to be able to return today to present your program *The Way of Righteousness*.

At this point in our study in the holy Gospel {*Injil*}, we have seen that the Messiah, Jesus, has **many names**. These names help us to know who He is. We have already heard that Jesus was called: *the Word which was with God in the beginning, the Son of the Most High, the Son of Man, the Lamb of God, the Savior, the Bread that gives life, the Light of the World, the Lord of Glory, the Gate of the Sheep pen*, and *the Good Shepherd*. Today we will see two additional names of Jesus: they are: "***the Resurrection***" and "***the Life***."

We have seen how Jesus traveled throughout the land of the Jews, teaching, doing good, healing the sick, the lame, the blind and the demon-possessed. A great crowd followed Him. However, the religious "experts," known as the Pharisees, were extremely jealous of Jesus. They could not deny **the wisdom** with which He spoke, nor could they deny **the miracles** which He did.

Today we plan to continue in the Gospel. We will see how **Jesus performed another supernatural wonder that revealed the glory of God in Him, so that people might believe in Him**. Reading in the Gospel of John, chapter eleven, the Scripture says:

> (John 11) [1]*Now a man named* ***Lazarus*** *was sick. He was from Bethany, the*
> *village of* **Mary** *and her sister* **Martha**. [2]*This Mary, whose brother Lazarus now*
> *lay sick, was the same one who poured perfume on the Lord and wiped his feet*
> *with her hair.* [3]*So the sisters sent word to* ***Jesus****, "Lord, the one you love is sick."*
> [4]*When he heard this, Jesus said, "This sickness will not end in death. No, it is for*
> *God's glory so that God's Son may be glorified through it."* [5]*Jesus loved Martha*
> *and her sister and Lazarus.* [6]*Yet when he heard that Lazarus was sick, he stayed*

where he was two more days. (Jesus knew that Lazarus would die. But Jesus planned to use the death of Lazarus to show the power of God which dwelt in Him, so that people would know that He came from heaven.)

[7]*Then [after staying for two days where they were, Jesus] said to his disciples, "Let us go back to Judea."* [8]*"But Rabbi," they said, "a short while ago the Jews tried to stone you, and yet you are going back there?"* [9]*Jesus answered, "Are there not twelve hours of daylight?...* [11]*..."Our friend Lazarus has fallen asleep; but I am going there to wake him up."* [12]*His disciples replied, "Lord, if he sleeps, he will get better."* [13]*Jesus had been speaking of his death, but his disciples thought he meant natural sleep.* [14]*So then he told them plainly, "***Lazarus is dead**, [15]*and for your sake I am glad I was not there, so that you may believe. But let us go to him."*

[17]*On his arrival, Jesus found that Lazarus had already been in the tomb for* **four days**. [18]*Bethany was less than two miles from Jerusalem,* [19]*and many Jews had come to Martha and Mary to comfort them in the loss of their brother.* [20]*When Martha heard that Jesus was coming, she went out to meet him, but Mary stayed at home.* [21]*"Lord," Martha said to Jesus, "if you had been here, my brother would not have died.* [22]*But I know that even now God will give you whatever you ask."* [23]*Jesus said to her, "***Your brother will rise again**." [24]*Martha answered, "I know he will rise again in the resurrection at the last day."*

[25]*Jesus said to her, "***I am the resurrection and the life. He who believes in me will live, even though he dies;** [26]***and whoever lives and believes in me will never die. Do you believe this?***" [27]*"Yes, Lord," she told him, "I believe that you are the Christ, the Son of God, who was to come into the world."* [28]*And after she had said this, she went back and called her sister Mary aside. "The Teacher is here," she said, "and is asking for you."* [29]*When Mary heard this, she got up quickly and went to him...* [32]*When Mary reached the place where Jesus was and saw him, she fell at his feet and said, "Lord, if you had been here, my brother would not have died."*

[33]*When Jesus saw her weeping, and the Jews who had come along with her also weeping, he was deeply moved in spirit and troubled.* [34]*"Where have you laid him?" he asked. "Come and see, Lord," they replied.* [35]*Jesus wept.* [36]*Then the Jews said, "See how he loved him!"* [37]*But some of them said, "Could not he who opened the eyes of the blind man have kept this man from dying?"* [38]*Jesus, once more deeply moved, came to the tomb. It was a cave with a stone laid across the entrance.* [39]*"***Take away the stone**," *he said. "But, Lord," said Martha, the sister of the dead man, "by this time there is a bad odor, for he has been there four days."* [40]*Then Jesus said, "***Did I not tell you that if you believed, you would see the glory of God?**" [41]*So they took away the stone. Then Jesus looked up and said, "Father, I thank you that you have heard me.* [42]*I knew that you always hear me, but I said this for the benefit of the people standing here, that they may*

> *believe that you sent me."* [43]*When he had said this, Jesus called in a loud voice, "***Lazarus, come out!***"* [44]*The dead man came out, his hands and feet wrapped with strips of linen, and a cloth around his face. Jesus said to them, "***Take off the grave clothes and let him go***."*

Before finishing this amazing story, it would be good for us to think a little about this mighty miracle Jesus did. From the creation of the world to today, nobody ever heard of anyone who could give life to a corpse that had already been four days in the tomb; a corpse that had begun to decay and stink. However, that is exactly what Jesus did when He raised Lazarus from the dead.

The power of death was not a problem for the Lord Jesus, because He is the Word of God; the very Life of God, who came from heaven. As God has life in Himself, so the Messiah has life in Himself. And as God can resurrect dead bodies and give them life, so also the Messiah can give life to whomever He wants, because He Himself is **the Source of Life**. That is why, when Jesus called Lazarus to come forth, the corpse came back to life, arose and came out of the tomb. That is also why Jesus could say to Lazarus' sister, ***"I am the resurrection and the life. He who believes in me will live, even though he die!"***

Now let us finish the story and find out what the Jews did after they saw Jesus raise Lazarus from the grave. The Scripture says:

> (John 11) [45]*Therefore many of the Jews who had come to visit Mary, and had*
> *seen what Jesus did,* ***put their faith in him****.* [46]***But some of them*** *went to the*
> *Pharisees and told them what Jesus had done.* [47]*Then the chief priests and the*
> *Pharisees called a meeting of the Sanhedrin. "What are we accomplishing?" they asked. "Here is this man performing many miraculous signs.* [48]*If we let him go on*
> *like this, everyone will believe in him, and then the Romans will come and take away both our place and our nation."*
>
> [49]*Then one of them, named* **Caiaphas***, who was high priest that year, spoke*
> *up,* ***"You know nothing at all!*** [50]***You do not realize that it is better for you***
> ***that one man die for the people than that the whole nation perish."*** [51]***He***
> ***did not say this on his own, but as high priest that year he prophesied***
> ***that Jesus would die for the Jewish nation,*** [52]***and not only for that nation***
> ***but also for the scattered children of God, to bring them together and***
> ***make them one****.* [53]*So from that day on they plotted to take his life.* [54]*Therefore*
> *Jesus no longer moved about publicly among the Jews. Instead he withdrew to a region near the desert, to a village called Ephraim, where he stayed with his disciples.*
>
> [55]*When it was almost time for the Jewish Passover, many went up from the*
> *country to Jerusalem for their ceremonial cleansing before the Passover.* [56]*They*
> *kept looking for Jesus, and as they stood in the temple area they asked one*

another, "What do you think? Isn't he coming to the Feast at all?" [57]*But the chief priests and Pharisees had given orders that if anyone found out where Jesus was, he should report it so that they might arrest him.*

(John 12) [1]*Six days before the Passover, Jesus arrived at Bethany, where Lazarus lived, whom Jesus had raised from the dead.* [2]*Here a dinner was given in Jesus' honor. Martha served, while Lazarus was among those reclining at the table with him.* [3]*Then Mary took about a pint of pure nard, an expensive perfume; she poured it on Jesus' feet and wiped his feet with her hair. And the house was filled with the fragrance of the perfume.* [4]*But one of his disciples, Judas Iscariot, who was later to betray him, objected,* [5]*"Why wasn't this perfume sold and the money given to the poor? It was worth a year's wages."* [6]*He did not say this because he cared about the poor but because he was a thief; as keeper of the money bag, he used to help himself to what was put into it.* [7]*"Leave her alone," Jesus replied. "[It was intended] that she should save this perfume for the day of my burial.* [8]*You will always have the poor among you, but you will not always have me."*

[9]*Meanwhile a large crowd of Jews found out that Jesus was there and came, not only because of him but also to see Lazarus, whom he had raised from the dead.* [10]***So the chief priests made plans to kill Lazarus as well,*** [11]***for on account of him many of the Jews were going over to Jesus and putting their faith in him.***

Our time is about up, but before we say goodbye, there is something we must consider. Did you see how the religious rulers reacted to the miraculous sign (proof) which Jesus showed them? None of them dared to deny the miracle Jesus did, because everyone could see for themselves the man who had been raised from the dead! But what did the High Priest and the other priests do? Did they repent of their sins and believe that Jesus was the Messiah who came from heaven? **No, they did not repent!** All the miraculous signs which Jesus performed did not cause the priests and their disciples to repent and accept Jesus as their Lord and Savior.

What did the High Priests do then? They hated Jesus even more and conspired together to devise a plan to kill Him! They also planned to kill Lazarus whom Jesus had just raised from the dead, because he was the reason that many Jews were turning away from the priests and following Jesus. How insincere and far from God were the hearts of those religious rulers! **They did not love God or the truth.** They ignored the obvious proofs (the many miracles) which Jesus had done before them. All they thought about was their own pleasure, their own position, their own advantage, and making money. Thus, they conspired together to kill Jesus, because they were afraid that if they allowed Him to continue, all the Jews would turn away from them and follow Jesus.

What do you think about those religious rulers? Who put the idea in their minds to kill Jesus? Satan was guiding them, because he hates God and His Messiah. Satan thought that if the Jewish leaders put Jesus to death, God's plan to save the children of Adam from his power would fail. What Satan did not realize was that **God planned to use the death of the Messiah to deliver the children of Adam from Satan's power!** Also, Satan and those who went along with him did not realize that the power of death could not hold the Lord Jesus. The earth could not decompose {Lit. eat} Him, because **Jesus is the Resurrection and the Life**. That is why Jesus could say to the sister of Lazarus, "***I am the resurrection and the life***. *He who believes in me will live, even though he dies…Do you believe this?*" (John 11:25,26)

This is where we must leave you today. We invite you to join us in the coming study as we continue in the Gospel and see how Jesus rode into Jerusalem on the colt of a donkey, thus fulfilling what God's prophets had written long beforehand concerning the Messiah....

May God Himself teach you as you ponder the blessed meaning of these words from Jesus the Messiah:

> ***"I am the resurrection and the life. He who believes in me will live, even though he dies...Do you believe this?"*** (John 11:25,26)

Lesson 79

Jesus Enters Jerusalem

Luke 18-20, etc.

Peace be with you, listening friends. We greet you in the name of God, the Lord of peace, who wants everyone to understand and submit to the way of righteousness that He has established, and have true peace with Him forever. We are happy to be able to return today to present your program *The Way of Righteousness*.

In our last lesson, we saw how **the Lord Jesus raised to life a corpse** that had been in the grave for four days. The power of death was not a problem for Jesus, because He Himself was (and is) the Resurrection and the Life. Today we plan to continue in the Gospel to see how Jesus entered Jerusalem where He was to be killed. **Jesus knew everything that was going to happen to Him**. He knew that the leaders of the Jewish religion would turn Him over to the Romans who would torture Him and nail Him to a cross. Still, that knowledge did not prevent Him from going to Jerusalem. Concerning this, the Gospel says: "*As the time approached for him to be taken up to heaven,* ***Jesus resolutely set out for Jerusalem****!*" (Luke 9:51) As He was walking, heading toward Jerusalem, Jesus said to His disciples, "*I have a baptism [of suffering] to undergo, and how distressed I am until it is completed!*" (Luke 12:50)

Why did Jesus resolutely set out for Jerusalem? He did this to give Himself up to those who wanted to kill Him! This is **amazing**! If you knew that, in a certain city, men wanted to torture and kill you, would you resolutely set out for that city? That is exactly what Jesus the Messiah did. Jesus knew that the reason He was born was to die as a sacrifice for the sins of the world. Jesus did not come into the world to seek His own pleasure, but **to fulfil what the prophets had written long before concerning Him:** that the Messiah would suffer and shed his blood outside Jerusalem on the mountain where Abraham offered the ram in place of his son. It was necessary that the symbolism of the sacrificial ram be fulfilled in Jesus. That was why Jesus went to Jerusalem, the city which, for Him, was like a den of hungry lions awaiting their prey.

Now let us continue our study in the book of the Gospel. The Scripture says:

"They were **on their way up to Jerusalem**, *with Jesus leading the way, and the disciples were astonished, while those who followed were afraid. Again* **he took the Twelve aside and told them what was going to happen to him**." (Mark 10:32) "*We are going up to Jerusalem, and* **everything that is written by the prophets about the Son of Man will be fulfilled**." (Luke 18:31) "*The Son of Man will be* **betrayed** *to the chief priests and teachers of the law. They will* **condemn him to death** *and will* **hand him over to the Gentiles** *who will* **mock him** *and* **spit on him**, **flog him** *and* **kill him**. **Three days later he will rise**." (Mark 10:33,34)

(Luke 18) [34]**The disciples did not understand any of this**. *Its meaning was hidden from them, and they did not know what he was talking about.* [35]*As Jesus approached Jericho, a blind man was sitting by the roadside begging.* [36]*When he heard the crowd going by, he asked what was happening.* [37]*They told him, "Jesus of Nazareth is passing by."* [38]*He called out, "Jesus, Son of David, have mercy on me!"* [39]*Those who led the way rebuked him and told him to be quiet, but he shouted all the more, "Son of David, have mercy on me!"* [40]*Jesus stopped and ordered the man to be brought to him. When he came near, Jesus asked him,* [41]*"What do you want me to do for you?" "Lord, I want to see," he replied.* [42]*Jesus said to him, "Receive your sight; your faith has healed you."* [43]*Immediately he received his sight and followed Jesus, praising God. When all the people saw it, they also praised God.*

(Matt. 21) [1]*As they approached Jerusalem and came to Bethphage on the Mount of Olives, Jesus sent two disciples,* [2]*saying to them, "Go to the village ahead of you, and at once you will find* **a donkey** *tied there, with her colt by her. Untie them and bring them to me.* [3]*If anyone says anything to you, tell him that the Lord needs them, and he will send them right away."* [4]**This took place to fulfil what was spoken through the prophet**: [5]*"Say to the Daughter of Zion, 'See, your king comes to you, gentle and riding on a donkey, on a colt, the foal of a donkey.'"*

[6]*The disciples went and did as Jesus had instructed them.* [7]*They brought the donkey and the colt, placed their cloaks on them, and Jesus sat on them.* [8]*A very large crowd spread their cloaks on the road, while others cut branches from the trees and spread them on the road.* [9]*The crowds that went ahead of him and those that followed shouted, "Hosanna to the Son of David!" "Blessed is he who comes in the name of the Lord!" "Hosanna in the highest!"*

(Luke 19) [39]*Some of the Pharisees in the crowd said to Jesus, "Teacher, rebuke your disciples!"* [40]*"I tell you," he replied, "if they keep quiet, the stones will cry out."* [41]*As he approached Jerusalem and saw the city,* **he wept over it** [42]*and said, "If you, even you, had only known on this day what would bring you peace–but now it is hidden from your eyes.* [44]*...because* **you did not recognize the time of God's coming to you**."

(Matt. 21) [10]*When Jesus entered Jerusalem, the whole city was stirred and asked,* "**Who is this**?" [11]*The crowds answered, "This is Jesus, the prophet from Nazareth in Galilee."* [12]*Jesus entered the temple area and drove out all who were buying and selling there.* **He overturned the tables** *of the moneychangers and the benches of those selling doves.* [13]*"It is written," he said to them,* **"'My house will be called a house of prayer,' but you are making it a 'den of robbers.'"**

[14]*The blind and the lame came to him at the temple, and he healed them.* [15]*But when the chief priests and the teachers of the law saw the wonderful things he did and the children shouting in the temple area,* "**Hosanna to the Son of David**," *they were indignant.* (They were angry because "*Hosanna*" means "*God save us*"— a word to be used for praising God alone.) [16]*"Do you hear what these children are saying?" [the priests] asked him. "Yes," replied Jesus, "have you never read, "'From the lips of children and infants you have ordained praise'?"*

"The chief priests and the teachers of the law heard this and began looking for a way to kill him, for they feared him, because the whole crowd was amazed at his teaching." (Mark 11:18)

(John 12) [23]*[Then Jesus spoke to his disciples, saying,]* "**The hour has come** *for the Son of Man to be glorified.* [24]*I tell you the truth, unless a grain of wheat falls to the ground and dies, it remains only a single seed. But if it dies, it produces many seeds…*

[27]*"Now my heart is troubled, and what shall I say? 'Father, save me from this hour'?* **No, it was for this very reason I came to this hour**. [28]*Father, glorify your name!" Then a voice came from heaven, "I have glorified it, and will glorify it again."* [29]*The crowd that was there and heard it said it had thundered; others said an angel had spoken to him.* [30]*Jesus said, "This voice was for your benefit, not mine.* [31]*Now is the time for judgment on this world; now the prince of this world will be driven out.* [32]*But I, when I am lifted up from the earth, will draw all men to myself."* [33]***He said this to show the kind of death he was going to die.***

Let us stop here briefly. We saw how Jesus entered Jerusalem, riding on a colt of a donkey, and how the crowd of Jews praised and applauded Him, wanting to make Him their king. However, the people did not understand why Jesus had entered Jerusalem. Even Jesus' disciples did not realize what was going to happen. They hoped that Jesus would save the Jewish people from the dominion of their enemy, the Romans. But that was not why Jesus came into the world. **Jesus did not come to destroy the empire of Rome, but to destroy the empire of Satan.** He did not come down to change this corrupt world, but **to change the hearts of people.** Indeed, one day, Jesus Christ will return to judge the people of the world and to restore the created world. However, when He came into the world the first time, **He came to die as a sacrifice**. He came to save the children of Adam from the penalty of their sin, as God had promised through His prophets long beforehand.

Continuing in the story, the Scripture says:

> (Luke 19) [47]*Every day [Jesus] was* ***teaching*** *at the temple. But the chief priests, the teachers of the law and the leaders among the people were* ***trying to kill him****.* [48]*Yet they could not find any way to do it, because all the people hung on his words.*
>
> (Luke 20) [1]*One day as [Jesus] was teaching the people in the temple courts and preaching the gospel, the chief priests and the teachers of the law, together with the elders, came up to him.* [2]*"Tell us by what authority you are doing these things," they said.* **"Who gave you this authority?"** [3]*He replied, "I will also ask you a question. Tell me,* [4]*John's baptism–was it from heaven, or from men?"* [5]*They discussed it among themselves and said, "If we say, 'From heaven', he will ask, 'Why didn't you believe him?'* [6]*But if we say, 'From men', all the people will stone us, because they are persuaded that John was a prophet."* [7]*So they answered, "We don't know where it was from."* [8]*Jesus said, "Neither will I tell you by what authority I am doing these things."*
>
> [9]*He went on to tell the people this parable:* **"A man planted a vineyard**, *rented it to some farmers and went away for a long time.* [10]*At harvest time he sent a servant to the tenants so they would give him some of the fruit of the vineyard. But the tenants beat him and sent him away empty-handed.* [11]*He sent another servant, but that one also they beat and treated shamefully and sent away empty-handed.* [12]*He sent still a third, and they wounded him and threw him out.* [13]*"Then the owner of the vineyard said, 'What shall I do? I will send my son, whom I love; perhaps they will respect him.'* [14]*"But when the tenants saw him, they talked the matter over. 'This is the heir,' they said. 'Let's kill him, and the inheritance will be ours.'* [15]*So they threw him out of the vineyard and killed him. "What then will the owner of the vineyard do to them?* [16]*He will come and kill those tenants and give the vineyard to others." When the people heard this, they said, "May this never be!"* [17]*Jesus looked directly at them and asked, "Then what is the meaning of that which is written: "'***The stone the builders rejected has become the capstone'?** [18]**Everyone who falls on that stone will be broken to pieces, but he on whom it falls will be crushed!"** [19]*The teachers of the law and the chief priests looked for a way to arrest him immediately, because* ***they knew he had spoken this parable against them****. But they were afraid of the people.*

Through the parable of the wicked farmers, Jesus warned those who were plotting to kill Him. Do you understand the meaning of this parable? Interpreting it is not difficult. In this parable, the Lord Jesus compares **God** to the owner of the field. The field of grapes (vineyard) is **the nation of Israel**. The evil farmers illustrate **the religious leaders of the Jews**. The servants that the owner of the field sent to collect the grapes, whom the farmers mistreated, are **the prophets**. The son of the owner of the field, whom the farmers killed, represents **the Messiah, Jesus.**

We can understand why the priests and the teachers of the law became very angry. They knew very well that Jesus was speaking about them! They understood that Jesus was comparing them to the wicked farmers who had harassed the servants of the owner of the field, and, in the end, killed his son. Thus Jesus denounced them as those who **ignored the words of the prophets**, and as those who would **kill the Messiah, the Son of the Most High**. Not only did Jesus tell them the parable, but He also quoted that which is written concerning Himself in the Psalms, saying: "***The stone the builders rejected has become the capstone***. *Everyone who falls on that stone will be broken to pieces, but he on whom it falls will be crushed!*" (Luke 20:17,18; Psa. 118:22) Thus Jesus warned the religious leaders that the **Savior** whom they refused and planned to kill, would, in the end, become their **Judge**!

Friends, our time is up. Thank you for listening. God willing, in the next lesson, we will continue with the amazing story of Jesus and the religious rulers....

God bless you as you think about what the Scripture declares concerning the Messiah:

> ***"He was in the world, and though the world was made through him, the world did not recognize him!"*** (John 1:10)

Lesson 80

Hard and True Words

Matthew 22-25

Peace be with you, listening friends. We greet you in the name of God, the Lord of peace, who wants everyone to understand and submit to the way of righteousness that He has established, and have true peace with Him forever. We are happy to be able to return today to present your program *The Way of Righteousness*.

In our last study, we saw how the Messiah, **Jesus, entered Jerusalem, fully aware** that Jerusalem was the city of the priests and the teachers of the law–the very ones who were conspiring together to murder Him! Jesus knew everything that would happen to Him, but that did not keep Him from going to Jerusalem. He knew that He had been born in order to die as a sacrifice for the sins of the world. Only a few days were left before the priests would arrest Him and have Him nailed to a cross.

Therefore fellow listeners, wherever you may be today, we ask you to pay careful attention as the Lord Jesus warns the religious rulers of the Jews, and admonishes them for their hypocrisy and their wickedness. The **words** which we will hear today are **hard**—and **true**. Sometimes it hurts to hear the truth. Today's lesson is full of such painful words. The (Wolof) proverb is true: "Truth is a hot pepper!"

As we saw in our last lesson, after Jesus entered Jerusalem, each day He went into the temple and taught the people. Every day the religious leaders and the teachers of the law sought an opportunity to catch Jesus in something He said so that they might have an excuse to put Him to death. However, they feared the people who were listening to Jesus attentively, not missing a word.

In the Gospel of Luke, chapter twenty, the Scripture says:

> (Luke 20) [20]*Keeping a close watch on him, [the chief priests] sent* ***spies****, who* ***pretended to be honest. They hoped to catch Jesus*** *in something he said so that they might hand him over to the power and authority of the governor.* [21]*So the spies questioned him: "Teacher, we know that you speak and teach what is right,*

and that you do not show partiality but teach the way of God in accordance with the truth. [22]*Is it right for us to pay taxes to Caesar or not?"* [23]*He saw through their duplicity [and their hypocrisy. "Why are you trying to trap me?" he asked. "Bring me a denarius and let me look at it." They brought the coin, and he asked them* (Mark 12:15,16)], [24]*"Whose portrait and inscription are on it?"* [25]*"Caesar's," they replied. He said to them,* **"Then give to Caesar what is Caesar's, and to God what is God's."** [26]*They were unable to trap him in what he had said there in public. And astonished by his answer, they became silent.*

(Matt. 22) [23]*That same day the* **Sadducees**, *who say there is no resurrection, came to him with a question.* [24]*"Teacher," they said, "Moses told us that if a man dies without having children, his brother must marry the widow and have children for him.* [25]*Now there were seven brothers among us. The first one married and died, and since he had no children, he left his wife to his brother.* [26]*The same thing happened to the second and third brother, right on down to the seventh.* [27]*Finally, the woman died.* [28]*Now then, at the resurrection, whose wife will she be of the seven, since all of them were married to her?"* [29]*Jesus replied,* **"You are in error because you do not know the Scriptures or the power of God.** (Luke 20) [34]*The people of this age marry and are given in marriage.* [35]*But those who are considered worthy of taking part in that age and in the resurrection from the dead will neither marry nor be given in marriage,* [36]*and they can no longer die; for they are like the angels. They are God's children, since they are children of the resurrection.* [37]*But in the account of the bush, even Moses showed that the dead rise, for he calls the Lord 'the God of Abraham, and the God of Isaac, and the God of Jacob'.* [38]*He is not the God of the dead, but of the living, for to him all are alive."*

(Matt. 22) [33]*When the crowds heard this, they were astonished at his teaching.* [34]*Hearing that Jesus had silenced the Sadducees, the* **Pharisees** *got together.* [35]*One of them, an expert in the law, tested him with this question:* [36]*"Teacher, which is the greatest commandment in the Law?"* [37]*Jesus replied: "'***Love the Lord your God with all your heart and with all your soul and with all your mind.***'* [38]*This is the first and greatest commandment.* [39]*And the second is like it: '***Love your neighbor as yourself.***'* [40]*All the Law and the Prophets hang on these two commandments."*

[41]*While the Pharisees were gathered together, Jesus asked them,* [42]**"What do you think about the Christ? Whose son is he?"** *"The son of David," they replied.* [43]*He said to them, "How is it then that David, speaking by the Spirit, calls him 'Lord'? For he says,* [44]*"'The Lord said to my Lord: "Sit at my right hand until I put your enemies under your feet."'* [45]*If then David calls him 'Lord', how can he be his son?"* [46]*No one could say a word in reply, and* **from that day on no one dared to ask him any more questions.**

(Matt. 23) [1]*Then Jesus said to the crowds and to his disciples:* [2]*"The teachers of the law and the Pharisees sit in Moses' seat.* [3]*...But do not do what they do, for* **they do not practice what they preach**. [4]*They tie up heavy loads and put them on men's shoulders, but they themselves are not willing to lift a finger to move them.* [5]*"Everything they do is done for men to see: They make their phylacteries wide and the tassels on their garments long;* [6]*they love the place of honor at banquets and the most important seats in the synagogues;* [7]*they love to be greeted in the marketplaces and to have men call them 'Rabbi'.* [8]*But you are not to be called 'Rabbi', for you have only one Master and you are all brothers.* [9]*And do not call anyone on earth 'father', for you have one Father, and he is in heaven.* [10]*Nor are you to be called 'teacher', for you have one Teacher, the Christ.* [11]*The greatest among you will be your servant.* [12]**For whoever exalts himself will be humbled, and whoever humbles himself will be exalted.**

[13]"**Woe to you**, *teachers of the law and Pharisees, you hypocrites! You shut the kingdom of heaven in men's faces. You yourselves do not enter, nor will you let those enter who are trying to.*

[15]"**Woe to you**, *teachers of the law and Pharisees, you hypocrites! You travel over land and sea to win a single convert, and when he becomes one, you make him twice as much a son of hell as you are.*

[23]"**Woe to you**, *teachers of the law and Pharisees, you hypocrites! You give a tenth of your spices–mint, dill and cummin. But you have neglected the more important matters of the law–justice, mercy and faithfulness. You should have practiced the latter, without neglecting the former.* [24]*You blind guides! You strain out a gnat but swallow a camel.*

[25]"**Woe to you**, *teachers of the law and Pharisees, you hypocrites! You clean the outside of the cup and dish, but inside they are full of greed and self-indulgence.* [26]*Blind Pharisee! First clean the inside of the cup and dish, and then the outside also will be clean.*

[27]"**Woe to you**, *teachers of the law and Pharisees, you hypocrites! You are like whitewashed tombs, which look beautiful on the outside but on the inside are full of dead men's bones and everything unclean.* [28]*In the same way, on the outside you appear to people as righteous but on the inside you are full of hypocrisy and wickedness.*

[29]"**Woe to you**, *teachers of the law and Pharisees, you hypocrites! You build tombs for the prophets and decorate the graves of the righteous.* [30]*And you say, 'If we had lived in the days of our forefathers, we would not have taken part with them in shedding the blood of the prophets.'* [31]*So you testify against yourselves that you are the descendants of those who murdered the prophets.* [32]*Fill up, then, the measure of the sin of your forefathers!* [33]*"You snakes! You brood of vipers! How will you escape being condemned to hell?...* [37]*"O Jerusalem, Jerusalem,*

you who kill the prophets and stone those sent to you, how often I have longed to gather your children together, as a hen gathers her chicks under her wings, ***but you were not willing****!*

(Matt. 24) [1]*Jesus left the temple and was walking away when his disciples came up to him to call his attention to its buildings.* [2]*"Do you see all these things?" he asked. "I tell you the truth,* ***not one stone here will be left on another; every one will be thrown down****."* [3]*As Jesus was sitting on the Mount of Olives, the disciples came to him privately. "Tell us," they said, "when will this happen, and what will be the sign of your coming and of the end of the age?"*

[4]*Jesus answered: "****Watch out that no one deceives you****.* [5]*For many will come in my name, claiming, 'I am the Christ,' and will deceive many.* [6]*You will hear of wars and rumors of wars, but see to it that you are not alarmed. Such things must happen, but the end is still to come.* [7]*Nation will rise against nation, and kingdom against kingdom. There will be famines and earthquakes in various places.* [8]*All these are the beginning of birth-pains.* [9]*Then you will be handed over to be persecuted and put to death, and you will be hated by all nations because of me.* [10]*At that time many will turn away from the faith and will betray and hate each other,* [11]*and* ***many false prophets will appear and deceive many people****....* [23]*At that time if anyone says to you, 'Look, here is the Christ!' or, 'There he is!' do not believe it.* [24]*For false Christs and false prophets will appear and perform great signs and miracles to deceive even the elect–if that were possible.* [25]***See, I have told you ahead of time.*** [26]*So if anyone tells you, 'There he is, out in the desert,' do not go out; or, 'Here he is, in the inner rooms,' do not believe it.* [27]*For as lightning that comes from the east is visible even in the west, so will be the coming of the Son of Man."*

[29]*"Immediately after the distress of those days 'the sun will be darkened, and the moon will not give its light; the stars will fall from the sky, and the heavenly bodies will be shaken.'* [30]*At that time the sign of the Son of Man will appear in the sky, and all the nations of the earth will mourn.* ***They will see the Son of Man coming on the clouds of the sky, with power and great glory****.* [31]*And he will send his angels with a loud trumpet call, and they will gather his elect from the four winds, from one end of the heavens to the other."*

(Matt. 25) [31]*"When the Son of Man comes in his glory, and all the angels with him, he will sit on his throne in heavenly glory.* [32]*All the nations will be gathered before him, and he will separate the people one from another as a shepherd separates the sheep from the goats.* [33]*He will put the sheep on his right and the goats on his left.* [34]*"Then the King will say to those on his right, 'Come, you who are blessed by my Father; take your inheritance, the kingdom prepared for you since the creation of the world....* [41]*"Then he will say to those on his left, 'Depart from me, you who are cursed, into the eternal fire prepared for the devil*

> *and his angels.'* [46]***Then they will go away to eternal punishment, but the righteous to eternal life****!"*

Fellow listeners, we must stop here today. We heard the Lord Jesus **admonish** the religious rulers for their hypocrisy and hardness of heart. We also heard Him **warn** His disciples concerning those who would come after Him, pretending to be prophets, but deceiving many people. Finally, we heard the Lord Jesus **announce** that He will one day return to earth, coming out of heaven with His mighty angels, to judge those who refuse to obey God's Good News about the Messiah, the Savior of sinners.

Yes, we have heard some **hard words** today, but they are also **good words** because they are **true words**. And they are **wonderful words** for all those who believe them, because the Lord Jesus said, *"You will know the truth, and* ***the truth will set you free****!"* (John 8:32)

Friends, thank you for listening. We invite you to join us next time to learn about one of Jesus' disciples who went to the High Priest in order to betray Jesus into the hands of those who wanted to kill Him....

God bless you as you consider what the Lord Jesus declared, saying,

> ***"You are in error because you do not know the Scriptures or the power of God!" But "the truth will set you free!"*** (Matt. 22:29; John 8:32)

LESSON 81

THE LAST SUPPER

MATTHEW 26

Peace be with you, listening friends. We greet you in the name of God, the Lord of peace, who wants everyone to understand and submit to the way of righteousness that He has established, and have true peace with Him forever. We are happy to be able to return today to present your program *The Way of Righteousness*.

As most of you know, in our journey through the Holy Scriptures, we are presently studying in the Gospel {*Injil*}, the holy book which tells the Good News about Jesus the Messiah. Jesus is the holy Redeemer who came into the world to deliver the children of Adam from the dominion of Satan. **The Redeemer was very different from all other men; He is the Word which was with God in the beginning who appeared upon earth as a man.** The Man Jesus was unique in His **birth**, because He was born of a virgin by the power of the Spirit of God. Jesus was also unique in His **character**, because He was born with a holy nature; He never sinned. His **works** were also unique; no one ever did miracles as He did. The Lord Jesus had power over Satan and his demons, the wind and the sea, and sickness and death. His **teaching** was also unparalleled; even His enemies said, "*No one has ever spoken like that man!*" (John 7:46)

Yes, Jesus Christ was unique in His birth, His character, His works and His words. But that did not cause everyone to recognize that He was the Savior who came from heaven. Most of the children of Adam did not understand who Jesus really was. They considered Jesus to be a prophet, but they did not realize that God Himself had come to visit them! As for the Jewish religious rulers, they not only failed to understand who Jesus was, but they even conspired together to have Him put to death! In our last lesson, we heard how Jesus rebuked the religious leaders and the teachers of the Law because of their hypocrisy and wickedness. But Jesus' words to them did not cause them to repent. In fact, the religious rulers were obsessed with one thought: **Jesus must be put to death!**

The Lord Jesus knew that He was going to die in Jerusalem, and that those religious rulers would be the ones who would put Him to death. Thus, we saw that Jesus informed His disciples that the Priests and the teachers of the Law would condemn Him to die. They would turn Him over to the Romans, so that they might mock Him, spit on Him, beat Him, and nail Him to a cross. But after three days He would arise again! Thus did Jesus predict His death on a cross and His resurrection from the grave. And Jesus not only announced **how** He would die, and **where** He would die, but in the chapter before us today, we will see that Jesus even announced **when** He would die!

Now let us continue in the Gospel of Matthew, chapter twenty-six, and hear how Jesus prepared for His crucifixion {Lit. death on a pole/cross}. God's Word says: (Matt. 26) [1]*When Jesus had finished saying all these things, he said to his disciples,* [2]*"As you know, the Passover is two days away–and the Son of Man will be handed over to be crucified."*

Did you hear what Jesus said to His disciples? He informed them that the sons of Adam would nail Him to a cross **on the day of the Passover feast**. This is very important. In our study in the Torah, we learned about the day of the Passover. The Passover took place in the first month on the Jewish calendar, which is in March and April (Easter). Every year, at that festival, the Jews recall what happened in the time of Moses when the Israelites were the slaves of the cruel king Pharaoh. Back then, God, in His righteous judgment and great plan, had condemned to death every first born male in Egypt. But God also provided a way of deliverance for those who believed Him and obeyed Him. God commanded every Israelite family to sacrifice a lamb without blemish and to stain the blood on the doors of their houses. God had promised them, saying, "***When I see the blood I will pass over you***!" (Exod. 12:13) The people of Israel did as God had commanded and, consequently, God delivered their firstborn sons from death. God redeemed them by **the blood of a lamb**.

For one thousand five hundred years, the Jews sacrificed lambs every year at the festival of the Passover, in order to remember how God had saved them from the plague of death that fell on the land of Egypt. However, God did not want them merely to **look back** and to remember what had happened. By means of those sacrificial lambs, God wanted them to **look forward** and anticipate the day when the Messiah would shed His blood on the cross. The blood which the Messiah would shed would save sinners from the plague that is worse than any other plague: the eternal fire of hell! The Redeemer's death on the cross would be the final and perfect sacrifice which God's righteous law required. God in His wisdom planned that the Redeemer would pour out His blood on the day of the Passover Feast and thus **fulfil the symbolism of the sacrificial lamb**. Thus, Jesus the Redeemer would finish the plan which God had designed to save sinners from His righteous judgment.

Now let us return to the Gospel, beginning with the verse we already read.

> (Matt. 26) [1]*When Jesus had finished saying all these things, he said to his disciples,* [2]**"As you know, the Passover is two days away–and the Son of Man will be handed over to be crucified**." [3]*Then the chief priests and the elders of the people assembled in the palace of the high priest, whose name was Caiaphas,* [4]*and they plotted to arrest Jesus in some sly way and kill him.* [5]*"But* **not** *during the Feast," they said, "or there may be a riot among the people."*... [14]*Then one of the Twelve–the one called Judas Iscariot–went to the chief priests* [15]*and asked, "What are you willing to give me if I hand him over to you?" So they counted out for him thirty silver coins.* [16]*From then on Judas watched for an opportunity to hand him over.*
>
> (Mark 14) [12]*On the first day of the Feast of Unleavened Bread, when it was customary to sacrifice the Passover lamb, Jesus' disciples asked him, "Where do you want us to go and make preparations for you to eat the Passover?"* [13]*So he sent two of his disciples, telling them, "Go into the city, and a man carrying a jar of water will meet you. Follow him.* [14]*Say to the owner of the house he enters, 'The Teacher asks: Where is my guest room, where I may eat the Passover with my disciples?'* [15]*He will show you a large upper room, furnished and ready. Make preparations for us there."* [16]*The disciples left, went into the city and found things just as Jesus had told them. So they prepared the Passover.*
>
> (Luke 22) [14]**When the hour came**, *Jesus and his apostles reclined at the table.* [15]*And he said to them,* "**I have eagerly desired to eat this Passover with you before I suffer**. [16]*For I tell you, I will not eat it again until it finds fulfillment in the kingdom of God."* (Mark 14) [18]*While they were reclining at the table eating, he said, "I tell you the truth, one of you will betray me–one who is eating with me."* [19]*They were saddened, and one by one they said to him, "Surely not I?"* [20]*"It is one of the Twelve," he replied, "one who dips bread into the bowl with me.* [21]*The Son of Man will go just as it is written about him. But woe to that man who betrays the Son of Man! It would be better for him if he had not been born."* (Matt. 26) [25]*Then Judas, the one who would betray him, said, "Surely not I, Rabbi?" Jesus answered, "Yes, it is you."* (John 13) [30]*As soon as Judas had taken the bread, he went out. And it was night.* (Mark 14) [22]*While they were eating, Jesus took* **bread**, *gave thanks and broke it, and gave it to his disciples, saying, "Take it; [this is my body given for you; do this in remembrance of me.]"* [23]*Then he took the* **cup**, *gave thanks and offered it to them, and they all drank from it.* [24]*"This cup is my blood of the covenant, which is poured out for many..."*

That is what is written in the Gospel concerning the last supper which Jesus had with His disciples, before He poured out His blood as a sacrifice that erases sin. Jesus made known to His twelve disciples that one of them would betray Him. It was Judas Iscariot. In the eyes of man, Judas was a faithful disciple, but in his heart, Judas only cared about money and the things of the world. That is why he went to the High Priests and said to them, *"What are you willing to give me if I hand him over to you?"* Thus the Priests counted out for him thirty pieces of silver. This took place to fulfil what the prophet Zechariah had predicted hundreds of years earlier, when he wrote that the Messiah would be betrayed for thirty pieces of silver. (See Zech. 11:12,13)

However, the most important thing in what we have just read is what Jesus said when He shared the bread and the cup with His disciples. Did you hear what He told them? Let's read it again:

> (Mark 14) [22]*While they were eating, Jesus took **bread**, gave thanks and broke it, and gave it to his disciples, saying, "Take it; this is my **body** given for you; do this in remembrance of me."* [23]*Then he took the **cup**, gave thanks and offered it to them, and they all drank from it.* [24]*"This cup is my **blood** of the covenant, which is poured out for many..."*

Thus we see how Jesus placed **two symbols** before His disciples: the symbol of **the bread**, and the symbol of **the cup**. The bread, which Jesus broke and gave to His disciples, **illustrated** His body, which He was going to give as a sacrifice. The cup with the juice of grapes **illustrated** the blood which Jesus the Redeemer would pour out to pay the debt of sin for the children of Adam so that they might live in the presence of God forever.

Thus, through **the symbol of the bread** and **the symbol of the cup**, Jesus taught His disciples that the reason He came into the world was **to give His life**–His body and His blood–as a sacrifice for sinners. Just as everyone on the earth must **take in** food and water in order to stay alive, so also, everyone who wants to live forever in heaven with God must **believe** that Jesus Christ gave His body and blood to give us eternal life. The Lord Jesus Christ is the only One who can give eternal life and the blood He shed is God's only remedy to redeem you and me from the curse which sin brought.

Ah, fellow listeners, if you remember only one thing from today's study, let it be this: **Jesus Christ came into the world to bear your burden of sin**. That is **the message** of God's prophets. That is the **meaning** of the ram which Abraham sacrificed in place of his son. The way of forgiveness is the way of the Perfect Sacrifice. God can forgive you of your sins through the sacrifice of the holy Redeemer, who poured out His blood for you. For thousands of years God required animal sacrifices so that He could pass over (cover, overlook) the sins of the children of Adam. That is the Old Covenant, which God entrusted to His prophets. However, Jesus the Messiah is the One who brought the New Covenant. He is the One who came to **fulfil the symbolism of the animal sacrifice**. Jesus Christ Himself is the final Passover Lamb that was slain, so that whoever believes in Him might be saved from God's righteous judgment. That is why the Holy Scripture says: "*[Jesus] Christ, our Passover lamb, has been sacrificed.*" (1 Cor. 5:7) "***God made him who had no sin to be sin for us, so that in him we might become the righteousness of God***." (2 Cor. 5:21)

The blood of Jesus is of infinite value. Listen to what the Word of God declares concerning the cleansing power of Jesus blood. The Scriptures say:

> "***The blood of Jesus [Christ]...purifies us from all sin***!" (1 John 1:7) "*For you know that it was not with perishable things such as silver or gold that you were redeemed from the empty way of life handed down to you from your forefathers,* ***but with the precious blood of Christ, a Lamb without blemish or defect****. He was chosen before the creation of the world, but was revealed in these last times for your sake. Through him you believe in God, who raised Him from the dead and glorified him and so your faith and hope are* ***in God***!" (1 Pet. 1:18-21)

May you carefully consider what you have heard today, because God wants to give you insight into these great truths. In the coming study we plan to complete the story about the last supper and see how the religious rulers arrested Jesus so that they might kill Him....

God bless you as you think about the deep meaning and great blessing contained in this verse from the Word of God,

> ***"The blood of Jesus [Christ]...purifies us from all sin!"*** (1 John 1:7; John 1:29)

LESSON 82

JESUS IS ARRESTED

JOHN 14; MATTHEW 26

Peace be with you, listening friends. We greet you in the name of God, the Lord of peace, who wants everyone to understand and submit to the way of righteousness that He has established, and have true peace with Him forever. We are happy to be able to return today to present your program *The Way of Righteousness*.

In the last program, we learned about **the last supper** which Jesus ate with His disciples before He was to die. We heard the Lord Jesus inform His twelve disciples that one of them would betray Him and deliver Him over to His enemies. We also saw Jesus pass the bread and the cup to His disciples, telling them that the bread which He broke illustrated His body which He was about to give as a sacrifice, and the cup containing the juice of grapes illustrated the blood which He was going to shed. Thus, Jesus again showed His disciples that His reason for coming into the world was to pour out His blood as a sacrifice that removes sin and imparts eternal life.

Today we plan to continue in the Gospel and hear more **profound and wonderful words** spoken by the Lord Jesus on **the night in which the temple guards came to arrest Him**.

We are reading in the Gospel of John, chapter fourteen. Jesus, knowing that the time for Him to lay down His life had arrived, spoke to His disciples, saying,

> (John 14) [1]*"Do not let your hearts be troubled. Trust in* **God**; *trust also in* **me.** [2]***In my Father's house are many rooms; if it were not so, I would have told you. I am going there to prepare a place for you***. [3]*And if I go and prepare a place for you, I will come back and take you to be with me that you also may be where I am.* [4]*You know the way to the place where I am going."*
>
> [5]*Thomas said to him, "Lord, we don't know where you are going, so how can we know the way?"* [6]*Jesus answered,* ***"I am the way and the truth and the life. No one comes to [God] the Father except through me.*** [7]*If you really*

knew me, you would know my Father as well. From now on, you do know him and have seen him." [8]Philip said, "Lord, show us [God] the Father and that will be enough for us." [9]Jesus answered: "Don't you know me, Philip, even after I have been among you such a long time? ***Anyone who has seen me has seen the Father****. How can you say, 'Show us the Father'? [10]Don't you believe that I am in the Father, and that the Father is in me? The words I say to you are not just my own. Rather, it is the Father, living in me, who is doing his work. [11]Believe me when I say that I am in the Father and the Father is in me; or at least believe on the evidence of the miracles themselves.*

[15]"If you love me, you will obey what I command. [16]And I will ask the Father, and he will give you ***another Counselor*** *to be with you forever—[17]****the Spirit of truth****. The world cannot accept him, because it neither sees him nor knows him. But you know him, for he lives with you and will be in you. [18]I will not leave you as orphans; I will come to you. [19]Before long, the world will not see me anymore, but you will see me. Because I live, you also will live. [20]On that day you will realize that I am in my Father, and you are in me, and I am in you. [21]Whoever has my commands and obeys them, he is the one who loves me. He who loves me will be loved by my Father, and I too will love him and show myself to him... [23]If anyone loves me, he will obey my teaching. My Father will love him, and we will come to him and make our home with him. [24]He who does not love me will not obey my teaching. These words you hear are not my own; they belong to the Father who sent me. [25]"All this I have spoken while still with you. [26]But* ***the Counselor, the Holy Spirit****, whom the Father will send in my name, will teach you all things and will remind you of everything I have said to you. [27]Peace I leave with you; my peace I give you. I do not give to you as the world gives. Do not let your hearts be troubled and do not be afraid."*

Thus the Lord Jesus comforted the hearts of His disciples and prepared them for what was about to take place. Did you hear what Jesus announced to them concerning **the Counselor** {Lit. Helper}? It is vital that you understand this, because some people today distort the words of Jesus and try to make men believe that He was announcing the coming of another prophet. But what Jesus said about the Counselor could not refer to a prophet, nor to any man, because Jesus said that this Counselor was an invisible spirit who would come to live inside of Jesus' true disciples.

Who is this Counselor? The Lord Jesus tells us plainly who the Counselor is. Listen again to what Jesus said,

"I will ask the Father, and he will give you another Counselor ***to be with you forever–the Spirit of truth****....He... will be* ***in*** *you. I will not leave you as orphans;* ***I*** *will come to you....the Counselor,* ***the Holy Spirit****, whom the Fa-*

> *ther will send* **in my name**, *will teach you all things and will remind you of everything I have said to you.*" (John 14:16-18,26)

Again, we ask the question: Who is the Counselor that Jesus promised to His disciples? He is **the Holy Spirit**, who comes from God and was in Jesus. He is the Spirit of God and Jesus. He is the Holy Spirit, whom God would place in the hearts of all who believe in Jesus as their Savior and Lord. Jesus promised His disciples that after He died, rose again, and returned to heaven, that He would send His Holy Spirit into their hearts, so that He might regenerate them, cleanse them, strengthen them, and "*guide them into all truth.*" (John 16:13; see also Titus 3:4-7) A few lessons from now, God willing, we will see how this is exactly what happened in Jerusalem, when (ten days after Jesus ascended to heaven) the Holy Spirit came down and began to live in the hearts of all of Jesus' disciples, just as He promised.

In a later program we will learn more about this Counselor, the Holy Spirit, who can transform a self-centered sinner into a person who loves God and desires to please Him. But now let us return to the Gospel to see what happened on that extraordinary night after Jesus ate the last supper with His disciples.

The Scripture says:

> (Matt. 26) 30*When they had sung a hymn,* **they went out** *to the* Mount *of*
> *Olives.* 31*Then Jesus told them, "This very night you will all fall away on account*
> *of me, for [the prophets have] written: "'I will strike the shepherd, and the sheep*
> *of the flock will be scattered.'* 32*But after I have risen, I will go ahead of you into*
> *Galilee."* 33*Peter replied, "Even if all fall away on account of you, I never will."*
> 34*"I tell you the truth," Jesus answered, "this very night, before the cock crows,*
> *you will disown me three times."* 35*But Peter declared, "Even if I have to die with*
> *you, I will never disown you." And all the other disciples said the same.*
>
> 36*Then Jesus went with his disciples to a place called* **Gethsemane**, *and he*
> *said to them, "Sit here while I go over there and pray."* 37*He took Peter and the*
> *two sons of Zebedee along with him, and he began to be sorrowful and troubled.*
> 38*Then he said to them, "***My soul is overwhelmed with sorrow to the point**
> **of death***. Stay here and keep watch with me."* 39*Going a little farther, he fell with*
> *his face to the ground and prayed,* ***"My Father, if it is possible, may this cup***
> ***be taken from me. Yet not as I will, but as you will."***

Let us pause here briefly. What is the cup of suffering which Jesus dreaded to drink? Why was Jesus overwhelmed with sorrow to the point of death? Jesus was in unimaginable distress because He knew that the time for Him to bear the punishment of sin for the children of Adam was at hand! **The hour of which all God's prophets had prophesied had arrived!** Men would torture the Redeemer and nail Him to a cross, but the most horrible thing for Jesus was knowing that God His Father in heaven, who loved Him, and whom He loved, was going to heap on Him the punishment of the sins of the whole world! That is the reason Jesus prayed saying: "*My Father, if it is possible, may this cup* (of unfathomable suffering) *and be taken from me. Yet not as I will, but as you will!*"

Next, the Scripture says:

> (Matt. 26) [40]*Then [Jesus] returned to his disciples and found them sleeping. "Could you men not keep watch with me for one hour?" he asked Peter.* [41]*"Watch and pray so that you will not fall into temptation. The spirit is willing, but the body is weak."* [42]*He went away* ***a second time*** *and prayed, "My Father, if it is not possible for this cup to be taken away unless I drink it, may your will be done."* [43]*When he came back, he again found them sleeping, because their eyes were heavy.* [44]*So he left them and went away once more and prayed* ***the third time****, saying the same thing.* [45]*Then he returned to the disciples and said to them, "Are you still sleeping and resting? Look, the hour is near, and the Son of Man is betrayed into the hands of sinners.* [46]*Rise, let us go! Here comes my betrayer!"*
>
> [47]*While he was still speaking,* ***Judas [Iscariot]****, one of the Twelve, arrived. With him was a large crowd armed with swords and clubs, sent from the chief priests and the elders of the people.* [48]*Now the betrayer had arranged a signal with them: "The one I kiss is the man; arrest him."* [49]*Going at once to Jesus, Judas said, "Greetings, Rabbi!" and kissed him.* [50]*Jesus replied, "Friend, do what you came for." Then the men stepped forward, seized Jesus and* ***arrested*** *him.*
>
> [51]*With that, one of Jesus' companions reached for his sword, drew it out and struck the servant of the high priest, cutting off his ear. [But Jesus touched the man's ear and healed him, and said to the one who wanted to protect him,* (Luke 22:50)*]* [52]*"Put your sword back in its place, for all who draw the sword will die by the sword.* [53]***Do you think I cannot call on my Father, and he will at once put at my disposal more than twelve legions of angels?*** [54]***But how then would the Scriptures be fulfilled that say it must happen in this way?***"
>
> (Matt. 26) [55]*At that time Jesus said to the crowd, "Am I leading a rebellion, that you have come out with swords and clubs to capture me? Every day I sat in the temple courts teaching, and you did not arrest me.* [56]*But* ***this has taken place that the writings of the prophets might be fulfilled****." Then all the disciples deserted him and fled.* [57]*Those who had arrested Jesus took him to Caiaphas, the high priest, where the teachers of the law and the elders had assembled.*

Thus we have seen today how Jesus delivered Himself into the hands of those who wanted to kill Him. Perhaps someone would ask: "Why did Jesus allow Himself to fall into the hands of his enemies? He who calmed the storm, drove out demons, healed the blind, and raised the dead–**why didn't He save Himself from His enemies**?" Jesus Himself told us why. When one of His disciples attempted to protect Him, Jesus told him,

> *"Put your sword back in its place....Do you think I cannot call on my Father, and he will at once put at my disposal more than twelve legions of angels?* ***But how then would the Scriptures be fulfilled that say it must happen in this way?***" (Matt. 26:52-54)

Why did Jesus allow Himself to be arrested by His enemies? He did so **to fulfil the Scriptures of the Prophets** who prophesied repeatedly that the Messiah must suffer and shed His blood as a sacrifice which takes away sin. The Righteous Redeemer had to die for the unrighteous in order to bring us to God. Jesus the Messiah came into the world to fulfil the words of the prophets. He came to fulfil the meaning of sacrificial sheep. He came to save you and me from our sins. That is why He allowed Himself to be arrested by His enemies. **Jesus gave up His life for you and for me.** Praise be to God for sending us such a Savior!

Friends, this is where we must stop today. We hope you will join us again in the next study to see how the chief priests and the people of Jerusalem and their leaders collaborated in judging Jesus and condemning Him, thus fulfilling the words of the prophets. . . .

God bless you as you remember what Jesus told His disciples, when He said,

> ***"I lay down my life—only to take it up again. No one takes it from me, but I lay it down of my own accord!"*** (John 10:17,18)

LESSON 83

JESUS IS CONDEMNED

MATTHEW 26,27; JOHN 18,19

Peace be with you, listening friends. We greet you in the name of God, the Lord of peace, who wants everyone to understand and submit to the way of righteousness that He has established, and have true peace with Him forever. We are happy to be able to return today to present your program *The Way of Righteousness*.

In our journey through the Holy Scriptures, we have heard how God's prophets announced **the plan of salvation** which God designed to save sinners from eternal punishment. What is that plan of salvation? It is the death of the Messiah on the cross. God's prophets testified that the righteous Messiah must die, shedding His blood for the unrighteous, bearing for us the punishment for our sins, like an innocent sacrificial sheep. This was the only way that God could forgive us of our sins and judge us as righteous without compromising His righteousness. In our chronological study of the Holy Scriptures we are nearing the most important story of all, that is, the historical account of the death and resurrection of the Messiah. In the will of God, today, and in the coming lessons, we will see how the Messiah, Jesus, offered His life to bear the sins of the world.

In our last lesson, we saw how the chief priests bought a betrayer who led them to the place where Jesus and His disciples were. We saw how they **arrested Jesus**, bound Him, and led Him away. **Amazing**! Why did Jesus, who was full of the power of God, allow His enemies to capture Him? He allowed them to capture Him so that He might **fulfil the Scriptures of the Prophets** which foretold how the Messiah must suffer and die and rise from the dead on the third day, so that whoever believes in Him will receive forgiveness of sins. Just as the prophets had prophesied, the Messiah would be *"led like a lamb to the slaughter."* (Isa. 53:7)

Now let us continue in the Gospel to see what happened on **that dark night**, after the religious rulers arrested Jesus. The Scripture says:

> (Mark 14) [53]***They took Jesus to the high priest, and all the chief priests, elders and teachers of the law came together.*** [54]*Peter followed him at a*

distance, right into the courtyard of the high priest. There he sat with the guards and warmed himself at the fire.

[55]The chief priests and the whole Sanhedrin were looking for ***evidence against Jesus*** *so that they could put him to death, but* ***they did not find any****. [5]6Many testified falsely against him, but their statements did not agree. [57]Then some stood up and gave this false testimony against him: [58]"We heard him say, 'I will destroy this manmade temple and in three days will build another, not made by man.'" [59]Yet even then their testimony did not agree. [60]Then the high priest stood up before them and asked Jesus, "Are you not going to answer? What is this testimony that these men are bringing against you?" [61]But Jesus remained silent and gave no answer. Again the high priest asked him, "Are you the Christ, the Son of the Blessed One?" [62]****"I am****," said Jesus. "And you will see the Son of Man sitting at the right hand of the Mighty One and coming on the clouds of heaven." [63]The high priest tore his clothes. "Why do we need any more witnesses?" he asked. [64]"You have heard the blasphemy. What do you think?"* ***They all condemned him as worthy of death.*** *[65]Then some began to spit at him; they blindfolded him, struck him with their fists, and said, "Prophesy!" And the guards took him and beat him.*

[66]While ***Peter*** *was below in the courtyard, one of the servant girls of the high priest came by. [67]When she saw Peter warming himself, she looked closely at him. "You also were with that Nazarene, Jesus," she said. [68]But he denied it. "I don't know or understand what you're talking about," he said, and went out into the entrance. [69]When the servant girl saw him there, she said again to those standing around, "This fellow is one of them." [70]Again he denied it. After a little while, those standing near said to Peter, "Surely you are one of them, for you are a Galilean." [71]He began to call down curses on himself, and he swore to them, "I don't know this man you're talking about." [72]Immediately the cock crowed the second time. Then Peter remembered the word Jesus had spoken to him: "Before the cock crows twice you will disown me three times." And he broke down and wept.*

(Matt. 27) *[1]Early in the morning, all the chief priests and the elders of the people came to the decision to put Jesus to death. [2]They bound him, led him away and handed him over to Pilate, the governor. [3]When* ***Judas****, who had betrayed him, saw that Jesus was condemned, he was seized with remorse and returned the thirty silver coins to the chief priests and the elders. [4]"I have sinned," he said, "for I have betrayed innocent blood." "What is that to us?" they replied. "That's your responsibility." [5]So Judas threw the money into the temple and left. Then he went away and hanged himself.*

(John 18) *[28][Thus,]* ***the Jews led Jesus*** *from Caiaphas* (the High Priest) ***to the palace of the Roman governor****. By now it was early morning, and to avoid ceremonial uncleanness the Jews did not enter the palace; they wanted to* *be able to eat the Passover.* [29]*So* **Pilate** *came out to them and asked, "What charges are you bringing against this man?"* [30]*"If he were not a criminal," they replied, "we would not have handed him over to you."* [31]*Pilate said, "Take him yourselves and judge him by your own law." "But we have no right to execute anyone," the Jews objected.* [32]*This happened so that the words Jesus had spoken indicating the kind of death he was going to die would be fulfilled.*

[33]*Pilate then went back inside the palace, summoned Jesus and asked him, "Are you the king of the Jews?"* [34]*"Is that your own idea," Jesus asked, "or did others talk to you about me?"* [35]*"Am I a Jew?" Pilate replied. "It was your people and your chief priests who handed you over to me. What is it you have done?"* [36]*Jesus said, "My kingdom is not of this world. If it were, my servants would fight to prevent my arrest by the Jews. But now my kingdom is from another place."* [37]*"You are a king, then!" said Pilate. Jesus answered, "You are right in saying I am a king. In fact, for this reason I was born, and for this I came into the world, to testify to the truth. Everyone on the side of truth listens to me."* [38]*"What is truth?" Pilate asked. With this he went out again to the Jews and said,* ***"I find no basis for a charge against him."*** (Luke 23) [5]*But they insisted, "He stirs up the people all over Judea by his teaching. He started in Galilee and has come all the way here."* [6]*On hearing this, Pilate asked if the man was a Galilean.* [7]*When he learned that Jesus was under Herod's jurisdiction, he sent him to Herod, who was also in Jerusalem at that time.*

(Luke 23) [8]*When* **Herod** *saw Jesus, he was greatly pleased, because for a long time he had been wanting to see him. From what he had heard about him, he hoped to see him perform some miracle.* [9]*He plied him with many questions, but Jesus gave him no answer.* [10]*The chief priests and the teachers of the law were standing there, vehemently accusing him.* [11]*Then Herod and his soldiers ridiculed and mocked him. Dressing him in an elegant robe, they sent him back to Pilate.* [12]*That day Herod and Pilate became friends–before this they had been enemies.*

[13]*Pilate called together the chief priests, the rulers and the people,* [14]*and said to them, "You brought me this man as one who was inciting the people to rebellion. I have examined him in your presence and have found* ***no basis for your charges against him****.* [15]*Neither has Herod, for he sent him back to us; as you can see, he has done nothing to deserve death."* (John 18) [39]*"It is your custom for me to release to you one prisoner at the time of the Passover. Do you want me to release 'the king of the Jews'?"* [40]*They shouted back, "No, not him! Give us* ***Barabbas****!"* (Luke 23) [19]*(Barabbas had been thrown into prison for an insurrection in the city, and for murder.)* [20]*Wanting to release Jesus, Pilate appealed to them again.* [21]*But they kept shouting, "****Crucify him! Crucify him!****"* [22]*For the third time he spoke to them: "Why? What crime has this man committed? I have found in him no grounds for the death penalty. Therefore I will have him punished and then release him."*

(John 19) [1]*Then Pilate took Jesus and had him* ***flogged****.* [2]*The soldiers twisted together a* ***crown of thorns*** *and put it on his head. They clothed him in a purple robe* [3]*and went up to him again and again, saying, "Hail, king of the Jews!" And they* ***struck him in the face****. [They* ***spat on him****, and took the staff and struck him on the head again and again. (Matt. 27:30)]* [4]*Once more Pilate came out and said to the Jews, "Look, I am bringing him out to you to let you know that I find no basis for a charge against him."* [5]*When Jesus came out wearing the crown of thorns and the purple robe, Pilate said to them, "Here is the man!"* [6]*As soon as the chief priests and their officials saw him, they shouted, "****Crucify! Crucify!****" But Pilate answered, "You take him and crucify him. As for me, I find no basis for a charge against him."* [7]*The Jews insisted, "We have a law, and according to that law* ***he must die, because he claimed to be the Son of God****."*

[8]*When Pilate heard this, he was even more afraid,* [9]*and he went back inside the palace. "****Where do you come from?****" he asked Jesus, but Jesus gave him no answer.* [10]*"Do you refuse to speak to me?" Pilate said. "Don't you realize I have power either to free you or to crucify you?"* [11]*Jesus answered, "You would have no power over me if it were not given to you from above. Therefore the one who handed me over to you is guilty of a greater sin."* [12]*From then on, Pilate tried to set Jesus free, but the Jews kept shouting, "If you let this man go, you are no friend of Caesar. Anyone who claims to be a king opposes Caesar."*

(Matt. 27) [24]*When Pilate [heard this and] saw that he was getting nowhere, but that instead an uproar was starting, he took water and washed his hands in front of the crowd. "I am innocent of this man's blood," he said. "It is your responsibility!"* [25]*All the people answered, "Let his blood be on us and on our children!"* (Mark 15) [15]***Wanting to satisfy the crowd, Pilate released Barabbas to them...and handed [Jesus] over to be crucified.***

Thus, everything took place just as the prophet Isaiah had prophesied some seven hundred years earlier, when he wrote concerning the Messiah: ***"He was oppressed and afflicted, yet he did not open his mouth; he was led like a lamb to the slaughter, and as a sheep before her shearers is silent, so he did not open his mouth."*** (Isa. 53:7) Isaiah also penned these words of the Messiah, ***"I offered my back to those who beat me, my cheeks to those who pulled out my beard; I did not hide my face from mocking and spitting."*** (Isa. 50:6)

Today we have seen how the religious leaders of the Jews fulfilled the Writings of the Prophets when they oppressed and afflicted the holy and righteous Messiah and condemned Him to death. Why did the religious rulers condemn the Messiah to death? They condemned Him because **they could not tolerate the light of the truth**. Jesus had told them the truth, and that truth revealed their hypocrisy and wickedness. Jesus Himself was the Truth! The Light had come into the world, but people preferred the darkness because of their evil deeds. And since the children of Adam could not tolerate the Light, their only solution was to attempt to extinguish it. That is what the Scriptures declare, saying:

> "*The light shines in the darkness, but the darkness has not understood it.…None of the rulers of this age understood it, for if they had, they would not have crucified the Lord of Glory.…He* (the Lord Jesus Christ) *was in the world, and though the world was made through him, the world did not recognize him. He came to that which was his own, but his own did not receive him.* ***Yet to all who received him, to those who believed in his name, he gave the right to become children of God.***" (John 1:5; 1 Cor. 2:8; John 1:10-12)

Friends, thank you for listening. Be sure to join us for the next program when we see how the children of Adam fulfilled the words which the prophet David wrote in the Psalms concerning the Messiah, saying: "*They have pierced my hands and my feet.*" (Psa. 22:16)…

God bless you as you ponder what the prophet Isaiah prophesied long beforehand concerning the sufferings of the Messiah:

> **"He was oppressed and afflicted, yet he did not open his mouth; he was led like a lamb to the slaughter, and as a sheep before her shearers is silent, so he did not open his mouth."** (Isa. 53:7)

Lesson 84

Jesus Is Nailed to the Cross

Matthew 27; Mark 15; Luke 23; John 19

Peace be with you, listening friends. We greet you in the name of God, the Lord of peace, who wants everyone to understand and submit to the way of righteousness that He has established, and have true peace with Him forever. We are happy to be able to return today to present your program *The Way of Righteousness*.

In our last lesson, we saw how the Jewish religious rulers arrested Jesus, led Him away to the house of the High Priest during the night, **tried Him** with false witnesses, **condemned Him**, and took Him to Pilate, the governor of the land, so that they might crucify Him. The soldiers viciously flogged Jesus, then twisted together a crown of thorns, and put it on His head, mocking Him, striking Him on the face, spitting on Him, taking a rod and striking Him on the head. **Thus, the children of Adam disowned the Righteous One, the Lord of Glory, who came from heaven.** The people who tortured Jesus did not know the words of the prophets; nevertheless they were fulfilling the words of the prophets which announced that the Messiah must suffer in this way at the hands of sinners.

Today we will continue in the book of the Gospel {*Injil*} to see how **Jesus the Messiah suffered and died** on the cross, **thus fulfilling God's great plan of salvation** which His prophets announced long beforehand. Before we begin today's study, you should know that when Jesus lived on earth, the Roman government would execute certain criminals by nailing them to poles, or trees or specially made crosses. Such a death is called *crucifixion*. This excruciatingly painful and shameful death was reserved for the worst criminals.

Perhaps some of you are wondering why God ordained that the righteous Messiah should die such a painful and shameful death. The reason Jesus had to die such a horrible death is because sin is such a horrible crime. **Sin is the problem of the world.** We are all sinners and our sins are an offense to a holy and righteous God! If God is going to forgive you and me of our sins without compromising His righteousness, then **God must judge our sins with a just and complete judgment**. He cannot forgive our sins in just any sort of way. God is a righteous Judge and must properly punish **every** sin. The penalty for sin is death and the eternal fires of hell. This penalty must be payed **in full**. The Good News is that God has sent us a righteous Redeemer to pay the full penalty of our sins. Jesus is that righteous and mighty Redeemer. He came to save us from God's wrath which should fall on us because of our sins.

Now dear friends, we invite you to listen with your mind and heart as we read from the Gospel **the sacred story of Jesus and His death on the cross.** The Scripture says:

> (John 19) [16]***Finally Pilate handed him over to them to be crucified***. *So the soldiers took charge of Jesus.* [17]*Carrying his own cross, he went out to the place of the Skull (which in Aramaic is called Golgotha).*
>
> (Luke 23) [26]*As they [were leading Jesus], they seized Simon from Cyrene, who was on his way in from the country, and put the cross on him and made him carry it behind Jesus.* [27]*A large number of people followed him, including women who mourned and wailed for him....* [32]*Two other men, both criminals, were also led out with him to be executed.* [33]*When they came to the place called the Skull, there they crucified him, along with the criminals–one on his right, the other on his left.* [34]*Jesus said, "**Father, forgive them, for they do not know what they are doing**!"...* [35]*The people stood watching, and the rulers even sneered at him. They said, "He saved others; let him save himself if he is the Christ of God, the Chosen One."* [36]*The soldiers also came up and mocked him. They offered him wine vinegar* [37]*and said, "If you are the king of the Jews, save yourself."*
>
> (John 19) [19]*Pilate had a notice prepared and fastened to the cross. It read:* JESUS OF NAZARETH, THE KING OF THE JEWS. [20]*Many of the Jews read this sign, for the place where Jesus was crucified was near the city, and the sign was written in Aramaic, Latin and Greek.* [21]*The chief priests of the Jews protested to Pilate, "Do not write 'The King of the Jews', but that this man claimed to be king of the Jews."* [22]*Pilate answered, "What I have written, I have written."* [23]*When the soldiers crucified Jesus, they took his clothes, dividing them into four shares, one for each of them, with the undergarment remaining. This garment was seamless, woven in one piece from top to bottom.* [24]*"Let's not tear it," they said to one another. "Let's decide by lot who will get it." This happened that the [word which the prophet David wrote in the Psalms]* ***might be fulfilled*** *which said, "They divided my garments among them and cast lots for my clothing." So this is what the soldiers did.*
>
> (Luke 23) [39]*One of the criminals who hung there hurled insults at him: "Aren't you the Christ? Save yourself and us!"* [40]*But the other criminal rebuked him. "Don't you fear God," he said, "since you are under the same sentence?* [41]*We are punished justly, for we are getting what our deeds deserve. But this man has done nothing wrong."* [42]*Then he said, "Jesus, remember me when you come into*

your kingdom." [43]*Jesus answered him,* **"I tell you the truth, today you will be with me in paradise."**

(Mark 15) [33]*At the sixth hour darkness came over the whole land until the ninth hour.* [34]*And at the ninth hour Jesus cried out in a loud voice,* **"Eloi, Eloi, lama sabachthani?"** *—which means,* **"My God, my God, why have you forsaken me?"** [35]*When some of those standing near heard this, they said, "Listen, he's calling Elijah."* [36]*[Another said,] "Leave him alone. Let's see if Elijah comes to take him down," he said.* (The people said that because they did not understand what Jesus had said, nor did they understand what was happening. The whole land became completely dark–-from midday until early afternoon. During those dark hours **God heaped the punishment of the sins of all the children of Adam upon the holy Redeemer**, so that whoever believes in Him will never perish! We cannot even begin to imagine the intensity of Jesus' sufferings for us.)

(John 19) [28]*Later, knowing that all was now completed, and so that the Scriptures would be fulfilled, Jesus said,* **"I am thirsty."** [29]*A jar of wine vinegar was there, so they soaked a sponge in it, put the sponge on a stalk of the hyssop plant, and lifted it to Jesus' lips.* [30]*When he had received the drink, Jesus said,* **"It is finished!"** (Luke 23) [46]*[Then] Jesus called out with a loud voice,* **"Father, into your hands I commit my spirit!"** *When he had said this, he breathed his last.*

(Mark 15) [38]**The curtain of the temple was torn in two from top to bottom**. [39]*And when the centurion, who stood there in front of Jesus, heard his cry and saw how he died, he said, "Surely this man was the Son of God!"* [40]*Some women were watching from a distance. Among them were Mary Magdalene, Mary the mother of James the younger and of Joses, and Salome.* [41]*In Galilee these women had followed him and cared for his needs. Many other women who had come up with him to Jerusalem were also there.*

(John 19) [31]*Now it was the day of Preparation, and the next day was to be a special Sabbath. Because the Jews did not want the bodies left on the crosses during the Sabbath, they asked Pilate to have the legs broken and the bodies taken down.* [32]*The soldiers therefore came and broke the legs of the first man who had been crucified with Jesus, and then those of the other.* [33]*But when they came to Jesus and found that he was already dead, they did not break his legs.* [34]*Instead,* **one of the soldiers pierced Jesus' side with a spear, bringing a sudden flow of blood and water**. [35]*The man who saw it has given testimony, and his testimony is true. He knows that he tells the truth, and he testifies so that you also may believe.* [36]*These things happened* **so that the scripture would be fulfilled:** *"Not one of his bones will be broken,"* [37]*and, as another scripture says, "They will look on the one they have pierced."*

[38]*Later,* **Joseph [a rich man from] Arimathea asked Pilate for the body of Jesus**. *Now Joseph was a disciple of Jesus, but secretly because he feared the*

> *Jews. With Pilate's permission, he came and took the body away.* [39]*He was accompanied by Nicodemus, the man who earlier had visited Jesus at night. Nicodemus brought a mixture of myrrh and aloes, about seventy-five pounds.* [40]*Taking Jesus' body, the two of them wrapped it, with the spices, in strips of linen. This was in accordance with Jewish burial customs.* [41]*At the place where Jesus was crucified, there was a garden, and in the garden a new tomb, in which no one had ever been laid.* [42]*Because it was the Jewish day of Preparation and since the tomb was near by, they laid Jesus there.*"

Friends, this is where we must end our reading today, although the story of the Messiah does not end with the tomb! How glad we are that we can invite you to join us in the next study called: "**Jesus is risen**!"

What we have heard today is truly astounding! We have seen how the children of Adam despised the Messiah, the Lord of Life, and killed Him by nailing Him to a cross. However, what we must remember is that the death of the Messiah was the fulfillment of the plan of salvation which God designed before the world existed.

Did you hear what the Lord Jesus announced from the cross just before He died? He said, "***It is finished!***" Why did Jesus say, "*It is finished!*"? He said,"*It is finished!*" because He had completed the work of salvation. Surely, the religions of the world do **not** say, "It is finished!" What they say is: "Nothing is finished! You must save yourself by your own good deeds! You must work to erase your own sins! Come on, get with it! Keep working! Nothing is finished! If you want to enter Paradise you must work, offer sacrifices, fulfil your religious duties, pray, fast, treat your body harshly, etcetera, etcetera!" That is the message of religion!

But God's Good News to man is: ***"It—is—finished!!!"*** Believe and be saved! The Messiah has paid your debt of sin with His own blood! The blood of Jesus can cleanse and change the worst of sinners! That is the reason Jesus could say to the dying, repentant criminal, "*I tell you the truth, today you will be with me in paradise.*" (Luke 23:43)

Dear friends, the work that can save you from sin's penalty is completely done. God is satisfied with Jesus' sacrifice. We no longer need to offer sacrifices of sheep as did our ancestors who lived before the time of the Messiah. Jesus Christ is God's perfect and final Sacrifice! Nothing remains for us, except to believe what God has testified concerning the Messiah and His sacrifice. ***"It is finished!"*** Jesus has fulfilled that which the prophets foretold about the sufferings and death of the righteous Redeemer! Seven hundred years before Jesus came into the world, the prophet Isaiah wrote:

> "*[The Messiah] was assigned a grave with the wicked, and with the rich in his death, though he had done no violence, nor was any deceit in his mouth....* ***But***

> ***he was pierced for our transgressions, he was crushed for our iniquities; the punishment that brought us peace was upon him, and by his wounds we are healed. We all, like sheep, have gone astray, each of us has turned to his own way; and the LORD has laid on him the iniquity of us all!*"** (Isa. 53:9,5,6)

You who are listening today, **do you really believe the prophets**? Do you believe that Jesus is the One who finished the work of Salvation of which God's prophets wrote? Do you now understand the reason for the death of the righteous Redeemer on the cross? **You and I** are the reason! It is because of **our sins** that He died, like a spotless sacrificial sheep. We deserve eternal punishment in hell, but God, out of His great love for us, sent Jesus (whom He calls His beloved Son) so that He might suffer our punishment and bear the penalty for our sins. That is what the Holy Scriptures declare, when they say:

> "*Very rarely will anyone die for a righteous man, though for a good man someone might possibly dare to die*. ***But God demonstrates his own love for us in this: While we were still sinners, Christ died for us!***" (Rom. 5:7,8) "*God made him who had no sin to be sin for us*, ***so that in him we might become the righteousness of God***." (2 Cor. 5:21)

Glory to God, the Merciful, the Compassionate…"***It is finished!***" God has fulfilled the symbolism of Abraham's Sacrifice {*Id al-Adha*}! For in the same location where Abraham sacrificed the innocent ram in his son's place, Jesus, the sinless Redeemer, allowed Himself to be sacrificed in our place —"*that* ***whoever believes in him*** *will not perish but have eternal life!*" (John 3:16)

Thank you for listening. If you have any questions concerning this perfect sacrifice which the Lord Jesus made for you, write to us....

God bless you as you ponder the deep and powerful words which Jesus announced from the cross just before He died. He said,

> "***It is finished!***" (John 19:30)

LESSON 85

JESUS IS RISEN!

MATTHEW 28; LUKE 24; JOHN 20

Peace be with you, listening friends. We greet you in the name of God, the Lord of peace, who wants everyone to understand and submit to the way of righteousness that He has established, and have true peace with Him forever. We are happy to be able to return today to present your program *The Way of Righteousness*.

In our last lesson, we saw how **Jesus the Messiah shed His blood** on the cross to which He was nailed, to pay for the sins of the world and **to open for sinners a door of everlasting peace**. Everything happened exactly as God's prophets had foretold it: The Messiah was mocked, scourged and nailed to a cross. Just as the innocent ram died in the place of Abraham's son, Jesus (the sinless Redeemer) died in our place. Before Jesus died, He shouted, ***"It is finished!"*** Praise be to God, the Lord Jesus had completed God's plan of salvation!

The death of the Messiah on the cross is the most important news in all the Holy Scriptures, because that death is the reason God can forgive us our sins without contradicting His righteousness. However, while the death of the Messiah is **the most important news**, what we are about to study is **the most wonderful news**, because we are going to hear how **God raised Jesus from the dead.**

As we already read, after Jesus died on the cross, a soldier took a spear and stabbed it into Jesus' side, bringing a sudden flow of blood and water which proved that He was dead. We saw also that a rich man took the body of Jesus and placed it in a new tomb that he had chiseled out of the rock for himself. A huge round stone was rolled over the tomb's entrance. Everything happened exactly as God's prophets had foretold it.

Thus, in the Gospel, it is written:

> (Matt. 27) [62]*The next day, the one after Preparation Day, the chief priests and the Pharisees went to Pilate.* [63]*"Sir," they said, "we remember that while he was still alive that deceiver said, '**After three days I will rise again**.'* [64]*So give the order for the tomb to be made secure until the third day. Otherwise, his disciples*

may come and steal the body and tell the people that he has been raised from the dead. This last deception will be worse than the first." [65]*"Take a guard," Pilate answered. "Go, make the tomb as secure as you know how."* [66]*So they went and made the tomb secure by putting a seal on the stone and posting the guard.*

(Matt. 28) [1]*After the Sabbath, at dawn* **on the first day of the week**, *Mary Magdalene and the other Mary went to look at the tomb.* [2]*There was a violent earthquake, for* **an angel of the Lord came down from heaven and, going to the tomb, rolled back the stone and sat on it.** [3]*His appearance was like lightning, and his clothes were white as snow.* [4]*The guards were so afraid of him that they shook and became like dead men.*

Thus when the women arrived at the cemetery, (Luke 24) [2]*they found the stone rolled away from the tomb,* [3]*but when they entered, they did not find the body of the Lord Jesus.* [4]*While they were wondering about this, suddenly two men in clothes that gleamed like lightning stood beside them.* [5]*In their fright the women bowed down with their faces to the ground, but the men said to them,* **"Why do you look for the living among the dead?** [6]**He is not here; he has risen**! *Remember how he told you, while he was still with you in Galilee:* [7]*'The Son of Man must be delivered into the hands of sinful men, be crucified and on the third day be raised again.'"* [8]*Then they remembered his words.* [9]*When they came back from the tomb, they told all these things to the Eleven and to all the others.* [10]*It was Mary Magdalene, Joanna, Mary the mother of James, and the others with them who told this to the apostles.* [11]*But they did not believe the women, because their words seemed to them like nonsense. [For the disciples still did not understand the Writings of the Prophets which said that Jesus had to rise from the dead. (John 20:9)]* [12]*Peter, however, got up and ran to the tomb. Bending over, he saw the strips of linen lying by themselves, and he went away, wondering to himself what had happened.*

[13]*Now* **that same day two of them were going to a village called Emmaus**, *about seven miles from Jerusalem.* [14]*They were talking with each other about everything that had happened.* [15]*As they talked and discussed these things with each other,* **Jesus himself came up and walked along with them;** [16]**but they were kept from recognizing him**.

[17]*He asked them, "What are you discussing together as you walk along?" They stood still, their faces downcast.* [18]*One of them, named Cleopas, asked him, "Are you only a visitor to Jerusalem and do not know the things that have happened there in these days?"* [19]*"What things?" he asked. "About Jesus of Nazareth," they replied. "He was a prophet, powerful in word and deed before God and all the people.* [20]*The chief priests and our rulers handed him over to be sentenced to death, and they crucified him;* [21]*but we had hoped that he was the one who was going to redeem Israel. And what is more, it is the third day since all this took place.* [22]*In addition, some of our women amazed us. They went to the*

tomb early this morning 23*but didn't find his body. They came and told us that they had seen a vision of angels, who said he was alive.* 24*Then some of our companions went to the tomb and found it just as the women had said, but him they did not see."* 25*He said to them, "***How foolish you are, and how slow of heart to believe all that the prophets have spoken!** 26**Did not the Christ have to suffer these things and then enter his glory?**" 27*And beginning with Moses and all the Prophets, he explained to them what was said in all the Scriptures concerning* **himself**.

28*As they approached the village to which they were going, Jesus acted as if he were going further.* 29*But they urged him strongly, "Stay with us, for it is nearly evening; the day is almost over." So he went in to stay with them.* 30*When he was at the table with them, he took bread, gave thanks, broke it and began to give it to them.* 31*Then their eyes were opened and they recognized him, and he disappeared from their sight.* 32*They asked each other, "Were not our hearts burning within us while he talked with us on the road and opened the Scriptures to us?"* 33*They got up and returned at once to Jerusalem. There they found the [disciples] assembled together* 34*and saying, "***It is true! The Lord has risen and has appeared to Simon!**" 35*Then the two told what had happened on the way, and how Jesus was recognized by them when he broke the bread.*

36*While they were still talking about this,* **Jesus himself stood among them** *and said to them, "Peace be with you."* 37*They were startled and frightened, thinking they saw a ghost.* 38*He said to them, "Why are you troubled, and why do doubts rise in your minds?* 39**Look at my hands and my feet**. *It is I myself! Touch me and see; a ghost does not have flesh and bones, as you see I have."* 40*When he had said this, he showed them his hands and feet.* 41*And while they still did not believe it because of joy and amazement, he asked them, "Do you have anything here to eat?"* 42*They gave him a piece of broiled fish,* 43*and he took it and ate it in their presence.*

44*He said to them, "This is what I told you while I was still with you:* **Everything must be fulfilled that is written about me in the Law of Moses, the Prophets and the Psalms."** 45**Then he opened their minds so they could understand the Scriptures.** 46**He told them, "This is what is written: The Christ will suffer and rise from the dead on the third day,** 47**and repentance and forgiveness of sins will be preached in his name to all nations, beginning at Jerusalem.** 48**You are witnesses of these things.**"

(John 20) 24*Now Thomas…, one of the Twelve, was not with the disciples when Jesus came.* 25*So the other disciples told him, "We have seen the Lord!" But he said to them, "Unless I see the nail marks in his hands and put my finger where the nails were, and put my hand into his side, I will not believe it."* 26*A week later his disciples were in the house again, and Thomas was with them. Though the doors were locked, Jesus came and stood among them and said, "Peace be with*

> *you!" [27]Then he said to Thomas, "Put your finger here; see my hands. Reach out your hand and put it into my side. Stop doubting and believe." [28]Thomas said to him, "**My Lord and my God!**" [29]Then Jesus told him, "**Because you have seen me, you have believed; blessed are those who have not seen and yet have believed.**" [30]Jesus did many other miraculous signs in the presence of his disciples, which are not recorded in this book. [31]**But these are written that you may believe that Jesus is the Christ, the Son of God, and that by believing you may have life in his name.***

What a thrilling story we have read today! **Jesus rose from the dead!** He conquered one of man's greatest enemies: death. The grave could not hold Him. On the third day, Jesus came right out of His grave clothes, like a butterfly leaving his chrysalis shell. Only the grave clothes remained where the body of Jesus had been lying. The Lord Jesus Christ arose in a glorious body like the body which everyone who believes in Him will one day receive! That is the reason the Scripture says:

> *"Christ has indeed been raised from the dead, the **firstfruits** of those who have fallen asleep. For since death came through a man, the resurrection of the dead comes also through a man. **For as in Adam all die, so in Christ all will be made alive!**"* (1 Cor. 15:20-22)

The resurrection of Jesus proves that He is the One He claimed to be. Do you remember that Jesus said, "***I am the resurrection and the life. He who believes in me will live, even though he dies!***" (John 11:25) Jesus promised to give eternal life to all those who believe in Him, but if He Himself had not conquered death, how could He save others from the power of death and sin and hell?

Perhaps **an illustration** will help. A child is playing in the waves along the seashore. Suddenly a strong current sweeps him out to sea. He desperately tries to get back to shore but cannot. The child will die unless someone rescues him. There is a man on the shore who sees the child and yells to him, "Don't be afraid. I will save you!" So the man swims out to where the child is, but, alas, the currents are too strong for him. Both he and the child drown. The man intended to rescue the child, but he lacked the power to carry out his intention. The ocean current was too strong for him. Similarly, we hear those who claim to be saviors, telling people, "Follow me, trust me, and you'll get into Paradise." Those who make such promises may have good intentions, but they cannot accomplish what they promise. They cannot even save themselves, because they are utterly unable to overcome the power of sin and death. The power of death is too strong for them, and when they die, they will be buried, their bodies will decay in the grave, and their souls will await the Day of Judgment.

But it was not that way with the Lord Jesus. **He is the One He claimed to be!** Everything took place just as He predicted. Jesus died as a sacrifice to take away sin, was buried, and then on the third day He came out of the grave! Never has there been anyone among the prophets who died, was buried, and then came out of the tomb never to die again! But that is what Jesus the Messiah did! He defeated death and the grave! He overcame sin and Satan and death and hell! And the most wonderful thing in all of this is that **whoever truly believes** this good news about the death and resurrection of Jesus Christ will share in His glory forever! That is what the Lord Jesus proclaimed after He had risen from the dead, saying, "***Do not be afraid. I am the First and the Last. I am the Living One; I was dead, and behold I am alive for ever and ever! And I hold the keys of death and Hades!***" (Rev. 1:17,18)

God raised Jesus to life, so that you might know for sure that He is the Savior and Judge of the world, whom God appointed. That is what the Scriptures declare, when they say:

> "***Salvation is found in no one else***, *for there is no other name under heaven given to men by which we must be saved!...[God] has set a day when he will judge the world with justice by the man he has appointed.* ***He has given proof of this to all men by raising him from the dead....If you confess with your mouth, 'Jesus is Lord,' and believe in your heart that God raised him from the dead, you will be saved!...Everyone who calls on the name of the Lord will be saved!***" (Acts 4:12; 17:31; Rom. 10:9,13)

Friends, thank you for listening. God willing, in our next program we will continue in the Gospel to see how the Lord Jesus ascended to heaven after He had appeared to His disciples over a forty-day period and showed them many convincing proofs that He was alive....

May God give you insight into all that you have heard today, and may you carefully consider this verse from His holy Word:

> ***"[God delivered Jesus] over to death for our sins and [raised Him back to life so that He might judge us as righteous]!"*** (Rom. 4:25)

Lesson 86

Jesus Ascends to Heaven

Matthew 28; Luke 24; Acts 1

Peace be with you, listening friends. We greet you in the name of God, the Lord of peace, who wants everyone to understand and submit to the way of righteousness that He has established, and have true peace with Him forever. We are happy to be able to return today to present your program *The Way of Righteousness*.

For a long time, we have been looking into the holy Gospel {*Injil*}, the book which contains the story of the Almighty Savior, Jesus Christ. As we have seen already, **Jesus** means *God saves*. **Christ** is a Greek word for *Messiah* meaning *Whom God has appointed*. Jesus Christ is the One whom God appointed **to save** the children of Adam from the dominion of sin.

However, as we have seen, **most people did not recognize who Jesus really was**. Some considered Him a prophet, but they did not understand that He was the very Word of God {*Kalimat Allah*} which came from heaven and appeared on earth as a man. Some, like the chief priests and the rulers of the Jews, were very jealous of Him and in the end they killed Him by having Him hung on a cross. However, God planned and knew about all these events beforehand. The Messiah's death on the cross was in perfect agreement with the plan God had announced long beforehand through His prophets. In our last program, we saw that God raised Jesus back to life on the third day. The resurrection of Jesus proves that God accepted the blood which Jesus shed as a full payment to redeem the children of Adam from the power of sin, the fear of death and the punishment of hell.

After Jesus came back to life, we saw that He appeared to His disciples, showing them the scars where the soldiers had pounded nails through His hands and feet. We also read that Jesus ate with His disciples to prove to them that He really was alive. The book of the Gospel {*Injil*} relates how Jesus appeared to His disciples over a forty-day period and spoke with them about the Kingdom of God. On one occasion, Jesus appeared to more than five hundred of His disciples at the same time. (1 Cor. 15:6) However, the greatest proof that Jesus is alive today is in the fact that He lives (by His Holy Spirit) within the hearts of those who believe in Him and submit themselves to His authority.

Today with the help of God, we will hear about **the great authority God has given to the Lord Jesus** and we will see **how Jesus parted with His disciples and ascended up to heaven**. We begin our study today in the last chapter of the Gospel of Matthew. The Scripture says:

> (Matt. 28) [16]*Then the eleven disciples went to Galilee, to the mountain where Jesus had told them to go.* [17]*When they saw him, they worshiped him; but some doubted.* [18]*Then Jesus came to them and said, "**All authority** in heaven and on earth has been given to me.* [19]*Therefore go and make disciples of all nations, baptizing them in the name of the Father and of the Son and of the Holy Spirit,* [20]*and teaching them to obey everything I have commanded you. And surely I am with you always, to the very end of the age."*

Did you hear what Jesus said to His disciples? He said to them, "***All authority** in heaven and on earth has been given* **to me***. Therefore go and make disciples of all nations*." Why did Jesus say that He had all authority in heaven and on earth?

In our studies in the Torah of Moses, we saw how God created the first man, Adam. We read that God gave Adam authority to rule over everything God had created. God wanted Adam to live with Him and rule with Him forever. But Adam forfeited that authority on the day he disobeyed God's command and ate of the tree of the knowledge of good and evil. Since Adam is our forefather, and since "an epidemic is not confined to the one from whom it originates!" {Wolof proverb}, we too have lost the privilege (authority) of living and ruling with God. Like Adam, we are all sinners, born into the kingdom of sin, far from God and His majestic glory.

However, we praise God, because the Writings of the Prophets show that God designed a plan to open for the children of Adam **a door** through which they could return to God and have a share in His glory and kingdom. That "Door" is **the holy Messiah** who came from heaven to pour out His blood as a sacrifice to cleanse people from their sins and to bring them to God. Jesus the Messiah was tested like Adam, but Jesus did not sin. He was perfect and holy, just as God is perfect and holy. That was the reason that God was not ashamed to call him **His Son**. Thus after Jesus gave His life as a sacrifice to take away sin, God raised Him from the dead, made Him the Lord of all and committed to Him "*all authority in heaven and on earth.*"

Perhaps some would ask the question, "If Jesus is Lord of everything, why is our world still so full of trouble and sin?" The Holy Scripture gives the answer when it says:

> *"For as* **in Adam** *all die, so* **in Christ** *all will be made alive.* **But each in his own turn**: *Christ, the firstfruits; then, when he comes, those who belong to him. Then the end will come, when he hands over the kingdom to God the Father after he has destroyed all dominion, authority and power."* (1 Cor. 15:22-24) *"He* **will** *wipe every tear from their eyes. There* **will** *be no more death or mourning or crying or pain, for the old order of things has passed away."* (Rev. 21:4)

From those verses, and from many other verses in the Word of God, we learn that God has committed all authority to Jesus so that He might take control of everything, and judge everyone. However, He has not yet taken actual control of everything, nor has He yet judged the people of the world. One day Jesus will return to earth. When He returns, He will take control of this world and make all things new again.

Therefore, whoever you are and wherever you are, God is commanding you to **repent** of your sins, turn to Him and **believe** the Good News of salvation based on the death and resurrection of the Lord Jesus Christ. If you truly believe, God will forgive all your sins in Jesus' name, make your heart new by the power of the Holy Spirit, and give you peace with God forever. If you believe in Christ, He will come to you by His Holy Spirit and establish **His kingdom in your heart**. Jesus Christ will not change the world until He returns in person to judge it. But He can change you today! Will you allow Him to establish His kingdom in your heart?

Dear friend, God has sent you a Savior who can take away your sins and give you a heart that is new and clean. You can **know** that you will spend eternity with God in the glory of Paradise, **if you believe** the truth about Jesus Christ, the Savior of the world! However, **if you ignore** the Savior whom God sent, He will finally become your Judge! That is what the Scripture speaks of when it says:

> *"The Lord Jesus [will be] revealed from heaven in blazing fire with his powerful angels.* **He will punish those who do not know God and do not obey the gospel of our Lord Jesus.** *They will be punished with everlasting destruction and shut out from the presence of the Lord and from the majesty of his power on the day he comes to be glorified in his holy people and to be marveled at among all those who have believed!"* (2 Thes. 1:7-10)

Friends, the Word of God is clear. It tells us that whoever truly **believes** the Good News about Jesus Christ's death on the cross and His resurrection from the dead will be **saved**! However, whoever does **not believe** it will be **condemned**! Jesus shed His blood as a sacrifice which can erase your debt of sin forever. But the blood which Jesus shed for you is of no value to you if you do not believe in it in your heart. Because the Scripture says:

> *"For God so loved the world that he gave his one and only Son, that* ***whoever believes in him*** *shall* ***not perish*** *but have eternal life….* ***but whoever does not believe*** *stands* ***condemned already*** *because he has not believed in the name of God's one and only Son."* (John 3:16,18)

Yes, if you believe the Good News of Jesus Christ, you will be **saved**, but if you do not believe it, you will **perish** in your sins. That is the word of salvation which God sent down to the children of Adam. That is the reason Jesus commanded His disciples, saying: "*All authority in heaven and on earth has been given to me. Therefore go and make disciples of all nations!*" (Matt. 28:18,19)

Now let us continue the story. Jesus appeared to His disciples for forty days after He had risen from the dead. The Scripture says:

> (Acts 1) [4]*On one occasion, while [Jesus was eating with His disciples], he gave them this command: "Do not leave Jerusalem, but wait for the gift my Father promised, which you have heard me speak about.* [5]*For John baptized with water, but in a few days you will be baptized with* ***the Holy Spirit****."*

Did you hear what Jesus said? We have already read (in the Gospel of John 14-16) how Jesus promised His disciples that His Father in heaven would send to them the Counselor, the Holy Spirit, who would live in their hearts, cleansing them, renewing them, strengthening them, and guiding them into all truth. Now we hear how He commanded His disciples to wait in Jerusalem for the Holy Spirit who was soon to come. In our next lesson, God willing, we will see how the Holy Spirit descended to fill the hearts of all the disciples of Jesus, just as He had promised.

Let us now read how Jesus departed from His disciples and ascended to heaven. The Scripture says:

> (Acts 1) [6]*So when [the disciples of Jesus] met together, they asked him, "Lord, are you at this time going to restore the kingdom to Israel?"* [7]*He said to them: "It is not for you to know the times or dates the Father has set by his own authority.* [8]*But you will receive power when the Holy Spirit comes on you; and you will be my witnesses in Jerusalem, and in all Judea and Samaria, and to the ends of the earth."*
>
> [9]*After he said this,* ***he was taken up before their very eyes, and a cloud hid him from their sight****.* [10]*They were looking intently up into the sky as he was going, when suddenly two men dressed in white stood beside them.* [11]*"Men of Galilee," they said, "why do you stand here looking into the sky? This same Jesus, who has been taken from you into heaven, will come back in the same way you have seen him go into heaven."*

Thus Jesus ascended into heaven, returning to His Father's house from where He had come some thirty-three years earlier. How majestic His departure was as He ascended into heaven before the eyes of His small band of disciples! There was no doubt—this Jesus whom they had been following over the past three years was truly the Messiah about whom all the prophets had spoken! In His birth, life, death, burial, resurrection and ascension–Jesus of Nazareth had **fulfilled everything** the prophets predicted concerning Him, even ascending into heaven as the prophet David had prophesied in the Psalms.

Friends, do you know where the Lord Jesus is today? The Scriptures tell us that *"Jesus Christ...has gone into heaven and is at God's right hand–with angels, authorities and powers in submission to him."* (1 Pet. 3:21,22) Yes, Jesus is in heaven, at God's right hand, where all created beings are in submission to Him. **All of God's true subjects are submitted to the Lord Jesus Christ.** How about you? Have you submitted yourself to Jesus the Messiah, the One chosen by God as the Savior and Judge of the world?

As we just read, after the Lord Jesus ascended back up to heaven, two angels appeared to His disciples and said to them, *"Why do you stand here looking into the sky?* ***This same Jesus, who has been taken from you into heaven, will come back in the same way you have seen him go into heaven***." Yes, one day Jesus Christ will return in the clouds. Are you ready for His return? **On that day everyone will behold Him, and everyone will know that He is the One whom God appointed as the Savior and as the Judge of the world!** That is what the Scriptures declare when they say:

> (Phil. 2) [5]*Christ Jesus* [6]*...being in very nature God, did not consider equality with God something to be grasped,* [7]*but made himself nothing, taking the very nature of a servant, being made in human likeness.* [8]*And being found in appearance as a man, he humbled himself and became obedient to death–even death on a cross!* [9]*Therefore God exalted him to* ***the highest place*** *and gave him the name that is* ***above every name***, [10]*that at the name of Jesus* ***every knee*** *should bow, in heaven and on earth and under the earth,* [11]*and* ***every tongue*** *confess that Jesus Christ is Lord, to the glory of God the Father!"*

Friends, this is where we must conclude today, but we hope you will join us in the next broadcast to discover how God sent down the Holy Spirit to live in the heart of every person who receives Jesus Christ as his Lord and Savior....

God bless you as you remember what the two angels told the disciples, saying,

> ***"This same Jesus, who has been taken from you into heaven, will come back in the same way you have seen him go into heaven."*** (Acts 1:11)

LESSON 87

THE HOLY SPIRIT HAS COME!

ACTS 1,2

Peace be with you, listening friends. We greet you in the name of God, the Lord of peace, who wants everyone to understand and submit to the way of righteousness that He has established, and have true peace with Him forever. We are happy to be able to return today to present your program *The Way of Righteousness*.

In our last few studies in the Gospel {*Injil*}, we have heard how **the Lord Jesus fulfilled all that God's prophets wrote long beforehand concerning the Messiah's death and resurrection**. We read that Jesus shed His holy blood on the cross to which He was nailed, to pay the debt of sin for the children of Adam. We saw also that He was taken down from the cross and placed in a tomb. However, on the third day, God raised Him up from the dead! After Jesus had risen, He appeared to His disciples for forty days, proving to them that He truly was alive. Then in our last lesson, we saw Jesus ascend into heaven while His disciples looked on.

Do you remember the last thing Jesus commanded His disciples, before He went up to heaven? Let us read again what He said:

> (Acts 1) [4]*[Jesus] gave them this command: "Do not leave Jerusalem, but* ***wait for the gift my Father promised****, which you have heard me speak about.* [5]*For John baptized with water, but in a few days* ***you will be baptized with the Holy Spirit****.* [8]*...**you will receive power when the Holy Spirit comes on you; and you will be my witnesses in Jerusalem, and in all Judea and Samaria, and to the ends of the earth.**"* [9]*After he said this, he was taken up before their very eyes, and a cloud hid him from their sight.* [10]*They were looking intently up into the sky as he was going, when suddenly two men dressed in white stood beside them.* [11]*"Men of Galilee," they said, "why do you stand here looking into the sky? This same Jesus, who has been taken from you into heaven, will come back in the same way you have seen him go into heaven."*

Thus Jesus parted with His disciples, returned to Paradise from where He had come, and sat down at the right hand of the Majesty on high. That is where He remains today, awaiting the moment when He will return to judge the world in righteousness.

Did you hear what Jesus commanded His disciples before He ascended to heaven? He commanded them to stay in Jerusalem until they were clothed with the Holy Spirit, who was to come from heaven. Perhaps some of you are still wondering: **Who is this Holy Spirit?** The Holy Spirit is the Spirit of God and the Spirit of Jesus. He is One with God the Father and Jesus the Son, yet distinct from them. He existed with God in the beginning when God created the world. He is the Spirit who inspired the prophets to write and to announce the Word of God in early times. The Holy Spirit is the Spirit of the Most High who descended on a virgin by the name of Mary and enabled her to conceive and give birth to the holy Child Jesus. He is the Spirit who was in the Messiah, Jesus. Also, the Holy Spirit is the Counselor, whom Jesus promised His disciples when He said to them,

> *"I will ask the Father, and he will give you another Counselor to be with you forever–the Spirit of truth. The world cannot accept him, because it neither sees him nor knows him. But you know him, for he lives with you and will be in you."* (John 14:16,17)

What Jesus promised His disciples concerning the coming of this Counselor (or *Helper*) is important for us to understand, because some today want to make people believe that Jesus was announcing the coming of another prophet. But the Counselor whom the Lord Jesus promised cannot be a human being, because Jesus stated clearly that the Counselor was **pure Spirit**, and that **no one could see Him**, and that **He would live inside Christ's disciples forever**. So who is this Holy Spirit? He is the Spirit whom God places in the hearts of all who believe in the Messiah. He regenerates them, {Lit. make them to be born again}, cleanses them, strengthens them, marks them as His own, and gives them a share in His holy presence forever.

Today we are going to see how God poured out His Holy Spirit on Jesus' disciples on the day of **Pentecost**. Pentecost was a festival God had established for the Israelites in the time of the prophet Moses. You can read about it in the Torah. On this day the Israelites would thank God for the prosperity which He had given them in the harvest of the wheat crop. However, there was an even more important meaning to the Pentecost festival. Pentecost was the day God chose long beforehand to send down the Holy Spirit to live in all who truly believe in the Messiah. Just as the Pentecost festival took place fifty days after the Passover feast, so God planned to send down the Holy Spirit fifty days after Jesus the Messiah died and rose again.

Now let us continue in the Word of God to see what happened after Jesus left His disciples and returned to heaven. The Scripture says:

449

s 1) [12]**Then [Jesus' disciples] returned to Jerusalem from the hill the Mount of Olives**, *a Sabbath day's walk from the city.* [13]*When they ed, they went upstairs to the room where they were staying. Those present re Peter, John, James and Andrew; Philip and Thomas, Bartholomew and Matthew; James son of Alphaeus and Simon the Zealot, and Judas son of James.* [14]*They all joined together constantly in prayer, along with the women and Mary the mother of Jesus, and with his brothers.*

(Acts 2) [1]**When the day of Pentecost came, they were all together in one place**. [2]*Suddenly a sound like the blowing of a violent wind came from heaven and filled the whole house where they were sitting.* [3]*They saw what seemed to be tongues of fire that separated and came to rest on each of them.* [4]**All of them were filled with the Holy Spirit** *and began to speak in other tongues as the Spirit enabled them.* [5]*Now there were staying in Jerusalem God-fearing Jews from every nation under heaven.* [6]*When they heard this sound, a crowd came together in bewilderment, because each one heard them speaking in his own language.* [7]*Utterly amazed, they asked: "Are not all these men who are speaking Galileans?* [8]*Then how is it that each of us hears them in his own native language?* [9]*Parthians, Medes and Elamites; residents of Mesopotamia, Judea and Cappadocia, Pontus and Asia,* [10]*Phrygia and Pamphylia, Egypt and the parts of Libya near Cyrene; visitors from Rome* [11]*(both Jews and converts to Judaism); Cretans and Arabs–we hear them declaring the wonders of God in our own tongues!"* [12]*Amazed and perplexed, they asked one another, "What does this mean?"* [13]*Some, however, made fun of them and said, "They have had too much wine."*

[14]**Then Peter stood up with the Eleven, raised his voice and addressed the crowd**: *"Fellow Jews and all of you who live in Jerusalem, let me explain this to you; listen carefully to what I say.* [15]*These men are not drunk, as you suppose. It's only nine in the morning!* [16]*No, this is what was spoken by the prophet Joel:* [17]*"'In the last days, God says, I will pour out my Spirit on all people. Your sons and daughters will prophesy...* [21]*And everyone who calls on the name of the Lord will be saved.'* [22]*"Men of Israel, listen to this: Jesus of Nazareth was a man accredited by God to you by miracles, wonders and signs, which God did among you through him, as you yourselves know.* [23]**This man was handed over to you by God's set purpose and foreknowledge; and you, with the help of wicked men, put him to death by nailing him to the cross.** [24]**But God raised him from the dead,** *freeing him from the agony of death, because it was impossible for death to keep its hold on him.* [25]*[The prophet] David said about him:*

"'I saw the Lord always before me. Because he is at my right hand, I will not be shaken. [26]*Therefore my heart is glad and my tongue rejoices; my body also will live in hope,* [27]*because you will not abandon me to the grave, nor will you let your Holy One see decay....*

[29]"Brothers, I can tell you confidently that the patriarch David died and was buried, and his tomb is here to this day. [30]But he was a prophet and knew that God had promised him on oath that he would place one of his descendants on his throne. [31]Seeing what was ahead, he spoke of the resurrection of the Christ, that he was not abandoned to the grave, nor did his body see decay. [32]God has raised this Jesus to life, and we are all witnesses of the fact. [33]Exalted to the right hand of God, he has received from the Father the promised Holy Spirit and has poured out what you now see and hear. [34]For David did not ascend to heaven, and yet he said,

"'The Lord said to my Lord: "Sit at my right hand [35]until I make your enemies a footstool for your feet."'

*[36]"**Therefore let all Israel be assured of this: God has made this Jesus, whom you crucified, both Lord and Christ!**"*

[37]When the people heard this, they were cut to the heart and said to Peter and the other apostles, "Brothers, what shall we do?" [38]Peter replied, "Repent and be baptized, every one of you, ***in the name of Jesus Christ*** *for the* ***forgiveness of your sins****. And* ***you will receive the gift of the Holy Spirit****. [39]The promise is for you and your children and for all who are far off–for all whom the Lord our God will call." [40]With many other words he warned them; and he pleaded with them, "Save yourselves from this corrupt generation."* Amen.

Fellow listeners, did you really hear Peter's sermon? In summary, he proclaimed to the crowd in Jerusalem that God had sent the Messiah, Jesus, just as He promised long ago through His prophets. Peter told them: You despised the Messiah whom God sent from heaven! You murdered Him by nailing him to a cross, but God raised Him from the dead! We are all witnesses of it! God has exalted Jesus to His right hand and has sent the Holy Spirit whom He promised! Repent and turn to God! Believe the message of God's prophets! Believe in Jesus whom God has appointed to be the Savior and Judge of the world! ***"All the prophets testify about him that everyone who believes in him receives forgiveness of sins through his name!"*** (Acts 10:43)

Thus did the apostle Peter proclaim **the Good News of salvation** through faith in Jesus the Messiah. When the crowd heard Peter's words, they felt great pain in their hearts because they now recognized that Jesus of Nazareth, whom they had nailed to the cross, was the Lord of Glory from heaven! This Jesus, whom they had scorned and hated, was the Messiah whom God had promised long ago through His prophets! Thus, on that day, many **repented** of their sins, turned to God, and **believed** in the name of the Lord Jesus Christ. These new disciples were baptized in water to give public testimony to the fact that they had been cleansed from their sin by faith in the death, burial and resurrection of Jesus Christ. Being baptized in water did not wash away their sin—it was only an **outward** sign of the cleansing that had already taken place on the **inside**.

Scripture says:

> *e who accepted [the message of the Gospel] were baptized, and about three sand were added to their number that day. They devoted themselves to the* ***apostles' teaching*** *and to the* ***fellowship****, to the* ***breaking of bread*** *and to* ***prayer****....and the disciples were filled with joy and with the Holy Spirit."* (Acts 2:41,42; 13:52)

Thus, on that day of Pentecost, **the church**—the assembly of those who believe in Jesus Christ—was born. The church of Jesus is not a building or a religion. The word for church in Greek is "*Ekklesia*" meaning "called out ones." Just as there are true believers and false believers in the world today, there is also a true church and a false church. The true church of Jesus Christ is composed of all who, since that day of Pentecost, have been transferred from **Adam's family** to **Christ's family** by sincere faith in Christ's perfect, finished sacrifice.

The events of Pentecost we have heard about today happened about two thousand years ago. Perhaps this will cause some to say, "This is of no concern to me! I was not one of those who crucified the Messiah! The Jews and the Romans did it! I didn't have a thing to do with it!" However, God's Word tells us that the Messiah "*was pierced for* ***our*** *transgressions, he was crushed for* ***our*** *iniquities!*" (Isa. 53:5) **Our sins** caused His death. **Our transgressions** were the reason God permitted man to nail His Beloved One to a cross! **Man crucified Jesus, but God raised Him from the dead** to be **the Savior** of all who **believe** and **the Judge** of all who do **not believe**. Thus, the Scriptures declare:

> *"[Whoever you are, wherever you are, God commands you] to repent. For he has set a day when he will judge the world with justice by the man he has appointed. He has given proof of this to all men by raising him from the dead!"* (Acts 17:30,31)

Think carefully about this word, because **your eternal destiny depends on how you respond to it.** Thank you for listening....

God bless you as you think about what the apostle Peter proclaimed, saying,

> ***"All the prophets testify about [Jesus the Messiah] that everyone who believes in him receives forgiveness of sins...and....the gift of the Holy Spirit!"*** (Acts 10:43; 2:38)

Lesson 88

Jesus Is Coming Back!

Revelation 19-22

Peace be with you, listening friends. We greet you in the name of God, the Lord of peace, who wants everyone to understand and submit to the way of righteousness that He has established, and have true peace with Him forever. We are happy to be able to return today to present your program *The Way of Righteousness*.

We have come today to the 88th lesson in our **chronological study of God's Word**. As we have seen, over several hundred years, the Spirit of God inspired more than thirty prophets to write the first part of the Holy Scriptures, that is, the Torah, the Psalms, and the books of the prophets. That first part of God's Book is called **the Old Testament**. In that part, all the prophets shared one message, telling us that God is holy and righteous and therefore must judge every sin. However, God is also full of mercy and does not want the children of Adam to perish in their sin. Thus we saw how God, through His prophets, promised to send a Redeemer, the holy Messiah, who would be born of a virgin, live a holy life and then shed His blood on a cross to pay for the sins of the children of Adam. All the prophets of the Old Testament wrote about this Messiah who was to come.

In the second part of the Holy Scriptures, **the New Testament**, the Book of the Gospel, we saw that, when the time which God planned had come, He sent forth the Messiah, the Savior of the world, just as He had promised through His prophets. The Messiah was Jesus of Nazareth—the only perfectly holy Person who ever lived. Jesus was full of the power of God, because He was the very Word of God in a human body. Of Him God declared, *"This is my Son, whom I love; with him I am well pleased!"* (Matt. 3:17) However, our fellow humans killed the holy One of God by nailing Him to a cross. But God raised Him to life on the third day. After Jesus was seen by many witnesses, God exalted Him to the highest place in heaven. But the story doesn't end there.

The wonderful story of God's righteous way of salvation has a beginning and an ending; a head and a tail. **This evil world has not yet seen the last of Jesus the Messiah!** The Word of God tells us that the Lord Jesus is going to come back to cast Satan and his evil angels into the lake of fire, to judge the children of Adam on Judgment Day, and to recreate this old world. Our lesson today is called **"Jesus is coming back!"**

We will be reading from the final section of the New Testament, from the book called ***Revelation***. Revelation is a profound and powerful book, because it announces what will happen at the end of time, when this present world will come to an end. The book of Revelation has twenty-two chapters, chapters which proclaim a glorious victory for all who believe. But for those who do not believe, these chapters contain great terror, because the book of Revelation reveals that if you refuse to accept Jesus Christ as your **Savior**, He will, in the end, be your **Judge**! If you do not accept **the Lamb of God**, you will meet **the Lion of God**, because the Lord Jesus, who died as a sacrificial lamb to take away sin, will return as a mighty lion to judge! That is what the Scriptures speak of when they say: *"The Lord Jesus [Christ will be] revealed from heaven in blazing fire with his powerful angels. He will punish those who do not know God and do not obey the gospel of our Lord Jesus!"* (2 Thes. 1:7,8)

Now, let us listen carefully to the excerpts taken from the book of Revelation. After the Lord Jesus had returned to heaven, He sent His angel to the apostle John, to reveal to him the events that will take place at the end of the world. In the first chapter, John wrote:

> (Rev. 1) 1***The revelation of Jesus Christ, which God gave him to show his servants what must soon take place***. *He made it known by sending his angel to his servant John,* 2*who testifies to everything he saw–that is, the word of God and the testimony of Jesus Christ.* 3*Blessed is the one who reads the words of this prophecy, and blessed are those who hear it and take to heart what is written in it, because the time is near.* 4*I, John, write to you…Grace and peace to you from him who is, and who was, and who is to come, and from the seven spirits before his throne…****To him who loves us and has freed us from our sins by his blood,*** 6***and has made us to be a kingdom and priests to serve his God and Father–to him be glory and power for ever and ever! Amen.*** 7***Look, he is coming with the clouds, and every eye will see him, even those who pierced him; and all the peoples of the earth will mourn because of him. So shall it be! Amen.*** 8*"I am the Alpha and the Omega," says the Lord God, "who is, and who was, and who is to come, the Almighty."*

In chapter nineteen, John wrote:

> (Rev. 19) 1*After this I heard what sounded like the roar of a great multitude in heaven shouting: "Hallelujah! Salvation and glory and power belong to our God,* 2*for true and just are his judgments…* 6*Then I heard what sounded like a great*

multitude, like the roar of rushing waters and like loud peals of thunder, shouting: "Hallelujah! For our Lord God Almighty reigns. [**The kingdom of the world has become the kingdom of our Lord and of his Christ, and he will reign for ever and ever!** (11:15)]

[11]*I saw heaven standing open and there before me was a white horse, whose rider is called* **Faithful and True**. *With* **justice** *he judges and makes war.* [12]*His eyes are like blazing fire, and on his head are many crowns. He has a name written on him that no one knows but he himself.* [13]*He is dressed in a robe dipped in blood, and* **his name is the Word of God**. [14]*The armies of heaven were following him, riding on white horses and dressed in fine linen, white and clean.* [15]*Out of his mouth comes a sharp sword with which to strike down the nations. "He will rule them with an iron scepter." He treads the winepress of the fury of the wrath of God Almighty.* [16]*On his robe and on his thigh he has this name written:* **KING OF KINGS AND LORD OF LORDS**.

(Rev. 20) [1]*And I saw an angel coming down out of heaven, having the key to the Abyss and holding in his hand a great chain.* [2]*He seized the dragon, that ancient serpent, who is* **the devil**, *or Satan, and bound him for a thousand years.* [3]*He threw him into the Abyss, and locked and sealed it over him, to keep him from deceiving the nations anymore until the thousand years were ended. After that, he must be set free for a short time.* [4]*I saw thrones on which were seated those who had been given authority to judge. And I saw the souls of those who had been beheaded because of their testimony for Jesus and because of the word of God.... They came to life and reigned with Christ for a thousand years.*

[7]*When the thousand years are over, Satan will be released from his prison* [8]*and will go out to deceive the nations in the four corners of the earth...to gather them for battle. In number they are like the sand on the seashore.* [9]*They marched across the breadth of the earth and surrounded the camp of God's people, the city he loves. But fire came down from heaven and devoured them.* [10]***And the devil, who deceived them, was thrown into the lake of burning sulphur, where the beast and the false prophet had been thrown. They will be tormented day and night for ever and ever!***

[11]*Then I saw* **a great white throne** *and him who was seated on it. Earth and sky fled from his presence, and there was no place for them.* [12]*And I saw the dead, great and small, standing before the throne, and books were opened. Another book was opened, which is the book of life. The dead were judged according to what they had done as recorded in the books.* [13]*The sea gave up the dead that were in it, and death and Hades gave up the dead that were in them, and each person was judged according to what he had done.* [14]*Then death and Hades were thrown into the lake of fire. The lake of fire is the second death.* [15]***If anyone's name was not found written in the book of life, he was thrown into the lake of fire!***

(Rev. 21) [1]*Then I saw* ***a new heaven and a new earth****, for the first heaven and the first earth had passed away, and there was no longer any sea.... [3]And I heard a loud voice from the throne saying, "Now the dwelling of God is with men, and he will live with them. They will be his people, and God himself will be with them and be their God. [4]He will wipe every tear from their eyes. There will be* **no more death** *or mourning or crying or pain, for the old order of things has passed away." [5]He who was seated on the throne said, "I am making everything new!" Then he said, "Write this down, for these words are trustworthy and true." [6]He said to me: "It is done. I am the Alpha and the Omega, the Beginning and the End.* ***To him who is thirsty I will give to drink without cost from the spring of the water of life.*** *[7]He who overcomes will inherit all this, and I will be* **his God** *and he will be* **my son**. *[8]But the cowardly, the unbelieving, the vile, the murderers, the sexually immoral, those who practice magic arts, the idolaters and all liars–***their place** *will be in the fiery lake of burning sulphur. This is the second death."*

(Rev. 22) [1]*Then the angel showed me the river of the water of life, as clear as crystal, flowing from* **the throne of God and of the Lamb** *[2]down the middle of the great street of the city. On each side of the river stood the tree of life, bearing twelve crops of fruit, yielding its fruit every month... [3]No longer will there be any curse. The throne of God and of the Lamb will be in the city, and his servants will serve him. [4]They will see his face, and his name will be on their foreheads. [5]There will be no more night. They will not need the light of a lamp or the light of the sun, for the Lord God will give them light. And they will reign for ever and ever. [6]The angel said to me, "These words are trustworthy and true. The Lord, the God of the spirits of the prophets, sent his angel to show his servants the things that must soon take place."*

[I, Jesus, I say unto you:] [12]..."**Behold, I am coming soon!** *My reward is with me, and I will give to everyone according to what he has done. [13]I am the Alpha and the Omega, the First and the Last, the Beginning and the End. [14]Blessed are those who wash their robes, that they may have the right to the tree of life and may go through the gates into the city. [15]Outside are...[those who love and practice] falsehood. [16]I, Jesus, have sent my angel to give you this testimony for the churches. I am the Root and the Offspring of David, and the bright Morning Star." [17]The Spirit and the bride say, "Come!" And let him who hears say,* "**Come!" *Whoever is thirsty, let him come; and whoever wishes, let him take the free gift of the water of life!***"

[18]I warn everyone who hears the words of the prophecy of this book: ***If anyone adds anything to them****, God will add to him the plagues described in this book. [19]And* ***if anyone takes words away from this book of prophecy****, God will take away from him his share in the tree of life and in the holy city, which are described in this book. [20]He who testifies to these things says,* "**Yes, I am coming**

> ***soon**." Amen. Come, Lord Jesus.* [21]*The grace of the Lord Jesus be with God's people.*

Thus, God concludes His marvelous Book, and promises that the Lord Jesus, whom the children of Adam nailed to a cross, will one day come back to earth. He will return to take those who believe Him to be with Him, and to judge those who do not believe Him! Dear friend, are you confident as you face the return of the Lord Jesus from heaven? Are you among those who have received Him as their Savior and Lord? Do you believe in your heart that God laid your sins on the Lord Jesus Christ, who never sinned, so that through Him, God can declare you righteous? **Is your name written in the Book of Life?** What is your relationship with Jesus Christ? Is He your **Savior**? Or will He be your **Judge**?

Are you ready for Christ's return? If you hear God's voice today, do not harden your heart, because the Scripture says:

> *"With the Lord…a thousand years are like a day. The Lord is not slow in keeping His promise, as some understand slowness. He is patient with you, not wanting anyone to **perish**, but everyone to come to **repentance**. But the day of the Lord will come like a thief. The heavens will disappear with a roar; the elements will be destroyed by fire, and the earth and everything in it will be laid bare!"* (2 Pet. 3:8,9) *"**Now** is the time of God's favor, **now** is the day of salvation!"* (2 Cor. 6:2) ***"We who have heard of this, how shall we escape if we ignore such a great salvation?"*** (Heb. 2:3)

Dear friends, thank you for listening so attentively. Our prayer to God is that every word that you have heard on *The Way of Righteousness* will be a blessing springing up in your life–leading you to God's "*great salvation*" which He freely gives to all who truly believe His Word. If you would like to have the entire book of the Gospel {*Injil*} from which we have read today, write to us….

Until next time, God bless you as you remember Jesus' final words in the Holy Scriptures. The Lord Jesus Christ said:

> ***"Yes, I am coming soon!"*** (Rev 22:20)

Part 4

The Way of Righteousness

Summarized

"How shall we escape if we ignore such a great salvation?"
Hebrews 2:3

Lesson 89
The Good News!

{Note: The first draft of lesson #89 in Wolof was written by Malick, radio voice of "Yoonu Njub"}

Peace be with you, listening friends. We greet you in the name of God, the Lord of peace, who wants everyone to understand and submit to the way of righteousness that He has established, and have true peace with Him forever. We are happy to be able to return today to present your program *The Way of Righteousness*.

In our study in the book of the *Injil* {Arabic for *Gospel* or *Good News*}, we heard the Lord Jesus Christ, after He had risen, command His disciples, saying, ***"Go into all the world and preach the good news to all creation."*** (Mark 16:15) And after Jesus was taken up into heaven, a man by the name of Paul (converted from being a brutal religious zealot to becoming a devout follower of Christ) wrote:

> *"[God called me to be his apostle, and gave me the task of making known His **good news**—the **good news**] he promised beforehand through his prophets in the holy Scriptures!...I am not ashamed of the [**good news** that I am preaching], because it is the power of God for the salvation of everyone who believes....For in the [**good news**] a righteousness from God is revealed, a righteousness that is by faith from first to last!"* (Rom. 1:1,2,16,17)

The good news, the good news, the good news! What is this **good news** that the Word of God tells us about again and again? Today, with the help of God, we would like to talk about this **Good News** which is proclaimed in the Holy Scriptures. But before we talk about **the Good News**, we need to remember ***the bad news***.

What is **the bad news**? You may recall that, in the beginning, after God created the heavens and the earth, God made Adam and Eve, placing them in the earthly garden of Paradise. God created them so that they might know Him, love Him, obey Him and glorify Him forever. However, to test them, God said to Adam: "You can take from all the trees of the garden, except from the tree in the middle of the garden. You must not eat from it, for in the day you eat from it you will die!" The bad news is that Adam and Eve listened to the serpent, that is, the devil, who tempted them to eat fruit from the forbidden tree. Adam and Eve's sin brought trouble and death into the world, contaminating them and all their offspring. As we often hear: "An epidemic is not confined to the one from whom it originates!" God's Word tells us the bad news when it says:

> *"Man is destined to die once, and* ***after that to face judgment****!...The Lord is coming–to judge everyone, and to convict all the ungodly of all the ungodly acts they have done in the ungodly way, and of all the harsh words ungodly sinners have spoken against him!"* (Heb. 9:27; Jude 15)

Therefore, the **bad news** is that **we are all sinners and we must face God's righteous judgment!**

However, **the Good News** is that right there in the garden of Paradise, God, who is full of mercy, proclaimed that He would one day send into the world a Person who would be unstained by sin, born of a virgin. This holy Person, this righteous **Redeemer**, would offer Himself to be killed as a sacrifice to pay for the sins of Adam and all his descendants. The punishment for sin which we deserve would fall on this sinless Redeemer. That is the Good News which God announced on the day that Adam and Eve sinned.

God used many men to announce the coming of this Redeemer, also called **the Messiah**. Each of God's prophets announced something about the Messiah, so that when He came, everyone could recognize that He was the One whom God had appointed. For example, the prophet Isaiah, who preceded the Messiah by about seven hundred years, prophesied how the Messiah would be born, saying: *"The virgin will be with child and will give birth to a son, and will call him Immanuel–which means, 'God with us.'"* (Matt. 1:23; Isa. 7:14) Another prophet, Micah, prophesied that the Messiah would come from heaven and be born upon earth in the village of **Bethlehem**. That is precisely where the Messiah was born. Yet Micah prophesied this hundreds of years before the Messiah's birth.

But the prophets did not merely announce the Messiah's birth. They also prophesied that **the Messiah would suffer and die** in the place of sinners. For example, the prophet David wrote that people would despise the Messiah, torture Him, pierce His hands and His feet, and kill Him. And David not only announced the death of the Messiah, he also predicted that **God would raise the Messiah** from the dead, thus proving that He was the one and only Savior whom God sent to save the children of Adam from the penalty of sin.

Little argument exists over the birth of the Messiah, but many stumble over His death and resurrection. They do not understand how could God just stand by and watch as men humiliated the Messiah whom He had sent. What most people fail to grasp is that God, who loves us, is the very One who purposed that the Messiah should suffer like that **for our sins**. Yet that is what the prophets proclaimed, saying: *"It was the Lord's will to crush [the Messiah–as a sacrifice* ***to pay for sin****]!"* (Isa. 53:10)

Do we believe the prophets? We say we believe them. If we really **believe the prophets**, we must also **believe what they wrote**. We must remember that the prophets did not speak their own ideas. God planted in their spirits what they were to say. Therefore, if we refuse to believe those prophets, who are we really rejecting? We are rejecting **God**–because He is the One who inspired the prophets to prophesy that the Messiah would die as a sacrifice to take away sin.

It is because God loves the world and does not want anyone to perish in sin that He planned the Messiah's death. It was necessary that a righteous Person die for unrighteous people to save them from God's judgment. That is what the offering of sacrifices of sheep and goats symbolized in earlier times. **Jesus Christ**, who was born of a virgin, by the power of God, is **the perfect and final sacrifice** which God gave. As it is said, "No need to draw picture of a dwarf (to depict what one is like), if one is standing before you." {Wolof proverb} Likewise, since we now have a perfect and permanent Sacrifice for sins, there is no need to weary ourselves by continuing to offer imperfect, symbolic sacrifices. Can you remember what the Lord Jesus declared on the cross just before He died? He said, *"It is* ***finished!****"* (John 19:30) He paid our debt of sin, once and for all time. The only thing that remains for us to do is **believe it!** As we already read, the Scripture says: The Good News of Jesus Christ's death and resurrection *"is the power of God for the salvation of* ***everyone who believes****!"* (Rom. 1:16)

Sadly, many refuse to believe in Him, saying that this whole thing about the death and resurrection of Jesus is just a made-up story. Yet when we study the Gospel, we discover that everything the prophets prophesied about the Messiah was **fulfilled** by Jesus Christ. **Everything**...concerning His birth, His life, His death, His resurrection and His ascension. Thus, the Gospel declares that *"Christ died for our sins according to the Scriptures [of the prophets], that he was buried, that he was raised on the third day according to the Scriptures [of the prophets]."* (1 Cor. 15:3,4) **Everything happened just as the prophets predicted**. Those who hated Jesus mocked Him, tortured Him and killed Him, and those who loved Him buried Him. But death could not keep Him in the grave. We saw that, on the third day after His crucifixion, some women got up at dawn and went to the tomb where Jesus was buried, and discovered that it was open and empty! After Jesus died and rose again, He showed Himself to His disciples over a period of forty days. Over five hundred people saw Him after His resurrection. It was true! The Messiah had conquered death, one of man's greatest enemies! Jesus' resurrection proved that God has accepted His sacrifice as a full payment for the sins of the children of Adam, so that whoever believes in Him might share in His eternal life.

That is the Good News. **The Lord Jesus Christ died to take away your sins, and He came out of the grave on the third day to give you eternal life.** The purpose of this Good News is to save all those who believe it. Therefore, the question that you must answer is: "**Do you believe it?**" The Word of God says: "Today is the day of salvation! If you hear the Good News, do not harden your heart! Believe!" Salvation is not a result of the works that we do, because **no one can do enough works to earn Paradise.** God will never **sell** you His great salvation; He wants to **give** it to you! Good deeds, prayers and fasting may give you a good feeling inside, but they do not satisfy God's righteousness! There is only one way for you to enter God's Paradise.

1.) You must first **recognize** that you are a sinner and that you have no strength to please God.

2.) Then you must **believe** that Jesus Christ is the Savior that God sent to die on the cross to take away your sins and that God raised Him from the dead to give you eternal life.

If you believe this Good News, **you can be sure that you will be taken to Paradise after you die,** because God Himself has promised us in His Word that we can **know** that we have eternal life, **if we believe** on the Name of the Lord Jesus Christ. (1 John 5:9-13)

{Following is Malick's personal testimony.} Let me pause here to tell you how I became a believer in Jesus Christ. As a young man I was faithful to pray five times a day and to observe the yearly fast, but I did not know where I would go after I died. I asked all around, but didn't receive a clear answer. But when I studied the Gospel {*Injil*}, I discovered that **I could know where I would go after I died,** because Jesus the Messiah Himself says in the Gospel: "*I tell you the truth, whoever hears my word and believes him who sent me* ***has eternal life and will not be condemned; he has crossed over from death to life.***" (John 5:24) He also said: "*I am the resurrection and the life. He who believes in me* ***will live****, even though he dies!*" (John 11:25) Thus, I repented of my own efforts to save myself and believed in the Messiah of whom all the prophets prophesied, saying, "***Everyone who believes in him receives forgiveness of sins through his name.***" (Acts 10:43) I took all my hope and hung it upon the Lord Jesus Christ. And from that time until now God has brought peace to my spirit. I no longer have a troubled conscience. My future is wonderfully bright because of the work of Jesus on the cross. In my life as a disciple of Christ, sometimes I face trouble and affliction because my faith differs from the opinions of my relatives and friends, but I have peace. The peace of God fills my heart and my mind. And Jesus who has given it to me says: "*If the world hates you, keep in mind that it hated me first.... Peace I leave with you; my peace I give you. I do not give to you as the world gives. Do not let your hearts be troubled and do not be afraid.*" (John 5:18; 14:27) And friends, what the Lord has done for me and in me, He can do for each of you. He asks one thing from you: **That you give Him your whole heart**. He will do the rest. For the Lord Jesus Himself has said, "*Come to me, all you who are weary and burdened, and I will give you rest. Take my yoke upon you and learn from me, for I am gentle and humble in heart, and you will find rest for your souls.*" (Matt. 11:28,29)

Are you weary and burdened because of your sins? Would you like to find rest for your soul? If you believe the Good News that the Messiah died for you and rose again for you, God will forgive you of your sins, judge you as righteous and write your name in the Book of Life. If you believe this Good News, God will mark you as His own and send the Spirit of Jesus into your heart. The Holy Spirit, who lives in you, will change your heart, your life and your way of living, because the Scripture says: "*If anyone is in Christ, he is a new creation; the old has gone, the new has come!*" (2 Cor. 5:17)

Friend, wherever you are, whatever your situation, whether you are a man or a woman, old or young, the Lord Jesus Christ can give you a new life–**if you believe in Him**. He died for you so that you might live with God forever. **Do you believe this Good News?**

Thank you for listening....

May God bless you. We leave you with a verse of Scripture that speaks about the wonderful assurance God gives to all who place their hope in God's Good News of salvation. The Scripture says:

> ***"[God] has saved us and called us to a holy life–not because of anything we have done but because of his own purpose and grace. This grace was given us in Christ Jesus before the beginning of time, but it has now been revealed through the appearing of our Savior, Christ Jesus, who has destroyed death and has brought life and immortality to light through the Gospel!"*** (2 Tim. 1:9,10)

Lesson 90

Man's Questions and God's Answers

Part 1

Peace be with you, listening friends. We greet you in the name of God, the Lord of peace, who wants everyone to understand and submit to the way of righteousness that He has established, and have true peace with Him forever. We are happy to be able to return today to present your program *The Way of Righteousness*.

Dear friends, we thank all of you who have written to us with questions about what the Holy Scriptures teach. We hope the letters, books and cassettes we have mailed to you have been helpful. We also want to thank those of you who faithfully listen to *The Way of Righteousness*, even if you have not written to us. May God bless each of you and help you to understand the righteous way of Salvation which He has provided.

Today and in the next program, we plan to do something a little different. We would like to share with you some **questions** we have received from you, our listening friends. To answer each question, **we will use only the Holy Scriptures**, since the Word of God is the only sure light that can guide us in the darkness. As it is written in the Psalms: "*Your word is a lamp to my feet and a light for my path!*" (Psa. 119:105)

Now…your questions. To help us today, a friend has joined us in the studio to read the questions.

1.) Thank you. The first question, received in a letter, is: **What is the religion of those who produce *The Way of Righteousness* programs?**

Long ago, God put it in our hearts to seek the truth—**His Truth.** We wanted to know for ourselves the Word of the one true God. We read the Bible carefully (which includes the Torah {*Taurat*}, the Psalms {*Zabur*}, the Books of the Prophets, and the Gospel {*Injil*}). We recognized that Jesus Christ is the Savior of whom all the prophets wrote. Jesus is the perfect and final sacrifice which God gave to erase the debt of sin of the children of Adam so that whoever believes in Him might live in the presence of God forever. Jesus Christ, who came from God, is the only One who can bring us to God. We have staked all our hope on Him.

Who are we then? We are **disciples of Jesus Christ**. The Qur'an calls us "*Ahl al-kitab*," which means *the People of the Book*. Others call us *Christians*, meaning *Christ's people*. In telling you that we are Christians, we remind you that many people call themselves Christians, but that does not mean that they are truly Christ's people. Just as a log does not become a crocodile by soaking in water {based on Wolof Proverb}, so a person does not become a Christian by merely doing the things that Christians do. Following a religion cannot give you a relationship with God. Only Jesus Christ can bring a person to God. How blessed we are to have Christ as our Savior, Lord and Friend! He has given us a wonderful relationship with God and confidence in the face of death. Every day He shows us His faithfulness and His love. In the Lord Jesus Christ, God has given us everything that relates to eternal life! In Him we have everything our hearts need!

2.) Thank you. The next question is important and deserves a clear answer. This person writes: **Something really troubles me. I have read in the Qur'an where our prophet, Muhammad, commands all Muslims to believe certain books contained in the Bible such as the Torah and the Gospel. I respect the Bible and have started to read it. However, my friends tell me that we cannot trust the Bible, because it has been corrupted and altered. They claim that the Bible I am reading is different from the original Bible. What do you say about this?**

Before answering this question, we have a few questions for those who claim that the ancient books of the prophets have been "corrupted and altered." What is the source of the idea that the Bible has been falsified? What is the basis for such a serious accusation? Tell us, **when** was the Bible altered? **Who** altered it? **Where** was it altered? **What** changes have been made? Can anyone give a single proof that the Holy Scriptures have been corrupted?

If you honestly search out the facts about the Bible, you will discover that God has protected His Holy Word which He inspired His prophets to write. Those who claim that the Bible has been falsified are simply believing rumors. There is no evidence to support the accusation that the Bible has been altered. There is much evidence however to prove that the Bible has **not** been altered.

Today, in the great museums and universities of the world, scholars have preserved thousands of ancient scrolls {Lit. in Wolof: *books*} of the Gospel Writings and the entire New Testament. Many of these scrolls existed hundreds of years before the time of Muhammad, as did the scrolls of the Old Testament. If you compare those ancient books with the ones we have in our hands today, you will discover how accurately God has preserved His Word for us. The Bible we read today is the same Bible that existed in Muhammad's day.

The prophets wrote God's words on scrolls made from animal skin or plant fiber. Jewish scribes copied God's Word onto new scrolls. These trained scribes were extremely careful to ensure that **the copies were the same as the original text**. The number of letters in a book was counted and its middle letter was given to ensure that the copy was the same as the original. If there was an error, the entire scroll would be destroyed! These Jewish scribes believed that to tamper with God's Word was to tamper with God Himself! Perhaps you have heard of the famous **Dead Sea scrolls** discovered in 1947. Did you know that these Old Testament scrolls were copied one hundred years before Jesus was born? Yet these ancient scrolls are consistent with scrolls copied one thousand years later! The Bible has not been altered!

No one can really alter the Bible. If someone wanted to change the Bible, he would have to change all the copies of the Bible. This would be impossible! In the period following the time of Christ, scholars began to translate the Bible from the original languages of Hebrew, Aramaic and Greek into **many different languages**. No one could change all the Bibles throughout the world! Today, the Bible (in part or in whole) is written in more than two thousand different languages. {Note: In English we are blessed with dozens of excellent translations.} God has preserved His Holy Word and His servants are translating it into the languages of the peoples of the world, because God wants everyone to hear it with their own ears, understand it in their own minds, receive it into their own hearts, and be saved.

Can the Lord God Almighty protect His Word from Satan and those who want to alter and corrupt it? Yes, He **can** preserve it and He **has** preserved it! *Allahu Akbar!* God is great! Of course we are aware that from the beginning of the world till today Satan has attempted to alter the Word of God—in the minds of people. For example, in the first book of the Bible, we heard God say to Adam, "*The day you eat of this tree* ***you will die****!*" But Satan denied what God had said, telling Adam and Eve, "*You will* ***not*** *die!*" Thus, Satan attempted to alter the Word of God. As you know, Adam and Eve chose to believe Satan and ate the forbidden fruit. As a result, their souls died and their bodies began to wither and die, just as God had said. Dear friends, God's Word is sure. The devil is a liar and a deceiver. Satan wants to deceive people and make them believe that the Bible has been altered. But the Lord Jesus Christ says, "*The Scripture* ***cannot*** *be broken!*" (John 10:35) "*Heaven and earth will pass away, but my words will* ***never*** *pass away!*" (Matt. 24:35)

3.) Thank you for that clear answer. Now, the third question. **Why do you call Jesus the Son of God? God does not beget and God was not begotten, therefore how can Jesus be His Son?**

We have answered this important question often, yet we will gladly answer it again. Ignorance in such an important matter can be deadly! As the (Wolof) proverb says: "Before you know it, ignorance will kill you!" The questioner asks, "Why do **you** call Jesus the Son of God?" First, we must remind our listeners that we did not give Jesus the title "*the Son of God!*" **God** is the One who calls Jesus **His Son**! Second, the name "Son of God" **does not mean** that God took a wife and had a son! As we have seen, Jesus has hundreds of names and titles in the Bible. These names help us to understand better who He is. For example, He is called "***the door***," but that does not mean that Jesus is a door of wood or of sheet metal. He is also called "***the Food which gives Life***" (Bread of Life) but that does not mean that Jesus is food, like rice with fish (national Senegalese dish) which we eat. God's prophets called the Messiah "***the Lamb of God,***" but that does not mean He is a sheep. Similarly, when God calls Jesus **His Son**, you should know that this does not mean that God took a wife and had a child by her! That is blasphemy! If I leave the country, they call me "a son of Senegal" because I come from Senegal. But that does not mean that Senegal took a wife and had a child! Similarly, God and the angels and the prophets called the Messiah "the Son of God" because He came forth from God. Jesus was born of a virgin. He had no earthly father. Even before He was born, He was living in heaven, because He is the "*Kalimat Allah,*" that is, ***the* Word** which was with God in the beginning. That is what the Scripture declares:

> "*In the beginning was the Word, and the Word was with God, and the Word was God. The Word became flesh and made his dwelling among us. We have seen his glory, the glory of the One and Only, who came from the Father, full of grace and truth....No one has ever seen God, but God the One and Only, who is at the Father's side, has made him known!*" (John 1:1,14,18)

Jesus is the Eternal Son of God, the Word of God that appeared on earth in a human body.

What is the Word of God? Perhaps you will answer that the Word of God is the Holy Scripture which God inspired the prophets to write. You are correct. The Writings of God's prophets are God's Word to us–like letters sent to us by God. But allow us to ask you about your good friend who lives in another town. Which would you prefer: that your friend merely writes you **some letters**, or would you rather he come and visit you **in person**? Of course you would prefer that he come in person, so that you can talk with him face to face. Similarly, since God is great and nothing is impossible for Him, and since He wants to make known to people what He is like and what His will is for us, do you think He would merely send us some letters or would He come in person to visit us? Friends, the good news which the prophets announced is that **God Himself would come to visit sinful humanity**!

In the Gospel, we discover that God has sent down His Word as a Man to live among people so that He might save them from their sins. That Man from heaven is Jesus Christ. Jesus is worthy to be called the Son of God, because He is the Word which was with God in the beginning. Jesus is God's Eternal Son, God's perfect representative—the One who has revealed God's character to man. We often say of a young man, "He is just like his father!" So it is with Jesus. Jesus bears the image of God. To know Jesus, is to know God and what He is like. Thus the Scripture says:

> "***In the past God spoke to our forefathers through the prophets*** *at many times and in various ways, but* ***in these last days he has spoken to us by his Son,*** *who he appointed heir of all things, and through whom he made the universe. The Son is the radiance of God's glory and the exact representation of his being, sustaining all things by his powerful word. After he had provided purification for sins, he sat down at the right hand of the Majesty in heaven.*" (Heb. 1:1-3)

One final word. God does not say that you must fully **understand why** He calls Jesus *His Son*—only that you must **believe it.** Remember that God is the One who inspired the prophet David to write in the Psalms: "*Kiss* ***the Son*** {give Him homage and submission}, *lest He be angry and you be destroyed in your way, for His wrath can flare up in a moment. Blessed are all who take refuge in Him!*" (Psa. 2:11,12) God is also the One who inspired the apostle John to write in the Gospel:

> "*Jesus did many other miraculous signs in the presence of his disciples, which are not recorded in this book. But these are written* ***that you may believe that Jesus is the Christ, the Son of God, and that believing you may have life in His name***." (John 20:30,31) ***"Whoever believes in the Son has eternal life, but whoever rejects the son will not see life, for God's wrath remains on him!"*** (John 3:36)

Thank you for listening. In the will of God, in the next broadcast, we will continue with more questions and answers....

God bless you as you consider this declaration from the Bible:

> ***"All men are like grass, and all their glory is like the flowers of the field; the grass withers and the flowers fall, but the word of the Lord stands forever!"*** (1 Pet. 1:24,25)

Lesson 91

Man's Questions and God's Answers

Part 2

Peace be with you, listening friends. We greet you in the name of God, the Lord of peace, who wants everyone to understand and submit to the way of righteousness that He has established, and have true peace with Him forever. We are happy to be able to return today to present your program *The Way of Righteousness*.

Today we will continue what we began in the last program–answering **questions** which we have received from you, our listeners. We thank each of you who have sent us letters. Before we begin, there is one thing that we need to make clear. In answering your questions, we dare not rely on our own knowledge or the knowledge of others. We rely on **God's Word alone**. We do not have the answers to your questions, but **God** has the answers and has given them to us in the Holy Scriptures. The Bible says: "*The word of God is living and active. Sharper than any double-edged sword, it penetrates even to dividing soul and spirit, joints and marrow; it judges the thoughts and attitudes of the heart.*" (Heb. 4:12) Now then, let us return to your questions. Again, we are glad to have a friend here to read the questions.

1.) Thank you. In this letter a listener writes: **You said in one program: "That which is evil cannot come from God." I disagree with that, because I believe that God first created what is evil before He made what is good.**

Allow us to answer this question with a question found in the Bible. "*Can both fresh water and salt water flow from the same spring? Never!*" (James 3:11) Just as a spring or a well does not give forth both fresh water and salt water, neither is God the source of both good and evil. The Holy Scriptures say:

> "*God is **light**; in him there is **no darkness** at all!*" (1 John 1:5) "*When tempted, no one should say, 'God is tempting me.' For **God cannot be tempted by evil, nor does he tempt anyone**; but each one is tempted when, by his own evil desire, he is dragged away and enticed...Don't be deceived, my dear brothers.*

> *Every* **good and perfect gift** *is from above, coming down from the Father of the heavenly lights, who does not change like shifting shadows. He chose to give us birth through the word of truth, that we might be a kind of firstfruits of all he created.*" (James 1:13,14,16-18)

God's prophet, Habakkuk, wrote: "*O LORD, are you not from everlasting?…Your eyes are too pure to look on evil;* ***you cannot tolerate wrong.***" (Hab. 1:12,13) Therefore if God cannot **tolerate** what is evil, we should not believe that He can **create** what is evil. God created the angel named Lucifer, but Lucifer became the devil by choosing to rebel against God. God created Adam, but Adam became a sinner by choosing to disobey God. The Word of God teaches us that the devil and the unrighteous heart of man are the source of evil and that God and His Word are the source of good.

2.) The next question is: **If God is holy and full of mercy, then why does He stand by and watch the quarrels and wars and murders and wickedness of the world? Can't He do something to help people who are in trouble?**

Indeed, God is the Lord of Mercy and what He should do to help people in trouble, **He has already done**! He sent the righteous Redeemer, Jesus Christ, to reconcile people to Himself and then to each other by dying for the sins of the world. However, before people can be truly reconciled among themselves, they must first believe in Jesus as the Savior whom God sent and submit to Him. When our relationship with God is right, then our relationship with people can be right. Only then will there be true peace. Everything depends on **our response** to God. We must take the remedy God has provided. Also, remember that God is going to judge this world for its wickedness. The Word of God says that the Lord Jesus Christ will return at the end of the age to judge everyone who refuses to accept and obey the truth. After the Lord Jesus has put down all of God's enemies, He will renew the whole creation. And then what is written in the Scriptures will be fulfilled, which says: "***No longer will there be any curse****….There will be no more death or mourning or crying or pain, for the old order of things has passed away.*" (Rev. 22:3; 21:4)

3.) The third question today is this: **Something troubles me. I've always believed that if I sin, that sin will affect me, but it will not affect my children because they did not commit it. But you say that the sin that our ancestor Adam committed in the Garden of Paradise spread to all of his descendants, and that God must punish them. How can this be?**

The Wolofs say: "An epidemic is not confined to the one from whom it originates!" and "The leaping gazelle doesn't produce burrowing offspring." This is true isn't it? We all agree that if you have a child, and you raise him in your own house, he will take on his character, good and bad, from you his parent. He will reflect your way of speaking, your way of living, your way of thinking, and your way of doing things. All of us belong to the family of Adam and Eve. We have descended from those who disobeyed God's commandment. Are we not like our ancestors? Who among us can say that we have never departed even once from the way of God's commandments? We are all guilty! We were born with a nature which disobeys God's commandments. From whom did we inherit this disobedient nature? **From Adam**. Like an awful disease, Adam's sin has spread to us all. Whether we like it or not, that is the way it is. That is precisely what the Word of God declares, when it says: "***Sin** entered the world through **one man**, and **death through sin**, and in this way **death came to all men**, because **all sinned**!*" (Rom. 5:12) However, all hope is not lost, because the Word of God also says: "*Just as the result of **one trespass** (by Adam) was condemnation for all men, so also the result of **one act of righteousness** (by Jesus Christ) was justification that brings life for all men.*" (Rom. 5:18)

4.) The next question is: **Why is the Bible divided into two sections, an *Old Testament* and a *New Testament*?**

In brief, everything that the prophets wrote in the *Old Testament*, that is, in **the First Covenant**, they wrote **before** the Messiah was born. Everything in the *New Testament*, **the New Covenant,** was written **after** the birth of the Messiah. Thus, the message of God's prophets who wrote the First Covenant was: "God **is going to send** the Messiah!" However, the message of the New Covenant is: "God **has sent** the Messiah, just as He promised through His prophets!" We thank God that the Bible has two sections—a First Covenant **and** a New Covenant, since in those two sections, we can see that what God promised so long ago, He has accomplished! God sent a Savior, Jesus Christ, just as He promised our ancestors in the Torah, the Psalms and the other writings of the prophets. As the rivers flow into the sea, so the Scriptures of the prophets find their fulfillment in Christ.

5.) Here's another question: **Many say that man cannot know whether he will go to heaven or to hell. God alone knows. But you say that you know that if you die today, you will go to heaven. On what do you base such a bold claim?**

Let us respond to that question with another question. **Can God go back on His word?** Is God faithful to keep His word? God's Word says:

> "*All the prophets testify about [the Lord Jesus Christ] that **everyone who believes in him receives forgiveness of sins** through His name.*" (Acts 10:43)
> "*I write these things to you who believe in the name of the Son of God **so that you may know that you have eternal life**.*" (1 John 5:13)

Since God Himself has said in His Word that you can know that you have eternal life, who are we to say that no one can know where he is going to spend eternity? Yes dear friend, **you can know** where you will go after death! The question is: Do you truly believe in the Lord Jesus Christ and His perfect sacrifice? Or are you trusting in your own "good works"? Only those trusting in Christ can honestly say, "I **know** that I have eternal life!"

6.) Thank you. This listener asks: **Jesus announced that the Counselor, the "Parakletos," would come after Him. Of whom did Jesus speak?**

"Parakletos" is a Greek word meaning *counselor, helper,* or *advocate.* In Scripture the name Parakletos is used both for Jesus (see 1 John 2:1) and for the Holy Spirit. As we have read in the Gospel, before the Lord Jesus returned to heaven He promised His disciples, saying:

> *"I will ask the Father, and he will give you* **another Counselor** *to be with you* **forever–the Spirit of truth**. *The world cannot accept him, because it neither sees him nor knows him. But you know him, for he lives* **with** *you and will be* **in** *you…* **the Counselor, the Holy Spirit**, *whom the Father will send* **in my name**, *will teach you all things and remind you of everything I have said to you.…He will convict the world of guilt in regard to sin…because men do not believe in me…" [Therefore] do not leave Jerusalem, but wait for* **the gift** *my Father promised, which you have heard me speak about. For John baptized with water, but in a few days you will be baptized with* **the Holy Spirit**." (John 14:16,17,26; 16:8,9; Acts 1:4,5).

The Lord Jesus said that the Counselor was **not a man**, but **a Spirit**—God's Holy Spirit—whom no one can see. Jesus told His disciples that after He returned to heaven, God would send the Holy Spirit down to live in their hearts. A few programs ago, we read how that is exactly what happened on the day of Pentecost, ten days after Jesus ascended to heaven.

In brief, the Counselor is the Spirit of Christ who comes to live in the hearts of all who accept the Gospel. If you sincerely believe, the Holy Spirit will cleanse and renew your heart, mark you as God's own child, and give you a share in God's holy presence forever. That is what the Scripture declares, saying:

> *"You…were included in Christ when you heard the word of truth, the gospel of your salvation. Having believed,* **you were marked in him with a seal, the promised Holy Spirit, who is a deposit guaranteeing our inheritance** *until the redemption of those who are God's possession–to the praise of his glory."* (Eph. 1:13,14)

For those of us who believe, the Holy Spirit is our helper, our guide, our strength, our teacher, and so much more. He does so many things for us that we cannot begin to mention them all. One way He helps us is in our prayers. There is a big difference between *reciting a prayer* and *truly praying to God!* The Holy Spirit helps us to pray true prayers to God. As it is written: "*The Spirit helps us in our weakness. We do not know what we ought to pray for, but the Spirit himself intercedes for us with groans that words cannot express.*" (Rom. 8:26) All who truly believe the Gospel of Jesus Christ have this heavenly Guest, the Holy Spirit living inside them. The Scripture says: ***"If anyone does not have the Spirit of Christ, he does not belong to Christ."*** (Rom. 8:9)

7.) The final questioner writes: **I understand from your teaching that I will go to Paradise if I receive Jesus Christ as my Savior. Does this mean I can live just as I please and do evil things and still go to Paradise when I die? What does the Bible teach?**

The Scripture answers this question clearly in the book of Romans, chapter six, when it says, "*Shall we go on sinning so that grace may increase? By no means! We died to sin; how can we live in it any longer?*" (Rom. 6:1,2) The message of the death of Jesus the Messiah on the cross and His resurrection from the grave is God's righteous plan **to deliver sinners** not only from **sin's penalty** but also from **sin's power**! If you accept that Good News in your heart with a sincere faith, the Word of God teaches that, in the instant you believe, God will accomplish two works in you:

First, God will forgive all your sins in the name of Christ, just as He has promised.

Second, God will renew your heart by the power of the Holy Spirit. Then you will begin to love righteousness and hate evil, because God will have placed in you His holy nature. Thus, the Scripture promises:

> "*If anyone is in Christ, he is a new creation; the old has gone, the new has come!*" (2 Cor. 5:17) "*Because…Christ…gave himself for us to redeem us* ***from all wickedness*** *and* ***to purify*** *for himself a people that are his very own,* ***eager to do what is good****!*" (Titus 2:14)

When someone truly believes in the Lord Jesus Christ, he will no longer continue to practice evil, because God has placed in him His ***Holy* Spirit**—and "*the fruit of the Spirit [in the life of the disciple of Christ] is love, joy, peace, patience, kindness, goodness, faithfulness, gentleness and self-control.*" (Gal. 5:22,23)

Our time is gone today, but, God willing, in the next program, we will look further into this question of how a follower of Christ should live.…God bless you. We leave you with this verse from the Psalms of the prophet David:

> ***"As for God, his way is perfect; the word of the LORD is flawless. He is a shield for all who take refuge in him!"*** (Psa. 18:30)

Lesson 92

How Should Christ's Disciples Live?

Peace be with you, listening friends. We greet you in the name of God, the Lord of peace, who wants everyone to understand and submit to the way of righteousness that He has established, and have true peace with Him forever. We are happy to be able to return today to present your program *The Way of Righteousness*.

As we promised in our last program, today we plan to look into **how those who follow Jesus Christ should live in order to please God**. The faith that a disciple of Christ has in his heart should be displayed in the way he (or she {neuter in Wolof}) thinks, in the way he talks, and in the way he acts–in his whole way of living.

Before we consider the way a disciple of Christ should live, let us review what makes a person a true disciple of Christ. As we have seen, the disciple of Christ is one who, first, admits that he is a sinner before God and that he has no hope of getting into Paradise by his own efforts. Second, he believes the plan announced by all of God's prophets–the plan by which God can forgive the sins of the children of Adam. That plan was the death of Jesus Christ on the cross. God delivered the sinless Redeemer over to death for our sins and raised Him to life so that He might judge us as righteous.

In summary, **the disciple of Jesus Christ is one who believes the Good News of Jesus the Messiah with all his heart** and knows for sure that all his sins have been forgiven, as God has promised in His Word. God adopts such a believer as His child. Thus it is written in the Gospel: To all who receive Jesus the Messiah and believe in His name is given "*the right* ***to become children of God****–children not born of natural descent...but born of God.*" (John 1:12,13) Dear friend, God wants you to know that if you become a child of God through faith in Christ and His sacrifice, you will never perish, and He will give you the right to live forever in His presence in Paradise!

Perhaps some would argue with this, saying: Ah, if entering Paradise is that easy for the disciple of Christ, then he can live as he pleases and commit sin as he pleases, without any fear of judgment, because God has forgiven him of all his sins already! Friends, this thought is **absurd**. Those who think this way do not yet know what sin is, nor do they know God the Holy One. Sin is a bad thing. Jesus Christ came **to deliver us** from the dominion of sin; He did not come to encourage us to continue in sin! Whoever believes in Christ is **no longer a slave of sin**. Truly, only those who belong to the devil can thoroughly enjoy sin. The person whom God saves and forgives has a changed heart. God washes his heart and makes it clean. The person for whom God has done this will avoid all uncleanness. That is what the Scriptures declare, saying: "*Therefore, if anyone is in Christ, he is a new creation; the old has gone, the new has come!*" (2 Cor. 5:17)

Tell us, if you are wearing a clean, white garment, will you sit or go where it is dirty? No, you will avoid anything that might stain your clothes. It is like that with everyone whom God has cleansed of his sins. You will no longer want to go along with anything that is not pleasing to God. You will **want** to please the Lord. If someone forgives you of a great debt of money, could you intentionally hurt him? No, you will do whatever you can to please him. Similarly, if the Lord God has forgiven you your great debt of sin and saved you from eternal punishment, should you not thank him and honor Him in thought and word and deed all your life long?

Listen to what the Gospel declares concerning those who belong to the Lord Jesus. It says:

> (Titus 3) [3]*At one time we too were foolish, disobedient, deceived and enslaved by all kinds of passions and pleasures. We lived in malice and envy, being hated and hating one another.* [4]*But when the kindness and love of God our Savior appeared,* [5]*he saved us, not because of righteous things we had done, but because of his mercy. He saved us through the washing of rebirth and renewal by the Holy Spirit,* [6]*whom he poured out on us generously through Jesus Christ our Savior,* [7]*so that, having been justified by his grace, we might become heirs having the hope of eternal life.* (1 Pet. 1) [14] *[Therefore] As obedient children, do not conform to the evil desires you had when you lived in ignorance.* [15]*But just as he who called you is holy, so be holy in all you do;* [16]*for it is written:* **"Be holy, because I am holy**."

How can we summarize the way of life of a disciple of Christ? Perhaps like this: God wants His children to show forth His character in their behavior here on earth. Simply put, **God wants His children to be like Him**. Well then, what is God like? In our studies in the Holy Scriptures we have seen that two prominent characteristics of God are **holiness** and **love**. God is the Holy One. He is also the God of Love. So what is His will for those of us who belong to Him? **He wants us to be holy as He is holy, and to love one another as He loves us.**

A holy life and a loving heart are what differentiates those who belong to God from those who do not. Concerning this, God's Word says:

(1 John 3) [10]*This is how we know who the children of God are and who the children of the devil are: Anyone who does not do what is right is not a child of God; nor is anyone who does not love his brother.* (Titus 2) [11]*For the grace of God that brings salvation has appeared to all men.* [12]***It teaches us to say "No" to ungodliness and worldly passions****, and to live self–controlled, upright and godly lives in this present age,* [13]*while we wait for the blessed hope–the glorious appearing of our great God and Savior, Jesus Christ,* [14]*who gave himself for us* ***to redeem us from all wickedness and to purify for himself a people that are his very own, eager to do what is good.***

(Eph. 4) [25]*Therefore each of you must* ***put off falsehood*** *and speak truthfully to his neighbor, for we are all members of one body.* [26]*"In your anger do not sin": Do not let the sun go down while you are still angry,* [27]*and do not give the devil a foothold.* [28]*He who has been stealing must* ***steal no longer****, but must work, doing something useful with his own hands, that he may have something to* ***share with those in need****.* [29]*Do not let any unwholesome talk come out of your mouths, but only what is helpful for building others up according to their needs, that it may benefit those who listen.* [30]*And* ***do not grieve the Holy Spirit of God****, with whom you were sealed for the day of redemption.* [31]***Get rid of all bitterness****, rage and anger, brawling and slander, along with every form of malice.* [32]*Be kind and compassionate to one another, forgiving each other, just as in Christ God forgave you.*

(Eph. 5) [1]***Be imitators of God****, therefore, as dearly loved children* [2]*and live a life of love, just as Christ loved us and gave himself up for us as a fragrant offering and sacrifice to God.* [3]*But among you there must* ***not be even a hint*** *of sexual immorality, or of any kind of impurity, or of greed, because these are improper for God's holy people.* [4]*Nor should there be obscenity, foolish talk or coarse joking, which are out of place, but rather thanksgiving.* 5*For of this you can be sure: No immoral, impure or greedy person–such a man is an idolater–has any inheritance in the kingdom of Christ and of God.* [8]*For you were once darkness, but now you are light in the Lord.* ***Live as children of light.*** (1 John 4) [7]*[Therefore] dear friends, let us love one another, for love comes from God. Everyone who loves has been born of God and knows God.* [20]*If anyone says, "I love God," yet hates his brother, he is a liar. For anyone who does not love his brother, whom he has seen, cannot love God, whom he has not seen.* [21]*And he has given us this command:* ***Whoever loves God must also love his brother.***

That is what the Scriptures say concerning the way of life for those who follow Jesus Christ. Does all this mean that the disciple of Christ can no longer sin, or that he always loves his neighbor as he loves himself? No! He still commits sin, but he no longer lingers in it. When he sins, he can put to use the promise in the Word of God that says: (1 John 1) [7]*...The blood of Jesus...purifies us from all* *sin.* [8]*If we claim to be without sin, we deceive ourselves and the truth is not in us.* [9]***If we confess our sins****, he is faithful and just and will forgive us our sins and purify us from all unrighteousness.* Amen.

Belonging to Jesus Christ is not just **a religion**—it is **a relationship**. When a person belongs to Christ, he is brought into **fellowship with the holy God of love.** That close relationship with God, which Adam and Eve lost because of their sin is restored to us through the blood which Jesus shed on the cross. God will no longer remember our transgressions because Jesus paid for us our debt of sin. Through our relationship with Christ, God is our heavenly Father, and we are His children. That is what the Scriptures speak of when they say: "*For through [Christ] we…have access to the Father by one Spirit. Consequently, you are* **no longer** ***foreigners*** *and aliens, but fellow–citizens with God's people and* **members of God's** ***household.***" (Eph. 2:18,19)

Those who belong to Christ can enjoy a close relationship with God on earth and look forward to an eternal inheritance in heaven. But one might ask, how can the disciple of Christ enjoy this relationship which he has with God on earth? How can we grow in our relationship with God? Concerning this, God's Word mentions **four responsibilities** (disciplines) which will help us know the will of God and live a life consistent with our position as children of God so that we might please Him in all things and increase in our knowledge of God.

1.) The first responsibility of the disciple of Christ is to **feed on the Word of God**—meditating on it daily and receiving it into his heart with a desire to obey it. The Holy Scriptures reveal God's will. God talks to us through His Word. God's Word is the food that nourishes and strengthens our spirit. It is wonderful food. Whoever really loves God should not need to be urged to read or listen to the Word of God, because he will hunger for it like he hungers for food. The prophet Job said, "*I have treasured [God's Word] more than my daily bread!*" (Job 23:12)

2.) The second responsibility is to **pray to God**, our Father who is in heaven. Whoever wants to grow in the relationship he has with God will want to talk to Him often. For the disciple of Christ, prayer is talking to God, as you would talk to your best friend. There is no specific time that we must pray. We can talk to our heavenly Father anytime of the day or night! There should not even be a moment when our minds are not conscious of God. He wants us to praise and thank Him continually for who He is and for all that He has done for us. He also invites us to tell Him about all our concerns. The disciple of Christ knows that prayer is powerful. The Lord Jesus Himself promised His disciples: "*You may ask me for anything in my name, and I will do it.*" (John 14:14) and: "*Do not be anxious about anything, but in everything, by prayer and petition, with thanksgiving, present your requests to God [your Father].*" (Phil. 4:6)

3.) The third responsibility is to **fellowship** with others who believe and love the Lord Jesus Christ. As a coal stays hot longer when left in the fire with other coals, so our fellowship with other believers will help us to live for Christ and to encourage others to do the same. God's Word says:

> *"Let us consider how we may spur one another on toward love and good deeds. Let us not give up meeting together, as some are in the habit of doing, but let us encourage one another–and all the more as you see the Day [of Christ's return] approaching."* (Heb. 10:24,25)

4.) The forth responsibility of Christ's disciples is to be **His witnesses**. Listen to what Jesus told His disciples before He ascended to heaven: "*This is what [the prophets have] written: The Christ will suffer and rise from the dead on the third day, and repentance and forgiveness of sins will be preached in his name to all nations...You are witnesses of these things.*" (Luke 24:46-48) Yes, Christ's disciples are to tell others about their Savior, explaining the Good News of Jesus Christ who died to give all who believe in Him a wonderful relationship with God forever. Of course, our witness should not be limited to mere words, but should be accompanied by a life of holiness and love. It is the change that Christ has made in our lives that will strengthen and confirm the message. For the Scripture says: "*The kingdom of God is not a matter of talk but of power!*" (1 Cor. 4:20)

You who are listening today, has there been a day in your life when you met the Savior, Jesus Christ, a day when He forgave your sins and renewed your heart? **Is your life full of the holiness and love of God?** Are you a true disciple of the Lord Jesus?

Thank you for listening....

God bless you as you consider what the Holy Scripture declares, saying:

> ***"God is light; in him there is no darkness at all. If we claim to have fellowship with him yet walk in the darkness, we lie and do not live by the truth."*** (1 John 1:5,6)

Lesson 93

Review #1
Adam, The Problem of Sin

Genesis 1- 4, etc.

Peace be with you, listening friends. We greet you in the name of God, the Lord of peace, who wants everyone to understand and submit to the way of righteousness that He has established, and have true peace with Him forever. We are happy to be able to return today to present your program *The Way of Righteousness*.

For a long time now we have been studying the Scriptures of the Prophets. We have seen that God inspired more than forty men (over a fifteen hundred year span) to write His Word–the Book that reveals the way of righteousness by which sinners can become righteous before God. We discovered that all the true prophets of God shared one idea and one message concerning that way of salvation. What they wrote did not flow from their own minds, but from the Spirit of God. With the help of God, **today and in the three coming broadcasts**, we plan to **review** and **condense** all that we have studied in the Holy Scriptures. Our lesson today is called: **"The Problem of Sin."**

Now let us return to **the foundation that God Himself laid**, the first part of God's Word, **the Torah**, which God put into the mind of Moses, His prophet. Can you remember the first verse? It says: ***"In the beginning God created the heavens and the earth."*** In this verse, we saw that, in the beginning, before the universe, angels and people were created, **only God existed.** God is the Lord of Eternity, the Eternal Spirit. He has no beginning and no end. He is the All-powerful One who sees everything and knows everything.

In the first chapter, we read how God, in six days, created the heavens, earth, oceans and all they contain. God prepared the earth for man, whom He planned to create. That is why, on the sixth day, God said,

> *"'Let us make man in our image, in our likeness, and let them rule over the fish of the sea and the birds of the air, over the livestock, over all the earth, and over*

> *all the creatures that move along the ground.' So God created man in his own image...*" (Gen. 1:26,27)

Man is **the most important of all the creatures** that God created. God created man in His image! God planned to have deep and wonderful fellowship with man. That is why He placed in the soul of the man and the woman a **spirit** so that they could know God, gave them a **heart** so that they could love God, and entrusted them with a **free will** so that they could choose between obeying God and disobeying God.

In chapter two, we read that God put the first man, Adam, in a lush garden, full of trees bearing fruits beautiful to behold, and delicious to eat. We also saw that God fashioned a woman out of a rib which He took from Adam and then presented her to him. Adam called her Eve. God blessed the man and woman and gave them everything they needed. Yet there was something God wanted to receive from them. What did God want from these two people He had created in His own image? He wanted them **to love Him** with all their mind, all their heart, and all their will, and thus to have a deep and wonderful relationship with Him forever. Consequently, we saw how God placed **a test** before them in order to reveal what was in their hearts. God gave Adam this command: "*You are free to eat from any tree in the garden; but you must not eat from the tree of the knowledge of good and evil, for [in the day that] you eat of it* ***you will surely die****!*" (Gen. 2:16,17) Thus God tested Adam, warning him that the consequence of straying from God's law would be death, that is, **separation from God forever**.

In chapter three, the Scriptures recount that one day, Satan, the angel who had rebelled against God, came to Adam and Eve as a cunning snake. He said to the woman,

> "*Did God really say, 'You must not eat from any tree in the garden'? The woman said to the serpent, "We may eat fruit from the trees in the garden, but God did say, 'You must not eat fruit from the tree that is in the middle of the garden, and you must not touch it, or you will die.'" The serpent said to the woman, "You will not surely die. For God knows that when you eat of it your eyes will be opened, and you will be like God, knowing good and evil.*" (Gen. 3:1-5)

What did God tell Adam and Eve would happen to them if they ate of the tree which He had prohibited? He said to them, "You will **die**!" What did Satan say? He said, "You will **not** die!" Whose word did Adam and Eve choose to believe and follow? Did they choose the word of God, or the word of Satan? **They chose the word of Satan, God's enemy!**

After that, what did God do? Did He just sit back and watch Adam and Eve? No. God did exactly what He warned them He would do. He summoned them, judged them, cursed them and the earth, then put them outside the lovely garden that He had created for them. On that sad day, Adam and Eve died in their souls. They became **separated from God**, the source of life. The only thing they could expect now was physical death and eternal punishment, because the payment for sin is eternal death, just as God said.

Truly, sin is a terrible calamity. Adam and all his descendants were separated from God by a single sin! Sin is somewhat like the disease called AIDS. As you know, AIDS is a sickness that people spread among themselves. It is a calamity that is all over the world. Once the AIDS virus enters a person's body, it will never leave him. Those who have AIDS can spread it to their children. AIDS is a killer, destroying all who have it. **Sin** is like that. Sin is everywhere, in everyone, and causes people to perish forever. But thank God, there is a difference between the disease of sin and the disease of AIDS. With AIDS, there is not yet a medicine to cure it, but there is **a cure** for people contaminated by sin! God Himself has provided a remedy, which, if we use it, will cleanse us from sin forever.

Can you remember **the wonderful promise** which God gave on the day that Adam and Eve sinned? Yes, on the same day that sin entered the world, God promised that He would send to the earth a holy Redeemer, who would redeem the children of Adam from the destructive power of Satan and sin. We also read that God announced that this Redeemer would be born uniquely of a virgin woman, because the Savior of sinners could not come from the descendants of Adam who were now contaminated by sin. He must come from the pure and holy Spirit of God.

Thus we saw in the Gospel {*Injil*} that thousands of years after God promised to send down that Savior, when God's appointed time had come, a perfectly righteous Man was born into the world; He had no earthly father; He was born of a virgin. His name was **Jesus**, which means *God saves*. Yes, Jesus Christ is the holy Redeemer whom God promised on the day that Adam and Eve sinned. He is the one and only Savior.

Let us now return to our review of what happened on the day that sin entered the world. Can you remember what Adam and Eve did after they had eaten of the tree of the knowledge of good and evil? They wove together fig leaves, tying them to their waists in an attempt to hide their shame, because before they sinned they were naked but were not ashamed. Did God accept the clothes which they had made for themselves? No! Why did God not accept those clothes? He wanted to teach them that there is nothing that man can do to cover the shame of his sin before God! However, God did something for Adam and Eve. We saw how God selected some innocent animals, slaughtered them, skinned them, and made clothes for Adam and Eve, putting them on them. In this way God taught Adam and Eve that **the payment for sin is death**! God not only sacrificed animals, but He commanded Adam and his descendants also to sacrifice animals without blemish as a sacrifice to cover sin, until the time when God would send down the Redeemer.

Thus God showed them clearly that there is **only one way of salvation: the way of the spotless sacrifice**. The way of righteousness which God decreed commanded that one must choose animals without blemish and slaughter them as sacrifices which cover sin. These sacrifices **illustrated the holy Redeemer**, who would come and shed His blood on a cross to pay the debt of sin for Adam's descendants. Thus, by those animal sacrifices, God put before sinners a shadow of Jesus the Messiah who would die as the perfect sacrifice to take away sin. In this way, God demonstrated that He is righteous, "*so as to be just and the one who justifies those who have faith in Jesus.*" (Rom. 3:26)

In the chapter following the story of Adam's sin and God's wonderful promise to send a Redeemer, we read about Adam's first two children, Cain and Abel. We saw that Abel offered to God a lamb without blemish and slaughtered it as a sacrifice which covers sin, just as God had commanded. Cain tried to approach God by his own efforts, bringing to God what he had cultivated in the cursed earth. Thus, the Scripture says: "*the* LORD *[God] looked with favor on Abel and his offering, but on Cain and his offering he did not look with favor.*" (Gen. 4:4,5) Why did God not accept Cain's sacrifice? As we have seen, the way of righteousness which God decreed declared that "***without the shedding of blood there is no forgiveness of sin.***" (Heb. 9:22) However, Cain disregarded the way of sacrifice which God had appointed. Cain pretended to believe God, but his deeds denied it, because he did not offer the blood sacrifice that God required. That is why God rejected Cain and his sacrifice. However, God looked with favor on the sacrifice of Abel, forgiving him all his sins, because Abel believed God's word and brought to Him the blood of a lamb.

Abel illustrates those whom God judges as righteous because of their faith in the Messiah, Jesus, who shed His blood to pay for sins. Cain illustrates those who try to be righteous before God by their own efforts, refusing to accept the sacrifice of the Redeemer, whom God sent from heaven. To this day, there are only these **two ways**: the way of Abel and the way of Cain. Which way are you following? Have you accepted the way of Abel, that is, **the way of righteousness**, which is founded on the sacrifice of the holy Messiah whom God sent down? Or are you still going the way of Cain, **the way of unrighteousness**, which is based on the works of man and the requirements of religion?

Fellow listeners, please know that **God is righteous** and cannot tolerate sin! God could not say to Adam and Eve, Cain and Abel, and all their descendants: "I know you've sinned, but that's O.K.! It's no big deal, I'll simply forget that you ever sinned!" Could God forgive sins like that? Never! If God did that how would sinners recognize His holiness? God is a righteous Judge and must punish sin.

The penalty for sin is death! That is why the holy Redeemer had to die for our sins. When He died on the cross He paid the penalty for my sins and yours.

Listen to what is written in the Gospel concerning **the way of righteousness** which God has ordained. The Scripture says:

> *"Just as sin entered the world through* **one man**, *and death through sin, and in this way death came to* **all men**, *because all sinned."* (Rom. 5:12) *"There is no difference, for* ***all have sinned and fall short of the glory of God***, *and are* ***justified freely by [God's] grace through the redemption that came by*** **Christ Jesus**. *God presented him as a sacrifice of atonement, through faith in his blood. He did this to demonstrate his justice, because in his forbearance he had left the sins committed beforehand unpunished–he did it to demonstrate his justice at the present time, so as to be just and the one who justifies those who have faith in Jesus."* (Rom. 3:22-26) *"For the* ***wages of sin*** *is* ***death***, *but the* ***gift of God*** *is* ***eternal life*** *in Christ Jesus our Lord."* (Rom. 6:23)

Thank you for listening. In our next lesson, God willing, we will continue to review the message of the prophets and recall how God called Abraham to be part of His wonderful plan to send the Savior into the world....

God bless you as you meditate on this statement from God's Word that can transform your life:

> ***"The wages of sin is death, but the gift of God is eternal life in Christ Jesus our Lord."*** (Rom. 6:23)

Lesson 94

Review #2
Abraham, Righteous by Faith

Genesis 6-22, etc.

Peace be with you, listening friends. We greet you in the name of God, the Lord of peace, who wants everyone to understand and submit to the way of righteousness that He has established, and have true peace with Him forever. We are happy to be able to return today to present your program *The Way of Righteousness*.

Today we continue our **review** of the message of God's prophets. The message of the prophets is a story…**God's Story**…God's wonderful story about what He has done to seek and to save the children of Adam who are lost in sin. In short, **the message of God's prophets is the Good News about how unrighteous people can be made righteous before God**. Our review lesson today is entitled: **"Righteous by Faith."**

Like every story, the story contained in God's book has a beginning and an end. In our last study, we reviewed the beginning of the story and saw how the first person, Adam, chose to follow Satan, the enemy of God. Adam's one sin caused all his descendants to be born in sin, on the path to hell. Some try to deny this, saying: "Adam's sin was his own problem! It doesn't affect us!" But those who say this ignore the Scriptures of the Prophets which declare: "***Sin entered the world through one man***, *and death through sin, and in this way death came to all men, because all sinned!*" (Rom. 5:12)

The Wolofs say: "An epidemic's effects are not confined to the one who caused it!" Similarly, the curse of Adam's sin did not stop with him alone, but spread to us all, like a contagious disease. Adam's original sin is the reason that all men are born with a sinful nature. "A rat only begets that which digs." {Wolof proverb}. Similarly, we have all inherited the nature of our forefather Adam. What is absolutely certain is that the sinful nature which is in us will condemn us forever–unless God provides a remedy for us. The good news is that the LORD God has provided **a remedy**. As we read in the Torah, on the same day that Adam and Eve sinned, God, in His mercy, made a promise. He promised to send down to earth a righteous Redeemer, who would be born of a virgin. This Redeemer would shed His blood as a sacrifice that would pay the debt of the sins of the children of Adam.

In our study in the book of the Gospel {*Injil*}, we saw that when God's appointed time had come, God sent down the One whom He had promised. Who is this Savior that God promised? He is the perfectly righteous Man, **Jesus Christ.** Listen to how the Word of God shows the difference between Adam who sinned and Christ who did not sin. The Scripture says:

> "*For if, by the trespass of the one man,* **death** *reigned through that one man, how much more will those who receive God's abundant provision of grace…reign in* ***life*** *through the one man, Jesus Christ. Consequently, just as the result of one trespass was* ***condemnation for all men****, so also the result of one act of righteousness was* ***justification that brings life for all men.*** *For just as through the disobedience of the one man the many were made* ***sinners****, so also through the obedience of the one man the many will be made* ***righteous***." (Rom. 5:17-19)

That is what the Scripture says concerning those who are **in Adam** and those who are **in Jesus Christ**.

We are all **born** in the likeness of Adam. But God is calling the children of Adam to be **born again** in their hearts, to put off the **likeness of Adam**, and to take on the **likeness of Christ**! How can this happen? It can only happen **by faith**! The Scripture says that if you believe in your heart that the Lord Jesus Christ paid for your sin, God will cause you to be born again by cleansing your heart and renewing you by the power of His Holy Spirit. You will become a new creation in Christ; you will no longer live for yourself, but for Him who died and rose again for you.

Now let us return to the Torah, and continue our review by recalling how God moved forward with **His plan** to send the Redeemer into the world. In our chronological lessons we saw the two first sons of Adam, Cain and Abel. Abel believed what God promised concerning the Redeemer, who would come to shed His blood as a sacrifice, but Cain did not believe it. God called Cain to give account so that he might repent, but Cain only got angry and killed Abel, his younger brother.

After that, we saw that most of the children of Adam followed in the footsteps of Cain, reveling in sin, which is why when we come to the time of Noah, the Scripture says: "*The* LORD *saw how great man's wickedness on the earth had become, and that every inclination of* ***the thoughts of his heart was only evil all the time***." (Gen. 6:5) We saw how God purposed to destroy the children of Adam with a flood. In that corrupt and crooked time, Noah was the only one who believed what God had promised concerning the coming Redeemer. Consequently, God commanded Noah to build a great ark, which would be a refuge for his family and many animals. For one hundred years God patiently endured sinners while Noah was building the ark. However, no one repented and believed God's word except Noah and his family. Thus in the end, God, who is faithful to His word, did everything He promised, wiping out all those who refused to enter the ark of refuge which He had provided for them.

After that, we saw that Noah's offspring gradually forgot the Word of God, because they too were children of Adam and sinners by nature. Then we read about the tower of Babel and how people tried to gather the peoples of the world to one place and to build a great city and a high tower in rebellion against God. However, God judged them by confusing their language and scattering them over the face of the whole earth.

Next, we came to the wonderful story of **the prophet Abraham**. Truly, Abraham had a very important place in God's plan to redeem the children of Adam from the dominion of sin. Abraham's father was an idol worshiper, and Abraham himself was a sinner, like all of Adam's descendants. However, we saw that God, in His wonderful design, appeared to Abraham and ordered him to move out of his father's house and to leave his country. God planned to make of Abraham a new nation, through which the holy Redeemer would come into the world. That is what we read in the Torah, in the book of Genesis, chapter twelve, when God called Abraham, saying to him,

> *"Leave your country, your people and your father's household and go to the land I will show you. I will make you into a great nation and I will bless you; I will make your name great, and you will be a blessing. I will bless those who bless you, and whoever curses you I will curse; and* ***all peoples on earth will be blessed through you****."* (Gen. 12:1-3)

Why did God command Abraham to move to another land? God wanted to make of him **a new nation**. **Why did God want to make of Abraham a new nation?** Through that nation, God planned to raise up the prophets who would write the Holy Scriptures. And through that same nation, God intended to send **the Redeemer** into the world. That is why God promised Abraham, saying, *"You will be a blessing...and all peoples on earth will be blessed through you."*

Did God fulfil what He promised to Abraham? Yes, He did! When Abraham was one hundred years old, and Sarah, his wife, was ninety years old, God gave them a son, Isaac, just as He had promised. Isaac had a son, Jacob, who had the twelve sons who formed the new nation of **Israel**. Those of you who know the Holy Scriptures, know that it was through the nation of Israel that the Redeemer came because Mary (Jesus' mother) and Joseph (Jesus' adoptive father/guardian) were both descendants of Abraham. Thus, the first verse in the Gospel says: "*A record of the genealogy of Jesus Christ the son of David,* ***the son of Abraham****.*" (Matt. 1:1) Concerning His earthly form–Jesus Christ came through the descendants of Abraham, Isaac and Jacob. But concerning His holy soul–He is the Son of the Most High, the very Word of God {*Kalimat Allah*} who came from heaven to be born upon earth.

However, let us return to the story of Abraham, because there is something else important to remember about him. We saw that Abraham was born in sin, like all the children of Adam. However, the Holy Scriptures tell us that today Abraham is in heaven, in the presence of God the Holy One, where he will be forever! Now we ask: **What did Abraham do for God to forgive him of his sins, judge him as righteous, and welcome him into heaven?** What does the Scripture say about this? It says: "*[Abraham]* ***believed*** *the LORD, and he credited it to him as* ***righteousness****.*" (Gen. 15:6)

Abraham believed **God**–God Himself. Abraham believed **what God said to him**. That is why God credited him with righteousness, counting him as righteous. You who are listening today, **do you believe the Word of God as Abraham believed it?** We are not asking if you believe that God exists, or whether God is One. The devil himself knows that God exists! What God wants is that you believe **what He says** concerning the way of salvation which He decreed, as Abraham believed it! Abraham told us what we must believe. Can you remember what Abraham announced on that distinguished mountain, the day he offered the sheep in place of his son? He said that "*God himself will provide the lamb for the burnt offering.*" (Gen. 22:8) And after he had slaughtered the sheep, he called that mountain *Jehovah Jireh* which means *the Lord will provide*. (Gen. 22:14) Why did Abraham name that mountain "*The Lord* ***will*** *provide,*" when God had already provided the sacrificial sheep? Abraham, as a prophet, was announcing what was yet to happen. When Abraham said, "*The Lord* ***will*** *provide,*" he was predicting what would happen on that mountain where the sheep replaced his son on the altar. He was looking ahead to the day when the Redeemer would shed His blood on that same mountain—**to save all who believe in Him** from God's righteous judgment.

In our study in the Gospel, we saw that Jesus Christ came into the world about two thousand years after the time of Abraham in order to fulfill Abraham's prophecy. Yes, outside Jerusalem, on the mountain where Abraham sacrificed the sheep in place of his son, there the Redeemer, Jesus, shed His blood to redeem the children of Adam. That is why, after they had nailed Jesus to the cross, before He died, we heard Him speak with a loud voice, saying, "***It is finished!***" The word *finished* means *completed.* Why did Jesus say "It is completed!"? He said that because **His death on the cross completed the plan of salvation**, which God had announced a long time previously through His prophets. **Jesus' death completed and fulfilled the symbolism of Abraham's sacrifice and of all animal sacrifices!**

You who are listening today, do you believe that Jesus Christ Himself is the perfect and final sacrificial {*Id al-Adha*} "sheep," whom God sent from heaven? **Do you possess the faith of Abraham?** Listen to what the Gospel says concerning Abraham's faith:

> (Rom. 4) [1]*What then shall we say that Abraham...discovered in this matter?* [2]*If, in fact, Abraham was justified by works, he had something to boast about–but not before God.* [3]*What does the Scripture say?* ***"Abraham believed God, and it was credited to him as righteousness."***... [22]*This is why "it was credited to him as righteousness."* [23]*The words "it was credited to him" were written* **not for him alone**, [24]**but also for us**, *to whom God will credit righteousness–***for us who believe** *in him who raised Jesus our Lord from the dead.* [25]*He was delivered over to death* **for our sins** *and was raised to life* **for our justification**. Amen!

Thank you for listening. We hope you will join us again for the next program. God willing, we will continue our review of the message of the prophets and see another great prophet whom God selected to prepare the way for the coming of the Savior of the world. That prophet is Moses....

May God bless you and give you a clear understanding of what the Scripture declares, saying:

> ***"Abraham believed God, and it was credited to him as righteousness."*** (Rom. 4:3)

LESSON 95

REVIEW #3
MOSES, GOD'S HOLY LAW

EXODUS 1-20, ETC.

Peace be with you, listening friends. We greet you in the name of God, the Lord of peace, who wants everyone to understand and submit to the way of righteousness that He has established, and have true peace with Him forever. We are happy to be able to return today to present your program *The Way of Righteousness*.

Today we plan to continue our **review** of the message of the prophets, the Good News which shows how sinners can become righteous before God. We are still reviewing the Torah, the book which God placed in the mind of His prophet, Moses. As we have seen, the Torah of Moses is of great value to all who desire to know the truth; it is the foundation which God established so that we might verify everything we hear to know whether or not it comes from God.

In the beginning of the Torah, we saw how our ancestor **Adam** sinned. His **sin spread** to all his descendants like a contagious disease, bringing sorrow, death and eternal punishment, as the LORD God had forewarned. But we thank God that the Scripture says: "*Where sin increased, [God's] grace increased all the more*." (Rom. 5:20) Yes, on the very day Adam and Eve sinned, God, in His grace, announced that He would one day send into the world **a Redeemer**, to redeem the children of Adam from the curse that sin brought.

In the last review lesson, we saw that God called **Abraham**, promising to make of him **a new nation** from which all the prophets and the Redeemer would arise. Thus Abraham had a son, Isaac, who had a son, Jacob, who had twelve sons from whom came the twelve tribes of **Israel**.

Now let us continue our review to see how God used Abraham's descendants, the Israelites, to teach mankind what the LORD God is like and which path sinners must take to escape God's righteous judgment. Our lesson today is called **"God's Holy Law."**

In our study in the Torah, we saw that God allowed the children of Israel to become slaves in the land of Egypt for four hundred years, as He had made known to Abraham long beforehand. When the time appointed by God arrived, He sent **Moses** to the Israelites. Moses was an Israelite who had grown up in the house of Pharaoh, the wicked king of Egypt.

God sent Moses to Pharaoh to say to him, "The LORD God says: '**Let my people go** that they may worship me!'" But Pharaoh refused and mocked, saying, "Who is the LORD? I will never let the people of Israel go!" Thus, God made His power and glory known to Pharaoh and the Egyptians by means of nine terrible plagues which fell on all the people of the land except the Israelites. However, the signs and wonders which God did before Pharaoh did not cause him to repent and obey the word of Moses. God said to Moses, "I will bring one more plague on Pharaoh and on Egypt. After that, he will let you go!" Do you remember what that plague was? Yes, it was **the death of the firstborn** in every household.

Thus, we saw that God killed the firstborn in the house of Pharaoh and in all the houses of Egypt. But He delivered the firstborn of the Israelites, because of **the blood of the lamb** which they, in obedience to God's command, had stained over the doors of their houses. God Himself had promised: "*The blood will be a sign for you on the houses where you are; and* ***when I see the blood, I will pass over you****. No destructive plague will touch you!*" (Exod. 12:10) Thus, because of the blood of the lamb, God passed over the houses of the Israelites, not killing their firstborn. This is how God saved the Israelites from the hand of Pharaoh.

As we have seen, the story of Passover day has **a deeper meaning** than the deliverance of the children of Israel from Pharaoh's dominion. For the Scripture says: "*These things happened to them as [illustrations]...for us, on whom the fulfillment of the ages has come.*" (1 Cor. 10:11) The story of the blood of the lamb which the Israelites stained over the doors of their houses so that God would spare their firstborns from death and deliver them from Pharaoh is an illustration. It **illustrates the way of salvation** established by God to save sinners from Satan, the taskmaster who is more wicked than Pharaoh.

The Word of God shows us that all the children of Adam are like **slaves**. Perhaps some of you are thinking, "Yes, we know that we are slaves of God!" But that thought does not agree with what the Lord Jesus declared in the Gospel {*Injil*}, saying, "*I tell you the truth, everyone who sins is* ***a slave to sin***." (John 8:34) And since all the children of Adam are slaves of sin, they are also slaves of Satan because Satan is the master of sin. What is absolutely certain is that whoever is Satan's slave has no way to free himself! Can a slave free himself? Can he give something to his master so that he will allow him to go free? That might work with a good master, but it will not work with a master like Satan. Like Pharaoh, Satan will never willingly allow his slaves to go free! Never! Oh, how we, the children of Adam, are cursed! Is there anyone who can deliver us from the dominion of Satan who has made us his slaves? Yes, praise be to God, **there is a Deliverer**! God has sent to us One who can liberate us! That One is the powerful and righteous Savior, Jesus the Messiah, who came from heaven, of whom all God's prophets bear witness.

In the **Torah**, we read how God promised to crush the head of Satan through the holy Redeemer who would be born of a virgin. In the **Psalms**, we heard how the prophet David wrote that this Redeemer, whom God calls His Son, would be put to death in a terrible way–that He would be tortured and that His hands and His feet would be pierced! In the book of the **Gospel**, we read much about this wonderful Redeemer. He is Jesus, the son of Mary, who lived a perfect life and then died on the cross for our sins and rose again from the tomb. Yes, Jesus is the One who fulfilled what God's prophets had written long beforehand about the Savior of sinners.

God's Word calls Jesus Christ **"the Lamb of God."** Like the lambs slaughtered on the day of the Passover–Jesus shed His blood to save us from judgment. Approximately one thousand five hundred years after God delivered the Israelites by the blood of a lamb at the first Passover, God allowed the sons of Adam to nail Jesus, the Righteous Messiah, to a cross. And it was on the day of the Passover feast that He was nailed to the cross. Thus, just as Jesus fulfilled the symbolism of Abraham's sacrifice {*Id al-Adha*}, so also, **Jesus fulfilled the symbolism of the Passover lamb.** The people who crucified Him on that day were acting in ignorance, but God had planned the sacrifice of the Messiah before He created the world. (See Revelation 13:8; Acts 3:17)

Jesus is the perfect and final Sacrifice for sin. The **blood of Jesus Christ is the legal price** that God required to redeem the children of Adam from the dominion of sin. Accordingly the Scriptures declare:

> "*Christ, our Passover lamb, has been sacrificed [for us].*" (1 Cor. 5:7) "*You see, at just the right time, when we were still powerless, Christ died for the ungodly. Very rarely will anyone die for a righteous man, though for a good man someone might possibly dare to die. But God demonstrates his own love for us in this: While we were still sinners, Christ died for us!*" (Rom 5:6-8)

Leaving the story of the Passover, let us now remember what we learned concerning the holy law, which God entrusted to the Israelites. In our research in the Torah, we saw how God revealed His holiness and glory to Moses and the Israelites in the wilderness, descending upon Mount Sinai in fire and thunder and lightning. Thus God passed on to the Israelites His Ten Commandments and many other commands, which is called *the Law of Moses*. God commanded them, saying: "**You shall love the Lord your God with all your heart, with all your soul, and with all your mind:** You shall have no other gods before me! You shall not make for yourself idols! You shall not misuse the name of the LORD your God! Remember the Sabbath day by keeping it holy! **You shall love your neighbor as you love yourself:** Honor your father and your mother! You shall not murder! You shall not commit adultery! You shall not steal! You shall not give false testimony against your neighbor! You shall not covet your neighbor's possessions!" And to these holy commandments, God added these words: "*Whoever keeps the whole law and yet stumbles at just* ***one point*** *is guilty of breaking all of it!*" (James 2:10) "*Cursed is everyone who does not continue to do* ***everything*** *written in the Book of the Law!*" (Gal. 3:10) That is what the holy law which God committed to Moses declares!

Listening friend, **have you kept this holy law of God which requires you to be absolutely perfect in thought and word and deed–from the day of your birth until the day of your death**? Every day and every hour, night and day, you must love the Lord your God with **all** your heart, **all** your soul, and **all** your mind. Also, you must love your neighbor **as you love yourself**! Have you fulfilled this holy law? You and I know that **we have not fulfilled it!** The Scripture says: "*There is no one righteous, not even one!*" (Rom. 3:10) "*If we claim to be without sin, we deceive ourselves and the truth is not in us.*" (1 John 1:8) None of us have ever fulfilled everything that God requires, because we were all born with a sinful nature.

Perhaps some would ask: If none of us can fulfil the law of Moses, why then did God give it to us? Is God Someone who wants everyone to perish? No. God is Love, and does not want anyone to perish! Then why did God give sinners His holy commandments, when He knew perfectly well that no one could keep them? What is the purpose of those commandments? God has answered that question when He says:

> "*No one will be declared righteous in [God's] sight by observing the law; rather,* ***through the law we become conscious of sin***." (Rom. 3:20) "*[The Law] declares that the whole world is a prisoner of sin, so that what was promised, being given through faith in Jesus Christ, might be given to those who believe.*" (Gal. 3:22)

Thus we discover that God entrusted His holy commandments to sinners, to show us our imperfection before Him, and to show us our need for Jesus Christ who bore for us the curse that sin brought. Among men, **the Lord Jesus Christ is the only One who kept the holy law** which God entrusted to Moses. As we have seen, Jesus was very different from the descendants of Adam, because He did not share their sinful nature. Jesus is the Eternal Word of God, who came down from heaven, to be born of a virgin. Jesus took on a body like ours, but did not take on our evil nature. That is why, when He was on earth, He could say: "*Do not think* *that I have come to abolish the Law or the Prophets; I have not come to abolish them but* ***to fulfil*** *them.*" (Matt. 5:17) Did you hear what Jesus said? It is a very deep and wonderful truth. Jesus said that He came into the world to **fulfil** the holy law which God entrusted to Moses! Do you understand what this means? **Jesus did for us what we, the children of Adam, could never do for ourselves!** He ful**filled God's holy law**, and after that, He shed His blood on the cross to **bear the curse of the law for us** and to save us from God's righteous judgment!

Jesus did not deserve to die, because He had never sinned. However, to complete the plan of salvation which God had promised through the prophets, the Lord Jesus, of His own will, gave His life for us. And after He shed His blood to pay our debt of sin, God raised Him from the dead on the third day! Listen to what the Holy Scripture declares concerning this. It says:

> "*[The holy law of God* ***cannot condemn]*** *those who are* ***in Christ Jesus****!...For what the law was powerless to do in that it was weakened by the sinful nature, God did by sending his own Son in the likeness of sinful man to be a sin offering. And so he condemned sin in sinful man.*" (Rom. 8:1,3)

Listening friend, on what are you hanging your hope? Are you relying on the Good News of God about the Righteous Redeemer who bore the punishment for your sins? Or are you are still relying on your own "good" works? Do not forget what the Word of God declares, when it says:

> "*All who rely on observing the law are under a curse, for it is written: 'Cursed is everyone who does not continue* ***to do everything*** *written in the Book of the Law.' [However, Jesus] Christ* ***redeemed us*** *from the curse of the law by becoming a curse for us...so that* ***whoever believes*** *in him shall not perish but have eternal life!*" (Gal. 3:10,13; John 3:16)

Thank you for listening....

In the coming study, God willing, we will complete our review of the Scriptures of the Prophets and see how Jesus the Messiah fulfilled everything which the prophets prophesied concerning Him, thus opening a door of salvation and peace for the children of Adam!

May God give you insight into what we have studied today and help you remember this promise from His Word:

> ***"[The holy law of God cannot condemn] those who are in Christ Jesus!"*** (Rom. 8:1)

LESSON 96

REVIEW #4
JESUS CHRIST, "IT IS FINISHED!"

JOHN 19, HEBREWS 10

Peace be with you, listening friends. We greet you in the name of God, the Lord of peace, who wants everyone to understand and submit to the way of righteousness that He has established, and have true peace with Him forever. We are happy to be able to return today to present your program *The Way of Righteousness*.

Three programs ago we began to review the message of the prophets of God. Today, with God's help, we plan to **conclude our review**. Our program today is entitled: **"It is finished!"**

As we have seen, God has divided His book into **two important sections**, the Old Covenant, and the New Covenant. **The Old Covenant** is the first section of God's wonderful Book. It contains the Torah {*Taurat*}, the Psalms {*Zabur*} and the other writings of the prophets. We saw in this first section of God's Book how our ancestor, Adam, disobeyed God, thus bringing all his descendants into the kingdom of Satan. However, we also learned that God promised to send down to the children of Adam a powerful Savior, to redeem those who believe and bring them back into the kingdom of God. This wonderful promise was an important part of the Old Covenant (agreement).

To set in motion His plan to send down the Savior, God called Abraham in his old age and said to him, *"I will make you into a great nation…and all peoples on earth will be blessed through you."* (Gen. 12:2,3) Thus we saw how God made Abraham the father of the nation of Israel. It was to that nation that God entrusted the Writings of the Prophets. For fifteen hundred years, God sent the Israelites His word, which He placed in the minds of many different men–from the prophet Moses to the prophet John. Through these prophets, God reproved the unrighteousness of the children of Adam and revealed to them the coming of the righteous Redeemer who would pour out His blood to pay their debt of sin.

As we have seen, the Old Covenant, which God established with sinners, required the sacrifice of animals. It declared that "without the shedding of blood there is no forgiveness of sin–because **the payment of sin is death**!" But the sacrifice of animals, which people carried out from the very first generation, could not really pay for sin, because the **value of an animal** and the **value of man** are unequal. For example, if I have a toy car, can I go to the car dealer, and exchange it for a real car, let's say, a Mercedes? Of course not! Why not? Because the value of my toy car is not equal to the value of a real car! Similarly, the sacrifice of animals, which God required in early generations, could not remove sin, because the value of an animal and the value of a man are unequal. As we have seen, animal sacrifices were only illustrations (symbols)–awaiting the time when God would send down the actual sacrifice: the Righteous Redeemer, who brought the New Covenant. Animal sacrifice could only cover sins for a time; they could not remove sins permanently.

The second part of God's Book is called **the New Covenant** or the Gospel {*Injil*}. It tells us about the covenant (agreement) which God established with man through the blood of the Redeemer who came from heaven. The book of the Gospel is the story of **Jesus** the Redeemer who **fulfilled the symbolism of all the animal sacrifices** when He shed his blood on the cross, so that we might receive forgiveness of sins. Why did the Redeemer have to come from heaven? Simply because every descendant of Adam bears the burden of sin. **A sinner cannot redeem a sinner**. To illustrate, can a woman who is carrying a basin of water on her head carry on her head a basin for someone else too? No. Similarly, a sinner cannot bear sin's punishment for another sinner. However, the Redeemer, Jesus Christ, whom God sent down, did not carry any burden of sin, because He was the pure Spirit Son of God, the Word that was with God in the beginning. He was born of a virgin. Thus, He had a body like ours, but He did not have our evil nature. He did not have the burden of sin upon Him. That is why God could place on Him the sin burden of us all. Jesus the Holy One died for our transgressions. Then three days later, He rose from the dead to give us new life. He overcame death, the grave, Satan and sin!

We have all been born in the deep pit of sin, and there is no one who can come to our rescue, except the Messiah who came from above. If you put your trust in Him, He will pull you out of the pit of sin. He came from heaven to rescue the children of Adam from their sins. And now He has returned to heaven, to mediate for those who believe in Him. That is what the Scripture says:

> *"There is one God and one Mediator between God and men, the man Christ Jesus, who gave himself as a ransom for all men!"* (1 Tim. 2:5,6) *"Such a high priest meets our need–one who is holy, blameless, pure, set apart from sinners...After he had provided purification for sins, he sat down at the right hand of the Majesty in heaven!"* (Heb. 7:26; 1:3)

As we saw in the Gospel, when Jesus the Messiah was on earth, some believed in Him. Those who recognized who Jesus was rejoiced greatly. They knew that for thousands of years God's prophets had been announcing the coming of the Messiah; now they were seeing Him with their own eyes! Among Jesus' disciples, we heard those who sought their relatives and friends, telling them, "***We have found the Messiah!...We have found the one Moses wrote about in the Law, and about whom the prophets also wrote!***" (John 1:41,45)

Tragically, most people living in Jesus' day **did not know who He really was.** Accordingly, the Scripture declares:

> "*The Word which was with God in the beginning...became flesh and made his dwelling among us....The light shines in the darkness, but the darkness has not understood it....He was in the world, and though the world was made through him, the world did not recognize him. He came to that which was his own, but his own did not receive him!*" (John 1:2,14,5,10,11)

As we have seen, many people witnessed the signs and miracles which the Messiah did. Jesus overcame diseases, storms, demons, sin and death, yet most people did not recognize who Jesus was because Satan had blinded their minds. The crowds touched Him and pressed in on Him but did not really know Him! They considered Him a prophet among the prophets, but they did not believe that all the fullness of God dwelt in Him.

As for the religious leaders of the Jews, we saw that they utterly rejected Jesus. They were extremely jealous of Him and, in the end, they killed Him by having Him nailed to a cross! But that is how God planned it from the beginning; the death of the Messiah on the cross was according to **His holy plan** which He had announced long beforehand through His prophets. That is why, on the night when the priests arrested Jesus to have Him put to death, Jesus said to Peter who wanted to protect Him, "*Do you think I cannot call on my Father, and he will at once put at my disposal more than twelve legions of angels? **But how then would the Scriptures be fulfilled that say it must happen in this way?***" (Matt. 26:53,54)

Jesus knew why He had come into the world. He came to give His life, to shed His blood for sinners, just as the prophets had announced long beforehand. Jesus came so that what Abraham's sacrificial sheep and all animal sacrifices symbolized might be fulfilled in Him. Can you remember the last thing that Jesus said on the cross before He committed His spirit to God? Yes, the Scripture says that Jesus cried out with a loud voice, "***It is finished!***" and died. When He died, the curtain of the holy place of the temple was torn in two from top to bottom. (John 19:30; Mark 15:37,38) Why did Jesus cry out, "*It is finished!*"? And why was the curtain of the temple torn in two, that is, the curtain of the Holiest Place, where they sprinkled the blood of the animal sacrifices to cover sin? God tore that curtain in two, and Jesus declared, "*It is finished!*" so that everyone might know that it is by **the blood of Jesus** that **God forgives** the children of Adam their sins and gives them the right to dwell in God's holy presence forever!

By His death, the Lord Jesus Christ fulfilled the words of the prophets and the symbolism of the animal sacrifices. And as we have seen, His resurrection on the third day was the clear proof that God accepted His sacrifice as **the full price** to pay for sin forever! Jesus Christ is the perfect sacrifice which God gave the people of the world, so that whoever believes in Him will not perish, but have eternal life!

Now then, to finish our review of the message of the prophets, we invite you to listen to some profound and wonderful verses from God's Word concerning the perfect and final sacrifice, which Jesus the Messiah gave when He shed His blood on the cross to pay for sins. The Scripture says:

> (Heb. 10) [1]*The law is only* ***a shadow of the good things that are coming–not the realities themselves****. For this reason it can never, by the same sacrifices repeated endlessly year after year, make perfect those who draw near to worship.* [2]*If it could, would they not have stopped being offered? For the worshipers would have been cleansed once for all, and would no longer have felt guilty for their sins.* [3]*But those sacrifices are an annual reminder of sins,* [4]*because* ***it is impossible for the blood of bulls and goats to take away sins.***
>
> [5]*Therefore, when [the Lord Jesus] Christ came into the world, he said: "Sacrifice and offering you did not desire, but a body you prepared for me;* [6]*with burnt offerings and sin offerings you were not pleased.* [7]*Then I said, 'Here I am–it is written about me in the scroll—I have come to do your will, O God.'"...* [9]*He sets aside the first to establish the second.* [10]*And by that will,* ***we have been made holy through the sacrifice of the body of Jesus Christ once for all****.* [11]*Day after day every priest stands and performs his religious duties; again and again he offers the same sacrifices, which can never take away sins.* [12]*But when this priest had offered for all time one sacrifice for sins, he sat down at the right hand of God.* [13]*Since that time he waits for his enemies to be made his footstool,* [14]***because by one sacrifice he has made perfect forever those who are being made holy.*** [15]*The Holy Spirit also testifies to us about this. First he says:* [16]*"This is the covenant I will make with them after that time, says the Lord. I will put my laws in their hearts, and I will write them on their minds."* [17]*Then he adds: "Their sins and lawless acts I will remember no more."* [18]*And where these have been forgiven, there is no longer any sacrifice for sin.*
>
> [19]*Therefore, brothers, since we have confidence to enter the Most Holy Place* ***by the blood of Jesus****,* [20]*by a new and living way opened for us through the curtain, that is, his body,* [21]*and since we have a great priest over the house of God,* [22]*let us draw near to God with* ***a sincere heart in full assurance of***

> ***faith**... [23]Let us hold unswervingly to the hope we profess, for he who promised is faithful. [24]And let us consider how we may spur one another on toward love and good deeds.... [26]If we deliberately keep on sinning after we have received the knowledge of the truth, no sacrifice for sins is left, [27]but only a fearful expectation of judgment and of raging fire that will consume the enemies of God. [28]Anyone who rejected the law of Moses died without mercy on the testimony of two or three witnesses. [29]**How much more severely do you think a man deserves to be punished who has trampled the Son of God under foot**, who has treated as an unholy thing the blood of the covenant that sanctified him, and who has insulted the Spirit of grace? [30]For we know him who said, "It is mine to avenge; I will repay," and again, "The Lord will judge his people." [31]It is a dreadful thing to fall into the hands of the living God.*
>
> "***We who have heard this, how shall we escape if we ignore such a great salvation?***" (Heb. 2:3)

With these words, God is warning each of you today not to neglect the one and only way of salvation, which is found in the blood of Jesus the Messiah. **Whoever disdains the Sacrifice which God Himself has given, needs to know there is no other sacrifice for sins**; there is nothing left except the judgment of God, which will be without mercy! Jesus Christ is the Perfect Sacrifice, which God Himself gave, so that **whoever believes in Him** will not perish but have eternal life. On the cross Jesus said, "*It is finished!*" and since Jesus is the Word of God–when Jesus said, "*It is finished,*" it was God Himself saying, "***It is finished!***" And three days later God raised Jesus back to life, proving to the world that He is completely satisfied with Jesus' sacrifice for sin.

Friend, do you realize that Jesus has paid for your sins? Do you believe that Jesus Christ finished the work of Salvation for you? Or are you still trying to save yourself by your own works?

Thank you for listening....

Until next time, may God bless you as you consider the deep meaning of the Messiah's triumphant proclamation from the cross, when He said,

> "***It is finished!***" (John 19:30)

LESSON 97
HELL!

LUKE 16

Peace be with you, listening friends. We greet you in the name of God, the Lord of peace, who wants everyone to understand and submit to the way of righteousness that He has established, and have true peace with Him forever. We are happy to be able to return today to present your program *The Way of Righteousness*.

The Holy Scripture says:

> *"The cowardly, the unbelieving, the vile…and all liars–their place will be in* ***the fiery lake of burning sulphur.***" (Rev. 21:8) *"[They] will be thrown outside, into the darkness…into the eternal fire prepared for the devil and his angels, where there will be weeping and gnashing of teeth."* (Matt. 8:12; 25:41) *"[These] will go away to* ***eternal punishment***, *but the righteous to eternal life!"* (Matt. 25:46)

Hell! No one likes to talk about it! We don't even want to think about it! Nevertheless, the subject of hell is what we plan to study today, because God has much to say about it. In the Holy Scriptures, God has given hundreds of warnings so that people might not go there. Today and in the next lesson, we plan to learn what the Scriptures teach concerning hell and heaven (Paradise), and how we can be sure that we will go to heaven and not be sent to hell. Many people think that no one can know what will happen in the hereafter, or where they will spend eternity. They think that way because they do not know the way of salvation which God has established, nor the wonderful promises of God, which give a confident assurance. Does the Word of God tell us how we can know for sure that we will go to Paradise? Absolutely! God's Word says: *"I write these things to you who believe in the name of the Son of God* ***so that you may know that you have eternal life!***" (1 John 5:13)

Listening friend, do you **"know"** that you have the eternal life that the Word of God proclaims? On the day that you die, do you **know** where your soul will go?

Are you **sure** that you will enter Paradise and not be sent to hell? If you do not have that assurance, our lesson today should be of great interest to you.

As we have seen in the Gospel, when Jesus the Savior was on earth, He often taught people about the place called **Heaven** and the place called **Hell**. However, Jesus taught more about hell than He did about heaven, because He knows about the horrible punishment of hell and does not want anyone to go there. Now then, let us return to the Gospel and hear how Jesus taught the crowds about hell. **Listen to this true story** about two people who died. In the Gospel of Luke, chapter sixteen, Jesus spoke to the crowd, saying:

> (Luke 16) [19]*"There was* ***a rich man*** *who was dressed in purple and fine linen and lived in luxury every day.* [20]*At his gate was laid* ***a beggar named Lazarus****, covered with sores* [21]*and longing to eat what fell from the rich man's table. Even the dogs came and licked his sores.*
>
> [22]*"The time came when the beggar died and the angels carried him to* ***Abraham's side****. The rich man also died and was buried.* [23]***In hell****, where he was in torment, he looked up and saw Abraham far away, with Lazarus by his side."*

Let us pause here. Did you understand what happened to the rich man and the beggar, Lazarus? Where did the beggar go when he died? Instantly, his soul was in **Paradise**, in the presence of God, where the prophet of God Abraham had been for a long time. And the rich man, where did he go? Instantly, his soul was in **hell**, where he was in torment.

Why did the beggar, Lazarus, go to Paradise and the rich man go to hell? First, know that being poor does not mean you will be saved, and having great riches does not mean that you will perish! Lazarus, the poor man, went to Paradise because **he paid attention to the way of salvation** which God announced in the Writings of the Prophets. As for the rich man, **he ignored the Word of God**. That rich man was like many people today who are outwardly religious. They know that there is one God and that the Writings of the Prophets exist, but they are on the path to hell, because they have never believed the way of salvation of which all of God's prophets testify in the Scriptures. Like the rich man in our story, having a good time and getting wealth is more important to them than listening to the Word of Truth, which can save their souls.

Let us continue with the story and hear how God allowed the rich man, who was in hell, to converse briefly with the prophet Abraham, who was in Paradise. God wants us to get insight from the words spoken by this man in hell. The Lord Jesus continued the story saying,

> (Luke 16) [23]*"In hell, where [the rich man] was in torment, he looked up and saw Abraham far away, with Lazarus by his side.* [24]*So he called to him, 'Father*

> *Abraham, have pity on me and send Lazarus to dip the tip of his finger in water and cool my tongue, because I am in agony in this fire.'*
>
> [25]*"But Abraham replied, 'Son, remember that in your lifetime you received your good things, while Lazarus received bad things, but now he is comforted here and you are in agony.* [26]*And besides all this, between us and you a great chasm has been fixed, so that those who want to go from here to you cannot, nor can anyone cross over from there to us.'*
>
> [27]*"He answered, 'Then I beg you, father, send Lazarus to my father's house,*
> [28]*for I have five brothers. Let him warn them, so that they will not also come to this place of torment.'*
>
> [29]**"Abraham replied, 'They have Moses and the Prophets; let them listen to them.'**
>
> [30]*"'No, father Abraham,' he said, 'but if someone from the dead goes to them, they will repent.'*
>
> [31]*"He said to him, '***If they do not listen to Moses and the Prophets, they will not be convinced even if someone rises from the dead.***'"*

This is where the story of the rich man and Lazarus ends. Truly, the place called Hell is a horrible place, where there is no mercy. The rich man in hell was in torment and no one could relieve his suffering by giving him even a drop of water! Even more awful, this same rich man is still there today! He is in hell awaiting the Day of Judgment when both his soul and body will be thrown into the place called **the lake of fire**. There he will be forever with **everyone who refused to obey the message of the prophets**—the Good News of Jesus the Messiah. That is what the Scripture declares when it says: "*If anyone's name was not found written in the book of life, he was thrown into the lake of fire…with burning sulphur…and the smoke of their torment rises for ever and ever. There is no rest day or night!*" (Rev. 20:15; 14:10,11) Think about it! Everyone who ignores the righteous way of salvation that God has established and enters hell, will **never** cease to exist, will **never** get out, and the fire will **never** be quenched! **Never**! **Never! Forever**!

Some think that after sinners have suffered for a time in hell they will get out and go to Paradise. But that idea is not in accordance with the Word of God, which describes hell as "***eternal** punishment.*" (Matt. 25:46) Consequently, there are no prayers for the dead in the Writings of the Prophets. Praying for the dead comes purely from man's traditions, but not from God's Word, which says, "*Man is destined to die once, and after that to face judgment!*" (Heb. 9:27) Praying for the dead cannot relieve the sufferings of those in hell, nor can it save them in the Day of Judgment. Concerning those who are in heaven, they do not need our prayers, because they are in the presence of God and in perfect bliss!

Fellow listeners, **do not allow anyone to deceive you with empty words.**

Some people say, "Ah, God is good! He would not create his servants and then burn them! He will have mercy on us all and receive us into Paradise!" Those who talk this way do not base their thoughts on God's Word. They only say this to appease their consciences since they are willfully ignoring the way of salvation which God has established. If they do not turn from their wrong ideas, turn to God and believe the way of righteousness through Jesus Christ, one day they will know that there really is a hell! But then it will be **too late** to repent!

Did you hear what the rich man asked of Abraham? He asked him to send Lazarus to his father's house to warn his five brothers who had not yet died, "*so that they will not also come to this place of torment!*" How did Abraham respond to him? He told him, "***They have Moses and the Prophets; let them listen to them!***" But the rich man said, "*No, father Abraham, but if someone from the dead goes to them, they will repent." Abraham said to him,* '***If they do not listen to Moses and the Prophets, they will not be convinced even if someone rises from the dead.***'"

Listening friend, do you know the Good News of God's prophets which can save you from hell? That Good News is the message you have been hearing on your program *The Way of Righteousness*. In summary, we have seen that the good news of the prophets is the Good News about the holy Redeemer, whom God sent down to die on a cross in order to pay for your sins, and to rise from the dead on the third day. **If you believe in your heart that He died for your sins, you will not go to hell!** That is the Good News which can save you from God's righteous judgment.

As we discovered in our first lessons, God did not create hell for man, but for Satan and his evil angels. However, the sin of our ancestor Adam is the reason we have all been born far from God, in the kingdom of Satan, on the wide path that leads to hell. Surely the sinful nature which is in us would cause us to **perish forever**, if God had not provided **a remedy** for us, since the payment for sin is death and eternal hell. In our own strength, we have no way of escaping hell! However, we thank God for designing a plan by which He can forgive us our sins! What is that plan? It is **the death of the holy Messiah**. God laid the punishment of our sins on Jesus when He died on the cross. As it is written: "*God made [Jesus Christ] who had no sin to be* ***sin for us****, so that in him we might become the righteousness of God!*" (2 Cor. 5:21)

We have seen how people tortured Jesus, flogging Him, putting a crown of thorns on His head, insulting Him, striking Him on the face, spitting on Him, and nailing Him to a cross! God allowed people to mistreat the sinless Messiah in order to display the punishment which our sins deserved. Everything that people did to Jesus–we deserve because of our sins. But God, because of His great love for us, laid the punishment for our sin on the holy Messiah, His Beloved, Eternal Son. And remember, the sufferings of Jesus on the cross were not limited to what men did to Him. The Scriptures of the Prophets show us that when Jesus was suffering on the cross, God Himself laid on Him a pain that the human mind cannot comprehend. God laid on Jesus the payment of our sin, that is, **our hell!** The prophet Job foretold the intense sufferings that the Messiah would endure from God when he wrote, "*God has turned me over to evil men and thrown me into the clutches of the wicked!...* ***God assails me and tears me in his anger and gnashes his teeth at me; my opponent fastens on me his piercing eyes!***" (Job 16:11,9)

The payment for sin is to die and to face God's wrath and to enter the darkness of hell, where God consigns all who refuse to believe the Gospel! However, Jesus endured God's wrath for us, so that we might receive God's grace. As we have read, when Jesus was dying on the cross the whole land became pitch-dark–just like hell—from noon until three o'clock. During those hours, Jesus called out with a loud voice, **"My God, my God, why have you forsaken me?!"** Why did God forsake the Messiah, His beloved, on the cross? **You and I are the reason!** Our sins are the reason! While Jesus was on the cross, God placed on Him the punishment for our sin, **our hell**! This is a profound truth which our minds cannot totally understand. However, what is absolutely certain is that **if you truly believe in the Lord Jesus, you will be saved, and you will never go to hell,** because God will count you as righteous based on the Redeemer's (substitutionary) sacrifice. Like the sacrificial sheep, which redeemed Abraham's son from death, Jesus the Messiah died to redeem you from the death which will never end in the place called **hell**!

God placed your hell on Jesus Christ. **Do you believe this?** Do you believe that Jesus Christ, the Righteous One, paid for you your debt of sin? Or will you go to hell to pay your own debt of sin throughout eternity? **It is up to you.** What do you choose? **Paradise**? Or **hell**?

Thank you for listening. We invite you to join us next time to look into a subject drastically different from what we studied today, because, God willing, we will study about the wonderful place called Paradise....

God bless you. We bid you farewell with these solemn words from the Lord Jesus:

> ***"Enter through the narrow gate. For wide is the gate and broad is the road that leads to destruction, and many enter through it. But small is the gate and narrow the road that leads to life, and only a few find it."*** (Matt. 7:13,14)

Lesson 98

Paradise

Revelation 21,22

Peace be with you, listening friends. We greet you in the name of God, the Lord of peace, who wants everyone to understand and submit to the way of righteousness that He has established, and have true peace with Him forever. We are happy to be able to return today to present your program *The Way of Righteousness*.

In our last lesson, we contemplated **hell**, the place where punishment never ceases. Hell is a horrible place, created for Satan and his angels. It is where everyone who neglects the way of salvation which God has established must go, forever separated from God! That is what the Holy Scripture declares, saying: "*If anyone's name was not found written in the book of life, he was thrown into the lake of fire!*" (Rev. 20:15)

Surely, hell is the most horrible subject that man can contemplate. However, today, we plan to look at one of the most wonderful subjects that the spirit of man can contemplate, the subject of **heaven**, also called ***Paradise***.

People have a great variety of ideas concerning Paradise, and what a person must do to enter it. For example, those who belong to eastern religions believe that there are many heavens (paradises) with varying degrees of pleasure and that where each person goes depends on his works. Others think that a person must first pass through hell and after he has paid his debt of sin, he will be transferred to Paradise. Still others think that Paradise is a place that God has reserved for those who are faithful in their religious duties and that it is a place where folks eat, drink, and pursue pleasure. Man certainly has many ideas about Paradise and how to get there. However, our concern today is not with **what people think** about Paradise, but with **what God says** about it in His holy Word!

The place of Paradise has many names in the Scriptures of the Prophets. It is called *Heaven; the throne of God; the presence of God; the house of God; the dwelling place of God the Holy One; the Holy City; the City of the Living God; the heavenly Jerusalem; the home of the holy angels and the Lamb; the presence of the Lord Jesus and His great glory; and the home of God's people, who have their names written in heaven.*

The Lord Jesus called Paradise, "My *Father's house*," because that was where He was before He was born on earth.

In summary, Paradise is **the dwelling place of God**. As we have seen, God is everywhere; nevertheless there is a specific place that is holy, radiant, and beautiful, far beyond the stars, where God dwells in His glory. That place is where the Son of the Most High, Jesus, sits on His throne, at the right hand of the Almighty, waiting until He returns to the world to judge it and to renew it. Also, Paradise is where thousands and thousands of angels surround the throne, together with the great multitude of people that God has redeemed for Himself through the blood of the Lamb, the Lord Jesus Christ.

In the end of the book of the Gospel, in the last two chapters of the book of Revelation, God gave John, His apostle, a vision to show him the Holy City of Paradise, which the Lord has made for those who have their names written in the book of eternal life. Listen to what the Scripture says about the City of Paradise.

> (Rev. 21) [10]*And he carried me away in the Spirit to a mountain great and high,*
> *and showed me* **the Holy City**... [11]*It shone with* **the glory of God**, *and its*
> *brilliance was like that of a very precious jewel, like a jasper, clear as crystal.* [12]*It*
> *had a great, high wall with twelve gates, and with twelve angels at the gates...*
> [16]*The city was laid out like a square, as long as it was wide...* [19]*The founda-*
> *tions of the city walls were decorated with every kind of precious stone...* [21]*The*
> *twelve gates were twelve pearls, each gate made of a single pearl. The great street*
> *of the city was of pure gold, like transparent glass.* [22]*I did not see a temple in the*
> *city, because* **the Lord God Almighty and the Lamb** (the Lord Jesus) *are its*
> *temple.* [23]*The city does not need the sun or the moon to shine on it, for* **the glory**
> **of God** *gives it light, and the Lamb is its lamp.* [24]*The nations will walk by its*
> *light...* [25]*On no day will its gates ever be shut, for there will be no night there...*
> [27]***Nothing impure will ever enter it, nor will anyone who does what is***
> ***shameful or deceitful, but only those whose names are written in the***
> ***Lamb's book of life.***
>
> (Rev. 22) [1]*Then the angel showed me the river of the water of life, as clear as*
> *crystal, flowing from* **the throne of God and of the Lamb** [2]*down the middle of*
> *the great street of the city. On each side of the river stood the tree of life, bearing*
> *twelve crops of fruit, yielding its fruit every month...* [3]*No longer will there be any*
> *curse [or death or mourning or crying or pain (Rev 21:4)].* **The throne of God**
> **and of the Lamb** *will be in the city, and his servants will serve him.* [4]*They will*
> *see* **his face**, *and* **his name** *will be on their foreheads.* [5]*There will be no more*
> *night. They will not need the light of a lamp or the light of the sun, for* **the Lord**
> **God** *will give them light. And they will reign for ever and ever.*

Thus did God show John the Holy City, which He is preparing for those who choose His way of Salvation. In the time that we have left today, let us think about what God says in His Word concerning **the way that leads to Paradise**. How can we be sure that we will go to Paradise and not go to hell?

Can you remember what the Messiah, Jesus, said to His disciples concerning the house of God and the way which leads there? He said to them:

> (John 14) [1]*Do not let your hearts be troubled. Trust in God; trust also in me.* [2]*In my Father's house are* ***many rooms****; if it were not so, I would have told you.* ***I am going there to prepare a place for you****.* [3]*And if I go and prepare a place for you, I will come back and take you to be with me that you also may be where I am.* [4]*You know the way to the place where I am going…* [6]*I am* ***the*** *way and* ***the*** *truth and* ***the*** *life.* ***No one comes to [God] the Father except through me.***

That is what Jesus the Messiah said. He Himself is **The Way**. Whoever does not come by the Son of the Most High, that is, the holy Redeemer, will never enter the holy presence of God! **Never**! That is what the Scripture declares when it says:

> *"Salvation is found in* ***no one else,*** *for there is no other name under heaven given to men by which we must be saved."* (Acts 4:12) *"For there is one God and* ***one mediator*** *between God and men, the man Christ Jesus, who gave himself as a ransom for all men…"* (1 Tim. 2:5,6)

The Mediator, Jesus Christ, who came forth from God, is **the Way of Salvation** that leads to Paradise. In order to bring sinners to God, Christ was born into the world, lived a holy life upon earth, shed His blood as the Perfect Sacrifice for sin, and then rose from the dead on the third day. No one comes to God except through Him. Do you believe that? Do you see that Jesus the Messiah is **the only Way** that brings sinners into the presence of God? Perhaps we can illustrate it with **a little story**.

A certain man lived in a small village far away in the bush. He belonged to a tribe of people who did not wear clothes. They only wore something like a belt around their loins. This man had a piece of land which he farmed, but someone more powerful than he came and stole his land so that he had nowhere left to farm. No one would help him to reclaim his land because he had no means of paying them.

One day he got the idea to go to the capital city to see the President, the ruler of the land, and ask him to help him, because he had heard that the Ruler was a just and compassionate man. Thus he got up and walked and walked and walked until he came to the big city and to the presidential palace. Oh, what a big and beautiful house! When he arrived at the gate of the house, and **attempted to**

enter with his filthiness and nakedness, a guard said to him: "Hey you! What are you trying to do?!" He replied, "I want to see the President." The guard said to him, "Ha! Do you suppose that anyone can just enter here as they please? Look at you! Don't you know that you cannot come in here naked and dirty? Get away from here, man, or I'll throw you in prison!"

Thus, the poor fellow turned and went away, but he was not discouraged. He went and begged from morning to afternoon. Then he bought some inexpensive clothes, bathed himself, dressed and went back to the Ruler's palace. Upon arriving back at the gate, the guard said to him, "You are wearing clothes, but the clothes are not good enough to allow you to come before the Ruler of the land. And even if your clothes were good enough, you couldn't enter, because **you must have special permission** to enter the Ruler's house. You have no right to enter! Now go!"

At this, the man became discouraged, saying, "What's the use? After all the trouble I've gone through, I still can't get near the Ruler of the land!" His hope gone, he sat at the side of the road in great dismay. However, while all this was happening, the Ruler of the land saw him. The Ruler's eldest son was there also. The Ruler said to his son, "Go and find out what that fellow wants." When the Ruler's son came up to the man, he squatted down and said to him, "Sir, can I help you with something? What has brought you here and why are you so upset?" The man said to him, "I want to see the Ruler of the land, but it is impossible. **All my efforts have been in vain**!"

The young man said to him, "I am the son of the Ruler of the land, and my father sent me out here to help you. Follow me." Thus, he accompanied him to the gate of the presidential palace. When they came up to the guard who had previously prevented the poor man from entering, the guard saluted them with great respect as they walked through the gate and into the court of the palace. The son gave the poor man a beautiful robe to wear, and together they entered the presidential palace. Thus, the man was able to enter the presidential palace and see the Ruler of the land, **because of the help and authority of the Ruler's son.**

Friends, that is how it is with those who want to enter Paradise, the palace of the King of kings. God, the Ruler of the Universe is high and holy. We cannot just enter His glorious presence in any sort of way! Our own efforts can never gain us access into His presence. We are all like that poor man who attempted to enter the presence of the President by his own feeble efforts. The Scripture says: "*All of us have become like one who is unclean, and all our righteous acts are like filthy rags.*" (Isa. 64:6) Paradise is a holy place, and "*nothing impure will ever enter it, nor will anyone who does what is shameful or deceitful!*" (Rev. 21:27) **No one can get us into that holy place except the Holy One who came from there!** That holy Person is **Jesus Christ,** the Eternal Son of the Most High, the Lamb of God, who came from Paradise, died as a sacrifice to take away sin, rose from the dead and returned to Paradise!

So then, who can enter Paradise? Only those who have been cleansed **through faith** in Jesus the Redeemer and in the blood that He shed. Only those will enter Paradise! That is what the Scripture declares when it says:

> "*There is no difference, for all have sinned and fall short of the glory of God, and are justified freely by his grace through the redemption that came by Christ Jesus. God presented him as a sacrifice of atonement, through faith in his blood.*" (Rom. 3:22-25) "*We accept man's testimony, but God's testimony is greater because it is the testimony of God, which he has given about his Son. Anyone who believes in the Son of God has this testimony in his heart. Anyone who does not believe God has made him out to be a liar, because he has not believed the testimony God has given about his Son.* ***And this is the testimony: God has given us eternal life, and this life is in his Son. He who has the Son has life; he who does not have the Son of God does not have life.*** *I write these things to you who believe in the name of the Son of God so that you may* ***know*** *that you have eternal life.*" (1 John 5:9-13)

You who are listening today, do you **know** that you have eternal life? Are you sure that you will enter Paradise and rejoice in the presence of God forever? Have you believed on the Name of the Son of God? Is your name written in the Lamb's book of life?

Think carefully about what we have read today, because God wants to give you insight into all of this....

God bless you as consider this thrilling verse from His holy Word:

> ***"No eye has seen, no ear has heard, no mind has conceived what God has prepared for those who love him!"*** (1 Cor. 2:9)

Lesson 99

What Do You Think About Jesus?

Part 1

{Note: Lessons #99 and #100 are adapted from a sermon presented by Charles R. Marsh in his excellent book, "Share Your Faith With A Muslim," Moody Press, 1975}

Peace be with you, listening friends. We greet you in the name of God, the Lord of peace, who wants everyone to understand and submit to the way of righteousness that He has established, and have true peace with Him forever. We are happy to be able to return today to present your program *The Way of Righteousness.*

For a long time now, we have been examining the Scriptures of the Prophets to see the righteous way established by God, by which sinners can become righteous before Him. We have seen how Jesus the Messiah fulfilled the words of God's prophets. **Today and in the next lesson**, we intend to review with you the glory of the One of whom all the prophets spoke. Thus, our final two lessons in our chronological study of the Scriptures of the Prophets are entitled, "**What do you think about Jesus?**"

In our study in the Gospel {*Injil*}, we heard Jesus ask people, "***What do you think about the Christ? Whose son is he?***" (Matt. 22:42) This is the most important question that each of us must answer in life. Our destiny in the hereafter depends on our response to this question! Soon Jesus the Messiah will return, and when He comes, He will question you as He questioned the people of His time, saying, "How about you, what do you think of me?"

Our goal is to make known to you who Jesus really is. Our greatest concern is that no one misleads you in this matter. We urge you not to assume that Jesus Christ was merely one of the prophets, or a good man among men. No, **He is unique!** He has no equal in this world or in the world to come. What do you think about Him? Who do you think He is? There are ten questions that we would like to ask you about Jesus the Messiah, five in this program and five in the next.

1.) **First, what do you think about His amazing birth?**

No one has ever been born like Him. He is Jesus *the Son of Mary*. You know that John was called *the son of Zechariah*, Solomon *the son of David*, Ishmael *the son of Abraham*. Everyone takes the surname of his father or adds his father's name to his own name. But in Jesus' case, why is the name of His mother attached to His name? It is because He did not have a father on earth. He was born of a young lady who was a virgin. He was born by the power of God. About seven hundred years before the Messiah was born, the prophet Isaiah predicted how He would be born, when he said, "*The* ***virgin*** *will be with child and will give birth to a son, and they will call him Immanuel (which means,"God with us)!*" (Isa. 7:14; Matt. 1:23)

It was from the dust of the ground that God created our ancestor Adam. We all are descendants of Adam, as were the prophets. We are of the earth. However, the Lord Jesus came from heaven. We are all like dirty soil because of our sin, but Jesus was like the rain which comes from heaven. He was pure and holy, just as God is pure and holy. The Gospel record declares: "*Jesus* ***came into the world*** *to save sinners*." (1 Tim. 1:15) Before Jesus came into the world, He was in the presence of God, because He is the Word of God and the Soul of God. He Himself chose to come and take on a human body, to save us from our sins. He came from above.

The story is told of two men who fell into a deep well. One said to the other, "Hey man, save me from this wretched place! Get me out of this slimy mud!" However, the other said to him, "Stupid, how can I get you out when you and I both are in this pit?!" They were both in it, and neither one could get the other out. Then they heard a voice from above telling them to grab hold of a rope that was being lowered into the well. **Only someone who had not fallen into the well could help them.**

The very best of the prophets could not save us from the deep, deep pit of sin, because they too were sinners. However, Jesus did not inherit the sinful nature that is in man. He came **from above**. He was born of a virgin. We also saw that God sent His angels, and that He placed a great star in the sky to announce the birth of the holy Messiah, the Savior of the world! How miraculous it all was! No man has ever been born like this Man. He is unique in His birth. He is incomparable! However, the greatness of Jesus does not end with His birth. Jesus is also unique in His character. Thus, our second question is:

2.) **What do you think of His holy character?**

Jesus was perfect. He never committed a single sin. He never asked for forgiveness, because He never wronged anyone. Every person who fears God must repent of His sin and ask for forgiveness. All the prophets did this. However, you can search the Word of God from beginning to end {Lit. in Wolof: *go around until you meet where you started*}, but you will not find a single verse which says that the Lord Jesus requested forgiveness. He did not need forgiveness since **He never sinned**. His friends and His enemies all testified that they could not find a single fault in Him. Friends, there is no one else who is without sin. The Lord Jesus is more than a prophet. He is the very Word of God that appeared upon earth as a man. Yes, Jesus is unique in His character. He is incomparable! But there is something else important to understand. Jesus is also unique in His words.

3.) **What do you think about His words?**

One day, His enemies sent soldiers to arrest Him. When they arrived and listened to His teachings, they returned without arresting Him. They were amazed and said, "*No one ever spoke the way this man does!*" (John 7:46)

Consider what He said about Himself. "*I am* ***the light of the world****. Whoever follows me will never walk in darkness, but will have the light of life.*" (John 8:12) The prophets are like the moon and stars that diffuse a weak light in the darkness. But Jesus is like the sun. Who needs the light of the moon and stars once the sun has risen? The prophets called the Messiah "the Sun of Righteousness." (Mal. 4:2) The waning crescent moon is like the prophets. But Jesus Christ is the sun. Have you ever seen the sun wane? No, it never goes out. It lights all the continents. Jesus Christ is like the sun. He will never pass away. He is for every nation of the world.

Jesus also said, "*I am* ***the way*****,** ***the truth*** *and* ***the life****.*" (John 14:6) Jesus is very different from the religious leaders who give orders, saying, "Do this, follow this teaching. This is the way. Keep these commandments…" The Lord Jesus said, "**I am** the way. Believe in me, come to me, and you will have the right to live in the presence of God forever." **Jesus Himself *is* The Way**. Let us try to illustrate what this means.

A small boy was lost in a big city. The child asked a police officer to explain to him the way back to his neighborhood. The officer said to him, "Go straight ahead, turn left at the second corner, take a right at the third corner, cross the bridge, take the traffic circle and then follow the second main road . . ." The child burst into tears. That police officer explained the way, but the child was too confused and afraid to follow what had been explained to him. Just then, a man from the same neighborhood came along. He took the child by the hand, and led him. When the child was tired of walking, the man carried him until they arrived at the house. The police officer **explained the way**. However, the other man **was the way**. Jesus said: **I am the way.** I am the way that leads to heaven, the house of God. "*I am the way and the truth and the life. No one comes to [God] the Father except through me.*" (John 14:6) No one ever spoke like the Lord Jesus Christ! He is unique. He is incomparable! However, the glory of Jesus does not stop at His birth, His character and His words. We can see it also in His works.

4.) **What do you think about the mighty works of Jesus?**

He can do anything. All power and all authority are given to Him. Whatever works God has done, the Lord Jesus did on earth, to show people where He came from and who He was. Who can still the wind but **God**? **Jesus** stilled the wind. Who can raise the dead to life but **God**? **Jesus** raised the dead to life. Who can open the eyes of the blind but **God**? **Jesus** did that too. He healed every kind of disease. He spoke one word and the demons fled. He changed the lives of many people and saved them from sin. God gave some of the prophets the power to do certain miracles. But the Lord Jesus did miracles by His own authority and power. He is the One who could stand over a paralyzed man, look him in the eyes and say, "***I tell you***, *Get up, take your mat and go home!*" (Luke 5:22) The man stood up and went home praising God! Jesus didn't heal with medicine or magic. By the power and authority of His word alone He healed the sick.

A man named Lazarus died and was buried. When Jesus arrived Lazarus had already been buried for four days. Jesus went to the tomb and said, "*Lazarus, come out!*" (John 11:43) The corpse came out of the tomb. Jesus has the authority to raise the dead which is why He could say, "*I am the* ***resurrection*** *and the* ***life****!*" (John 11:25) The day is coming when all who are in the tombs will hear His voice and arise to stand before Him. Listening friend, you too will come out of the tomb if you have died. Even now, the Lord Jesus can give you a new life and the authority to live forever in paradise, if you believe in Him as your Savior and Lord. Jesus is still transforming the lives of many people around the world. **He can transform your life too.** What do you think about Jesus? What do you think about His works? He is unique. He is Almighty. He is incomparable! Before we leave today, let us ask you one more question about Jesus:

5.) **What do you think about His names and titles?**

As we have seen in the Writings of the Prophets, Jesus has hundreds of names and titles. These names help us to better understand who He is. For example, He is called: *Immanuel…the Word…the Son of Man…the Lamb of God…the Redeemer…the Savior…the Bread of Life…the True Vine…the Good Shepherd…the Light of the World…the Lord of Glory…the Resurrection…the Alpha and Omega, the First and the Last, the Beginning and End…the Door…the Way, the Truth and the Life*…and ***the Son of God****!*

We saw that God's prophet, Moses, was called *the man of God*. The prophet Abraham was called *the friend of God*. But only One Person is called **The Son of God.** Tell us, who has the closest relationship to a man, his friend or his son? Speak the truth that is in your heart. Yes, Jesus was called the Son of God. God called Jesus His Son to distinguish Him from all others. We read in the Gospel that God declared of Jesus, saying, "*This is my Son, whom I love; with him I am well pleased. Listen to him!*" (Matt. 17:5) What did God mean? We say that the Son is the shadow of the father. The son reflects the image of the father. Jesus shows us what God is like. That is what the Scripture declares when it says: "*No one has ever seen God, but God the One and Only, who is at the Father's side, has made him known.*" (John 1:18) Do you want to know God, and have a wonderful relationship with Him forever? Then come to the Lord Jesus, whom God called His Son. A son can speak in the name of his father. That is what Jesus did when He was among men. That is why He was called Immanuel which means ***God with us.***

Some assume that God cannot appear on earth in a human body. However, anyone who thinks this way does not yet understand the plan which God designed to save sinners. His plan required that the Eternal Son of God appear upon earth in a human body, to make Himself known to the children of Adam, and redeem them from the hand of the devil. Friends, **God is great** and He can do anything. God wants everyone to know Him. That is why He became a man and lived on the earth.

What do you think about the names and titles of Jesus the Messiah? He is incomparable. What do you think about His birth, His character, His words and His works? Whom do you consider Him to be? "*What do you think about the Christ? Whose son is he?*" (Matt. 22:42)

Our time is up for today. God willing, in the next study we will ask and answer five more questions about Jesus and complete our journey through the Holy Scriptures....

God bless you as you ponder this verse of Scripture:

> ***"In Christ all the fullness of the Deity lives in bodily form, and you*** **(who believe)** ***have been given fullness in Christ."*** (Col. 2:9,10)

Lesson 100

What Do You Think About Jesus?

Part 2

Peace be with you, listening friends. We greet you in the name of God, the Lord of peace, who wants everyone to understand and submit to the way of righteousness that He has established, and have true peace with Him forever. We are happy to be able to return today to present your program *The Way of Righteousness*.

Today we are going to continue with the talk we began in the last program, called "**What do you think about Jesus?**" This question is intensely important, because where we will spend eternity depends on what we think about Jesus the Messiah. In our last program, we asked what you thought about **His miraculous birth, His holy character, His wonderful words, His mighty power and His lofty titles.** Today we have five more solemn questions we want to ask you about Jesus. The first question is:

6.) **What do you think about His death?**

Do you know **where** you will die? Or **how** you will die? Do you know **when** you will die? You and I must admit that we know nothing about these things. But Jesus was not like us. He knew **where** He would die and announced it. He would die in Jerusalem. He also foretold **how** He would die. He told His disciples,

> "*We are going up to Jerusalem, and everything that is written by the prophets about the Son of Man will be fulfilled. He will be handed over to the Gentiles. They will mock him, insult him, spit on him, flog him and kill him. On the third day he will rise again.*" (Luke 18:31-33)

He also told His disciples **when** He would die, that is, on the same day the Jews would be killing a lamb to celebrate the feast of the Passover. It was on that day that He must die as the Lamb of God, as a sacrifice to take away the sin of the world.

The death of Jesus was different from all other deaths, because He Himself

chose to die. We heard Jesus say, *"No one takes [my life] from me, but I lay it down of my own accord. I have authority to lay it down and authority to take it up again."* (John 10:18) Jesus never sinned; that is why He could have bypassed death. He could have simply ascended to heaven from where He came, without passing through death. But He chose to die because of His obedience to His Father's will and His love for sinners. He gave His life for us by allowing men to nail Him to a cross. He died to provide for us forgiveness of sins and guarantee a place for us in Paradise. About seven hundred years before the Messiah came into the world, God's prophet, Isaiah, declared why the Redeemer must die, when he said:

> *"But he was* ***pierced for our transgressions****, he was* ***crushed for our iniquities****; the punishment that brought us peace was upon him, and by his wounds we are healed. We all, like sheep, have gone astray, each of us has turned to his own way; and* ***the LORD has laid on him the iniquity of us all.****"* (Isa. 53:5,6)

You and I are the reason that Jesus the Messiah died. He is the Good Shepherd who willingly gave His life for His sheep. No man has ever died like Him. He is incomparable. He is unique among men.

Another important question to which everyone must respond is:

7.) **What do you think about His victory over death, that is, His resurrection?**

Jesus died and was buried. His enemies did everything they could to guard the tomb. They rolled a huge stone to close the tomb, then sealed it tight. They placed soldiers there to guard the tomb. However, all their efforts did not hinder Jesus from rising from the dead. Indeed, the Lord Jesus rose from the dead on the third day and appeared to His disciples. After that, He appeared to more than five hundred witnesses at once. Those people saw Him, touched Him, and ate with Him after His resurrection. He showed them the wounds in His hands, His feet and His side. Yes, He rose from the dead exactly as He predicted! God raised Jesus from the dead to prove to the whole world that He is satisfied with the work of Jesus on the cross as the perfect and final Sacrifice which pays for sins.

Death is a great enemy. Our ancestors died. The prophets also died, and their corpses remain in their graves. We too will die some day. But praise be to God, **Jesus Christ conquered death**! He is a living Savior and can save all who come to God through Him, because He is alive and intercedes for all who believe in Him. Is any other prophet alive today after having died? No, not one. Jesus Christ is the only One who conquered the grave. He is alive today, which is why those of us who believe in Him are not afraid to die. To die is merely to go to be with our Lord above. Yes, Jesus is unique and incomparable. He has no equal on earth or in heaven. What do you think about His victory over death? Another question is:

8.) **What do you think of His ascension to heaven?**

After the Lord Jesus arose from the dead, He appeared to His disciples for a period of forty days. Then we saw that He bid them farewell, ascended to heaven, and sat down at the right hand of God, the place of supreme honor, thus showing that He is greater than the angels, the prophets, and all humankind! That is what the Scripture declares, saying,

> "*God exalted him to* ***the highest place*** *and gave him the name that is* ***above every name****, that at the name of Jesus every knee should bow, in heaven and on earth and under the earth, and every tongue confess that Jesus Christ is* **Lord**, *to the glory of God the Father.*" (Phil. 2:9-11)

Yes, Jesus is unique. He is incomparable! In relation to this, another question you must answer is:

9.) **What do you think about His return to the earth?**

Jesus Christ is going to come back. He declared it. The prophets announced it. The angels also said so. All true disciples of Christ await His return. He will return and take His people to heaven. He will judge the world in righteousness and reign over all the earth. He will be the King of the world. He must reign for one thousand years until all His enemies bow at His feet. Yes, He is coming back soon. Everyone will confess that He is the King of kings, the Lord of lords. He is coming and you will stand before Him, the Great Judge. On the day in which you will be face to face with Him, He will ask you, "**What did you think of me?**" What will you answer? If you answer, "I thought You were one of the prophets," then He will ask you why you did not sincerely believe Him—and you will be condemned, because you did not believe what He said about Himself, nor what the prophets wrote about Him—that He is **the Son of God from heaven, the one and only Savior**. Who is coming back to reign? Will Abraham, Moses, David or some other prophet return to reign? No. The Lord Jesus Christ is the One who is coming back. He will be **the Judge**. God has given proof of this fact by raising Him from the dead. He will return. Every eye will see Him. Every knee will bow. Every tongue will declare that "*Jesus Christ is Lord!*"

Now we come to the final question:

10.) **What do you think about His demands on you?** {Lit. what He wants you to do}

The Lord Jesus says, "***Come to me****, all you who are weary and burdened, and* ***I will give you rest****. Take my yoke upon you and learn from me, for I am gentle and humble in heart, and you will find rest for your souls.*" (Matt. 11:28,29) This very day He is calling you. When He called the first disciples to follow Him, they left everything: their homes, their families, and their work. He wants you to do the same. This does not mean that you must abandon your home and your job to follow Jesus, but you must surrender your whole life to Him and give Him first place in your heart. He wants you to trust Him, believe in Him, and receive Him as your Savior and Master. **He wants all of you**–your mind, heart, body and soul. If He is the One He claims to be, then everything He demands is logical.

As we have seen, Jesus Christ is unique and cannot be compared with anyone else. He is unique in **His birth**, in **His character**, in **His teachings**, in **His works**, in **His names and titles**, in **His sufferings and death**, in **His resurrection**, in **His ascension**, in **His return**, and in **His power to change the hearts of the children of Adam**. He is alive today. He is with those who believe in Him. Soon He will return. There is no one like Him in heaven or on earth. That is why He has the authority to be the King and the Lord of your life! The Lord Jesus Christ wants to be your Savior and your Lord. That is why He died on the cross and came back to life! He has the power to take away your sins and give you a deep and wonderful relationship with God forever. He can give you new life, wash your heart clean, and renew you in the power of the Holy Spirit, but you must **trust** {Lit. hang your hope on} Him and His sacrifice.

Tragically, so many consider Jesus Christ to be a great prophet, but they have never received Him as their Lord and Savior. To believe that Jesus was a great prophet is not enough! **You must agree with God that Jesus is the Lord of *all* and that when He died on the cross, He died in *your* place**. All of us children of Adam have a serious problem: it is **sin**. God, in His great mercy, has provided a **remedy** for our problem, but **we must take it.** If I am sick and go to the doctor, he writes me a medical prescription. So I go and buy the medicine, return home, place it on my table, look at the medicine and the medicine looks at me. Will that make me get well? No! To get well, I must **take** the medicine, and swallow it **as prescribed**. The medicine of God is the Lord Jesus Christ and the blood which He shed on the cross.

Perhaps someone is asking, "How can I take God's remedy for my sin?" Very simply, you must **confess to God** that you are a sinner, that your "good works" are like filthy rags before Him, and that you have no means of saving yourself from His righteous judgment. Then you must **believe in your heart** that the Lord Jesus Christ bore the punishment for your sins. Jesus the Messiah satisfied completely God's every demand for judgment. If you believe that Christ died and rose again to save you, then God will forgive your sins, clothe you in the righteousness of Christ, send His Holy Spirit into your heart, and give you the right to live in His presence forever! Glory to God, you can be made righteous today—if you will believe!

Listening friends, have you taken "God's medicine" which can heal you of the disease of sin and save you from the eternal fires of hell? Whoever despises God's medicine, that is, **the blood that Jesus shed**, must know that there is **no other**

medicine to cure you of sin. None whatsoever! God has no other way to cleanse sinners and make them righteous before Him. There is **no other way** to Paradise.

Listen carefully to what the Holy Scripture declares concerning **the one and only way of righteousness** which God has provided for sinners to be made righteous before Him. The Scripture says:

> (Rom. 3) [20]***No one will be declared righteous*** *in his sight by observing the law…* [21]*But now* ***a righteousness from God****, apart from law, has been made known, to which the Law and the Prophets testify.* [22]***This righteousness from God comes through faith in Jesus Christ to all who believe.*** *There is no difference,* [23]*for all have sinned and fall short of the glory of God,* [24]*and are justified freely by his grace* ***through the redemption that came by Christ Jesus****….* [27]*Where, then, is boasting? It is excluded. On what principle? On that of observing the law? No, but on that of* ***faith****.*
>
> *"For it is by grace you have been saved, through* ***faith–and*** *this* ***not from yourselves, it is the gift of God–not by works****, so that no one can boast."* (Eph. 2:8,9) *"If you confess with your mouth, 'Jesus is Lord,' and believe in your heart that God raised him from the dead,* ***you will be saved****….for 'Everyone who* ***calls*** *on the name of* ***the Lord*** *will be* ***saved****!'"* (Rom. 10:9,13)

Dear friend, have you called on the name of the Lord? Have you received God's gift of salvation? Or are you still trying to save yourself by your own works? We plead with you not to reject God's righteous way of Salvation. God knows your heart. Admit to Him that you are a sinner, that you have broken His holy laws. Tell Him you know you deserve His fiery judgment. Then thank Him for sending you a sinless Savior who willingly suffered in your place—taking your eternal punishment and then rising triumphantly from the grave!

Friend, you must come to God by **the way of righteousness that He has established**—or you cannot come at all. God, the Merciful, the Compassionate, invites you to come. Come to Him today and be saved. *"Believe on the Lord Jesus Christ and you will be saved—you and your household."* (Acts 16:31)

If you have put your trust in the One of whom all the prophets bear witness, write to us and tell us about it…

Today is the one hundredth (and final) lesson in our journey through the Holy Scriptures. Thank you for joining us. We bid you farewell with this wonderful prayer found in the Word of God:

> ***"To him who is able to keep you from falling and to present you before his glorious presence without fault and with great joy–to the only God our Savior be glory, majesty, power and authority, through Jesus Christ our Lord, before all ages, now and forevermore! Amen."*** (Jude 24,25)

Appendixes

"Do you believe the prophets?"

(Acts 26:27)

Appendix A

Basic Truths Taught In Each Lesson

with Audio-Cassette Groups

The Way of Righteousness 100-lesson radio-series fits on 20 audio-cassettes. A 60-minute tape contains four lessons; a 90-minute tape contains six lessons. On cassette #8 and #18 we suggest that the unused 15 minutes be filled with some appropriate music. Listed to the right of the lesson title is the Scripture reference on which the lesson is based followed by a brief description of some basic truths taught in the lesson.

Cassette 1: The Beginning

1. **God Has Spoken**—The Way of Righteousness. What is a prophet? God wants to speak to you.
2. **What Is God Like?** *Genesis 1*— God's eternal greatness. He wants us to know Him.
3. **Satan and the Angels** *Isaiah 14; Ezekiel 28* — Satan's origin. God's holiness.
4. **How God Made the World** *Genesis 1* — God's wisdom, power, faithfulness, and goodness.
5. **Why God Created Man** *Genesis 1, 2* — Man: created in God's image. God's exalted purpose for mankind.
6. **Adam and Eve and the Garden of Paradise** *Genesis 2* — God's command. Sin's penalty. Sin and death defined.

Cassette 2: Sin's Entry

7. **How Sin Entered the World** *Genesis 3* — Human race led into sin. Satan is a liar and a deceiver.
8. **What Adam's Sin Produced** *Genesis 3* — Dead in sin. Separated from the Source of Life.
9. **The Wonderful Promise** *Genesis 3* — First promise of the Redeemer. First animal sacrifice. God's holiness.
10. **Cain and Abel and the Way of Sacrifice** *Genesis 4* — God's uncompromising law of forgiveness. First false religion.
11. **Unrepentant Cain** *Genesis 4* — What is sin? What is repentance? A solemn warning.
12. **The Prophet Enoch** *Genesis 4, 5* — Righteousness v. unrighteousness. Faith.

Cassette 3: **The Prophet Noah**

13. **The Prophet Noah: God's Patience and Wrath** *Genesis 6* — God's righteous anger. God's grace.
14. **Noah and the Great Flood** *Genesis 7* — One door of salvation. God's fearful judgment.
15. **Noah and the Faithfulness of God** *Genesis 8, 9* — Noah's faith. God's faithfulness.
16. **The Tower of Babel** *Genesis 10, 11* — Man's Pride and Rebellion. God's judgment.

Cassette 4: **The Prophet Abraham**

17. **Review of "The Beginning"** *Genesis 1-11* — God is righteous. Man is unrighteous.
18. **Why God Called Abraham** *Genesis 12* — God's plan of redemption advances.
19. **Abraham, God's Friend** *Genesis 13-15* — Righteous by faith. What is true faith?
20. **Abraham and Ishmael** *Genesis 16, 17* — Abraham's unbelief. God's faithfulness.
21. **Sodom's Ruin and Isaac's Birth** *Genesis 18-21* — God's judgment and faithfulness.
22. **Abraham's Sacrifice** *Genesis 22* — Abraham's prophecy of the Redeemer's Greater Sacrifice. Jesus' fulfillment.

Cassette 5: **Jacob and Joseph**

23. **Esau and Jacob: The Temporal and the Eternal** *Genesis 25* — Eternal values.
24. **Jacob Becomes Israel** *Genesis 28-32* — The Ladder. Man's failure. God's faithfulness.
25. **Joseph's Humiliation** *Genesis 37-39* — Joseph: a youth who walked with God. No one can serve two masters.
26. **Joseph's Exaltation** *Genesis 40-42* — Joseph: a picture of the promised Redeemer.
27. **Joseph: The Rest of the Story** *Genesis 42-50* — God's sovereignty. Death's certainty.
28. **Review of the First Book of the Torah** *Genesis 1-50; Exodus 1* — God's perfect Plan.

Cassette 6: THE PROPHET MOSES

29. **THE PROPHET MOSES** *Exodus 1, 2* — Moses' birth. God's greatness, mercy & faithfulness.
30. **MOSES MEETS GOD** *Exodus 3, 4* — God reveals His awesome character (holy, faithful, merciful) & His unique Name!
31. **PHARAOH: WHO IS THE LORD?** *Exodus 4-7* — Religion v. relationship. Do not harden your heart.
32. **THE PLAGUES** *Exodus 7-10* — Satan's imitations and limitations. Folly of fighting against God's Word.
33. **THE PASSOVER LAMB** *Exodus 11, 12* — The value of the blood of the sacrificial lamb. The Redeemer.
34. **A PATH THROUGH THE SEA** *Exodus 13-15* — Man is helpless to save himself. God's Salvation.

Cassette 7: GOD'S HOLY LAW

35. **FOOD IN THE DESERT** *Exodus 16, 17* — Man's unbelief. God's goodness. The Bread of Life.
36. **FIERY MOUNT SINAI** *Exodus 19, 20* — Man's presumption. God's terrifying holiness.
37. **TEN HOLY COMMANDMENTS** *Exodus 20* — The Ten Commandments interpreted: Guilty!
38. **PURPOSE OF THE COMMANDMENTS** *Exodus 20* — God's "X-Ray." Man's sin. Way of forgiveness.
39. **BROKEN COMMANDMENTS** *Exodus 32* — The Golden Calf. Vain religion. True worship.
40. **THE TENT OF MEETING** *Exodus 24-40; Leviticus 16* — God's holiness and way of Salvation portrayed.

Cassette 8: ISRAEL'S UNFAITHFULNESS AND GOD'S FAITHFULNESS

41. **THE ISRAELITES' UNBELIEF** *Numbers 13, 14* — Leviticus condensed. Sin of unbelief and its result.
42. **THE BRONZE SNAKE** *Numbers 20, 21* — Sin's penalty. God's remedy: Look and live.
43. **MOSES' FINAL MESSAGE** *Deuteronomy* — Brief review of Torah. Moses' final exhortations. The Greater Prophet.
44. **JOSHUA AND THE LAND OF CANAAN** *Joshua* — God's faithfulness. Believing God and His Word.
45. **JUDGES AND RUTH** *Judges; Ruth* — The choice: God's Way or man's religion?

Cassette 9: THE PROPHET DAVID

46. **SAMUEL, SAUL, AND DAVID** *1 Samuel 1-16; Psalm 8, 23* — God looks at the heart.
47. **DAVID AND GOLIATH** *1 Samuel 17; Psalm 27* — The need to know God personally.
48. **KING DAVID AND GOD'S PROMISE** *1 Samuel 18–2 Samuel 7* — "David's" Eternal Kingdom.
49. **DAVID AND BATHSHEBA** *2 Samuel 11, 12; Psalm 51, 32* — David's sin and repentance. God's forgiveness.
50. **THE PROPHET DAVID AND THE MESSIAH** *Psalms 1, 2* — Prophesied: Messiah, King, Son of God.
51. **MORE FROM THE PSALMS** *Psalms 22, 16* — Prophesied: Messiah's crucifixion and resurrection.

Cassette 10: THE PROPHET SOLOMON TO THE PROPHET ISAIAH

52. **THE PROPHET SOLOMON** *1 Kings 2-10; Psalm 72* — Seeking the One who is greater than Solomon.
53. **THE PROPHET ELIJAH** *1 Kings 6-18* — The Choice: Empty religion or the living God.
54. **THE PROPHET JONAH** *Jonah* — Salvation is from God. No favoritism with God. Man's choice.
55. **THE PROPHET ISAIAH** *Isaiah* — Prophesied: Messiah's Person and Work. Bad news and Good News.

Cassette 11: THE PROPHET JEREMIAH TO THE PROPHET MALACHI

56. **THE PROPHET JEREMIAH** *Jeremiah* — God's prophet rejected. False prophets believed. Captivity.
57. **THE PROPHET DANIEL** *Daniel 1, 6* — Daniel's prophecies. Sincere faith. Fear God, not man.
58. **THE PROPHET ZECHARIAH** *Ezra, Zechariah* — Messianic prophecies. Heed the prophets' Message.
59. **THE MESSAGE OF THE PROPHETS SUMMARIZED** *Malachi* — Review: God, Man, Messiah. The New Covenant foretold.

Cassette 12: THE MESSIAH'S ARRIVAL

60. **THE PROPHET JOHN** *Luke 1* — Why an Old & a New Testament? Why four "Gospels"? Introduction to the "*Injil.*"
61. **THE ANNOUNCEMENT** *Luke 1: Matthew 1* — His name: Jesus! Why is He called the Son of God?
62. **THE MESSIAH'S BIRTH** *Luke 2: Matthew 2* — More than a prophet. No one born like Him.
63. **THE HOLY SON** *Luke 2, Matthew 3, 4* — His sinless nature. His distinction as the Son of God.

Cassette 13: THE MESSIAH'S WORKS AND WORDS

64. **THE LAMB OF GOD** *John 1* — John's testimony of Jesus. John's distinction as a great prophet.
65. **THE GREAT HEALER** *Mark 1, 2* — Jesus' power and authority. Sin, the worst disease.
66. **THE GREAT TEACHER** *Matthew 5-7* — The unparalleled Sermon on the Mount.
67. **YOU MUST BE BORN AGAIN** *John 3* — God requires a pure heart. Mere religion will not suffice.
68. **THE SAVIOR OF THE WORLD** *John 4; Luke 4* — Accepting and rejecting the Messiah.
69. **JESUS' AUTHORITY** *Matthew 12; John 5* — To believe Jesus is to believe the prophets.

Cassette 14: THE MESSIAH'S POWER AND GLORY

70. **JESUS' POWER** *Mark 4-6; Matthew 9, 10* — The Messiah's Deity. No need to fear the spirits.
71. **TWO IMPORTANT PARABLES** *Luke 8; Matthew 13* — Man's heart condition. Coming Judgment.
72. **THE BREAD OF LIFE** *Mark 6; John 6* — Only Jesus can satisfy the hungry soul.
73. **JESUS CAUSES DIVISION** *Matthew 15, 16; John 7* — Jesus v. religion. On whose side are you?
74. **THE LIGHT OF THE WORLD** *John 8, 9* — The religious "experts" and the blind man. The worst kind of blindness.
75. **THE LORD OF GLORY** *Matthew 16, 17* — Who is Jesus? Son of God. Why did He come?

Cassette 15: THE MESSIAH'S WISDOM AND MISSION

76. **THE GOOD SHEPHERD** *John 10* — Jesus: One with God, the Door & the Good Shepherd.
77. **THE HEART OF GOD** *Luke 18, 15* — Two Parables: God's mercy is for the repentant. Slave or Son?
78. **THE RESURRECTION AND THE LIFE** *John 11, 12* — Many believe. The religious leaders plot.
79. **JESUS ENTERS JERUSALEM** *Luke 18-20, etc.* — Jesus' approaching death. Warnings.
80. **HARD AND TRUE WORDS** *Matthew 22-25* — Jesus' wisdom and warnings. End times.
81. **THE LAST SUPPER** *Matthew 26* — The bread and the cup. The infinite value of Jesus' blood.

Cassette 16: THE MESSIAH'S SACRIFICE AND CONQUEST

82. **JESUS IS ARRESTED** *John 14; Matthew 26* — Comforter promised. Why Jesus gave Himself up.
83. **JESUS IS CONDEMNED** *Matthew 26, 27; John 18, 19* — Jesus' tried and tortured. Like a lamb.
84. **JESUS IS NAILED TO THE CROSS** *Matthew 27; Mark 15; Luke 23; John 19* — "It is finished!"
85. **JESUS IS RISEN** *Matthew 28; Luke 24; John 20* — Positive proof: Jesus is who He claimed to be!

Cassette 17: GOOD NEWS

86. **JESUS ASCENDS TO HEAVEN** *Matthew 28; Luke 24; Acts 1* — Christ's absolute authority.
87. **THE HOLY SPIRIT HAS COME** *Acts 1, 2* — Who is the Holy Spirit? The Gospel preached.
88. **JESUS IS COMING BACK** *Revelation 19-22* — Will Jesus Christ be your Savior or Judge?
89. **THE GOOD NEWS** — The Gospel of God. You can know you are saved. Personal testimony.

Cassette 18: MAN'S QUESTIONS AND GOD'S ANSWERS

90. **MAN'S QUESTIONS; GOD'S ANSWERS (#1)** — Has the Bible been altered? Why "Son of God"?
91. **MAN'S QUESTIONS; GOD'S ANSWERS (#2)** — Why evil? O.T./N.T.? Holy Spirit? Faith alone? Etc.
92. **HOW SHOULD CHRIST'S DISCIPLES LIVE?** — Christ's purity and love in the believer. Four disciplines.

Cassette 19: GOD'S PLAN OF REDEMPTION

93. **REVIEW #1: ADAM, THE PROBLEM OF SIN** *Genesis 1-4* — Sin's entry and God's remedy.
94. **REVIEW #2: ABRAHAM, RIGHTEOUS BY FAITH** *Genesis 6-22* — God's Way of justifying sinners.
95. **REVIEW #3: MOSES, GOD'S HOLY LAW** *Exodus 1-20* — The Law and the Lamb.
96. **REVIEW #4: CHRIST, "IT IS FINISHED!"** *John 19; Hebrews 10* — God's great Salvation.

Cassette 20: YOU MUST CHOOSE

97. **HELL** *Luke 16* — The reality of hell. God laid our hell on Christ. Heaven or Hell: The choice is yours.
98. **PARADISE** *Revelation 21, 22* — The glorious place called Heaven and how to get in.
99. **WHAT DO YOU THINK ABOUT JESUS? (#1)** — Christ is incomparable in His Person.
100. **WHAT DO YOU THINK ABOUT JESUS? (#2)** — Christ is incomparable in His Work. Believe and be saved!

Appendix B

Wolof Proverbs

Storytelling is an important part of Wolof culture and tradition. The Wolofs use proverbs {"*léebu*"} to give a moral lesson to the story and to make it memorable. Some like to quote proverbs in everyday conversation and circumstances. In *The Way of Righteousness* we have used sixteen Wolof proverbs to illustrate and apply God's Eternal Truth. We have listed the proverbs below with their approximate English translation. The numbers in parentheses show the lessons in which the proverb has been used. The phrase in brackets gives the main Scriptural truth the proverb illustrates. The proverbs are listed according to their frequency of use in the lessons.

1. *"Musiba du yem ci boppu boroom."*
   "An epidemic is not confined to the one from whom it originates." (#7, 9, 13, 28, 86, 89, 91, 94)
   [Adam's sin with its consequences has spread to all his descendants. See Romans 5:12]

2. *"Nen du bëre ak doj!"*
   "An egg should not wrestle with a rock!" (#1, 3, 12, 16, 32, 33, 60)
   [Man cannot oppose the Word of God and win. 2 Peter 3:16]

3. *"Dëgg, kaani la."*
   "Truth is a hot pepper." (#3, 9, 68, 80, Appendix D)
   [God's Truth is not always easy to accept nor is it appreciated by all. Romans 3:23]

4. *"Lu bant yàgg-yàgg ci ndox, du tax mu soppaliku mukk jasig."*
   "Even if a log soaks a long time in water, it will never become a crocodile." (Preface, #67, 72, 90)
   [Man's religious rituals will never make him righteous. John 3:6,7]

5. *"Ku bëgg lem, ñeme yamb."*
   "Whoever wants honey must brave the bees." (#23, 45, 73, Appendix D)
   [Whoever follows God's Way of Righteousness must be prepared to be mis-

understood by family and friends. Hebrews 11:24-27]

6. *"Bala nga koy xam, xamadi dina la rey!"*
"Before you know it, ignorance will kill you!" (#50, 51, 74, 90)
[Ignorance concerning God's Way of salvation is deadly! Hebrews 2:3]

7. *"Janax du jur lu dul luy gas."*
"A rat only begets that which digs." (#8, 16, 61, 94)
[We are born sinners. Psalm 51:5]

8. *"Kéwél du tëb doom ja bëtt."*
"The leaping gazelle does not produce burrowing offspring." (#7, 12, 91)
[We have inherited the sinful nature of our forefather Adam. Ephesians 2:1-3]

9. *"Ku yaag ci teen, baag fekk la fa."*
"A water pail will find the person who waits diligently at the well." (#1, 9)
[God rewards those who diligently seek Him. Hebrews 11:6]

10. *"Ndànk-ndànk, mooy jàpp golo ci Ñaay."*
"Slowly, slowly one catches a monkey in the forest." (#1)
[Be patient. Don't expect to grasp all of God's truth in one lesson. Isaiah 28:10]

11. *"Sa xaritu noon, sa noon la."*
"Your friend's enemy is your enemy." (#8)
[When Adam and Eve sided with the devil they forfeited their relationship with God. James 4:4-8]

12. *"Nag wéq na doomam, waaye bañu ko."*
"The cow kicks its calf but does not hate it." (#11)
[God deals severely with people so that they might repent and follow His way of righteousness. 2 Peter 3:9]

13. *"Fukki nit gas pax mu xoot, fukki nit suul ko, pënd mi bare na, waaye pax amul."*
"Ten men dig a deep hole, ten men fill it—there is plenty of dust, but no hole." (#53)
[Religious rituals–no matter how zealously performed–do not produce the righteousness required by God. Romans 10:1-4]

14. *"Bala ngay fél gémmiñu sàmm, nga xam lu mu walis."*
"Before you slap the shepherd on the mouth, you should find out what he is whistling about." (#61)

[Before you criticize and condemn the teachings of the Bible, you should learn their meaning. Jude 10]

15. "*Garab gay doon pénc, lawbe du ko gis ba di ko gor.*"
"The woodcutter does not cut down the main tree in the village (under which folks meet)." (#68)
[Jesus the Messiah is God's "main tree." How foolish and evil of men to scorn or ignore the One whom God has appointed as the Savior and Judge of the world! Acts 4:10-12]

16. "*Tungune du teew ñuy nataal.*"
"No need to draw a picture of a dwarf (to depict what one is like)**, if one is standing before you."** (#89)
[There is no need to waste your energy on symbolic animal sacrifices when the Perfect and Final Sacrifice has been provided for you by God! Hebrews 10:1-25]

APPENDIX C

THE TEACHING METHOD

"LINE UPON LINE"

A preschool teacher does not start her students with $x^2 + 2x + 1 = (x + 1)^2$. She begins with *1 apple + 1 apple = 2 apples*. Her goal is to lay a foundation upon which her little pupils can build. Similarly, God's revelation to the children of Adam is progressive, ***"precept upon precept, line upon line...here a little, there a little."*** (Isaiah 28:10) God's Book begins with *"In the beginning God"* and goes on to reveal His complex Person and His categorical plan by which He can count sinners as righteous.

The Way of Righteousness radio series presents the message of God's prophets in consecutive order. Through the narratives of the people, patriarchs and prophets of the Holy Scriptures, listeners can discover for themselves God's uncompromising system of forgiveness—how He has provided a way by which the fallen children of Adam can be delivered from sin's curse and restored to happy fellowship with their Creator.

Taking into consideration the Muslim's understanding of God and the prophets, this series employs a "modified chronological approach"— carefully drawing from all the Scriptures as it proceeds through them chronologically. The lessons put a premium on repetition, especially since many listeners may not hear every program. Each lesson begins with a review of the previous one.

WHY THE CHRONOLOGICAL METHOD?

The Messiah Himself taught the Gospel chronologically. For example, on the day of His resurrection, He said to two of His incredulous followers, *"O foolish ones, and slow of heart to believe in all that the prophets have spoken!...And* ***beginning at Moses and all the prophets****, He expounded to them in all the Scriptures the things concerning Himself!"* (Luke 24:25,27)

Similarly, all Muslims should be given **the opportunity** to hear and understand what the prophets (whom Muslims profess to believe) have written so that they can give an honest answer to the question, *"Do you believe the prophets?"* (Acts

26:27) An unhurried journey through the Torah, the Psalms, the Prophets, and the Gospel affords them this opportunity.

Like all who are religious, Muslims need **time** to rethink much of what many have unquestioningly accepted as truth. Teaching from the whole of Scripture can help people to see that when we preach *"Jesus Christ and Him crucified"* (1 Corinthians 2:2), we are *"saying no other things than those which the prophets and Moses said would come— that the Christ would suffer, that He would be the first to rise from the dead, and would proclaim light to the Jewish people and to the Gentiles* [which includes all Muslims!]." (Acts 26:22,23)

Another good reason for presenting God's Word chronologically is that the Old Testament stories of the unbelieving nation of Israel and the New Testament stories of the hardhearted religious leaders of the Jews encourage honest **self-examination**. These stories have caused many to ask, "Is my heart also hard? Will I, like the Israelites, also spurn the message of God's prophets and the Messiah God sent from heaven?"

The best of seed will not germinate in hard, unprepared soil. The "Good Seed" of God's Word can only produce eternal fruit in **prepared hearts**. The Holy Torah is an effective plough. Remember the rich young ruler who came running to Jesus and asked, *"Good Teacher, what good thing shall I do that I may inherit eternal life?"* (Matthew 19:16; Mark 10:17) To the crowd, the young man's question seemed good, but not to the Lord. Jesus knew that this religious man had not yet grasped the foundational truths concerning God's infinite holiness and man's utter sinfulness. This self-righteous man imagined that he could earn his way into paradise. (He was like a child holding out a grimy fistful of copper coins to the world's wealthiest man, and asking him, "How many shall I give you that I may inherit your estate?") How did Jesus answer the man? He directed him back to the Torah and the Ten Commandments to show him that he could never, in his own strength, satisfy God's perfect standard of righteousness. There is no *"eternal life"* for those who think they can merit it by doing some *"good thing."*

Avoid Unnecessary Offense

In *The Way of Righteousness* series we strive to define misunderstood terms and use familiar terms whenever possible. For instance, we refer to God's written Word as the Holy Scriptures, the Writings of the Prophets, the Torah, the Gospel...but rarely do we call it *the Bible* (Latin for *the Book*). We do this because many Muslims associate *the Bible* with Roman Catholicism—a religion that erroneously bases salvation on human achievement rather than on Divine accomplishment.

Being careful with *terms* does not mean toning down the *truth*. We seek to avoid unnecessary offense, but never at the cost of compromising the Truth of the Gospel. (Galatians 2:5,14; 1 Corinthians 9:22,23) The *methods* of presenting God's way of Salvation will vary depending on the hearers, but the essential *message* remains the same. The Lord Jesus' *method* of presenting the *message* of salvation to a religious man like Nicodemus (John 3) was quite different from the way He presented it to the immoral woman of Samaria (John 4). Like their Master, the apostles were sensitive to people's perceptions and prejudices, seeking to lead their hearers from where they were to where they needed to be. (Compare: Acts 2:14-39 with 10:34-43; Acts 17:1-3 with 17:16-31)

SIMPLE ENGLISH

The Way of Righteousness is written in a simple, spoken style, suitable for radio. While this English version is not an exact word-for-word translation from the Wolof series (this would make for very uncomfortable reading!), it maintains a similar simplicity of structure and style. This makes for easier translation into other languages. Obviously, the illustrations and Wolof proverbs used in these lessons will need to be adapted to express God's truth effectively in the local culture and language.

RECYCLABLE

These one hundred programs may be presented on a daily or weekly basis. We have been careful not to date the lessons in any way. Each program is approximately fifteen minutes in length when spoken at a normal conversational speed. As a weekly broadcast, the series lasts about two years (100 weeks). When broadcast five days a week, it takes less than five months. These programs, which present the living, powerful, penetrating and never-outdated Word of God, are intended to be broadcast over and over again. Lesson #1 follows #100.

SERVE WITH GREEN TEA

In addition to radio broadcasts, the audio-cassettes of the lessons can be played for small discussion groups or informal gatherings of men and women (around a pot of steaming green tea with plenty of froth, sugar and mint, of course!). The cassettes can also be lent out or given away like a tract. Even in poorer nations, most taxi drivers, restaurant and boutique owners have cassette players. Record these messages over those old tapes that are collecting dust in the closet and pass them on!

GOD'S WORD, NOT OURS

In each of these one hundred programs, we present God's infallible Word. If anyone is offended by what is taught, they should talk to God about it, since it is His Word, not ours. In teaching God's truth, we have not used the *mechanical-academic-apologetic* approach so much as the "*God's-Word-is-a-Lion-and-will-defend-itself*" approach. When handling the living Word of the living God—the best defense is a good offense. To hear God's holy Book taught chronologically is to come face to face with the Almighty Himself!

When our Senegalese friends ask us, "Why do you not also teach the Qur'an?", our answer is simple. "In every town and village you have men teaching the Qur'an, but how many are teaching the Torah, the Psalms and the Gospel? Our unique purpose is to make known the Good News of the prophets which you seldom hear."

God's Theme, Not Ours

The theme of God's Word and the theme of these one hundred lessons are identical: "***The Gospel of God** which He promised before through His prophets in the Holy Scriptures*." (Romans 1:2) That is what these lessons are about: the Gospel of God—the righteous way of salvation established by God—the only system of forgiveness that satisfies both God and man. Man's efforts may give him temporary feelings of satisfaction, but they can never satisfy the uncompromising righteousness of God. Only the Gospel satisfies both man and God. "*The Gospel...is the power of God to salvation to everyone who believes...For in it the righteousness of God is revealed*." (Romans 1:16,17)

God's Power, Not Ours

The Scripture says that "*the natural man does not receive the things of the Spirit of God, for they are foolishness to him!*" and that "*the message of the cross is foolishness to those who are perishing*." (1 Corinthians 2:14; 1:18) These lessons by themselves will never reveal God's truth to a soul. Only the Spirit of God can do that. We count on Him to reveal His way of righteousness to those who listen to these programs. "*For the weapons of our warfare are not carnal but **mighty in God** for pulling down strongholds, casting down arguments and every high thing that exalts itself against the knowledge of God!*" (2 Corinthians 10:4,5)

Our Heartfelt Prayer

God is at work in the hearts of Muslims around the globe. Many are seeking, finding, and submitting to *God's way of righteousness*. For those continuing in *man's way of self-righteousness*, we offer to God this prayer penned by the apostle Paul:

> "*Brethren, my heart's desire and prayer to God...is that they may be saved. For I bear them witness that they have a zeal for God, but not according to knowledge. For they being ignorant of **God's righteousness**, and seeking to establish **their own righteousness**, have not submitted themselves to **the righteousness of God.** For Christ is the end of the law for **righteousness** to everyone who believes*." (Romans 10:1-4)

Appendix D

Insights Into Islam

Muslims are My Friends

With so much media attention given to radical, violent Muslim groups, we need to remind ourselves that most Muslims are friendly, hospitable, peace-loving people. They are our neighbors and our friends. In general, I feel more comfortable speaking with Muslims than with secularized Americans. Unlike so many in the West, most Muslims fear God, sense His impending judgment, and are willing to talk about God and the prophets. For those unfamiliar with a Muslim's basic beliefs and practices, the following observations may be helpful.

Islam, Muslims and Allah

Islam is the religion of Muslims. The Arabic word *Islam* means *submission* (to Allah). *Muslim* (or Moslem) means *one who submits*. *Allah* is the Arabic word for *God*.

Islam's fundamental concept of God is that God is one. God is great, indescribable, almighty, and compassionate—especially to Muslims. Everything that happens in the world has been predetermined by God. Muslims believe that God has revealed His will, but not Himself, to humankind. Muslims view their relationship to God as a master-slave relationship, with no possibility of a more intimate father-son relationship.

Five Pillars

The roughly one billion Muslims around the world find themselves in widely differing socio-economic-cultural circumstances—ranging from the wealthy oil sheiks of the Persian Gulf to the rural farmers of West Africa. While local culture and perspectives affect Muslim beliefs considerably (Eg. see note in Preface under the subtitle: *The 'very religious' Wolofs*), all Muslims assent to Islam's "Five Pillars." Most Muslims believe that they must fulfill these five duties to atone for their sins and merit a place in paradise.

llars of Islam are:

ness (*Shahada*): *La illaha illa Allah, wa Mohammed Rasul*
ere is no god but God, and Muhammad is the prophet of

.) **Ritual Prayers** (*Salat*): Five times daily at hours specified, in the Arabic language, facing toward Mecca, preceded by a ceremonial washing of face, hands and feet.
3.) **Alms** (*Zakat*): Sharing 2.5% of one's wealth with those in need.
4.) **Annual Fast** (*Saum*): An obligatory, dawn-to-dusk, month-long fast which takes place during Ramadan, the ninth month on the Islamic lunar calendar.
5.) **Pilgrimage to Mecca** (*Hajj*): Required of all able-bodied Muslims who can afford it, at least once in a lifetime.

The Prophets and the Qur'an

Most Muslims profess belief in **the prophets** of the Bible. The Qur'an names more than twenty Bible prophets, including Abraham (*Ibrahim*), Moses (*Musa*), David (*Dawud*), John the Baptist (*Yahya*) and Jesus the Messiah (*Isa al Masih*). Muslims consider Muhammad (born in Mecca, Saudi Arabia, in 570 A.D. and buried in Medina in 632 A.D.) to be the last and greatest prophet.

Muslims maintain that God revealed His will through **four holy books**: the Torah ("*Taurat*") of Moses, the Psalms ("*Zabur*") of David, the Gospel ("*Injil*") of Jesus, and the Qur'an (also spelled *Koran*) of Muhammad. Many Muslims assert that the Qur'anic revelation annuls the earlier revelations, but this assertion has no clear support from the Qur'an. They believe that Muhammad (who never learned to read or write) received the Qur'anic verses over many years from the angel Gabriel in a desert cave near Mecca. Muhammad recited the verses to his followers who wrote them down. Years after Muhammad's death, these verses were collected into a single book known as *the Qur'an*—which means "*recitation*."

The Qur'an has 114 chapters (*suras*) and is about two-thirds the length of the New Testament. Muslims venerate the Qur'an and are profoundly affected by its Arabic language and poetic style. Though most Muslims have never read the entire Qur'an, it is their point of reference for every area of life: religion, family, health, ethics, economics and politics. Like the Bible, the Qur'an affirms the reality of God and Satan, angels and evil spirits, a coming day of resurrection and judgment, a hell to shun and a paradise to gain. But the similarity ends there. The Qur'an's descriptions and definitions of these realities differ greatly from those recorded by the prophets of the Bible.

God

The Qur'an presents God as a single entity. "*Say not, 'Three.' Forbear, it will be better for you. God is only one God! Far be it from His glory that He should have a son!*" (4:172) {Note: "4:172" means chapter 4 and verse 172 of the Qur'an. However, the verse may be as many as five verses away in different versions of the Qur'an.} This and other Qur'anic verses (5:116), combined with the Roman Catholic Church's unscriptural practice of praying to Mary, have caused many Muslims to think that Christians believe in three gods–God, Mary and Jesus. This is a serious misunderstanding of what a true Christian believes. The Bible says: "*There is* ***one God*** *and* ***one Mediator*** *between God and men, the Man Christ Jesus.*" (1 Timothy 2:5)

The Bible clearly condemns polytheism and idolatry, and consistently confirms the oneness of God, declaring: "*You shall worship the LORD your God, and* ***Him only*** *you shall serve!...The LORD our God, the LORD is* ***one****!*" (Matthew 4:10; Deuteronomy 6:4,13; Mark 12:29) Oneness, however, does not preclude depth and dimension. The Qur'an reveals God as unknowable and *one-dimensional*. The Bible reveals God as self-revealing and *tri-dimensional*—Eternal Father, Eternal Son and Eternal Holy Spirit.

Satan, Sin and Man

The Qur'an teaches that Satan became the Devil (*Iblis*) when he stubbornly refused to bow down to Adam at God's command (7:11-18). Adam is said to have been in a heavenly Paradise before he ate the forbidden fruit. After Adam transgressed, God sent him down to earth. The Qur'an views Adam's disobedience as *a minor slip* rather than *a major fall*. According to many Qur'anic scholars, all Adam had to do to get back into God's favor was to learn and recite certain prayers (7:18-30; 2:30-40).

While the Bible portrays God as absolutely holy and man as totally depraved, the Qur'an portrays man as weak and misguided. In the Muslim view, man does not need redemption, he only needs some guidance so that he might develop the inherently pure nature with which the Creator has endowed him. If he will be faithful in his prayers, almsgiving and fasting, God is likely to overlook his sins and usher him into Paradise, a garden of sensual delights.

Jesus

Every Muslim professes to believe in *Isa* (the Qur'anic name for Jesus). They believe that Jesus is one of 124,000 prophets, that he was sent uniquely to the

Jews, that he denied the Trinity, that he predicted the coming of Muhammad, that he was not the Son of God and that he was not crucified! The Bible calls such a Jesus *"another Jesus."* (2 Corinthians 11:4)

The Qur'anic profile of Jesus presents Muslims with a difficult paradox. While certain verses declare that Jesus was *"no more than a prophet"* (4:171-173; 5:75; 2:136), others ascribe to him characteristics and titles never attributed to any other prophet. For example, the Qur'an affirms that Jesus was born of a virgin, that he was righteous and holy, and that he possessed the power to create life, open the eyes of the blind, cleanse the lepers and raise the dead (3:45-51; 5:110-112; 19:19). Furthermore, the Qur'an calls him the Messiah (*Al Masih*), the Word of God (*Kalimat Allah*) and the Spirit [Soul] of God (*Ruh Allah*) (4:171,172). These supernatural descriptions and titles have caused many Muslims to seek the truth about who Jesus really is.

One day, a devout Muslim man said to me, "The Qur'an calls Jesus *Ruh Allah*. If Jesus is the Soul of God, then He must be God!" This Muslim was beginning to grasp one of the most basic truths of Holy Scripture—not that a man became a god—but that God became a Man in order to reveal Himself to the children of Adam and save them from their sins. Some time later, at the cost of being cast out by his family, this same Muslim boldly acknowledged Jesus as his Savior and Lord.

THE SON OF GOD

The ultimate sin in Islam is *"shirk"* (Arabic for *association*). *Shirk* is the sin of regarding anything or anyone as equal to God. The Qur'an rejects Jesus' title as the Son of God. *"They say: 'Allah has begotten a son. God forbid!"* (2:110) *"Say: 'If the Lord of Mercy had a son, I would be the first to worship him.'"* (43:81; 4:172; 5:72.73) Unfortunately, many Muslims interpret "Son of God" in a carnal sense. They understand the term to mean that God took a wife and had a son by her! In several *Way of Righteousness* lessons (including #50, 61, 63, 75, 90, and 99), we explain from the Bible ***why*** the prophets, the angels, and God Himself call Jesus *the Son of God*. These simple explanations have helped many Muslims so that they no longer say, *"Astaghferullah!"* ("God forgive you for this blasphemy!") when they hear Jesus called by His rightful title as *The Son of God*.

The Bible gives **three main reasons why Jesus is called *the Son of God***. Interestingly, the Qur'an contains verses that appear to affirm all three reasons.

1.) The Bible calls Jesus the Son of God because ***He came from God*** (Isaiah 7:14; Luke 1:34,35). Similarly, the Qur'an teaches that Jesus came directly from God, that He was born of a virgin, that He had no earthly father (3:47; 19:20). Also, the Qur'an sets Jesus apart from all other prophets by calling Him *the Messiah* (*the Anointed One*) (4:157,171,172). Unlike Adam, who was formed from dust, the Messiah came from Heaven.

2.) The Bible calls Jesus the Son of God because **He is like God**. He has God's holy and sinless character and all of God's mighty attributes. Like Father, like Son (Hebrews 1:1-9; Matthew 17:5). The Qur'an calls Jesus *"a holy son."* (19:19; 3:46) While the Qur'an speaks of the other prophets' need of forgiveness (38:24; 48:1), it never attributes a single sin to Jesus. Also, it ascribes to Jesus supernatural powers that God alone possesses (3:45-51; 5:110-112).

3.) The Bible calls Jesus the Son of God because **He is One with God**. He is the Eternal Word who *"was in the beginning with God."* (John 1:1-18; Philippians 2:5-11) Similarly, the Qur'an calls Jesus *the Word of God* and *the Soul/Spirit of God* (4:171,172). Just as, in some mysterious way, a person is one with his words, spirit, and soul—so God and Christ are eternally One.

THE CROSS

All the prophets of the Bible, in one way or another, foretold the Messiah's sacrificial death. But the Qur'an says: *"They denied the truth and uttered a monstrous falsehood against Mary. They declared: 'We have put to death the Messiah, Jesus the son of Mary, the apostle of Allah.' They did not kill him, nor did they crucify him, but it appeared so to them."* (4:157) While Qur'anic scholars interpret this verse in a variety of ways, most Muslims fervently deny the historical and Scriptural records concerning Jesus' death on the cross. They believe it inappropriate that a great prophet like Jesus should die such a shameful death. Thus, Muslims dismiss the central message of the prophets of the Bible—that Jesus the Messiah *willingly* offered Himself as the final sacrifice to pay the sin-debt of the world *"that the Scriptures of the prophets might be fulfilled."* (Matthew 26:56)

The Qur'an omits the Good News of atonement through Jesus' shed blood by which God *"might be just and the justifier of the one who has faith in Jesus."* (Romans 3:26) The Muslim sees no need for the sin-bearing death of the sinless Messiah. The Qur'an says, *"No soul shall bear another's burden."* (6:164; 17:14-16; 39:7) Islam teaches that God excuses sin based on man's repentance and good works (42:26,31; 39:54,55). The Qur'an bases salvation on **what man can do for God**. The Bible bases salvation on **what God has done for man**, saying, *"not by works of righteousness which we have done, but according to His mercy He saved us..."* (Titus 3:4)

ISLAM'S SACRIFICE

While Islam denies the Messiah's death on the cross—it faithfully commemorates an Old Testament sacrifice which prefigured the Messiah's sacrificial death. Every year, on the tenth day of the last month of the Islamic calendar, Muslims celebrate **the Feast of Sacrifice** (*Id al-Adha*). On this day Muslims around the world slay carefully selected rams (or lambs, male goats, cows or camels) in commemoration of the ram that God provided on the mountain to die in the place of Abraham's son. Tragically however, they overlook the fact that, about two thousand years after God provided the ram for Abraham, **God fulfilled the symbolism of Abraham's sacrifice**. For on the same mountain (not far from where the Dome of the Rock is located today), Jesus the Messiah willingly shed His righteous blood as God's sufficient and final payment for sin. And three days later God raised Jesus from the dead—the triumphant Savior and Lord of all who believe.

Through Jesus' voluntary substitutionary sacrifice, God has revealed His great love and mercy to humankind. The Messiah's death and resurrection perfectly fulfilled God's plan of salvation about which the prophets wrote—thus eliminating the need for continued animal sacrifices. Yet millions persist in sacrificing animals while ignoring the purpose, meaning and fulfilment of the animal sacrifice.

THE QUR'AN SAYS...

Many are surprised to learn that the Qur'an commands Muslims to believe the Torah, the Psalms and the Gospel. The Qur'an says:

> "*If you are in doubt concerning what we revealed to you, then* ***question those who read the Scripture that was before you***." (10:94) "*We sent down* ***the Torah*** *in which there is guidance and light*." (5:44) "*We have revealed to you* ***as we revealed to Noah and the prophets after him****, and as we revealed to Abraham, Ishmael, Isaac, Jacob, and the tribes; to Jesus, Job, Jonah, Aaron, Solomon and David, to whom we gave* ***the Psalms***." (4:163) "*We sent forth Jesus, the son of Mary, to follow in the footsteps of the prophets,* ***confirming the Torah*** *which was before him, and we gave him* ***the Gospel*** *with its guidance and light,* ***confirmatory of the preceding Torah****; a guidance and warning to those who fear God.* ***Therefore let the people of the Gospel judge according to what God has sent down therein.*** *Evildoers are those that do not judge according to God's revelations*." (5:46) "*Those who treat the Book, and the message we have sent through our apostles, as a lie, will know the truth hereafter: when, with chains and collars around their necks, they shall be dragged through scalding water and burned in the fire of hell*." (40:71)

The Qur'an contains dozens of similar verses.

THE DILEMMA

Such Qur'anic verses confront sincere Muslims with a serious dilemma: **How can one accept both the Bible and the Qur'an when they clearly contradict each other?** Furthermore the Qur'an emphasizes the high risk involved: to treat any of the Writings of the Prophets as a lie is to be "*burned in the fire of hell*."

Many attempt to resolve their dilemma by contending that the original Bible has been lost or falsified and is no longer reliable. Yet this explanation does not satisfy those who know their Qur'an, which says: "*The Word of God shall never change. That is the supreme triumph.*" (10:64) "*None can change the decrees of God.*" (6:34) The Qur'an claims that it was given **to confirm and guard** the preceding Scriptures. Muslims must ask themselves, "Would the Qur'an confirm a corrupted, unreliable book?"

Some suggest that Christians and Jews falsified the Bible after the time of Muhammad. This argument is disproved by the fact that today's Bibles are translated from ancient manuscripts which date to a time long before Muhammad. The Bible we are reading today is in harmony with the Bible of Muhammad's time. "*Allahu Akbar!*" ***God is great*** and has preserved His eternal Word for every generation.

Those who read the Bible with a desire to understand it will discover that it defends itself. The best defense is a good offense. "*The Word of God which lives and abides forever*" presents an awesome offense.

"*All men are like grass, and all their glory is like the flowers of the field: the grass withers and the flowers fall, but* ***the Word of the Lord stands forever****!*" (1 Peter 1:23-25)

The Way of Righteousness

Wolofs say, "Truth is a hot pepper" and "Whoever wants honey must brave the bees." Similarly, the penetrating power of *God's Truth* and everlasting sweetness of *God's way of righteousness* makes going after it worth every possible risk—even ostracism, persecution, and physical death.

The prophet Solomon wrote: ***"In the way of righteousness is life*** *(a relationship with God)****, and in its pathway there is no death*** *(separation from God)!*" (Proverbs 12:28) Does this claim sound too good to be true? Friends, with God—nothing is "too good to be true." *Allahu Akbar!* God is great!

To all who submit to God's *way of righteousness*, He promises to give freely that which religion can never provide: Salvation from the penalty and power of sin, a credited-righteousness, assurance of sins forgiven, a cleansed conscience, a deep peace, an untouchable joy, a new nature, a personal relationship with God, an eternal home with Him in Paradise, and infinitely more!

To all who read or hear these one hundred lessons—we commend you to God, the Compassionate, the Merciful, ***the Righteous***—who extends this life-giving and life-transforming promise to all who will claim it:

> ***"You will seek Me and find Me, when you search for me with all your heart."*** (Jeremiah 29:13)

*"Blessed are those who hunger and thirst
for righteousness,
for they shall be filled."*
(Matthew 5:6)